ADMIRAL JOHN H. TOWERS

Library of Congress Cataloging-in-Publication Data

Reynolds, Clark G.
  Admiral John H. Towers : the struggle for Naval air supremacy /
Clark G. Reynolds
    p.   cm.
  Includes bibliographical references and index.
  ISBN 0-87021-031-9 (alk. paper)
  1. Towers, John H. (John Henry), 1885–1955.   2. Admirals—United
States—Biography.   3. United States. Navy—Biography.   4. United
States. Navy—Aviation—History.   I. Title.
V63.T68R49   1991
359′.0092—dc20
[B]   91–14694

Printed in the United States of America on acid-free paper ⊗

2   4   6   8   9   7   5   3

First printing

Frontispiece: John H. Towers. (Copyright 1941 Time Warner Inc. Reprinted by permission.)

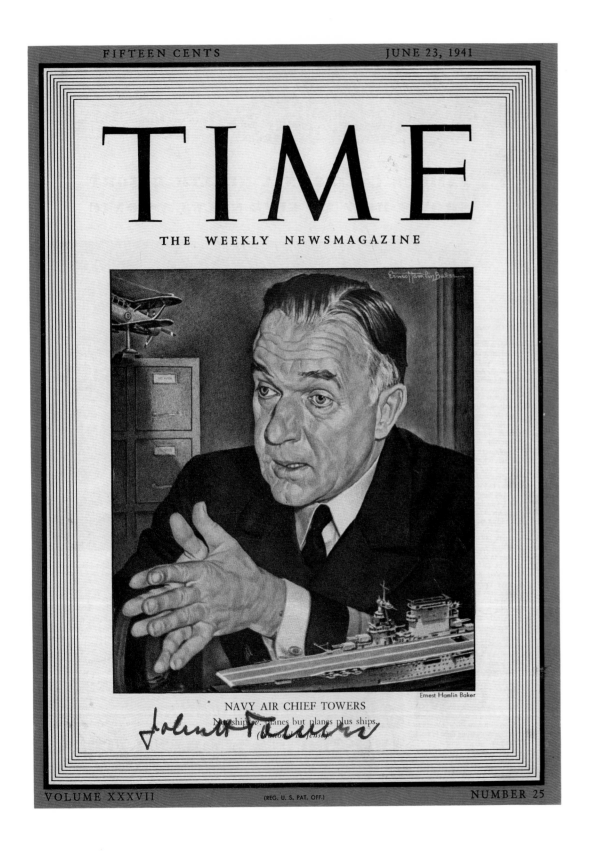

ADMIRAL JOHN H. TOWERS

The Struggle for Naval Air Supremacy

Clark G. Reynolds

NAVAL INSTITUTE PRESS   ANNAPOLIS, MARYLAND

FIFTEEN CENTS   JUNE 23, 1941

TIME

THE WEEKLY NEWSMAGAZINE

Ernest Hamlin Baker

NAVY AIR CHIEF TOWERS

Not ships or planes but planes plus ships.

(National Defense)

VOLUME XXXVII   (REG. U. S. PAT. OFF.)   NUMBER 25

ADMIRAL JOHN H. TOWERS

The Struggle for Naval Air Supremacy

Clark G. Reynolds

NAVAL INSTITUTE PRESS   ANNAPOLIS, MARYLAND

© 1991
by the United States Naval Institute
Annapolis, Maryland

Library of Congress Cataloging-in-Publication Data

Reynolds, Clark G.
  Admiral John H. Towers : the struggle for Naval air supremacy /
Clark G. Reynolds
    p. cm.
  Includes bibliographical references and index.
  ISBN 0-87021-031-9 (alk. paper)
    1. Towers, John H. (John Henry), 1885–1955. 2. Admirals—United
States—Biography. 3. United States. Navy—Biography. 4. United
States. Navy—Aviation—History. I. Title.
  V63.T68R49 1991
  359'.0092—dc20
  [B]   91–14694

Printed in the United States of America on acid-free paper ∞

2 4 6 8 9 7 5 3

First printing

Frontispiece: John H. Towers. (Copyright 1941 Time Warner Inc. Reprinted by permission.)

TO THE MEMORY OF MY DAD,
BILL REYNOLDS,
WHO POINTED THE WAY

CONTENTS

vii

Contents

PREFACE

An event of symbolic importance in the annals of navies took place on board a powerful aircraft carrier moored at Pearl Harbor the morning of 1 February 1946. For the first time in history, an aviator assumed command of the United States Pacific Fleet. It was still, five months after the end of World War II, the largest fleet in the world. The change-of-command ceremony was held in the hangar bay of the veteran combat carrier *Bennington*.

Admiral John H. Towers stepped to the podium at 1000 and read his orders before an audience of officers and sailors. He had reached the pinnacle of his career, one highlighted by the difficult struggle to win acceptance of the airplane and its carriers in the U.S. Navy. The crusade had begun thirty-five years before, when he learned to fly as the navy's third pilot. And the man he now relieved, Admiral Raymond A. Spruance, had been one of the battleship men who had resisted him.

Historians would best remember Spruance, and rightly so, for Spruance had had the good fortune to command during the great Pacific battles against Japan—Midway, Truk, the Philippine Sea, and Okinawa. But it was Towers who, more than any other single individual, had given Spruance the weapons—the carriers, the planes, the trained pilots—and the tactical and logistical doctrines with which to fight and win these victories. The battleships in which Spruance had served and trained played a relatively minor role.

In assuming command of the new carrier-oriented Pacific Fleet, Towers represented the future. It was a future long in the making. When he entered the U.S. Naval Academy in 1902, mankind had not even conquered the air.

At the time of his birth, seventeen years before that, the modern steel battleship had yet to grace the oceans of the world. Alone among his peers, Towers provided the continuum of leadership in naval aviation from its earliest days in the shadow of the battleship to the dawn of the nuclear age.

Indeed, no U.S. naval officer in aviation attracted more public attention during the world war periods 1912 to 1921 and 1939 to 1942 than John H. Towers. Following the short flying careers of Spuds Ellyson and John Rodgers, he became the navy's number one pilot. He was the first career aviator in the navy to rise to the ranks of rear, vice, and full admiral. During the war against Japan, he shared distinction as a key architect of the Pacific victory with only five other men—King, Nimitz, Spruance, Turner, and Mitscher. The complete professional, Towers commanded the respect of these men and other admirals, of generals in the army and its air forces, and of civilian, industrial, and foreign leaders. But his dogged determination to elevate aviation in the navy earned the animosity of many, notably King, Nimitz, and Spruance, who together prevented him from attaining the wartime seagoing command he richly deserved. Yet none could deny his major role in achieving victory in the greatest sea war in history.

Among career aviators in the navy—those who earned their wings shortly after being commissioned and who stayed in aviation billets—Jack Towers remained the acknowledged leader from 1912 until his retirement thirty-five years later. His career was therefore more than the history of naval aviation during those critical years; it was the history of the navy itself as it slowly but inexorably transformed itself from a battleship- to an aviation-centered fleet.

A biography of this man based entirely on official records and documents would reveal the breadth of his role in this area. Its depth, the author found, was apparent in personal letters, abbreviated reminiscences, and daily diaries that Towers dictated to a secretary or yeoman throughout his eight years as a flag officer. Oral interviews of fellow officers, family relations, and aviation pioneers by oral historians at the U.S. Naval Institute and Columbia University and by the author corroborate and enhance Towers' papers.

What has emerged are heretofore unknown or inadequately understood aspects of major events in twentieth-century American history. Towers' technical and managerial expertise during the infancy of American aviation enabled him to survive not only early air crashes but political infighting that eliminated all the other naval pioneers in the field. In World War I he was posted as a virtual spy for the navy in London, and during this time he surreptitiously saw combat over the Western Front. A detailed log of the

NC-3 has illuminated neglected aspects of his flight in the first transatlantic seaplane expedition. As the first career aviator captain of the *Langley,* he left a rich and unparalleled record of life and progress aboard the navy's earliest carrier in the 1920s. And now we know that Towers provided the real brains for Admirals William A. Moffett and Harry E. Yarnell ashore and afloat as their carriers revolutionized warfare in the Depression-era navy.

No mere air tactician, Towers mustered his considerable intellectual powers at the Naval War College, where his advanced and uncommon strategic writings are carefully preserved. Most significantly, his elevation to Chief of the Bureau of Aeronautics in 1939 brought him into intimate contact with President Franklin D. Roosevelt, Congressman Carl Vinson, Army Air Corps chief "Hap" Arnold, and the captains of the aircraft industry; through these associations Towers played a key role in shaping the two-ocean navy and mobilizing Allied air power for World War II. The details of such developments have been only superficially chronicled until now.

Towers' strategic and administrative acumen and forthright leadership not only provided the aeronautical tools for the wartime navy but antagonized Secretary of the Navy Frank Knox sufficiently to result in the aviator's transfer—and virtual exile—to the Pacific. Once there, however, Towers seized the initiative. He instituted doctrinal reforms that at first irritated his boss, Admiral Nimitz, but over time won Nimitz's respect, to the extent that Towers became one of Nimitz's inner circle of advisers in the war against Japan. This story, told broadly as part of my 1968 book, *The Fast Carriers,* is here treated in detail for a more thorough understanding of the great Pacific War. Nimitz would keep Towers on his team to shape the cold war navy along the general strategic lines that it has maintained down to the present.

Jack Towers, an outwardly shy individual, was branded a crusader and upstart by many of his shortsighted contemporaries. But beyond adhering to his beliefs and principles, he rarely blew his own horn, working instead within the system to forge what he envisioned as the inevitable consequence of technological change, the air navy. Towers was its first and foremost admiral.

ADMIRAL JOHN H. TOWERS

I

TO MAKE AN ADMIRAL

TO 1909

John Henry Towers knew nothing of manned flight during his youth. His awareness of all-steel battleships came about only through reading exciting newspaper accounts of the U.S. Navy's victories in the Spanish-American War of 1898. But he did know something about land warfare from tales of the Civil War told him by his elders. These accounts probably planted the seeds of his eventual attraction to aviation.

From the "Hill City" of Rome in northwest Georgia's Floyd County, paternal grandfather Colonel John Reed Towers had led the 8th Georgia Infantry Regiment in most of the battles of Robert E. Lee's Army of Northern Virginia, while maternal grandfather Reuben Smith Norton had watched Confederate and Union forces move in and out of Rome. But it was the experiences of his father, William Magee Towers, that most impressed him. In late 1863, as a teenager, "Billy" Towers had joined the personal escort of the celebrated Southern cavalryman Nathan Bedford Forrest. He remained with Forrest for the duration of the war.[1]

"Get there the fustest with the mostest," the brazen Forrest had declared, sharply defining the very tactics of surprise, flexibility, and concentrated firepower that would become the hallmark of military aviation in the next century. "General Forrest," Billy later told his sons, "adopted much the same tactics in all of his battles, that is to charge vigorously in the front, and at the same time to have a detachment . . . attack the rear around both the right and left flank with orders to make as much noise as possible, charging the

1

Jack's grandfather, Colonel John Reed
Towers, Confederate States Army, who
commanded the 8th Georgia Infantry in
Lee's army through most of the Civil War.
He died in 1903 when Jack was eighteen
years old. (Courtesy Lynne L. Riley)

wagons and into the rear. . . ."[2] Young John Towers and the family would
host Billy's wartime comrades at home in 1904 and hear the stories. The
memories of Forrest's exploits and those of other celebrated horsemen led
early military flyers to regard their airplanes as the "cavalry of the sky."[3]

The Southern defeat tested the mettle of these transplanted New England settlers, who before the Civil War had founded the Hill City among the
rolling farmlands of Georgia's Coosa Valley. But they endured the privations
of Reconstruction to raise the next generation in the same virtues of hard
work and no nonsense. Billy Towers became a blacksmith, took the nickname
"Captain Billy," courted and in 1875 married the pretty daughter of Reuben,
Mary Caroline Norton, five years his junior. They moved in with the sixty-

Jack's father, William M. "Captain Billy"
Towers, about 1895, when Jack was ten years
old. (Courtesy W. T. Maddox)

nine-year-old widower Norton to raise a family of seven children in the
big two-story white frame house near the center of Rome. In that house, on
30 January 1885, their sixth child and fourth son was born—John Henry
Towers, named after his grandfather, then keeper of the Georgia State
Penitentiary.

All the Towers children were short like their parents but otherwise
robust from the bracing, healthy climate and abundance of farm products.
Young John survived the usual childhood illnesses and, having entered the
world near the bottom of the family hierarchy, was toughened by the teasing
and roughhousing of his three older brothers, Reuben, Will, and Fullton, "the
Major." One thing he could not overcome, however, was a minor eye
defect—weak color perception, potential trouble in the navy.[4]

Young John also inherited his parents' tireless energy and resourcefulness as they struggled to make ends meet, Captain Billy as owner of a farm
implements company, collector of minerals and rainfall figures, and city
elder. He learned discipline from the white-whiskered patriarch Reuben,

Reuben S. Norton at age eighty-six in 1894
with his brood of Towers and Norton
grandchildren. John is second from right.
(Courtesy W. T. Maddox)

being forced to cut a sturdy branch from a bridal wreath tree for punishment over misdemeanors but earning the old man's respect as a lad who was "all set for fair." John only tolerated his three sisters, Jessie, Nanie, and Ruthie; when asked the number of children in the family, he answered, "Seven, that is, if you count the girls!" Throughout his childhood, he savored the attention of "Big Sue" Griffith, the family's black maid and cook of good and warm heart who plied him with "wet hash"—hash mixed with milk.[5]

In such a stable and loving home environment, Towers soon became self-reliant, disciplined, and meticulously punctual. He was so reserved, however, that he would cross a street to avoid speaking with someone. In 1890, at the age of five and to his mother's horror, he solved a toothache by taking a dollar from his piggy bank and paying a quack dentist at the fair grounds to pull it out. Fortunately, it was only a baby tooth. He earned dimes doing chores for his brothers and enjoyed the companionship of the family's three pet dogs.[6]

A lover of the outdoors, the diminutive child earned a reputation as a "water dog"—one of the first kids every spring to jump into the old water-hole off the Oostanaula River just behind his home. Once Jack fashioned a make-believe ship, replete with cabins and flag, against a side of the barn. Later he was allowed to handle one of the four oars in the family's old life boat, obtained from one of the river steamers still plying the Oostanaula. This craft was eventually replaced by a motorboat, the very first on the river. Jack became an expert at tinkering with its balky engine—a skill that would pay dividends when he worked with naval guns and early aircraft. An expert swimmer and diver, the youngster was unfazed the one time he was swept over the falls. He enjoyed camping every summer with his father and brothers and developed a keen interest in astronomy—which would reap handsome dividends when he navigated ships and aircraft by the sun and stars.[7]

Intelligent, studious, and inquisitive by nature and upbringing, Towers profited greatly from Rome's school system. From the day he entered the first grade, in 1892, he attracted the notice of his teachers. One of them, J. C. Harris, remembered young John as "a very quiet, very modest, very lovely child . . . distinguished from the average boy by a quietness of movement and a steadiness of application that made him the joy of the teachers at once." In fact, Harris recalled in 1919, "he was awarded the first honor in every class of which he was a member," owing to his punctuality as well as his mind. John missed only one day of class in nine years and that to attend Grandfather Norton's funeral in 1897. His "habitual mood" was one of seriousness and sedateness, like that of a grown man, and he spoke in a low voice. But all his teachers remarked on his "fine sense of humor" and great capacity for joy.[8]

The family broadened the children's range of experience by taking them on summer trips. In Rome such family concern for learning was not universal; Towers once remarked that many of his childhood acquaintances probably drank themselves to death in due course, having wasted their lives. Captain Billy instilled a hatred of strong drink in his offspring and told John that if he refrained from drinking or smoking until his twenty-first birthday, he would give him a gold watch. Towers refrained, got the watch, and for the rest of his life partook of alcohol only socially (but then with *potent* martinis!). Once in the navy, he did pick up the cigarette habit.

Friends and family considered John, in spite of good looks that would earn him the sobriquet Handsome Jack in the navy, downright bashful. Part of the problem was his size. Still growing when he graduated from Rome's schools in 1901, he continued to fill out even through his years at Annapolis and aboard his first ship. As late as 1909, on the eve of his twenty-fourth birthday, he wrote his mother that at 5 feet 10 inches and 150 pounds, he was "almost the heaviest member of the family." Yet his erect bearing added inches to his appearance.[9]

Although detractors would later criticize Towers for being solemn and unsmiling, he shed his reserve when an occasion arose for fun. He differed little in expression and manner from his outstanding naval contemporaries during the Pacific war. He was not ornery like Ernest J. King, no more taciturn and colorless than Raymond A. Spruance, and not nearly as quiet and wizened as Marc A. Mitscher. Neither was he downright mean, like Richmond Kelly Turner, nor less forthright than Chester W. Nimitz, though Nimitz projected a more pleasant, affable disposition. These five future giants of naval leadership, like Towers, came from the hard-working middle-class stock of inland, agrarian America, as indeed did the vast majority of future flag officers who attended Annapolis in the first decade of the twentieth century—boys who dreamed romantically of going to sea.[10]

Many of them sought naval or military careers—it often did not matter which—only as a means of obtaining a superior and cost-free education at whichever federal academy would admit them. Towers certainly had no aspirations toward a naval career. He wanted to be a civil engineer, "to learn to become a great bridge and dam builder in faraway countries." But a professional education at a leading school in the North cost more than a middle-class family of the bankrupt South could afford, and though Captain Billy insisted his children obtain a college education, John could only dream of a place like Princeton University. And so following in the footsteps of brothers Reuben and Fullton, he attended Georgia Tech.[11]

At the not unusual age of sixteen, Towers reported to Tech at the end of the summer of 1901. Unfortunately for his engineering aspirations—but fortunately for the U.S. Navy—his roommate turned out to be a slovenly Yankee, several years older, rough, loud, a tobacco chewer who not infrequently missed his spittoon. Jack endured these indignities for months, studied hard, and received acceptable grades. But at the beginning of the third term of the freshman year, his letters to Captain Billy betrayed his unhappiness. One particularly bad day in the room, he received a telegram from Billy, "My friend Congressman Maddox has an open appointment to the Naval Academy. Do you want it?"

Jack took a long look at his messy roommate, eyed the big spittoon, and went downstairs to send off a one-word reply: "YES." Then he returned to the room and started packing, not bothering to complete the term. He was seventeen years old "and had never even seen the sea, but decided to take a chance."[12]

Captain Billy had arranged the whole thing with daughter Jessie's future father-in-law, Congressman John W. Maddox. Over the spring and summer of 1902 Jack helped his father harvest mountaintop fruit to augment the family's income while listening to the former cavalryman extol the virtues of a naval career. On 11 August, he took the formal entrance examination to the Naval Academy and passed.[13]

The newsworthy event was lauded by the state press, which had always followed the doings of the Towers clan, "one of the best families in Georgia." John was hailed as "a splendid young man" with "a very bright future before him," beginning with a salary of $500 a year at Annapolis and $1,400 once commissioned as ensign. "These officers of the Navy are the special pride of the government, and Mr. Towers will no doubt write his name in honor in his country's history." No doubt, as events would prove.[14]

The U.S. Navy was the shining monument of dynamic President Theodore Roosevelt, whose philosophy of American leadership and involvement in world affairs inspired Towers' generation of naval officers. The growing fleet of battleships required more Naval Academy graduates to officer them, and when Towers arrived by rail from Rome that August of 1902, he discovered his class of 1906 to be the largest yet enrolled—170 plebes. Each midshipman (the new rank replaced naval cadet), unless "turned back" for low performance, would spend four years at Annapolis, graduate in the rank of passed midshipman, then serve a two-year apprenticeship at sea before final commissioning as ensign.

On 29 August a medical board found Towers physically fit despite a "somewhat feeble color sense," which it disregarded. Outright color blindness was grounds for rejection mainly because the navigation lights on ships were red (on the port or left side) and green (starboard, right side). But the fleet needed good men, and Towers' slight red-green deficiency seemed minor. Next day, he was sworn in for an eight-year hitch "unless sooner discharged by competent authority."[15] After drawing his uniforms, Towers repaired to his room, an austere two-man space in the so-called New Quarters, an overcrowded five-story building dating from 1869.

A bright, soft-spoken extrovert from Butte, Montana, turned out to be his roommate. Lew Morton Atkins was nicknamed Tommy Lew not only for the British army sobriquet Tommy Atkins but because his older brother Arthur of the Class of '05 was already Tommy. For his good looks Towers soon received the moniker Hattie, a common name for Southern ladies. He was also called by his given name, John Henry. Jack developed over time.

Despite rather different personalities, Towers and Atkins soon became a perfect match. Tommy Lew would attain the post of company lieutenant, lead the choir, serve as cheerleader, play class football, sit on five extracurricular committees, and excel academically. By contrast, Jack, in the words of the *Lucky Bag* classbook, "lived with Tommy Lew for four years and never turned a hair." Towers avoided all extracurricular activities and concentrated on his studies. His classmates respected his reserved manner, quoting Fielding, "Thy modesty's a candle to thy merit." It was probably roommate Atkins, serving on the *Lucky Bag*'s staff, who wrote the prescient profile of Towers: "Has a handsome figure, walks and runs with a modified slit-bar motion. His true worth has never been appreciated."[16]

Towers took to the sea as avidly as he had to the Oostenaula River as a boy, deftly handling the academy's rowed and sailing cutters and steam launches, manning the yards of the new square-rigged bark *Chesapeake* (renamed *Severn* in 1905), and cruising in the coastal monitor *Terror*. The academic work required more effort, especially mathematics. Tommy Lew tutored him in it, and through hard work John established himself in the upper third of his class in his plebe year, the upper fourth in succeeding years.

Towers and his classmates were "run" and hazed by the midshipmen of the preceding classes. Foremost among future World War II leaders in '05 was Chester W. Nimitz, as well as two rambunctious roommates destined to join Towers in early naval aviation, Theodore G. "Spuds" Ellyson and Kenneth Whiting. Ellyson, who would "stop at nothing in search of a good time," said his classmates, was one of the first upperclassmen to report Jack for a disciplinary infraction—unauthorized "visiting."[17] Of the first-class seniors of '03, who commanded the four-company battalion of midshipmen, the most colorful was future pilot and Towers colleague John "Jang" Rodgers. Unlike Towers, Rodgers was a prominent athlete and bold, happy extrovert. The last in a long line of renowned naval officers, he "can see a joke ten minutes after it is perpetrated." Academically undistinguished, Jang Rodgers was a six-year man, having been turned back two years. He stood near the bottom of his class.[18]

In February 1903, when '03 graduated five months ahead of schedule to fill new battleship billets, the second classmen (juniors) of '04 took over the battalion. Their number included future luminaries William F. Halsey, Jr., and Husband E. Kimmel. Low academic performance and poor conduct reduced the size of Towers' class, but Jack and roommate Atkins accumulated very few demerits. The only time Jack suffered more than a five-demerit offense was when he was caught during study hours indulging in his favorite passion, bridge. Only occasionally did he report others once he became an upperclassman.[19]

Vice admirals of the Academy Class of '06 outside Pacific Fleet headquarters at Pearl Harbor in November 1943, with midshipmen photos superimposed. *Left to right:* William L. "Calliope Bill" Calhoun, Commander Service Force Pacific; John H. "Hattie" Towers, ComAirPac; Robert Lee "Eagle Beak" Ghormley, Commander Hawaiian Sea Frontier; and Aubrey Wray "Jakey" Fitch, Commander Air Force South Pacific. (Nimitz Library, U.S. Naval Academy, and Naval Historical Center)

The Class of '06 began to take on its own character during plebe year, foreshadowing the eventual wartime leadership of many members. Among the "brains" was W. L. "Calliope Bill" Calhoun, who generously helped the "wooden" men in their studies, especially the five-sport class athlete, Aubrey Wray "Jakey" Fitch. Another scholar was the erudite Robert Lee Ghormley, whose unusual facial characteristics earned him no fewer than one dozen nicknames, among them Eagle Beak and Hawk Eye. Frank Jack "Flap Jack" Fletcher was admired for his "sunny disposition and a hearty laugh" and for talking "forcibly with his hands." Ladies' man Leigh Noyes was there, along with Arthur L. "Bris" Bristol, W. A. "Tubby" Glassford, Isaac "Cap" Kidd, and John Sidney McCain, "the skeleton in the family closet of 1906." Fitch, Fletcher, Noyes, and McCain would command carrier forces in battle, and Bristol would lead them before that war.[20]

In June 1903 the dreaded "ans"—annual final exams—further whittled the class down until there were only 152 of the original 170 men. Towers did so well in these and in conduct that he ranked forty-second in the class. The survivors of plebedom then joined the other two classes for the summer cruise with the Coast Squadron to Bar Harbor, Maine, and points in between. They went on board the "Cheesebox" (the *Chesapeake*), the veteran Civil War steam frigate *Hartford,* and the *Indiana,* the navy's first modern battleship. Parades, dances, and lawn parties with New England girls offset their full work schedule.[21]

During the next academic year the battalion of four midshipman companies was increased to two such battalions, with the 267-man Class of '07 producing wartime leaders Raymond A. Spruance and aviators P. N. L. "Pat" Bellinger, J. H. "Johnny" Hoover, A. C. "Putty" Read, and Ernest D. McWhorter. Towers endured a case of the mumps but in March 1904 got his first career scare when the medical examiners ruled his weak perception of green to be unacceptable. Given the manpower needs of the navy, however, the Surgeon General overruled these findings and in May ruled Jack "physically qualified. Nothing abnormal detected." Towers was not the only midshipman with this affliction. To gain admittance to the academy, the brightest member of '06, Allan Chantry, had faked his eye test by memorizing the chart. Later he required waivers.[22]

Their second year gave greater social freedom to these mids, though Towers' classmates chided him for his apparent shyness with the ladies. In the class yearbook they said he "went to a hop [dance] once but has since lost his nerve. Never fusses [chases girls] in Annapolis, but writes letters on Sundays [to his family], laying grave suspicion on his actions during midshipmen's wooing times, otherwise known as leave. . . ."[23]

Such needling masked the truth. Towers was not a "Red Mike," a woman hater. His weekly letters home, especially after graduation, showed his delight at the chase. Once in 1908 he instructed his brother Will to "give my love" to a particular damsel in Georgia "(if she will take it!)—also to the other (No, belay the last, it might cause trouble!).)." His adventures during the summer cruises to New England ports kept him socially active.[24]

Towers served on the same three vessels of his first summer cruise during the second in 1904 but saw little more than the Chesapeake Bay. The open ocean, the mids griped, "was sighted twice, whereupon all hands straight way fell sick."[25] On the last day of leave, 24 September, a banquet at the New Willard Hotel in Washington marked the Class of 06's halfway mark at the academy. Towers sewed a "buzzard" on his sleeve as a cadet second class petty officer in the brigade, now enlarged with the admission of 284 plebes from the Class of '08. This group would produce major wartime luminaries in Marc A. Mitscher, Richmond Kelly Turner, Willis A. Lee, and Thomas C. Kinkaid, as well as future aeronautical engineer Jerome C. Hunsaker.

The first class graduated early on a snowy day in January 1905. Teddy Roosevelt himself gave the formal address, leaving the Class of '06 as first classmen in everything but name. Towers kept his grades up, but his annual physical in February gave him another "unsat" for color blindness. The academy medical board waived his disqualification until a final pregraduation physical to let him at least finish the course, but the possibility of a medical discharge hung over his head during that final year.[26]

Embarking in the two windjammers, four monitors, and two protected cruisers, the midshipmen on their third summer cruise enjoyed the best exercises to date. During nine days of rough seas, however, the low-freeboard monitors seemed to roll "through 365° at every swell, and all the old standbys manned the lee rail"—away from the wind. Half the ships went on to Maine, the rest to the eastern end of New York's Long Island. They rendezvoused next at New London, Connecticut, proceeded to Newport, Rhode Island, for instruction in torpedoes, then to the Washington Navy Yard for lessons in ordnance at the gun factory—preparations for the first classmen's entry into the line. Finally, on 31 August 1905, "we came in sight of Annapolis, that garden spot of the world," which most midshipmen loathed until they became alumni. "Tain no mo' cruise for 1906!" rejoiced Towers and his mates.[27]

After a diphtheria epidemic that delayed their return to the academy until mid-October, the first classmen learned they too would be graduated five months early, in February 1906. In jockeying for the coveted "striper"—cadet officer—positions in the brigade, Tommy Lew Atkins got transferred to another company to be a cadet lieutenant, and because roommates were supposed to stay together, Towers had to transfer with him as a cadet petty officer.[28]

Midshipman First Class Towers anticipated "big doings" as the chill winds of autumn penetrated his spacious room in newly completed Bancroft Hall. The staff kept the mids warm enough with what they called campaign drills—an entire week of "many long marches through [the] woods." Tailors measured the first classmen for their new navy uniforms, though Towers decided not to order his until the final physical examination since his color blindness might scotch his career altogether. "We are kept very busy now," he wrote to his mother, "as they are crowding things up for graduation" in mid-February. Just how busy no one could ever have anticipated, given the sorry events about to unfold.[29]

The seamier side of academy life centered around the hazing of the plebes, a code of social initiation enforced by little more than tradition and during Towers' years practiced in utter defiance of federal law. Of late, physical abuses had been intensifying, leading to a twenty-eight-round boxing match on 5 November between bitter foes, misfit James R. Branch '07 and a gentle Louisiana lad, Minor Meriwether, Jr., a turnback to '08. First classman Leigh Noyes, a friend of Towers, and Jakey Fitch acted as timekeeper and referee respectively while the two squared off in a secluded room in Bancroft Hall.

Both men knocked down the other several times, Branch once falling and bumping his head against a radiator. When an officer showed up, Fitch ended the affair as a draw and the fighters were put to bed. Later Branch could not be awakened. Surgeons were called in to operate, but the midshipman died, probably from bumping the radiator.[30]

A public uproar followed. Meriwether was arrested but allowed to resign. When the hazing continued the enraged superintendent, Rear Admiral James H. Sands, meted out severe punishment. Among the punished was future airman Pete Mitscher, turned back two years to the Class of '10. Jack Towers had other concerns. As feared, he failed his final physical examination. Fortunately, according to his *Lucky Bag* classbook entry, he had "all the doctors guessing as to whether or not he knows green from pink, but managed to get the benefit of the doubt." The navy needed good young officers.

Despite this, Admiral Sands remained determined to eliminate the hazers as undesirables. "If the Superintendent is not detached," Towers wrote to his mother, "I really believe that half of the second class will be driven crazy before they are through with him."[31] Sands, he observed, was a Catholic and "almost a fanatic about religion. His ideas of duty are almost beyond mortal comprehension. . . ." The duty Sands demanded was that all first classmen report every infraction of the rules, even on themselves for unintentional slips like not hearing reveille. If a mid did not report himself, then his roommate or another was to report him. Tommy Lew Atkins reported roomie Towers for infractions twice. Jack did not reciprocate.[32]

"Isn't that a nice state of affairs?" complained the future air admiral. "It puts us even below the plebes. . . . How we are going to live through it, I don't know. As an old officer remarked yesterday, if we live up to those ideas, we will sprout wings. Our Class is suffering now for the sins of all who have gone before." In the midst of the hysteria, Annapolis began to fill up with families and other visitors weeks in advance of the scheduled 12 February graduation. The first class counted the days. In Towers' words, "I am afraid there will not be very much weeping in our Class, not because of a lack of feeling but the joy of getting out overpowers everything else."[33]

Towers performed handsomely on his last tests, scoring 150.29 points of a possible 192. Top man Chantry scored 180.42. This placed Jack thirty-first—in the top 20 percent—in a class of 116 graduates, enabling him to graduate with distinction. Though 54 of their mates had passed along the wayside since the opening day of classes in 1902, the Class of '06 was still the largest yet to graduate. Twenty-two men of the class would attain flag rank, five in the four-star rank of admiral, nine with the three stars of vice admiral, and eight with the two stars of rear admiral, though several of these final flag ranks would be "tombstone" promotions, one grade up at retirement in recognition of wartime services.[34]

After "Sob Sunday"—in which midshipmen displayed the customary mock grief at leaving—the brigade held the graduation ceremony in the new Armory on the wintry Monday afternoon of 12 February. The Farewell Ball took place that evening in the Armory, brightly decorated with '06's colors of green and white. A legacy to navy tradition was provided by navy Bandmaster Charles A. Zimmerman, who composed a new march for the class to replace the customary "Home Sweet Home." As the local newspaper explained,

"When the 1906 March is played, only the graduates will dance with their partners, no other dancers being allowed on the floor. The new class march composed by Professor Zimmerman is entitled: 'ANCHORS AWEIGH.'" A member of '07 later provided lyrics, and it became the official navy song. The Class of '06 was the last one to be graduated early as a body, except in wartime.[35]

The academy experience had taught Towers and his comrades navy life, and its severe regimentation would be crowded out of memory by the inevitable sentimentalism with which they would view their formative years. Towers seems just to have been glad it was over, probably sharing the view of one midshipman who commented on "the sense of power and poise one feels one has attained as the result of one's training at the Naval Academy . . . , priceless possessions that one cherishes, but never mentions."[36]

The boy from Rome, Georgia—turned twenty-one two weeks before graduation—went home on leave, where he soon received orders to report to the battleship *Kentucky* for two years of sea duty in the rank of passed midshipman. He had all the makings of an excellent naval officer. If he continued his performance, he could reasonably expect to earn the two stars of rear admiral within thirty to thirty-five years after his graduation. Yet obstacles lay in the path of flag rank, among them his color blindness. Only time would tell whether he would make the grade.

The *Kentucky* was one of the navy's finest capital ships. Towers and three classmates took a mail steamer from New York to Guantanamo Bay, Cuba, the navy's Caribbean base where the battleship lay during the fleet's winter maneuvers. Reporting aboard 7 March 1906, they handed their orders to the officer of the deck (OOD), Lieutenant Stafford H. R. "Stiffy" Doyle. Head of the ship's prize-winning Third Division gun crews, Doyle would one day become the first captain of the navy's very first aircraft carrier, the *Langley*. Jack was assigned to the Powder Division.[37]

A proud and innovative ship commissioned in 1900, the 11,540-ton "Old Kentucky Home" was manned by 37 officers and 591 enlisted men who lived by the motto "Always Ready." Their skipper, Captain Edward B. Barry, exhorted them to practice "industry, success, and happiness." The *Kentucky* and her sister ship the *Kearsarge* were the first battleships in the world to feature superimposed turrets: the two main turrets each housed two 13-inch guns, topped by a smaller turret with twin 8-inch guns. The turrets were arranged along the centerline of the ship to deliver "superfiring" salvos, augmented by seven 5-inch/40 caliber rapid-fire secondary batteries in each

The battleship *Kentucky* in 1907. Note the forward turrets of 8- and 13-inch guns along the centerline and the seven 5-inchers of the portside battery. Towers commanded the starboard side battery and spotted ship's fire from the forward crow's nest. (National Archives)

broadside. Towers learned that new sleeve patches with the letter E worn by the best gun crews had been awarded upon recommendation by one of their officers, Lieutenant Harry A. Baldridge, and just been adopted throughout the fleet as a standard award. The E stood for Excellence, Expertness, and Efficiency.[38]

Towers plunged into his work with alacrity and quickly won the plaudits of Captain Barry for making "an excellent beginning. He is zealous and attentive." He improved so much during spring record target practice—the 5-inch-gun crews of each ship competed at ranges to 1,600 yards—that the captain transferred him that summer to Stiffy Doyle's champion Third Division starboard 5-inchers. "Mr. Towers," Barry wrote in Jack's fitness reports, "is quiet, attentive and systematic, . . . a good drill officer" who "never blusters, but he gets good results at all times. He has in him the makings of a fine officer."[39]

Although the *Kentucky* had a spotless safety record, Towers and all hands in the fleet were shaken when an electrical short circuit in a main turret of the *Kearsarge* caused a fatal explosion. Jack's nervousness after this incident proved well founded, for on 14 December 1906, while the *Kentucky* was undergoing routine repairs at her home port of Norfolk, she had her first accident. Towers was standing watch in the dynamo room when a large electrical switch short-circuited, the fault of a careless navy yard worker. The heavy shock jolted Jack and burned his right eye, blinding him for several minutes. As he recalled years later, an eye specialist in Washington decided that his "vision was not permanently affected but that a small scar would remain on the periphery lens, and much later in life, that the scar might cause trouble." Like his poor color perception, it would.[40]

Towers performed so well in Stiffy Doyle's Third Division that when Doyle was transferred in June 1907, Captain Barry gave Jack command of it. In addition, Towers proved so adept at spotting the fall of shot from guns that Barry's relief, Captain Walter C. Cowles, gave him the duty of permanent gunfire spotter for all 5-inch guns. Cowles further assigned Towers to regular watchstanding duties as a junior OOD. These skills prepared him for his final examinations, which he took at New York in November 1907 as the last step toward formal commissioning as ensign.[41]

Promotions of junior officer talent in the battleships were essential before the Atlantic Fleet departed on what would be a voyage around the world. The *Kentucky* received a new executive officer in Lieutenant Commander Henry A. Wiley—"small in stature but very erect and stern," recalled Earle Johnson. Though Towers did not care for this future admiral, Wiley was a skillful manager who soon found his most adept gunnery officers in Lieutenants Baldridge and Thomas T. Craven. The latter would eventually push to completion the first carrier, the *Langley*. Tommy Lew Atkins' brother Arthur also reported aboard.[42]

The *Kentucky* was one of sixteen Atlantic Fleet battleships at Norfolk that President Roosevelt formed into the Battle Fleet of the United States Navy in December 1907. Its endurance was to be tested on a voyage around South America, during which it would touch at major ports until it reached Baja California to conduct semiannual target practice before continuing to the U.S. West Coast. The fact that American relations with Japan were worsening, however, led to suspicions about ulterior motives for the fleet's dispatch to the eastern Pacific. After Japan's stunning defeat of Russia just two years before, American anti-immigration sentiments against the Japanese had raised their ire; bad blood was brewing.

"Everyone realizes," a suspicious Towers wrote to his mother on the eve of departure, "there is more behind the [fleet's] movements than is given out, but no one has facts. Great excitement was caused by the orders to immediately transfer all Japs. We lose our cook and wine boy today, and it is a hard blow. It seems to me to be rather bad policy, to do this in a lump, this way." But it reflected widespread American paranoia and fears over Japanese intentions; Japan had, after all, begun its late war against Russia with a sneak attack on the anchored Russian Far Eastern Fleet.[43]

In fact, President Roosevelt planned to send his aptly nicknamed Great White Fleet of gleaming white, ochre, and gilded battleships and escorting destroyers westward into the Pacific and around the world. It was commanded by the famous Rear Admiral Robley D. "Fighting Bob" Evans. Along with gauging the fleet's operational capabilities, the voyage would demonstrate American naval prowess to imperial Japan, a fact unknown to the crews when the ships sortied from Hampton Roads on 16 December 1907. The *Kentucky* brought up the rear. Supervising her Third Division, Jack Towers lamented the fact that the ship had "almost an entirely new crew." Of the seventy-three enlisted sailors under him, Jack wrote home that "two thirds of these 'men' are boys."[44]

As the Great White Fleet headed into Latin American waters, Towers continued to worry over "why we are really making this trip." Admiral Evans soon announced that the fleet would circle the globe after reaching California. This left Towers and his mates with no inkling of the strategic applications of naval power. He certainly knew nothing about the naval theories of the great savant of sea power, Admiral Alfred Thayer Mahan, who preached the necessity of keeping the fleet concentrated rather than divided between oceans in order to assert command of the sea. Late in life Towers would remember senior officers of the day regarding Mahan "as somewhat of a crackpot."[45]

All the name Mahan meant to the handsome bachelor was the admiral's niece, Denise, whom he had recently begun to pursue. Her father, Captain Dennis Hart Mahan, was the admiral's brother. "A very fine girl, and a very pretty one," Jack wrote of her to his mother. Her family "treated me finely ever since I met them," he had reported from Norfolk, "and Miss Mahan is the most attractive girl in the [navy] yard (to me at any rate and I think to all the others)."[46]

After spending Christmas at Trinidad, the fleet steamed at eleven knots to buck tropical heat and a bad storm in the run south. On the morning of 6 January 1908 Neptunus Rex and his court of *Kentucky* Shellbacks carried

Ensign John H. Towers in formal dress
uniform, with fore-and-aft hat, about 1909
(Towers collection)

out the traditional crossing-the-equator ceremonies for novice Pollywogs. Towers exercised the officer's option of buying a forfeit from the rough physical hazing with two dozen bottles of beer. He was content merely to look on during the riotous frolic, while the ship's band played such memorable tunes as "There's Room for All of Us on the Trolley" and "A Lemon in the Garden of Love." Jack noted that the role of venerable recorder, Davy Jones, was filled by "a man who has served 22 years in the British and 21 in the U.S. Navy!"[47]

By day, Towers had his division overhaul its seven 5-inch guns. Off watch he slept through the heat in his bunk in a two-man stateroom below decks, thanks to blasts of cool air from the ship's blowers and an electric fan turned directly on him. By now he felt "so accustomed to the sea routine . . . that I rather hate to see us going into port." When the fleet did arrive at Rio de Janeiro on 12 January, it was to rumors of sabotage and spies. Towers noted the ominous presence in the harbor of one German and one Italian cruiser. Next to Japan, imperial Germany seemed the most likely future foe of the United States.[48]

On 22 January, after the Brazilian navy passed in review, Fighting Bob Evans led his fleet to sea through a "fierce, driving rain." Three nights later, reported Towers, four cruisers of "the crack Argentine squadron met us and cruised along some one hundred miles with us, while a wireless confab was held." Jack knew something about the new technological marvel of radio electronics; when he had first reported aboard, the *Kentucky* had had a "Kentucky Junior" wireless boat rigged for experiments, and Jack had since become rather adept at handling the equipment.[49]

As the fleet headed for the Straits of Magellan, Towers boasted in a letter that the American warships "will be absolutely ready for anything that comes along, when we get at and pass the Straits. Nobody knows the game, but everybody is ready to play." The fleet entered the straits on 31 January, the day after Towers' twenty-third birthday. "Of all the bleak, dreary, wild and desolate places, this wins," he observed. "This whole part of the' world is strewn with wrecks." After coaling at Punta Arena the fleet proceeded to Valparaiso, Chile, firing salutes to the gathered throngs on 14 February, then headed north to Callao, Peru.[50]

"This is indeed a formidable fleet now," Jack decided, "ready at all times to cope with any emergency. . . . Personally, I have worked too hard, and, on the quilt, weigh less than I have before in six years." He now received his reward: assignment as a regular OOD, "in complete charge of the handling of the ship during my watch, and responsible for the lives of everyone on board. It is thrilling to stand there and say, 'Full speed!,' and feel her jump like a horse!"[51]

After visiting historic places in Callao with the well-known war correspondent Frederick Palmer, Towers was happy to be under way again, especially since Captain Cowles moved him from his double room to a single "wardroom stateroom . . . living with the older officers of the ship" near the wardroom dining spaces, "in closer touch with whatever may be coming." When the *Kentucky* anchored at Magdalena Bay on Mexico's west coast on 12 March, Captain Cowles assigned Towers, his best gunfire spotter, to report the ship's main battery fire during the gunnery competition. A floating canvas target was placed between 7,000 yards—the maximum effective range—and 10,000 yards away, roughly five miles, for the 13- and 8-inch guns to bombard simultaneously, while the 5-inchers aimed at targets placed at 1,600 yards. Towers "sat in a big chair on the fore-and-aft bridge, with a pair of $128 big field spotting-glasses, a midshipman with a range-board and telephone on each side, a timekeeper and two recorders behind." As the *Kentucky* made each firing run, three guns of one set of superimposed turrets fired simultaneously. Jack had to separate the plunging shells while they were in the air, "observe where all three struck, call out changes of ranges and deflections (different for 8″ and 13″), and call out to the recorders in what forefront square they struck."[52]

The Old Kentucky Home easily lived up to her reputation, shooting so well that she placed a very close second to the defending champion *Illinois.* Captain Cowles applauded Jack's performance as spotter and was pleased to inform him that he had passed his November exams and that his commission as ensign was in the mail, backdated to 12 February. When it arrived on 3 April, Jack put on his ensign's bars.[53]

Hastening to California, the fleet spent two months visiting West Coast ports prior to crossing the Pacific. At Los Angeles, Ensign Towers marveled that "nearly everybody owns motor cars, there being few horses." He led his division in a "grand parade" at San Francisco but otherwise suffered keen disappointment. The *Kentucky* was then overhauled at Puget Sound Navy Yard, Washington, where Denise Mahan's father was stationed. "I am a regular white-haired child with Mrs. Mahan," he informed his mother, "and always have been, also with the Captain, and their Navy Yard homes have always been a regular second home to me." But Denise now rejected any idea of courtship.[54]

Early in July 1908 the Great White Fleet, now under the command of Rear Admiral Charles S. Sperry, set forth from San Francisco for a nine-day run to Honolulu. There Towers surfed at Waikiki and went for a swim at Pearl Harbor, a place he would later know intimately but which had yet to become a naval base. The ships then consumed no fewer than seventeen days cruising from Hawaii to Auckland, New Zealand, and thence to Sydney and Melbourne, Australia. The American crews were wildly greeted by British colonials fearful of the Japanese menace.[55]

The printed program for the stay at Melbourne, 29 August to 5 September, was provided by the Continental Rubber Company and included advertisements not only for "motor tyres" but for airships and balloons as well. Boasting that the company had "the only specialists in the world engaged in the building of craft for navigating the air," the ad stated that Continental had produced over three hundred "balloons of various types" for Count Ferdinand von Zeppelin of Germany, for French "aeronauts," and for "the aero clubs of Paris, London, Berlin." In mid-1908 aviation generally meant dirigibles, the so-called aeroplane having yet to be perfected into a serious challenger to the airship. Towers no doubt read this ad, which would have reinforced a slowly growing interest of his in the notion of manned flight.[56]

Lacking sufficient coal, the fleet plodded north to the American Philippines, where Towers dreaded the possibility of being reassigned to gunboat duty. After the fleet arrived at Manila on 1 October, planned festivities had to be canceled because of a cholera epidemic.[57] Weighing anchor for Japan on 10 October, the ships ran smack into a violent typhoon with waves so high that a sailor swept overboard from the *Illinois* was lifted alongside the *Kentucky,* whose crew rescued him easily. The "exceedingly rough trip up" ended on the eighteenth when the fleet was escorted into Tokyo Bay by units of the Imperial Japanese Navy. With daytime fireworks exploding overhead, each vessel dropped anchor next to a Japanese escort ship, the *Kentucky* abreast of the brand new cruiser *Ikoma,* the first oil-burner in Japan's fleet.[58]

The visit of the Great White Fleet provided an unusual opportunity for observations of their future enemy by the young officers who, a third of a century hence, would lead the U.S. Navy in the epic struggle of the Pacific war. Their initial impression was one of a wily host. The sampans and solicitors who surrounded the warships "all appear very glad to see us, but who knows!"[59] Although Jack had to stand watch and do "code work for the Captain" until 22 October, his initial fears quickly subsided. "In the first place," he reflected at the end of the week-long visit,

> we have been treated as heroes, or kings, or something of the sort, all the time. We have been smothered with gifts, cheered everywhere we went, and with every want supplied. . . .
> Everyone thought, at first, that the reception was merely good acting, but towards the last, it was realized that it was really genuine. The children—and there are millions of them apparently!—were cheering all the time. It was "Banzai! Banzai!" from morning till night, and even then, they would wait outside any place where we were being entertained till late at night, to greet us with cheers when we came out.

The jubilant cheer, which would later become the shrill cry of defiant Japanese troops on Pacific atolls, meant "10,000 generations" (forever), and was uttered with both arms raised.[60]

The attention the average Japanese lavished on the seafaring Americans took some getting used to. Each officer, reported Lieutenant Tom Craven, was given free rides about the city in an "Imperial carriage at the sight of which all business in the street is suspended and everything comes to a standstill."[61] Towers went ashore and attended a party at the Imperial Garden given by Admiral Count Heihachiro Togo, famous for Japan's watershed victory over the Russian fleet at Tsushima in 1905, followed by constant entertainments hosted and attended by "all the celebrated men of Japan." At one affair Jack received a personal tour of the grounds from Field Marshal Prince Oyama, commander in chief of the victorious armies in the recent war with Russia. And he went to dinner "with a Japanese officer, the son of Admiral [Gombei] Yamamoto," chief architect of Japan's naval expansion.[62]

Amidst the flurry of activity, officers alert to the new phenomenon of aviation read in the Tokyo English-language press of dramatic flying demonstrations by the pioneer airman Orville Wright for the U.S. Army at Fort Myer, outside of Washington, D.C. These accounts awoke in Towers the possibilities of putting the aeroplane to use in the navy.

One story told of a flight in which Wright's passenger, a young army officer friend of Tom Craven's, was killed. "Tom Selfridge's death was most unfortunate," wrote Craven, especially for the apparent future of aviation. Towers recalled many years later that wardroom discussions on the *Kentucky* "were to the general effect that the accident proved the impracticality of flying. I was only a brand new ensign at the time, and my somewhat different views were received with polite disdain. Nevertheless my inherent interest in aviation was aroused. . . ."[63]

The grand visit to Tokyo ended with mutually hosted meals on the paired-off ships, including the *Kentucky* and the *Ikoma,* and considerably eased relations between the two nations. Only one incident marred the affair for the *Kentucky*: the death of a crewman from a lethal intoxicant drunk in defiance of a strict no-liquor rule.

While half the fleet departed for the Philippines, the *Kentucky* and the rest made a goodwill visit to Amoy, China, where Jack's shipmates won solid gold and silver Chinese trophies for taking first prize in baseball and second in a boat race with the natives and foreign residents. But the men were getting restless. Several were caught raiding Captain Cowles' liquor closet. So Towers kept his division busy preparing for gunnery drills at Manila, to which the ship returned on 7 November. "We don't expect to win any trophy at battle practice this Fall, as the range is too long for the guns, compared to the newest ships!" The days of the Old Kentucky Home were numbered.[64]

As were Ensign Towers' days aboard her, for he and "all the officers of the broadside divisions" now received their long-anticipated orders for three-year tours of duty with vessels on the Far Eastern station. His high performance meant a relatively choice assignment as navigator and ordnance officer on the flagship there, the cruiser *Rainbow.* Little did he know that the incumbent in the job, Ensign T. G. "Spuds" Ellyson, would before long become the navy's first pilot. Ellyson and two other future airmen, Ken Whiting and Jack's classmate Jakey Fitch, had been playing hard-drinking mischief-makers in the otherwise comfortless region of the Philippines and China.

Towers, however, was reluctant to spend three long years in the Far East. Moreover, he would have hated "to give up the 3rd division for I have practically raised that bunch." Fortunately, Captain Cowles refused to relinquish his skilled gunfire spotter and personally visited Admiral Sperry to obtain permission for Towers to trade orders with another officer who wanted to remain in the Far East. So Jack did not have to share in the "great deal of moaning and groaning throughout the Fleet."[65]

The *Kentucky*'s superb forward turret officer, Harry Baldridge, was being transferred to Washington to become assistant director of target practice. Towers' hopes of replacing him were dashed because Jack was the "junior commissioned officer on the ship now." The *Kentucky* did not win anything in the shooting at Manila, although Towers led sixty men through the surf to work the 3-inch field guns the ship carried, "and we made beautiful scores." On 1 December the fleet departed for Ceylon, a two-week run that enabled Towers to indulge in his favorite pastime of playing bridge "nearly every evening after dinner, at sea, when not on watch."[66]

Since mail often took three or four months to travel between the fleet and the States, Towers shared the crew's enthusiasm when thirty-three bags of it were waiting for the *Kentucky* at Colombo, Ceylon, where she dropped anchor on 12 December. A fine puckish side of Jack's personality shown forth in his recounting the swimming and water sports at a Colombo beachfront hotel, where, through some misstep, "I shortened my neck about 2 inches against a brick wall . . . !" He found the Malay vendors to be "great swindlers," and as OOD he refused to allow the snake charmers on board.[67]

With her homeward-bound pennant flying, the *Kentucky* headed westward across the Indian Ocean at the end of the month. The fleet held a signaling competition en route to the Red Sea, with the *Kentucky* and the *Nebraska* emerging as finalists. On Christmas Day the brazen Kentuckians asked the *Nebraska* officers if they could raise $500 to sweeten the kitty. They did, but when the *Nebraska*'s semaphore men, led by Passed Midshipman Newton H. White, Jr., won hands down, the *Kentucky* sent over a worthless collection of various foreign coins collected on the voyage. The *Nebraska* nevertheless celebrated Christmas Day with the jovial Lieutenant (jg) John Rodgers playing Santa Claus. White and Rodgers both shared futures with Towers in aviation.[68]

When the fleet reached the Suez Canal, Towers went ashore to see Cairo and make the arduous climb to the top of the great Cheops Pyramid on 4

January 1909. A major earthquake and tidal wave had devastated parts of Italy only the week before, forcing the fleet to scatter to different ports of call. The *Kentucky* went first to Tripoli in Ottoman Libya for two days, then on to French Algiers for eleven. Towers and a shipmate spent a glorious week with two millionaires, a newlywed American couple they met there.[69]

Coaling at British Gibraltar on 6 February, the *Kentucky* and the rest of the fleet then headed home, turning down a visit to England out of embarrassment; America's obsolete battleships paled alongside Britain's ultramodern *Dreadnought*. The crossing of the Atlantic turned out to be a voyage "of continual horror" through successive storms in which sailors were washed overboard. Towers had the conn as OOD when, after midnight on 22 February, the *Kentucky* dropped anchor outside the Chesapeake Bay.

Shortly after sunup, the Great White Fleet moved into Hampton Roads, having completed a journey of forty-six thousand miles. That day the ship passed in final review before the man who had sent them off, Teddy Roosevelt, and fired him a salute. In Washington on 4 March, Towers took a company of *Kentucky* sailors ashore and with twenty-four hundred other sailors marched in the inaugural parade of President William Howard Taft.[70]

Jack Towers' career had gotten off to an excellent start in the battleship navy. He had one of the most important jobs on one of the very best warships. He proved himself to be serious, steady, and not given to wild ideas or departures from the normal demands of his profession. Thus no one—least of all Towers himself—could have imagined that he would risk everything on an experimental toy like the aeroplane. Future admirals were simply not made of such irresponsible deviations from sanity.

2

TO MAKE AN AVIATOR

1909–12

The newspapers that Ensign Towers and the men of the Great White Fleet devoured once they were home again revealed a new excitement abroad in the land—aviation! Five years of successful powered flights by the Wright brothers had gone relatively unnoticed until 1908, when Wilbur in France and Orville at Fort Myer gave public exhibitions of maneuverable, sustained flying in their aeroplanes. One naval officer, Lieutenant George C. Sweet, took a ride aloft with Orville and pronounced that aircraft could act as "a scouting and dispatch unit . . . , to be launched and to alight on a ship's deck." Mirroring gunfire spotter Towers' ideas, Sweet believed that the fall of shells from ships' guns "might be reported from the aeroplanes and the range corrected to secure more accurate hitting."[1]

This need became especially apparent in the U.S. Navy's new dreadnoughts nearing completion. Unlike "predreadnoughts" such as the *Kentucky,* these behemoths, starting with the 16,000-ton *Michigan,* would have all big guns—eight 12-inchers—superimposed along the centerline for massed salvo fire and eliminating the need for medium-caliber 8-inchers. Towers, like his peers, sought assignment in the new ships. Late in 1908, while still in the Far East, he had "put out a few feelers in Washington about getting a new job, . . . and hope for the *Michigan.*" Moreover, there was "talk of putting a new billet in, that of 'spotter without a gun division' because she has such a big battery that the spotter, to organize things properly, should have no other duties. This has never yet been done, and the man that gets it will be a small celebrity. There are so many senior to me that are trying that my chances are small. . . ."[2]

For a lowly ensign Towers did indeed have high aspirations, and in his enthusiasm he let his hopes soar even higher. By mid-January 1909, though fearing assignment to a gunboat "doing Haitian duty," he had planned to apply for service on board the newer and larger 21,000-ton *North Dakota*. He intended to "try to get a temporary job on some ship till the *North Dakota* is ready, and then make a big try for her." He courted the officer detailers at the Bureau of Navigation (BuNav) to keep him in battleships.[3]

In the meantime, Towers helped put both the *Kentucky* and the *Kearsarge* into mothballs at the League Island Navy Yard, Philadelphia. He cast covetous eyes on the *Michigan* at a nearby berth. To maintain his special skills as a gunfire spotter, he requested and received temporary assignment to the Atlantic Fleet's battle practice during August and September.[4] In all probability, this initiative caught the attention of the assistant chief of BuNav, Captain Nathaniel R. Usher, who had choice orders of his own as prospective commanding officer of the *Michigan*. The captain surely met Jack during their mutual visits to the ship during her outfitting, for by September 1909 he had arranged for Jack's assignment to her first crew. That month Towers moved his gear temporarily to the old *Indiana*, lying next to the *Michigan*, where he found "a very congenial crowd" of fellow *Michigan* officers. Usher was a backslapping extrovert and veteran skipper whose enthusiasm to get his ship into service was infectious. Wrote Jack, "I can't see why they will wait so long. The Captain wants to walk aboard and steam right out to sea."[5]

In mid-October the *Michigan*'s crew learned that, after commissioning, their ship would rendezvous with the Atlantic Fleet at Guantanamo Bay over the winter. Usher included Towers in the first list of watch officers—"a bunch of the best young officers in the fleet," in Jack's view. He was the youngest by two years. His busy social life that fall included dances, bridge, tennis, Tommy Lew Atkins' wedding at Annapolis, and shopping at the new Wanamaker's department store in Philadelphia, "the largest in the world. . . . They sell aeroplanes there! . . ." This first mention of aviation in Towers' correspondence hints at his growing interest in the subject.[6]

The *Michigan* was commissioned on 4 January 1910. She featured improved gun directors that increased the effective range of heavy guns from the usual five nautical miles to thirteen (21,000 yards), just over the horizon. And scuttlebutt proved correct that she was the first ship in the navy to be assigned an officer solely as chief gunfire spotter. That individual was none other than Ensign John H. Towers, which made him, in his own words, "a small celebrity."

Wardroom discussions about guns became so intense that they had to be banned at mealtime. The concentration of effort put a heavy load on Towers, who was therefore glad to be joined by another spotter, Ensign Bruce L. Canaga '05. In Canaga's words, he and Towers "were stationed as far aloft as possible so as to judge the fall [of the shell] better, this for both day and night practices." Positioned in the crow's nest atop the towering newfangled cage masts, 130 feet above the waterline, they could shift ranges "to put the shell on the target"—a responsibility for the spotter, as Towers put it, that "could make or break his ship's record."[7]

Understandably, the *Michigan* did not win any gunnery trophy in her first year of competition; her gun crews were simply too new. But as Towers recalled, Captain Usher fashioned "a happy ship, brand new, fine spirit, earmarked to be the crack gunnery ship at the next target practice." The wardroom ban on shop talk proved difficult to honor. To muzzle one officer from talking of nothing but planting mines from the ship's boats, according to Canaga,

> Jack built a miniature model of a ship's mine from a cigar box and a tennis ball, painted the miniature a funeral black and tipped off the officer of the mess. That evening, when the band was playing the evening concert on the quarter deck, Jack led a white thread from the head of the table to the foot where the "mine" was, and on signal, each officer reached in front of him at the table, removed the silver and glass from the center of the table, and while the band played the "Dead March," the mine was slowly paraded the length of the table. That did, very noticeably, reduce the "shop talk" at the table for some time.[8]

That the *Michigan* tolerated such antics was borne out by "another of Jack's pranks" that Canaga never forgot. This was "to temporarily cross-connect the telephones of two of the senior officers during a very serious drill, so that they could talk to no one but each other. The story goes that, after the drill, a person could have written an entirely new dictionary of profanity from the conversation between the two officers on the phone!"[9]

Young Jack was feeling his oats as the proud new dreadnought operated between New England and Caribbean waters throughout 1910. At Guantanamo Bay, he never missed an opportunity to indulge in his pastime of swimming. During his tenure there with the *Kentucky,* he had even given swimming lessons to fellow junior officers. One morning he insisted that Canaga join him in a swim across the bay, which took an hour. When they

Ensign Towers (*inset*) and the officers of the *Michigan* in 1910. For some reason, he missed the group photo. *Center:* Captain Nathaniel R. Usher; *front row, third from left:* Lieutenant Commander Clarence S. Kempff, gunnery officer; *fourth from left:* Lieutenant Commander A. B. Hoff, executive officer; *sixth from left:* Lieutenant Commander David F. Sellers, navigator; *standing, far left:* Passed Midshipman Charles H. Maddox, radio expert; and *fifth from left:* Ensign Bruce L. Canaga, assistant gunfire spotter. (Naval Historical Foundation and Towers collection)

reached the far shore, Jack showed Canaga "a place on his instep where for about eight inches there was no skin. He had apparently kicked a shark."[10]

Between his spotting duties and leave periods in Rome pursuing local girls, Towers turned his eyes on the aviation mania now sweeping both America and Europe. Aeroplanes commanded the popular attention by day that Halley's comet got by night during that spring of 1910; American aircraft builder and flyer Glenn Curtiss proclaimed that "the battles of the future will be fought in the air."[11] The U.S. Navy tried to ignore such grandiose claims, but in September the Navy Department yielded slightly to mounting inquiries and offers of aircraft by assigning an officer, Captain Washington Irving

Chambers, the collateral task of acting as a clearinghouse for information on aviation matters.

As so often happens with military innovation, however, the seeds of change germinated not from the high command but at the grass-roots tactical level. The chief spotter of the *Michigan,* for example, found the range of her guns too great to allow him and Bruce Canaga to do their work effectively. They could observe to 16,000 yards under ideal conditions, but the shells landed as far away as 21,000. "It was clear," Towers said late in life, "that ordnance had outgrown the ability of the personnel to use it in that it fired over the horizon, out of sight. We couldn't get high enough in the ship to see where we hit. That was the real beginning of my interest in aviation."[12] In other words, Towers merely envisioned utilizing aeroplanes to *improve,* not overtake, the battleship. Spotters borne aloft could sight the fall of shell and correct the aim of gunners.

Just when Towers first contemplated actually entering the field of aviation is a matter of conjecture. The idea probably had grown on him from reading about achievements in aviation. Later he would reminisce that "in the autumn of 1910" he "had been thinking about it for several months." That he mulled it over for so long was entirely in keeping with his deliberate and no-nonsense way of doing things. In any case, that fall "the aviation bug, which had been nibbling at me, really bit me," in spite of the fact that "the old conservative Navy Department took a very dim view of flying."

The thinking of the high command and of Ensign Towers gradually converged. On the eve of the *Michigan*'s departure from Boston to visit European ports, 1 November 1910, her officers were sitting around the wardroom drinking wine and coffee. Suddenly, Towers recalled, "I announced to Bruce Canaga . . . that I intended to apply for assignment to Aviation duty. Bruce said: 'Fine, but there isn't any such thing!' We had quite a conversation, and I did admit I had been thinking about it for several months. It would be boasting to say I had visions of the future of flying and of what Aviation would mean to the Navy. It was entirely foreign to my character for me to plunge off into the deep simply for the thrill of a new venture, yet there was an urge somewhere. . . ."

Towers' conversation with Canaga was overheard by other junior officers, who passed the word from their end of the table up to the senior officers' end, where it reached the navigator, Lieutenant Commander David F. Sellers, a future commander in chief of the U.S. Fleet. Sellers "left his seat and, bringing his glass of port—the Navy was more civilized then—came down and sat alongside me: 'Are you really serious about this?!' he asked. At that time, I really did not know whether I was or not. I had never flown . . . , but there was something that made me say 'Yes.'" Sellers warned Jack "to be awfully careful because many an officer had ruined his career by trying to be a little too progressive."

Next morning, 2 November, Jack wrote a letter to BuNav asking "to be assigned to duty for instruction in aeroplaning. . . in case of the adoption of aeroplanes by the Navy [and to] be assigned to that service." Just as he finished, Bruce Canaga "passed my door with a paper in his hand and said, 'I am applying for Aviation too!'"—apparently convinced by Towers' arguments of the previous evening.[13]

Jack took his application to the executive officer, Lieutenant Commander Charles F. Preston,

> who simply initialed it and dismissed me with a gesture, and I left his office with a clear impression that he thought I was crazy, and perhaps the ship was well rid of me. Then I took it to the Commanding Officer, Captain Usher, who tried to argue me out of it. He was a delightful gentleman who would argue about anything, but he finally agreed to put on a favorable endorsement with the proviso that I should not be detached until after the Spring Target Practice. This was disappointing.

The letter was forwarded to the Navy Department, where the detailers at BuNav, never having received such a request for duty in a specialty that did not exist, made the only possible reply: "You are informed that your request has been noted and placed on file." This was dated 28 November 1910. Bruce Canaga was similarly turned down. Meanwhile, on the fourteenth, the part-time director of naval aviation, Captain Chambers, had managed to have one of Glenn Curtiss' flyers, Eugene Ely, take off from a ramp on the cruiser *Birmingham* in the Chesapeake Bay. It was the first time an aircraft had flown from a ship.[14]

The tremendous impact of this news on the British and French only heightened their enthusiasm over the visit of the Atlantic Fleet's sixteen ships to their shores. In the *Michigan*'s wardroom, however, talk remained all business, even at lunch, as a visiting French naval officer discovered. "Jack had fallen heir to a cowbell," Bruce Canaga recalled, "and when anyone talked too much 'shop,' the bell would be rung. This happened several times during lunch until, finally, the French officer said in a loud tone: 'Oh, I see, an American custom! When one talks too much, zey ring zee bell, yes?'"[15]

The fleet spent most of December at Cherbourg, and Jack took some leave time to visit the French aviation center at Issy-les-Moulineaux, the aerodrome in the suburbs of Paris. Never having even seen an aeroplane before, "I was very thrilled. Nobody was flying, but these French pilots were strutting around in extraordinary flying costumes, wearing those caps backward, and being followed around by crowds." Being "young and impressionable," Towers reaffirmed his desire to become an aviator, and he began writing to civilian flyers asking for their assistance in getting him into aviation. Though sympathetic, they could do nothing. Canaga remembered that Jack then applied monthly to be assigned to a civilian flying instructor.[16]

Meanwhile, on 16 December 1910, back at Norfolk, Lieutenant Spuds Ellyson applied for "duty in connection with aeroplanes as soon as such duty becomes available," to which request eight days later the BuNav detailers gave him the same answer they had given Towers. Yet, by sheer happenstance, Ellyson's application proved to be more timely than Towers', for Captain Chambers needed an available officer to receive free flying instructions from Glenn Curtiss in California. Ellyson was available, whereas Towers—still in Europe—was not, so Spuds got into aviation ahead of Jack.[17]

No sooner had Towers returned from Europe with the *Michigan* than headlines electrified the aviation and naval communities. On 18 January 1911, Gene Ely took off in another Curtiss aeroplane from a field near San Francisco. He landed on a makeshift platform aboard the armored cruiser *Pennsylvania,* anchored in the bay, then flew ashore. A week later Curtiss himself flew a pontoon-equipped "hydro-aeroplane" from the water at San Diego—the second person ever to do it. A witness to these events was the assistant engineer of the *Pennsylvania,* the colorful Lieutenant John Rodgers, who then went aloft in tethered box kites to spot ship's fire by telephone. Congress was impressed enough by these events to allocate funds for the purchase of three experimental aeroplanes for the navy, one from the Wright brothers and two from Curtiss. The suppliers agreed, at Chambers' insistence, to train one pilot and at least one mechanic with each plane. Spuds Ellyson was already with Curtiss, so John Rodgers and a mechanic were ordered to the Wrights' plant at Dayton, Ohio.[18]

In April, the question over which other officer to assign to Curtiss was answered when he decided to return from California to his headquarters at Hammondsport, New York, for the summer months. Captain Chambers had Jack Towers' application, among many others now coming in, and obviously saw in him the same steady qualities Ellyson had. With Towers serving on an East Coast battleship, he could easily report to Hammondsport to begin training. Unfortunately for everyone concerned, Towers could not be spared just yet. As Jack saw it, the well-meaning Captain Usher held up his orders for several weeks and spent "most of that time trying to persuade me from what he regarded as sure suicide."

Promoted to lieutenant (jg) on 13 February 1911, Towers directed his considerable spotting talents toward the *Michigan*'s efforts in the March gunnery competition in the Caribbean. Years later one of his sailors remembered his inspiring "kindness—yet strong leadership—and courage." In the last days of Towers' life, former Coxswain John Scanlan wrote to him, "Your leadership and understanding exerted tremendous influence on me in civil life. I learned much from your teachings, patience, fairness. In my book, Sir, you are a great man."[19]

That he was, for when the *Michigan*'s 12-inch guns blasted away at targets, "Jack placed the ship an easy first," as fellow spotter Canaga put it, earning the *Michigan* not only the gunnery trophy but also the very first battle-efficiency pennant ever awarded. In fact, the *Michigan* won "by such an overwhelming score," an almost perfect 99.929, Jack recalled, that she was selected to conduct a firing demonstration for members of Congress in the Chesapeake, further delaying his detachment. Only three officers from the *Michigan* received letters of commendation from President Taft and Secretary of the Navy George von L. Meyer for the ship's high scores—Captain Usher, executive officer Preston, and Ensign Towers.[20]

Captain Usher stubbornly refused to endorse Jack's transfer until mid-May. Spuds Ellyson observed ruefully to Chambers that of the five *Michigan* officers ordered detached on 23 May, the first two to leave, rather than Towers, were two of Ellyson's classmates assigned to the navy's rifle team! The interests of aviation, it seemed, came last. Then Jack required a week of sick leave for a phimosis operation to correct a minor birth defeat, leading Ellyson to fire off a letter himself to BuNav on 14 June urging that Towers be detailed at once to Hammondsport.[21]

Towers had discussed his application for flying duty several times with his father. Old Captain Billy enthusiastically encouraged him to go ahead with it, believing that "aviation would play a big part in the wars to come." Yet, when the rest of the family found out about it, in the words of brother Reuben, "we all thought he had prepared to commit suicide."[22]

Jack finally received his orders for "Aviation Instruction, Hammondsport, N.Y." on 20 June, just as the *Michigan* steamed into Newport. Captain Usher joined his officers in throwing a big farewell dinner on board for their chief spotter. "I am sure many of my shipmates thought it *was* really and finally Farewell and that a small allowance should be put aside for later flowers," remembered Jack, for the primitive flying machines were claiming the lives of many daring aeronauts. The menu even proclaimed, in large block letters, "TO THAT RISING YOUNG AVIATOR"—a barb aimed at the fact that even getting off the ground was considered an achievement! On 26 June, "to the tune of 'Auld Lang Syne,' I left my ship to catch a night boat to New York. . . ."[23]

Towers' departure from the big-gun battleships was almost permanent. He would not return to them for another third of a century, then to hoist his flag aboard the *New Jersey* as commander of the U.S. Fifth Fleet in Tokyo Bay.

Looking to the future with some trepidation, the twenty-six-year-old lieutenant (jg) made his way to the Finger Lakes region of New York state. "I had read," he admitted later, "what I could find about aviation, and it was practically nothing, because nothing was published, except, of course, the experiments of the Wright brothers and meager reports of what Curtiss was doing. I had a very clear picture in my mind as to the manner of man Glenn Curtiss would be," given his notable achievements first as a motorcycle racer and then at air meets alongside other aerial showmen.[24]

Recalling the flamboyant French pilots strutting around at Issy-les-Moulineaux, Towers anticipated that the thirty-three-year-old Curtiss would be "a dynamic sort of man with goggles on his forehead, wearing a cap backward, dashing about and followed by throngs. So I expected great things when I went to Hammondsport. I arrived there, a lovely little village on a beautiful lake, late one evening," 27 June 1911, though presuming it to be "a big place, because it was where Curtiss built his airplanes. I didn't know that he only built one or two."[25] Spuds Ellyson met Towers at the lakefront station and took him to the only boarding house in town, Mrs. Lulu Mott's, a two-story white frame house a block from the town square. Jack was "full of enthusiasm and resolved not only to become a pilot but also to fulfill my collateral responsibility which was that of inspector of construction" for Curtiss' two navy hydros.[26]

Next morning Ellyson took Towers down to the Curtiss factory near the lake. None of the students were flying because of high winds, so Ellyson sought out Curtiss to introduce him to Jack. Towers remembered the flyers in Paris,

> and I couldn't believe it when I met this modest, retiring man in an ordinary business suit. He didn't wear any uniform and was a very reticent sort of a fellow . . . who looked as though he had never been on anything faster in his whole life

than a tricycle. I was rather diffident myself, and that, coupled with my upset mental picture of him, did not put me completely at ease.

He did his best to make me feel at home, taking me around the shop and explaining what was going on, particularly in the way of improvements in design. As I hardly knew one end of an aeroplane from the other, this did not help matters much. I asked him if he would let me see the plans and specifications for those two Navy airplanes he was building. The contract specifications were absurdly simple. They covered about four lines. The plans were something else, and he took me to see them. He had sketched them himself with a carpenter's pencil on the white-washed wall of the shop. Those were the *only* plans, and that's what they were using to build those aeroplanes! The men would come in and look, and go back, and that's the way they worked.

[Later] Curtiss took me across the road to his little frame cottage to meet his wife, Lena, and he'd said something about having a drink. They make awfully good champagne in those hills, and it was a hot day. I'd accepted eagerly. . . . Finally he went into his house and being hospitable offered me a great big glass of buttermilk. Now, if there is anything in the world I loathe, it's milk, and buttermilk only more so.

. . . I didn't believe I could swallow the stuff, but I thought I had to try. . . . Fortunately, I made the porch rail just barely in time, and there was Curtiss laughing like mad, saying, "Why didn't you say you didn't *like* buttermilk?!" Anyway, that broke the ice and established a relationship between us that lasted the rest of his life.

Ellyson took Jack down to the field called Kingsley flats where the training planes were kept in an old barn. The two men looked at several odd-shaped flying machines being built on civilian contracts. The training aeroplane looked like the pictures Towers had seen. "Even to inexperienced eyes, it was a weird affair of doubtful mechanical ability. It was built largely of bamboo and wire, with linen cloth stretched over the tops of the ribs to form the wings!" It did not weigh more than 500 pounds. To Towers' amazement, it had only one seat, positioned in front with a four-cylinder engine behind it. Some of the students were tinkering with Lizzie, as the aeroplane was called. Students were also mechanics.

Towers, asking how a student got instruction when there was only one seat, was told how the throttle could be wedged to prevent the aeroplane from getting off the ground. After the student got the feel of the machine moving, "the wedge was replaced by a smaller one, and he could make hops across the field, and later, without the wedge, could get up high enough to circle."

Ellyson had Jack up three hours before dawn on 29 June. In addition to giving them exclusive use of the trainer, their early hour avoided the dis-

Glenn Curtiss

turbed airs of midday. Jack was surprised to find that Ellyson, not Curtiss, was going to instruct him; Curtiss was too busy putting the final touches on the two hydros he was building for the navy. At first light, "we pulled Lizzie out of the barn, and Spuds whittled a little wedge and put it under the throttle. Then with rocks under the wheels, he pulled the propeller through, and the engine started. He made what was called a 'grass-cutting' run hopping up the field, [got out,] lifted Lizzie up by hand [turning her around] and came back."

Ellyson then told Jack how to steer the craft. At the end of the quarter-mile airstrip at the other end of the lake lay a stone wall and high trees. Towers

> was afraid to step on the throttle, but equally afraid not to, so I pushed it down as far as it would go. The plane bumped across the field like a scared rabbit. When I was about halfway up the field, a little zephyr came along, and the next thing I knew I was twenty feet in the air and headed for those trees. I didn't stay there very long. Before I even had time to think, the left wing dropped and we hit the ground with quite a thud. I tried to roll myself into a ball like a tumble bug, but the plane also rolled completely over, and Lizzie and I went into a beautiful cartwheel. I ended up rolling the plane up into a mass of bamboo, wire and linen, [tore some ankle ligaments], and got all bruised up.

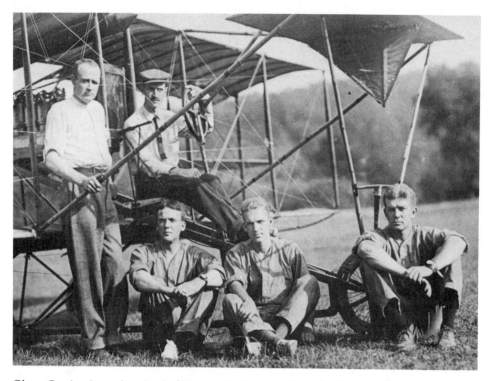

Glenn Curtiss sits at the wheel of Lizzie with his 1911 class of military students. *Left to right:* First Lieutenant John W. McClaskey, USMC (inactive); Captain Paul W. Beck, USA; Lieutenant (jg) Towers, USN; and Lieutenant T. G. Ellyson, USN. (T. G. Ellyson collection, Naval Historical Foundation)

What Ellyson had overlooked was that at 170 pounds, he outweighed Towers by a good 20; with the lighter load, the 500-pound machine had lifted off easily. After Spuds realized Jack hadn't been killed, he and the other students gave Jack "very little sympathy." Not until Lizzie was repaired would they be able to fly again. Jack, on crutches from his banged-up ankle, could not help much with those repairs, which took several days, but he did what he could. He also exercised with daily swims in the cold lake and, more importantly, used the opportunity to inspect the two planes Curtiss was building for the navy.[27]

Towers observed that Curtiss had added retractable landing wheels to his basic hydro, making it into what he called a triad (land-sea-air), the first true amphibian in history. The navy's contract in May 1911 had called for two hydros with greater lifting power so that the first of them could carry two persons. The first was named the Triad, though conceived primarily as a hydro, and was officially designated the A-1. Its single-seat sister was the A-2.[28] The two seater A-1, 29 feet long with a 37-foot wingspan and a 16-foot pontoon, had a "pusher" eight-cylinder, 75-horsepower engine designed to propel the 1,575-pound plane 60 mph, fast for the day. But it now failed on the engine block and had to be substituted with a standard four-cylinder, 50-horse motor.[29]

The A-2 was still under construction, the workers guided by the pencil sketches on the wall of Curtiss' shop. Unfortunately during Towers' first weekend there, a newly hired janitor "decided he'd really clean up, and the first thing he did was to wash all that stuff off the wall! When they came in Monday morning, there weren't any plans left for the plane that they were building, and Curtiss couldn't remember what they were like!" The result was a two-week delay on the A-2.

The navy's first plane, the Curtiss A-1 Triad, seen with its hydro float on the day of its initial acceptance trials, 1 July 1911, at Hammondsport. *Left to right:* Curtiss exhibition flyers C. C. Witmer and John D. Cooper; Dr. A. Francis Zahm, Smithsonian Institution; Marine Lieutenant John McClaskey; mechanic Jim Lamont; Glenn Curtiss; Lieutenant Spuds Ellyson; Captain Washington Irving Chambers, USN; Lieutenant (jg) Jack Towers; Curtiss publicity man Bill Pickens; and another mechanic. Towers' crutches are hidden from view. (Navy Department)

That Saturday, 1 July, Captain Chambers arrived to witness the acceptance trials, accompanied by Dr. Alfred Francis Zahm of the Smithsonian Institution and Aero Club of America, who would simultaneously judge Ellyson's eligibility for an Aero Club license. The Aero Club's standards were based on those of the Federation Aeronautique Internationale (FAI), and Ellyson's makeshift training syllabus for Towers was patterned on the Aero Club rules. Anxious for Towers to start his flying training, Chambers had laid plans for the navy's first "aerodrome," at Greenbury Point, Annapolis, across the Severn River from the Naval Academy. He planned to transfer Ellyson, Towers, and John Rodgers there later in the summer.[30]

Although the A-1 balanced perfectly in the air and on the water that day, Ellyson did not qualify until next morning, after which he convinced Chambers to let him and Towers remain at Hammondsport several more weeks so that Jack could learn to fly before they moved to Annapolis. Jack cast away his crutches on 5 July and the next day went for his first ride in the A-1 with Curtiss, a ten-minute hop that increased his determination to get on with the lessons. Ellyson shared his desire but made him wait because of Jack's stiff ankle. In fact, the injury would bother Towers the rest of his life. Another delay threatened on the tenth when Towers received orders to report to Washington nine days hence to take his promotion exams for senior-grade lieutenant. Such an acceleration in rank after only five months as a junior grade was common in the growing fleet. After getting these orders delayed, Towers climbed into Lizzie on 10 July for his first successful grass-cutting runs along the field.[31]

He slept little that night and was back in the pilot's seat again at 0400 for several hours of practice ahead of the other students. "If the weather stays good," Ellyson wrote Chambers, "I will start him on jumps tomorrow and I feel sure he will be flying before we leave here."[32] Jack mostly lived up to Ellyson's expectations. Once, however, he "overran the rough beach ground at the lake end of the field, was bounced off the seat and run over by the plane—actually being dragged along with my face rubbing the ground, held down by a cross member running from one of the rear wheels to the center axle. My injuries did not extend beyond losing several square inches of skin on one side of my face."

The morning of 12 July Ellyson took Towers up in the A-1, now rigged as a triad with a "land chassis" of three wheels. They made four short flights at varying heights to 300 feet to familiarize Jack with the sensation of being airborne, after which Ellyson turned him loose with Lizzie for his first solo "jumps." Towers made such swift progress in Lizzie that Ellyson reported on the seventeenth that Towers "now makes jumps the whole length of the field. I may put him in our machine tomorrow but I am trying to wait until I have the permission to accept the machine."[33] "Our machine" was not the A-1 but the A-2 landplane trainer, turned over to the navy on the thirteenth. For two days, Ellyson let Jack use it to make two dozen straight jumps of about a minute's duration to heights up to 40 feet.[34]

Engine troubles in both navy planes forced Towers to confine his training to reliable old Lizzie. He quickly progressed from straight jumps to "half turns," "taking off diagonally and heading towards one side of the field, then turning sufficiently to get back and land at the other end." Without much time to climb, and because Lizzie had too little climbing power, none of the

Towers and Ellyson share the hinged dual control of the A-1, rigged with her "land chassis" (wheels), mid-July 1911. This photograph appeared on the cover of *Aero* magazine, 5 August 1911. (Navy Department)

students attained more than 30 feet of altitude, though each had to scrape by a large tree at the edge of the field where he turned. "From the half-turn stage, we went to the full turn which meant taking off straight down the field, going out over the water, then turning and coming back to land [on] the field." At this point, the student had mastered Lizzie's capabilities. Jack hoped to reach this goal during August.

Because of continual breakdowns and winds over 10 mph, the young men had time to enjoy their summer. With fellow students Gink Doherty, Mac McClaskey, Becky Havens, and Ellyson, Jack relaxed at quaint lakefront Hammondsport, attended band concerts in the park and lounged at the new Park Hotel, on such occasions sporting a three-piece suit, derby, and spats and carrying a cane, which favored his sore ankle.[35]

For mobility, Towers and Ellyson purchased their own Curtiss-built motorcycles or borrowed Curtiss' cars or speedboat. Though generous in the lending of these vehicles, Curtiss insisted that any repairs to the speedboat be carried out by the following morning so it could be used as a crash boat. More than once, the men walked or swam several miles to find spare parts for the boat, then worked all night on it. That and repairs to plane engines made them into decent mechanics.

Curtiss' talented shop foreman Henry Kleckler remembered Towers as "serious-like, bound he was going to learn himself to fly. Quiet, too, just minded his own business, he did, not like Mr. Ellyson who was a boozer and more than once tee-totally blotto when he shouldn't have [been]."[36] When Ellyson drank heavily everyone grew apprehensive, for then he usually decided to go for a ride in his motorcycle. But Towers or one of the others would soon locate him "snoring away peacefully in a ditch."

Although Ellyson's drinking rarely affected his general performance, foreman Kleckler remembered half a century later that Spuds' flying "was erratic, sometimes. And Mr. Towers, he was junior, he couldn't say much. But once, he said he never knew what to expect when he was up with Mr. Ellyson." Ellyson himself was generous in his praise of Jack, once informing Captain Chambers, "I do not think that there are two 'safer and saner' pilots than Towers and myself," and later he observed how "Towers and I have confidence in each other . . . , something I fear I wouldn't have in 4 out of 5 men in the air." The fact was they had to do nearly everything for themselves, including paying work-related expenses out of pocket when the navy failed to provide sufficient funds.[37]

After passing his promotion exam to lieutenant in Washington on 1 August (backdated to 1 July), Towers dropped by Annapolis to see the navy's

Ellyson, Towers, and McClaskey pose for Curtiss while relaxing on the foot pier at the edge of Lake Keuka. Towers' two-piece swimsuit reveals his upper arms and shoulders, made strong from regular swimming and which would save his life during the celebrated crash in 1913. (T. G. Ellyson collection, Naval Historical Foundation)

first aerodrome at Greenbury Point, then returned to Hammondsport to make both right- and left-hand circles. Joining Ellyson for a trip to an "aviation tournament" in Chicago, he observed American and foreign aircraft, conferred with John Rodgers for the first time, and watched John's cousin, C. P. "Cal" Rodgers, perform masterful stunts.[38] Over four days, 15–18 August, Jack met other members of the rival "flying camp" run by the Wright brothers. The Dayton and Hammondsport schools were rivals because the Wrights had filed a lawsuit against Curtiss, insisting that their wing-warping system of lateral aircraft control had been stolen. Along with John Rodgers, the Wright gang included two young army lieutenants whom Jack met for the first time, T. D. "Tommy" Milling and H. H. "Harry" Arnold. Thus began a lifelong friendship between Towers and Arnold, for their careers ran parallel courses.

Towers wanted to fly in a Wright. Though the pilots didn't mind, Towers knew the Wrights' antipathy toward Curtiss men and so used "a little skulduggery," passing himself off to the brothers as "a wealthy young man who wanted to learn to fly." Orville Wright thereupon instructed one of his pilots, Frank T. Coffyn, to take Towers up. Jack regarded the series of maneuvers by

Coffyn as his "first real flight" in an aeroplane. When the Wrights learned Jack's true identity, they regarded Coffyn as little more than a traitor. At least no army or navy flyers were killed at the meet. Two civilians were less fortunate. The meet was an education to him.[39]

On 21 August, back at Lake Keuka, Ellyson decided to accompany Towers for a long run over the lake before letting him fly the A-1 alone. They took off and climbed to an altitude of about 200 feet when the engine suddenly quit, which was not unusual, Jack recalled, though generally preceded by "a little warning sputter." Expecting a jolt when the wheels slammed into the water, Ellyson told him to hold tight and dive upon landing. Recalled Towers,

> We glided down to sit on the water, and when we hit in a landing which would have been very good on land, I was shot out of my seat like the man comes out of Ringling's circus gun and straight through the front elevator. The shock of landing threw Ellyson forward, and he went under water with the plane which promptly turned over.
>
> We got to the surface at about the same time, neither of us hurt except that the front elevator, pretty strongly built, had taken a few pieces off me as I went through. The water was pretty cold and as everyone had been at the field watching the take-off, there were no boats ready. I swam in the lake every day and was used to the cold water. Not so Spuds. We were in up to our necks, holding on to the floating plane, and his teeth were chattering.
>
> A young fellow paddled out in a canoe and said he had telephoned the field, and could he help in any way? Spuds said, "Yes! Bring us some whiskey!" And he returned in a few minutes with a half-pint of Bourbon. I hardly drank, and Spuds was feeling the cold more than I was, so I told him to keep it all.
>
> Eventually the rescue boat arrived and took us back. They had built a big fire on the beach to warm us up, but we hadn't stood before it more than a minute before Spuds toppled over. He fell face first right into the fire [and was yanked out]. The combination of that near-freezing water, the liquor, and the heat right on top of it was just too much for anyone.[40]

Before the two men could proceed with their two aeroplanes to the new aviation camp at Annapolis, Towers faced licensing tests given by the Aero Club of America. The candidate had to fly a closed circuit of 5 kilometers twice and past buoys or posts separated by not more than 500 meters, to execute "an uninterrupted series of figures 8" around the markers, to do it all at a minimum altitude of 50 meters, and to land and cut the motor within 50 meters of a preselected point. A representative of the Aero Club arrived to act as judge.[41]

Lieutenant Towers on the cover of *Aero* magazine.

For Towers' test, Ellyson installed an eight-cylinder engine borrowed from Curtiss in the A-2, rigged with wheels. The weather stayed fair enough for Jack to practice in the single-seat plane on 10 September. Next day, after one unsuccessful try, he made the first of the two prescribed flights, reaching 450 feet in the sixteen-minute hop, but did not fulfill the requirement in two subsequent tries. Early autumn winds prevented another try until the thirteenth, when he decided to try in spite of gusts. After one unsuccessful attempt, he soared up to 300 feet and completed his figure 8s in fifteen minutes. According to *Aero* magazine, he "handled the machine with exceptional skill in a strong wind that would have taxed the ingenuity of the most skillful aviator."[42]

That evening Ellyson fired off a telegram to Captain Chambers: "TOWERS WON LICENSE THIS AFTERNOON." Aero Club aviator certificate number 62, issued under FAI rules, was officially awarded the next day, 14 September. And *Aero* put him on the cover of its 23 September issue, lauding him as "a young man of exceptional skill in mechanics."[43]

Exuberant, Jack took the A-2 up again on the sixteenth and spent more than five hours aloft in no fewer than eighteen hops on the seventeenth, once pushing the machine up to an unprecedented altitude of 2,100 feet. Then he departed for Annapolis with two navy mechanics and both planes, Ellyson to follow later. Towers left the Curtiss school with some regret, for he had been privileged to work closely with so many pioneers.[44] Having learned to fly in just ten weeks, during much of that time beset with malfunctioning or grounded flying machines, he was nevertheless ready to initiate formal training and testing as administrative control of the tiny aeronautical contingent passed directly to the navy.

Towers and his generation of officers represented a new breed in the U.S. Navy: managers and specialized engineers, not outside the traditional surface line but part of it, as Towers would always insist. These first flyers—and their peers in submarines, diesel propulsion, and communications electronics— were innovators willing to experiment with new technologies, integrate them into the operating fleet, and wage political struggles to gain acceptance by more conservative seniors, the Congress, and the public. A "skill group" formed, at first consisting only of Chambers, Ellyson, Rodgers, and Towers, the elite nucleus around which would gather an ever-widening circle of experts. Elitism of any kind breeds suspicion in those outside it; this would prove to be a source of service tension.[45]

Annapolis received the airmen with mixed feelings. The Engineering Experiment Station adjacent to the aviation camp at Greenbury Point could help in limited ways thanks to its elitist engineers—Captain Thomas W. Kinkaid, its head, and the executive officer, Lieutenant Ernest J. King. In contrast, the superintendent of the Naval Academy across the Severn River, Captain John H. Gibbons, utterly disinterested in aviation, provided the airmen only with a temperamental old motorboat to transport them between their in-town quarters at Carvel Hall and Greenbury Point. Worse, the aviation camp was still little more than a cornfield, which Towers and his two enlisted men had to clear away.[46]

The transfer to Annapolis enabled Ellyson and Towers to mix socially and professionally with their army counterparts based at College Park, Maryland, near Washington. Towers and Arnold became especially close. Arnold called Towers by his academy nickname Hattie, while Jack called him Harry, although Arnold's rosy personality soon had most people addressing him as Hap. Jack once invited him to a formal affair in Annapolis at which the fun-loving two, being of similar size and feeling playful after several cocktails, swapped uniforms to the displeasure of their superiors.[47]

On 30 September 1911 Towers and his mechanics pushed the A-1 Triad down a specially constructed ramp into the Severn for a short solo hop. Three more solos, made on 3 October, impressed Captain Kinkaid: "Lieutenant Towers made a very pretty trip around the harbor, coming down to the water at intervals, and skimming along."[48] Ellyson checked in next day and flew the Triad the following week in his new role as instructor, with Jack as assistant instructor. John Rodgers would operate as instructor in the Wright B-1 landplane, though he was absent at this time helping cousin Cal in a cross-country flying marathon.

On Wednesday afternoon, 4 October, when Ellyson and Towers were seated in the A-1 in the doorway of the hangar, "we heard something strike the radiator directly behind us. Turning quickly we saw water spouting from a hole in the metal . . . caused by a bullet which had passed directly between us. With this clue it did not require much to discern that the hangar had been located in a dead line with the Naval Academy rifle range so that any shots passing over the butts pierced the wooden walls." As a result, flying had to be suspended each Wednesday and Friday when the midshipmen held target practice.

Also ominous were the stiff autumn breezes. Captain Chambers, anxious to test the A-1 for endurance with a 147-mile flight down the Chesapeake to Hampton Roads, had Ellyson and Towers take off on 10 October. But they were forced down and had to be rescued—plane and all—by the torpedo boat *Bailey*. On board, Towers encountered a former *Michigan* shipmate, Ensign Charles H. Maddox, a pioneer in shipboard radio communications. The two men used the occasion to discuss the possible marriage of their separate technologies in an airborne wireless set for communication with ships.[49]

After repairing their aircraft, Ellyson and Towers took off again on 25 October for Hampton Roads, taking ten-minute turns at the controls because the 20-mph winds taxed their arms. Making 60 mph, they flew at 500 feet for two hours, landed near the Rappahannock River to repair a leaky radiator, then reascended for another half hour. Only six miles from their destination the radiator forced them down into an eight-foot surf, which damaged their pontoon. They spent a cold night at Buckroe Beach. Needing a short takeoff run to miss the breakers, Ellyson let the lighter Towers continue alone next day while he hired a car. The long flight made headlines and proved the durability of the A-1.[50]

Getting back to Annapolis was another story altogether. With a new radiator and pontoon, and after several frustrating delays, the flyers took off on 30 October only to come down twenty minutes later with a steaming radiator at the mouth of the York River. An oysterman took them in tow and filled both hungry aviators with his mollusks. A damaged water-pump shaft drove them to spend two nights in humble rural cabins. They fashioned four new shafts on a local blacksmith's lathe before getting one to work. Next day, they covered forty-nine miles before the radiator forced them to alight at Fleeton, Virginia. "When we taxied up on the beach," Towers remembered, "all the Negros working in the fields ran to the woods when they saw us." It was Halloween day, and the fieldhands, never having seen an aeroplane, thought the pilots were supernatural beings. They refused to help pull the hydro up on shore. Two further hops were abbreviated by a broken pump shaft and carburetor and gale-force winds, and they did not reach Annapolis until late on the third. "We pulled up on our little beach and waited for the mechanics to come out," Towers recalled. "We wondered, Well, why doesn't somebody come? We are heroes! Then all of a sudden, we saw two spurts of sand right in front of us. The midshipmen were at it again. So we cleared out."

This hair-raising adventure of the A-1 tested and demonstrated Towers' and Ellyson's skills not only as pilots but as mechanics as well, and experimental ones at that. The flyers also made night landings, using two rowboats anchored well out in the Severn, each boat containing a bucket of flaming gasoline. Towers was the first one to take off and land the hydro between the lighted boats.[51]

The onset of winter meant the camp would have to be moved to warmer climes, but Captain Chambers had begun to harbor doubts about his two senior pilots, Ellyson and John Rodgers. Ellyson "has got a bit of competition fever and wants to break records," Chambers confided to Glenn Curtiss. Rodgers was "a fine fellow with the pluck of the devil, . . . but his zeal . . . to do something more startling than his rivals is apt to get him off on the wrong tangent."[52] Needing more aviators with a mite less flair, men like Towers, Chambers accepted the application of Ensign Victor D. Herbster to join the camp at Greenbury Point. Nicknamed Spigetti or Spig by his classmates of '08 for his dark Mediterranean complexion, Herbster had been accurately pegged as "small of stature, but obstinate of mind and strong in body. When he commands, he speaks in a tone that is truly Napoleonic." Wanting to keep the Ellyson-Towers "Curtiss team" together, however, Chambers assigned Herbster to take flying lessons from Rodgers in the Wright B-1 landplane.[53]

On 15 November Towers made a left turn in the A-1 at 70 feet, whereupon a gust of wind sent the plane banking steeply. With its vertical rudder jammed, the machine turned sharply to the left and plunged down in a spiral. Jack tried to right the craft but lacked the altitude. The A-1 smacked into the river at a 45-degree angle. Towers, who had tried to jump clear, got caught in the wires and went under with the plane. When it bobbed to the surface upside down, Jack struggled clear of the wires and climbed onto the upturned pontoon, to which he fastened himself with his belt. The impact had given him a puffed-up black eye, wrenched ankle, badly bruised thigh, and several minor cuts. He had to wait forty-five minutes before the slow-starting motorboat could reach him. But he stayed in the hospital only three days.[54]

This and a crash by John Rodgers on 11 December enabled Ellyson to convince Captain Chambers that the budding aviation unit was not ready to operate with the fleet in the Caribbean; all three machines and four aviators should spend the winter at San Diego to work with Curtiss. Chambers, still concerned about the reckless Rodgers, who was senior to Ellyson, ordered two separate camps established at Curtiss' North Island field, Towers and Ellyson in one, Rodgers and Herbster in the other.[55]

On 20 December Towers, still limping from his crash, took Ensign Maddox and an experimental wireless set aloft five times to trail out a wire aerial antenna, but each time it snapped off in the slipstream. When the bitter cold frustrated further attempts, Ellyson gave up trying to fly at Annapolis. On the morning of the twenty-ninth, with the thermometer standing at 26°F and a fifty-mile wind blowing, he, Towers, and their mechanics broke down and crated the planes and spare parts for shipment by rail to San Diego. They eagerly packed their bags and departed for sunny San Diego—four pilots, four mechanics, and one dog, a fox terrier mascot that had attached itself to Jack.[56]

Ellyson headed straight for California, while Towers took emergency leave to go home to Rome. There Captain Billy lay dying of stomach cancer, and Jack was able to spend ten days with his beloved father before the old Confederate passed away the morning of 16 January, one day shy of his sixty-sixth birthday. Two days later, Jack boarded the train. As for John Rodgers, he remained in Annapolis, having become engaged to a local girl who tried in vain to talk him out of flying. They had not even set the date, when without any announcement he married her and whisked her off to the West Coast.[57]

During the unit's transfer, Captain Chambers expressed worry to Glenn Curtiss about the Wright brothers' use of levers for aircraft control, a much more demanding system than Curtiss' wing-tip aileron, which warped only part of each wing. Wilbur Wright so vigorously fought Curtiss in the courts over rights to any warping system that it damaged his health and he soon succumbed to typhoid fever. Brother Orville never forgave Curtiss and harbored such animosity toward Curtiss-trained flyers that he refused to accept Jack Towers as a bona fide aviator for another twenty years. Yet, according to one observer, Orville eventually admitted "that Towers had one of the finest minds in the Service. . . ." Taught to fly by Curtiss, Towers had naturally been biased in favor of Curtiss.[58]

Chambers insisted his pilots learn both types of pilot control. He informed Curtiss that he wanted Rodgers "to teach others than Herbster, and I particularly want him to teach Towers to fly that Wright machine. In my own opinion the Wright control must be very tiresome to the arms in fluky winds, aside from its unnatural features, but . . . I am extremely anxious to settle upon a *standard* control for the Navy. . . ."[59]

The competition between the Wrights and Curtiss Chambers saw as affecting their respective students, his pilots. "Of course there is jealousy among aviators. . . . [W]e have *got* to curb that feeling. . . . I begin to fear that Towers is a little jealous of Ellyson and I shall try in future to assign each of them more or less definite tasks, although I want them to fully exchange ideas and all to work together in harmony like Nelson's 'band of brothers.'" Lord Horatio's ship captains had trained to fight Napoleon's navy with one tactical method, thinking and acting with initiative and resourcefulness.[60]

Ellyson arrived at San Diego in mid-January 1912 to find that Curtiss had flown his first flying boat, a hull with wings and engine. The reverse of the hydroaeroplane, it tended to float nose down. Ellyson erected a tent hangar and wooden runway for the Curtiss camp, dubbed Camp Trouble by its inhabitants. Three-quarters of a mile away lay the Wright camp of John Rodgers. Overland communications between them, remembered Towers, was "by a circuitous path through the cactus and brush. Ellyson and I used motorcycles," and "the trip along this path required a degree of skill comparable to that of a tightrope walker." They gave destroyer officers short hops to gain support within the fleet and helped Curtiss test his planes and teach civilian students. Towers in fact took over most of Curtiss' own flying chores, since Glenn's pregnant wife had gotten nervous about his flying.[61]

Ex-marine Mac McClaskey handled overall instruction in the Curtiss school, ably assisted by an exuberant newcomer, J. Lansing Callan. Two Japanese civilian students reported in, Motohisa Kondo and Takeshi Kono. In teaching them, Towers showed himself to be an excellent and patient instructor. He acted as their Aero Club licensing judge in the spring and passed them both. Unfortunately, Kondo, Japan's very first licensed pilot, would perish in a crash before the end of the year. Japan's interest in the military potential of aviation became apparent when two naval officers were soon ordered to the Curtiss school.[62]

With the A-1 and A-2 undergoing repairs, Towers and Ellyson spent much of their time learning to operate the Wright B-1. Whichever planes they flew, the two pilots performed well and safely. One thing that bothered Jack, however, was the front elevator in the Curtiss planes. "It was much in the way and was frequently damaged. One morning I decided to leave it off and see what would happen. Nothing at all happened. In fact, the plane controlled even better without it, so they were then and there abandoned for both seaplanes and landplanes."[63]

Jack never failed to see the humor in spectacular crashes, especially those of the B-1, whose twin floats, of inferior design, tended to nose the plane over "on the slightest provocation. Every flight was an event, and we always stood on the beach and watched for the inevitable crash of one kind or another. On one occasion Rodgers was flying close to the water with a stop watch strapped close to his wrist timing the speed of the plane," the "notoriously underpowered" B-1, which never exceeded 35 mph. "He got too close to the water, the floats touched, and the plane turned a complete somersault. Rodgers swam all the way ashore, a distance of some 300 yards, holding his left arm out of the water. Then one of us enlightened him: 'Great work, John, the water wasn't over waist deep all the way!' "

Naval Constructor Holden C. "Dick" Richardson arrived at North Island full of ideas for hydroplane pontoons he had built along the lines of torpedo and ship hull designs. He wanted to learn to fly, a task Towers undertook with some dismay, for Richardson was a difficult student. Part of the problem was Richardson's size. Broad-shouldered and weighing 195 pounds, he could not fit inside the shoulder yokes of the pilot's seat. Tagged Big Dick, he was allowed to learn with his shoulders outside the harness and could only be taken up in the morning, the one time of day there was a sufficient breeze for lifting him.[64]

On 14 March Big Dick was ready to solo in a grass-cutting single-seat landplane, but since the air was unusually hot and bumpy Ellyson and Towers decided to test the flying conditions before letting him go up. They took the A-2, rigged as a landplane, on its first flight in six months, and each man had trouble. A whirlwind swept the plane halfway around before Towers could land. They waited nearly an hour, then Ellyson took off at noon. Only 25 feet over the Curtiss field, the A-2 dropped without warning. Ellyson recovered momentarily, whereupon a second "hole in the air" sent the plane plunging earthward at a 45-degree angle. It crashed and turned over in the field.[65]

Jack jumped on his motorcycle and sped out to the wreckage, where he found his friend draped over the plane, unconscious and covered with dirt. In a few minutes he regained consciousness and complained he couldn't see because of the dirt in his eyes. Towers "got some water from the radiator and washed them out." Soon the flyer fainted again. As it turned out he had landed on his head, protected by his helmet, but his neck was so badly twisted that it would plague him for the rest of his life. Under constant nurse's care for a week, he remained laid up at home a month longer and could only listen to Towers' nightly reports of events at North Island. Ellyson would never again be quite the same.[66]

The accident convinced Chambers to have the wrecked A-2 rebuilt purely as a hydro, while Towers and Richardson received the latter's "much advertised new float" as the hoped-for answer to the pontoon question on their three aircraft. Recalled Towers, "When it was unboxed I took one look at it and pronounced it useless. It [looked as if it had] been evolved by expanding the dimensions of a toothpick, having a regular knife edge, bow and stern, and very little beam. Richardson was very indignant and informed me that it was the result of months of calculations by some of the best hull designers in the Navy, among which he inferentially included himself." When Towers refused to fly with it, Richardson prevailed upon Herbster to try it in the B-1, whereupon Herbster promptly crashed.[67]

On 25 March Towers began instructing Richardson and Mac McClaskey in the repaired A-1. On 3 April they installed a Curtiss double-control wheel mechanism. They also installed the repaired wireless set, although it still failed to work. All the while Richardson urged Towers to try his toothpick-shaped float on the Triad. Reluctantly, Jack agreed:

> Foolishly I started the engine and pushed off from the beach without first having the plane shoved into deep water to try out the balance of the float. As soon as I opened the throttle the bow went completely underwater and the plane started into a nice submarine dive. When I eased up on the throttle, it started to rear over backward like a trained dog. I was out of reach of the men on the shore and there was no boat.
>
> There was no longer any question in my mind of testing the float but only of getting the plane back safely without turning over one way or the other, wetting the engine and delaying our flying for a week at least as we had no spare engine. Eventually I did get back right side up. Richardson had disappeared, and I found him in a tent busily working a slide rule to find out what was the matter with the float. "Throw that slip stick away, and I'll tell you what the trouble is," I said and proceeded to enlighten him in no uncertain terms.[68]

With the original float reattached, Towers and Richardson flew the A-1 throughout April, Big Dick learning rapidly.

For John Rodgers the month began with tragedy. On the third, his fearless cousin Cal, showing off in his plane over Long Beach, had ridden it to his death into two feet of surf. The official speculation was that Cal's deafness, the result of a childhood illness, had affected his sense of equilibrium: he hadn't been able to hear the engine to know when it wasn't "right." Towers and Ellyson were less charitable. In the postscript of a letter to Captain Chambers, Jack remarked, "Too bad about Cal Rodgers. He was trying to do a foolhardy thing, and I have heard, on good authority, that he had been drinking." To which Ellyson added that Cal had been known to belt down a few before several flights at Long Beach. The fact that Cal Rodgers' death was aviation's seventeenth fatality of the year underscored the constant dangers of the flying art.[69]

On 1 May the naval airmen broke their camps, crated the planes into boxcars, and shipped them off to Annapolis for the summer. In spite of mishaps and problems, the navy's four pilots had flown a great deal and had tackled, if not completely solved, several technical problems plaguing their three aircraft. Their mechanics had become highly skilled, which greatly enhanced the efficiency of the entire program. Best of all, none of the four had been killed.

As for Towers, he had admirably filled in for the injured Ellyson and matured as a test pilot and instructor. Naval aviation had survived its birth pangs, and Jack looked forward to returning to the fleet to prove the utility of the naval aeroplane.

3

SENIOR AVIATOR

1912–14

Of the four men who pioneered the navy's aviation program in 1911–12, Towers was surely the steadiest. Like Captain Chambers, he knew very well that the aeroplane was no miracle weapon—then or for the foreseeable future. But he formed his judgments about aircraft from hands-on experience at the controls, while Chambers tried to make decisions with secondhand data. The captain's young charges viewed his ignorance as downright dangerous where the design of their machines was concerned, and all three—Ellyson, Rodgers, and Towers—clashed with him. Only Towers remained determined to stick with it.

But even he failed to appreciate Chambers' delicate political position as a subaltern within BuNav who had to orchestrate aeronautical developments with other bureaus. Thirty-four years later, Towers recalled his and Ellyson's view that "Captain Chambers unnecessarily permitted himself to be pushed around." Though Towers "had a great admiration" for Chambers, he never forgave him for failing to get the navy to reimburse him and Ellyson for travel, repair, and other expenses.[1]

As for John Rodgers, he was so depressed by the fatal crash of his cousin Cal that he had his detailers inform his mother he had quit flying. Although Chambers kept him flying when the unit returned to Annapolis, Rodgers resented the captain's high-handedness and preference for Ellyson, junior to him in rank by two years. Seeing little future for himself in aviation, Rodgers decided to transfer back to the general line several months hence.[2] Towers never understood Rodgers' motives, "as we were not particularly close friends; certainly it was not fear, for he had not even the slightest comprehension of the meaning of the word."

Rodgers' decision was ill-timed, for the department, with an eye toward the next annual winter fleet maneuvers, ordered another hydro and two new flying boats. Ellyson spent much of the summer and fall of 1912 at Hammondsport testing the new Curtiss machines, leaving Towers in charge of the Curtiss camp at Annapolis. Jack instructed interested Washington-based officers in the A-1 and A-2. In fact, he took charge of all instruction and of writing the required weekly report to Chambers. He and Ellyson managed to move their aerodrome away from Greenbury Point and the midshipmen's rifle range to a safer beach adjacent to the Experiment Station. The change also solved their supply problems, for whatever the station did not provide them over the counter, their mechanics obtained through twilight requisitions. Also, Towers recalled, "by this time we had developed a nice scheme to obtain gasoline and oil. We would write to the various companies and suggest they send a barrel or so of their best products for test. A barrel of gas went a long way; average aircraft consumption was about eight gallons an hour. An average flight, more often than not determined by a forced landing, was about twenty minutes."

Towers and friend in the Triad at Annapolis in April 1912. This was the dog that helped save Towers' life in his crash one year later. (Navy Department)

When newlywed Rodgers departed in August he left behind a group of carefree bachelors who worked hard, played hard, and believed nothing serious could happen to them. Nothing did—yet. They were joined by Marine First Lieutenant Alfred A. Cunningham, who had taught himself the Wright method before reporting to Annapolis to practice in the B-1 and receive instruction from Towers in the Curtiss method.[3]

When Towers and Ellyson were not teaching at Annapolis, they flew for practice and to sell aviation to interested passengers. Jack took up old ship-mate Bruce Canaga and Senator James A. Reed of Missouri. During June he soloed in the A-1 over fleet units anchored off Annapolis, "saluting each ship by gliding," flew the Triad with Spuds thirty miles round trip across the Chesapeake, and with a student flew the rebuilt A-2 to Baltimore.[4] Towers' students learned quickly that his expertise, steadiness, and meticulous standards at the controls accounted for his zero accident rate. Ellyson was not so successful. On 31 July he sent the A-1 spilling into the Severn while testing a compressed-air catapult of Dick Richardson's; Towers helped the two men modify the system for another try in the fall.[5]

Towers flew so often over the summer of 1912 that by the end of August he had totaled 202 flights and 2,035 miles to Ellyson's 200 and 2,227 respectively. In August he made the second of two summer trips to Hammondsport, both at his own expense, to help test-fly the new Curtiss C-1 flying boat. The plane took off with an extra load of 360 pounds and handled well in rough weather, which impressed him greatly.[6]

Hoping to observe the latest developments in aeronautics at home and abroad, Towers prevailed upon Captain Chambers to have him sent to the Gordon Bennett air meet in Chicago in mid-September, accompanied by two students. Of the American entries, the Curtiss and Wright machines, along with Glenn Martin's, dominated the meet.[7] It was a French aeroplane, however, that enthralled Towers. "The Deperdussin is the most wonderful machine I have ever seen, and it is extremely simple," he reported. "The stream lines are almost perfect, and the whole finish is so far ahead of anything in this country that there is no comparison." The simplicity to which Towers referred was the single system of pilot control; the plane was steered with a foot rudder bar, as opposed to the Curtiss steering wheel or Wright levers. Jack thought some of the entries "of the tractor type"—propeller in front—"appeared rather good, but very rottenly constructed and braced." But Chambers was not prepared to adopt new-fangled European ideas or tractors over pushers.[8]

Towers was anxious to begin instructing officers at Annapolis while the good flying weather held. He and Ellyson began with another marine, Second Lieutenant Bernard L. "Barney" Smith, training him in the A-2. To delegate responsibility for the equipment, in October Ellyson assigned each plane to one of his pilots: Towers took charge of the A-2, Alfred Cunningham the B-1, while an enterprising Vic Herbster prevailed upon Chambers to let him construct another Wright hydro from spare parts of the single-motor B-1. The new B-2 had two engines and became Herbster's sole responsibility. Barney Smith was to have taken over the A-1, but on the sixteenth Ellyson managed to pile up the newly repaired Triad during a landing. Nearly a total loss, the navy's very first plane had to be scrapped.[9]

Unlike Ellyson, Towers kept performing without mishap. While his roommate's plans had a way of leaking to the press, publicity-shy Jack decided to try to set an endurance record for hydros—"to test endurance of operator, motor and structural part[s] of Curtiss aeroplanes"—without fanfare. The previous record had been established at two and a half hours in December by the civilian Harry Atwood. Jack set his sights on doubling that time aloft, which would also beat the navy record of two hours, two minutes.

He fitted regular extension panels onto the upper wing of the A-2 for an extra 17 square feet, giving added lift. He mounted an extra 10-gallon gas tank over the existing two tanks for a total fuel capacity of 42 gallons for the Curtiss 80-horsepower engine. In addition, to prevent the radiator from overheating in flight as was its custom on long hops, he placed a 1-gallon rubber water bottle on top of it. All these devices could be reached and thus regulated from the pilot's seat. His only instrument was an aneroid barometer, forerunner of the altimeter; he attached it to a cord around his neck.

At 0650 on 6 October 1912, Jack lifted the A-2 off the Severn and coolly piloted the machine through the hazy skies over Annapolis at altitudes between 600 and 700 feet and at an average speed of 62 mph for two hours and fifteen minutes. When he could not cut in the reserve fuel, he stood up and made the switchover manually, during which the hydro dropped several hundred feet. He then calmly regained his cruising altitude and droned on in circles amidst clearing skies and 12-mph winds for four more hours. Finally, at 1300, the motor stopped at 500 feet. His gas spent, Jack landed the A-2. He had stayed aloft a phenomenal six hours, ten minutes, and thirty-five seconds. Even the radiator had cooperated, never requiring reserve water.

Not only had Towers beaten Atwood by almost four hours and set a new world's endurance record for hydros—which would stand for two and a half years—but he had even bested army Captain Paul Beck's endurance record in any American aircraft, set the previous April, by almost two hours. Furthermore, he had covered around 389 miles in his circular odyssey, which more than doubled the American distance record of 176 miles. Since his mileage count was unofficial, however, he made no claim to this honor.[10]

Most importantly, Towers had impressed the admirals with the staying power of a naval aircraft. The same month he demonstrated the A-2's utility to two officers destined to play key roles in the future of naval aviation. On 11 October he took up Captain Kinkaid's executive officer at the Experiment Station, Lieutenant Ernest King. King tried his hand at the controls and thoroughly enjoyed the ten-minute flight, though he was not ready to buy Jack's arguments about the importance of aviation for the navy. On the twenty-third, Jack's passenger was Captain Noble E. Irwin, later to administer naval aviation during World War I. As the campaign for aviation escalated, Towers became a leading if unobtrusive advocate.[11]

The question of the aeroplane's ability to detect submarines was tested over the month commencing the last week in October. During this time Towers was brought into direct contact with his future boss in the war against Japan, Chester Nimitz. In command of the Atlantic Fleet submarine flotilla, Lieutenant Nimitz met with Towers to plan maneuvers with the underwater boats at the entrance to the Severn River. The subs submerged while Towers, in the A-2, and Herbster, in the B-2, flew at different altitudes trying to sight them. The two planes occasionally carried submarine officers, who picked out the periscopes and escaping bubbles of gas but, in the clouded water of the Chesapeake, only once discerned the shape of a sub.

Meanwhile, more officers were accepted as pilot trainees, some after taking demonstration hops. One of these was the enthusiastic Lieutenant Pat Bellinger, another Ensign Godfrey de C. Chevalier. Word came that instead of the anticipated Pat Bellinger one Ensign William Devotie Billingsley would be assigned. A BuNav detailer had confused the two names, which Bellinger quickly corrected, though Billingsley told the detailer he'd like to stay on as well. So Towers taught Barney Smith, "Chevy" Chevalier, and Pat Bellinger in the A-2. Herbster shared the B-2's controls with Billingsley, while "Cunny" Cunningham spent the fall overhauling the B-1.[12]

Spuds Ellyson remained so busy testing new aircraft and Dick Richardson's improved catapult that he was prevented from finally accompanying the aviation unit to winter maneuvers with the Atlantic Fleet in the Caribbean. Operational command therefore fell to Towers. Ellyson's new bride, with whom he had eloped in mid-November, did not like Jack when she met him

Naval aviation camp at Fisherman's Point, Guantanamo Bay, Cuba, early in 1913, with a battleship (*left, background*) and assorted fleet units at anchor. Towers' command included four tent hangars. The two in the center contain the Wright B-1 and B-2 plus twenty-one berthing tents, two mess tents, and one tent each for headquarters, stores, carpentry work, and cooking. (T. G. Ellyson collection, Naval Historical Foundation)

and suggested to her husband that Jack had done him in. Ellyson did not buy this; he continued to regard Jack as a friend. But Ellyson's disappointment at being kept in Washington further soured his relations with Chambers.[13]

Towers, with his first command one month shy of his twenty-eighth birthday, loaded the A-2, B-1, B-2, and new A-3 onto the collier *Sterling* for the passage south; the C-1 flying boat would follow later. Jack boarded the new battleship *Utah* and departed three days later, his orders being to get the senior officers of the Atlantic Fleet "interested" in aviation. He hoped to do it by proving the utility of his seaplanes as scouts and by taking the admirals aloft as passengers. He had a lot of selling to do. The fleet commander, Rear Admiral Charles J. Badger, "considered aviation a game for fools and nitwits and wanted no part of it."[14]

Arriving at Guantanamo Bay, Cuba, on 10 January 1913, Towers found that Smith and Chevalier had already set up camp at Fisherman's Point, using four large tents as hangars and twenty-six smaller ones for working and living. As senior aviation officer, Towers ran the camp from a headquarters tent. Almost immediately, officers crowded in for rides; he tried to accommodate all of them when he was not instructing his charges. Following a hot-weather work schedule of 0530 to 1130 and 1530 to 1800, at midday they could test equipment, swim, or zip around in an old Curtiss motorcycle. The entire fleet was present, and all hands joined in the usual recreation of smokers, movies, baseball games, and tennis. Jack also played with the unit's mascot, a fox terrier. One day it bit him on the cheek so hard that the wound required a dressing.[15]

The unit made its fleet debut late on the afternoon of 14 January with Towers soloing in the A-3. The other three hydros immediately began flying, and on the twenty-second all four took off together for the first time, which suitably impressed fleet observers. That day the collier *Vulcan* delivered the C-1 flying boat from Washington, and five days later all five planes roared into the sky together, Towers at the controls of the C-1 with Chevalier as copilot. The machines sparked interest throughout the fleet. For the next six weeks they flew as much as wind, inferior gasoline, and the usual mechanical difficulties permitted. By early February Towers could boast to Ellyson, "We . . . have made a great many converts."[16]

As senior aviator, Jack placed himself in charge of the flying boat, named Chevalier his assistant and copilot, and assigned the A-2 to Barney Smith and the A-3 to Bellinger. Cunningham kept the B-1 and Herbster his B-2, assisted by Billingsley. But mechanical difficulties, which plagued all the hydros except the B-1, forced Towers to shift personnel around so that they could get adequate time in the air. The energetic New Englander Chevalier overcame an initial nervousness in the A-3 to emulate his able mentor Towers.[17]

Jack found Pat Bellinger, a perpetually smiling South Carolinian with an appropriate drawl, "the hardest man, except Richardson, that I have ever undertaken to teach. I spent thirteen hours and twenty-seven minutes in the air with him" before he was able to solo on 1 February. But, reported Jack, once "he learns how to do something, he never forgets." Bellinger especially appreciated Jack's landing technique of looking at the horizon rather than at the forward end of the pontoon. Once Bellinger had the rudiments, he developed into a master pilot. The two men became fast friends.[18]

Vic Herbster was the troublemaker, anxious to excel and jealous of nearly everyone, especially Towers. He resented having to share his B-2 with another pilot, usually Billingsley, even for instructional purposes. When he wrote directly to the Wright company, Towers ordered him to route all letters through him, Towers. Herbster demanded a second pontoon for the Wright machine before either of the two on hand had even been tested. Then he offered to build a complete plane (he had built the B-2) just for Billingsley to fly. Jack turned him down, unanimously supported by the others, because of the lack of hangar space, spare parts, and mechanics for another machine. Irate over this refusal, Vic quarreled with Jack, to no avail, and later complained that Towers controlled all the purse strings and, being pro-Curtiss, refused to allocate enough money for the Wright machines. Apparently Herbster was also jealous of Cunningham.[19] Such troubles Towers poured out in long letters to both Chambers and Ellyson, part of his exceedingly heavy paperwork. By mid-February he complained to Ellyson that he was spending six hours a day at his desk between flying chores.

Towers was pleased that the marine Cunningham had not been uncooperative, as Chambers had feared; he not only worked with Towers and performed well but also helped him court marines in the fleet. On one occasion Jack took up another marine, Lieutenant Colonel John A. Lejeune, destined for fame in World War I. He made friends with two marine sergeants, later recalling that during midday siesta breaks they "would guide us up the Guantanamo River to large wooded areas where there was fine wild guinea shooting and also to a fresh water lake alive with ducks" to enhance the unit's already famous cuisine.[20]

Among the many officers in the fleet who went hunting with the aviators but who had no interest in flying with them was the executive officer of the battleship *Arkansas*, Lieutenant Commander William A. Moffett. Recalled Jack, "While trudging back to camp, well-laden with wild guineas and ducks, he once said to me, 'Towers, you're such a nice chap, why don't you give up this aviation fad? You'll surely get yourself killed. Any man who sticks to it is either crazy or else a plain damned fool!'" Moffett would ultimately go on to lead naval aviation.

With Chevalier as copilot, Towers usually flew the C-1 flying boat, which struck a visiting lady journalist as resembling "a huge wooden shoe in front with the tail of a fish in the rear." In spite of minor problems he was satisfied with the C-1, remembering that it "did not have much reserve power and was not very stable in the air, but it was something different and we were very enthusiastic about it." They flew it as far as forty miles out to sea—considered hazardous over the temperamental Caribbean—and to extraordinary altitudes for a seaplane, first to 1,300, then to 1,600 feet. Pat Bellinger, wanting to be the record-setter, went higher in the A-3; he reached 2,075 feet.[21]

In spite of the usual maintenance problems, the planes performed several experiments with general success—detecting mines and Lieutenant Nimitz's submerged subs in sixty feet of clear water and making night flights by guiding on the light and reflection of the full moon. Towers was pleased to report to Chambers that the flyers had also "become fairly accurate at dropping missiles, using a very simple device, gotten up by one of the men, at a small box floating in the bay."[22]

Sidestepping an unenthused Admiral Badger, Towers seized on political unrest in the Caribbean to promote the cause of naval aviation. Civil war in Mexico threatened to bring chaos to the region, which was now becoming vital to American interests, especially with the anticipated completion of the Panama Canal. Talk of possible American naval intervention at Vera Cruz began to grow. On the morning of 4 February Jack flew the C-1 out to meet the incoming Third Division of battleships, and he began quietly to lobby Admiral Badger's staff for aircraft participation in fleet maneuvers and for the use of planes as reconnaissance scouts if there were a landing at Vera Cruz.[23]

At 1300 on 19 February, Admiral Badger dispatched a boat to fetch Towers from the camp and bring him out to the flagship for a personal chat. "When I got there," Jack wrote Ellyson afterwards, "he had the whole place littered with maps and told me that he was figuring on the question of taking aeroplanes with the Fleet to Vera Cruz in case they were ordered to proceed there." Jack guessed that his efforts with Badger's staff had won over the admiral.[24]

Badger questioned Towers closely on how the planes might be used,

Lieutenant Towers poses with his men and a goat and dog mascot in front of a tent hangar and a Curtiss A-type hydro early in 1913. The flyers are, *left to right,* Lieutenant (jg) Pat Bellinger, Marine First Lieutenants Barney Smith and Alfred Cunningham, Towers, and Ensigns Vic Herbster, Bill Billingsley, and Chevy Chevalier. (T. G. Ellyson collection, Naval Historical Foundation)

especially from a land field. Jack explained that the flying boat could be rigged with wheels (though he did not like such an arrangement), adding that he had enough gear to rig one of the hydros as well. He pointed out, however, that his planes could operate from the water and "still scout several miles over land in comparative safety." As he later confided to Ellyson, "I think . . . I persuaded him that we were absolutely indispensable." That he did, for the admiral now ordered Towers to get two planes ready. Badger cabled the Navy Department for permission to use them for "shore service" in any landing operation in Mexico, in which they were "likely to be valuable." Since only the two most reliable machines would go, his own C-1 and Cunningham's B-1, a jealous Vic Herbster could only complain.[25]

Alas, given all these preparations, the Taft administration decided not to intervene in Mexico, thus postponing naval aviation's combat debut. The battleships departed for two weeks on maneuvers, which left Towers free to work with Nimitz's sub flotilla and to force the disgruntled Herbster to "give up a lot of prospective joy rides and [to] take Billingsley out."[26] At the beginning of March Jack turned over all instruction to the other officers in order to concentrate exclusively on Lieutenant Commander Henry C. Mustin, executive officer of the battleship *Minnesota* and new convert to aviation. And all the airmen gave demonstration hops to win over the doubters.[27]

Finally, at 1700 on 6 March 1913, Admiral Badger ordered Towers to prepare for an air search for a "hostile fleet" of approaching battleships—the first tactical maneuver involving aircraft. Because of 20-mph winds and rough seas, Jack planned to use only the flying boat, taking Chevalier along as observer. Loaded on board the C-1 were an Aldis signal lantern, eight-power Zeiss binoculars, a megaphone, a notebook, some simple instruments, and a few spare parts. For over a month the mechanics had been working on a wireless transmitter for a demonstration during this exercise, and it was taken along too.

When the appointed time came the air was full of moisture from a solid hour of rain, and squalls were visible around Guantanamo Bay. Badger insisted that for safety's sake a destroyer follow the C-1 and keep it in view during its search.[28] The two flyers nevertheless took off at 1745 and with Towers' steady flying climbed through no fewer than three rain squalls as the sun set. At 600 feet, just outside the bay, they sighted five battleships some fifteen miles distant. Jack headed towards the ships, taking the C-1 up to 1,150 feet while Chevalier jotted down the course, approximate speed and distance, and bearing of the "enemy." Some 10,000 yards away, just outside the light gun range of the ships, Jack turned the C-1 around and headed back. Chevy keyed the wireless to make the report, whereupon, in Towers' words, "the damn radio broke down!"

The battleships had not seen the plane, whereupon Towers landed alongside the flagship at 1815 and personally reported to Admiral Badger what they had observed. The flagship sent a radio message to the defending destroyers, which immediately got under way and attacked the enemy an hour later. Although the wireless had not worked, for the first time an aeroplane scout had demonstrated the usefulness of aviation to the main battle fleet.[29]

To follow up this success, Towers impressed the battleship commanders with the durability of the flying boat. On 10 and 11 March he went on a relatively long flight of forty-five miles along the south coast of Cuba from Guantanamo to Santiago and back. The performance made good copy in the aviation press, Jack having bested Pat Bellinger's high-flying record for the Caribbean deployment by reaching 2,700 feet. Late on the eleventh he made a short hop with Congressman Lemuel P. Padgett, eminent chairman of the House Naval Affairs Committee, who was pushing important naval appropriations through the House.[30]

Perhaps convinced by such demonstrations of the naval potential of seaplanes, one of the admirals finally consented to be taken up. Rear Admiral Cameron McR. Winslow, second in command of the Atlantic Fleet and "a very bold officer indeed" in Towers' opinion, reported to the aviation camp early on the morning of 12 March. Jack and Winslow climbed into the flying boat and soared up to 575 feet over the anchorage on a fourteen-minute hop. It was the climax to the aviation unit's successful initiation in the fleet. Afterwards the planes were loaded onto the *Minnesota* and the collier *Neptune* for the return to Annapolis. Jack carried with him his first formal orders, having been assigned to "duty as actual flier of heavier-than-air craft," a designation conferred upon him on 5 March.[31]

Not only had the unit's overall performance and Towers' own handling of the flying boat been a success, but Jack emerged from the experience for the first time as something of a public figure. Among many local and national news journals, the Philadelphia *Public Ledger* and *Leslie's Illustrated Weekly Newspaper* published photographs of him in feature stories on the unit's activities in the Caribbean. *Leslie's* hailed him "as one of the most efficient air experts," while the *Ledger* labeled him "head of the Navy Aviation Corps."[32]

The latter label proved immediately prophetic, for Spuds Ellyson suddenly quit aviation, leaving Towers in permanent command of the aviation detachment and school. He also inherited Ellyson's problems with Chambers.[33] But changes were in the wind. Rear Admiral Bradley A. Fiske had become senior administrative officer in the navy; not only a champion of aviation, he had patented a design for a torpedo-launching aeroplane. And the new president, Woodrow Wilson—whose wife was from Towers' hometown—appointed newspaperman Josephus Daniels to be secretary of the navy. Under the sympathetic leadership of Daniels and Fiske, naval aviation made important gains that spring of 1913. Pilot's pay was increased, more trainees were enrolled, and they would be guided by a training syllabus, for the navy now took over licensing its own aviators. Henceforth, naval air pilot certificates would be issued to those who could meet seaplane standards worked up by Chambers and Ellyson, replacing the less-demanding FAI–Aero Club landplane test. Towers received the first certificate.

At Annapolis, Jack got his planes uncrated and back into the air. Pat Bellinger, responding to a casual remark by Jack that "anyone who gets above 3,000 feet will get his name in the papers," pushed the A-3 to an altitude of over 6,000 feet by mid-June, over twice Towers' mark in the C-1. The inferior Wright B-2 was markedly improved with the installation of a Curtiss motor; Towers took his first hop in it, as passenger with Vic Herbster, on the twenty-sixth. Among the many officers Towers took aloft in the A-2 on 3

Towers (*right*) and copilot Chevalier in the C-1, Curtiss' first navy flying boat, in 1913. (Naval Historical Center)

May was his old *Kentucky* shipmate, Lieutenant Commander Tom Craven, now occupying the key post of director of target practice and engineering competitions at the Navy Department.[34]

Captain Chambers had Towers ship the C-1 over to the Washington Navy Yard for public exhibition flights during ceremonies on 6 May honoring the late Samuel P. Langley, Smithsonian's pioneer aeronautical experimenter. There, the new assistant secretary of war, Henry S. Breckinridge, himself "trying to make propaganda for an air force," made a hop with Towers despite his fear of heights. Breckenridge recalled that he never forgot Jack's remark, "Mr. Secretary, under proper conditions aviation is the safest means of transportation." Another passenger that day was the inventor of some crude aerial bombs, J. B. Semple, who carried five of the seven-pound "areo-granades [*sic*]" in his lap. "Apparently," remembered Jack, "he didn't have any more confidence in them than I did, because we'd hardly got off the water [of the Potomac River] before he began to chuck them overboard. They didn't have time to arm, and they struck the water and broke apart. None of them went off."

On 9 May Towers and Chevalier returned to Annapolis in the C-1 by a circuitous route down the Potomac and back up the Chesapeake Bay, covering 171 miles in three hours and five minutes at 2,200 feet—the longest nonstop flight yet by military pilots in a seaplane.[35]

Such sustained cross-country flights became the main task for the rest of the spring and summer, notably on 21 May when Secretary Daniels, on his first visit to Annapolis, stopped by the aviation camp. When Daniels agreed to go for a ride in the flying boat, Towers had his sailors fashion a miniature four-star secretary's flag of blue silk and attach it to the machine. After Jack had Daniels don an overcoat and stuff cotton in his ears, they took off in late afternoon for a flight of eight minutes over the *Illinois,* which fired a nineteen-gun salute—the first ever to an airborne secretary. The two men got along famously; Daniels recalled in his memoirs, "It was a fine experience and I returned to Washington more enthusiastic about the future of aviation." Jack presented him with the flag as a souvenir.[36]

Daniels asked Towers to come to Washington and discuss how best to integrate aviation into the navy. While there, Jack also helped make "a staunch supporter out of the Assistant Secretary of the Navy, who helped us out greatly, I may say, regardless of politics. He was a smart young fellow named Franklin Roosevelt," then age thirty-one. Towers may have first met FDR when the latter visited Annapolis on Sunday, 25 May.[37]

Still a bachelor, Jack pursued the ladies relentlessly from his Annapolis quarters at Ogle Hall. A fairly typical week began on Monday, 26 May, when, as he recounted to his mother, he "motored to Washington" for a date with a woman named Mary, then returned to Annapolis in time to leave on a four-day trip to the Curtiss plant at Hammondsport. Back at Ogle Hall by noon on Saturday, he went to Washington for dinner and a dance that night at the Chevy Chase Club, where he had "several dances with Miss Eleanor Wilson." The following afternoon, Sunday, "I took Emily Munroe out for a long motor trip. . . . Laura leaves tomorrow for Louisville. I hate very much to see her go."[38]

Jack obtained Chambers' permission to take leave in July to fly a Curtiss F boat, the same as the C-1, in a major seaplane competition. Sponsored by *Aero and Hydro* magazine, the "Great Lakes Cruise" was to cover 900 miles between Detroit and Chicago. During his short stay at Hammondsport in late May, Jack not only discussed the race but observed Curtiss' work in tractor (front-engine) planes, notably for the army.

During June, with the race several weeks away, Towers remained in Annapolis flying the C-1 on cross-country flights and instructing students in the A-2. He did not plan to make a flight scheduled for the twentieth across the bay to St. Michaels, Maryland, because he wanted Chevalier to get more experience in the C-1, with a student as passenger. The only other plane scheduled for the junket was the two-seat Wright B-2. Jack gave it to Bill Billingsley, who had become a very good pilot. Billingsley was supposed to take Herbster along as his passenger to navigate, observe the operation of the machine, and measure the altitude with an aneroid barometer. The presence of an officer was standard procedure in test flights. But Herbster missed the ferry launch from Annapolis to the camp, so an enlisted mechanic was assigned as Billingsley's passenger.

Just as Billingsley was taxiing out into the water preparatory to takeoff, Towers approached in a boat, flagged him down, then climbed aboard and traded places with the mechanic. Since this was only his second flight in the troublesome Wright, he was still a relative stranger to its controls. Taking off at 0923, Billingsley piloted the machine across the Chesapeake to Claiborne without incident, turned around, and headed back.

As the B-2 neared Annapolis, a rain squall stood in its path. Billingsley maneuvered around the edge and dropped his altitude, though the "strong unsteady following wind" of the squall blew behind the craft. Jack busied himself searching for the C-1 in the mist as Bill leveled off at about 1,625 feet.

65

Then, about six or eight miles from their destination, the B-2's tail was suddenly lifted by a gust. The plane took "an uncertain dive forward. The angle was about 65 degrees at first—pretty bad."[39]

The plane bucked, and after it had fallen about 130 feet "Billingsley was thrown forward out of his seat, against the elevating lever," which disabled the lateral rudder planes and increased the throttle. This pushed the machine into a faster, steeper dive "at express train speed," whereupon Billingsley went hurtling into the air and fell about 1,500 feet to the bay. He no doubt lost consciousness as he twisted and turned violently.

As for Towers, he "was hurled from my seat, but I caught an upright and managed to hold on" with both hands, swinging clear of the gearing. "The strain on my arms and fingers was awful. I tried to kick the steering gear back into working order, but I could not make it go" because "the machine began to dive straight down." In the midst of his predicament Jack looked down at Billingsley, arms spread and whirling through space.

> The machine seemed to take quick darts, shifts of direction, now and then. I don't know how I ever held on. At first, my instinct, or whatever it was, told me to let go. . . . I had more fear of the machine's falling on me than I had of hitting the water. Then I recovered presence of mind enough to believe that I was going to certain death anyway. Falling from that height, if I fell by myself, I might never come to the surface. . . .
>
> Just as I decided to hold on, the machine checked suddenly with a vicious twist, slacking its speed somewhat, and turning almost bottom up in a complete somersault. This twist tore away the grip I had with my right hand, although I held on with every ounce of strength I had [with my left]. . . .
>
> The muscular strain of keeping my grasp of the upright tore one of my ribs from the breastbone. . . . The machine must have been going off on a . . . more slowly descending slant, like a piece of cardboard that is spun into the air. . . . I suppose I was about 800 feet above the water when the machine took this first long dash sidewise . . . it was the only thing that saved my life, for otherwise I should have gone down almost as fast as Billingsley. . . .
>
> After the machine turned upside down it shot down at least 400 feet, not straight, but at an angle of about 50 degrees. Then it flattened against the air resistance. It was poised for a fraction of a second, stopping partly and turning. Then it started down again on another dash in the opposite direction. It was about 400 feet high when it began the last dive. This time it took a sharper angle.
>
> I was still holding on with my left hand, unable to get a better grip. The machine was still upside down. The motor was now in a position to strike the water ahead of me instead of crashing down on me. It was the best place for me—another strange piece of luck—because there were no heavy weights above me except the beams of the plane.
>
> Then came the crash.

66

Jack heard the lower wing strike the water, then lost consciousness. When he came to he realized he might never be found in the afternoon mist, should he pass out again. Using his handkerchief, he lashed his good arm to the pontoon and soon heard the crash boat approaching. It passed by without spotting him and started off in the other direction. Then Jack heard barking, whereupon the two crewmen turned the boat around. Towers' dog was aboard and must have seen or smelled him. He had been in the water some forty-five minutes by the time the sailors turned off the motor and hauled him into the launch.

Towers kept his wits about him, in spite of the pain, to direct the recovery of Billingsley's body. After a twenty-minute search in vain, the sailors refused to obey Towers' entreaties to keep looking, fearful lest they lose him too in the absence of prompt medical attention. Meanwhile, the launch was joined by the torpedo boat *Stringham,* commanded by Lieutenant Ernie King.

Upon reaching the academy dock, Towers was able to walk unassisted up the hill to the Naval Hospital, where reporters saw him "almost in a state of nervous collapse, his entire body trembling and his head piteously." Nevertheless, he made his report before being given a sedative that put him to sleep. Though he was severely hurt, his body bruised all over from hitting the water, fears of serious internal injuries proved unfounded. The Experiment Station's derrick raised the B-2, a total wreck aside from the Curtiss engine and pontoons. The second Wright hydro had ceased to exist.[40]

Ensign Richard E. Byrd, like most serving officers, learned of the incident from the newspapers, in his case when a shipmate rushed in exclaiming, "For God's sake, listen to this! Jack Towers has fallen fifteen hundred feet in an aeroplane and lived to tell the tale! . . . Think of the nerve of the man!" Byrd, along with the rest of the naval community, was impressed.[41]

Billingsley's body surfaced about a week later. The board of inquiry absolved the dead man of any fault for the crash, while Vic Herbster strongly defended the airworthiness of his machine. But he could not explain away the constant technical troubles that had plagued both Wright hydros—not least the lack of shoulder straps (which the Curtiss machines had) to keep occupants secure in their seats in just such circumstances as this. Only days before this flight, orders had been issued for pilots to use the strap on high flights—a preventive measure forgotten on this occasion. Inflatable life jackets had also been left behind. Official blame for naval aviation's first fatality was laid to the erratic winds, the so-called holes in the air, or downdrafts.[42]

Had Billingsley and Towers been strapped into their seats, they would at least have been able to work the controls to prevent their nosedive, perhaps even to recover before striking the water. Several persons had fallen to their deaths in this manner, but since none survived to tell the tale, everyone assumed they had merely lost consciousness, then fallen out. Towers' report now changed this, and when Glenn Curtiss arrived from Hammondsport to check on his condition the two men agreed that some sort of buckled lashing had to be installed in all navy aircraft. Whereupon Curtiss returned to his plant to develop one. The result was the safety belt, with a simple link and cam buckle, that quickly became standard equipment in all aircraft, not just the U.S. Navy's. This development was the single greatest result of Bill Billingsley's death and Jack Towers' ordeal.[43]

Jack's excellent physical condition minimized his injuries, though navy doctors insisted he take three months' sick leave to recuperate. Secretary Daniels paid him a visit in the hospital on 2 July to ask if he wanted duty other than flying. Jack assured him that he had no doubts about wanting to remain at the Annapolis camp. Discharged from the hospital on 8 July—the day he was to have competed in the Great Lakes seaplane race—he left immediately for Bar Harbor, Maine, and Newport, Rhode Island, to spend the summer with friends regaining his strength.[44]

Billingsley's death cast a pall over naval aviation. The B-1 was grounded, its pilot Cunningham left aviation at the behest of his fiancée, flight applications were suspended, and Captain Chambers had to bring in a newcomer to replace Towers as head of the camp, Lieutenant (jg) James McC. Murray. What American aviation needed to prevent similar accidents was a theoretical grounding in aerodynamics. Assistant Naval Constructor Jerome C. Hunsaker was dispatched to Europe to observe progress in the field and to initiate a navy program. That Jack Towers survived his early aeroplane flights without the benefit of such knowledge bears testimony to his uncanny savvy as a pilot. He had also become expert in the problems of float design, now being pursued vigorously in Washington by Dick Richardson.[45]

Meanwhile, on 1 July, without any warning, Admiral Fiske retired Captain Chambers from active duty, wanting new blood to run the program, which meant Towers. Jack's absence on medical leave proved timely, for Chambers, shattered by this defeat, lashed out in frustration at his senior aviator. On the Fourth of July the captain penned a long letter from his home to Towers concerning "the *solar plexus* blow that I have just received. . . . Confidentially, some of my newspaper friends have given me a hint that reflects upon you, but I refuse to entertain any suspicions because I have always relied on your integrity and frankness. I may have differed with you in matters of policy but it has never shaken my faith in you. . . . I gather that he

[Secretary Daniels] has you in view for my relief." Chambers explained how he had always intended that Ellyson should replace him. But with Ellyson gone, "I am not going to stand in the way if you have any desire for the billet. . . ."[46]

No reply survives. Towers probably used his convalescence as an excuse not to answer, thus giving Chambers a chance to cool off. That he did very quickly may be owing to the fact that Admiral Fiske could not find any officer in the rank of captain to replace him; Chambers, though retired, stayed in charge of naval aviation. In a lengthy summary report that August, Chambers generously observed that "great credit is due to Lieutenant John H. Towers . . . for his competent management, under difficulties," of the aviation camp at Annapolis. Of the 2,118 flights made in navy aircraft since the first one on 1 July 1911, Towers had piloted over a fourth of them, 546, and of these 110 solo hops, in addition making 40 as a passenger himself. This gave him 151 hours and 53 minutes total time aloft, nearly twice as much as the next man. His records far outdistanced those of the remaining active navy pilots, which now numbered thirteen.[47]

Not only was Towers the most experienced pilot in the Navy, he was the best one, the best teacher, and the best administrator of flying activities. His talent for running the Annapolis camp was made conspicuous by his absence in the summer of 1913. At its end, Chambers wrote to him, "I think the camp has suffered somewhat by not having a man of your ability in charge. . . ." Chambers wanted Towers to return in that role and eventually offered to nominate him as the next director of naval aviation.[48]

Replied Jack, "It is certainly fine of you to give me that chance, but I do not feel that I have rank enough for the position. I think the officer who holds that position should be one who would carry enough weight to be heard in the Department." Towers preferred resuming command at Annapolis to prove himself after his injury. For without him, aviation activities there only limped along. An August hurricane finished off the B-1, from the wreckage of which Vic Herbster fashioned another Wright, the B-3. Chambers still disliked having two control systems, both of which had to be mastered by all the navy pilots, but he was glad to receive the D-1 flying boat, built by the Burgess subcontractor of the Wright company. In spite of lingering lawsuits, Wright was losing credibility with both services; five of the newest Wright pushers had already killed five army pilots and seriously injured Hap Arnold.[49]

Admiral Fiske, anxious to bring the navy's air arm closer to European standards, authorized the appointment of four new student officers. When thirty-three applied, Chambers lamented Towers' absence; he needed the aviator's input, without which he had to "rely on the records and the judgment of the Detail Officer." Unfortunately, the latter had the "idea that a close corporation or 'clique' is apt to result if the advice of aviators is taken exclusively." This was a problem Towers would encounter throughout his career, as conservative "Gun Club" personnel officers tried to prevent airmen from selecting aviation trainees. Chambers implored Jack to make recommendations for selection.[50] This was one of Towers' first acts upon resuming command at Annapolis on 30 September 1913, his health restored. Of the several officers he recommended, Ensign Clarence K. "Buck" Bronson headed the list.[51]

The aviation camp slowly rejuvenated under Towers' leadership. Although he flew again, he concentrated on getting his machines in condition for the new students and participating in a new long-range study of naval aviation. On 7 October, Acting Secretary Franklin Roosevelt appointed a special board to draw up a list of specific requirements for the future. Chambers headed it, with Towers as member and recorder; flyers Alfred Cunningham and Dick Richardson respectively represented the Marine Corps and the Bureau of Construction and Repair (C&R), responsible for inspecting and establishing specifications for new planes. Three nonflyers were also appointed.

For six weeks, Towers shuttled between Annapolis and Washington gathering data for the Chambers board as it studied aeronautical developments in Europe and in the U.S. Army. He visited the army aviation camp at College Park, where he flew hydros and renewed his friendship with Hap Arnold. Inevitably, the expertise of the qualified pilots on the board led them again to disagree with their nonflying administrative boss, forcing Towers to confront Chambers over diverging interpretations of policy. Towers took exception to the idea that persons with no experience handling aircraft—by inference, Chambers—should design planes that others had to fly. Still smarting from the fatal Billingsley crash, Towers recommended to the board that "the designs of prospective machines be submitted to a board of aviation officers before purchases of such machines are made." Furthermore, he noted, the "great many risks" run by flyers "are no longer necessary provided that [they] have an opportunity to take part in the design of the new machines."[52]

Having solicited ideas from the small cadre of pilots, Towers specifically attacked a new amphibian design by Chambers, the conversion of the A-2 into the E-1 OWL (over land and water), while marine Barney Smith argued for army-style tractor aircraft over pushers. Stung by these initiatives against two of his pet preferences, Chambers lamented Towers' notion that aviators be "the originators of design." Towers, however, by now established as the acknowledged expert on naval aviation, found his advice sought on all related matters. It was a mantle he would not give up for the remainder of his career. Critics would call him ambitious. But in 1913 his first thought was to save the necks of flyers by obtaining decent machines and reliable men to operate them—a worthy if simple cause.[53]

By mid-November, the members of the Chambers board overcame their differences with a unanimous report of sweeping recommendations. Those accepted by the navy were the creation of the Office of Naval Aeronautics, directed by a captain; the establishment of an aeronautical center; and the assignment to it of the training battleship *Mississippi*. Unable to obtain the Annapolis site for the center, the board requested and got the naval station at Pensacola, which had been closed the year before as an economy measure. At the very least, flying conditions on the west coast of Florida should be good year-round.

Admiral Fiske prevailed upon ordnance expert Mark L. Bristol to accept the position of director of the new office. Towers' student Lieutenant Commander Henry Mustin was assigned as skipper of the *Mississippi*. Towers would direct the actual flight training. Under the navy's new certification policy, effective 1 January 1914, Towers ranked as navy air pilot no. 2 after Ellyson, followed by Mustin, a sequential rating system so obviously full of omissions and inconsistencies that it would not last long.[54]

Upon the arrival at Annapolis of the *Mississippi* and the collier *Orion*, planes, equipment, and personnel were moved aboard for passage to the Gulf of Mexico. Towers had charge of five flying boats and two hydros, the most impressive force of American naval aircraft yet assembled.[55] The *Mississippi* carried Mustin, Towers, four other flyers, and representatives from the key aircraft companies—Starling Burgess, Grover Loening from Wright, Lanny Callan from Curtiss, "and a most extraordinary fellow named Reid," remembered Jack. "[W]e were supposed to have technical discussions on the way down, but this old battleship wallowed all the way and everybody was seasick in his bunk, except Mr. Reid. I don't know what aviation company he was supposed to represent, but it should have been Haig and Haig or Old Grandad, I think." Marshall E. Reid was a private stunt flyer and customer of Curtiss who would earn his wings as a naval aviator during World War I. He was also Mustin's brother-in-law.

The *Orion* unloaded the planes at Pensacola on 20–21 January 1914, while the officers and mechanics established living quarters aboard the *Mississippi*. Their arrival proved timely, for Admiral Badger again hoped to use them should American intervention in strife-torn Mexico become necessary. For the moment, Towers busied himself training his "squabs"—student pilots— and experimenting with equipment. He and Mustin hammered out a formal training syllabus, which included the task of spotting mines in offshore waters. With the Pensacola facility in a state of disrepair, the unit's tent hangars offered the only shelter, and high winds and choppy seas often prevented the planes from operating.[56]

Although officer in charge of the flying unit, Towers found himself part of an extremely awkward command arrangement. Mustin had charge of both the *Mississippi* and of the shore facility, but to get the operation there under way, Captain Bristol spent most of February on the scene. Keen and abrupt, he was a sound administrator who found Towers "so burdened with paper work" as to have little time for anything else. Bristol tried to get Mustin to streamline his system of reporting, but with little success. The three officers labored amidst an incredibly tangled logistical system to make Pensacola into a viable installation. Needed requisitions went directly to the office of Assistant Secretary Franklin Roosevelt, where they were often rejected outright by the frugal "confidential clerk" there, one Louis Howe. Towers and his men therefore had to jury-rig equipment from leftover parts of the former naval base, which, however, was jealously guarded by the Bureau of Yards and Docks and a force of resident marines.[57]

Then there were the planes, temperamental as ever, with the new ones still relatively untested. In light of his own crash and survival, Jack insisted that all the flyers know how to swim and personally wrote out nine pages of safety instructions for them. Lanny Callan of the Curtiss Company lived with the officers in the *Mississippi,* worked closely with Towers, and helped reassemble and maintain the flying boats. Within days they had the C-1, C-2, and C-4 as well as the A-3 hydro flying. The Wright and Burgess planes were less reliable, and Lanny Callan confided in his diary, "Towers is not at all in favor of the 'Owl' type of machine and says that it is only an idea of Capt. Chambers." Jack, regarding this, the E-1, as too heavy and in need of a longer hull, warned Callan to have Curtiss tone down publicity over it, since the truth would come out eventually and reflect unfavorably on the company.[58]

On the morning of 16 February, the transport *Hancock* brought marines Barney Smith and Mac McIlvain with the C-3 and E-1 from Puerto Rico to work at Pensacola. That afternoon Jimmy Murray took up the Burgess D-1

A pensive Jack Towers, in life jacket, on the
beach at Pensacola. Note the cotton in his
ears to protect them from the noise of the
pushers. (Navy Department)

for its second flight at the camp. Towers, concerned over the new flying boat's
poorly performing motor in 20-mph winds, questioned Murray after he had
landed and taxied back to the hangar ramp. Murray told him "that the air was
rather bad but that he did not consider it unsafe" and "that the motor still
lacked power," whereupon Towers tested the plane's controls. Murray took
the pilot's seat again, "appeared to strap himself in" as he had done on the first
flight, then took off alone.

Towers went into a nearby workshop. Reemerging ten minutes later, he
saw several people in the lookout tower; they informed him that Murray "had
fallen" into the bay. By the time Jack flew to the scene in the C-4, the flyer's
body had been recovered and removed by Pat Bellinger and R. Caswell
Saufley. Coming in to land, the D-1 had apparently lost power and plummeted 200 feet into the water. In fact, Murray did not use the waist strap.

Jack insisted on swimming proficiency for his seaplane
pilots. Scene probably at Guantanamo Bay, early in 1913.
Left to right: Bellinger, Towers, Cunningham, Billingsley,
Herbster, and Smith. (Towers collection)

Thrown out of the plane and probably knocked unconscious, he drowned
face down in the water—naval aviation's second fatality. The D-1 was a total
wreck. Rather than risk another life in Burgess or Wright planes, Towers had
an A-4 Curtiss hydro built from spare parts to help meet his needs. This plane
was also necessary because the float of the E-1 soon wrecked, ending that
unpopular plane's usefulness.[59]

The navy's only hope for reliable seaplanes lay in Glenn Curtiss, who
returned from a European trip in February with a fantastic scheme for a
long-range flying boat to cross the Atlantic. Former British navy Lieutenant
John Cyril Porte, who had talked him into it, would be pilot, and department
store heir Rodman Wanamaker would put up the money, encouraged by the
London *Daily Mail*'s promised £10,000 sterling ($50,000) to anyone who
could accomplish the incredible feat. Wanamaker's only stipulation was that if
Britisher Porte was pilot, an American naval aviator be copilot. Curtiss had no
doubt who this should be—his friend and former student Jack Towers.[60]

Curtiss contacted Captain Chambers, who agreed enthusiastically; if
Towers did not actually make the flight, he could at least help test-fly the giant
boat. As Captain Bristol hold his superiors, "the flight across the Atlantic is
not a wildcat scheme, and Towers will not be in favor of it unless it is a
practical scheme. . . . Towers is the best man to represent us, I think."
Bristol also wanted to get the very latest information on aeronautical progress
in Europe from Curtiss. So on 19 February 1914 he had Towers ordered to
New York to meet with Curtiss and Wanamaker.[61]

On the twenty-third he arrived in New York City, where he and Curtiss met Cyril Porte. With Wanamaker, the men repaired to the offices of the New York Aero Club to scrutinize the plan. Jack convinced Curtiss to change the original design by rejecting the notion that the flying boat should soar high above the clouds for a possible nonstop crossing. Instead of 10,000 feet, he said it should fly low, under 1,000 feet. Jack remarked that he had had trouble seeing destroyers from 4,000 feet. From a low altitude, the two pilots would see not only ships but also the waves, by which they could measure the plane's drift in relation to the force and direction of the wind. Said Towers, "Stick close to the water, to study the compass, to watch the course of ships, and be ready to alight and make repairs if necessary."[62]

Back in Washington, Admiral Fiske and Captains Bristol and Chambers (who had stayed on as technical adviser) were interested in what Towers had to report on Curtiss' latest intelligence concerning aeronautical developments in Europe. As he related, Germany was producing a new generation of aircraft engines and starting to develop naval aircraft "on a very broad and substantial basis" that might put the Germans in the lead. All the

To keep their feet dry in the air, Towers and a passenger are carried to the A-3 by enlisted men at Pensacola early in 1914. (Navy Department)

major countries were getting into the field, with Russia and Italy relying completely on a handful of Curtiss-built planes. Britain and France were each experimenting with a "hangar ship," lowering seaplanes into the water and hoisting them back aboard. And all the nations, save the British, now favored the single-wing monoplane over the biplane. This information substantiated the relative backwardness of American aviation.[63]

As construction of the big flying boat got under way, Towers returned to sunny Pensacola to continue his teaching and experimental duties with the half-dozen aircraft still in working order.[64] He also helped the Pathé motion picture company take films from the air. The silent-film industry was intrigued with flying. Indeed, in that spring of 1914 one company released a single-reel feature, "The Naval Aviator." Press accounts in all likelihood were referring to this film when they identified Jack as

> the young man who played the part of the ardent young lover in the motion pictures produced by the navy department some time ago—pictures for which $20,000 worth of powder was used and seven warships employed in a great battle scene. In the picture, the young hero, the naval aviator, comes upon the scene to bid a tragic farewell to his lovely sweetheart. His lips move slowly and with effort. The girl looks up at him in sadness. It is easy to imagine what tender words fall from his lips.
>
> According to those who saw the pictures made, what he actually did say at this juncture was: "Let's hurry and get this over and go out for something to eat. I'm starved."

That was typical Towers humor, although years later he recalled he had only been an unpaid stand-in for the star of the film.[65]

When the executive officer of the *Mississippi* was detached for medical reasons in March, Rum Mustin made Towers acting exec of the battleship. Mustin soon reported him "doing well" in the post and creating "much better harmony" than his predecessor between the ship's company and the airmen, although Mustin harbored a certain jealousy toward Jack as Secretary Daniels' fair-haired boy in aviation. "Towers says he likes the opportunity for getting the experience and as he has been so long in aviation work only, I think it is doing him a lot of good." Bristol, however, disapproved, since Towers was busy enough keeping the school going. Jack turned over the exec's job to a permanent relief in late April.[66]

The relative isolation of the Pensacola facility from the mainstream navy was alleviated only by occasional visits of warships, notably the scout cruiser *Birmingham,* flagship of Captain William S. Sims, the fleet's torpedo destroyer commander, and some destroyers that arrived on 10 April as the

The navy and marine flyers at Pensacola, posing before a Curtiss C-type flying boat early in 1914. *Left to right:* Godfrey Chevalier, Caswell Saufley, Pat Bellinger, Towers, Mac McIlvaine, Mel Stolz, Barney Smith, and Vic Herbster. (Navy Department)

situation in Mexico worsened. On the ninth, Mexican police had arrested and detained an American naval party putting ashore at Tampico for gasoline. When the Mexican authorities steadfastly refused to fire a salute to the flag over this indignity, the Wilson administration decided to intervene in the Mexican civil war. Mustin and Towers persuaded Captain Sims "that he would need some aeroplanes down there, and the Navy Department authorized placing three on board the *Birmingham*."[67]

On the nineteenth Towers had the C-4, C-5, A-4, and much of the E-1 for spare parts placed aboard the cruiser, which sailed next morning with him, Smith, Chevalier, and twelve enlisted men as passengers. No sooner had the *Birmingham* weighed anchor than Mustin received orders to embark the five hundred Pensacola marines and the A-3 and C-3 on the *Mississippi* for immediate passage to Vera Cruz. Pat Bellinger went aboard with ten mechanics and several trainees. To prevent arms from being landed by a German merchantman for the current Mexican dictator, the Atlantic Fleet assaulted and occupied Vera Cruz before dawn of the twenty-second, the day the *Birmingham* arrived off Tampico.

Mustin had instructed Barney Smith to make a "land chassis" for the A-4. Mustin did the same for the A-3. Both were to use a makeshift airstrip ashore.[68] Towers assisted Smith by "taking wheels off handling trucks, raiding the ship's storeroom for iron rods, etc. . . ." But Captain Bristol frowned on seaplanes converted to land use, because the army, unable to get its own planes to Vera Cruz, was agitating for the navy's planes to be placed under tactical army control.

For the first time American military aircraft were going into a combat situation, an event preceded only by the Italians and Spanish in their North African colonies and by the Greeks in the Balkans. The American press made the most of it. Journalists duly reported the sensation caused in Vera Cruz on 25 April when thousands of people rushed outdoors to get their first glimpse of an aeroplane. Pat Bellinger had been lowered over the side of the *Mississippi* in the C-3 to scout for mines, though in vain. Next day, Bellinger took off from the beach. Reporters mistook him for Towers, who consequently got his portrait on the front cover of the 2 May issue of *Aero and Hydro*.[69]

Towers and his contingent in the *Birmingham* had nothing to do for an entire month, since Captain Sims had to keep the ship off Tampico to prevent a threatened clash between British and German vessels. Bellinger, encamped ashore at Vera Cruz with the land-rigged A-3 hydro, monopolized the action. His A-3 received two bullet holes in the wings, another first for American military aviation.[70]

Mustin and Towers chafed at the boredom of being in the subordinate role of supporting ground forces. Bristol shared their frustration, writing to Mustin at the end of April, "We must never lose sight of the Navy's real work at sea—one fleet against another." Towers just wanted to fly, and when his appeals to Bristol to order his section either to Vera Cruz or back to Pensacola came to naught, he tried the direct approach, to the dismay of Mustin. In May Towers personally approached Rear Admiral Frank F. Fletcher, in command at Vera Cruz, and Fletcher agreed to his request. On the twenty-fourth Captain Sims transferred Towers' men and machines to the *Mississippi* for flight training.[71]

The airmen operated both of the hydros from their Vera Cruz airfield and the three flying boats from the water throughout late May and early June 1914. Towers shared in the scouting chores when he was not instructing. On

The *Mississippi* en route to join the fleet off Vera Cruz during the intervention, April 1914. Lashed down, *left,* is the C-3 flying boat and, over the 12-inch guns, the A-3 hydro. (National Archives)

27 May he took a Secret Service man over Mexican positions to ascertain that no Mexican artillery was aimed at the American outposts, and the next two days he and Barney Smith engaged in bombing practice. Testing the planes in open seas, the airmen agreed that the hydros got airborne more easily than the longer-hulled flying boats—unfortunately, since Bristol had already decided to opt for flying boat purchases. Meanwhile the fighting between warring Mexican armies seesawed as the latest strongman was gradually dislodged.[72]

The activity at the shoreside camp was not all drudgery. "We had a great deal of fun," Towers commented, since the camp "soon became the gathering place of all the war correspondents." Among them were the celebrated Jack London, Frederick Palmer, Richard Harding Davis, and old Jimmie Hare, photographer for *Collier's.*[73] On 28 May Towers

> took Jimmie on a photographic flight well over behind Vera Cruz. We were flying in a Curtiss pusher seaplane, and how he managed to handle a large camera and get fine pictures without any protection from the wind is still a mystery to me. But he did. We got a photograph of the Mexican outposts and on our way back the engine started missing, and to me it looked like a seaplane landing in No Man's Land. Jimmie was so busy looking for something to

photograph that he did not even notice the trouble, and I then and there decided that he was one of these people you often hear about but rarely find, a man who had no idea of the meaning of fear.[74]

The journalists, starved for real news, sensationalized every move the airmen made. One day Towers found a hole in a plane he had just flown inland. He was sure it had been made from a screwdriver wielded by his mechanics, jealous of the bullet punctures received by Bellinger's machine. Thereafter Jack and Bellinger became the focus of the reporters' attention, a notoriety utterly rejected by Towers. A homesick, ill-humored Mustin resented the attention directed at the others, although reporters praised him as being a "high type." The press also wrote about the airmen enjoying the company "of fine looking women among the refugees," swimming in the saltwater pool, and dancing at "turkey trot parties" at the Hotel Universal.[75]

Though few dramatic results were obtained from the Vera Cruz aeronautical experience, the worth of naval aviation was definitely proved to the navy hierarchy. Admiral Badger praised the airmen, while Secretary Daniels proclaimed, "Aeroplanes are now considered one of the arms of the Fleet the same as battleships, destroyers, submarines, and cruisers." Jack Towers' image continued to soar in the public press.[76]

With the situation ashore stabilized, the aviators departed in the *Mississippi* on 12 June, just missing the greatest drunk of American naval history. On the night of the thirtieth, the wine messes were emptied for good by order of teetotaler Josephus Daniels. Upon his return to Pensacola, Towers received a telegram from the Navy Department ordering him to Washington for talks on the proposed transatlantic flight of Glenn Curtiss' big flying boat. He would then proceed to Hammondsport to work on the plane and to help Curtiss redesign new hydros.[77]

Towers was enthusiastic about being copilot to Cyril Porte on a transatlantic crossing. There were difficulties, however, as Curtiss had explained in a letter in May:

> It has been my idea all along that owing to the difficulty of devising a plan whereby you and Lieut. Porte could co-operate in this undertaking, that you should operate entirely independent of him. As the matter now stands, it would seem that the best plan is for you to keep the matter in mind with a view to undertaking it in case Lieut. Porte is unfortunate enough not to accomplish it. This would give you a distinct advantage, as you would have the benefit of his experience. . . . Mr. Wanamaker has all along been very keen on your going into this thing and is anxious to have an American accomplish the flight, although he must, of course, give Lieut. Porte his opportunity because of his early connection with the enterprise.[78]

By the time Towers arrived in Washington, Curtiss had announced that instead of a risky, direct Newfoundland-to-Ireland route, the transatlantic flying boat would take a southerly route along regular shipping lanes with a stopover in the Azores islands. Wanamaker announced from England that the boat would be named *America*. Jack reported to Admiral Fiske, who queried him about the possibilities of success. "I told him that I thought that there was a reasonable chance of accomplishing the flight successfully, provided the flying boat could take off with a sufficient amount of gasoline to go from Newfoundland to the Azores and that this could not be determined until the plane was completed and tried out. He . . . stated that if I reported to him after the tests that the flight was practicable he would recommend to the Secretary that I be permitted to make it." And, if the flight was approved, Fiske promised to "do all in his power to arrange for adequate cooperation of surface vessels" posted along the flight path.[79]

During Towers' absence in Mexico, Curtiss had assigned civilian mechanic George E. A. Hallett to be the probable copilot. Lanny Callan was sent ahead by ship to the Azores to relieve Hallett on the second leg of the flight.

Towers, Curtiss, and John Cyril Porte stand in front of the enclosed cockpit of the *America* on her day of christening at Hammondsport, 22 June 1914. Porte's floppy straw hat became all the rage of vacationers up from New York to witness the trials of the transatlantic flying boat. (Glenn H. Curtiss Museum)

81

During the summer of 1914 the red-painted flying boat *America* makes a full-powered test run along Lake Keuka, propelled by two 90-horsepower Curtiss OX pusher engines. Two men can be seen standing, one kneeling, and two sitting behind the enclosed cockpit to increase the payload. (Glenn H. Curtiss Museum)

Rumors were already circulating that Towers would replace Hallett as co-pilot, though Jack denied them. Another rumor emerged when Towers made his appearance in Hammondsport for test flights. Curtiss was building a duplicate of the *America,* leading reporters to speculate whether Tower would be the prospective pilot for this second transatlantic boat.[80]

Towers found normally sleepy Hammondsport "seething with excitement" over what the press called the airboat. Among the many reporters grasping at tidbits of information were Norman G. Thwaites of the London *Daily Mail* and Herbert Bayard Swope of the New York *World*. The newspapermen found Jack Towers, like tight-lipped Curtiss and Porte, adding nothing substantial to their inquiries. Nor did Dick Richardson, also assigned to observe the *America* and two new Curtiss navy seaplanes.[81]

Towers witnessed the christening of the bright-red *America* on 22 June. Porte had to smash the stubborn ceremonial bottle of champagne with a hammer after the sponsoring teenage girl failed to break it against the fragile hull in five attempts. Launched into the waters of Lake Keuka, the big plane was a pusher whose 74-foot-long upper wing, 35-foot-long hull, and enclosed cabin were powered by two 90-horsepower engines. It housed the latest aeronautical instruments, including dual controls with a Deperdussin-style footbar for the ailerons and a Curtiss steering wheel for longitudinal control.[82]

Next day, the twenty-third, Curtiss and Hallett flew the *America* on a ten-minute hop before yielding the controls to Porte and a mechanic for the first scheduled test flight. Towers then joined Curtiss in his "scooter," "a small, very fast [50-mph] speedboat [constructed] for the specific purpose of running alongside the *America* and watching the action of the hull. . . ." With the speedboat racing parallel to it, the lightly loaded *America* "took off very nicely" but not quickly enough to satisfy Towers, who was convinced it could never get off with its full load. Otherwise, the machine flew magnificently. Over succeeding days sandbags were gradually added, and "long before anything like a full load had been reached the *America*'s hull was so submerged that it simply wallowed through the water." Since the plane would carry a load of 2,600 pounds of mostly gasoline, design changes had to be tried and tested.

The 1 July front page of the *Hammondsport Herald* featured the *America* story and several photographs of Towers, Curtiss, and Porte, along with the news that sparked World War I, the murder of Archduke Francis Ferdinand of Austria-Hungary. While modifications to the *America* increased the payload, the great flying boat still refused to lift the required 2,600-pound cargo. Curtiss held a long discussion on 18 July with Porte, Towers, Richardson, Hallett, and marine airman Mac McIlvain to consider alternatives. They decided to add a third 90-horsepower engine, a tractor, over the top wing. This and other additions consumed four days and nights. On the morning of the twenty-third Jack, Richardson, and McIlvain piled into Curtiss' scooter to run alongside the sleek *America* as Curtiss lifted her off the water. He brought the flying boat back around to play "in hundred-yard bounds along the surface," in the words of one observer. The *America* was "followed at [an] even pace by the strenuous scooter and the three naval officers, their hair streaming and shirt sleeves fluttering. It was a novel sight, this saucy sea dog straining at terrific pace, as if to devour the great red-winged whale, frolicking along without effort a yard or two above the water."[83]

A few more flights that day and the next were equally successful, achieving the necessary lift capacity without the additional engine. Unfortunately, the need for two new propellers and other alterations meant that the *America* could not be shipped to Newfoundland before the onset of the storms of mid-August and September, which would have made the flight hazardous. Curtiss announced on 25 July that it would be postponed until 1 October.[84]

Towers, realizing he and his navy colleagues would not be needed until the reconfigured plane was ready for testing, requested permission to go home on leave. By the time he reached Rome, war had broken out in Europe. Britain began to mobilize, which meant that Cyril Porte was recalled to active duty, whereupon Wanamaker and Curtiss decided that Towers should replace him as the pilot of the *America*. But, due to the war, the navy could no longer spare a picket line of destroyers for the flight. On 3 August, the day after Germany invaded Belgium, Jack read in the papers that the flight had been postponed indefinitely.[85]

The same day Towers, knowing that the latest aeroplanes could best be observed in wartime Europe, fired off a telegram to the Navy Department: "IF ANY OFFICERS WILL BE SENT EUROPE OBSERVE WAR, DESIRE VOLUNTEER THAT DUTY." Next day, when Britain went to war against Germany, to Towers' surprise and joy, he received a dispatch ordering him to proceed immediately to New York and report aboard the armored cruiser *Tennessee* for passage to Europe.[86]

What Towers did not know was that Bristol had earlier decided to send him abroad and thus to have him on board a warship going to Europe in the expectation that he would be available and on the scene when the Navy Department made the decision to assign observers to the capitals of the warring powers. Bristol justified Towers' orders by claiming to route him to Paris for the inspection of a French aeroplane the navy was considering purchasing. Virtually all the other navy pilots sent similar letters applying for duty in Europe as observers, though Mustin wanted to continue their work at Pensacola. Bristol, who could accommodate only two other requests, assigned Barney Smith to Paris and Vic Herbster to Berlin.[87]

The suddenness of Towers' orders, received on 4 August, left him a margin of only thirty hours in which to reach New York by rail. All of his "uniforms were in Pensacola, and there was no time to wait for them, so I telegraphed to New York and had another lot made." He arrived on the late afternoon of the fifth only to find that the *Tennessee* had already left the Brooklyn Navy Yard and moved to the quarantine station at Staten Island. Enterprising as ever, he picked up his new uniforms, "caught a boat at the New York Yacht Club landing and got aboard the *Tennessee* in the lower harbor" an hour before she was scheduled to sail.[88]

The navy was frantically pressing two armored cruisers into the task of rescuing American citizens vacationing in Europe. The old *Tennessee*, supposedly at the end of her seagoing days, not only was "not properly fitted out for the trip but also had its officers and crew literally thrown aboard, and most of them had never been on the ship before." The cruiser earmarked to accompany the *Tennessee* was the *North Carolina,* Mustin's new aviation training ship, which hastened to Boston, where her aviation equipment was put ashore; her hapless pilots remained on board to make up for the shortage of watchstanders.[89]

Similarly, Towers was to be "available for ship's duties when not occupied by regular duties" during the *Tennessee*'s transatlantic voyage. On the morning of 6 August the ship fired a fifteen-gun salute to the assistant secretary of war, Henry Breckinridge, as he came aboard. He had charge of a special cargo that arrived late in the day: no less than $4.5 million in gold coins furnished by private banks and Congress to buy passage home for the stranded Americans. The *Tennessee*'s departure was delayed while the money was being insured.[90]

The bullion-laden *Tennessee* upped anchor that evening and headed to sea to rendezvous with the *North Carolina*, out of Boston. The two cruisers shaped their course for Falmouth, England.[91] That Towers was crossing the Atlantic by ship rather than flying boat was irrelevant, since the flight of the *America* had been scratched. George Hallett eventually admitted that the plane probably would have gone down anyway because of excessive engine vibrations. He also believed the wings would have iced up, though this seems unlikely at the planned cruising altitude of under 1,000 feet. But the two big *America* flying boats would prove important, not only in the war but in paving the way for the first transatlantic flight five years later.[92]

The posting abroad of the U.S. Navy's most proficient and experienced aviator did no real detriment to his career or to the growth of American naval aviation. For the state of the art in the United States was downright inferior, and despite proddings by Congress during the two years Towers was absent, the navy, doubting the country would be drawn into the conflict, did not expand its air program significantly. One admiral who disagreed was Bradley Fiske: "With the advent of practical aircraft, command of the air becomes just as important as command of the sea, both for land and sea warlike operation." His outspokenness led to his forced retirement, and Mustin would struggle along with the minuscule training program at Pensacola.

During Towers' absence, one matter festered among the navy's airmen—their rating as qualified aviators on the basis of seniority. The system of numbered naval air certificates proved unsatisfactory. On 22 March 1915 Towers and his fellow pilots were given the designation naval aviator, but it took three more years before they would finally be rated in a satisfactory sequence—Spuds Ellyson as naval aviator no. 1, John Rodgers as 2, and Towers as 3, with others following roughly according to the dates they earned their licenses.[93]

Though Jack Towers had left Hammondsport for global horizons, he never forgot his affection for the idyllic proving ground on the shores of Lake Keuka where he had established his aeronautical roots with Glenn Curtiss.

Late in life Jack recalled how he and Ellyson had routinely frequented the Gent's Club, that "little barber shop on main street." In the summer of 1939, during his tenure as chief of BuAer, he rented a cottage on Lake Keuka for his family. One weekend he saw the old barber shop and decided he needed a haircut.

> So I walked in—a two-chair place. . . . The barber that had the back chair had a customer, and he said, "Sit down, the boss will be in." I sat down and began to think of what had happened to me during the intervening years. I thought of World War I when I was abroad, the NC flight, commanding the *Saratoga,* becoming Chief of the Bureau of Aeronautics.
>
> And sitting in this chair I was beginning to think, "Well, maybe you're getting somewhere." Just then the second barber came in, walked up behind my chair, and then came around to look at me, and he said quietly, "Well, hello, Lieutenant! Where *have* you been?!"

4

LEARNING FROM
THE BRITISH
1914–16

The outbreak of World War I in mid-1914 stimulated both naval and aeronautical progress, giving Lieutenant Towers a unique perspective as an observer for the neutral United States. Ostensibly, he and a dozen other navy officers in the *Tennessee* and the *North Carolina* were to help Assistant Secretary Breckinridge distribute funds to stranded American tourists. But the presence of naval officers, Breckinridge confided in his diary, "is really a subterfuge to enable the Navy to place these officers as observers with the British fleet, if possible. I am to use every effort to accomplish this upon arrival in England."[1]

The *Tennessee*'s skipper, Captain Benton C. "Uncle Benny" Decker, had been "a well-known character" at the Naval Academy, handling severe infraction cases during Jack's years there. Towers' skills in the use of the wireless led to his assignment as radio officer, while future aviator Johnny Hoover was placed in charge of the kegs of gold stowed throughout the ship. Breckinridge had the navy and army officers give talks in their leisure time on specialized topics.[2]

On 13 August Towers was thus called upon to speak about the state of American naval aviation, an address that so impressed Captain Decker that he wrote up a lengthy report for the Naval War College. Towers' state-of-the-art observations emphasized the readiness of the navy's seaplanes. Each battleship and cruiser could be equipped with two to four planes, along with a "launching device" (catapult) to send them off on scouting missions of up to five hours' duration and in winds up to 40 mph. He reviewed all the instruments then available, notably Elmer Sperry's new course indicator and automatic stabilizer; only the problems plaguing radio remained to be solved. Jack's own experiences had proved the aeroplane's ability to spot submarines and mines, while ships would have difficulty spotting and hitting a plane further than two miles away. A faulty engine or wing could usually be replaced in one hour.[3]

The *Tennessee*'s only anxious moments on this cruise occurred in midafternoon of the last day, 16 August. Two cruisers, one French and one British, bore down on the American ships until they had identified them, whereupon gun salutes were exchanged. Then at 1800 the *Tennessee* followed the *North Carolina* into Falmouth harbor on the southwest tip of the English coast, welcomed by a throng of private boats jammed with cheering spectators waving handkerchiefs to their American cousins. Secretary Breckinridge's orders were to stay only briefly, visit the embassy in London, then proceed with the monies to the continent.[4]

Towers' orders were to accompany Breckinridge to London, which they reached by rail the next morning. They proceeded immediately to the embassy and reported to the ambassador, Walter Hines Page, who, appearing to resent the presence of Breckinridge, wanted him to hasten to the continent.[5] So the party returned to Falmouth on the all-night train, Towers toting $1,700 in gold in a money belt around his waist, fearful lest he be separated from a regular paymaster. Thus "when I arrived back at the ship I had on my hip a blister the size of my fist."

On 20 August the *Tennessee* set course for the Hook of Holland. From there Breckinridge and his keg-toting army officers departed to the capitals of Europe with their gold. Towers and several colleagues visited Rotterdam during the ship's four-day visit to neutral Holland. He found the city

in a state of great suppressed excitement. The Dutch are a phlegmatic people, but even they were visibly stirred by what was taking place. The great German drive through Belgium and northern France was in full swing and at night the noise of the guns could be heard. Thousands of refugees were pouring over into Holland, and the Dutch were by no means sure that their country would not be overrun by the Germans at that time.

A Zeppelin raid was made on Antwerp [Belgium], only fifty miles distant, the night we were in Rotterdam, and the next morning thousands of Belgians came pouring in with the wildest kind of stories as to what had happened. In reality it was ascertained later that very little damage had occurred.

The aerial attack on a major city by a German dirigible had introduced strategic bombing into the annals of war. Though the bombs had accomplished little, they added to the general conflagration that the German armies inflicted on helpless Belgium during the drive into France.

Returning with the *Tennessee* to Falmouth, Towers received orders en route to report to Ambassador Page in London for duty as assistant naval attaché. Apparently Cyril Porte, now lieutenant commander in the Royal Naval Air Service (RNAS), had urged Jack's assignment to London instead of Paris. Figuring that Jack "preferred England" because of this recommendation, Captain Bristol approved the assignment. Towers left the *Tennessee* to her relief tasks, Breckinridge eventually returning home in the liner *Lusitania*.[6] Meanwhile Henry Mustin, Pat Bellinger, and Barney Smith went to Paris to witness sleek tractor-style French warplanes—"so far ahead of us," wrote Mustin, "that it looks like an impossibility ever to catch up. . . ."[7]

When Towers arrived in London again the last week in August, he had no idea that he would be staying there until September 1916. The naval attaché at the embassy was Commander Powers "Pete" Symington, ordered to report European naval operations to the Office of Naval Intelligence (ONI). Towers would handle all intelligence on British aircraft, assisted by Lieutenant Commander Frank R. McCrary, a shy visionary who obtained permission to undertake flight training in England before returning home to become the U.S. Navy's first blimp and free-balloon pilot. Naval Constructor Lewis B. McBride observed weaponry in general.[8]

Though little more than a week separated Towers' two arrivals in London, he now found the great city

> in a very tense state. The Battle of Mons had been fought and lost [on 23 August]. The flower of the British Army had resisted that great German drive. Everyone you met had a son, brother, or a husband in that Army, and none had any news except the general news that there had been terrible losses. There was no hysteria, however, and the man in the street was confident that Mons was only a temporary setback and that the war would be won within three months. The war drums of England were sounding, and tens and tens of thousands of volunteers were pouring in; the Grand Fleet was nobody knew where, but wherever it was it was there and England was safe.

The British Grand Fleet was in fact ensconced at Scapa Flow in northern Scotland, blockading the entire North Sea against a possible breakout by the

German High Seas Fleet. Towers' job was to find out all he could about the British fleet's newly created air arm, the RNAS, first by contacting Cyril Porte, about to take command at the Hendon naval aerodrome north of London. A fighter and training facility, Hendon became Jack's own headquarters for gathering intelligence. He began his duties by flying there once or twice a week in British planes made available to him by Porte.[9]

Within two weeks Towers had seen enough to conclude "that the Navy Air Department was *not* prepared for war, being short of machines, spares and general equipment. They took over everything in the country that was any good," part of the policy of the First Lord of the Admiralty, Winston Churchill, to expand the RNAS from a nucleus of sixty-four aircraft into a powerful arm of the Royal Navy.[10]

At first Towers was caught up in the frenzied evacuation of American tourists, "just about like shovelling the tide back with a spoon." The departing liners did not seem to put a dent in the thousands of Americans pouring into London from the continent—along with the first casualties. Jack found it hard to believe that less than a month after they had all been together at Hammondsport, he and reporter Herbert Swope found themselves "sitting alongside a hospital bed in London in which lay Norman Thwaites just brought over from France, badly wounded." By mid-September the worst of the tourist crisis was over, and Towers could turn his full attention to gathering aeronautical intelligence.[11]

On 5 September Jack went to the Admiralty to call on the officer in charge of the Royal Navy's growing 200-man aviation arm, Captain Murray F. Sueter, who told him he could visit any of the navy's air stations, or depots. But two days later he received a letter from the Admiralty saying that that would not be "expedient at present." Also finding access to aircraft manufacturers difficult, Jack nevertheless used his personal connections and the argument that he was interested in purchasing planes for his government to visit T. O. M. Sopwith on the tenth. Britain's leading aircraft manufacturer was polite and let him see the company's production lines but informed him that British companies were now forbidden to build for foreign countries.[12]

Towers wrote to Bristol that "the individual officers have been fine," but that the Royal Navy "very strictly enforced orders not even to *talk!*" And when he tried to arrange an inspection trip to Paris, the embassy sent his army counterpart instead. In fact, Britain's lack of cooperation was deliberate. As Towers remembered it, "At first they resented the evincing, on the part of the Americans, of any interest in what was going on. It was their war. They were fighting it and America was simply taking the gate receipts."[13]

Towers was not to be deterred quite so easily, however. Officially forbidden to venture outside London, he informed the local police that it was time for him to take his annual physical, an endurance test in which he had to walk fifty miles over three consecutive days. He took it outside London, trailed by bobbies. Johnny Hoover recalled, "He led them a merry chase for three days."[14]

Official British bitterness toward the neutral Americans was underscored as German successes mounted on land and even at sea. In October Antwerp and the Belgian coast finally fell to the Germans, and the Western Front was established as a network of trenches. The fear of Belgian-based Zeppelin dirigibles bombing London, Towers informed Bristol, caused insurance rates to soar, blackouts to be imposed at night, and searchlights and skywatchers to be placed around London. "Machines are kept in readiness for night flights at Hendon but there are few pilots available to operate them."[15] Though no attacks occurred that fall, Towers knew from Vic Herbster in Berlin that "aviators and officers of various corps all believe that the reconnaissance work of the Zeppelins has been of immense value. Their greatest service is yet to come (they say)—namely against England. This war is going to last some time yet, about one year more, and they mean to win it. . . ."[16]

Poking about Hendon, Towers watched Cyril Porte test the two modified Curtiss *America* flying boats just brought over from Hammondsport but was prevented from observing a new Sopwith speed scout (fighter). Acting virtually as a spy, he gleaned news from conversations about improved designs at the Farnborough Royal Aircraft Factory and by visiting the Teddington National Physical Laboratory, where he was allowed to examine in detail the newest of three wind tunnels. Early in November Captain Reginald Belknap, impressed by Jack's intelligence-gathering successes, informed Bristol that Towers "seemed to share in the disgust the others [at the embassy] felt at the cold shoulder which the British are giving us. It would be a pity to take him away."[17]

Hoping to remedy the situation, Assistant Secretary Franklin Roosevelt wrote to Commander Symington suggesting that he, Roosevelt, be allowed to come over to study the British naval organization and to bring more officers with him to act as observers. But First Lord Churchill refused even to discuss the idea. Symington informed FDR, "The lid is down tight and we get almost nothing. With Towers and McBride we can keep an eye on things and they are gradually working up an acquaintance that will produce results if anything ever happens."[18]

So Captain Bristol had Towers, Vic Herbster (in Berlin), and Barney Smith (in Paris) collecting "some very interesting and useful information," though Towers' being furthest from "the field of action" was perhaps least useful. Homeward-bound student pilot Ensign Mel Stolz carried to Bristol a recommendation from Towers "that the development of an anti-aircraft gun should be immediately considered."[19]

Towers became more active at the end of November 1914, when Tom Sopwith invited him to his factory to observe an impressive output of one seaplane per day. In his attempt to obtain data on building rights in England Jack had difficulty, although the Vickers company provided him with dirigible blueprints. "I know now quite a lot of the British flyers and have been taken on some trips (on the q.t.!) about England by them." But he could say little about what he had learned "for fear of getting the officers in trouble." Rather, he intended to keep moving between air stations, talking aeronautics with everyone he met, then to sum up his intelligence when he felt sure of the data. Bristol appreciated this need for restraint and approved it.[20]

One individual Towers befriended was Lieutenant Commander Spenser D. A. Grey, commander of a Royal Navy squadron. Grey wanted Jack to accompany the squadron to the continent but instead was ordered to make a quick trip to the United States in December to obtain more Curtiss flying boats. There Grey briefly visited with Bristol, who then wrote Jack, "I hope you will get a chance to go to the Continent with him when the [flying] season opens. This chap is very interesting and we enjoyed meeting him." But when Grey returned to London in March 1915, he was placed in charge of conducting the flying boat experiments at Hendon. So Jack did not go to France.[21]

The flaws in British aeronautical policy did not escape Towers' probing questions, especially the fact that Royal Navy air stations were indiscriminately commanded by navy or marine officers who lacked knowledge of aviation; Towers personally observed particular cases of resulting mismanagement. He learned that the six small British naval airships were being used with trawlers to search for mines, but he told Bristol that "regular flyers rather look down" on the lighter-than-air craft.[22]

By the Christmas season Towers admitted being homesick, but gradually his successes mounted, as in December when he learned that the Admiralty had had a forty-eight-hour advance warning of a German battle cruiser bombardment of the British coast—evidence of Britain's code-breaking skills. And he reported the first seaborne air attack when seven British seaplanes were lowered into the water from specially converted seaplane carriers and took off to attack the Zeppelin sheds at Cuxhaven, Germany, on Christmas Day. This epochal operation in the history of navies inflicted little damage, but it inspired the RNAS to try again later—and Towers to suggest that his own navy "ought to be taking up the question of seaplane-ships."[23]

In mid-January 1915 naval attaché Symington wrangled a permit from the Admiralty to operate regularly as an observer on board ships of the Grand Fleet, "a deep secret" that Towers did not convey to Bristol for another six months—"so deep that officers actually in ONI in Washington do not know it, and very few people here. . . . We tell the story that he [Symington] is in America." Such subterfuges demonstrated how the British were beginning, ever so subtly, to court American favor. Commander Symington's absence did not turn out to be temporary. Except for short visits to the embassy he remained with the operating fleet for most of the remaining twenty months of Jack's tour of duty in London. This left Towers as senior U.S. line officer and acting naval attaché in Britain, greatly increasing his responsibilities.[24]

Indeed, his intelligence gathering suffered from severe lack of funding for both him and his fellow "spy," Lewis McBride. Towers told Bristol in February that he could "only hope . . . to hold out financially until they make us some sort of an allowance: McBride and I are having rather an expensive time of it and have finally succeeded in getting a temporary magnificent allowance of $17.00 to cover costs of 'acquiring information.' He has submitted a test claim, but I do not think anything will come of it. It is the necessary entertaining of officers that mounts up." The allowance was later increased.[25]

Early 1915 proved momentous as Britain attempted, disastrously, to turn the German flank by attacking through Turkey at the Dardanelles, and Germany initiated a U-boat blockade of the British Isles. Many of Towers' contacts left Britain for the Dardanelles, and in March he warned Bristol of the danger to Sperry agent William L. Gilmore, who was carrying samples of the most recent British aeronautical compasses aboard the British liner *Lusitania* to America.[26]

The diplomatic ramifications of Germany's new submarine policy became plain on 1 May when the American gasoline tanker *Gulflight* was torpedoed off the Scilly islands, to which she was then towed. When the Germans claimed the *Gulflight* had struck a British mine, the Admiralty "left no stones unturned to supply proof" to the Americans that she had been deliberately torpedoed. A destroyer placed at Towers' disposal took him and McBride to the Scillys to inspect the ship. There Jack "was overwhelmed by the evidence supplied by the British that she had been torpedoed."[27]

Then came the afternoon of 7 May 1915. Ambassador Page sent for Towers and informed him "with tears in his eyes" that the *Lusitania* had been torpedoed and sunk. To obtain details, Towers went directly to the Admiralty and presented himself to the First Lord.

He found Churchill anxiously awaiting further information. "At his invitation, I remained in his office and was given reports as they came in. At first the Director of Transportation, Captain [Richard] Webb, insisted that there was some mistake, as the Admiralty had known that a German submarine was awaiting the *Lusitania* at Kinsale Point and had specifically directed the captain to take a course which would avoid the area. Alas, the captain had disobeyed those orders and had cut straight across the danger area in order to save time and make the favorable tide in the Medway." The cost was 1,198 lives, including 128 Americans.[28]

"It was evident that afternoon as I sat in the office of the First Lord of the Admiralty that he [Churchill] thought that this tragedy was not without its reward and that he believed that it would result in an American declaration of war on Germany." It did not, but "the Admiralty from that time on changed its attitude from one of resentfulness about our curiosity to one of helpfulness," giving us "every opportunity to see that the Germans were waging war in fact on America as well as England." And Secretary Daniels ordered that intelligence henceforth be transmitted to ONI in code.[29]

On 26 May, before the furor over the *Lusitania* could die down, yet another American merchantman experienced a "mysterious" explosion off the coast of Ireland—the *Nebraskan.* Three months later a U-boat sank the British liner *Arabic,* killing two Americans. Strong American diplomatic protests prompted Germany to announce an outright ban on liner sinkings on 1 September, but three days later a torpedo struck the British liner *Hesperian,* and a piece of the projectile was afterward found on her deck. She sank trying to make port, taking over fifty lives. When the Admiralty refused to let American naval officers see the evidence, Ambassador Page obtained permission for Towers to be shown everything the British had relating to the incident. They gave Towers the piece of metal, which Page mailed home directly. The Germans were guilty again.[30]

Despite the provocation by German subs, the Wilson administration's stance toward Britain was complicated by the fact, uncovered by the New York *Tribune*'s London correspondent Philip H. Patchin, that Japan, since 1902 allied to Britain, had received British acquiescence in occupying the German islands in the central Pacific. Notable was Yap in the western Carolines, important as a cable station. The official word was that an Australian expeditionary force had taken Yap, and everyone in London, except the Japanese ambassador (privately), denied that it was Japan that had done it.

When Patchin "was brushed" by Ambassador Page, he took the news to Towers, who also found that Page "had little interest" in the matter. Jack thereupon reported directly to ONI, which already had the information from its attaché in Tokyo. The Japanese had taken, and meant to keep, the German island groups in the Pacific—the Carolines, Marianas, and Marshalls.[31]

Towers' ability to report on aviation in Britain declined sharply as the Royal Navy shifted its training activities from Hendon to Chingford, twelve miles from London—"and whereas anyone could go to Hendon," he told Bristol in June, "it takes almost an Act of Parliament to get into Chingford. Commander Porte has permanently moved to Felixstowe [sixty miles northeast of London, on the North Sea coast] where he is commanding the [naval air] Station that is continually being enlarged, and while every time I see him, he tells me he is going to let me know when would be a good time to come down, he never names the day!"

On 19 June Towers got a promise in person from the new First Lord, Arthur J. Balfour, for a meeting at which Jack planned to request "the run of all the stations in England and . . . permission to get on one of the 'aeronautic ships.'" The Royal Navy's air arm now included no fewer than 1,500 officers, 11,000 men, and over 1,000 aircraft, and Jack meant to see as much as he could. But Balfour, like Porte, kept fending off his requests, including one to ascend in one of the navy's new captive kite balloons, which had just become operational. Porte sat at the center of British seaplane developments and was surely reluctant to disclose secrets to any foreign officer. The Admiralty did not trust the U.S. Navy with such data. "We would be pleased to give you more information," the director of naval intelligence, Captain W. R. Hall, once remarked to Towers, "but we feel over there that the Navy Department is a kind of Press Bureau, and that such secret information might soon appear in one of the American newspapers."[32]

British intransigence can be explained partly by the Royal Navy's failure to operate its seaplanes with much success in the heavy weather of the North Sea. Also, its landplanes had failed completely to intercept the Zeppelins that had begun to drop bombs on southeastern England at night, even on the outskirts of London. Towers learned details of the attacks from his American newspaper friends, "who 'under run' all these raids." He knew damage was light, but the psychological effect was "demoralizing," especially since "the War Office has published notices in all the papers urging people to supply themselves with 'respirators' in case the Zeppelins come armed with gas-bombs! Some of the weirdest things come from the War Office, to the great amusement of the Germans, I hear."

Towers reflected in June,

I do not see why the Germans do not come right up every night, almost, for so far as I can see, the only serious danger they run is on their return when they reach the Belgian coast [and Allied fighters based in adjacent France]. It is a hopeless proposition to aeroplanes to attempt to find them [Zeppelins] in the dark, and the two pilots who may have were recently killed in night landings after this hopeless search. The whole thing seems to be rather stupidly run for even after it was known that the Zeppelins had left the vicinity of London and were making for the coast, [the British] would not permit any lights to be turned on at Hendon or Chingford and the several pilots in the air had no possible way of telling where those places were.[33]

Towers regarded dirigibles as "an unknown quantity, but I believe we will find when this war is over that they have been of great help, especially in the use against submarines." By midsummer, however, he had yet to meet a British dirigible officer. As for aircraft, he knew the Royal Navy was seeking larger flying machines with bigger engines, to achieve up to 300 horsepower, but such engines were still in the experimental stage. He admired the strides made in aeronautical instruments, which he wanted for American planes, for it was "criminal to let a machine go up without them." He submitted a detailed report of recommendations, partly based on the organization of the army's Royal Flying Corps, and he sent Bristol a set of RNAS training manuals.[34]

The captain pressed Towers on the question of engine location for aircraft. The issue of tractor versus pusher engines for seaplanes plagued Bristol, since it was of fundamental importance for future development. Whereas in April he thought tractors "doomed for military purposes," by June he was asking Curtiss to build them and soliciting Towers' advice on the relative merits of the two types of engine. Jack would not commit himself on the issue in July, except to reject U.S. pusher flying boats in favor of the British Sopwith and Short tractors, which added strength to the growing American preference for the front-engine plane.[35]

Needless to say, Bristol was pleased to receive such thorough intelligence and advice, which he used to push enlarged appropriations for naval aviation through Congress. "Your ideas for getting news is the right one. Keep knocking about and always keep your ear to the ground," he encouraged Jack. Not only was Towers kept abreast of aviation developments at home by Bristol, but Chevy Chevalier, Earle Johnson, and others wrote to him of their work at Pensacola. And in May he learned that the Aero Club had awarded him an expert certificate and that Mel Stolz had perished in a hydro-pusher crash at Pensacola.[36]

Jack complained anew in June about being homesick, though he knew he could not leave until he had his long-anticipated interview with the First Lord or until Pete Symington returned to the embassy; Towers was simply too valuable in London. Fearful lest his complaints had struck Bristol the wrong way, Jack started his July report, "I don't want you to think that I am growling about staying over here, for I still think that I am earning my pay." Bristol reassured him: "[W]hat you are accomplishing is of more service to us than you really think yourself."[37]

Towers offset his homesickness with social events, theater, and daily exercise. The talented budding English stage actress Lynn Fontanne later recalled to him "that long supper table down at the Manners' house on the Thames, and Phil Lidig striding about saying, 'Russia! Russia has done her dirty bit!' " in the war. Jack stayed fit by playing tennis and golf, the latter occasionally with Ambassador Page. Ever the dapper civilian with British bowler, spats, and cane, he maintained his moderate eating habits, though he smoked cigarettes steadily and drank martinis to relax. Unlike his navy peers, he generally shunned coffee. "Save it for when you need it!" was his motto.[38]

Having reached the age of thirty in January 1915, the handsome bachelor longed for a mate, and opportunity knocked during a dinner at the residence of Ambassador Page. He found himself seated next to the attractive daughter of prominent American art dealer Charles Stewart Carstairs, who had offices in New York, London, and Paris. Elizabeth Haseltine "Lily" Carstairs was twenty-three years old, almost seven years younger than Jack. Among her illustrious forebears, and the man for whom her father was named, was the famous commodore of the early American sailing navy, Charles Stewart of Philadelphia. Though from the upper crust and quite spoiled, Lily came from a family with a worthy reputation for social responsibility. Two of her three older brothers had plunged into war work, Hake with Belgian Relief, Carroll enlisting in the British Grenadier Guards. Given the family's naval heritage, her father and the other members could only regard Jack Towers' profession—and post at the embassy—with respect. Before long, Jack was actively courting the only Carstairs daughter. She reciprocated his affection.[39]

Ever since becoming an aviator, Towers had been concerned about the navy's attitude toward flyers being married. When insurance companies had decided to cease coverage of aviators, he supported the issuing of flight pay "as a form of insurance to which they are justly entitled, and not in the nature of a prize or reward."[40] This being especially important for a surviving widow, flight pay would eliminate one of the obstacles to flyers marrying. Though an initial bias by BuNav against married pilots had softened, Towers was not going to take chances. He told Captain Bristol nothing of his proposal of marriage to Lily, which she accepted. The date was set for the autumn.

Towers' joy was augmented at the end of July 1915 when Cyril Porte finally allowed him to visit Felixstowe—which resulted in two lengthy reports to ONI on Porte's work—and when First Lord Balfour at last granted him an interview. At this "long conference," Jack "asked for all sorts of privileges, such as visiting all the stations in England, and the advanced bases in Flanders, seaplane-ships, and the various factories which are now closed to me." On Bristol's instructions he particularly wanted to bid on British aircraft engines. Balfour seemed receptive to Jack's entreaties and followed up with a note saying he was discussing them with his admirals.[41]

But still the Royal Navy stalled. For meanwhile, on 1 August, a reorganization of the RNAS took effect, aimed at putting air policy on a more efficient footing. An office of director of air services was created, headed by a rear admiral, C. L. Vaughn-Lee, whose favor Towers immediately began to court. Training was centralized at one depot. And a senior airman was given control of naval air patrols over the U-boat–infested English Channel. Otherwise, trained pilots were too junior to command these forces and had to be content with jobs on the staffs of their nonflying chiefs. "The general tone of everything," Towers reported later, "is that of a temporary affair," owing largely to the "lack of sufficient regular naval officers of aeronautic training. . . . All of which seems to me a good lesson for us." It was a lesson he would spend much of his career trying to teach his own superiors.[42]

Jack and Lily were married on 5 October 1915 and took a home in Surrey, a suburb of London. The news swiftly reached Captain Bristol, who two days later congratulated Jack: "You will be a better man for having a charming helpmate." Bristol reassured the newlywed pilot that his being married would not affect his career. Bristol regarded aeronautical duty as "a temporary detail" like duty on any type of ship. If naval aviation were otherwise—"a special sort of service"—then "you would never look forward to commanding a fleet" of all classes of vessels, submarines and aviation units included. By endorsing Jack's marriage, he was subtly warning him not to stay too close to aviation.[43]

The couple had to endure blackouts as bombing Zeppelins penetrated the heart of the city. Many pedestrians were run over by motor cars and killed in the darkness. And it was a mixed blessing when Lily quickly became pregnant, an unwanted development that made the fun-loving bride furious. The wartime marriage was off to a rocky start, and the situation was exacerbated by Jack's leaving his wife to visit Paris in November for talks with Barney Smith. For five busy days Towers and Smith compared notes about events of the past year and visited French air stations and factories, which impressed Towers in most respects. He returned to England with aircraft manufacturer Tom Sopwith, who while crossing the channel expressed interest in building machines for the Americans, though the British government still refused.[44]

Doors finally began to open when Towers visited Sopwith's factory for the first time in months. Then Balfour granted him permission to inspect eight naval air stations, including Felixstowe, Chingford, and the three depots around Dover. His pass was personally signed by Admiral Vaughn-Lee. Jack lost no time in making the rounds in mid-December. He marveled at Cyril Porte's "enormous" new flying boats at Felixstowe and reaffirmed the superiority of Sopwith's "speed scouts" (fighter planes). His mobility was greatly facilitated by the availability of an automobile, "though with petrol at two shillings and a penny a gallon, it is rather expensive since the car uses a gallon every 8 miles!" Heavy rains and gale-force winds caused delays in his inspection trips until mid-January 1916, when he got down to Dover for his first look at British dirigibles.[45]

German Zeppelins and seaplanes had been increasing their attacks on London and the Kentish coast over recent months, even in heavy weather; one of the most successful Zep raids that Towers witnessed was made "in a blinding snowstorm." Jack "plotted the fall of the bombs" to ascertain the exact targets and was invariably satisfied that the Germans were aiming only at military objectives, usually arsenals. Occasionally, the bombs started fires, one inflicting $10 million of damage. But the greatest effect, in Towers' opinion, was indirect—the closing of all businesses and industries between 2100 and 0400 whenever a raid was reported to be approaching the coast.[46]

Since the pilots defending the homeland felt they could not reach 9,000 feet to stop the Zeps, the Admiralty in January 1916 finally approved their request to carry out systematic bombing attacks on German airfields along the Belgian and German coasts. The raids consumed most of the spring with uneven results and thus were postponed in May. Towers continually urged the Admiralty to let him go to the continent to observe these operations but without success. His enthusiasm hardly impressed wife Lily, since their baby was due in midsummer.[47]

Busy as Towers was providing crucial data to ONI and Bristol from his visits to factories and naval air stations, he had professional concerns, namely over his inability to draw the sea duty necessary for advancement. "I am still worrying about staying over here so long," he wrote Bristol at the end of January. "I do not feel that I should leave while things are coming my way so fast, but I should like to know that my staying is with the *entire* approval of the Department." Bristol assured him that it was, in fact that he must stay on, although he could file a letter requesting sea duty just for the record. Meanwhile, jested Bristol, "Hope you keep clear of the Zeppelin bombs. . . ."[48]

During the spring of 1916 Towers' boss Pete Symington managed to land an observer's berth on the battle cruiser *Indefatigable* with the British Grand Fleet, enabling him to make extensive observations and notes on the fleet's use of kite balloons, airships, and aircraft over several months. He shared his impressions with Towers, including what he saw on visits to the seaplane carrier *Campania:* twenty-three wheel-rigged Short seaplanes with 225-horsepower engines and folding wings for efficient stowage. In lieu of catapults, which the British had not yet developed, Symington noted that a "starting deck" allowed for a maximum powered takeoff run of 197 feet over the bow; the pilot aimed at "a jet of steam" at the forward end of it. The wheels were jettisoned after clearing the ship, enabling the returning plane to land alongside on its pontoons and be hoisted back aboard by boom and derrick.[49]

Symington was privy to nearly everything, including printed comments of fleet battle tactics and gunnery that Admiral Sir John Jellicoe, commander in chief of the Grand Fleet, issued to his vice and rear admirals on 15 April 1916. The American naval attaché noted that, in the event of a naval engagement, Jellicoe wanted his flag officers "being independent and taking the initiative . . . after the battle is joined . . . in accordance with his general instructions." Jellicoe was anticipating a clash with the German High Seas Fleet, though he by no means cared to take unnecessary risks against the Germans. When nothing happened, Symington went ashore for the last weekend of May, which he spent visiting Jack and Lily.[50]

Thus Symington missed the only major naval battle of World War I. The two battleship fleets collided off the Jutland Peninsula in the North Sea. According to Jellicoe's guidelines, the commander of his battle cruisers, Vice Admiral Sir David Beatty, opened the action by seizing the initiative. He tried to use his battle cruisers to cut off their German counterparts, but instead three of his thin-skinned vessels were blown to bits. The *Indefatigable* was one of them. Symington was lucky to have missed sailing with her, for all

but 2 of her complement of 1,017 men were lost. Then the German battleships hove into view, and Beatty's force was only rescued by the arrival of
Jellicoe with his dreadnoughts. By smart, daring seamanship, the German
fleet escaped Jellicoe's snare during the night. The Battle of Jutland therefore
ended in a tactical draw, and Britain's command of the North Sea remained
unchanged.

Jutland generated much discussion and criticism within the Royal Navy,
since the one opportunity to destroy the German High Seas Fleet had been
missed. To Pete Symington, who on 15 July was able to pay his respects to
Jellicoe, he admitted that the German ships "are considerably faster than the
book shows" and that therefore "he would probably not let the B.C.F. [Battle
Cruiser Fleet] get so far afield again." That is, Jellicoe regretted the initiative
he had encouraged and that Beatty had seized.[51]

The debate over the battle extended to the U.S. Navy and would last
twenty-five years. Towers and his fellow attachés were impressed by the
Germans' use of long-range naval Zeppelins in reconnoitering British fleet
movements. Had the Grand Fleet had adequate aerial reconnaissance,
Jellicoe and Beatty might very well have won the battle decisively. But
seaplane carrier *Campania* was inadvertently left behind on the fleet's sortie,
while poor visibility hampered the one seaplane carrier, rigged only with
boom and derrick and no "starting deck." One seaplane, lowered over her
side, had played a small role in the action.

If the outcome made Jellicoe more conservative in his tactics, it also
made American battleship admirals take heed. As far as Towers and the naval
aviators were concerned, however, aircraft might have made a difference, a
view actually shared by Jellicoe, who now endorsed the development of two
true aircraft carriers. The wheeled landplane with its better speed and rate of
climb thus began to supplant the shipboard seaplane in the British navy.[52]

By contrast, the Germans turned increasingly to their submarines to try
and strangle Britain's maritime trade, increasing the ire of the American
people. Ordered by ONI to get more data on British airships, now deemed
important for antisubmarine work, Towers inspected and rode in them at
Dover. And he continued to press the Admiralty to allow him to visit its air
stations along the French coast.[53]

Suddenly, in mid-July, his efforts bore fruit. The Admiralty granted him
permission to inspect RNAS fields around Dunkirk. At the same time, Lily's
pregnancy reached its climax. Jack followed the practice of British high
society by renting a suite of rooms at Claridge's Hotel for the delivery. The
night of 29 July Zeppelin airships resumed their strategic bombing campaign

after a hiatus of three months, adding to Lily's anxiety. Next day she gave birth to a girl, Marjorie Elizabeth. And the day after that Jack received orders to return home in September. If this came as welcome news to the young mother, unwelcome to her was the determination of her husband to see combat. On 26 August the Admiralty gave him a letter granting passage by rail to Dover, thence by warship to Dunkirk. He left immediately.[54]

At Dunkirk, the main Royal Navy air station in France, "it appeared that I was to be permitted to go no further, but on the second day my old friend Squadron Commander Spenser Grey, commanding [Wing No.] Five at Coudekerque, not far behind the front lines, hearing I was at headquarters, came in to Dunkirk and after about an hour's argument [with his superiors] obtained permission to take me out to his [wing]." Grey's wing consisted of two squadrons, one the two-seat Sopwith $1\frac{1}{2}$ Strutter fighters (so named for their wing-strut arrangement) that Towers admired, the other the French-built twin-engine Caudron bombers. In August the bombers, escorted by the fighters, had resumed bombing German airfields in Belgium, mainly to draw enemy air strength away from the fighting along the Somme River. The fighters were also involved in defending their own bases and in driving away German reconnaissance planes from Allied lines.[55]

At Coudekerque, Towers was assigned comfortable quarters with Grey, located no less in the large discarded packing case of a Farman aircraft. These consisted "of a sitting room, two bedrooms and bath—small, of course, but quite livable. The bath was rather ingenious. On top of the case they placed a fifty-gallon gasoline drum filled with water, plug side down. There was a hole cut in the top of the case, and in the middle of the floor beneath sat the bath, under which was another hole to let the water out. I spent two very pleasant, and at times rather exciting, weeks there."

Towers observed the sturdy 100-mph Sopwiths and the slower, lumbering Caudrons take off and land for raids on 2 and 3 September, followed by rainy weather that prohibited aerial operations. Jack chafed to go aloft himself. "Although I had asked several times, it was not until the day before I was due to leave that Grey permitted me to go on a raid. I was assigned as machine gunner in a Sopwith $1\frac{1}{2}$ Strutter which was to form part of the escort detachment.

"Looking back upon the episode, it seems rather a harebrained idea, for had we been forced to land in the territory occupied by the Germans the situation to say the least would have been embarrassing for both Grey and myself. I was an official representative of a neutral country sitting behind a Lewis [machine] gun in a British aeroplane. Grey had no authority whatever to send me on the trip. Fortunately for both of us there was no forced landing."

On 7 September 1916 wings no. 4 and 5, in conjunction with units of the Royal Flying Corps, were ordered to bomb the German aerodrome at St. Denis Westrem in Ghent, Belgium. Normally raids were started before daylight to give the slow, bomb-laden Caudrons time to get across enemy lines before daylight exposed them to accurate German antiaircraft fire. This raid was different, however, being set for a noon departure, probably because of lingering rains.

Twelve Caudrons and six Sopwiths were armed with 65- and 16-pound bombs; each plane carried but one occupant, the pilot. Providing fighter escort were two Sopwiths, each with an observer also on board. Another $1\frac{1}{2}$ Strutter was added but not logged as a participant in the raid. This was Towers' plane, flown by Flight Lieutenant Frank G. Anderae.[56]

The two fighter escorts, probably along with Anderae's plane, took off last at 1232 and followed the two squadrons up the coast through generally clear skies. Though two Caudrons had to turn back with engine trouble, the others flew on. Some of the Sopwiths climbed as high as 15,000 feet, others remaining with the Caudrons at around 9,000. Passing over Ostend, the flyers saw light British warships offshore, and over Zeebrugge they spotted three German planes far below them—too distant to attack. At this point the six bomb-laden Sopwiths and one escort turned inland, while the others, probably including Towers' plane, proceeded beyond Zeebrugge with the Caudrons.

Sopwith $1\frac{1}{2}$ Strutter fighter, 110 horsepower. This is the type in which Towers flew on the only combat mission of his career, against the St. Denis Westrem airdrome, Belgium, 7 September 1916. His participation as an observer was a violation of American neutrality. (Imperial War Museum)

At 1400, opposite the neutral Dutch border, Caudron Flight Commander Newton-Clare turned his planes inland, whereupon the weather worsened and accurate antiaircraft fire licked up at the intruders. One of the Caudrons was apparently shot down; this was not witnessed, but the plane did not return and the flyer's body was found at sea two weeks later. Two others managed to land on friendly beaches with engine trouble. Several planes were hit by fragments. The remaining seven Caudron pilots turned for home, blaming high winds. Newton-Clare was aware of none of this, for at about 1410 he encountered heavy banks of clouds that obscured both the ground and the other planes.

All Newton-Clare could see was a lone escorting Sopwith that flew alongside, its observer pointing below, meaning the other Caudrons had dropped. Newton-Clare spiraled down in pursuit of them but could find no one, for the other Caudrons were already heading back. The Sopwith followed him to 2,500 feet, then lost sight of him. But Newton-Clare found the target in spite of a driving rain and unloaded his four 65-pound bombs. He heard them hit though saw nothing. Five of the six Sopwiths also bombed blindly.

Lieutenant Anderae and his American observer turned for Coudekerque directly over land and rendezvoused with the other returning planes, all at 14,500 feet. Still behind the lines, they approached German positions at Dixmude and Ypres. There, in Towers' words, they "came under fire again, and this time it was much too close for comfort. Several explosions were so close aboard that I could feel the shock and smell the pungent odor of the explosion gases." The high-explosive flak was bursting at an altitude of 18,000 feet; Jack could see the flares of the 6-inch guns one mile distant.[57]

"Only two German aeroplanes were sighted. One of them [a Fokker] came rather close to us, and as our formation was very open it looked as though he was about to take a chance and come in on us. I hardly knew what to do, because I fully appreciated my position as a neutral." Jack sat behind his Lewis gun, mounted on a ring, while the pilot had a fixed forward-firing gun. As it turned out Towers did nothing, because the other escort planes closed in and the Fokker turned away.

After passing over no-man's land, the returning planes landed at Coudekerque, Anderae and Towers in midafternoon, following a three-hour flight. Damage was impossible to assess, but the head count was not. The missing pilot turned out to be the popular exec of the Caudron squadron, Flight Commander George H. Beard. His fate unknown, Newton-Clare and another pilot took off in separate planes to search for him. Then, a German plane flying high was sighted headed directly toward the field. He made a dive and when over the field dropped a package with streamers attached. Everyone knew it was news of Beard. There was contained in the package a brief message from the German squadron commander stating that with regret he informed the British squadron commander that Lieutenant Beard's plane had been shot down, and he had been killed. In their typical way the officers made no further mention of this little tragedy, except that when the pre-dinner cocktails were poured Grey raised his glass and said, "To his memory."

Next day Towers left Coudekerque for London and home. With Lily and seven-week-old daughter Marjorie, he boarded a liner at Falmouth for the crossing on 22 September. His invaluable experience of having intimately witnessed the world's greatest naval power mobilizing and employing the first major wartime naval air force in history would provide the U.S. Navy with a unique perspective. In addition, Jack had tasted real combat for the first time. Little did he know that it would be the only time he would ever come under fire.

The British bombing campaign of Belgian targets continued but failed in its objective of forcing the Germans to divert their own machines away from the Somme battlefield. Like the Battle of Jutland, it changed nothing.[58] Neither did the stalemate on the Western Front break. All the Allies could hope for was intervention by the United States. At least they had a firm friend in the American camp in the person of Lieutenant Jack Towers.

5

TOWERS AT WAR
1916–18

Upon returning to America in September 1916, Towers quickly discovered that the Woodrow Wilson administration refused to face reality and streamline military planning for total war along European lines. He found American naval aviation in "a rather chaotic condition. A certain number of officers had been ordered to Pensacola for flight training, but aviation had not been accepted by the higher command as an integral part of the Navy and was still regarded as a side issue to which they were willing to assign those officers who were foolish enough to apply but for which there was no policy and about which there was no real interest."

He reported to the State-War-Navy Building in Washington on 3 October, however, determined to prepare naval aviation for the war he believed the United States would soon enter. His task was monumental, since the chief of naval operations (CNO), Admiral William S. Benson, had succeeded in reducing the aviation program to near impotence. It was administered by a lowly lieutenant (jg), Buck Bronson. This amiable pilot that Jack had taught to fly at Vera Cruz reported to material director Captain Josiah S. McKean, who, however, desired a more experienced aviator. Henry Mustin was the logical choice, but his many clashes with Captain Bristol scotched his chances, and Bristol himself returned to sea.[1]

The obvious man to hold down the aviation desk and restore the sagging morale of the flyers was Towers. Though he preferred sea duty, he was acutely aware of the importance of tooling up for war and thus had no objection when ordered to relieve Bronson on 17 October, taking over two days later. Bronson had only begun briefing him on his new duties when on 8 November an experimental bomb the youngster was carrying over the Potomac prematurely exploded, killing him. This latest tragedy deprived Towers of Bronson's expertise; for several months, he was unassisted in the office.[2]

Under congressional pressure for military preparedness, particularly in aviation, the navy sought Towers' expertise from his two years in Britain. On 6 October he was called before the executive committee of the advisory General Board, chaired by Admiral Badger, who asked most of the probing questions. Jack gave the board an earful in no uncertain terms.[3]

The British, Towers revealed, "do not consider that they could get along without it [naval aviation] and they are extending the use of it more and more." The RNAS had swollen during Towers' time in London from 200 to more than 2,000 officers and 25,000 men by drawing on the reserves—most importantly, on "very young lads" who became "fairly good officers." Their output in an average three-month preliminary training course was heady stuff for the academy-weaned admirals. Enlisted mechanics had been brought in from the automotive industry. By implication, the United States could do the same.

The principal interest of the General Board was the optimum use of aircraft for scouting. Badger revealed that the navy, to enhance gunfire spotting, planned to place two hydros on board every battleship and four on each of six new battle cruisers just authorized. This Jack regarded as "the ultimate solution to the problem." Although the British had not yet made such a move, he believed they would eventually. One radical idea they had was launching "a small land machine" from each capital ship that would ditch at sea. The British considered all aircraft to be munitions and thus expendable, which raised the eyebrows of these penny-pinching American admirals.

To date, the Royal Navy had tried to solve its aerial scouting problems with shipboard captive kite balloons near the shore, a few light airships, and the special "aeroplane ships." At nineteen knots, however, the latter could not "keep up with the fleet" of twenty-five-knot battleships. Towers believed, wrongly, that specially built fast aircraft carriers for launching landplanes were too expensive in the eyes of the British.

Long-range patrol missions seemed to be the province of the large, rigid Zeppelin, which Towers strongly advocated and toward which the British seemed to be turning. Towers thought Cyril Porte's huge flying boats would not be able to match the sea-patrolling qualities of the Zep for another five years. The Zeppelin, with its "higher speed, much better vision," and cheaper cost, "can do many things in a much better manner than a light cruiser."

Entirely new to the board were Towers' observations of British naval air operations along the Belgian coast, where kite balloons spotted naval gunfire and Sopwith's fighters escorted bombing planes over the western end of the front—an offensive role. The 95-mph fighters, best in the Allied inventory, could cruise four hours, climb rapidly, and send out wireless reports to fifty miles. They also flew cover for photographic planes, which took clear pictures of German ships, subs, and army positions.

The only point on which Towers and the board disagreed was the exact type of aircraft to be assigned to battleships. The board—on the advice of other American naval airmen—endorsed a large, 4,000-pound shipboard flying boat. But Towers argued for a smaller 1,200- to 1,300-pound machine that was faster and more maneuverable, more easily stowed on board, and lighter for hoisting aboard by the ship's crane. Only when Admiral Badger countered these arguments did he back down. However, on 6 November, after Henry Mustin supported the small scout, Towers was recalled before the committee. He made his strongest arguments yet for the small shipboard scout, augmented by kite balloons, with the rigid Zeppelin to provide long-range reconnaissance until better flying boats could be developed.[4]

The board acceded to Towers' basic argument for the small fast scout. But the admirals were not about to sacrifice landplanes by ditching them at sea in a cavalier manner; they ruled that shipboard scouts be seaplanes of the hydro variety. Large flying boats were to be further developed for coastal patrols of up to six hours from shore stations and for possible use as bombers, while work would go forward on the Zeppelin-type dirigible. The Navy Department adopted these recommendations—for 564 front-line aircraft plus a handful of trainers, kite balloons, and airships.[5] Most were those of Glenn Curtiss, including the N-9 seaplane version of the army's new trainer, the JN-4B or Jenny, with a front-end tractor engine. The return home of Curtiss' old friend Towers strengthened the navy's relations with his company, now enlarged with new factories at Buffalo and on Long Island and schools in Miami and Newport.[6]

Finding pilots to fly the new planes had been addressed by the Naval Appropriations Act of 29 August 1916, which authorized a naval flying corps and the Naval Reserve Flying Corps. The former could not be implemented, being too small, and Towers agreed with the admirals that in any case aviation should play an integral role in all fleet operations—a position from which he would never waver. The Naval Reserve Flying Corps, however, provided

Towers the means to obtain the services of men already skilled in the flying business. Until it could be developed, makeshift preparedness organizations provided ready expertise.[7]

Towers became aware of a dozen well-heeled Yale University undergraduates trained to fly as Volunteer Aerial Coast Patrol Unit No. 1 when their leader, F. Trubee Davison, begged him to take them into the navy. Jack was "tremendously impressed by his enthusiasm" but doubted whether Secretary Daniels would be receptive to the idea. When Davison assured Towers that they had the support of the college president, Jack told him to shoot off a formal request for enrollment. The letter went out but got lost, and a frantic telegram from Davison prompted Jack to send him a personal invitation to come to Washington.[8]

"Well," Towers replied after hearing out Davison's plea, "I don't see why you should have to fiddle around any longer. If you're all set, why not join up in the Naval Reserve?" Jack obtained Assistant Secretary Roosevelt's approval and had the Yale men enlisted as a body in the Naval Reserve Flying Corps on 24 March 1917. Rather than further taxing the resources at Pensacola, they were allowed to continue their own training in West Palm Beach, using seaplanes purchased by their wealthy fathers under the tutelage of a navy pilot. The so-called First Yale Unit, remembered Towers, "became the backbone of our Naval Reserve during the War" and inspired more college men to form units. Sadly, Trubee Davison was badly injured during training and left crippled.[9]

The almost haphazard procurement of machines and personnel in the waning months of American neutrality reflected the absence of national strategic planning. In October 1916, however, the Joint Board on Aeronautic Cognizance was established, with three aviation-wise army officers and three naval officers of unequal talents—Captain McKean of CNO Benson's office, Captain Hugh Rodman representing the General Board, and Lieutenant Towers. Jack exerted considerable influence in the two months he sat on the board, pushing through his recommendation to have a Zeppelin and other airships built. But when the board was given wider responsibilities in February, Benson replaced Towers with a senior captain. All three captains continued to consult Towers for technical advice.[10]

Towers' closest connection with the aviation community centered on the National Advisory Committee for Aeronautics (NACA), established in 1915 to pool civilian and military technical information. The navy was represented by the air-minded chief of C&R, Rear Admiral David W. Taylor, and Jack's former student, Commander Dick Richardson. Early in the new year Towers himself was appointed to the twelve-member committee. Also, during the autumn of 1916 Towers and aeronautical engineer Jerry Hunsaker were appointed to a NACA subcommittee to inspect the army's Langley Field near Hampton Roads as a possible site for an experimental station. Both men rejected the site "because of lack of deep water access for ships," although NACA established its aeronautical laboratory there, and the navy decided to build a naval air station at Hampton Roads for its new planes. The army elected Dayton, Ohio, as the site for its testing. Towers later chaired the NACA subcommittee on "aero torpedoes." [11]

American military aviation could not progress until the Wright Company's long-festering lawsuit against Curtiss was settled; the threat of legal action even discouraged new companies from entering the industry. NACA was charged with resolving the issue and turned for guidance to the automotive industry, because it had solved a similar deadlock on behalf of auto tycoon Henry Ford. Auto maker Howard E. Coffin suggested that the aeronautical industry make a cross-licensing agreement, by which the federal government could buy up patents and thus allow their use by all aircraft builders. NACA members accepted the proposal, and Congress rushed through enabling legislation during February and March 1917. The aeronautical industry, for its part, simultaneously organized into the Aircraft Manufacturers Association. On 8 March, now free to bargain with the companies in dispute, NACA appointed a four-man subcommittee on patents, with Towers as navy representative, and the legal logjam was soon removed. [12]

Towers' prodding for dirigible development contributed to the creation in January 1917 of the Joint Army and Navy Airship Board under the chairmanship of Admiral Taylor. As naval representatives Taylor selected Towers, Hunsaker, and new pilot Lieutenant W. G. Child, later succeeded by Arthur Atkins. The board immediately decided to let Hunsaker's section in Taylor's bureau do the design work while drawing heavily on the knowledge Towers had gained from airship flights in England. In mid-March Towers, as de facto director of naval aviation in the CNO's office, contracted with the Goodyear Company in Ohio to train additional lighter-than-air (LTA) pilots and with Hunsaker and Taylor arranged for sixteen B-type dirigibles from five separate companies for their construction and assembly. [13]

Occupying the aviation desk at the Navy Department, sitting on NACA, and serving with several boards (including one on submarine warfare), Towers became the major spokesman for naval aviation. He "commented . . . vehemently" on Henry Mustin's transfer to a battleship, noted an observer, and sought to repair the sagging morale of the navy's few airmen by imitating the Royal Flying Corps to create a special insignia for their uniforms. In late 1916 Jack contracted Henry Reuterdahl, the famous marine artist, to come up with a basic design, then got the idea and the design—golden wings— approved by BuNav. He also won approval for a special uniform, forest green being selected for winter wear because of a surplus of Marine Corps forest-green fabric. These were tailored to match dress whites.[14]

The best stimulus for developing naval aviation was the sinking by German U-boats of Allied merchantmen off the Atlantic seaboard. A navy study chaired by Rear Admiral J. M. Helm recommended new coastal stations for air and antisubmarine patrol craft. Only Towers, from his experience in Europe, knew how to organize such bases and to employ their aircraft. Strategically, he advised the Helm board on 3 November, dirigibles, kite balloons, and seaplanes should help defend operating bases. Tactically, he envisioned them flying from ships and shore stations for reconnaissance, "fighting patrols," "offensive operations against [the] enemy," and training. He recommended ten large airship stations, plus seaplane bases, with at least two machines to cover each hundred miles of the American coastline. The Helm board reflected the navy's general passivity toward aviation, making no proposals other than to strengthen Pensacola.[15]

This nonpolicy was shattered on 31 January 1917 by Germany's sudden announcement that it would wage unrestricted submarine warfare against *all* ships—including neutrals—in the war zone. Four days later President Wilson broke diplomatic relations with Germany, and U-boats began attacking U.S. merchantmen. A frantic CNO Benson immediately called upon Towers for a definite proposal regarding defensive air stations. Jack instantly recommended eight new naval air facilities: north to south, Massachusetts Bay; Newport, Rhode Island; New York City; Cape May, New Jersey; Hampton Roads; Key West, Florida; Galveston, Texas; and the Panama Canal. Each station should have two dirigibles and four to six seaplanes. Benson rushed the proposal to Secretary Daniels on 5 February, calling for immediate approval. In addition, Towers devised a plan to beef up the faltering enrollments of student pilots at Pensacola—only thirty were on board—and to get more mechanics. Daniels approved the personnel request at once and let the Joint Army-Navy Cognizance Board develop interservice aerial responsibilities for coast defense, using three regional panels. Towers was appointed to study the needs of the mid-Atlantic naval districts, especially the third, headquartered at New York under his beloved old *Michigan* skipper Rear Admiral Usher.

On 30 March Towers' list was incorporated into a plan for eleven stations that corresponded closely with the thinking of the Cognizance Board. Importantly, the list included an air station at Pearl Harbor in Hawaii; the navy intended to keep its eye on Japan. For the moment, though, the only air station in operation was Pensacola, for training, experimentation, and now offshore patrol. Jack's contacts there were the station exec, Frank McCrary; the senior aviation officer afloat, new pilot Lieutenant Ken Whiting; the head of research, Dick Richardson; testing director Pat Bellinger; and Jack's former copilot, Chevy Chevalier.[16]

The luxury of peacetime planning came to an end on 6 April 1917 when Congress, in response to the U-boat sinkings, declared war on Germany. The U.S. Navy entered the war with a formidable battle fleet but only a few antisubmarine vessels and a pitifully small navy-marine air component of 54 planes (mostly trainers), 48 aviators, and 239 other personnel.[17] Within days, however, the admirals assigned subchasers and escorts for a new convoy system being implemented by the British. Naval aircraft and airships would augment this new mission.

The strenuous efforts of Lieutenant Towers had laid the administrative foundation for a mushrooming wartime program that would in effect become a superbureau in which all the regular bureaus were to focus their aviation work. Although he would be promoted to lieutenant commander on 13 October (to date from 1 July), he still lacked adequate rank to wield such responsibility. So on 17 May Captain Noble E. Irwin was appointed director of naval aviation in the material branch of the CNO's office, with Towers as his assistant. Described as "a huge man, over six feet and built like a prize fighter," "Bull" Irwin was a superb administrator who allowed the more knowledgeable Towers to run the operation—even after July 1917 when aviation was made a section directly under the CNO. Later, in March 1918, the section was upgraded to the Division of Naval Aviation under CNO, with Towers as assistant director and acting director in Irwin's absence.[18]

The aviation arm of the navy—and the larger Army Air Service—faced acute manning problems. For the sake of efficiency, Towers wanted his office to handle its own personnel affairs rather than BuNav, given the normally rigid peacetime bureaucratic system. The talented Leigh C. Palmer had recently been jumped from commander to rear admiral to be chief of BuNav. Towers, who had spotted gunfire for Palmer in the *Vermont* during the ship's award-winning shooting at Magdalena Bay in 1908, went to see him and found in Palmer "a friend in court." Very quickly, recalled Towers, "he and I cooked up the scheme of having me given additional duty under the Bureau of Navigation as Supervisor of the Naval Reserve Flying Corps." That occurred officially on 15 May.

"I built up a special section in offices adjacent to mine, the officers of which were attached to the Bureau of Navigation. In that section, we used BuNav stationery and ran aviation personnel matters entirely." Palmer gave full authority to Jack in addition to his regular aviation duties. Since the arrangement bypassed Captain Irwin, he succeeded in having himself named supervisor in August, though he too let Towers run everything. Similarly, the navy's training division allowed Jack to control aviation training, and the other bureaus coordinated their aviation activities through his office. The key bureaus represented were steam engineering (BuEng), responsible for aircraft engines, and C&R, responsible for air frames.[19]

Staffing the many agencies held the key to success. In some cases, Towers had to follow the new policies of wartime BuNav, one being that all regular navy officers would be kept in the surface line for the duration to help fill the immense manpower needs of the fleet. This prevented defrocked airmen Ellyson, Rodgers, Mustin, and Vic Herbster, now back at sea, from returning to aviation duties; thenceforth only reservists would be enrolled as new pilots. On the other hand, from his new role in BuNav, Towers could obtain men of calibre to assist him, for example, Barney Smith, who returned from Paris to coordinate aircraft design and procurement in Towers' office.[20]

Mobilizing such talent took months, meaning that Towers was virtually alone during the first weeks of war, even while inspecting new training units. At one visit to the Massachusetts Naval Militia at Squantum, he attended a large dinner at which

one young man in particular made quite an impression on me. I . . . found out that his name was Gordon Balch, that in Naval life he was a carpenter's mate of the Reserve, third class, but that in civilian life he was a man of very considerable standing in the [banking] firm of Stone and Webster. I decided that I could use him in Washington and upon my return the next day had telegraphic orders issued for him to report there for duty.

He arrived promptly, and I gave him a desk and made him my immediate assistant. Nobody in Operations knew who he was or what he was, [everyone still dressed in the civilian attire of peacetime Washington] except that his efficiency was immediately apparent and he was soon in the inner circles of the admirals and captains of Operations. Then, bang, came an order that everyone in the Navy Department would from the next day wear a uniform. Alas, Balch was only a carpenter's mate. Something had to be done about this immediately, so I sent him out to obtain an ensign's uniform and told him that I would endeavor to have him commissioned before the next morning. This I finally did manage, and Balch stayed with me as my assistant until the end of the War, with the final rank of lieutenant commander.

Harvard graduate Balch then assumed the title of assistant supervisor of the Naval Reserve Flying Corps and twelve months later earned his own wings as a navy pilot.

This experience taught Towers the efficacy of recruiting men of finance for naval aviation, a policy he would follow on a larger scale in World War II. Bankers, stockbrokers, and corporation executives relieved him of much of the tedious work of figuring and computing budgetary requirements for aviation. Meanwhile, he was plagued by requests from Assistant Secretary Roosevelt and his private secretary Louis Howe to admit friends of theirs into naval aviation, applications that Towers treated like any others. He encouraged individuals to apply only on the basis of merit.[21]

Towers learned to appreciate the value of women in government service during World War I. Here he poses with some of his associates and female clerks at the Division of Naval Aeronautics early in 1919. *Top row, left to right:* Lieutenant Commander George D. Murray, commanding officer, NAS Anacostia; Gladys Pierce; Towers; Hilma Johnson; Lieutenant Commander Pat Bellinger, transatlantic flight section; unidentified clerk; and Major Barney Smith, transatlantic section. *Front row, left to right:* Margaret Burns, Catherine Macdonald, Hallie Allen, Inez Brown, Alice Hungerford, Margaret Shellhorn, and unidentified clerk. (Navy Department)

The French government, anxious to shore up the morale of its people, requested that a token force of American naval aviators be sent over immediately, a full year ahead of the fully trained American Expeditionary Force. Jack could only scrape together six available aviators at Pensacola and sent them off before the end of May, along with a hundred mechanics. Arriving in France early in June, this first American military force to reach Europe began to train in French aircraft.[22]

But the loss of such a large chunk of talent, Towers advised CNO Benson, "could only be undertaken . . . by discontinuing aeronautic work on ships of the fleet, and utilizing the aeronautic personnel in the handling of the training and in general expansion work." With manpower shortages acute, on 1 June he urged that seaplane activities from three catapult-equipped cruisers be postponed and that equipment and personnel be removed for more pressing tasks. Benson agreed, and over the summer the three vessels were stripped of their aviation detachments, their pilots distributed among the several new training stations. The number of pilot trainees was so great and of qualified instructors so few that the Canadian government agreed to absorb some of the load. A unit sent from Princeton University to Toronto included James V. Forrestal, whose administrative abilities led Towers to bring the young lieutenant (jg) into the aviation division a year later.[23]

On 20 April 1917 Towers' estimates for more training planes resulted in orders for 442. He quickly discovered that most of the contracted companies were ill-equipped to meet the navy's needs, or the army's. The new Aircraft Production Board set the quantity of aircraft to be procured, while the Joint Army-Navy Technical Board on Aircraft ascertained aircraft types and standardized designs. When Congress reorganized the Aircraft Production Board in October, dropping the word *production* from the title, Irwin and Atkins were made additional navy members; this had the effect of strengthening Towers' influence on the board because of his intimate working relationships with both men.[24]

The Joint Army-Navy Technical Board included Towers, Hunsaker, Atkins, and two army captains—all of them experts on aircraft design and capabilities who would make the crucial decisions regarding the nation's embryonic air armada. In fact, this board established aviation policy, although neither it nor any army or navy agency was issued directives on the strategic and tactical uses of aeroplanes. As a result, one of the great evils of modern machine warfare—of which Captain Chambers had warned long before—was being institutionalized: the weapon was dictating doctrine, rather than the reverse. Such material determinism was and remains something to which advocates of new weapons have always been particularly susceptible. In this case, since Hunsaker and Atkins were engineers, the only pilot on the board who really spoke for naval air doctrine was Towers. Over time, the high commands of the two services assumed the heavy responsibilities of the Technical Board, and it would pass out of existence by mid-1918.[25]

At the end of May 1917, acting on the advice of Towers and General Benny Foulois of the Army Air Service, the board called for a massive army-navy total of ten thousand trainers and twelve thousand combat planes, phenomenally large figures that left the CNO's office and the Army General Staff aghast. The conservative admirals and generals vehemently opposed them, lest such an outlay of funds undermine the traditional needs of the two services. But as members of the Technical Board, Towers and Foulois reported directly to their respective secretaries, bypassing the uniformed chain of command. Jack spent most of June working up facts and figures. Assuming that 500 aviators would operate abroad "on ship and coastal and insular patrol," he called for 500 "school" planes, 400 service/scout machines, and 100 large flying boats, plus 100 coastal dirigibles, 40 kite balloons, and 12 free balloons—all to the tune of over $29 million. Assistant Secretary Roosevelt, after slightly reducing the number of school planes and airships to save $5 million, approved the plan. Foulois worked up figures for landplanes in the army: 4,900 trainers, 4,000 scouts, 6,667 fighters, and 1,333 bombers. The need was there, and Congress approved. The total package, costing $640 million, was enacted into law on 24 July 1917.[26]

While authorizing aircraft was simple enough, Towers shared the general belief that their designs would have to be borrowed from the Allied powers. Neither army, navy, nor the aeronautical industry could develop fresh designs for needed aircraft types soon enough to help achieve victory. Only Glenn Curtiss had done anything original with his seaplanes, but his company had been unable to produce a superior airplane motor. So in late June, acting on the Technical Board's recommendation, Towers suggested that the navy secure examples of four Allied seaplanes for possible production by new American companies and thereby complement Curtiss' boats, all of which had Allied engines. However, during the single month of June, the automobile industry designed the brand new superior Liberty aircraft engine, which quickly went into mass production as the nation's greatest single contribution to the Allied aviation effort.[27]

Aside from the large Curtiss flying boats, the Navy and War Departments lacked firsthand knowledge of exactly what types of aircraft the United States should produce along European lines. During the summer, the navy merely authorized more training planes and construction of the Naval Air-craft Factory in Philadelphia to augment production. But an aeronautical mission returned from Europe with the expected conclusion that only European combat planes should be produced for American aviators. Irwin and Towers assembled their experts to deliberate on which plane types the navy should adopt. Their basic decision was to reject four seaplane designs in favor of the best in the world, those of Glenn Curtiss, a move influenced by a recent decision of the Allies to do exactly the same thing. The Towers-Curtiss connection greatly facilitated the navy's seaplane program for antisubmarine operations, and during the summer plans were laid to establish fifteen U.S. naval air stations in Britain, France, and Italy to combat enemy U-boat and surface forces.[28]

In spite of these crucial overseas arrangements, Towers found himself handicapped by America's home-defense mania. Congress insisted that top priority in naval air base construction be for coastal patrol stations in the continental United States, requiring a building and manning program of colossal proportions. This placed Towers in a quandary: he opposed the priority, believing that the war would be won in Europe rather than off the Atlantic seaboard, yet if home bases were to have any value their development had to be expedited. So Jack urged the Bureau of Yards and Docks (BuDocks) to keep moving and then had to spend a great deal of time inspecting the stations.[29]

One stateside base was particularly important and brought Towers his first opportunity to speak before the legislators on Capitol Hill. In July 1917, the army and navy were authorized to purchase and share North Island in San Diego Harbor as a major training facility. The army was already there, leasing the land, when the order came for it to turn over half of the 1,200 acres to the navy. Negotiations dragged on for nearly a year, and when Captain Irwin was bedridden from the flu epidemic in February 1918, Towers acted in his stead. Pressed by Congressman Fred A. Britten to explain delays in the transfer, Jack remained typically calm during this baptism under political fire. By June North Island was on the way to becoming the West Coast equivalent of Pensacola.[30]

Moved in July 1917 from the State-War-Navy Building to the Navy Annex in northwest Washington, Captain Irwin's and Lieutenant Commander Towers' staff had grown to twenty-seven officers and dozens of enlisted personnel and civilian secretaries by the following March, when it became the Division of Naval Aviation under the CNO.[31]

Though many reservists accepted their boss's policies uncritically, some personality conflicts inevitably developed. Forrest Wysong, a directly commissioned Curtiss pilot, complained: "I'd say things Towers didn't approve of, and he'd get me out in the hall and bawl the hell out of me. I was an ensign and he was a commander, so I didn't say anything. I had this training: aye-aye, sir, no back talk. One day the commander comes in and says, 'I've heard you were fraternizing with enlisted men!'" Wysong also locked horns with Jack over the importance of kite balloons, the less informed reservist challenging their utility at a Technical Board meeting, for which Towers also called him down. Such were the petty frustrations the regular navy endured in running the vast wartime program.[32]

In November 1917 the navy obtained a license from the army to operate its planes from the army field at Anacostia across the Potomac from Washington, improving accessibility by air to the newly opened Hampton Roads Naval Air Station experimental facility. At Jack's instigation, Lieutenant Gink Doherty took command of the navy's operations at Anacostia, Jack welcoming this former Hammondsport crony and his wife as house guests for several months. Located in northwestern Washington, the house was a wedding present from father-in-law Charlie Carstairs.

The heavy demands of war considerably strained Towers' family life. During a work day that usually lasted beyond six o'clock, plus all-night duty watches "on a cot by a telephone" in the CNO's office, Towers, Earle Johnson, Barney Smith, and Tobey Balch would grab a quick sandwich and coffee across the street at the Ohio Lunch Room or devour littleneck clams at the New Willard Hotel.[33] Lily took a dim view of her husband's absences from home. Accustomed to London high society, she found navy life exceedingly confining, especially when she had to kowtow to wives of Jack's seniors whom she considered socially inferior. At parties she resented being left in a corner with them while the men gathered to talk aviation. Lily poured out her frustrations to Gink Doherty's wife Tommie, who at least could help her entertain and care for baby Marjorie. Lily and Tommie agreed they were "aviation widows." Jack, when not at the office or away on inspection trips, did manage to make short trips with his wife and baby to visit her relatives in Philadelphia.[34]

In December 1917 Jack suffered a personal blow: his mother, Mary Caroline, quietly succumbed to pneumonia at age sixty-six. Jack could not be with her in Rome, nor could brothers Fullton, in Gary, Indiana, producing steel for the war effort, or Will, serving in France with the YMCA. Both parents were now gone, and his marriage was shaky; Towers' demeanor changed from reserved to somber.

The severe winter of 1917–18 exacerbated Towers' heavy workload. Foot-deep snow and subzero temperatures kept Lily snowbound at home, and the flu incapacitated Captain Irwin. Apologizing to his brother Will for not writing more often, early in the new year Jack assured him, "I never worked so hard in all my life. Am at it all day, not usually even going out for lunch and generally work late at night. It is now nearly eleven, and my offices are filled with clerks getting out mail." With Irwin absent, "I am the whole works. . . . My office organization is better now, for I have 28 officer assistants and about fifty-five clerks, but I can't seem to get it arranged so [that] I have nothing to do. . . . I am beginning to think the Kaiser has got the ear of God on this weather business. . . ."[35]

Meanwhile Germany's armies, air forces, and U-boats hammered away on the Western Front and in the North Atlantic, trying to break Allied resistance before the new American army could be sealifted to the continent. U.S. naval aviation faced one primary mission, in Towers' words, "the destruction of the enemy submarine, wherever it could be found, and second only to this was the protection of supply and troop ships. The primary mission was purely offensive"—to seek out and destroy or at least neutralize the U-boat, from the new stations on the East Coast and in Europe. In January 1918, the Helm board recommended additional stations and refueling stops to fill in gaps along the coast, an expansion that greatly taxed naval aviation resources and increased Towers' problems outfitting and manning them.[36]

As the first U.S. Navy pilots entered the fight, the new year brought an immediate threat from German bombers in Belgium threatening to destroy seaplanes at the new American naval air station at Dunkirk. Towers endorsed a recommendation from Alfred Cunningham, just back from Europe, that Marine Corps fighters be assigned to defend Dunkirk: "No matter how many bombing machines we put out" to strike the U-boat bases in Belgium, "if there are no fighting machines there to protect them it is a useless sacrifice." He wanted two hundred pilots trained and sent over to operate fighters in the Dunkirk area, first for airfield defense, then for a "maximum effort" against German targets.

Since the Navy had agreed to let the army have exclusive jurisdiction for overland operations, Towers first checked with his new army counterpart in the War Department, Colonel Hap Arnold, for approval. Arnold saw no problem with marine and navy planes operating over land against naval targets but thought the request should go from Admiral William S. Sims, the U.S. Navy commander abroad, to General John J. Pershing, commanding army forces. Jack was more concerned over opposition to the idea within the navy. He reminded the General Board in February that the RNAS had been so heavily committed to operations on the continent early in the war that it had been sadly deficient in antisub planes when the U-boat menace had escalated.

The board not only agreed with Cunningham and Towers, it gave high priority to flying land-based fighters on these missions, the planes to be obtained from the U.S. Army. Sims went further by asking for fast unescorted land-based bombers rather than the slow, vulnerable seaplanes; well-armed landplanes would be able to defend themselves during round-the-clock bombings of both sub pens and German airfields. General Pershing, not wanting his plans saddled with the task of attacking naval installations, was perfectly willing to let the navy do it.[37]

Nevertheless, in April 1918 the army and navy air arms erupted into a bitter rivalry that was to characterize much of their relationship over the next three decades and during Towers' career. In tactical roles, the army's airmen insisted on a monopoly over all continental operations in support of the ground forces, especially to resist the terrible spring offensive now being unleashed by the German army. The navy countered that naval base targets belonged to its planes, working in tactical support of fleet operations. Indeed, the RNAS had been so heavily employed assisting the Royal Flying Corps along the Western Front and in handling home defense against air raids that that very month the two merged into one service, the Royal Air Force (RAF), in order to simplify their operations. The British suggested that the Americans do the same, a recommendation utterly dismissed by its recipients. Furthermore, the founders of the RAF wanted to promote the new concept of strategic bombing—that is, to have heavy bombers pound German cities until the empire surrendered, a view echoed by a senior U.S. Army aviator, Colonel William "Billy" Mitchell.[38]

Before the month was over, the top-priority U.S. Naval Aviation Northern Bombing Project was approved, for which Admiral Sims wanted 240 day and 120 night bombers, 100 Curtiss-style trainers, 527 officers, and 5,097 men to operate and service them. The desire for fighters was dropped, since the British de Havilland bombers that the Americans would fly had enough machine guns to defend themselves.

Such a burgeoning role for aviation caused the army and navy to upgrade the positions of air leadership and to promote deserving officers like Towers. The navy made this possible by waiving its peacetime requirement of sea duty in grade before promotion to the next rank, though only with the direct approval of Secretary Daniels and Admiral Benson. Since both men prized

Towers' role, they opened the way for his temporary advancement to full commander. He was promoted on 6 September (effective from 1 July).[39]

By the beginning of June, with American ground and air forces moving into the forward sectors of the Western Front, the RAF begged the U.S. Navy to provide replacements for its mounting pilot losses. The task fell to Towers' staff, which promptly agreed to send them, in addition to the regular American squadrons abroad, now starting to receive the first small Curtiss HS-1 seaplanes and big H-16 flying boats. On top of this, Towers had to press student pilots into airship service to search for U-boats attacking East Coast shipping. Dick Byrd was sent to Nova Scotia to open two U.S. naval air stations. The staff also set to work devising a methodical air patrol plan covering the area from Maine to Panama, while the General Board looked forward to establishing additional major air bases in Alaska, Hawaii, Guam, and the Philippines—a hedge against Japan.[40]

The United States was flexing its strategic muscles, and none too soon. The German spring offensive pushed the British and French armies back against the airfields around Dunkirk until the first U.S. Army ground and air reinforcements checked the advance. American naval pilots were assigned to British and French squadrons; in addition, regular patrols by U.S. Navy squadrons and bombing raids by U.S. Army squadrons began in mid-June. Despite deficiencies in the Allied aircraft assigned to the navy-marine bombing project, at least the overseas administration of U.S. naval aviation had become well organized by summer's end. Captain Irwin went over on an inspection tour, leaving newly assigned Captain G. W. Steele, Jr., and Towers to administer the sprawling air arm from Washington.[41]

As the great American-spearheaded offensive of September 1918 was being readied, the General Board carefully studied the lessons being learned in Europe and called upon Towers and his colleagues for advice. Remembering the impact of the Zeppelin bombings on London, Jack advocated the utilization of long-range flying boats to bomb Berlin as well as Germany's naval bases. None of the existing boats had the necessary range, but a new design called the NC was under development for such distances and would be ready by mid-1919. For the northern bombing campaign against U-boat pens, the H-16s might well need fighter escorts; Towers proposed the development of a small, high-speed navy fighter, which was undertaken by Curtiss.

The two British aircraft carriers nearly completed, Captain Irwin endorsed the idea for the U.S. Navy. Towers suggested that a merchant ship converted into a carrier would be of "material advantage for experimental purposes." The General Board, however, preferred to build carriers from scratch. On 10 September it recommended a construction program over the next six years to yield no fewer than six fast 35-knot carriers with clear 700-foot flight decks, each capable of operating forty-five planes! The admirals also wanted a huge array of flying boats, dirigibles, and ship-based kite balloons.[42]

This ambitious program, which heralded the complete acceptance of aviation by the high command, turned out to be premature for wartime purposes. For on 12 September the Allied counterattack began at St. Mihiel, supported by nearly 1,500 planes under Colonel Billy Mitchell; it was followed two weeks later by the Meuse-Argonne offensive in which most of the 821 participating aircraft were flown by U.S. Army pilots. The fledgling navy-marine Northern Bombing Group inflicted much damage on German installations and ships as the enemy evacuated its Belgian submarine bases. The all-out attack shattered the German war machine.

Germany sued for peace by agreeing to an armistice on 11 November, well before the full weight of American arms could be brought to bear, including four thousand naval aircraft by the spring of 1919. The introduction of American arms and manpower to the Western Front had proved crucial, a victory subtly but decisively made possible by the Allied convoy escorts and air patrols that had neutralized the U-boat. The Northern Bombing Group had dropped over 125,000 pounds of small bombs, while American-flown seaplanes from French, Irish, and English bases had claimed five U-boats—questionable claims, the much larger British naval air arm having sunk a mere six—and damaged perhaps as many as fourteen. This was a tiny number against the total wartime Allied U-boat kills by ships (eighty-three), mines (forty-three), and other subs (twenty). But the presence of the ubiquitous seaplanes and airships had seriously intimidated enemy sub skippers; in 1918 not one U-boat had dared attack a convoy covered by naval aircraft.[43]

Most remarkable had been the stupendous wartime expansion and administration of naval aviation, the major credit for which belonged to Jack Towers. First alone, then as de facto manager of naval air under Captain Irwin, Towers had molded an efficient staff of both regulars and reservists to create a massive air force over the nineteen months of America's participation in the fighting. From 54 planes and fewer than 300 personnel, the U.S. Navy had gained 1,865 flying boats and seaplanes, 242 landplanes, 15 dirigibles, 205 kite balloons, 10 free balloons, 6,998 officers (half still student pilots), and 32,882 enlisted men. And there was no longer a lone air station at Pensacola: 570 planes and 17,544 people were abroad at eighteen stations in France, five in Ireland, three in Italy, two each in England and Canada, one in the Azores, a refueling stop in the British West Indies, and Allied units and overseas training bases. The rest were at home: at the Navy Department, thirteen coastal patrol stations, eleven flight training facilities, and ten ground, enlisted, and technical schools. Operational losses in Europe totaled 11 officers and 8 men killed and 2 pilots captured, plus 187 training casualties.[44]

These statistics reveal better than any other index the managerial and organizational revolution that had swept through American government and industry. None of the regular uniformed officers had entered the conflict prepared to become expert managers on a grand scale. Jack Towers was among those who had learned quickly and contributed materially to the final victory.

A thirty-three-year-old full commander when hostilities ended, Towers was equipped with an administrative ability indispensable for the U.S. Navy, which emerged from the world war equal in strength to the Royal Navy. He could not know that his two-year tour heading the air program would ultimately turn out to be a dress rehearsal for an identical role two decades later when the nation entered World War II.

6

BRIDGING THE ATLANTIC
1918–19

The wartime NC (Navy-Curtiss) flying boats had been earmarked to fly the Atlantic via the Azores in order to eliminate the risk entailed by transporting seaplanes on ships vulnerable to submarines. Towers had endorsed the scheme, "convinced that the effect on the morale of the Germans of a successful flight across the Atlantic would more than justify the cost of diversion of energy from other war efforts." Seeing the sudden approach of the armistice, however, he submitted a proposal to the CNO on 31 October 1918 recommending such a flight by the first four NC boats during the immediate postwar period. Eager to resume the dream of the 1914 *America* project, he nominated himself to command the expedition. The CNO appointed a board under Captain John T. Tompkins to study the idea and made Towers a member of it.[1]

Towers' proposal proved most timely. It coincided with the recent completion of the prototype NC as well as with a sudden resurgence of public interest in a transatlantic flight, stimulated by cash prizes for civilians. When British contenders came forward, Towers could appeal to America's national honor: "The prestige gained . . . by the United States in [the] early stages of aviation, and now being regained, should be held. . . ."[2]

The Tompkins board was favorably stacked, the only other member besides Tompkins and Towers being Chevy Chevalier. Secretary Daniels favored the idea, as did the acting CNO, Jack's wartime material boss Rear Admiral Josiah McKean. But the NC boats held the key. They were the product of many Towers associates: main designer William Gilmore and manager Henry Kleckler, navy hull designer Dick Richardson, wing designers Commander G. Conrad Westervelt and Ensign C. J. McCarthy, engine supervisor Arthur Atkins, and overall project supervisor Lieutenant Commander Garland Fulton. So all Towers would have to do would be to join an established team already constructing the four NC flying boats on Long Island.[3]

Towers said that the British would probably try to be the first to bridge the Atlantic by air. Britain certainly had the capability with Cyril Porte's supreme achievement, the Fury or "Super Baby"—a five-365-horsepower-engine triplane flying boat, which, however, was wrecked in a crash. The NC-1 design closely resembled Porte's: three 400-horsepower Liberty tractor engines; an upper wing span of 126 feet; a length of 68 feet 5½ inches; a hull of 44 feet 9 inches; and a lift of 22,000 pounds, including a crew of five.[4] Colossal for its day, the NC, in Towers' words, "appeared rather queer, and there were many officers, including myself, who did not like it." But when the NC-1 first flew in October 1918 it attained speeds in the water up to 60 mph and cruising in the air to 85 mph. Its range was 1,400 nautical miles.[5] One by one, the other three boats were assembled at Rockaway over the winter of 1918–19. Nicknamed Nancies by the press, they embodied state of the art aeronautics.[6]

For Towers, the NC study was almost as if he were picking up where he had left off with the *America* project four and a half years before. He rejected the 1,675-mile direct Newfoundland-to-Ireland route in favor of the Newfoundland-Azores route—1,320 nautical miles, with more predictable weather. Navigation and rescue along the Azores route could be assisted by the 1914 scheme of a line of patrolling destroyers. The addition of a fourth engine to the NCs would extend the "radius of action" to 1,420 miles for a comfortable margin to the Azores with a payload of 28,000 pounds.[7]

The Tompkins board made its report on 4 February 1919: "Four of the best seaplanes available" should fly from Rockaway Naval Air Station (NAS) on Long Island to Newfoundland about the first of May, after the ice had broken up at the latter place, thence to the Azores, then Portugal and Plymouth, England. The board estimated that the longest leg of the trip, Newfoundland to the Azores, would take perhaps twenty hours. Most of this hop would have to be done at night, in order that the planes make the safer daylight landings off the Azores. And, equally important, the anticipated difficulties of flying several hours in the darkness had to be minimized by making use of the full moon. This would occur on 14 May. Therefore, departure from Newfoundland had to take place on or about that date.

Towers inserted the proviso that "a line officer of the Navy be detailed to command this expedition," someone "authorized to select the personnel . . . , collect all data, assemble all material, direct experiments, and carry the entire project to completion." Jack was writing his own ticket, for Admiral McKean endorsed, and Secretary Daniels approved, the report immediately. On 12 February Towers received orders placing him in command of the transatlantic or TA section of the aviation division under operations. It was generally understood that the principal aviators in TA would also make the flight.[8]

The whole project was supposed to be a secret, but the press got wind of it when a notice of Towers' new assignment was routinely published, and Jack was saddled with the unwelcome task of keeping the ubiquitous reporters "satisfied and happy, but not telling them anything."[9] He planned to utilize six officers and six clerks in two rooms at the division, plus a sprawling

Officers of the transatlantic section stand behind Towers during the planning of the NC flight, spring 1919. *Left to right:* Lieutenant Commander Godfrey deC. Chevalier, liaison and assistant in charge of operations; Commander Holden C. Richardson, construction; Lieutenant (jg) Roswell F. Barratt, aerographer; Lieutenant Commander P. N. L. Bellinger; Lieutenant Commander Richard F. Byrd, navigation; and Major B. L. Smith, USMC, material. (Navy Department)

organization from the bureaus and the fleet.[10] As director of naval aviation, Captain Irwin would have overall control until relieved in the spring by Jack's old shipmate Captain Tom Craven. In late April Towers' title would change to commander, Seaplane Division 1, the equivalent of a destroyer division flag officer; not bad for an officer who had never commanded his own ship!

He was not, however, given free rein in the selection of participants in the flight. He especially wanted his planning staff to take part, notably Lieutenant Commanders Dick Byrd and Chevy Chevalier and Major Barney Smith, the latter in charge of material and equipment. But Captain Irwin, possibly on Towers' advice, issued an edict forbidding any personnel who had had foreign, including Canadian, wartime duty. It was a fair enough policy, giving wartime desk-bound and stateside men an opportunity to enhance their careers, but it eliminated Byrd. When the latter, laid up with the flu, heard the news, he telephoned Jack from his sick bed and obtained an endorsement to remain at least during the planning stages—and Captain Irwin agreed.[11]

On 15 February Towers convened a meeting of his staff and engineering specialists to consider the NCs' engines. The men not only settled on the latest high-compression Liberty engine but considered alternatives to the three-tractor arrangement of the NC-1. Though the NC-2 was being constructed experimentally with two tractors and a center pusher, they decided to modify it with two nacelles, each with engines in tandem, one tractor and one pusher. After this was tested, a third possibility would be tried, a single two-engine center-tandem nacelle with one tractor on each wing. Over the ensuing weeks of tests, the latter system proved optimum, so the NC-3 and NC-4 were completed as such and a pusher was added to the center tractor nacelle of the NC-1. The NCs thus became four-engine machines. Though supposedly self-starting, each engine still used the old hand crank, "geared down so that it stuck out the side."[12]

Navigation provided perhaps the greatest challenge of all, particularly since flying machines had rarely ventured even 150 miles beyond sight of land (the wide-ranging Zeppelins had been guided by radio from shore stations). The destroyers stationed every fifty miles along the route would provide easy visual signals by making smoke in daylight and at night firing star shells and "torching"—spewing flames from their smokestacks. During February and March Pat Bellinger successfully tested this arrangement in navigation exercises with several F5L flying boats and two destroyers at Hampton Roads.

Yet Towers and his planners decided to play it safe by assuming that no destroyers would be available. The planes must be navigationally self-sufficient to meet any crisis. This meant developing and testing instruments and training the navigating officers to operate them, a considerable task facing Dick Byrd. In addition to special compasses, charts, and watches, Byrd had to come up with wireless sets, a radio compass/direction finder, a sextant, and drift and course indicators and flares. It would be the largest array of navigational instruments yet carried aloft by any heavier-than-air craft.[13]

Towers wanted no part of airborne radio equipment. His experience with the bulky sets had been frustrating as far back as Charles Maddox's experiments at Annapolis, and he did not believe their added weight was worth it. He was convinced by navy experts, however, to include such equipment on each boat in order to enable the crews to communicate with and home in on the prepositioned destroyers. Assigned to work with Byrd as aircraft radio specialist was Lieutenant Commander Robert A. Lavender, who installed 500-watt wireless arc transmitters on the flying boats. Equipped with a long trailing wire antenna of 250 feet, each plane's receiver had an incredible 1,200-mile range while airborne, a far cry from the fledgling sets of prewar days. If forced to land en route, the plane could utilize a fixed-antenna transmitter with a seventy-five-mile range. Amplifiers increased the incoming Morse code signals fifty times beyond any other set.[14]

Each plane was also equipped with a 5-watt antinoise radiotelephone headset and microphone that acted as an intercom between the plane commander/navigator and his pilots and as an interplane communications net out to twenty miles. Partly developed by the navy's first officer to have been taken aloft, Lieutenant Commander George Sweet, this system enabled the crews to maintain their proper cruising intervals and thus to keep on course.[15]

The radio compass—an instrument for pinpointing radio signals from ships and shore stations up to fifty miles away—Lavender mounted in the stern of each hull after it was tested in Bellinger's F5Ls. But at the last moment, in late April, a wiring change had to be made in all the boats that, in Towers' words, "resulted in such an increase of the ignition noises [from the engines] in the compass that signals could not usually be heard for more than ten miles," at least in the plane Towers would command. With the departure date fast approaching, Lavender lacked the time to correct the fault.[16]

Beyond the radio gear, Towers, himself adept at navigating a ship, directed Byrd to devise instruments and methods that were as simple and swift to use as they were economical in size and weight. These were essential, given the fact that celestial navigation had rarely been tried by anyone aloft, pilots being preoccupied with flying their planes.

At Byrd's request, navy hydrographer George H. Littlehales prepared a special chart of the open North Atlantic to speed up the determination of a plane's line of position, though tests quickly demonstrated that the familiar Marc St. Hilaire method of plotting position was "easier and faster," that is, it established altitude, azimuth, and hourly angle diagrams for four key celestial reference points before departure. Charts of the North Atlantic were thus prepared based on the probable date of departure from Newfoundland, the assumed track of the flight, and the relative positions throughout of the sun and the stars Arcturus, Vega, and Deneb. The navigators had only to "shoot" the altitude of these objects, observe the Greenwich sidereal and mean times on the two torpedo boat watches provided each plane, and compute their position using specially prepared slide rules and tables.[17]

Observing the precise altitude of a star or the sun with a sextant required a sharply defined horizon, day and night. This was unlikely, given the ocean hazes that usually obscured the horizon from the 1,000-foot altitude at which Towers planned to fly. So a ship's sextant would not suffice. Fortunately, Byrd had already invented a bubble sextant that simulated its own artificial horizon, and the Naval Observatory helped to refine Byrd's invention—a major advance in the art of aerial navigation. In addition, Byrd installed standard navy conning tower compasses and provided Sperry vertical-card aircraft compasses. As for severe fog and storms, Towers kept his meteorological officer, Lieutenant (jg) Roswell F. Barratt, hard at work establishing a weather-reporting and -analysis network between U.S. and British armed services and governmental agencies.[18]

Previously, airspeed had usually been registered by a pitot tube and pressure gauge, which, however, gave low-pressure readings and succumbed to the effects of rain and spray. Dr. A. F. Zahm solved this problem by inventing a waterproof venturi nozzle to replace the pitot tube. Jerry Hunsaker's navy designers also illuminated the standard inclinometer measuring a plane's trim, and a Sperry gyroscope was installed as the turn indicator.[19]

Looming large was the factor of wind, which caused planes inevitably to drift off course. Surface wind speeds would be transmitted by wireless from the picket destroyers. An Italian ground-speed indicator for airships was modified by the Naval Gun Factory into a drift indicator; eight were delivered to the expedition, two per plane. In tests, one of these successfully measured wave actions to obtain drift angles from 1,000 feet over smooth water and up to 5,000 feet over disturbed seas. A duplicate instrument measured the plane's speed over water by noting the distance from the plane of a smoke bomb or nighttime magnesium flare dropped into the water. These drift flares, developed by the Bureau of Ordnance (BuOrd) with help from the army, were delayed-action affairs mounted on two-foot-long floats. The army also provided two magnesium flares per plane for night landings.

Finally, a large, improved type of course and distance indicator was built for tying together the foregoing data. Dick Byrd coordinated all these developments, wrote the navigating instructions for the trip, and instructed the plane commanders in the new science of aerial navigation.[20]

Jack Towers proved more than equal to the multitudinous tasks of mobilizing Seaplane Division 1 for the transatlantic crossing. Captain Harris Laning, chief of staff of the U.S. Fleet's destroyer force, visited Jack in Washington to coordinate ship movements with the flight. Completely ignorant of aircraft, he recalled that he "had to learn from the aviators and base everything on that." The patrol line would be comprised of no fewer than sixty-six destroyers, with four battleships making weather reports from positions 400 miles apart for the long Newfoundland-to-Azores leg. Tenders and supply vessels were designated and equipped for the several stations where the NCs were to land—Halifax, Nova Scotia; Newfoundland; Horta and Ponta Delgada in the Azores; and Lisbon, Portugal.

Pat Bellinger and the Coast Guard's first aviator Lieutenant Elmer F. Stone braved wintry Newfoundland in a destroyer during March to select Trepassey Harbor as the best point for departure. There they encountered the first of several British contenders who had arrived to challenge the NCs. Pat wrote Jack, "We certainly have got to work at high pressure, else we are going to be left behind." The race was on.[21]

By the end of March—only five weeks before the target date—none of the four planes had flown on four engines, while two had not flown at all. The NC-1 lost its entire port wing riding out a storm at anchor at Rockaway on 27–28 March, and since the subcontractor of the wings could not furnish a replacement, Towers had to make the decision to scratch one plane from the flight. On 1 April the NC-2 flew the first of many test flights with its new twin-tandem engine arrangement, once with visiting Assistant Secretary Franklin Roosevelt aboard as passenger.

This engine system proved unsatisfactory, leading Lieutenant Commander Marc A. "Pete" Mitscher, just assigned to the project, to suggest that the port wing of the NC-2 be cannibalized to repair the NC-1, thus eliminating the NC-2 instead of the NC-1. Towers approved, and conversion commenced on 23 April, the day Jack moved the TA section from Washington to New York; he could now supervise the preparations directly. Also on the twenty-third the NC-3 flew for the first time. Soon after, as the station ships began to depart for the mid-Atlantic, Towers swooped down over the weather-reporting battleship division standing out of New York. "They gave us a wonderful cheer, wished us good luck by wireless, then headed out."[22]

Personally selected for the expedition by Towers because of his navigational skills was Lieutenant Commander Albert C. "Putty" Read. After completing the immense task of collecting and loading all the necessary equipment for the planes, crews, and support ships, Read came to Rockaway as prospective skipper of one of the flying boats. Standing five foot four, the quiet, unassuming, and unemotional New Englander had been admired by his '07 classmates for his "proud record of patience and good nature"; they had nicknamed him for his puttylike face. With his businesslike demeanor Read was like Towers and Mitscher; all three could ward off pesky reporters more easily than the affable Dick Richardson and Pat Bellinger.[23]

By the end of April, the TA section was settled in at NAS Rockaway, adjacent to Jamaica Bay, complete with a mascot dog that had become a Towers fixture. The three-boat Seaplane Division 1 was ready to be commissioned, "the first time," boasted a proud Jack Towers, that aircraft would be commissioned in the navy "and given a real individuality, like a ship." Few ships had been rushed into major service quite so rapidly; the NC-4 flew for the first time only on 1 May, four days before the earliest possible departure date from Rockaway. The race was not only against the British challengers but to meet the 14 May departure date from Newfoundland. A veritable armada was timing fuel supplies around that date, and the new moon waxed larger each night toward its full brilliance on the appointed evening.[24]

On the eve of the formal commissioning ceremonies, scheduled for Saturday, 3 May, Towers assigned the crews. He himself would command not only the entire expedition but the flagship NC-3 as well. Lieutenant Commanders Bellinger and Read would command the NC-1 and NC-4 respectively. Since the three boat commanders would do all their own navigating, each would have two pilots, a radio operator, and two engineers. Towers arranged to have Dick Byrd accompany him in the NC-3 as far as Newfoundland to help test the navigating instruments.

For chief pilot of the NC-3 Jack selected Commander Dick Richardson, the man he had taught to fly and key designer of the NC hulls. Second pilot was Lieutenant David H. McCulloch, a skilled civilian and wartime airman. Towers wanted them both because of their experience from the beginning flying the NC-1. To handle the flagship's wireless he assigned Lieutenant Commander Robert Lavender. His engineer was Chief Boatswain Lloyd Ray

Crew of the NC-3 with their plane at NAS Rockaway. *Left to right:* Towers, plane commander and navigator; Commander Dick Richardson, pilot; Lieutenant David H. McCulloch, pilot; Lieutenant Commander Robert A. Lavender, radio officer; Chief Boatswain Lloyd R. Moore, engineer; and Lieutenant (jg) Braxton L. Rhodes, reserve engineer later bounced from the flight at Trepassey, Newfoundland. (Towers collection)

"Dinty" Moore, highly recommended by Mitscher as the best aviation mechanic available and also a qualified naval aviator. For reserve engineer Towers chose Lieutenant (jg) Braxton L. Rhodes, who knew the engines from having served at the navy's wartime Liberty motor school.[25]

The three sparkling, yellow-winged, gray-hulled flying boats and green- and blue-uniformed crews mustered before their hangars at Rockaway the morning of the third for the commissioning ceremony. Reading Jack's commissioning orders was the chief of staff of the Third Naval District, none other than his former London boss, Captain Pete Symington. Everything seemed to be ready for the Monday flight to the Canadian Maritimes.

While Towers had the utmost confidence in his ability to fly, navigate, and lead this monumental expedition, his wife Lily had her doubts. Jack told friends that "she was too loyal and patriotic to ask me not to make the attempt. I'm supremely confident that we'll make it all right." Still, the strain on Lily would tell. Their marriage was not working out, and they tried to strengthen it with another child; Lily was in her first month of pregnancy.[26]

While the expedition was under pressure to leave, hazards mounted. Several spring storms broke out, and about two hours after midnight on the fifth, Towers was awakened "by excited calls." A fire had ignited during fueling of the NC-1, destroying its starboard wing and damaging parts of the NC-4. Towers jumped up and got repairs under way immediately. The NC-1 seemed lost for the flight, though Pat Bellinger assured Jack his crew would get it airworthy by further cannibalizing the idled NC-2. Because of the fire the flight could not leave that day. Jack decided to have Bellinger follow the NC-3 and NC-4 to Canada whenever his crew had the NC-1 ready. But rain delayed the two boats' departure. Preparations were also marred on the fifth by the fatal crash at the station of an HS-1 seaplane, which killed both of its occupants.[27] Spirits dropped with the repeated delays. Franklin Roosevelt, acting secretary while Josephus Daniels was in Paris with the peacemakers, took the opportunity to have four letters given to Towers for personal delivery to key dignitaries at the several destinations along the route.[28]

The general gloom deepened the afternoon of the seventh. Just after another fire was narrowly averted, an NC-4 crewman accidentally stuck his hand into one of the boat's big whirring propellers, which whacked it off. Chief Special Mechanic E. Harry Howard had the presence of mind to grab the stump and walk the three hundred yards to the first-aid station, where corpsmen checked the bleeding and bandaged him up. Before transferring to the hospital, he reappeared at the hangar and manfully called out to Towers, "I'm all right, sir. I hope there is bad weather for two weeks, for if there is I'll make the trip with you yet." But, of course, he had to be replaced.[29]

The delays at least enabled Bellinger and his workers to have the NC-1 in flying trim by the time the sun rose bright and clear over Rockaway on Thursday, 8 May. Weather reports for the coast were optimistic. All hands eagerly awaited Towers, who appeared at 0930 and announced with a smile, "Well, boys, let's go." Captain Irwin handed out four-leaf clovers to each crewman as they hastened toward their machines—the NC-1 and -3 tied up, tails into the beach, the NC-4 still perched on the marine railway leading to the water. Jack told the gathered reporters, "Guesses aren't worth much, but if you want mine, here it is: we'll get there!"[30]

As the plane commanders climbed into their open cockpits in the bows, five hundred spectators focused on the beaming, exuberant Bellinger—he always beamed!—while Towers and Read predictably kept their emotions buried inside their flight suits. At 0957 Dick Richardson brought the motors of the NC-3 to life, warmed them up briefly and taxied her out into Jamaica Bay, followed closely by the NC-4 and NC-1. From his open navigator's perch inside the bow of the flagship's hull, Jack stood erect and gave the navy yardarm snap, the signal for takeoff.

Richardson "jammed on power," and the NC-3 sped across the water until it got airborne at 1015, followed quickly by the other two planes. After the rendezvous in a V formation, NC-3 in the lead, Seaplane Division 1 turned east just south of Rockaway. Next stop—Halifax, Nova Scotia, 540 nautical miles to the northeast.[31]

Climbing above the morning haze into a brilliant Long Island sky at 1,800 feet, the three boats headed eastward along the south shore. Robert Lavender immediately established wireless contact with his two airborne counterparts and with Rockaway. One hundred miles out he communicated with NAS Chatham on Cape Cod, toward which the flight turned, cruising speed 85 to 90 mph. Just past noon the faster-running NC-4 edged well ahead of the flagship near Martha's Vineyard and had to circle around once to resume its proper station astern.

In the NC-3 Dick Richardson and Dave McCulloch traded off, taking half-hour "tricks at the wheel." At 1347, 3,500 feet over Chatham lighthouse, the flying boats headed seaward. "The air was smooth and warm," recalled Jack, "and everybody aboard was wearing a big smile." A clear Morse code message of congratulations from Franklin Roosevelt revealed the radios to be working well.[32]

The excitement of leaving on this unprecedented adventure stimulated everyone, though Dick Byrd confessed that the attention of the NC-3's crew "was riveted more on the thunder of our engines than on any other single factor," for everything depended on them. Towers' cockpit was small, especially with the charts, chart desk, sextants, drift indicator, and chronometers, as well as all the telephone wires trailing from his helmet. When Byrd wedged into the forward cockpit, the wires enmeshed both men. "Byrd and I were continually getting all mixed up like a couple of puppies on leashes," noted Towers.[33]

Over the open sea in early afternoon, Towers and Byrd practiced determining their drift with smoke bombs and taking sights on the sun. Course was shaped for Seal Island off the southwest tip of Nova Scotia, 250 miles and three hours away, the longest flight yet of any airplane out of sight of land. Rhodes and Moore kept steady eyes on all the machinery, while Lavender manned the radio. Everything worked well, except that Towers and Byrd made an error in calculating drift—3,500 feet was too high for an exact reading of the waves—and were twelve miles off course to the east when the first picket destroyer was spotted. Telephoning the pilots of all three planes, Jack ordered them to descend to 2,000, whereupon they spotted black and white puffs of smoke from the *McDermut* to the northward. The brand-new four-stacker could be seen steaming in the direction of the next destroyer, enabling the planes to check and correct their courses. As they passed over, Jack trained his binoculars on the NC-1 and saw Bellinger looking at him. They waved to each other.

Just then, Putty Read informed Towers that the NC-4 was having engine trouble. One motor had quit and another was missing. The men in the NC-3 soon lost sight of the -4, enveloped in a dark haze well to the northward. When Read reported he would probably have to land, Towers crawled back to talk with Richardson, the NC hull designer who assured him that the hull, once down, could withstand the seas. Towers figured Read would put the NC-4 alongside the *McDermut,* so the -3 and -1 pressed on.

Dave McCulloch now took the controls, enabling a hungry Dick Richardson to crawl aft for sandwiches and a thermos of coffee, which he took forward to Towers and Byrd. There Jack showed him the chart and their course change to starboard, eastward, of the second destroyer, the *Kimberly.* Haze obscured that vessel, but the men could see her smoke by 1510. The fate of the NC-4 was unknown. Continuing on his corrected course toward the third destroyer, the *Delphy,* Towers at 1530 spotted her dead ahead over his drift indicator sights. The changing light of late afternoon made her difficult to see, even though she was making smoke, so Jack had her transmit radio compass signals as he took the NC-3 directly overhead at about 1600.

Twenty minutes later both planes approached a sharp wind squall. Towers had his pilots take the flagship down to within 50 feet of the water, while Bellinger took the NC-1 upward. When the NC-3 struck the squall and was severely buffeted, Towers gazed back anxiously at his two pilots. But it only lasted about ten minutes and did not affect their course. They climbed higher again, altogether missing the fourth destroyer, the *Ludlow.* For this reason, Towers told Richardson he wanted to stay at 1,000 feet to better determine the drift. But then they sighted land, first Seal Island, then Cape Sable. They passed over the latter at 1710.

Although visibility was now good for the final run up the Nova Scotia coast, sharp squalls buffeted the NC-3 all the way, and the NC-1 was no-where to be seen. McCulloch and Richardson had to man the controls together. Nevertheless, the NC-3 handled well, generally displaying its inherent stability and good balance.

Radio officer Lavender received favorable weather reports from Halifax, with the winds gusting and the sun still high as the NC-3 approached its first destination. Suddenly they sighted "a huge rainbow," which Richardson described in a letter as "an enormous column dead ahead, reaching from the earth to the clouds, about 4 times as high as it was thick," about 2,000 feet up. The pilots headed straight into Halifax Harbor, since the wind was blowing directly in their faces, and landed precisely at 1900 New York time, 2030 locally. The trip had lasted just under nine hours—a magnificent display of endurance.

The NC-3 taxied up to its moorings as boat and factory whistles blew a welcome in the harbor, which was bathed in glorious colors from crimson sunlight reflecting off the clouds, hills, and water. The NC-1 landed ten minutes later. Towers led the two crews aboard the minelayer *Baltimore*, station ship for the stop, for happy welcomes, "a fine, hot meal," and conversation with her officers and assorted reporters. Inquiring about the NC-4, Jack was startled to learn that Read and his crew were missing somewhere off Cape Cod, where the picket destroyers were hunting for them. The anxious flyers refused to turn in until, in the words of Richardson, "lookouts reported a plane over the city. This sounded fine and we all rushed out on deck. Although many of us thought we could see the lights move, and through glasses we could see the red and green lights, it finally turned out to be a star low down in the haze. We finally turned in with some misgivings." Not until morning did word come that the plane had alighted and taxied all night to Chatham. Following repairs, she would resume the mission.[34]

The bright prospects of the expedition were now underscored by a telegram from Towers' former patron of the *America*, Rodman Wanamaker, who called Jack "Conqueror of the Wind and the Sea on this memorable crossing which will make true the dream I had hoped for you long ago."[35]

Daylight of 9 May revealed cracked propellers on both flying boats. Replacements were obtained from the *Baltimore*. But fresh propeller hubs were not available until Dick Byrd remembered a supply of them he had left the Canadians upon relinquishing the two wartime Halifax stations. He used a speedboat to fetch the hubs. The NC-3 then took a short test hop at sundown. The two boats were ready to take off for Newfoundland on the morning of the tenth. But when the NC-3 finally got her engines going in the cold, the starter on her pusher engine broke. Jack ordered the NC-1 to proceed on to Trepassey alone.

The broken part replaced, the NC-3 took off at 0910 Halifax time, but the pusher continued to malfunction and so thirty-eight miles out Towers had Richardson set her down. Although the engine was found operable, a close examination of the Olmstead-made propellers revealed that the tip of the starboard tractor's prop was cracked. The crew used their emergency transmitter to inform the *Baltimore.* Then on three engines they flew back to Halifax, where the reliable center tractor prop was installed in place of the derelict, and another put in its place. But Jack was not about to cross the ocean with such fragile airscrews; he radioed the Navy Department for twelve new props made of oak.[36]

The NC-3 again cleared Halifax harbor at 1245, all hands expecting the five-hour, 460-mile flight to be fairly easy until they encountered heavy winds. The four picket destroyers proved easy enough to see, but the cold was numbing when erratic winds began to buffet the plane. McCulloch and forty-one-year-old Richardson, the latter already plagued by sore muscles from the first leg of the journey, had to battle the controls in search of a favorable altitude.

Passing to seaward of Cape Canso, the plane was suddenly blown off course by a heavy northeast wind. Gravity seemed to disappear; in an abrupt downcurrent, Dick Byrd hit his head and worried "that Towers was going to fly out of the cockpit." Recovering, Jack handed Byrd a note calling the draught "the roughest air I have ever felt." He had his pilots take the plane above their 2,500 feet only to encounter winds "dead against us." So he ordered it down to 1,000 feet; there running into a heavy northwest wind.

Over St. Pierre Island they turned toward Newfoundland. Byrd used his drift indicator to discover that they were now 30 degrees off course and asked Towers to check him. Jack took a sighting on the water and confirmed Byrd's reading. Deciding to trust the new instrument, they changed course accordingly and were delighted to make landfall on the Newfoundland coast right on the mark. Said Byrd later, "I knew then that at last an airplane could be navigated without land marks."[37]

Towers had his pilots ascend toward 4,000 feet, where they found the air, in Richardson's words, "as smooth as a billiard table." Over the coast, tailwinds pushed their air speed up to 112 knots, and they climbed to 5,000 feet for the final approach to Trepassey Bay. But at that altitude the temperature dropped to near zero. Suddenly Byrd handed Jack a note saying he thought the plane might be on fire. Byrd crawled aft and to his great relief saw that it was only a cigarette McCulloch was smoking.[38]

Icebergs were the next thrill. Hundreds loomed up, looking to Towers like "sheep in pasture" and to others like a fleet of sail-driven fishing boats. The NC-3 also passed the fourth destroyer, the *McKean*. When Towers sighted Trepassey Bay, he likened it to "a small pond" surrounded by high hills but whipped by near-gale-force winds. Taking no chances landing in a harbor new to them, he and Byrd abandoned their nest in the bow and crawled aft to the cockpit.[39]

With Richardson at the controls, they tried a long glide down to the five-mile-long anchorage. At 2100 feet the flying boat started getting pounded by gusty crosswinds that steadily increased to 50 mph, so they avoided the narrow half-mile-wide inner harbor and headed toward the harbor's entrance. After a sharp descent that threw Towers off balance, the NC-3 touched down, completing a flight of six hours and fifty minutes from Halifax; the landing alone had taken forty minutes. Racing a "heavy brown fog settling over the headlands to the east," Richardson taxied the machine at high speed toward its intended moorings. Puffs of wind made the boat skid and lift clear of the surface. Only by great exertions were he and McCulloch able to use the ailerons to keep the lee wing above the water.[40]

The plane taxied by the NC-1 to its own moorings alongside the mine-layer "mother ship" *Aroostook*, whose skipper, Captain J. Harvey Tomb, greeted the men. The 3,800-ton converted coastal steamer became their headquarters, and after a hearty supper they gave to reporters the bare facts of their most recent leg. Interviews were not supposed to be granted, because several newspapers had already given exclusive contracts to many of the airmen. Towers had one with the New York *World*. Excluded editors had protested so vigorously to the Navy Department that Acting Secretary Roosevelt had banned further interviews until the flight was over.[41]

A glance around cold, blustery Trepassey revealed the old cruiser *Chicago*. Surprise of surprises, Towers and his men now learned for the first time that a brand new dirigible, the C-5, was about to make an attempt to cross the Atlantic ahead of the NCs. The *Chicago* would be its tender after the airship arrived at Trepassey. The LTA boys were going to show their stuff too, with a direct nonstop flight from Trepassey to Ireland, kept secret until now in the event the preparations miscarried.[42]

As the sun set on this tenth day of May 1919, Trepassey Bay turned dark from a heavy overcast. The two flying boats had to be carefully secured for

Warming up the engines of the NC-3 with a steam connection from the destroyer tender *Prairie* at cold, wind-swept Trepassey Bay, Newfoundland. Being a commissioned flying boat, the plane displays an ensign aft. (Navy Department)

riding out the 61-mph gusts, and overnight refueling was called off lest the boats drag their moorings. In fact, this weather would last for days, which at least made possible the careful but time-consuming refueling as the gas was strained of impurities. And the power plants could be overhauled and tuned up, the controls checked and rechecked. All these preparations were completed in two days. Filling the radiators would be a last-minute operation, for fear the water would freeze during the frigid nights.[43]

The men had comfortable, dry quarters after their wet landings. Towers and Richardson, as the most senior officers, were given the pilot house on the *Aroostook,* "built largely of glass" and hence offering "the privacy of the proverbial goldfish," wrote Towers. But two brass beds had been installed for their comfort. They enjoyed these amenities, for each man would be allowed a mere five pounds of personal baggage on the leg across the Atlantic.[44]

Far away, at the Paragon propeller factory in Baltimore, an incredible feat of production took place that very weekend, 10–11 May. Inspired by Towers' urgent call to replace the defective Olmstead props in record time, Paragon workers delivered the oaken props to the navy Monday morning for passage to Trepassey in the destroyer *Edwards.* They would not arrive before the fourteenth, which was just as well since weather across the North Atlantic remained unsettled and Trepassey bitterly cold; the *Aroostook* had to blow steam on the planes' engines to keep the oil from congealing. During sunny intervals, Towers with Richardson, and Bellinger with Mitscher, flew the *Aroostook*'s two small Curtiss MF seaplanes over the harbor to determine the best takeoff route. The delay also bought time for Putty Read's NC-4, still undergoing repairs at Chatham.[45]

The layover gave the division commander the opportunity to modify his planes based on lessons thus far learned. The only navigational difficulty had been seeing the picket destroyers; Towers radioed Captain Laning to have them display their searchlights day and night—a successful measure, since the lights would be seen from fifteen miles even during daylight. Fuel requirements were studied and restudied until Jack decided that the plane loads, now up to 29,000 pounds, should each be reduced by 700; extra spare parts, tools, and rations were accordingly removed. Jack and Bellinger continued taking practice sightings on the sun, moon, and stars, while Dick Byrd received the final word from Captain Irwin that he could not accompany the flight to the Azores.[46]

Towers and Bellinger spent 13 May discussing the projected route and every possible detail of the flight, while the meteorologists sent up sounding balloons. Towers decided to aim for an afternoon departure two days hence, one day later than originally scheduled. He "hated the thought of starting without Read," still stuck at Chatham, but "the weather people advised a start" while the weather held.[47]

Events began to move quickly on Wednesday the fourteenth. In the morning the *Aroostook*'s radios crackled with news that the blimp C-5 had left NAS Montauk on Long Island for a 1,200-mile nonstop flight to Trepassey, and that the NC-4 had departed Chatham for Halifax. Putty Read reached Halifax before noon and replaced a cracked prop, but a clogged carburetor kept the NC-4 there overnight. Meanwhile, at midday on the fourteenth, the destroyer *Edwards* put in to Trepassey with Towers' much-needed oaken propellers. Though the weather over the course was now reported to be clearing, Jack decided to wait the additional day in hopes that the NC-4 would arrive in time to make a full-division flight.[48]

Midmorning of the fifteenth brought another round of frustrations, starting with word that the NC-4 was down at sea an hour out of Halifax. Then, just before noon, the 196-foot-long Goodyear gas bag lumbered into Trepassey. At forty-five knots, the C-5 and her crew of six had covered the 1,177 miles from Montauk in twenty-five hours and fifty minutes, setting the dirigible record for distance nonstop. Perhaps the airship might yet depart for

Towers in his flight gear, probably on board the tender *Aroostook,* just before the departure from Trepassey. (Towers collection)

Europe first, though with the afternoon came word that the NC-4 had completed oil and gas line repairs and was heading for Newfoundland. Then Towers learned that one of the tankers that was supposed to refuel the destroyers had broken down; the "small boys" might be recalled to port if they could not be serviced on station.

In addition, the winds were making up, so much so that at about 1700 a furious gust tore away the mooring lines of the C-5, whose handlers had been straining all day to keep it secured. Though all hands jumped clear, a loose line struck and killed a young civilian volunteer. The abandoned airship blew out to sea and destruction.

The field was now open to the NCs, despite several British challengers in various stages of unreadiness.[49] Towers still wanted to wait for the NC-4, reported by the picket destroyers to be edging closer to Newfoundland. His two crews were suited up in fur-lined boots and hoods, leather flight suits over their uniforms, with two layers of socks, when Jack made his decision. They must go now, immediately, before the weather worsened; Read would have to follow whenever he could. The night of the full moon had just passed. With each additional day, it would rise nearly an hour later and with less than a full disk, meaning fewer hours of light and reduced brilliance.[50]

Towers' NC-3 led Bellinger's NC-1 into the harbor, then commenced a full-power run for the takeoff. Jack stood up in the bow, his back to a mighty crosswind blowing spray into the faces of pilots Richardson and McCulloch. The pervasive spindrift not only soaked the men but got into the engines. Worse, Richardson could not coax the plane into the air—waves created by a heavy swell refused to unleash their suction hold on the hull. After two and a half hours of trying, Towers had no choice but to abort the attempt before the plane reached the choppy seas beyond. Pilot Mitscher had the same trouble in the NC-1. They would taxi back and try again.

Just then the drenched flyers looked up to see their sister ship winging its way over the harbor. Read had made it, everybody was wet through, and Jack wisely decided to postpone the attempt until the morrow. The NC-4 got the full treatment overnight, assisted by the crews of its sister boats. The aviators dried out, rested, and decided to reduce the fuel supply of each 28,300-pound plane by 90 pounds to 1,800 for a lighter takeoff. Meanwhile reports were received of excellent meteorological conditions over the Atlantic. The flyers' desire to be off was reinforced by their British competitors, visiting from St. John's to rib them for their failure. After a final conference before midnight, the men relaxed over poker.[51]

And so Friday, 16 May 1919, became the history-making date. Towns-folk jammed the shore and fishing boats in anticipation. The three plane commanders practiced their navigating with Byrd, who still tried in vain to convince Jack to let him accompany them.

Early in the afternoon, lingering winds and swells abruptly quieted down, leaving a calm, hazy atmosphere, and more glowing weather reports were received. Then W. R. Gregg of the weather bureau handed Jack a handwritten note pushing for immediate departure; partial low clouds and possible occasional showers would begin at destroyer no. 8, light winds after no. 12. Gregg advised Towers to fly over the clouds. Jack, glad that he had waited, now met with Bellinger and Read to go over their procedures one last time, while the radiators were topped off and coffee and sandwiches placed on board. Skippers from the several anchored warships visited the *Aroostook* to offer words of good luck, and the three crews assembled topside.

"If hard work on the part of everybody counts for anything," Towers told the reporters, "we ought to make a go of it. The machines are in excellent shape and the crews are fine, capable fellows." The plane commanders thanked Captain Tomb for everything and said they'd see him at Plymouth, England, where the *Aroostook* would bring the crews' baggage. Tomb jokingly bet Jack that he'd get there first.[52]

Delivered by launch to their planes, whose engines had already been warmed up, the crews settled in and were ready for departure by 2030 Greenwich mean time (4:30 PM eastern daylight time). They cast free of their mooring buoys. Towers stood up in the bow of the flagship, shouted "Let's go!" to his pilots, and waved his arms to the others. Richardson turned over the four big engines and new oaken propellers of the NC-3 at 2036 and began taxiing into the harbor, although the other two planes took longer starting their engines.[53]

Whatever optimism Towers had vanished when the speeding NC-3 failed to lift off in the outer harbor. To the rear, Read decided to keep going and roared into the sky over the NC-3. Jack had Richardson try again, to no avail. Meanwhile, Bellinger kept the NC-1 on the water and Read circled, waiting. Obviously, the NC-3 was still too heavy; Jack ordered it back to the *Aroostook*. When Read saw this, he landed. As the flagship taxied, Jack told reserve engineer Braxton Rhodes, who weighed 185 pounds, that he would have to leave. Though Richardson's bulk of 243 pounds might have been a greater saving, as flagship pilot he was indispensable to the mission. Rhodes protested but had to obey. Jack patted him gently as he climbed out and said, "I'm sorry, boy."

In fact, the NC had been designed to carry only a five-man crew "for an endurance flight." The aggregate crew weight was supposed to be 850 pounds. This was included in the theoretical figure of 12,126 pounds for crew, supplies, and fuel. The extra man now dispensed with, other sacrifices would have to come from the 524 pounds of spare parts, food, and water and/or the 250 pounds of radio gear. Towers had his men tear up floorboards and remove a bag of mail for stamp collectors, along with extra tools and extra radiator drinking water. And as events were to prove, he made a fateful decision, namely, to eliminate the emergency radio transmitter, which weighed 26 pounds. This brought fervent protests from radio officer Lavender, who reminded Jack of its usefulness when the NC-3 had landed off Halifax. But Towers had to make tradeoffs to break clear of the water and lead the expedition. And with Rhodes gone, Boatswain Dinty Moore had to handle the engineering chores alone.[54]

After a delay of exactly ninety minutes, the lightened NC-3 roared back down the harbor against the difficult crosswind and into the sky at 2206, followed a minute later by the NC-4 and at 2209 by the -1, the latter time the official moment of departure recorded by the navy. The next stop would be the harbor of Ponta Delgada in the Azores islands, some 1,300 miles to the southeast. Expected flying time according to navy weather forecasts was nineteen hours.[55]

Because of the heavy load and "very rough air," which made Towers uneasy, Richardson and McCulloch manned the controls together as the NC-3 passed low over the Canadian shoreline and a sea spotted with icebergs. The sky got steadily hazier as the planes climbed 50 feet per minute toward the designated cruising altitude of 1,000 feet. Towers meant to keep the flagship in the lead of the V formation but had difficulty making out the other two boats astern in the haze. The prescribed interval was between 400 yards and three miles, with all three planes helped along by a twelve-knot tailwind for an average cruising speed of ninety knots. Ere long, everything seemed to be running smoothly, although the fast running NC-4 inched slightly ahead of the -3. Towers' nervousness disappeared as he navigated toward the position of the destroyer on station no. 1, the *Greer*.[56]

The crews watched one another and at 2245 spotted the smoke and searchlight of the *Greer* in the overcast dusk. The NC-3 approached slightly south of her, so Towers corrected his course. About sundown, when the planes were just over the ship, Towers lost sight of the NC-4 and sent his first radio message to Read asking if it was "just astern." Read could not see the NC-3 either and asked Towers to turn on his running lights—red and green (port and starboard, as on ships), plus one white light in the front center of the top wing. The crew of the NC-3 had already tried, but the lights had failed to respond, a fact Robert Lavender conveyed to Read's radioman. Playing it safe, Read took the NC-4 in a wide circling arc over the *Greer* to restore a proper interval well behind the NC-3. NC-1 brought up the rear.

The haze in the darkening sky obscured all but a few stars, which meant they had to depend mainly on their instruments to maintain the correct altitude. This was unfortunate, for moments later the lights on the NC-3's instrument panel began to fail. Apparently moisture from the previous after-

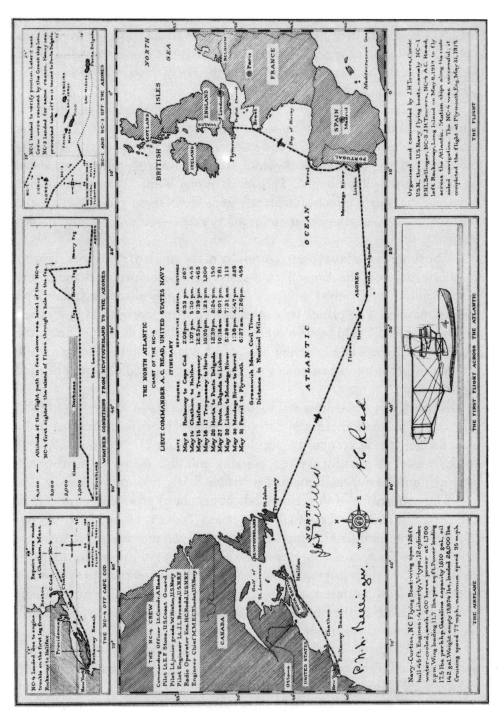

Transatlantic flight of the NC-4

noon's wet takeoff attempt was the cause. Pilots Richardson and McCulloch traded off piloting chores and pointed a flashlight at the instruments, while Moore aft in the hull kept his flashlight at the ready to warn off either of the other planes should they get too close.[57]

A few stars came out above the overcast, and, according to one contemporary account, "a swift narrow stem of flames runs up the sky," where at 4,000 feet it "bursts into flower, and scatters petals across the night." This was the expected star shell, greenish-white, from the destroyer fifty miles ahead on station no. 2, Raymond A. Spruance's *Aaron Ward*. At intervals of five minutes, the ship's 3-inch antiaircraft guns fired these projectiles to the northwest at a 75-degree elevation for safety's sake—they didn't want to hit a plane.

The three flying boats passed carefully to the south of the bursts. Towers presently made out the *Aaron Ward*'s searchlight beam, two truck lights, and a large illuminated canvas stretched over the fantail displaying the ship's station number. The planes flew over her cheering crew at 2335.[58] Then another star shell could be seen off to the eastward from destroyer no. 3, the *Buchanan*. All the while Lavender had been having difficulty running out the NC-3's 250-foot trailing antenna wire; he did not succeed until well beyond the *Buchanan*.

At 0019 of 17 May, recalled Richardson, "the moon rose red as fire and much distorted dead ahead, and instead of being of much assistance was really a menace[,] for on account of peculiar dispositions of the clouds and fog banks it gave us a badly skewed horizon, and also it blinded us to some extent[,] making our instruments less visible."

The appearance of the thin clouds hours ahead of schedule concerned the navigator-commanders of all three boats. Towers realized he could not use the magnesium flares, supposed to be dropped into the sea to measure drift. Unless the planes went down to within 50 feet of the water, the flares could not be seen for making measurements. It being too risky to fly that low in the dark, Towers stayed at 1,000 feet where he could guide by the easily visible star shells in the distance. And he spotted two steamers, one a brilliantly illuminated passenger liner, heading west.

Star shells from destroyers nos. 4, 5, and 6—the *Upshur, Boggs,* and *Ward*—guided Towers easily, but just after he'd sighted bursts from the *Palmer,* no. 7, his view was obscured by heavy overcast. Near the *Boggs* and cruising around 2,000 feet, Jack, Dick, and Dave saw the NC-1 loom up from behind and below, out of the fog, flying faster and dangerously close. Boatswain Moore frantically waved his flashlight astern, whereupon the plane abruptly veered away. Then the NC-3 got into the slipstream of the -4's powerful engines, whereupon Towers instructed Bellinger and Read to abandon formation flying and maneuver independently.

McCulloch and Richardson now called Jack over the phone to recommend that they take the NC-3 above the rapidly approaching fog bank. In the clear they would be able to utilize the moon and stars as reference points. Towers concurred, and as they ascended he sighted the *Palmer* slightly to the north. Correcting his position, he also spotted the star shells of the next "tin can," the *Walker*. When he lost sight of the NC-1 in the fog bank, however, he realized the -3 lacked the speed to get above it, so he ordered his own pilots back down to 1,000 feet. There, nearer the surface, the air was clear but turbulent, and they had to climb again.

At 2,000 feet the air was better, and the wind helped push the plane along. Passing over destroyer no. 9, the *Thatcher,* at 0410, the NC-3 broke into the clear, where the crew beheld the pale-white disk of the nearly full moon high in the eastern sky.[59]

"It was beautiful up there," remembered Jack, "like sailing over a sea of snow, and through an occasional rift [in the clouds] we could see the One and Four below us, each on one side. The star shells exploded above the clouds, so there was no difficulty about keeping on course," the bursts being "plainly visible for sixty miles." He would remember "these hours above the clouds over the mid-Atlantic at night . . . as the most impressive" of his life. "The engines were running beautifully, all forty-eight cylinders spitting short purplish flames, with a roar. . . ."[60]

Dinty Moore occasionally crawled up to give Towers details regarding radio messages and the fuel supply he had not relayed over the intercom. The three planes "worked" each other's radios, those of the destroyers, and the navy's transmitter at Bar Harbor, out to 700 miles—a record for a wireless—though the NC-3's equipment was not performing as well as the others'.[61]

With the planes abeam the *Crosby,* destroyer no. 10, at 0445, the clouds thickened, and the NC-3 began climbing to 3,500 feet where the air was completely smooth. On approaching the shell bursts from the *Kalk,* no. 11, Towers realized the NC-3 would pass slightly north of it instead of the safer south. "Foolishly," he admitted later, "I thought it was out of position, and I didn't want to change course. Besides, I could see it, and thought they could see us through the thin clouds, so I kept right on. . . . I knew they were due to fire just about when we were in line." The shells were set to burst at 4,000 feet, 500 feet below where Jack thought his plane was. The *Kalk* fired "right on the second," for he saw the flash of the gun. "The shell exploded just under us. I looked back and both Richardson and McCulloch looked as though they would like to take the navigating out of my hands."[62]

By now a grey dawn was breaking. As they passed destroyer no. 12, the *Meredith,* at 0545 this seventeenth of May, the NC boats were eight hours out of Trepassey. But when a high thick cloud mass obscured no. 13, the *Bush,* about 0623, Towers had Lavender call ahead for weather reports, star shells, and radio compass signals to assist his navigation. The clouds blotted out no. 14, the *Cowell,* however, leading Towers to alter his course, descending to try and spot no. 15, the *Maddox.* He had his pilots plunge 2,000 feet through "a small hole" in the clouds at 0707. Instead of the *Maddox,* the NC-3 encountered heavy rain squalls that fouled his theretofore steady navigating.[63] The station ship *Rochester* waiting in the Azores now began to receive reports of bad weather from the destroyers, but Towers heard nothing. He noted later, "Had there been any intimation made to me that such weather might be encountered, no start would have been made from Trepassey on the afternoon of the 16th."[64]

With the NC-3 down to 1,500 feet and Towers looking north for the *Maddox,* his pilots called him up. One had spotted the shape of a vessel to the southwestward. Jack "could not believe we had been set to the northward, but a look through the glasses showed that the ship was war-colored. . . ." Assuming the *Maddox* was in proper position, "I changed course 20 degrees to Southerly to pass within sight of No. 16 and pass over No. 17," the *Hopewell* and Harry Baldridge's *Stockton* respectively. Towers and Baldridge later decided that in fact the vessel sighted had been the American gunboat *Marietta,* heading home from European duty and some fifteen miles south-southwest of the *Maddox.* So the NC-3 was actually heading off to the southeast, well away from the destroyer line.[65]

Towers had Lavender transmit position reports every half-hour. Unknown to the crew, however, the radio's ground wire broke just after the plane had passed beyond the *Stockton.* Though they could receive, their own transmissions were no longer being heard. The rain squalls became "so bad that we had to turn and run before them. We made frequent attempts to get above them, but they seemed to extend all the way up to the heavens." With visibility less than a hundred yards, even the wing tips could hardly be seen. Jack now admitted he did not know whether the NC-3 "was north or south of No. 17, so changed course ten degrees to northward to run parallel to the proper course, hoping that the weather would clear and No. 18 would be sighted," the destroyer *Craven.* The plane "side-slipped" once, but stability was easily restored. It had to detour around what were now impenetrable rain squalls, flying at about 1,000 feet.[66]

After eight hours of steady night flying, the men of all three flying boats were faced with many more hours in horrendous weather. Lavender reported that Read and Bellinger were having equal difficulties. Towers had his pilots try different altitudes, "but as soon as we escaped the fog we struck clouds" and then bursts of rain. Richardson and McCulloch, already tired, now worked together. Richardson kept an eye on the wing tips while working the ailerons to keep the plane in trim, while McCulloch stayed on course by manipulating the rudder and elevator.[67]

Eventually, the constantly pelting rain made the pilots drowsy. "The medical officer at Rockaway had both forewarned and forearmed me for such an emergency," said Towers, who administered two doses of strychnine an hour apart to Richardson. "I cannot describe," Richardson reported later, "the mental agony this condition caused, fully realizing the seriousness of my condition and the responsibility resting on me, yet in spite of that unable to control my physical condition." The second dose of strychnine relieved his distress, however, and he returned to the controls. Meanwhile forward visibility deteriorated to less than 100 yards.[68]

All morning Jack strained his eyes trying to spot the mountain peaks of the three highest islands of the Azores—Flores, Corvo, and Pico. The island farthest beyond them in the 280-mile chain was San Miguel, the NCs' destination. At its port, Ponta Delgada, the tender *Melville* awaited them.

An hour before noon local time, a sudden lull in the storms gave Towers a glimpse of the sun. He took a quick sighting with his sextant, although the air being rough rocked the bubble for the artificial horizon, and got a line of position passing through Pico, near which the small island of Fayal offered the harbor of Horta as an emergency landing place. There also lay the old cruiser *Columbia,* moored as an emergency tender.

Discounting his hasty sighting of the sun, Towers figured they were fifty miles southwest of Pico and decided to head 60 degrees to the northward. In hindsight, he remarked, "Had I trusted in my snap sight taken aloft and continued on the course of 90 degrees which I laid we would have landed right at Fayal, but the visibility was so bad it was probable that we would have actually flown into one of the mountains."

All hands kept a sharp lookout as the haze closed in again. Dinty Moore announced that they had only two hours of fuel remaining. Towers pondered his options, among them "the advisability of landing, stopping our engines, getting a radio bearing, and proceeding again." The more he thought about it, this seemed to be the most sensible course of action to take.

He left his perch in the bow and crawled back to the cockpit, where he wrote his idea on a pad, holding it up for McCulloch to read. Detailed discussion was impossible over the roar of the engines. Richardson assured Jack that he and McCulloch had easily landed one of the NC-3's sisters in waters off Delaware. From 500 feet it looked as if the surface of the sea, though only faintly visible, would be sufficiently calm for a landing and takeoff.

Towers decided to land. After more than five hours battling the storms, any respite would be welcome. Having consumed most of the fuel, the plane would be light enough to take off again. Lavender began transmitting SOS signals and their position, but with the radio ground disconnected none of his appeals were picked up.

They spiraled around and approached the surface with caution, throttling down the wing engines, then the center engines. In Towers' words, "we realized just as we were about to touch that there was a big sea running. It was too late to pull up. We touched the top of a big roller and jumped from that wave to another, then slid down the face of the second one with high velocity, and took the approaching wave with a very heavy blow, hitting with a crunch that left no doubt as to the seriousness of the damage done." Jack expected the hull would give out, but Richardson's design proved its sturdiness.[69]

Coming to a stop at 1300, the five men scrambled forward over their flying boat to discover the center tractor-engine support struts bent "like a bulldog's legs" and the hull seriously damaged above the waterline, with a slight leak under the cockpit. By no stretch of the imagination could the NC-3 be expected to take off again, even in smooth seas, let alone in the ten- to twelve-foot waves then running. The crew took a few minutes to rest and consider their options. The transatlantic flight of the NC-3 was over.[70]

Towers shot the sun again, and Lavender got a radio bearing on the *Columbia*, fixing their position 34½ miles southwest of Horta. Lavender also discovered and reconnected the parted radio ground wire. They moved the wind-driven wireless generator to a position behind the port engine, which gave it wind power to continue sending SOS signals and their position out to 100 miles, but none was acknowledged. At 1800 Lavender learned from the busy air waves that the NC-4 had landed safely in the Azores but that the -1 was also down north of the course. A search was under way for her. He also heard inquiries about the NC-3 and found out that destroyer searches were being undertaken 400 miles too far to the west, between stations no. 16 and 18. Jack reckoned instead that the -3 was down opposite station no. 23. But no one seemed to be listening in on his frequency.

In the meantime the running of the port engine in the wind-whipped waves caused the plane "to plunge . . . heavily into the approaching seas," so that Jack finally had it shut down. Without it, radio signals could not be sent out, only received. Jack's unloading of the small emergency radio to lighten ship before takeoff from Trepassey now took its toll.

The truth dawned on them that "if we were to be saved, we would have to do it ourselves." First, stock was taken of supplies for survival: a few water-soaked jelly sandwiches that had fallen into the bilge upon the impact of landing, five chocolate almond bars, and six small tins of emergency rations, all nourishing but unsavory. Even less tasty was the water from the eleven-gallon radiators, "thick with iron rust" and engine oil. This additional weight-saving economy measure, the discarding of extra water, had also come to grief.

Then they set their course, toward the shipping lane between Fayal and San Miguel to the northward, in hopes that a passing ship might sight them. Failing that, the east winds might push them toward San Miguel, over 200 miles away. Towers "now had the interesting job of navigating a sailing seaplane 205 miles on the water, in a storm." This called for seamanship of the highest order.[71]

At 2000 Towers established two-hour watches for himself and each of his four crewmen, assigned duties to them, and had everything secured. He put the precious Very pistol and flares in his pockets lest they be lost should the plane suddenly sink. Wires loosened during the landing were tightened, and the crew rigged the American flag upside down as a distress signal. Although no one had slept during the long night flight, "all hands turned out" in this struggle for survival, trying with little success to snatch a few minutes of shuteye between watches and emergencies. The wind was estimated running at between 65 and 70 mph, varying from the southwest to northwest. Towers decided to sail the boat stern first, with the hull acting as centerboard.

To keep it headed up into the approaching seas he played out two canvas buckets from a wire cable. He did not use the plane's regular heavy-sea anchor for fear it would cause too great a strain, snap the wire, and disappear. The drift did not exceed 15 mph, enabling Richardson and McCulloch to use the controls to head off the wind as much as four points. Given the high winds and more than twelve-foot seas, plus "the general wrecked condition of the wings, great care had to be exercised to avoid getting too far off wind and getting swamped by the seas, and all the big rollers had to be met head on."

Here was proof positive of the correctness of Towers' philosophy that a naval aviator had first to be a naval officer, at least when it came to seaplanes. Fortunately, Naval Academy products Richardson and Lavender were also trained navigators and seamen. Moore was a seasoned sailor, while McCulloch had been in hydros long enough to have learned the sea.

The overcast day ended with increasing winds, and during the night waves and rain pounded the NC-3. Exhausted, Towers took his turn on watch. Off watch, he was awakened by his mates the several times that the moon and stars were visible so he could take sights on them. In spite of gale-force winds, he made sightings through holes in the clouds. These gave him a good fix, from which he could see that the boat was making progress, but eastward rather than northward.

Dawn of 18 May brought a heavy storm out of the north-northwest, with 45- to 50-mph winds, a driving rain, and swells up to thirty feet. The flying boat began to yield to the pounding. First the ribs of the lower left wing broke, then the tail went under and the lower elevator snapped. Richardson and Moore crawled out and punched holes in the wings through which water could pass instead of collecting in the fabric cavities and dragging them under. The two men also inched themselves out to cut away the broken lower wing and control column, the latter because it was banging against the hull, threatening to cause a puncture.

Towers and Moore used the plane's hand pump to clear the water from the leaking hull. At one point they attached the hose from the pump to the center oil tank to pour oil over the side and "smooth out the seas." This worked, but the oil drifted away too fast so they stopped doing it. Jack also wanted to conserve oil for possible use in the engines.

Then at 0900 "a heavy cross sea carried away our port wing pontoon. It looked then as though we were surely gone." Stability would be jeopardized should the plane roll to port. Dinty Moore's lineman's harness, used when he had crawled about the plane in flight, was broken out, and each man took turns wearing it, strapped to the outer starboard wing "to keep that down and the port wing tip clear of the water. . . . [T]he starboard pontoon might go at any moment." Between this, standing watch, and continuously pumping out the hull, there was no break.

Towers conceived the idea of using the wooden ribs of the lower wing, broken off by the high seas, as flotsam to determine the speed of the flying boat. He began "by dropping a piece of rib or other wreckage over . . . and taking the time it required for the hull to drift past. Knowing the length of the hull [just shy of forty-five feet], speed was then computed in knots." It worked.

Half an hour after that the violent waves broke off the second canvas bucket, a fate already suffered by the first one. In its place they put their big sea anchor, but it "tore to pieces at once." A section of torn wing fabric used as an anchor also carried away, whereupon the men employed a smaller section, using the doubled-up trailing antenna wire of the radio as an anchor cable. This held. Then at midday the lower elevator disintegrated from the force of a steep wave. Pieces from it threatened the guy wires and hull until it was swept away completely.

At 1237 the air cleared sufficiently for Dick Richardson to notice the dim outlines of Pico's 7,600-foot peak through clouds to the northwest. To compute their position Towers got a bearing and sextant altitude of the peak, plus a meridian altitude of the sun. It jibed with his dead reckoning from earlier sightings and estimated drift: they were forty-five miles southeast of Pico. Rigging up Lavender's radio, and starting the port engine to give it power, they transmitted their position but without success. And the powerful engine caused the boat to turn around and almost capsize from the cross seas. Some of the men wanted to use the engines to buck the sea and head north, but Jack overruled this, reasoning that it "would have undoubtedly swamped us."

Then the 60-mph wind shifted more to the northwestward, blowing them farther from land. If they missed San Miguel the next land was Europe, a thousand miles beyond. The five men decided to take "advantage of every lull in the waves to head off a little [to leeward] and make a course slightly across the wind." The more experience that pilots Richardson and McCulloch gained doing this, the more successful they became at it. But the thought of losing sight of land, Pico, and spending another night of uncertainty was unsettling.

As the second nightfall approached, high winds continued to blow, up to forty-five knots, and the seas remained enormous, again cresting at thirty feet. Some waves even curled, sending the boat coasting like a surfboard at a twenty-knot clip. None of the men expected to live through the night. After moonrise near midnight, Towers was able to use the sextant to get "a good cross between Arcturus and the Moon, and checked it with sights of Vega, Deneb, and Polaris," the north star. Then he took his turn on the starboard wing, the wires and bolts of which had to be continually tightened against the sea's heavy blows.

The cold-water spray and smoking cigarettes kept those on duty awake, and none of the men got more than four hours' sleep during the entire odyssey. Towers

> crawled down under the pilot's seat, but sleep was hopeless when you were one minute standing on your head, the next plunging feet first down steep sloping waves and expecting to have the whole plane disintegrate. Eventually the water got so deep in the hull that I was flooded out, and Moore, Lavender, and I spent the next six hours pumping. The water was nearly two feet deep in the hull. One man had to lie in the water down under the gasoline tanks to keep debris from stopping up the suction while the others pumped, then we would change so the wet man could get warm.

Their hands became badly swollen from this endless task.

With better control over the craft's stability, a man did not always have to be kept on the right wing. "This was important," reported Richardson later, "for . . . it was dangerous for the man on the wing tip if he should fall asleep, as . . . he could be washed overboard with almost no chance of recovery. . . . We found that each wave crest had to be tackled individually and square to the crest," most difficult since the wind changed continuously and the waves could not be seen far ahead in the darkness. The phosphorescence of the white caps made the men think they were seeing searchlights from ships.

In the midst of these labors dawn of 19 May broke, a little clearer but with winds and seas only slightly moderated. Realizing they were within striking distance of San Miguel, Towers told the pilots to steer a course for the island. A two-hour squall detoured them southward. Carefully manipulating the controls, they gradually worked their way northward. Towers knew he was on course after obtaining a good longitude line from the sun at 0930 and by computing their speed at six knots.

Forty-five minutes later Moore sighted land astern—that is, ahead, for the NC-3 was stern-first—which Jack calculated to be forty-four miles away. It had to be San Miguel.

> The effect on all hands was astonishing. After two days without seeing any sight of a vessel and expecting to go down any moment, to have land in sight! I saw that if the wind held in direction, and we could continue to head three points off, slightly more to the north, we could make it. It was still rough, and we didn't know if the old wreck would hold together long enough to make shore. But there was hope, spelt with a great big H.
> The first thing I did was to go down in the hull and rescue my uniform hat from the bilge where it had fallen two days before. I had seen no further use for

it, so I had just let it stay there and float about. The next was to unload from my pocket the waterproof package of Very's signal cartridges, and the Very's pistol. . . . We continued to pump, but with a different spirit. All hands suddenly realized hunger and thirst. Realization of fatigue was to come later. Unanimous vote decided on bacon and eggs as the best food in the world. I took some photographs of the personnel and of the NC-3. . . . [We] . . . hoisted our flag right side up . . . and hoisted our pennant.

Lavender tried transmitting again, without success, but was astonished to pick up radio signals from the *Baltimore,* all the way back at Halifax.

Despite the return of heavy rain squalls, the crew worked slowly to within seven miles of the coast of San Miguel, whereupon Towers laid course down to Ponta Delgada. This took most of the day, during which the men admired the vineyards, trees, sugar factory, and houses on the shore. Finally, at 1612, Lavender stuck his head out and announced, "They have seen us!" His radio receiver had erupted with messages "flying about like mad." No one on shore or at the anchorage had imagined the NC-3 to have been so far to the east. The appearance off the harbor entrance was a dramatic climax to its ordeal.

Moments later, at 1625, the flyers saw "a big smudge of smoke and spray, as the *Harding* came dashing out." Jack grabbed the plane's Aldis lamp and blinked out a signal "for her to stay clear, but to be ready to render assistance if called upon." The destroyer answered, "It's a miracle! It's a miracle!" But the ship passed so close that her wash created waves, sending McCulloch and Moore scrambling over the wings to keep the plane balanced. Just then the starboard pontoon was dislodged by a big wave, and the plane almost went under. The pontoon was finally cut free of the wire that was dragging it.

Richardson started the center pusher engine. When Lavender emerged near the whirring pusher, a frantic yell from Towers saved the radio officer from the prop. Then Richardson skillfully maneuvered the remaining controls. Towers recalled: "We crabbed in under the eastern end of the breakwater and into the harbor. That place was perfect bedlam. Whistles were blowing, flags flying everywhere, and boats chasing about like mad. It looked like a comic moving picture. . . ." Under a twenty-one gun salute from the Portuguese citadel, and with rockets and bombs bursting in the air, the NC-3 barely escaped capsizing in the harbor. Towers accepted the help of two clumsy whaleboats from the tender *Melville,* which, however, became fouled in the surviving jury-rigged sea anchor. The NC-3 reached its moorings at 1830 Greenwich mean time. An admiral's barge whisked the men ashore.

The NC-3 at the end of its epic 205-mile voyage, stern view, showing extensive wing damage from the pounding of storms at sea, 19 May 1919. A dinghy is approaching to lend assistance. (Navy Department)

The crew had already learned by radio that the NC-4 had succeeded in reaching the Azores by air, whereupon fog had forced Putty Read to put it down at Horta, 153 nautical miles shy of Ponta Delgada and 1,206 out of Trepassey. Towers and the NC-3 had achieved 1,240 miles before landing at sea. Read had landed seven minutes before Towers, and Bellinger and the NC-1 in waters off to the northwest just before that. So the NC-3 had set the record for nonstop distance and endurance—fifteen hours, twenty-four minutes in a 1,240-mile flight, plus fifty-three hours afloat over a course of another 205 miles.

The NC-3's crew had performed magnificently, still managing to reach Ponta Delgada first; the NC-4 remained fogbound at Horta. Jack Towers had proved himself to be as able a seaman as he was an aviator.[72] Still in all, the NC-3 had failed to reach the Azores by air and was too wrecked to go on. Only the NC-4 would be able to continue, for after Bellinger and his crew had been rescued by a passing Greek merchantman the battered NC-1, wallowing for several days under tow, finally sank.[73]

The main reasons for Towers' failure to reach the Azores by air had been the inaccurate weather forecast and his consequent dependence on the star shells for guidance rather than his own navigating. Had Towers managed to stay airborne and on course in the murk, the NC-3 might well have plunged into one of the Azores' clouded mountainsides; before sighting land Read had

An exhausted Jack Towers reports to Rear Admiral
Richard H. Jackson (*right*), U.S. naval commander in
the Azores, and Captain Ward K. Wortman of the
destroyer tender *Melville* just after landing, 19 May
1919. Towers has written in the margin, "This is
terrible looking, I'll admit, but I'd been 74 hours
without sleep or food." (Towers collection)

nearly done just that in the NC-4. The big lesson was that the errors were due
to guidance, not the flying machines themselves. Aircraft could bridge the
oceans!

Towers and his crew were greeted ashore near Admiralty House by Rear
Admiral Richard H. Jackson, American naval commander in the Azores;
Captain Ward K. Wortman of the *Melville;* a group of local dignitaries; and a
crowd of cheering citizens. The flyers were so unsteady on their feet that they
had to be assisted. Photographers caught Jack and the others looking suitably
haggard after seventy-four hours without real sleep or food. Towers, fulfilling

a promise to Lily, immediately fired off a telegram via the Navy Department: "MRS. TOWERS, 1715 19TH STREET. SAFE AND WELL.—JACK."[74]

When the NC-3 was reported missing, the evening *Washington Post* had run large pictures of Jack and Lily alongside the alarming news. Lily kept vigil for two days at her Washington home, telling pesky reporters, "Given up hope? Why, my faith and confidence in my husband is even strengthened. I am dreadfully worried, naturally. But I just know he's all right. . . . He told me he'd make it—and that's all there is to it." Friends dropped by the Towers home during the evening to offer encouragement and saw two-and-a-half-year-old Marjorie brought in by the maid to be kissed goodnight. With big eyes the child had lisped to the callers, "Did oo all know my daddy is flyin' to En'land?" All the world had known it on the morning of 19 May. The headlines of the *New York Times* blared, "NO WORD FROM TOWERS AND MISSING NC-3."[75]

Despite Lily's realistic understanding of her husband's abilities, her distress over the ordeal did nothing to strengthen their marriage. Secretary Daniels informed her of Towers' arrival, and thankfully both his and Jack's messages were received ahead of a bizarre crank letter. A New Yorker, emotionally unbalanced from the recent death of his wife and believing himself to be in spiritual communication with "the other side," wrote to Lily that Jack had spoken to him through his late wife on the evening of the nineteenth. This was Jack's message: "My dear wife, I was burnt to death by an explosion of gasoline caused by a leak in the gasoline tank. . . ." He instructed Lily to tell their daughter "Ruthie" to "be a good girl and grow up to be a good woman." Curiously, though their daughter's name was Marjorie, Ruth had been the name of Jack's late younger sister. An apologetic letter from the man who shared lodgings with the letter writer soon explained everything.[76]

On the evening of 19 May, while stories of the conquerors of the Atlantic made grand news for a war-weary world, Jack and his men were hailed at Ponta Delgada. Before they could clean up, eat, or sleep for the first time in more than three days, they had to brave the formal accolades and ecstatic crowds. Taken immediately to the Portuguese Admiralty's reception room for refreshments, the five flyers were described by a local reporter as "healthy and hearty men in the prime of life" whose "faces and hands were bronzed from the wind and rain and gasses expelled from their motors." They exhibited "a touch of sadness" for not completing the journey by air, but they were admired for their steady courage. Towers "quietly and naturally narrated, as if of no more consequence than a pleasant auto trip, briefly to

Admiral Jackson the trip of the NC-3."[77] After a hot shower and nap on board the *Melville,* they were wined and dined by the governor of the Azores.

Although the NC-3 and NC-1 were out of the running, the NC-4 was still in the race to be the first plane ever to reach Europe by air. News flashes told Towers that two British challengers had taken off from Newfoundland the day before, the eighteenth, bound for Ireland, though one plane had crashed on takeoff. Neither pilot was hurt. And the other plane was now missing and long overdue; its two flyers were presumed lost, but in fact they had been rescued at sea by a freighter without a radio.[78]

Seaplane Division 1 was now down to one effective flying boat, yet Towers as its commander would still be able to complete the crossing to Lisbon and on to Plymouth as a passenger on the NC-4. For his operational instructions had stated explicitly that if the flagship were forced to land, another of the flying boats was to "take aboard the Division Commander in case Flag will not be able to resume flight." This was standing procedure for all ships of war. After a welcome night's sleep, early on 20 May Jack ordered the battered NC-3 to be disassembled for shipment to New York aboard the *Melville.* Then he radioed a preliminary report to the Navy Department, concluding it with the simple statement, "I will proceed to Lisbon in NC-4."[79]

Happily, the weather had cleared, enabling Putty Read to take off from Horta just after noon of the twentieth to fly to Ponta Delgada for the next leg of the flight. The NC-4 made the 176-mile hop without difficulty and upon landing was greeted by Jack in a launch. Towers, pumping Read's hand, observed, "I got here first, Putty, but you made it the way we had planned." Learning the fate of the flagship, Read remarked that he "presumed" Jack "would continue in NC-4 as Division Commander." Jack replied "in the affirmative." For the much shorter legs to Europe, Jack's weight would take the place of some of the gasoline no longer required. Putty concluded his report to Washington with the matter-of-fact statement: "Expect leave for Lisbon 21 May, weather permitting, with Division Commander on board." Towers even hoisted his flag on the -4.[80]

Late in the afternoon, as all hands were preparing for a grandiose dinner and dance in their honor at the governor's palace, Towers was stunned to receive an inexplicable message from the Navy Department: "While Secretary recognizes full merit Commander Towers services for which he should be rewarded[,] in justice to all concerned does not approve his sailing in NC FOUR." Only then did Jack learn that early in the day Admiral Jackson, the local U.S. Navy commander, thrilled at the "most remarkable exhibition of pluck and skill and seamanship" aboard the NC-3, had on his own initiative wired the CNO, Admiral Benson, in Paris. He recommended that Towers be allowed to proceed to Lisbon aboard the NC-4 "as a reward for his remarkable energy and skill in bringing NC-3 safely into port." Jackson had forwarded a copy to the department in Washington. Benson had answered, "I will in no way interfere with this expedition except to render assistance," leaving the decision up to the secretary.[81]

Unknown to Towers, Josephus Daniels, though sharply opposed by Assistant Secretary Roosevelt, Acting CNO McKean, and the other admirals, had seen better publicity for the navy in having the diminutive Read go on to Lisbon and Plymouth without Towers. Putty had, after all, enabled the lame duck NC-4 to keep up with the flight to Trepassey and therefore should complete the crossing as senior officer in his own plane. Daniels used the phrase "in justice to all concerned" in his reply, meaning to Read. A newspaperman by trade, Daniels milked the hoopla of Read's success to push for appropriations before the House Naval Affairs Committee then in session. Admiral Jackson, though acting with the best of intentions, had been utterly ignorant of Towers' original orders and had thereby unwittingly alerted the secretary to the newsworthiness of Read continuing on without a superior officer.

Those in the Azores could not comprehend Daniels' thinking. Admiral Jackson allowed Towers to send another message requesting "reconsideration . . . and permission [to] sail in NC-4 not in command [of] that seaplane." Vice Admiral Harry S. Knapp, commanding U.S. naval forces in European waters, rallied to Towers' support with a similar message. But to no avail, for late in the evening Daniels reaffirmed his decision. In Jack's own view, he had been virtually relieved of his command in the middle of an operation for no apparent reason. Normally the kiss of death for any naval career, this move however was purely political and reflected not in the least on Towers' performance. But Jack could not know this; he had no choice but to swallow the bitter pill. So much for the flight he had sought for over five years.[82]

Needless to say, Towers was furious over the decision. Putty Read sympathized with him: "I know how long you've had your heart set on this flight. I know that without you it wouldn't have left the ground in the first place. I'm sorry." Jack did not blame Putty for the decision, but his bitterness was obvious during the brief stay at Ponta Delgada. Read worried about encountering him again, though Jack withdrew to endure his agony alone and retrieve his flag from the NC-4. Richardson, McCulloch, Pat Bellinger, and Pete Mitscher all counseled Putty to forget about Towers and carry on. Putty tried.[83]

Luckily, Towers' administrative chores and fresh orders soon removed him from the Azores. He ordered Dinty Moore to supervise the transportation of the battered NC-3 on the *Melville* to New York, recommending that it be decommissioned. Instead, it would be repaired. Towers planned to proceed to Plymouth for the rendezvous with the *Aroostook,* which was carrying his personal effects. A sympathetic Admiral Knapp issued the order, and destroyer commander Rear Admiral C. P. Plunkett made the *Stockton* available to him. An equally disappointed Robert Lavender had no interest in going on, so Towers allowed him to return home in the *Columbia.* The rest of the NC-3 crew and Bellinger's NC-1 crew would accompany Towers to Plymouth.[84]

Jack wished Read good luck for the next leg of the flight, then boarded the *Stockton,* which departed Ponta Delgada just after midnight on 22 May. On board, Towers renewed his acquaintance with her skipper Harry Baldridge, who was suddenly ordered by Admiral Jackson to proceed to Lisbon. Himself miffed at the treatment Towers had been given, Jackson made certain that the airman not be deprived of sharing in the victory of the NC-4 when it arrived there. Though the destroyer reached Lisbon late on the twenty-third, the NC-4 was still at Ponta Delgada, socked in by weather. Towers, Bellinger, and their crews transferred to the cruiser *Rochester,* where Jack found a most sympathetic ear in Admiral C. P. Plunkett.

While waiting for the NC-4 to arrive, the men went sightseeing and attended many parties. The fact that Towers had been bumped from the NC-4 now became apparent to the press, and suspicious reporters began to speculate why. They guessed that somehow Read had appealed to Daniels to keep Towers from sharing the glory, and without grounds they faulted Jack's behavior over the affair. Their criticisms surprised both Towers and Read. Daniels' decision was causing a minor furor that marred the otherwise superb expedition; the secretary admired Jack for doing nothing to contribute to the uproar.

The NC-4 completed its transatlantic crossing on 27 May 1919, nineteen days late. After the weather over the Azores finally cleared, Read took off in midmorning, flew the 780 nautical miles to Lisbon, and landed offshore after dark. Towers followed his progress from radio messages received in the *Rochester* and warmly pumped Read's hand as soon as the launch delivered him on board. After the ship's band had played "The Star-Spangled Banner," the Portuguese naval minister presented the Military Order of Tower and Sword to the pilots and crewmen of all three flying boats.

Next day, while Lisbon celebrated, Towers warned the local U.S. Navy meteorologist to be absolutely certain of his forecasts, anxious that the weather that had scotched the efforts of the NC-1 and -3 not also torpedo the -4 on its last leg to Plymouth. Then the *Rochester* departed for Plymouth. When she arrived late on 29 May Towers recovered his personal effects from the *Aroostook,* already there a week; Jack had lost his bet with Captain Tomb over which one would reach Plymouth first.[85]

Early on the thirtieth the NC-4 lifted off from Lisbon, bound for Plymouth, but had to set down twice in Iberian coastal waters because of engine trouble. Then it bucked foul weather again before reaching its destination during midafternoon of the next day. Since leaving NAS Rockaway on 8 May, the NC-4 had flown 3,936 nautical miles—total flying time fifty-two hours, thirty-one minutes. Again Towers had tracked the flight over the *Rochester*'s radio, again he greeted Putty, and again they braved the cheering crowds and generous entertainment. At last the mission was over; Seaplane Division 1, minus the NC-3 and -1, had crossed the Atlantic.[86]

Without further responsibilities, Towers could now enjoy the honors for the flight he had conceived and commanded, despite his irritation over the press's concocted feud with Read. After a ceremony with British dignitaries at the spot where the Pilgrims had departed for America, on 1 June Admiral Plunkett took Towers, Read, and Bellinger by train to London, where jubilant American doughboys surrounded and pushed the car from the station to the Royal Aero Club. With many of Jack's old London friends, they witnessed an air show at Hendon and were feted by admiring Londoners before taking the ferry to France on 3 June.

In Paris they were entertained at dinner by Admiral Benson, the CNO. Next morning Benson presented them to President Wilson and the Allied prime ministers at the Hotel Crillon, where the Versailles peace settlement was being finalized. Putty Read remained the center of attention, and justly so. Admiral Benson took Jack aside to tell him that he "had been unintentionally treated unfairly" by Daniels, to whom Benson promised to register a complaint.[87]

Whisked back to London, the flyers were taken to the House of Commons on 5 June for a luncheon given in their honor by Major General J. E. B. Seely, British air minister. Among the many dignitaries were Towers' wartime friends and acquaintances Tom Sopwith, Winston Churchill, and espe-

The NC flyers share a laugh with their British hosts after a luncheon at the House of Commons, 5 June 1919. In front of the Terrace House, overlooking the Thames River, *left to right:* Ensign H. C. Rodd and Lieutenant James L. Breese of the NC-4; Pat Bellinger; Lord Reading, former British ambassador to the United States; Towers; Admiral Sir Rosslyn E. Wemyss, first sea lord; the Prince of Wales (later the Duke of Windsor); Putty Read; and Major General J. E. B. Seely, RAF, undersecretary for air. Out of the picture to the right were Lord Birkenhead, the lord chancellor, and Winston Churchill, secretary of war. (Towers collection)

cially Colonel Cyril Porte, with whom he could compare notes on the original *America* project. On 9 June the Air Ministry awarded the RAF Cross not only to Read and his crew but to Towers as well. In London Jack threw a big party for the men of the NCs, at which they agreed to send a telegram to Dick Byrd congratulating him for his bubble sextant. Admiral Knapp then sent them back to Paris on the tenth for a week of leave.[88]

There the flyers learned that two of their British challengers, John Alcock and Arthur W. Brown, had just flown the Atlantic direct from St. John's, Newfoundland, to Ireland. The fact that the 1,950-mile flight was accomplished nonstop—sixteen hours, twenty-seven minutes in a twin-engine Vimy biplane—tended to overshadow the achievement of the NC-4 with its many stops and vast logistical support. Nevertheless, Towers and Read both lauded the flight, Jack telling reporters it was "a splendid feat." But no one could ever dispute the fact that the NC-4 had been the first![89]

At long last, on 17 June, the men of the NC boats embarked on the navy transport *Zeppelin* at Brest for their return to the United States. They were accompanied by several thousand Yank soldiers and escorted to sea by French seaplanes in a shower of rockets and Very lights. The NC-4 had meanwhile been disassembled and placed aboard the *Aroostook* for transit home. After an inevitably stormy crossing, the *Zeppelin* entered New York Harbor on 27 June, escorted into port by two F5L flying boats, an airship, and a de Havilland army bomber that dropped message packets onto the deck inviting the airmen to a banquet in their honor at the Commodore Hotel. It was being given by Glenn Curtiss, builder of the NCs. He, Admiral Bradley Fiske, and several aviation enthusiasts greeted the flyers from one of two navy patrol boats. The other carried the NC wives, including Lily Towers, and a band playing "Hail, Hail, the Gang's All Here."[90]

Jack led his "division" ashore for the last time, at Hoboken, where another excited crowd delayed the men from being reunited with their families. The men were especially touched when greeted by Harry Howard, their shipmate who had lost his hand in the prop of the now famous NC-4. To reporters, Towers and Read both pooh-poohed the story of a rift between them and endorsed the airship as the most likely hope for sustained transatlantic flight, weather and uncertain navigation being the greatest handicaps for aircraft. How prophetic they were became evident the following week, on 6 July, when the British dirigible R.34 reached Mineola, Long Island, after a four-day nonstop flight from Scotland. The R.34 then flew back on the first round-trip crossing of the Atlantic by air.[91]

On 30 June the crews went to Washington for awards and were there joined by Dick Byrd. The affable Josephus Daniels informed his gallant flyers that a special NC-4 medal would be awarded them, though only Putty Read's would be made of gold, those of the rest of NC-4's crew and Towers' to be in silver, Bellinger's and the others' in bronze.[92]

The Curtiss banquet on 10 July honored Read and Byrd in particular. The hall was sumptuously decorated like the cabin of a huge futuristic seaplane. Curtiss presented each of the flyers with a medallion he had had personally struck for them and gave the three plane commanders specially made gold wristwatches. The faces were inlaid with the intertwined initials

N.C. During the dismantling of the NC-4, its fabric had been lovingly cut up for souvenirs, and one piece was given each guest at the dinner.[93]

The navy and the government quickly forgot not only the medals but the epic flight in the rush to unwind from the trials of the wartime period. The flight was not brought to public attention again until the wake of Charles Lindbergh's monumental 1927 solo flight from Long Island to Paris. Only then, in February 1929, did Congress authorize gold medals for the men who undertook the first transatlantic crossing, the following August awarding a prize of $1,000 for their design. On 23 May 1930 Jack and several of his NC comrades received theirs personally from President Herbert Hoover. Five years after that they were authorized to wear miniature NC medals on their formal dress uniforms, with the procurement of these, however, to be "at the expense of the individual." The ribbon consisted of the national colors of the United States and Portugal—red, white, blue, green, and red.[94]

Towers' feelings toward Secretary Daniels that summer of 1919 were surely ambivalent, not only because of the latter's sudden refusal to allow Jack to proceed to Lisbon on the NC-4. On 30 June, the secretary counseled the House Naval Affairs Committee against passing a bill to promote Towers and Read to the permanent rank of commander and Bellinger to permanent lieutenant commander. Their honors must be conferred in other ways, said he, for such promotions would unfairly upset the list of commanders; Towers would have jumped 203 numbers. So Congress killed the proposed bill, though it did convey its official thanks to the crewmen.[95]

Admiral Cy Plunkett, determined to set Towers' record in order, wrote a long report on 16 July setting forth the details of the case. He concluded, "As a matter of fact Commander Towers' attitude was one of simple devotion to duty and of carrying out his orders. . . . Furthermore, the wonderful exhibition of grit, skill, seamanship, navigation, and devotion to his mission shown by Commander Towers in successfully taking NC-3 to Ponta Del Gada stands out as the greatest accomplishment of the flight, and clearly demonstrates that Officer's exceptional ability even under the most trying circumstances." The issue subsided only slowly, with several congressmen on the House Naval Affairs Committee adopting a distinctly adverse view of Jack's role in the flight based on reporters' guesswork. Towers therefore wrote an extensive memorandum to Secretary Daniels in September, explaining his conduct and that of Putty Read in hopes of offsetting the criticism.[96]

Admiral Benson voiced the navy's general view by endorsing Towers' memo and recommending further that this endorsement be placed in the official records, that the secretary write to the misinformed congressmen, and "that a statement correcting the false impressions already made be given out to the press." The CNO appealed to the secretary's sense of fair play. Daniels could hardly refuse such a strong appeal, particularly since he had been in the wrong and was having a difficult time explaining why he had bumped Towers from the NC-4. He denied any criticism of Towers, commended him for his performance, and thus conveniently rejected the necessity of making a public statement. One year later he awarded Jack the Navy Cross "for distinguished service in the line of his profession as Commanding Officer of the seaplane NC-3, and of the NC Division, which made a long overseas flight from New Foundland to the vicinity of the Azores, in May 1919." Daniels awarded all the NC pilots and crewmen Navy Crosses—except for Read, who only got the Distinguished Service Medal. Justice was thus done, Daniels style.[97]

As for Towers' relationship with Putty Read, the press-generated controversy would spark speculation over the years that Towers' bitterness led him to thwart Read's advancement in the navy. This idea Read completely rejected. Vindictiveness, especially unwarranted, was simply not in Towers' nature. Though never close friends, before or after the flight, the two men shared respect for each other and would in future meet socially at each other's homes. Indeed, Jack would assure Putty's promotion to rear admiral in 1942. That Jack was jealous, however, can hardly be denied—a perfectly human reaction.[98]

Reunited with his pregnant wife and his daughter, Towers finally went on leave for a much-needed rest after almost continuous active service for three years. After being officially detached from command of his now-defunct seaplane division on 19 July, he took a family trip to Lake George in the Adirondacks. While there, he wrote a long account of the expedition, "The Great Hop," for *Everybody's Magazine*. In it he concluded that he was "just happy to be alive. . . ."[99]

His relatives and friends in Rome, Georgia, were planning to honor him with a special day. When a Georgia senator asked Daniels to grant special leave for Towers to be there, the secretary jumped at the chance to further right the wrong he had done Jack: "I wish to express to Commander Towers' people my warm regard for him and the high esteem in which he is held. There is no honor which can come to him which is too high. He is one of the best officers in the navy and has rendered great service."[100]

Tuesday, 7 October, was set aside as homecoming day for all the soldiers and sailors of Floyd County, with Towers as guest of honor. To open the annual North Georgia Fair, a new airfield on the grounds was dedicated that

Lily and Jack, probably mid-1919 (Navy Department)

afternoon as Towers Field, and army and civilian flyers put on an air show. The proud citizens of Rome gave their hero a huge ovation as they presented him with a gold medallion commemorating the NC flight. That night they honored him with a big banquet.[101]

In many ways this hometown event marked the culmination of the long wartime era, for Towers had not been to Rome since before his departure for England at the outbreak of war. It had been an era in which the American and British peoples had joined in common cause, a union that Jack Towers had helped to forge, culminating in a project of his own design, the flight of the

NC boats. Despite lingering differences, the two English-speaking democracies already faced another common threat, this one in the Pacific: a new naval arms race with the truculent empire of Japan. But this time international tension took a back seat to the excitement generated by the dawn of the Air Age.

7

PEACETIME BATTLES AND
BILLY MITCHELL
1919–25

After more than eight years in the public eye Towers had become famous, and he would remain so because he was an aviation pioneer, whether or not he did anything else in his career. By contrast, his World War II contemporaries would remain completely unknown outside a service that traditionally eschewed publicity. Towers' administrative skills during World War I had shown him to be an effective organizational leader, while his personal heroism aboard the NC-3 had demonstrated that individualism still counted in the modern machine navy. And as far as the hierarchy was concerned, Towers was its most knowledgeable expert on aviation, a heady mantle indeed. He steadfastly believed the fleet must retain control of its own air component, in contrast to army General Billy Mitchell, who during 1919 initiated a public crusade to establish an independent air force modeled after Britain's RAF. As expectations over what warplanes could do mounted inversely to appropriations, interservice fighting erupted.[1]

At thirty-four Towers was in robust health and could endure the rigors of the cockpit and the boardroom; he fully expected thirty more years until mandatory retirement at sixty-four. Daily calisthenics, swimming, tennis, golf, a light diet, and eight hours of dreamless sleep (so he claimed) kept him fit; his only physical problem was dental. His smoking habit grew to fifteen or twenty cigarettes a day, often inhaled through a long holder, which added to his air of urbanity. Acquired English manners suited his dapper civilian attire, cane, and straw hat or bowler, and he ordered his uniforms from Rice and Duval of New York for their smart wide-wale fabric. Bridge remained his off-duty passion, next to a new wire-haired terrier puppy he named Mr. Delmont Tyke.[2]

The onset of prohibition in 1919 did not deter Towers from relaxing over martinis; two cocktails enabled him to "talk much better" in social gatherings. "It isn't anything more than a relaxation on the reins. I am really myself, then. Why can't I be always, for I can't go around drinking two cocktails every time I want to talk, now can I?" Like most "wet" Americans, Jack would manufacture his own bathtub gin and court resourceful friends for imported French vermouth. Thus he roared through the Twenties with the rest of the country, enjoying the prestigious New York Yacht Club, the Aero Club of America, New York's University Club, and the Racquet Club of Philadelphia, in all of which he was a member.

Towers' politics were virtually nonexistent, as were his religious convictions; the navy, if anything, was his religion. The hazards of flying, in fact, he treated rather stoically. When one of his pilots once grieved over the loss of a comrade in an accident, Jack told him simply, "There's just no accounting for it. Some of us survive and some of us don't. Nobody knows why."[3]

A voracious reader, Towers consumed history, biography, and novels, all of which sharpened his intellect. "It seems that I am always reading about four books at once," he wrote in 1926. An unusually fast reader, he could quickly absorb the essence of any piece of material, including operations orders, a feat that impressed subordinates.[4]

Towers continued to suffer from an unhappy marriage. Lily still liked parties and was less than an attentive mother, and Jack's professional demands prevented him from being a doting father. Nonetheless they had made the decision to have another child. Born on 20 January 1920, Charles Stewart Towers was named after Lily's father and the War of 1812 commodore; the parents called him Chas or Chassie. Dick Byrd was the boy's godfather.

Like all but a few of his classmates of '06, Towers chose to remain in the postwar navy. His temporary rank of full commander would become permanent on 13 January 1922 and ultimately date from the previous 25 June. Most of the wartime reservists returned to civilian life, leaving regulars to resume flight training. Two returnees to the fold were naval aviators no. 1 and 2, Commanders Spuds Ellyson and John Rodgers. Postwar naval aviation strength was set at five hundred officers and five thousand enlisted men, a major increase over the prewar era yet barely adequate to meet the newly accepted missions of scouting and spotting for the fleet.

The most vexing problem for the navy was trying to decide exactly how to use its aviation, a dilemma Towers addressed in a speech to the Society of Automotive Engineers late in 1918. He saw four types of naval aircraft for the immediate future: small catapult-launched airplanes or seaplanes for spotting gunfire and for fighting, medium-sized planes launched from high-speed ships with "flying-off decks" to scout and to drop bombs and torpedoes, towed kite balloons for spotting, and shore-based flying boats and airships for long-distance reconnaissance. Land-type airplanes were easier to launch and better for fighting, he believed, but he was uncertain about methods of recovering them on board.[5]

Towers was flirting with the idea of a flight-deck aircraft carrier. He had not witnessed the two recent British carriers, as had Kenneth Whiting, Chevalier, and Hunsaker. Back in August 1917 Towers had testified before the General Board that "it could be a material advantage" for the U.S. Navy to have such a vessel "to experiment with," and in October 1918 the board had urged conversion of one collier into such a carrier.

The following March it called on him—"a better prophet than we are," said the chairman—for his thoughts on future developments in this area. Towers declared that control of the air in a naval battle was an absolute necessity. Unless the navy had "an air fleet of the largest size . . . your surface fleet won't be of any great value by 1925, . . . because if the enemy has superior air scouting forces and has gone in for tremendous construction of torpedo and bombing planes and fighting planes to keep your own scouts down, your fleet is not much use and you stand a good chance of losing it."[6]

Many of his ideas were not well formed. He spoke with most authority on the rigid airship and the big flying boat, with which he had the greatest experience and to which he now assigned immediate priority. The problem of operating smaller planes from ships troubled him most, because of the difficulty of recovering them. Flying airplanes from ships in wartime seemed to him suicidal; the preferable solution would be the seaplane "or else some form of craft that can practically hover and land on [scout cruisers]."

Thus Towers regarded the aircraft carrier only as a makeshift solution, "nothing more than a floating platform," necessary for the immediate future but not beyond 1925. "[I]ts use is justified now . . . to develop . . . aircraft for spotting and scouting." A collier should be converted into a flying-off ship, as the board had recommended, in order to "give us valuable information for application in the building of a real airplane carrier." He agreed with the board's proposal that the latter should be a fast, 35-knot vessel with a 700-foot flight deck, probably converted from one of the projected battle cruisers. But he did not think planes could operate from carriers if such ships mounted 8-inch guns, as the board wanted.

Once there were suitable shipborne scout planes, Towers believed, the functions of the capital ship—battleships and battle cruisers—and of the airplane carrier would merge. Aviation was becoming such an integral part of the fleet that, by 1925, "it will be quite possible that ships will all become more or less aircraft carriers and be so designed." That is, air and gunnery would be equal components of each major warship. Such "a compromise ship," he admitted, "is merely an idea of mine"—"the development of aviation is so startling that any one is foolish if he attempts to lay down a six year's aviation program."

Towers furthermore fantasized that the NC-type flying boat would be succeeded by an even larger version "turned into a battle cruiser of the air or perhaps a battleship carrying an enormous amount of explosives. These big craft will be followed [in the air] and surrounded by smaller scouts [i.e., fighters], for keeping down enemy scouts, and ahead of that will be the rigid airships for general overseas scouting before any contact is made." Finally, he held to the utility of the kite balloon, now on its way out. So Towers made some wrong guesses, based on the limits of technology in 1919.[7]

In spite of reduced congressional appropriations and the dogged conservatism of CNO Benson, the navy was authorized to convert the collier *Jupiter* into the experimental carrier *Langley* and to develop two rigid airships. While Captain Tom Craven and Commander Ken Whiting superintended work on the carrier, Towers cast his lot with the flying boats he knew so well. And since the fleet's fourteen frontline battleships were being transferred to the West Coast in response to the growing arms race with Japan, Jack managed to get an assignment to the Pacific Fleet's air detachment. From Navy Department headquarters he coordinated the transfer to NAS San Diego of eighteen seaplanes, two airships, six kite balloons, fifty-six officers, and four hundred enlisted men. Then he headed west and on 31 October 1919 reported as aviation officer to air detachment commander Captain Harvey Tomb, also as executive officer of the NC tender *Aroostook,* which Tomb still commanded. On 8 December Tomb was relieved in both posts by Captain Henry Mustin. Thus Mustin and Towers were reunited after more than five years since the Vera Cruz affair.[8]

Towers set about organizing the air detachment to impress the high command with its utility. Although the Pacific Fleet commander in chief,

Admiral Hugh Rodman, was only lukewarm, his chief of staff Rear Admiral Nathan C. Twining believed that any naval battle would begin in the air and should include torpedo-launching planes. Another convert was the skipper of the battleship *Mississippi,* Captain William A. Moffett, who many years before had counseled Towers to get out of aviation. Moffett made the *Mississippi* the second ship to have a flying-off ramp erected over one of its turrets, and he arranged to have Mustin and Towers spot for her gunfire.[9]

After an absence from the oceangoing navy of five years, Towers got back his sea legs when the *Aroostook* cruised to Mare Island Naval Shipyard, San Francisco, in mid-December. In February 1920 Mustin let him command the ship for a run down to Santa Barbara for operations with the seaplanes. Mustin flew back to San Diego, leaving Towers to bring back the *Aroostook*— the first time he had ever captained a warship by himself. Jack always enjoyed being at sea, and the crew liked him and admired his professionalism. He was finally in his element, with his aircraft at sea and working effectively with Mustin. He gave a ride to his old *Kentucky* exec Admiral Henry Wiley and was pleased when two former bosses, Captains Pete Symington and Harvey Tomb, qualified as pilots. The message was spreading.[10]

The social whirl in San Diego gave Lily Towers many opportunities to attend and give parties, especially with the Mustins and Lieutenant Commander E. W. "Win" Spencer and his wife, the former Wallis Warfield, a distant cousin of Corinne Mustin. Jack and Lily hosted one memorable masquerade party that made the society pages in August 1920, and they were among the aviators and wives at a reception on board the British battleship *Renown* that April to meet the visiting Prince of Wales. Little did any of them know that commoner Wallis would eventually marry the prince, and that he would have to give up his throne as a result. Like Wallis, Lily had an independent nature; the roaring Twenties saw the birth of the free-spirited flapper.[11]

During May and June 1920 Mustin and Towers exercised their F5Ls, Jennys, and Sopwiths in spotting gunfire, especially for Captain Moffett's *Mississippi,* off the southern California coast. Markedly effective were wireless Morse code transmissions of ranges from the planes to Moffett's gun boss, Jack's classmate Commander Bill Calhoun; the *"Missy"* was able to blast targets at a range of 22,000 yards. Twice on 10 June alone, Moffett signaled the *Aroostook,* "Your aeroplanes were our salvation. We thank you." Indeed, the *Mississippi* made such record scores that they nearly equaled those of the other battleships combined. The two assigned blimps operated during the summer, though one was wrecked, and the kite balloons saw their last service. Parachute experiments were conducted, since heretofore the only prescribed

At San Diego in August 1920, Lily and Jack Towers threw a costume party that made the society pages then and again years later when one of the guests of that evening married King Edward VIII, resulting in his abdication. The future Duchess of Windsor, Wallis Warfield Spencer and at the time wife of pilot Lieutenant Win Spencer, is sitting in the middle of the second row (no headdress). Jack Towers is the clown on the floor. Lily is on the floor, third from the left. Standing behind and to the right of Wallis is Captain Henry Mustin; standing behind him to the right is Spig Wead, fighter pilot and future screenwriter. (Towers collection)

means of survival had been to ditch a malfunctioning or damaged plane. And as backup for the radios, homing pigeons were employed, but with mixed results.[12]

In July 1920 Mustin's air detachment was upgraded to Air Force, Pacific Fleet, and conversion of the destroyer *Mugford* into a seaplane tender for NC boats was rushed to completion. Hoping to make a good showing in fleet maneuvers over the autumn, Mustin had Towers, Win Spencer, and Charles P. Mason rehearse planes in scouting the fleet as it headed back to California after a visit to Hawaii. Early in October the seaplanes intercepted the fleet in exceedingly foul weather 165 miles off San Pedro, winning praise from Admiral Rodman himself. Mustin and Towers then developed a tactical aviation manual for the Pacific Fleet commander, thus laying groundwork for the first carrier operations as soon as the *Langley* was ready.[13]

Until then, naval aviation's punch lay in the flying boats, whose long-distance capabilities were now to be tested in a major overwater flight as part of a joint fleet exercise on both sides of the Panama Canal. For the Pacific Fleet's air force of two NC boats and twelve F5Ls, this meant a flight of 3,019 miles along the Central American coast, with stops along the way for refueling, rest, and maintenance. The Atlantic Fleet's planes would fly to Panama from Hampton Roads. Towers was given two hats on 10 December: commander Seaplane Division 2, in charge of the NC-5 and NC-6, completed as trimotors, and captain of the seaplane tender *Mugford,* his first ship command, with five other officers and some one hundred men. Seaplane Squadron 1 under Charlie Mason consisted of two six-plane F5L divisions, while Rum Mustin gave acting command of the *Aroostook* to veteran combat pilot Lieutenant Commander Hugh Douglas. Mustin would accompany the planes.[14]

On the afternoon of 29 December 1920, Towers conned the *Mugford* from the dock and the *Aroostook* fell in 1,000 yards astern, destination Magdalena Bay in lower California. Next day the F5Ls flew 325 miles to Bartoleme Bay to refuel, thence to Magdalena Bay, 257 miles beyond. The *Mugford* lost three of her four boilers en route but joined the F5Ls and the *Aroostook* late on the thirty-first. That evening all hands tried to enjoy a Western film that kept breaking; in the words of Mustin, "the pilot of this cinema machine is inexperienced and had many forced landings, so to speak." The late-starting NC boats caught up with the F5Ls 445 miles down the coast at Banderas Bay on 3 January 1921, but Mustin ordered Towers to head straight for Acapulco in his crippled ship, accompanied by the tug *Kingfisher.*[15]

During the evening of 4 January, as the two ships lumbered along, Towers felt a slight pain in his abdomen and experienced diarrhea. His condition quickly worsened and appeared to be acute appendicitis. The NC-5 flew one of the *Aroostook*'s two medical officers to Acapulco to meet the *Mugford.* When the ship arrived there Jack was transferred to the oiler *Cuyama,* whereupon his temperature dropped from 104° to 99°, convincing the surgeons that an operation was unnecessary. But en route to Salina Cruz his condition worsened. The surgeons moved him to the *Aroostook* on the ninth. The high winds in "this detestable Gulf of Tehuantepec," as Mustin put it, made the ship roll, preventing the surgeons from operating.

Hugh Douglas took the *Aroostook* to sea for a three-day run to Bahia Honda, Panama, during which Towers' condition remained stable, with the flying boats proceeding 485 miles to La Union Harbor, El Salvador, in the Gulf of Fonseca. Towers, feeling better when the *Aroostook* dropped anchor at

Bahia Honda on the 14 January, witnessed the arrival of the F5Ls after their five-hour, 243-mile jump from Punta Arenas, Costa Rica. The hospital ship *Mercy* took him aboard on 15 January, "very weak and emaciated" from his ailment. When the doctors operated, they found and removed two intestinal blockages, leaving his appendix intact. The F5Ls made the last 243-mile hop to Balboa, Panama, but both NC boats went down and finally disintegrated while under tow. Worse, the *Mugford* lost her last boiler and also had to be taken in tow.

Nevertheless, the long flight of the F5Ls was widely heralded as a great achievement, along with the flight of nine F5Ls and the NC-10 from Norfolk (the NC-9 had broken up in heavy seas). Mustin had reached Balboa exactly on schedule, having flown 3,019 miles from San Diego, actual time aloft fifty-one hours, forty-eight minutes. He took his twelve planes across the isthmus to NAS Coco Solo for overhaul, then repeated his achievement by retracing his steps to San Diego between 23 February and 10 March, though at the cost of one plane. The round trip of 6,076 miles had been a dramatic demonstration of the strategic range of flying boats in conjunction with the operations of the fleet.

For Towers, however, the whole affair had been a disaster, between his illness, the destruction of his seaplane division, and the breakdown of the first ship he had ever commanded. He spent six weeks recuperating before rejoining the *Mugford* briefly and finally returning to the *Aroostook* on 8 June to resume his duties as Mustin's senior aide. His bad luck notwithstanding, Towers' performance in shaping fleet aviation policy had been exemplary, and Mustin recommended him for command of another and more important ship, a recommendation endorsed by Admiral Twining. Unfortunately, his ten years of service in aviation, especially being desk-bound during the war, had deprived him of real sea duty, and he was refused a ship command. His career prospects suddenly began to darken.[16]

For the time being, Towers could only continue to perform his current duties. Over the summer of 1921 he and Mustin reorganized the Pacific Fleet air force into squadrons of fighters and patrol planes. For practice in carrier landings, construction began on an 836-foot raised wooden platform at North Island that would simulate the *Langley,* soon to be commissioned.[17]

Naval aviation's steady progress, however, was overshadowed by the public crusade of Billy Mitchell for a unified air force, alarming even the conservative admirals to create the navy's own Bureau of Aeronautics (BuAer) in mid-1921. Captain William A. Moffett became the first chief of bureau in the rank of rear admiral, giving the airmen a full-time flag officer to fight their battles. The legislation also required that 70 percent of all officers in aviation qualify either as naval aviator or naval aviation observer, the latter to navigate and spot for the pilot. Moffett ordered an observer's course implemented at Pensacola and promptly enrolled in it himself.[18]

Wanting the highest-ranking pioneer navy pilot to be his assistant chief of bureau, Moffett ordered Captain Mustin to the post. Captain Henry V. Butler, a student of aviation at the Naval War College after the Armistice, took command of the fleet's air force, with Pat Bellinger as his senior aide. Moffett also brought in the legendary Commander Spuds Ellyson to head the plans division at BuAer. These shifts did not include Towers. In September he received orders to Pensacola Naval Air Station to be executive officer and captain of the yard until a sea command became available for the current commandant early in the new year. At that time, Jack could fleet up to command of the air station. A 1919 directive had ruled that the commandant of the navy's only aviation training station could be a nonaviator. The incumbent, one Captain Harley Hannibal Christy, forty-nine and a very popular four-striper, was so enthusiastic about his command that Jack would soon discover that he had no intention of vacating his post or seeking sea duty.[19]

As a thirty-six-year-old commander, Towers was indeed setting his sights high. At Pensacola he was clearly to be the brains of the operation, in charge of the flight school. His task was to produce the many pilots that Admiral Moffett believed essential for the future of naval aviation. "It is a good job," Jack wrote to his brother Will, "but I am not at all anxious to go to Pensacola. . . . We will have lots of perquisites . . . such as a big car, big house, servants, boats, etc., and be 'big frogs' but the puddle is rather small."[20]

Towers' plans to leave San Diego for a vacation in New York were shattered at the end of September when he and his five-year-old daughter were stricken with the flu. He recovered in three days, but Marjorie's condition quickly worsened into a serious case of pneumonia. Lily and the hired cook also contracted it, and when Lily took a prescribed steam bath she fainted and suffered a violent heart attack. A doctor who lived nearby arrived within three minutes, probably saving her life. As if this calamity weren't enough, Marjorie developed emphysema and had to be rushed to the hospital for an operation. Jack prevailed upon BuNav to delay his detachment until late November. Marjorie's medical bills greatly strained his resources, but the extra time at San Diego enabled him to break in Admiral Butler and Pat Bellinger to their new jobs.[21]

After a trip to visit Lily's family in New York, Jack finally got his family to Pensacola. The $1,000 spent on train fare further taxed his finances, as did Lily's extravagances, which included two more trips during the new year. He tried to satisfy her needs, but the tension in the marriage only deepened.[22]

From the small aviation fraternity Towers was able to have assigned to Pensacola some of the best men he knew, notably Charlie Mason as superintendent of training schools. Among the first postwar Annapolis men who had earned their wings and now stayed on as instructors were future carrier commanders Lieutenants Donald B. "Wu" Duncan, Ralph E. Davison, and Arthur W. Radford. Towers also supervised the training of Admiral Moffett to become an aviation observer and in the process got to know him better.[23]

The fifty-nine regular Pensacola students for 1922 included future World War II aviation leaders Lieutenant Forrest P. Sherman, Ensign A. K.

Towers accompanies an unidentified admiral and captain (H. H. Christy?) on an inspection of pilot instructors and student pilots at NAS Pensacola. Curiously, he is not wearing his golden wings. (Navy Department)

Doyle, and naval constructor Commander Emory S. "Jerry" Land, with whom Jack roomed for a time while Land qualified as a naval observer. Towers made only one speech to them after they reported: "Don't drink during the week. Don't drink and try to fly. Don't drink except on Saturday night, and don't do much of that . . . Try to be the oldest, not the boldest of pilots." They all had to sign the "Bevo" list, promising not to touch the hooch twenty-four hours before a flight. Towers' penchant for flight safety made a lasting impression on them.[24]

Towers was building a following of talented flyers that would strengthen the navy's air arm. They would become loyal to him, and he to them, as their careers intertwined over the years. The ship that would unite them was the aircraft carrier. Its development received a major stimulus over the winter of 1921–22 at the Washington Naval Conference, which defused the arms race between the United States, Japan, and Great Britain. In addition to limiting battleship strength, the three powers, at the instigation of Admiral Moffett, agreed that in place of new battle cruisers each navy could convert two uncompleted battle cruiser hulls into mammoth 34-knot, 36,000-ton carriers. For the United States, this meant the *Lexington* (CV-2) and *Saratoga* (CV-3), *V* being the new navy symbol for aircraft. Until their long conversion was completed, the tiny 11,000-ton *Langley* could be used to solve many problems.

Commissioned at Norfolk in March 1922, the *Langley* was commanded by Captain Stafford Doyle, to whom Towers had first reported in the *Kentucky* in 1906; Ken Whiting was exec. That October, Lieutenant Commander Chevy Chevalier, her senior flight officer, made the first successful landing aboard. Three weeks later, however, the popular flyer crashed, suffering injuries that proved fatal. The price of progress continued to claim Towers' comrades and former students. The *Langley* proceeded to Pensacola for the winter to have additional equipment installed. With her there, Jack began to see how the problems of recovering a landplane on board a ship were being remedied.[25]

Towers did not like his Pensacola duty because as captain of the yard he oversaw the physical plant, a job for which he was not qualified. The most trying episode occurred on 5 July 1922 when his boss, Captain Christy, was away on leave and Towers was left in command of the station. The tug *Allegheny* was docking the collier *Orion* when the latter's propeller chewed into the tug, causing it to sink. Jack called on constructor Jerry Land to help him direct the tedious salvage operation and had nothing but sleepless nights thereafter until she could be raised. He wanted a transfer.[26]

Meanwhile the marriage deteriorated almost to the breaking point. Not only did Pensacola offer nothing for Lily, but other couples refused to play bridge with the Towers because they won virtually every time. Jack the athlete swam and played golf, even winning one tournament, whereas Lily enjoyed none of this. She longed for the high life of her adopted home, London, where her parents still resided. Jack therefore requested attaché duty there again, which Moffett approved.[27]

Then, more trouble. During a routine eye checkup in 1922, the examiner discovered the old scar on the rear of the lens of Towers' right eye caused by the flash burn in the dynamo room of the *Kentucky* sixteen years before. His vision was normal, for the scar had not spread, but in an annual physical in February 1923 the scar was seen to have become a slight astigmatism that weakened his depth perception. The doctors rated him as unqualified for flying duty. "Owing to the past record of this officer," they added, "and his very evident value to the Aviation branch of the Naval Service, it is recommended that the above defects be waived and he be continued on aviation duty," though minimally and, "as far as possible, with a second pilot." The waiver was granted.[28]

For intelligence-gathering duties as assistant naval attaché Jack first underwent indoctrination at ONI, now headed by the dynamic Captain Luke McNamee. Jack's posting in London brought concurrent duty in the capitals of France, Italy, and the Netherlands. A restricted budget meant one officer had to do the work of several, and he would be on the move again, away from his family. They all departed by ocean liner for England on 6 March; only Mr. Tyke, the dog, stayed behind. Towers reported to the embassy at the Court of St. James on the seventeenth.[29]

During his time abroad, which would again last more than two years, Towers missed little of significance in the progress of U.S. naval aviation, since BuAer was still getting started and much of its effort was devoted to countering General Billy Mitchell's attempts to have a separate air force absorb naval aviation. Rum Mustin stayed on as Moffett's assistant chief until July 1923 when ill health caused him to be relieved. On 23 August his heart failed him. Jack Towers and all the navy had lost a great colleague and innovator.[30]

The naval attaché in the Western European capitals, Captain Charles L. Hussey, kept Towers' work concentrated in London. In spite of the Washington arms control agreements, ONI director McNamee instructed his attachés to be alert to any intelligence about Japan, America's potential foe. Thus Towers met often with Colonel Sir William F. Forbes-Sempill and the members of his mission, just back from two years in Japan helping the Imperial Navy to create its own air arm. Towers reported on its first carrier, the uneven quality of Japanese naval pilots, and the fact that the Japanese were still copying Western technology.[31]

In August four of Towers' former top *Aroostook* flyers arrived in London, including Lieutenants Frank W. "Spig" Wead and David Rittenhouse, representing the navy in the prestigious international Schneider Cup speed race for seaplanes. With Towers observing, two CR-3 Curtiss Racers performed handsomely on 28 September 1923. Dave Rittenhouse won the cup at a top speed of 177 mph, followed by Rutledge Irvine at 173, achievements that garnered important data for the navy's first postwar planes, then under development.[32]

Towers participated in the trial flights of the dirigible ZR-3 (Z meaning airship), built by the Germans for the U.S. Navy as a war reparation. On 6 September he was joined by several American flyers as guests of the dirigible's builder Hugo Eckener for a successful 475-mile, nine-and-a-half-hour flight over southern Germany. The other American officers then rode the great ship across the Atlantic to NAS Lakehurst where it was commissioned the *Los Angeles*. The Navy built the rigid *Shenandoah* (ZR-1), commissioned in October under the command of Captain Frank McCrary. Unfortunately—or perhaps fortunately, for McCrary—he was relieved after the airship broke away from its mooring mast. Recalled Towers in 1925, "They tried to make me" take the *Shenandoah*. But instead "poor Zach Lansdowne" wanted the job and got it. He would perish when the dirigible crashed. Jack in any case was strictly a heavier-than-air pilot.[33]

Meanwhile Lily's reunion with her parents in London had not helped the marriage, even though Jack had rented a house and provided her with two servants and a maid, all of which taxed his modest navy salary. Neither spouse was happy after almost eight years together. They agreed on a divorce, obtained in Paris before the end of the year; it could not help Towers' career, for divorce carried a stigma in the U.S. Navy.

Needless to say, the breakup caused unhappiness to all, especially the young children. The thirty-two-year-old mother at first kept custody of seven-year-old Margie and four-year-old Chas. She was relieved to be freed from navy life but soon found herself incapable of handling parental responsibilities. She plagued Jack to enroll both children in English preparatory schools but was unsuccessful. Though on good terms with her family, he soon found himself in growing debt from her extravagant ways.[34]

A miserable, lonely thirty-eight-year-old divorcé, Towers chanced to meet a young French woman at a party in London one Saturday evening that fall of 1923. At twenty-one, Marie-Louise-Anne-Pierrette Chauvin de Grandmont, Pierre for short, was alert, intelligent, attractive, and such a good dancer that Jack would not let go of her at the party. She found him to be "a very nice, different sort of person" whose company she enjoyed, and she accepted his invitation to visit the zoo next day with him and the children.

Other dates followed, a dazzling experience for Pierre. Descended from landed gentry, she had been raised as an army child, and her world had been shattered when her father was killed at the head of his regiment on the Western Front in 1914. She had learned English at the Sorbonne after the war, then studied briefly at Oxford. Her stylish figure led to her employment by a leading Paris dressmaker, whose collection Pierre successfully displayed on visits to London.

Whenever Towers visited the embassy in Paris, he took Pierre to lunch. He liked her mother immediately, leading Pierre to assume that he was courting Madame Chauvin de Grandmont herself! She soon caught on, however, for he would telephone her immediately upon arriving at the train station and ask her out for a martini. When he picked her up, he was invariably carrying an enormous and impressive diplomatic bag full of documents, and off they'd go to the Ritz. Their fondness for each other grew over the months, in spite of the age difference of seventeen years. Unlike Lily, Pierre as an army offspring understood the sacrifices military families had to make and thus had no difficulty appreciating Jack's professional situation. He taught her to play bridge, which she did not enjoy but was willing to share with him. By the time his European tour of duty ended, they were very much in love.[35]

Commander Towers gathered intelligence on British military aviation and even managed to get in flight time on the de Havilland that the embassy kept at an airfield at Kenley. He learned how the Royal Navy had fought and lost the postwar battle to regain control of its own air arm from the RAF, and that the government was trying to compensate by making concessions to the navy. In fact, the Air Ministry designed all naval aircraft with virtually no navy participation, except that the navy had to foot the bill. At the Admiralty, only a tiny air section survived from the huge wartime RNAS, headed by a nonflying captain. Indeed, all that the Royal Navy controlled were the planes deployed aboard carriers. Whatever happened to British naval air, Towers believed, correctly, that the RAF had become a permanent institution.

Towers found the navy's aerial spotting poor but only because it had been conducted by RAF pilots ignorant of naval operations. The British had developed the torpedo plane to the total exclusion of the naval bomber, and Towers personally observed dismal bombing tests against the target ship *Agamemnon* by pilots from inland stations who knew nothing about attacking a ship under way. He admired British defensive fighters and short-range tactical scouts and learned that the military had virtually abandoned airships.

Towers' responsibilities grew in April 1924 when he was given additional assistant attaché duty in Berlin. "This place is ruining me financially," he wrote to Garland Fulton. Captain Hussey in London had refused to cover his extensive travel expenses, and he had to live in a hotel. At least that fall he was able to dispose of his responsibility as assistant attaché to Rome. Pierre visited him several times in Berlin. Upon returning to London Towers earned flight pay piloting the embassy's de Havilland, and in September he took leave to accompany Glenn Curtiss on a "shoot" in Scotland. Back again in London, he was pleased to find attaché Hussey relieved by Captain Luke McNamee, now "Captain Mac" to Towers.[36]

After representing the United States at the International Commission of Aerial Navigation in London in April 1925, Towers received orders to rejoin the fleet on the West Coast as soon as his relief reported. Although anxious to return to sea duty, he would have to leave Pierre, now residing in London as a dressmaker and spending all her free time with him and the children, who had grown fond of her. Hopelessly in love, they spent Sunday evenings by the fireplace in her flat and other days met for a drink at the Cafe Royal. So devoted to her had he become that for the first time in his career he seriously entertained the notion of leaving the navy and entering the business sector. Money, as always, was a problem: he had to support his children, custody of whom Lily was all too happy to grant him for the foreseeable future, as well as hire an English nurse to accompany the three of them on the trip home. Until Jack and Pierre could be certain of their love, and until Jack was more financially secure, Pierre would retain her job in London.[37]

Meanwhile Towers, awaiting his relief, kept at his work, which included a startling interview with an English officer just back from Japan who reported having seen many good Japanese flyers. This contradicted the intelligence Towers had garnered from the Sempill mission. The man explained that student aviators worked at it hard, and "the ones that didn't make good flyers usually broke their necks."[38]

Pierre helped Jack and the nurse, a Miss Pearce, pack for their departure by rail for Southampton the morning of 25 August; they sailed in the *Leviathan* that afternoon. Pierre hated to see him go, except that one month later his replacement perished while flying the embassy's plane; it could have been

Jack. On the hot, stormy crossing, he entertained his children between social activities and conversations with two other officers important to his career, Captain Henry V. Butler and Rear Admiral Mark Bristol. Though his personal future was uncertain, he continued to advance his professional goal of promoting aviation.[39]

When the *Leviathan* docked in New York on 31 August 1925 Towers was met by his brother Fullton, now vice president of the Ford, Bacon and Davis engineering firm and anxious to find Jack a good position in banking. Fullton's entreaties only compounded the sheer chaos of getting children, luggage, and "Nurse," as he called Miss Pearce, to Washington and into the apartment of Captain Jerry Land, head of BuAer's material division, while Land was away on vacation. One night Towers turned down an invitation to dinner to sup with Nurse, fearful lest she get homesick and desert him and the children. "If she left," he wrote Pierre, "I would be in a pickle!" Small wonder he felt "lonely and forlorn" and missed his Pierre.[40]

His travails were only beginning. He could not head west to rejoin the fleet until Admiral Moffett returned from San Francisco to hear the report about his experiences abroad. Moffett had gone to California to witness a nonstop long-distance flight to Pearl Harbor. Taking off on 31 August, one of the flying boats washed out early, but the leader, Commander John Rodgers, pressed on in the other, a twin-engine, four-man PN-9.

Towers was scheduled to testify before a special hearing of the General Board on 2 September. The papers that morning announced the alarming news that Rodgers and his plane had gone down somewhere short of their destination, position unknown. Shades of the NC-3! So the hearing was delayed until the third. That morning the Navy Department and the nation were stunned by worse news. During the night the navy dirigible *Shenandoah* had crashed in a storm over Ohio. Zach Lansdowne perished with thirteen others of the crew. Glad that he had avoided that command, Jack wrote Pierre, "The ghastly accident . . . will be the finish of lighter-than-air, or airships, I believe."[41]

In spite of the twin catastrophes, Rear Admiral Joseph Strauss conducted the General Board hearing on the third to find out what Towers had learned of the "united air force in England." The political atmosphere was already highly charged because of Billy Mitchell's by-now furious crusade for an independent American air force as well as several recent studies of army and navy aeronautics. Admiral Strauss himself had been highly critical of what he considered waste in the aviation budget. Several times during Towers' interview Strauss went off the record, notably when Jack asserted that the U.S. Navy had "faith in aviation." Strauss asked him if he still entertained the strong views about "the importance of aircraft in warfare" he had had before going to England.

"Yes, sir," replied Jack firmly, "I think it is [important] and I have always regarded myself as a very conservative officer when it comes to aviation." Compared to Mitchell he certainly was, but that was not the point; the admirals were irritated by the festering controversy about what they considered to be an auxiliary weapon. Nevertheless, the board could not ignore Towers' conclusion about the RAF continuing as a separate air force.[42]

This informed opinion of the navy's most experienced aviator contributed to the newest alarm for the navy two days later, when Billy Mitchell made the most dramatic attack of his crusade. He alleged that the two naval air accidents were "the direct result of incompetency, criminal negligence, and almost treasonable administration of the National Defense by the Navy and War Department." President Calvin Coolidge immediately ordered the army to institute court-martial proceedings against Mitchell for his insubordinate attack on the government. And Admiral Moffett rushed back to Washington to launch a counterattack on Mitchell.[43]

Towers was immediately plunged into the maelstrom. Setting up a temporary office in the Army and Navy Club, he found himself appointed to a special board to investigate the *Shenandoah* disaster—"a compliment, but a bore." Coolidge appointed his own aircraft board under the highly respected banker and lawyer Dwight W. Morrow to study all aspects of the nation's aviation, whereupon Moffett assigned Towers to help prepare the navy's position. On 17 September he complained to Pierre, "I am terribly busy here, I am on three Boards now, and everybody is saying: See Towers." This meant several more weeks, if not months, before he and his children could go to the West Coast.[44]

Jack's spirits plummeted; he worked late each night all month long. He engaged a maid to clean and cook for the household, though she had to depend on him to do the shopping. He avoided socializing and drinking but did play enough bridge to win pin money. Meanwhile he had to borrow from a bank and his brother Fullton to make ends meet. His loneliness deepened when he sent Marjorie, Chas, and Nurse to visit friends near Boston and an entire month passed without a letter from Pierre. Then he attended the funeral of the *Shenandoah* victims at Arlington National Cemetery, "rather sad on account of the young widows and kiddies." At least there was some

185

good news: John Rodgers and his crew suddenly sailed their PN-9 into Hawaii after a ten-day, 450-mile odyssey, having run out of gas while off course. All the while Towers cultivated his banker and broker friends with a view toward possibly leaving the navy.[45]

The *Shenandoah* investigation required his presence at Lakehurst, the navy's dirigible base in New Jersey, beginning 21 September. Rear Admiral Hilary P. Jones headed the three-man court of inquiry, which also included Jack's wartime colleague, Captain Lewis McBride of the Construction Corps. "This *Shenandoah* business is occupying the front page of the papers every day," Jack wrote Pierre on 1 October. "We three 'learned officers of the Navy,' as we have been described, sit each day and all day, surrounded by experts, professors, newspaper men, photographers, etc. in a big room filled with people and listen and question, and listen, while a telegraph instrument ticks out every word to the country."[46]

The *Shenandoah* inquiry shared headlines with the Morrow Board, which had begun its public hearings in Washington the same day, 21 September. President Coolidge had appointed a board of individuals with unassailable credentials, among them senators, congressmen, and technical advisers, to deal with both the Billy Mitchell challenge and the future of aviation in general.[47]

Towers was informed he would be summoned before the board to testify later in October. On the fifth, as soon as he got off the train in Washington, he was "besieged by a lot of people, some of whom wanted the latest on the *Shenandoah,* and others who were trying to find out what I proposed to tell the President's Committee in regard to reorganizing aviation. I didn't tell them much about either. . . ." Also arriving that evening, all the way from London, were Commander Jerry Hunsaker and Captain Luke McNamee. "You can imagine the importance of the situation if they bring people [from] so far! Hunsaker is to defend the *Shenandoah* and Captain Mac to testify about [the] Royal Air Force (all he knows is what I told him, so he says!)."[48]

No sooner had Towers reported back to the Navy Department next morning than he was summoned by the Morrow Board "for a private hearing, which was continued through dinner and until late at night." Admiral Moffett was perfectly willing to let his most informed associate, Towers, contribute his expertise. As the admiral wrote to Captain Pete Symington, by challenging Billy Mitchell's facts and inferences and bringing out more information, "the fallacies will be shown up in their true light." Mitchell had already had his day—rather, two days—in court the week before to make his extremist and undocumented statements. His new "Air Force," he declared, should have charge of continental coast defense out to the 200-mile range limit of its bombers, presumably to protect against a hostile Great Britain![49]

The Morrow Board, representing the president and his service secretaries, had to refute Mitchell's facts carefully and at the same time counter the conservatism of senior officers. Its goal was to establish once and for all an effective long-range aviation policy, thus putting an end to the controversy. The board could not have found a better man than Jack Towers to present counterarguments to Mitchell's testimony and to propose solutions. "It is all very difficult and complicated for me," Jack wrote Pierre after an exhausting long night with the committee. "They seem to be endeavoring to get me to make the main assault against Col. Mitchell . . . and also to make the big attack against the older admirals in the Navy who are hampering progress in aviation. It is not quite fair to me, for it involves risks [to] my professional career, but I think I may do it."[50]

Despite this delicate position, Towers was his own man, confident that his wartime and more recent experiences gave him a unique perspective. Like the rest of the navy he opposed an independent air force, but he could not accept either of the two extreme points of view offered by other navy witnesses who came before the board. Younger aviators like Pat Bellinger wanted a separate naval air corps in charge of its own personnel, the goal more moderate army flyers wanted for the Army Air Service. Indeed, the key personnel test, in the minds of most naval airmen, would be whether their senior man, Jack Towers, would be promoted to captain when his time came. Most feared he would not. Allied against them were the older admirals represented by the chief of BuNav, Rear Admiral William R. Shoemaker, who resented having to draw manpower away from existing ships to man the two big carriers when they joined the fleet. In addition, he bitterly attacked the airmen's exclusive privilege of drawing flight pay.[51]

Towers therefore viewed the problem within the navy as basically one of personnel, and he did not agree totally with Admiral Moffett, who waffled over endorsing a separate naval air corps before deciding against it. Following his prepared remarks before the board, he fumbled a response to Congressman Carl Vinson by endorsing the airmen's desire to control aviation personnel. Moffett argued that naval aviation observers rather than rapidly promoted aviators should command aviation units; younger airmen should reach higher ranks through the normal selection process. In fact, the admiral believed that among the existing aviators, only Towers deserved a carrier command in the near future. The secrecy of Towers' own meetings with Morrow and other members of the board indicates that most of his views were carefully kept from Moffett.[52]

Morrow instructed Jack to appear officially before the board on 14 October, giving him time to prepare a statement and to coordinate his plans with certain members of the board. He worked late into the evenings, met and dined often with Dwight Morrow, and gained two extra days when his appearance was postponed to Friday the sixteenth. He spent the preceding day listening to other witnesses and entertaining some anxiety over his own appearance: "It will be rather exciting, for my speech is going to be very frank and will arouse the anger of some of the old admirals. However, it must be done. How glad I will be when it is all over."[53]

The testimony of Towers, one of ninety-nine witnesses to appear over four weeks of hearings, was saved until the very end. Chairman Morrow introduced Towers by asking him if he were in the line of the navy before learning to fly in 1911. Jack replied coldly, "Yes. I am *still* in the line of the Navy."[54]

Rather than acknowledging Billy Mitchell's arguments, Towers focused his prepared remarks exclusively on the navy's personnel policies. He recounted the immense problems he had had mobilizing wartime naval aviation personnel. The situation in 1925 was the same as it had been in 1917, except that the new BuAer lacked authority to develop its programs. As a result, "a distinct feeling of disquiet" existed within BuAer, whose grievances, "real or imaginary," its personnel aimed at BuNav. The current ad hoc cooperation between the two bureaus depended on each side's good will, "not always a sound foundation to build upon. I do not believe it will work under stress of a great war. . . ."

Changes would have to be made not simply internally, Towers asserted, but also through the passage of new legislation. In this he was echoing Admiral Moffett's testimony. "The Navy, if it proposes to keep up with world progress, is committed to a policy of extensive development of aviation," revolving around "a very large increase in the number of naval aviators within a rather short space of time." Aviators almost uniformly wanted a separate corps, "with full control of personnel" by BuAer, whereas BuNav and most nonaviators were equally adamant about preserving the status quo.

Unlike the other witnesses, Towers deftly rejected both extremes: "[T]he proper course must lie somewhere between. . . ." From his own point of view as an aviator, he admitted, a separate naval air corps "would undoubtedly work well within itself. Close-coupled organizations usually do." People within it would know where they stood. Indeed, his "own professional future would be more or less secure, whereas under the present system it looks extremely precarious." Nevertheless, the idea of a separate corps disturbed him.

Then he hammered home his own controversial conviction: "Aviation is not only the eyes of the Navy but also its good right arm. It does not require a great deal of vision to see the day when it may be *both* arms. Even now a theoretical battle between a fleet of fast carriers on one side and a fleet of battleships on the other makes the most interesting study." Jack followed this understatement with a remark to placate the old admirals: "I am firmly convinced that aviation must remain an integral part of the main fighting organization, and that is the line." In short, aviators had to be recognized as full-fledged line officers and promoted on that basis, not treated by BuNav as second-class specialist officers.

The first step was to straighten out the differences between BuAer and BuNav. Either bureau could be charged with handling all aviation personnel, though he thought BuNav with its traditional centralized system was better suited. In any case, he recommended the appointment of "an additional Assistant Secretary of the Navy, to be charged with the responsibility of aviation and aviation only . . . to coordinate the bureaus concerned with aviation. . . ." This idea was Towers' own. Then he went into the detailed problems of better integrating existing naval aviators into the promotion system, giving them "general naval duty" aboard battleships and cruisers, and enrolling more officers and enlisted men as pilots.

Finally Towers addressed the ticklish problem of inadequate numbers of senior officers qualified to command aviation units. His solution was twofold: assign some senior men to aviation billets and advance several lower-grade aviators to higher ranks. Needless to say, Towers had his own predicament in mind as well as that of other aviators; some changes were necessary if he was ever to command at sea and advance to higher grades.

In closing his prepared testimony, Towers stated his opposition to a "unified air force which would include naval aviation."

During the questioning that followed, he refused to comment on any aspect of aviation outside the navy, thus protecting himself from the charge, leveled at Billy Mitchell, of meddling in matters beyond his own area of expertise. Dwight Morrow, however, got him to refute one of Mitchell's claims by alluding to Towers' experience leading the transatlantic flight and asking if he felt the country was in danger from any airplanes "that exist in the world today?" "Not in the slightest degree," said Jack. A peacetime attack on either coast, if opposed by American armed forces, "would be entirely ridiculous."

Senator Hiram Bingham was the first to challenge Towers. He wondered why virtually all army aviators favored and all navy airmen opposed a united air force. Towers used his knowledge of circumstances in Britain to explain that the RAF had swallowed up naval aviation and rendered it "insignificant." Still, a separate air force was necessary for England because of that nation's proximity to potential foes. Unlike the United States, insulated by two large oceans, the nations of Europe "think they need a defensive air force. They think also that they need an offensive air force to strike first. But the arguments that apply to the Royal Air Force in England do not apply to an air force in this country. . . ."

This was the crux of Mitchell's faulty reasoning. He was advocating the strategic bombing theories being touted by Air Marshal Sir Hugh Trenchard of the RAF and the Italian pundit General Giulio Douhet, both based on purely European models. The short range of bombing planes in the 1920s and indeed for the foreseeable future could not serve a country so geographically insular as the United States. Heavy-laden bombers would simply not be able to bridge the Atlantic with current or anticipated technology. America's only logical enemy being Japan, the U.S. Army had no interest in fighting another European war anyway.

When Army Air Service veteran Bingham pressed Towers to comment on the specific disadvantages of a united air force, Towers replied, "Very few war operations in history requiring complete cooperation of the forces of Army and Navy, representing two units, have been successful." This being so, "it would be practically impossible to ever get complete cooperation among three forces." He reiterated his belief that the navy's air arm "must be run by the Navy. It does not cooperate with the Navy, it *is* the Navy. . . . In 10 years it may be one-third of it, and in 20 years it may be all of it." (That would be 1945, a sage if somewhat exaggerated forecast.)

Naval aerial scouts provided the same functions as scouting ships, and naval bombing and torpedo planes the same as naval guns, Towers asserted. Their pilots had to be trained in the navy by men who understood sea and naval conditions, not by air force–trained personnel ignorant of such matters. He saw no point in having a united air force that detailed naval aviators back to the navy, as the RAF was doing. "I could give you a great many objections to a plan for a united air force, sir," he concluded with a devastating remark to Bingham, but as a proposition it was "so fundamentally unsound I had not even prepared any argument on it."

Congressman Vinson took up the matter of aviators feeling their naval careers jeopardized and addressed possible solutions to Towers. The problem was the nine-admiral selection boards that passed on all promotions. Towers recommended modifying the law to allow each aviator to be judged like any line officer who specialized, giving him special due for his performance in aviation as well as in nonflying duties. Dwight Morrow went further, asking Towers if he thought an aviator who "kept up in general fleet duties, is better able to command a ship, and perhaps ultimately to command a fleet, because he is an aviator." Jack replied yes, "in the very near future." Morrow wondered if the system was "defective" because the navy regarded aviators as unfit for command of a ship. "I not only believe it, sir, but I know it," Towers responded, citing his own case of having been turned down for a ship command in 1921 despite the recommendations of his immediate superiors.

Admiral Frank F. Fletcher, the only naval officer on the board, suggested aviators "be carried on the Navy Register with extra numbers," which Towers rejected. "I should rather have all or nothing," he said, and "take my changes with the rest. I would not want to see whether or not I was passed over [for promotion as a line officer] and then have the consolation prize, an extra number, passed out to me."

Professor William F. Durand of NACA questioned Towers about the pilot manpower problem. Since Towers had stated he believed in "short-service commissions" for "a limited number of university graduates," Durand wanted to know how well such men had performed as naval pilots during the war. Jack answered that they had been "very good" though "not as good as if they had come through the professional school," Annapolis. Durand, more interested in the problem of aviators as line officers, asked Towers flatly whether he'd "rather go along as a regular number or an extra number." Jack naturally cited his preference for the former, calling for "drastic action" to remedy the situation, that is, "a change in the law. . . ."

Towers yielded the stand to Jerry Hunsaker, who made a few brief comments, whereupon the formal Morrow Board hearings came to a close. Towers had clearly defined the problems of aviation within the navy, exposed the weaknesses of Mitchell's unified air force scheme, and offered workable compromise solutions designed to strengthen naval aviation. Having done his duty, Jack became a passive observer, unsure of the reaction to his speech by the members of the board and senior admirals of the navy.

Quite frankly, Jack's thoughts were elsewhere. Remembering his happy times in London with Pierre, he agonized at having heard precious little news from her. "How wonderful life can be when two people love each other," he wrote to her, "but it is Hell when those two people are separated by an OCEAN! . . . I still have a little sense and I wouldn't ask you to marry me until I thought I saw enough ahead to keep you happy, or until I was sure you really would be happy on what little there is. This must be a trial for both of us. It won't hurt. If it is real, it will survive." He still contemplated going into business—"a very momentous decision to have to make, and I must be sure of myself." Brother Fullton now wanted to take him into his engineering firm as an aviation consultant. Or Towers could work with Glenn Curtiss, who was making a fortune in Florida real estate.[55]

Ex-wife Lily was back in town, clearing out her things from their old house, and both children returned from their New England trip only to be put into bed with the flu. Jack had to help Nurse care for them in the small austere apartment he had leased. His spirits remained low, as he wrote Pierre: "Nothing seems to go right. I have been working terribly hard, and am mentally tired and dull." Thankfully, he was able to get away for a hectic weekend to watch the Schneider Cup races in Baltimore.[56]

The hearings of the Morrow Board were over by the time Billy Mitchell's army court-martial trial began on 28 October, freeing Towers to make a 350-mile round-trip seaplane flight from Washington to Hampton Roads, "a lovely flight, over Virginia with lots of rivers and islands." He used the weekend to move more things into the apartment, hire another cook, and fend off social invitations from his neighbor, Captain Henry Butler, and others. On the thirty-first Morrow informed Jack that he had "made a very favorable impression" in his first hearing, and that the board was proposing "to adopt most" of his recommendations.[57]

Indeed the board was, for bright and early Monday morning, 2 November, Towers was summoned to "a long secret session" during which he was questioned at great length about his schemes. The members leaned so heavily on Towers' advice that the following week he was able to write Pierre, "The latest rumor is that the President's Aircraft Board is adopting my report as the basis for its own recommendations. It is rather exciting waiting for their report, and my stock is going up rapidly!" Not only with the Morrow Board, but with Admiral Moffett, who recommended that he be given command of the navy's only carrier, the *Langley*. Obviously, his calculated risk of speaking frankly and dispassionately before the board was beginning to pay handsome dividends.[58]

Such news acted as much-needed balm, but Towers continued his hermitlike existence in the drab apartment and yearned so much for Pierre that alarmed friends descended on the apartment one evening and forced him to accept several dinner invitations. He flew as often as possible, though the cold, wet November weather took the joy out of even that; returning from a long open-cockpit flight to North Carolina in a driving rain, his "poor face was so pounded that it was the color of a beet." Jack desperately wanted to move the family to San Diego for a happy California Christmas; it looked as if his work would tie him down in Washington.[59]

The navy did not know that its increasingly valuable pioneer aviator was receiving many job offers from the business world. During November Towers was interviewed on several trips to New York, which he financed with lucrative winnings at high-stakes bridge. On one visit he stayed overnight at the home of Chance M. Vought, manufacturer of navy fighters, spotters, and trainers. He deposited Miss Pearce and the children at the apartment of Charlie Carstairs so they could spend time in New York with Lily, and he returned a week later to fetch them and attend a gala formal affair in Manhattan. Former father-in-law Charlie continued to hold Jack in high esteem, entertaining him at the swank Links Club and offering to back him in business as well as to help out with the children's expenses. Towers, though grateful, could not accept.[60]

Towers did not spend the full week in New York, for the pro-Mitchell "yellow" press was launching fresh attacks on the *Shenandoah* investigation. The weary, unpleasant proceedings taxed Towers' energies, and, in need of a break, on the evening of 17 November he "went to see the Ziegfield [*sic*] Follies with another man. They were very good. He knew two of the girls and got them and brought them to my flat. We had a bottle of champagne, and they cooked eggs and bacon. They were very nice and very pretty, but I think they thought it rather strange that I didn't make love to them." This he confessed in a letter to Pierre, which was softened by an assurance that he'd dreamt of her after the ladies left. His candor elicited a strong response from an equally lonely Pierre. She wanted to come to America, marry her "Jackie," and tend the children. All of which only caused him further agony, for he would never permit this, he told her, until he was financially secure.[61]

While his days were spent at the tedious *Shenandoah* hearings, the rest of his time was taken up with certain members of the Morrow Board, "secretly working at night." The final report was being written, and they needed the input of their leading expert. The board could not lose a minute if it was to meet the president's deadline for completing the report before the Mitchell court-martial ended. Jack added his final thoughts to the last draft of the report, completed before the Thanksgiving holiday on 26 November.[62]

His work on the Morrow Board done and the *Shenandoah* court recessed, Towers took the train to New York the day after Thanksgiving to see the Army-Navy football game, the first time, he reflected, that he had ever been to the big event without the company of "a girl." Brothers Fullton and Will joined him, and he saw a lot of friends among the large crowd. Unfortunately Navy lost, 10–3. The three brothers attended the theater that evening, and Jack spent Sunday with Charlie Carstairs at the Links Club playing bridge. He won enough to cover the expenses of his trip.[63]

The Sunday papers revealed "what was reported to be an advance report of the President's Aircraft Board, and stated that the Army battle had been lost through following Mitchell, and that the Naval Aviators had won through following Rodgers and Towers." Jack told Pierre, "Of course, it is largely 'bosh'—but rather amusing!" Towers tore out a clipping from the New York *World* whose headline blared, "MITCHELL AIR PROGRAM THROWN IN DISCARD BY MORROW INQUIRY BOARD." The headline was not what amused him but rather the reporter's speculation that he and Rodgers might be made rear admirals and placed in command of the carriers *Lexington* and *Saratoga* upon their completion. Whatever happened, he told Pierre, admirals did not command individual ships, and "there isn't a chance of my being made a rear admiral for YEARS, so don't get excited." Rodgers had been singled out for praise largely because of his heroic survival on the PN-9 flight.[64]

What the Morrow Report to the President, officially dated 30 November 1925, did say closely followed Towers' testimony and recommendations. It even quoted him directly on how "ridiculous" an enemy air attack on the United States would be. He was the only person quoted by name except for Orville Wright, who had made some remarks on civil aviation. The report repudiated the concept of a unified air force, thus rejecting Billy Mitchell without mentioning him by name, and instead called for the strengthening of the air components within the existing services.

Most importantly, it recommended that specialized assistant secretaries of war, navy, and commerce be established to coordinate aviation in and between the three respective spheres. The Army Air Service should be upgraded to a semiautonomous air corps and more aviators assigned to the Army General Staff. Since naval aviation was integral to the navy and that service already had its own BuAer, more aviators should be assigned to the CNO's office and to BuNav. In particular, such men "must be of the temper of mind to appreciate not only the special needs of aviation but the needs of" the army and navy "as a whole." Aviation commands in both services should be held only by qualified aviators, who might be given temporary higher ranks if necessary, and Congress should allocate more and improved aircraft over the next five years.[65]

These carefully measured recommendations reflected the like minds and temperaments of Dwight Morrow and Jack Towers. Although Towers opposed the granting of extra numbers to speed the promotion process, a solution he regarded as a stigma, he was willing to compromise. Captains, commanders, and lieutenant commanders in aviation could be given extra numbers "at their own request," which would enable Towers to try and advance on his own ability and thus pave the way for aviation eventually to take over the navy itself. In any case, the board specified that only qualified aviators should command carriers, seaplane tenders, and other flying units. No mention was made of aviation observers for top aviation commands.[66]

President Coolidge, not taking time even to ponder the report, accepted it in toto and instructed the board members to draw up enabling legislation. "Now that the smoke of battle has cleared away," Towers wrote Pierre on 1 December, "things are beginning to quiet down." Dwight Morrow continued to rely on him to help draft the new laws, and the two spent one Sunday afternoon discussing who the new assistant secretary of the navy for aeronautics should be. Towers had just the man for the job and Morrow concurred: a technical adviser to the Morrow Board itself, Professor Edward P. Warner of M.I.T. The thirty-six-year-old aeronautical engineer's credentials were unassailable, and he would get the job the following July.[67]

In one final dispute, after Towers had left Washington, Admiral Moffett streamlined the naval observer's course by requiring all candidates, even captains the age of fifty, to log a minimum of 100 hours in the cockpit with a pilot at the controls. By contrast, a qualified pilot needed 200 hours aloft, including soloing. Neither the airmen nor the admirals liked such a compromise solution. Moffett agreed with his fellow admirals that air station commanders need not be qualified aviators, but the Morrow-influenced congressmen insisted on it, to the satisfaction of Towers and the pilots.[68]

The Naval Aircraft Act of 1926 embodied all the above reforms and was matched within days by similar laws creating the Army Air Corps and the post of assistant secretary of war for aeronautics. Each act established a five-year thousand-plane procurement policy for both services. The monumental achievement of the Morrow Board and of ensuing legislation was to remove the major logjams for promotion and sea commands, though relations between the uniformed "brown-shoe" flyers and the "black-shoe" traditionalists of the "Gun Club" would still fester. Jack Towers had been a major catalyst of and contributor to the new program.

Both Towers and John Rodgers, though still relatively junior as commanders, were the senior-ranking pioneer aviators to whom Moffett now assigned captain's billets for their recent successes. Rodgers became Moffett's assistant chief of bureau, while Towers was promised command of the *Langley*. First, however, Jack had to prove his mettle for sea-going command by serving a year or so as the carrier's executive officer. That suited him fine, and in mid-December 1925 he turned down another job offer in New York.[69]

Much to his chagrin, Towers could not join his ship at San Diego until after Christmas, because the *Shenandoah* court would not hear Billy Mitchell again until the completion of his court-martial trial. On 17 December, the army found Mitchell guilty of insubordination and ordered him suspended from active duty at half-pay for five years. He then testified before the *Shenandoah* court and early the next year resigned from the service. His ideas on strategic bombing were years ahead of their time, and he had sealed his fate by his tactless manner. The *Shenandoah* court ended on Christmas Eve with opinion divided over the causes of the airship disaster. The navy's LTA program would continue because Admiral Moffett believed in it, and he was able to convince Congress and the navy that the *Shenandoah* disaster would probably not be repeated, for that airship had only been experimental.[70]

The Christmas season was thus a hectic one for Towers, and he planned a happy holiday for his children with friends in New Jersey. He was sabotaged by a homesick Nurse—without her, said Jack, "the whole organization would break down"—and he had to discharge his cook for "insolence." Matters improved as invitations to Christmas parties came in, including one at the home of T. Douglas Robinson, the assistant secretary of the navy. Jack had a long talk with him and found him to be a supporter.[71] Towers needed all the political support he could get after stepping on the toes of the uniformed hierarchy.

He spent the night before Christmas decorating a large tree for his children and wrapping their gifts. Nurse went to the movies with a girlfriend and the children retired, leaving Jack alone by the tree pouring out his heart in another long letter to his beloved across the ocean. "It is rather cold and the wind is whistling outside, and downstairs, some girl is playing and singing 'All Alone'," Irving Berlin's hit tune of 1924. "She sings very well, but why do you suppose she sings that song? It is hardly fair to lonely people. . . ."[72]

Towers devoted the next few days to "camping" in the apartment with Miss Pearce and the children and packing their six trunks for the transcontinental trip. On 29 December they boarded the train for Chicago, and from there went to California on the Sante Fe Limited. New Year's Eve found them racing across the Rockies, while a letter on board an ocean liner carried his next mailing address to Pierre: "Air Squadron, Battle Fleet, San Diego."[73]

8

CARRIER TACTICIAN

1926–28

The aircraft carrier seemed to hold the key to the future of naval aviation when Towers reported aboard the *Langley* as executive officer on 4 January 1926. After relieving Commander Gerry Child, however, he could only regard the uncomfortable 11,500-ton former collier as "this poor comic old ship." The girder-supported flight deck had been superimposed over the bridge, so that its occupants could not see to navigate; everything had to be done by telephone or orderly. She was therefore aptly nicknamed the Covered Wagon.

Worse, Towers' cabin sat high on the fantail, over which planes passed as they landed. "The cabin is the result of the efforts of two idiots," Jack complained to Pierre, "first, one who thought it would be a clever thing to carry homing pigeons on the ship (of course, if the ship moved, the poor things got lost) and the other who, when the pigeon idea was at last given up, decided to convert the pigeon house into the Executive Officer's Quarters! I really live in a pigeon cote, complete with sitting-room, bedroom and bath, all about the size of your hat. . . ."[1]

The captain of the *Langley,* only her second, Edward S. Jackson, had relieved Stiffy Doyle in mid-1924 and was due for a transfer; Towers expected to relieve him.[2] Although commissioned four years earlier, the ship had been operating with the fleet for only one. The carrier was the nucleus of Aircraft Squadrons, Battle Fleet, the so-called eyes of the battle line. Admiral S. S. Robison, the new commander in chief, U.S. Fleet, had his doubts about aviation. He had lost his staff gunnery officer in a plane crash the year before. An impressive performance by the *Langley* in fleet war games did not dispel Robison's anger at the airmen's demands that only they should command aviation units, and he apparently rejected Admiral Moffett's request to allow the junior Towers to succeed Captain Jackson in command of her. This forced Moffett to elicit a fresh promise from BuNav chief Shoemaker to give Towers the carrier under Robison's successor. Robison's staff tactical officer happened to be Commander Chester Nimitz, whose later distaste for Towers' political maneuvering may have stemmed from this period.[3]

As Towers knew all too well, the best way to sell aviation to the chain of command was by superior performance, and he could hope for no better person to demonstrate this than the new commander Aircraft Squadrons, Captain Joseph Mason Reeves. A hardboiled, demanding officer known as Bull since football days at the academy and as Billygoat for his goatee, he had decided at the Naval War College that inasmuch as the United States refused to match British battleship strength, aviation might make up for it. So he had taken the naval observer's course at Pensacola during the summer of 1925. At first, the pilots did not care for him, but gradually he won their respect and admiration by personally briefing squadron commanders. A superb and knowledgeable speaker, he would delight them with allusions to "those old coots who command battleships." As a type commander, he was entitled to be addressed as commodore.[4]

Finding Aircraft Squadrons too loosely run, and preoccupied with technical problems, Reeves had demanded a new operating doctrine from his pilots and increased the *Langley*'s operating complement from eight to fourteen planes. When the battle fleet conducted convoy-escort exercises off San Diego that month, January 1926, Towers was impressed. The morning of the first day out, for example, Lieutenant Spig Wead led six other fighters off the deck to intercept an incoming bombing strike, and this was followed by a second launch of equal strength. The battle fleet commander, Admiral C. F. Hughes, was equally impressed.[5]

That morning of 15 January the *Langley* chugged along at a standard speed of 9.3 knots. The former collier could only reach a top speed of 14 knots, sufficient for operating the aircraft of the day but not for keeping up with the 21-knot battleships. The 200-horsepower Vought UO-1 fighters of Wead's Fighting Squadron 2 (VF-2) produced a top speed of only 124 mph and a landing speed one-third of that. The *Langley*'s two hinged smokestacks were lowered to their horizontal position in order that the stack gases not create air disturbances over the flush deck when she turned into the wind to launch planes. Their speed of launch was important for effective defense of the ship, and Wead got the seven fighters off in a remarkable forty-one seconds, just under six seconds per plane. When a plane landed, its tailhook grabbed one of several horizontal arresting cables, while its cross-axle hooks caught wires stretching fore and aft to prevent the plane from going over the side or crashing into planes spotted (parked) forward on the 520-foot deck. One of the *Langley*'s tasks was to devise an effective crash barrier to prevent such calamities.[6]

Towers intended to learn the ropes firsthand. Ten landings and takeoffs were required to qualify as a carrier pilot. "No officer of my age [forty-one on 30 January] has ever landed an aeroplane on the deck of a carrier successfully (two crashed trying!)—but I believe I can fool them if I can just get a little practice," he confided to Pierre. "The old guard is still holding on and would be delighted, I know, if I broke my neck and got out of the way (naturally). However, I don't intend to do that." But the attempt would have to wait, for the *Langley* was scheduled to participate in the annual winter fleet problem in Central American waters.[7]

Towers rented a bungalow from an old friend for Nurse and the children, while another returned his pet terrier to him. "We have Tykie back!" Jack announced in a letter. After nearly three years of separation, "he knew me and nearly went wild with joy." After passing his annual physical and receiving another waiver for his inferior depth perception, he pushed the crew to prepare for the day- and nighttime carrier-pilot-qualification operations off San Diego.[8]

Appointed one of the umpires for Fleet Problem VI, Towers flew to San Pedro for the final planning conference on 26 January. Separate elements of the U.S. Fleet were to attack each other in various tactical situations, this to be followed by a general fleet attack on the defenses of the Panama Canal. Commodore Reeves was determined that his ship and her planes would make an impressive showing. During the voyage south, the *Langley* was integrated with the battleships in a relatively new and successful circular defensive formation devised by Commander Nimitz. As "enemy" cruisers and destroyers attacked the battleships and carrier over several days, the Covered Wagon retaliated with her UO scout-fighters. Escorting destroyers provided an antisub screen around the *Langley* at night. The duties of umpiring forced Towers to remain at his post almost continuously, day and night, until the games ended. On 16 February the ships anchored together at steamy Balboa for a week of tactical analysis, upkeep, and liberty.[9]

The combined U.S. Fleet sortied again on 23 February. On the twenty-sixth the *Langley* and the gunships headed back in for a dawn "bombardment" of the canal, Towers expecting sure defeat at the mercy of the many defending army bombers. The battleships and carrier planes executed their attacks without difficulty, however, then headed in to anchor. At the critique, Admiral Robison concluded that a surface bombardment could not overcome the canal's defenses, but that combined with an aerial bombing attack it might very well succeed—a noteworthy kudo.[10]

The regimen in the tropics proved exhausting to the exec of the *Langley*. The greatest irritation of his grueling schedule was an utter lack of privacy. Even Towers' mail stimulated the curiosity of his shipmates. When a bundle of European letters was handed to him during a meeting with Captain Jackson and visiting army officers, "the Captain said with a smile, 'I see you have not severed foreign relations!' "[11]

On the leisurely return voyage to San Diego, word was received of Captain Jackson's impending transfer but nothing yet about who would relieve him. The most important thing for Jack to do was to qualify as a full-fledged carrier pilot, and he immediately began refresher training at North Island. The first step was learning to handle a single-seat fighter, since most of his flying had been in seaplanes. After a few days at it, he noted, "For an 'ancient mariner' I am really getting along pretty well! None of my contemporaries are allowed to fly fighters. I may 'bust' it, but I won't get hurt!"[12]

Between the ship's business and flying, Towers settled into a busy but well-ordered life. The *Langley* normally put to sea early four mornings a week to qualify pilots, then returned late in the day. Towers spent Sundays swimming and taking car rides with his children, sometimes to the cinema. Aside from an occasional Saturday night dance at the local country club, however, he preferred to keep his own social company, even rejecting invitations to play bridge, and continued his long letters to Pierre. In addition to his endless financial woes, he now learned that her family preferred that she remain in France and marry there instead of relocating in the United States to be close to him. He liked the idea of her coming but feared marriage: "I have been so miserable because of my first mistake that I want absolutely not to drag you into another. . . ." He warned her of how much older he was than she, all the while needing her desperately.[13]

Towers' devotion to his children governed his personal actions. At sea he missed them and at home tried to fill the parental vacuum. In the fall he would have to return them to Lily in New York, much against their wishes. If anyone would cheer him up, it was his ebullient old friend Pat Bellinger, Admiral Hughes' aviation officer, who flew down from San Pedro in mid-April to spend a few days. They celebrated Jack's first solo in a single-engine Vought on the nineteenth, then grieved when Spig Wead, skipper of Fighting 2, fell down some stairs and broke his neck, leaving him a paraplegic. The injury did not impair Spig's upper body, though, and he would soon receive his discharge and begin a successful career as a Hollywood screen writer for aviation films.[14]

As April drew to a close, Towers got wind of Admiral Robison's efforts to deprive him of his promised *Langley* command. He told Pierre, "They are trying apparently to keep me from getting command of the LANGLEY, because they say I am 'too young'! Of course, they want to give it to some Captain!. . . . I don't see how they can go back on their promises. . . ." He sent telegrams to friends at BuAer seeking information. Finally, on 12 May, "I discovered there is a regular conspiracy from the higher-ups of the Fleet . . . 'to protect the Navy from the movement to put aviators in command of carriers.' If it were not so serious, it would be comic!"[15]

Loyalty was being interpreted differently by different parties. Towers believed that by working for change within the system he was demonstrating his loyalty to the navy, fleet commander Robison felt the perpetrators of change were disloyal, while Admiral Hughes remarked to his aviation adviser Pat Bellinger, "When I first took command of this fleet [in October 1925] I thought aviation was disloyal and could not be trusted to do any job. I now feel that aviation is one of the most loyal forces in my command and that it will do its best to do the job no matter what it is."[16]

Towers learned that Admiral Moffett was going to work out an arrangement on his behalf, but in his frustration he wrote Pierre, "I shan't compromise this time! I would rather resign, but I cannot do that on account of the children. . . . [A]ll this hard work has been thrown away! . . . I seem to make a complete and utter failure of it, although they all say, 'He is an unusually capable officer!'" Embittered, and under the constant pressure of operations at sea, he sought a scapegoat in Bull Reeves, accusing him privately of building "a reputation for himself so that he will make rear admiral." Then Jack admitted, "If I didn't have something to complain about, I would be equally unhappy!" Under the circumstances, it wasn't easy for him to laugh at himself.[17]

Moffett did work a deal with the chief of BuNav, Admiral Shoemaker, about which Towers learned at the beginning of June: "They have done me out of command!—and said that they will give it to me in six months more, regardless of what opposition is offered. . . . The older officers advise me to stick on, the younger ones are very anxious for me to precipitate a crisis. What shall it be . . . ?" At least he learned that after Captain Jackson's transfer the interim skipper would be a good friend from wartime London days, Frank McCrary. According to Towers he did not want the job but was compelled to take it, being the "only captain aviator." But McCrary was a superb officer, idolized by many who served under him, and the other captains were still undergoing flight training or were primarily LTA men.[18]

Meanwhile, Pierre responded to Jack's letters of despair by scolding him for his negative attitude and seeking details about the alleged "conspiracy": "And where is that man Rodgers, who is in the same case as you, more or less?" In fact, John Rodgers, assistant chief of BuAer, had just been selected for captain, being four years senior to Towers; he was to be promoted as soon as a vacancy occurred in the list of captains. Rodgers was planning another long-distance flying boat trip, first cross-country to San Francisco in the fall, then to Honolulu the next summer, his second try. Tragically, he would crash while landing at Philadelphia late in August and die from his injuries the next day.[19]

Towers decided to stick it out for the time being. In May his friend Dick Byrd became the first person to fly over the North Pole, an immense achievement. On the twentieth his old compatriot from NC days, Lieutenant Commander Pete Mitscher, reported aboard the *Langley* as senior flight officer. The ship continued to qualify pilots, several destined to command carriers in World War II, notably VF-1 skipper Lieutenant G. F. "Jerry" Bogan.[20] On 5 June Towers threw a farewell cocktail party for Captain Jackson a week before his relief.[21]

Soon thereafter, despite a hectic schedule, Jack decided to attempt to qualify as a carrier pilot, fearing only "the mortification if I don't get away with it. No Commander has ever done it, so I really should not mind (but I WOULD!)." On 15 June he went up with Lieutenant (jg) Andy Crinkley for a run-through. Two mornings later, he followed Pete Mitscher in making two successful landings on the *Langley* to become "the only Commander who has got away with it, the young pilots thinking that it was something they only had the skill and courage to try!" Over the next two days he completed his ten required arrested landings to become "a qualified carrier pilot, the oldest and most senior in the world!"[22]

The many carrier takeoffs and landings proved the soundness of the newly fashioned wire crash barrier and also resulted in continuing improvements to the ship's arresting gear. During July Captain McCrary took accrued leave time, Towers assuming command of the *Langley* during the intensive qualification operations of two observation squadrons. The qualifying pilots comprised a who's who of future wartime carrier leaders and part of the Towers team: Lieutenants Arthur Radford, Donald Duncan, Thomas Sprague, Calvin Durgin, Jock Clark, and Miles Browning. And reporting aboard for a month to learn the ropes was Towers' old compatriot Commander Spuds Ellyson, prospective exec of the *Lexington*.[23]

Commodore Reeves hoped to increase speeds of launch and recovery in order to enhance the carrier's ability to protect herself from enemy planes and to rearm and refuel quickly for continuous scouting and attacking operations. It was grueling work. Towers spent day and night on the flight deck with Mitscher observing everything, impossible from the masked bridge. Movie cameramen filmed crashes to help analyze their cause, and Jack hurt his knee jumping into a net "when a pilot let his plane get away from him and nearly knocked us off the flight deck!" But he could report by the end of July that they had broken "all records for landing on board."[24]

The days when the *Langley* was not at sea, Towers sharpened his own skills by flying from the air station at North Island. He flew solo, in direct violation of his medical ruling to fly with a second pilot. Yet even at age forty-one he was as good a pilot as ever, dodging fog and strong winds on one particularly hair-raising hop. In more typically clear San Diego skies, the trouble was dodging planes: "About 200 . . . are flying here off this island, and one has to keep . . . a close watch to avoid collision. . . ."[25]

Progress in aviation was rapid. The *Langley* was suddenly ordered to prepare for departure to join the battle fleet at Seattle, then to return via San Francisco, conducting air operations throughout. Early in the new year, the carrier would accompany the battle fleet to the Caribbean and then to the East Coast. By that time Towers should be in command and reunited with Pierre if she could come to America. Though he feared he would have to remain on sea duty for at least two more years to get his promotion, he wrote, "Let's start thinking about it, darling." "It" was marriage. Meanwhile he devoted time to his children before they rejoined their mother in New York and socialized with well-to-do acquaintances at Rosarita Beach in Mexico, thirty miles south of San Diego and where liquor was still legal.[26]

On 6 August, in a "grand rush," the Covered Wagon took on "dozens of aeroplanes, tons of stores, hundreds of men," and even Towers' dog Tyke, then shoved off. Two of the planes were Curtiss F6C-2 Hawks, the newest and fastest navy fighters—400 horsepower for 150 mph. Bull Reeves wanted to see if the *Langley* could handle such powerful planes. The ship, in Towers' words, was "a perfect mass of men and aeroplanes. It is almost impossible to walk about the decks, on account of the congestion." Planes were launched on the seventh, the commodore timing each takeoff and landing with a stopwatch. Launch intervals were beginning to average fifteen seconds, the landings ninety—longer than hoped but still admirable.

Two days later, Reeves told Pete Mitscher and VF-1's Jerry Bogan that he wanted to set a record for one day's operations. Bogan protested that the ship was pitching too badly from high winds across the bow, but the attempt was made anyway. Several planes were damaged in the process and one crashed at sea, the pilot being rescued. Late in the day, as the *Langley* approached a heavy mist, twelve planes rushed aboard in twenty-one minutes. The record was set—127 landings in a single day. Only terrier Mr. Tyke was unimpressed, Jack wrote to Pierre—"the aeroplane engines frighten him to death."[27] Reeves, delighted with the *Langley*'s achievement, recommended that her official status as an experimental ship be changed to that of a full-fledged combatant, believing she could double her aircraft component to twenty-eight machines. Jack thought such crowding was too dangerous.

After arriving in Seattle, Towers avoided official parties and the pilots' makeshift saloon at a local hotel, unlike the fun-loving Spuds Ellyson, preferring to remain aboard and read. At San Francisco the *Langley* received a new navigator, Lieutenant Commander D. C. "Duke" Ramsey, a pilot with a sound intellect and tactfulness that were already paying dividends for naval aviation. Ramsey would soon become another member of the Towers team.[28]

Secretary of the Navy Curtis Wilbur spent 1 September on board observing flight operations off San Pedro, which underscored the high command's increasing interest in carrier aviation. Three days later Admiral Hughes relieved Robison as commander in chief, U.S. Fleet, clearing the way for Towers to get command of the *Langley* at the end of the year. The new battle fleet commander was Admiral Richard Jackson, Jack's old admirer from the NC flight. In the midst of air operations during September, Admiral Moffett arrived from Washington with Ed Warner, the new assistant secretary (aeronautics), to observe tactical exercises, and Admiral Hughes spent a day aboard. Frank McCrary, Pat Bellinger, and Duke Ramsey all qualified as carrier pilots.[29]

In the meantime Jack was juggling personal crises: food poisoning from bad clams, a sick son, a Tykie "nearly killed by three dogs who jumped on him all at once," and worst of all, a nurse who confessed that during his recent absence she had married her boyfriend because she was pregnant. Towers counseled her to seek an annulment and flew ashore to testify in court on her behalf. The annulment went through, and Miss Pearce had an abortion.[30]

Ordered north to Monterey Bay to participate in Navy Day festivities on 22 October, Aircraft Squadrons made a deep impression on the fleet as the battleships sortied from San Pedro. Eighteen new F6C-2 Hawks of Fighting 2 came screaming down in nearly vertical dives from 12,000 feet, a dramatic demonstration of dive-bombing led by Lieutenant Commander Frank D. Wagner, who had been working on the technique for months. Since defense against it seemed impossible, dive bombing now progressed alongside fighting and torpedo-launching as carrier missions.[31]

Towers began to put his life in order. He scraped up money to send the children and Miss Pearce to live with Lily in her Central Park apartment in New York, although Miss Pearce soon quit in a huff over Lily's difficult ways. No longer burdened by her wages, and having given up his Coronado house to live on board, Jack saved enough to start paying off his debts. He repaid social obligations by throwing a big cocktail party for Admiral and Mrs. McNamee, making his own bathtub gin for the occasion. His two comforts were his books and the scrappy Tyke, whose dogfight wounds were unfortunately reopened when he was run over by a bicycle. The good news was that Pierre was definitely coming to New York in the new year to see if the old fire was still there.[32]

Progress in carrier aviation continued steadily with the arrival of an improved F6C-4 Hawk. Its 400-horsepower air-cooled radial Pratt and Whitney Wasp engine would replace the existing liquid-cooled in-line affair. Such new and heavier models required structural changes to the *Langley,* and she went to the Mare Island shipyard in San Francisco during late November and December.[33]

Towers finally received word that he would relieve McCrary in command of the *Langley* on 4 January 1927. "I will be in command for the big winter cruise and the trip to New York," he rejoiced. It will "be rather good fun and not nearly so much work if I get a good officer for the job I now have (as good as I am in it!)." This would be Lieutenant Commander R. R. "Rip" Paunack, an aviator since 1916. After a round-trip Christmas trip to San Diego, he proclaimed to Pierre, "This is going to be a good year. I take command in four days, and you will be coming to New York!"[34]

Though he lacked captain's stripes, Towers was ably qualified for command of the 11,500-ton carrier. Commander Eugene E. Wilson, soon to join Reeves' staff, recalled Towers' reputation as "one of the best ship handlers in the whole service." While exec under Jackson and McCrary, Jack had streamlined the *Langley*'s administration and insisted on shipboard smartness and cleanliness, reflecting his own ordered mind, habits, and personal appearance. And Jack knew how to delegate authority. Anticipating the day he would finally get the *Langley,* he had observed in March, "I won't be able to do all the details just as I want them, for a skipper must not meddle too much with details." His executive officer and department heads had that responsibility, especially navigator Duke Ramsey and air officer Ralph E. Davison.[35]

The fourth of January 1927 was the big day for Towers. He took the *Langley* to sea at dawn and assembled her crewmen aft on the flight deck for the change-of-command ceremony at 0900. Then he settled into new and better quarters, which confused Mr. Tyke, who kept trotting back to the other cabin. Jack plowed through a mass of confidential papers and made several official calls "wearing the comic 'chapeau' "—the fore-and-aft hat in use since the founding of the navy. Jack Towers finally had his first major seagoing command.[36]

The *Langley* made a long run up to Seattle in mid-month. Still without an exec, Towers had to take the ship through the dangerous waters of Puget Sound in the midst of a raging storm. He underwent his annual physical exam on board and eventually received the usual waivers for his eyes. In the course of the three-day visit, twenty-seven brand-new FB-5 fighters were ferried out to the ship on lighters from the shoreside Boeing factory. Assigned to VF-1 and VF-6, the staggered-wing planes could cruise at 150 mph and were capable of operating at altitudes to 19,000 feet.[37]

Back at San Diego, a torrential winter storm greatly inhibited the loading of a record thirty-six aircraft, men, and supplies, but Towers met the schedule and sortied with the battle fleet on 17 February, bound for New York. The *Langley* was carrying sixty-five officers and over six hundred men. After a wardroom dinner at which Jack was the guest of his officers, he darkened ship and commenced maneuvering in antisubmarine night formations, throughout which he had to remain on the bridge. Before dawn on 3 March the *Langley*'s Vought and Boeing fighters protected the battleships against defending army planes and attacked the defenses of the Panama Canal. Both missions succeeded admirably. The ships then anchored in Panama Bay for German beer and parties at the Union Club in Balboa.[38]

Towers wryly noted the presence of interested foreign eyes. He dined with the Italian naval attaché, "down here spying on the Fleet" for Mussolini's fascist regime. There was also a British cruiser there. The Royal Navy, as usual, was everywhere.

Jack was disturbed when Jerry Bogan of VF-1 reported one morning sporting "a beautiful shiner." Explained the pug-nosed Bogan to his skipper, "Some little matter had to be attended to, sir." In fact, he had acquired the black eye after replying physically to another officer's disparaging remarks about Towers. The closely knit team of carrier airmen was fighting for recognition at every level.[39]

Towers took the *Langley* through the canal on 7–8 March and proceeded to Guantanamo Bay in Cuba to join the seaplane tender *Wright,* aviation flagship of the scouting fleet. While the *Langley* was operating with the battle fleet out of "Gitmo" and from Gonaives, Haiti, tragedy struck: Commander Cabby Cabaniss, skipper of the tender *Aroostook* and Jack's classmate, was killed in the crash of a PN-9 flying boat. He was replaced by Commander Vic Herbster.[40]

Fleet Problem VII, conducted in these Caribbean waters during March and April, was witnessed by Assistant Secretaries Robinson and Warner. The *Langley* provided air cover for the Blue Fleet as it escorted a large convoy setting out to capture an enemy base. Everything went smoothly until the last day when, after the *Langley* had just recovered her planes, a force of twenty-five planes from the Black Fleet attacked the blue force with a crippling blow. U.S. Fleet commander Hughes was suitably impressed by such naval air power, and Bull Reeves demanded more tactical freedom.[41]

The fleet and its lone carrier proceeded thence to New York. As the *Langley* entered the harbor on 29 April an exhaust generator exploded, temporarily disabling the vessel but not injuring anyone. Towers' excitement mounted when he received word of Pierre's anticipated arrival by ocean liner on 3 May. Regrettably, he had to attend an official dinner that evening at the Hotel Astor. So he sent a wire to her ship instructing her to contact his friend Grover Loening when she arrived. Upon reaching the hotel, however, he entered the revolving glass doors and saw Pierre on the opposite side. Their eyes fixed on each other for the first time in over twenty months, and they went round and round in the revolving door. The magic, it seemed, was still there.[42]

Jack arranged for Pierre to stay at his brother Fullton's apartment. Over the next few days they attended Broadway shows and visited with his children. They decided to continue their courtship; Pierre would move to a hotel. With her credentials as a high-fashion model and dress designer, she got a job designing costumes for the Gershwin-Astaire hit show "Funny Face," then

The *Langley* is anchored among no fewer than seven battleships of the Battle Fleet at Port Culebra, Panama Canal Zone, March 1927. (National Archives)

joined Saks Fifth Avenue. Later she would open a French salon for Gimbel's department store. They agreed that Jack should remain in the navy and return with his ship to the West Coast; they would stay in touch by mail and occasional long-distance telephone calls. Their relationship would be a difficult one, to be sure, but at least now only a continent would separate them.[43]

With the *Langley* in dry dock at New York, Towers testified before a navy board to confirm many policies already being instituted at the tactical level, such as the priority of fighters over other carrier plane types. He met with Moffett and BuAer's assistant chief Jerry Land, whose cousin Charles Lindbergh left North Island on 9 May for a cross-country flight in his single-engine plane to Long Island. From there Lindbergh took his monumental solo flight across the Atlantic on 20–21 May—eight years to the week after the NC expedition. Not far behind was Dick Byrd, who would fly across the "great moat" at the end of June.[44]

After maneuvers off Newport, Rhode Island, Towers began the return voyage to San Diego. The *Langley* stopped at Hampton Roads for test landings and takeoffs by Jerry Bogan in the experimental Boeing XF3B-1 single-seat fighter and Martin XT4M-1 three-seat torpedo-bomber, prototypes of the planes for the big new carriers. On 4 June the *Langley* launched ten planes as she passed in review before Calvin Coolidge in the presidential yacht *Mayflower*. After transiting the Panama Canal, she rejoined the battleships for a dull cruise to San Diego. "Mr. Tyke," Towers wrote, "is getting as bored as his master with so much ocean. His new rubber balls have all bounced overboard, which has been a great cause of grief to him!" It was a relief to reach North Island on 27 June for a summer of daily flight operations, some with Jack in the cockpit.[45]

Towers enjoyed the chance to resume swimming and purchased a new swimsuit, shirt and shorts being the fashion, so brief that two girls "tried to persuade me to exchange with them as they like mine better than their own!" Beach parties at Ensenada south of the border, dances, and golf brought Towers much-needed relaxation—and outrage when county prohibition officers raided a party he attended in San Diego. When Pierre complained about the heat in New York, Jack responded that in America "the climate just goes to extremes, like the people." This offhand observation was about as political as Towers ever got. He did make a singular reference to President Coolidge: "He is a dull dog."[46]

On 17 August Towers was at a private cocktail party in the Hotel Del Coronado when an officer from the ship rushed in with orders from the fleet to return aboard immediately. When he arrived, he found the *Langley* already preparing to get under way on urgent instructions from the fleet commander, as Jack put it, "to look for the fools that tried to fly to Honolulu." Two out of fourteen planes racing from Oakland to Hawaii for prize money offered by the Dole pineapple company had disappeared en route. The *Langley* was to help find them.

Exec Rip Paunack was aboard, but navigator Duke Ramsey and 60 of the 410-man crew could not be located, in spite of urgent appeals over commercial radio. Worse, the navigational charts had been locked up and the keys to the chart locker were ashore with their custodian. But Towers knew the channel by heart. He had six *Langley* Vought scout-fighters and two Loening amphibians from the battleship *Colorado* hoisted aboard. Then he eased the ship away from the dock an hour before midnight, "flanked by *large* and continuous pots of coffee." It was a black night and the channel was narrow, but he managed to make it without a navigator.[47]

Running continuous air searches along the Great Circle course of the eastern Pacific from dawn to dusk each day for an entire week, Towers made all his available officers do double duty. Even the new air officer, Lieutenant Commander Robert P. Molten, Jr., flew searches, while the Loenings had to be hoisted aboard by crane after each patrol. Towers' own energy was strained when seven destroyers arrived to form a small task force. He was made its commodore but had no staff and got no more than three hours of sleep a night. By 25 August, Towers ended the futile search. The four aviators and one aviatrix of the two lost planes were never found, although two racers did reach Hawaii.[48]

On 30 August Jack welcomed Bull Reeves back from the abortive Geneva naval conference and in the rank of rear admiral. Secretary Wilbur arrived as well and so admired the *Langley*'s operations that he later sent Jack a letter praising her performance. For the first six months of Towers' command, said he, the *Langley* had "attained an improvement in merit in engineering of 1.349 over that of the previous year. This is the second highest improvement factor attained by any eligible vessel of the Tender Class."[49]

Four carrier fighter squadrons at North Island not only operated the improved Boeing FB and Curtiss F6C but also initiated the Boeing F2B and F3B into fleet operations. The only torpedo squadron traded in the old Martin SC for the new Douglas T2D, capable of dropping a 1,000-pound "fish." A few of the new planes crash-landed aboard but without fatalities, an unprecedented safety record that reflected favorably on the captain of the ship. Such progress drew curious eyes, as one July day when a British cruiser anchored very close by. Like all hands, Jack suspected correctly that Japanese agents were gleaning what data they could for the one *Langley*-size carrier they had and for two large conversions of the *Lexington* variety on the way.[50]

In mid-October 1927 U.S. Fleet commander Hughes, known because of his big handlebar mustache as the Walrus, inspected Aircraft Squadrons with Towers as senior officer present.[51] All went well. Then the *Langley* exercised in fog off Long Beach for three days before heading back to the harbor on the twenty-second. "It was too foggy to come in," Jack wrote Pierre, "even though I knew it was clear inside, for the Channel is very narrow. I was the first one to make the attempt, and when we got in, about fifty other ships followed." Towers' seamanship gave the lie to the oft-heard accusation that aviators could not perform as line officers. His crewmen liked and admired him for his cool professionalism. No fair judge could deny he was earning the right for promotion to captain when the time came for the Class of '06.[52]

Bull Reeves, determined to improve the striking power of his carrier planes, transferred dive bombing innovator Frank Wagner from command of VF-6 to be his tactical and gunnery officer, a newly created post. He also accepted as his chief of staff Commander Gene Wilson, a bright engineering specialist rushed through flight training before this first assignment to an aviation unit. His technical expertise proved essential, for Reeves wanted to increase the size of the flight deck to accommodate more aircraft—two full squadrons of eighteen planes each, plus some scouts. He wanted to lengthen the deck from 520 to 542 feet and to widen it by 10 feet to 65.[53]

Reeves' scheme brought him into direct conflict with Towers, who had not liked having thirty-six planes aboard during the East Coast trip. Though favoring increased bombing missions for fleet aviation, Jack thought that no more than twenty-seven planes could be operated from the *Langley* with safety, even if the flight deck was lengthened. The October day Wilson had reported aboard Towers told him, "The allowed complement is 12 aircraft. He [Reeves] insists that we've got to carry three times that many. Now, if he persists in that course, we'll have an accident, and the first time we kill somebody on *Langley,* the aircraft carrier development will go down the drain." To emphasize his point, he showed Wilson the films taken of crackups on the ship.[54]

When Towers urged Wilson to persuade Reeves to change his mind, Wilson demurred, saying his job was "to help the Old Man carry out his program, not hinder him." Wilson really had no choice. Since he was a Johnny-come-lately to aviation, the younger pilots decided to haze him by requiring him to take his carrier quals. They thought he would fail. Instead he succeeded handily after only a week of training at Ream Field. The young bloods were not amused. Neither was Admiral Reeves when he learned of Jack's entreaties to the new chief of staff. But having high regard for his flag captain, Reeves decided to bring Jack around by experimenting gradually.[55]

Reeves' decision to have the flight deck enlarged also foiled Jack's plans to take a long leave and spend Christmas in New York with Pierre and his children. The *Langley* would now require his presence at the Mare Island Navy Yard throughout December, which meant a lot of headaches. At least Pat Bellinger flew down for a "last fling" before being detached. Jack's affection for his old pal was undiminished. "One of the nicest men I ever knew," Jack wrote Pierre, then added wryly, he "has a wife and two children, but contrary to a lot of people, still enjoys life immensely."[56]

The *Langley*'s departure for Mare Island was suddenly delayed a month. Towers hoped to wrangle orders for himself "to get East in January for consultation on new designs of aircraft carriers" but was turned down since the *Langley* continued qualifying pilots.[57]

One thing that bothered Towers about the *Langley* was her gasoline system, which he regarded as faulty and therefore dangerous, a fact he reported several times. For the ship carried up to 140,000 gallons of high-test aviation gas.[58] At 0946 the morning of 20 December, while several men were departing for liberty, a huge explosion suddenly rocked the ship and flames shot up through vents on the port side of the flight deck. The blast burned crewmen and knocked several unconscious and others overboard. It tore a hole in the side of the ship above the waterline, ruptured and dented bulkheads, and caused a bulge in the flight deck between frames 43 and 50. Fire call sounded the alarm.

One of the topside fuel tanks had exploded, and the burning oil and gas sent clouds of black smoke billowing from the puncture. Towers sprang into action to direct the rescue work, while alert firemen managed to plug a burst six-inch pipe leading to the main fuel tank. Since that tank contained 60,000 gallons of aviation gas, this quick thinking saved many lives and possibly the ship. Three navy tugs moved alongside and played steam, chemicals, and finally water on the fire and smoke, and rescue parties from the *Aroostook* and the air station rushed to the stricken carrier. The firefighters "had to stand on top of the tanks to fight the fire," Jack reported, "and I really expected any instant to see a flash and know nothing more."[59]

Thankfully, no additional explosion occurred, and at 1100 the ship secured from fire quarters. One man died from burns, and four others were burned severely. The danger was not over, however, since all remaining gasoline had to be drained from the ruptured tanks and it leaked into adjacent spaces, spreading fumes through the ship. For two whole weeks men descended into the big tanks wearing gas masks.

When the task was finally completed, damage control experts swarmed over the *Langley* seeking the cause of the explosion. It was never determined, for there had been "no wires, nor fires, and no men around." The crew, however, believed that a sailor had inadvertently tossed a lighted cigarette that had touched off escaping gas fumes. In any event, the ship's gasoline stowage would now be reduced to 50,000 gallons and the system converted to the safer arrangement used on battleships. Reflecting on his eye injury from the *Kentucky* accident and his several mishaps in aviation, Jack wrote, "Certainly, I am unusually lucky. . . ."[60]

The court of inquiry, consisting of four pilots, absolved Towers of any blame for the explosion, for indeed he had often warned of the danger of gasoline fumes in the *Langley*. When the evidence was finally accepted by the Navy Department a lamentably long eighteen months later, Towers was in fact recommended for a commendation. Unaccountably, this paperwork was lost until 1935, at which time he was finally praised "for the measures you took immediately after the explosion to fight the fire and to prevent further explosion. Your coolness and courage in the face of danger, combined with your vigorous action in suppressing the fire, are responsible to a high degree for the prevention of a catastrophe."[61]

The departure to Mare Island had to be delayed again while emergency repairs were made. These, along with the *Langley*'s overhaul and modification, were vitally important, for the newly completed carriers *Saratoga* and *Lexington* were due to arrive on the West Coast early in the new year. Admiral Reeves was still determined to increase the *Langley*'s regular air complement from the paltry twelve preferred by Towers to forty-two, over half the size of each of the big carriers' aircraft complements. And he wanted it done in time for Fleet Problem VIII in April 1928, for he intended that the Covered Wagon operate as a full-fledged battle line carrier instead of an experimental vessel. So before the ship left for Mare Island, the admiral had Gene Wilson instruct Towers to make certain that the shipyard install accommodations for the additional air crews for forty-two planes.[62]

After a run north during which a potentially dangerous fire erupted and a storm tossed the *Langley* about, Towers brought her into San Francisco on 23 January 1928. Next day his flight physical revealed that the vision in his right eye had dropped below normal, and a civilian specialist thought a cataract might be forming. Over the next two months the flight deck was lengthened twenty-three feet and widened and the ship overhauled and repaired. Additional arresting wires were added, and indirect lighting was installed for flight-deck operations at night. Additional berthing spaces, however, were not installed for the air crews. Though Towers would blame C&R for this oversight, he was surely dragging his feet to frustrate Reeves' program for increased planes.[63]

In answer to a suggestion from Pierre that she leave New York and join him in California, Jack replied that his days in southern California were numbered. He expected to be transferred to Washington during the summer, since "my time on the *Langley* is already up, and several other Captains want my job. . . . Besides," he said, his high-style tastes showing, "I hate Los Angeles, and so would you. It is a poisonous place, full of poisonous people, newly rich." So while Pierre remained in the East, Jack played golf in the San Francisco Bay area, often with shipyard commandant, Rear Admiral John H. Dayton. One day Jack made the mistake of taking Mr. Tyke to the links. The frisky terrier chased rabbits and Jack's ball, "sneaked over to a tee where another group was about to drive off and stole one of their balls, and brought it to me! It was Admiral Dayton's. . . ." Out came the leash.[64]

Towers flew down to San Diego late in February to coordinate plans for the *Langley*'s part in the forthcoming fleet problem and to meet with the officers of the *Saratoga,* which had just arrived in southern California. There he learned that Admiral Henry Wiley, the new commander in chief U.S. Fleet, had approved Bull Reeves' proposal to put two fighting squadrons and several scouts on the *Langley.* According to Duke Ramsey, aviation officer to Wiley, there was concern that her flight-deck extension might not hold. Jack discussed matters with Reeves' staff and the *Saratoga's* officers. Their deliberations were marred by the shocking news that early on the twenty-seventh Commander Spuds Ellyson, exec of the *Lexington,* had disappeared over the Chesapeake Bay in a Loening amphibian; his body was not found until forty days later. He had perished on his forty-third birthday. Towers, a month older, was now the senior surviving aviator of the earliest pioneers.[65]

Going aboard the *Saratoga,* Jack saw for himself the first major evidence of the offensive potential of carrier aviation. Her 36,000-ton displacement dwarfed the mere 11,500 tons of the *Langley.* Driven by 180,000-horsepower engines, the "Sara" had a top speed of thirty-three knots, making her a truly fast carrier; the Covered Wagon could not keep up at even half that speed. With a flight deck stretching 888 feet and flanked by a towering island superstructure, the *Saratoga* could operate seventy-two planes (compared with the *Langley's* new 542 feet of flush deck and only twelve to forty-two planes, depending on whether Towers or Reeves had his way). With no fewer than eight 8-inch guns, the *Saratoga* had considerably more defensive clout than the *Langley's* paltry four 5-inchers. Her crew exceeded two thousand men, quadruple that of the *Langley.* And sister ship *Lexington* was now en route to California to match the *Saratoga's* power.[66]

When Mare Island completed its work on the *Langley,* Towers brought her back to San Diego at the end of March and had to report to Gene Wilson that Reeves' desired accommodations for the enlarged air crew had not been added. A few days later, Towers and his officers were surprised to see "a procession of bluejackets" pushing fighters and scouts down the street toward the *Langley's* dock. Bull Reeves supervised the hoisting aboard of exactly forty-two and had Wilson and Frank Wagner park them tightly together. Then he announced, "Captain Towers, there is your complement." Before Jack could object that he lacked accommodations for the additional personnel, Reeves ordered every available carpenter at the air station to come aboard and build them.[67] Needless to say, Towers did not take kindly to Reeves' action.[68]

Admiral Wiley and Duke Ramsey agreed that the increased number of planes stretched the *Langley's* resources but decided to let Reeves try it. So the two fighting squadrons, totaling thirty Boeing F2Bs, plus six new Vought 02U Corsairs and six older scouts, were kept aboard for the upcoming war games. During all this hectic activity, on 4 April, as Jack was "going over the gangway to drive . . . to the golf course, who should I see strolling aboard but

Towers' *Langley* at San Diego in 1927, with thirty-four planes crammed topside, as Admiral Reeves preferred. (Towers collection)

Lindbergh." The now-famous but shy transatlantic solo flyer had landed at North Island to avoid a crowd waiting for him at the city airport. "I showed him over the ship and had quite a long talk with him, then we smuggled him over to San Diego in a boat."[69]

Next day the *Lexington* appeared off San Diego, then proceeded to San Francisco with the *Saratoga*. The *Langley* took two days to reach the Golden Gate, launching twenty-six planes outside the harbor for an aerial show, with VF-1 landing ashore when fog and rain shrouded the ship. The following day the carrier anchored. Her air crews were optimistic, part of the reason being increased safety measures during the forthcoming operations en route to the Hawaiian islands. There would be two plane guard tenders, inflatable flotation gear on each plane, one plane equipped as an airborne radio link between the *Langley* and her fighters, and a Corsair specially rigged for air-sea rescue. The two big carriers stayed in San Francisco, too new to join the war games.[70]

The *Langley* and the battle fleet comprised the Blue Fleet, which sortied from San Francisco on 18 April for the ten-day Fleet Problem VIII. The objective was to seize Honolulu, defended by the Orange Fleet, the air component of which consisted only of cruiser-based scouts and some Hawaiian-based patrol planes. The *Langley*'s singular mission was to scout for battleships, astern of which the Covered Wagon had to steam, much to the mortification of Bull Reeves. But the planes performed superbly, taking off each morning at daylight and leaving the ship "charging around at full speed," a mere fourteen knots. The fleet, darkened at night, swung to the southward to evade detection by Orange until the very end of the cruise. The high command admired the effective air cover provided by the *Langley*'s planes.[71]

As usual, Jack loved operating at sea and joined his crew on the flight deck each afternoon for ninety minutes "of strenuous exercise, all hands in bathing suits. . . . I never felt better, and should be in good shape to tackle the surf board riding at Waikiki. . . ." Jerry Bogan's VF-1B (the *B* now added for battle fleet) considered itself so special that it had adopted a high hat as its emblem. VF-6B, sporting a Felix the Cat emblem, was led by Lieutenant D. W. "Injun Joe" Tomlinson and was working up the navy's first aerobatic team, the Sea Hawks.[72]

On 29 April the *Langley* docked at Ford Island to commence almost daily operations around the islands. The only mishap occurred when a Vought UO spun in after clearing the deck, killing its pilot. This was the ship's first and only flying-related fatality under Towers' command. The airmen tended to blame it on the crowded conditions imposed by Admiral Reeves, but passions finally cooled; it was the price of progress in the deadly business of war. A near-disaster occurred when Bogan and nine fighters got lost during a Kona wind, which whipped up yellow volcanic dust that obscured the sea; they found the carrier only after the battleships made smoke.[73]

In mid-May Towers learned that, with the two new carriers unable to join the fleet officially, Reeves wanted him to remain with the *Langley* through the annual summer fleet concentration. The admiral did not want an inexperienced flag captain running his only carrier and advising him. This at least would enable Jack to enjoy his children, who were coming west for the summer.

Reeves ordered the *Lexington* to make a high-speed run from San Francisco to Hawaii, the progress of which all hands in the *Langley* followed with great interest. When she pulled into Pearl Harbor on 12 June, seventy-two hours and thirty-four minutes later, she had set a record for ships traveling 2,225 miles, having averaged nearly thirty-one knots. Reeves shifted his flag and the *Langley*'s planes to the *Lexington* and took her 250 miles to sea for an exercise against the army's defenses. She ran in at night and launched a dawn attack, taking Pearl Harbor completely by surprise—a harbinger of things to come.[74]

In Hawaii Towers was able to enjoy flying and other recreations, yet one may assume he also wrote discreet letters to Admiral Moffett urging his early detachment. For over strenuous objections, Bull Reeves soon received word that Towers would indeed be transferred ahead of schedule to Washington. Relations between the two men remained formal, especially after the scrappy Tyke had a run-in with Punch, Reeves' bull terrier. "Mr. Tyke is in disgrace," reported Towers, for he won the fight. "The Admiral is very annoyed. . . ."[75]

In late June the *Langley* returned to the West Coast with the fleet, whereupon the intensive summer concentration began. Anxious to beef up the offensive capabilities of his new three-carrier force, Reeves reshuffled his squadrons, designating two of his four fighting squadrons as light-bombing units (VBs) and assigning them and the torpedo squadrons (VTs) to the big carriers. He kept the carrier-based scouts in scouting squadrons (VSs) and left the spotters on the battleships and cruisers as observation units (VOs). So to Towers' relief the *Langley* was reduced to eighteen fighters and six scouts.[76]

Reeves then trained his squadrons relentlessly, mostly off the *Langley*. Beginning early in July and continuing for five straight weeks, Towers took her to sea early and returned late each weekday. No fewer than 945 landings were made, one-sixth the total landings since her commissioning in 1922. Ninety-four novices qualified after ten landings, eleven of them fledglings who did it all in a single day. Whereas one crash per thirteen landings was the average from 1925 to 1927, during these five weeks it was only one per 28.6 landings. Towers' safety consciousness had paid off, earning him a letter of commendation. Admiral Reeves added his own congratulations: "You . . . were responsible for the splendid performance" of the *Langley*, "due largely to your zeal, iniative [*sic*] and high qualities of leadership."[77] As for the ship, she received the Engineering Trophy and Efficiency Pennant.[78]

Jack occupied the Coronado bungalow of a friend to spend time with Marjorie and Chas during a few days' leave. The children had a new Swiss governess, along with a horse and another wire terrier that came with the house. Mr. Tyke teamed up with this worthy to pick fights with nearly every dog in the neighborhood.

One of Towers' last activities while in command of the *Langley* was making the ship and her planes available for movie makers at San Diego. He welcomed back Spig Wead, down "from Hollywood as Technical Director in a large motion picture concern, drawing a big salary and enjoying life though he is partially paralyzed." Spig had written the screenplay for "The Flying Fleet" and provided technical advice during the shooting that summer of 1928. "I knew all the cast intimately of course," Jack later told his brother Will, which included the star of the film, Ramon Navarro.[79]

On 19 August Towers received orders detaching him from the *Langley* for assignment as head of the plans division at BuAer, an interesting job but one fraught with the political infighting he loathed. Handing over the reigns of the Covered Wagon to Rip Paunack without ceremony a week later, he took his leave, began packing, and attended a round of farewell parties in his honor. Leaving the nine-year-old Mr. Tyke with friends to live out his last days, Jack boarded the Santa Fe Chief with his children on 11 September, bound for New York and Pierre.[80]

In thirty-two months aboard the *Langley,* twenty as her captain, Towers had remolded the navy's first carrier from an experimental platform into a clean, efficient, first-class fighting ship. His clash with Bull Reeves over the size of her aircraft complement had been both unfortunate and understandable, Jack having safety uppermost in his mind. He had been wrong, as events showed. Reeves was shaping the navy's fast carrier tactics, even though that meant pushing the old *Langley* to the limit. Still, Towers had proved equal to the task. Their combined efforts were already bearing fruit. Just four months later, in January 1929 during Fleet Problem IX, Reeves used the *Saratoga* in independent operations to launch a revolutionary surprise air attack on the defenses of the Panama Canal.

The age of the aircraft carrier had begun.

9

CHIEF OF AIR STAFFS,
ASHORE AND AFLOAT
1928–33

According to Commander Gene Wilson, Jack Towers "had a natural flair for politics," a view shared by others. "However, like many pioneer aviators he tended to believe that once he'd learned to fly, he'd taken on angel's wings, become a different breed from the common run. In some cases it was true, and in other cases it wasn't. Towers was a man of very great ability" who "liked to play politics."[1]

Wilson was only partially correct. Through the many struggles Towers had had to wage since taking to the air, by 1928 he had developed a keen sense of political savvy, within the navy and outside it. That he enjoyed political battles was not true. "I detest the thought of office work," he wrote Pierre immediately upon his arrival in Washington, "and the necessary intrigue which usually accompanies it." In fact, he later admitted to Admiral Moffett that he had reported to his job as head of the BuAer's plans division very reluctantly.[2]

His new boss lacked Towers' style as a meticulous, adept manager and left details to subordinates to concentrate on political and policy battles, exuding both charm and toughness in his dealings with congressmen and admirals alike. Moffett rarely explained his decisions to his officers; conversely, he signed virtually anything they put in front of him. He instilled supreme confidence in all who served under him, Towers included.[3] "I cannot recall any man who loved a fight and who could think of more ways to win one" than Moffett, remembered Towers. "His effectiveness . . . was due in large part to the fact that his opponents soon learned to be afraid of him, backed as he was by a host of friends who nearly always rallied to his support." This included presidents, congressmen, industrialists, journalists, and airmen. For Moffett was, according to Towers, "beloved by all who had the privilege of really knowing him."[4]

Moffett and Towers shared one overriding ambition—to integrate aviation into the navy so thoroughly that it would eventually become the striking heart of the fleet. They agreed that the primary vehicle was the aircraft carrier, though for long-range scouting roles Moffett favored the dirigible, Towers the flying boat. And they shared another ambition—to remain at the helm of naval aviation. Moffett had forsaken sea duty to accept a second four-year term as bureau chief in 1925; with this tour now drawing to a close, he intended to seek a rarely granted third term. Towers wanted to fill the post eventually, though as a commander he was still too junior. Moffett made clear to all that he was grooming Towers to be his successor.

In terms of service, experience, ability, and seniority as a flyer, Towers plainly deserved the post. Moffett consciously exploited his fame, especially from the NC expedition and from his survival in the Billingsley crash of 1913, to advance the cause of naval aviation. In January 1929 Congress finally authorized the issuing of the gold medals to the crew of the NC-4, whereupon Moffett had Towers added as a recipient. The month before that, when President Coolidge convened an international civil aeronautics conference in Washington to commemorate twenty-five years of heavier-than-air flight, Moffett sent Jack as the navy representative.[5]

When Towers reported to the bureau, 17 September 1928, he became privy to the old guard's attempt to rid the capital of Moffett. Admiral Hughes, the CNO, and Rear Admiral R. H. "Reddy" Leigh, chief of BuNav, were jealous of Moffett's political power and wanted to replace him with Bull Reeves. Naturally, if Moffett lost this fight, it might jeopardize Towers' future, for his disagreements with Reeves had not particularly endeared the two men to one another.[6]

Towers was among several officers Moffett asked for comments on a highly critical study headed by the assistant CNO, Rear Admiral William H. Standley. It singled out a fatal crash involving the commanding officer of NAS Pearl Harbor to condemn naval aviation for poor discipline. The Standley Report recommended abandoning the Morrow Board's requirement that aviators command aviation units and hold the key posts at BuAer. Towers replied to Moffett that no naval activity should be subjected to detailed examination "by a party so obviously hostile to the activity being investigated." The slack discipline at Pearl Harbor had been corrected, while the attack on the Morrow laws, as Towers suspected, served to reopen Billy Mitchell's drive for a separate air force under a unified department of national defense.[7]

Moffett and Towers were of one mind on practically everything, including their contempt for the crusty old guard. Since civilian attire was worn during working hours he could only guess the ranks of unknown men seen in the corridors of the Navy Department. "It will be rather amusing," he told Pierre on the eve of Navy Day, when all hands would be in uniform, "I will probably discover that some of the moth-eaten old fellows I have been seeing around the Navy Department and thinking were old civil service clerks, are Medical and Supply officers with the rank of Rear Admirals!"[8]

In three appearances before the General Board during his first month at the bureau, Towers faced his conservative seniors and with mixed results. When his advocate from NC days Admiral Jackson called on him to comment about increasing the number of spotting planes on battleships, Jack not only wanted to raise the two-plane complement per ship but resurrected his 1919 idea of a composite capital ship. The board cut him off. During a hearing on torpedo design he challenged Rear Admiral Frank H. Schofield, head of the war plans division, who wanted to stop inferior torpedo plane development on the grounds that it was wasteful; Jack asserted that even current torpedo planes could get in close to attack under cover of an aerial-laid smoke screen. The war plans division, however, did want more carriers, and Towers was called back to discuss the relative merits of single- versus two-seat fighters. He tended to favor the latter because of the additional rear-seat gun, but much depended on the performance of new experimental planes.[9]

Naval aviation welcomed the November election of Republican Herbert Hoover, seemingly disposed to reappoint Moffett. But within days Moffett learned of a two-year-old letter by Admiral Robison attacking the airmen for their role in the Morrow legislation, a blast Moffett regarded as indicative of navy attitudes toward aviation. Regarding Robison's criticism of Moffett for insisting that only aviators command carriers, Moffett explained to Duke Ramsey that he had never advocated this, "except in the case of Towers, who I thought in every way capable of performing the line duties in connection with it." The Morrow laws had not ended the controversy within the navy.[10]

Towers remained sensitive to all of Moffett's frustrations and maintained his own political contacts in the navy-wide struggle, among them Assistant Secretaries T. Douglas Robinson and Ed Warner and his former London boss Admiral McNamee, now director of fleet training. The *Saratoga's* highly publicized attack on the Panama Canal in Fleet Problem IX helped Moffett and Towers give persuasive testimonies for more funding before the House Naval Affairs Committee in mid-February 1929. Indeed Moffett even suggested the use of enemy carriers "in raiding operations . . . against docks in Pearl Harbor." And only days after Hoover's March inauguration, the new president recommended Moffett's reappointment as chief of BuAer, a decision approved by the new secretary of the navy, banker Charles Francis Adams, and Moffett's friends in the Senate.[11]

Even within the brown-shoe flying community, a serious political division existed between the younger pilots and the officers they regarded as mere opportunists—the naval aviation observers and those already in mid-career when they earned their pilot's wings. Needless to say, Towers was regarded as the "crown prince" of aviation by the "genuine" flyers. The more vociferous young bloods called the observers Kiwis—the Australian birds with no wings—and the latecomers Johnny-Come-Latelys (JCLs) and synthetics. The fact was, an aviator became a real pilot only *after* learning the rudiments of flying at Pensacola, namely, by engaging in aerial navigation, scouting, dogfighting, and squadron techniques, which the senior students had never done. Moffett defended these observers, among them Rear Admiral Bull Reeves, as a temporary expediency. The most promising JCL was Moffett's own assistant chief of bureau, Captain Ernie King. With enough senior men wearing observer's wings, Moffett terminated the observer program in 1930 and placed the future of naval aviation in the hands of a few more JCLs and the experts epitomized by Towers.[12]

The Moffett-Towers preference for qualified aviators over observers partly accounted for the strain between Moffett and Reeves. In addition, Reeves' outspokenness on naval disarmament and on locating a West Coast dirigible field brought him into direct conflict with Moffett and the Navy Department, leading to a year of virtual exile on the General Board. Towers shared Moffett's suspicions about advancing officers belonging to Reeves' team. One of these was Gene Wilson, a JCL and engineer who, convinced that Towers would block his advancement, resigned late in 1929 to become a senior executive of the United Aircraft Corporation.[13]

Indeed, the endless infighting gave rise to several cliques, the Moffett-Towers team being one of the most determined. The naval aviation house had to be kept in order if it was to survive the relentless opposition of the Gun

Club, and Jack developed as strong a position as possible to remain at or near the helm. His zeal created another strain, between him and assistant BuAer chief Ernie King, that would cost him dearly in the future. Though a late-comer to the cockpit, King was a boon to BuAer's relationships with the other bureaus. The two men got along well enough within BuAer, though King had no use for the Towers group. Not surprisingly, he would recall that "Towers was an able man, but hard to work with." Coming from King, this was a backhanded compliment, since the very same criticism was leveled at him by his contemporaries.

King became an example of Moffett's insistence on unanimity within the bureau; when the two men disagreed over BuAer's relationship with BuNav, King asked to be reassigned. Moffett, admiring King's intelligence and ability, gave him command of NAS Hampton Roads in April 1929 and elevated Towers to King's vacated post as assistant chief of bureau. Not only was the job normally a captain's billet, but, Towers boasted to his brother Will, he became "the youngest officer who has ever had it and the youngest Assistant Chief of any Bureau in the entire Navy Department. . . ." The advancement alerted King to the extent of Towers' ambition.[14]

Jack renewed his social contacts in Washington and traveled often to New York to see Pierre and the children. The financial burden of voluntarily providing child support was lifted when Lily remarried in February, enabling him to pay off his debts and even to purchase a sporty LaSalle convertible—the same make car that Admiral Moffett drove. He missed Pierre terribly and ran up large telephone bills with calls to her in New York. Towers spent a good deal of time with Commander Wilder D. Baker, a submariner and destroyerman, making official calls on local dignitaries and attending navy football games in Annapolis. He found liquor flowing as freely as ever in prohibition Washington.[15]

In January Commander Frederick A. Ceres, a leading navy flight surgeon, passed Towers on the depth-perception test but since the vision in Jack's right eye seemed to be worsening suggested that he wear corrective goggles to fly solo. Admiral Moffett came to Jack's defense by pointing out that he didn't need to fly solo anyway (although he did). BuNav voiced concern about this issue, a hint that trouble might be expected on future physicals. Towers sought out a civilian eye specialist, who thought the trouble might be attributed to infection from a dead tooth in the upper jaw. Jack had it extracted, painfully, but no infection was found; his vision continued to deteriorate.[16]

In Towers' three years at the bureau he performed as Admiral Moffett's alter ego—as head of plans (1928–29), assistant chief (1929–31), and acting chief during Moffett's absence at the London Naval Conference (the first third of 1930). Together and individually, they attended air races, inspected naval air facilities, and promoted their cause inside the navy, to sister services, before the public at large, and with key members of Congress.

One sensational battle erupted early in 1930, while Moffett was in London, when BuNav chief Leigh ordered Moffett's favorite racing pilot Lieutenant Al Williams to sea duty. Williams loudly protested, and Towers was compelled to mollify several senators irritated by his stance. After the pilot vociferously resigned rather than accept his fate, Moffett had no choice but to accept the loss. Leigh, however, was soon succeeded by Rear Admiral F. Brooks Upham, who along with the new CNO himself, Admiral William V. Pratt, was friendly to aviation.[17]

Moffett and Towers molded BuAer into such an efficient team that Jack could observe in 1930, "The Bureau has encountered an attitude of mutual helpfulness in attacking common problems. . . . A free exchange of ideas, techniques, experiences . . . a recognition of the fact that aviation, as a science, an industry, or a service, is greater than the individual aspirations, ambitions, or interests that serve it. To that spirit the Bureau of Aeronautics is committed by its very nature." A large measure of this success was due to the expertise of the two assistant secretaries for aeronautics, Ed Warner and David S. Ingalls. Ingalls, the navy's only wartime ace, flew and tested all the navy's planes himself and was a delightful coworker and boss.[18]

Towers counseled Moffett on the best men for heading and staffing BuAer's several divisions and sections, among them Commander Richmond Kelly Turner, who replaced Towers as head of the plans division and was assisted by Lieutenant Commanders Pete Mitscher and Charles Rosendahl, the leading dirigible officer. The material division's engine section was headed by Charles A. Pownall. Donald Duncan took over the radio section. The several divisions promulgated information in BuAer's newsletter, edited by Joy Bright Hancock, twice widowed by dirigible pilots and now courted by the able Lieutenant Commander Ralph W. Ofstie, head of flight testing at Anacostia; Towers found her services invaluable.[19]

The most crucial Washington billet for a naval aviator outside BuAer was head of the aviation section in the ship movements division, Office of the Chief of Naval Operations. When the incumbent, Ralph Davison, came due for reassignment in 1930, CNO Hughes rejected the officers recommended by Towers and Moffett. Eventually the new CNO, Admiral Pratt, brought his own U.S. Fleet aviation officer to the post, Lieutenant Commander Calvin T.

Durgin.[20] For duty assignments in aviation, Towers worked closely with the director of officer personnel in BuNav, Captain J. O. Richardson, although Moffett had the final say for aviation flag and ship recommendations to BuNav. In some cases Moffett and Towers were successful, getting aviators to relieve observers in command of the two big carriers in mid-1930: Frank McCrary replaced Frederick Horne on the *Saratoga*, Ernie King doing the same for Frank D. Berrien on the *Lexington*. Moffett was less successful at the fleet level. Instead of getting observer Rear Admiral John Halligan as head of the fleet's air squadrons, he was forced by Hughes to accept Bull Reeves' return to the job.[21]

The biggest overall problem BuAer faced, especially after the stock market crash, was fulfilling its many requirements under an increasingly tight budget. Moffett's and Dave Ingalls' powers of persuasion actually resulted in an increase in aviation personnel, although there never seemed to be enough men to shoulder the increased workloads. Early in 1930, for example, Captain Ernie King protested a plan by Kelly Turner to temporarily shift thirty-five mechanics from King's NAS Hampton Roads to Anacostia for help testing new planes. Towers reassured King that the bureau would find other mechanics, especially from the Marine Corps airfield at nearby Quantico. Incidentally, the closing salutations in their correspondence over this matter were friendly, indicating that these two men respected one another. They handled each other carefully.[22]

When Towers reported to the bureau in mid-1928, the projected five-year program for a thousand modern planes authorized by the Morrow legislation was two years along. In spite of the Depression the pace of production accelerated, purchases staying well under budget due to economy, lower aircraft prices, and fewer wrecks; planes had stronger metal construction and better safety records. The total navy inventory of useful planes increased so rapidly that the goal of a thousand was reached during the summer of 1930, one year ahead of schedule. Towers actively consulted with the executives of Curtiss–Wright, United, Consolidated, Martin, and the new Grumman company, personally inspecting their handiwork.[23]

Theoretical work in aerodynamics became Towers' direct concern. In July 1929, after a ten-year absence, he was reappointed to the National Advisory Committee for Aeronautics, in October he was made a member of the executive committee, and in November he was appointed to Admiral David Taylor's Committee on Aeronautical Inventions and Designs. He inspected the training course at Pensacola with Ingalls and supported a plan for a base modernization program, only to have it dashed by the sinking economy. He also testified before the Bureau of the Budget in March 1930 that the army should give up its half of San Diego's congested North Island to the navy; the War Department refused, loath to surrender anything to its sister service.[24]

Towers' responsibilities grew steadily. He served on the Board for Development of Navy Yard Plans and was a member of the Naval Academy's Postgraduate Council. He lectured at the Marine Corps school at Quantico and the Air Corps tactical school at Langley Field and witnessed ordnance tests at the army's proving ground near Baltimore. A promoter of the fledgling naval air reserve program, he attended the opening of the reserve field at Miami in June 1930.[25]

Whenever Anacostia hosted air shows or races, Moffett and Towers could conveniently attend them together. One of the two men generally stayed at the bureau while the other traveled, Towers often with Ingalls, their appearances all part of Moffett's promotional campaign. In August 1929 the three men attended the air races in Cleveland, Ingalls' home turf, and the following May Jack and Ingalls flew first to New York for an aeronautical exhibition, then to Norfolk for the presidential review.[26]

Most of Moffett's absences from Washington were related to his unending struggle for the airship program, a project Towers generally left to the admiral. But when the admiral was abroad early in 1930 Towers became embroiled in the stormy battle in the navy and in Congress for its development. Of particular concern to him was "Mr. Dirigible," Lieutenant Commander Charles Rosendahl, who tried to force the retention of an unqualified airship officer. When Jack notified Moffett that Rosendahl had lied outright to him, the admiral merely shrugged it off: "Whatever he [Rosendahl] says in criticism goes in one ear and out the other." The sour relationship between Towers and Rosendahl would intensify.[27]

The aircraft carrier remained the pride and joy of BuAer, whose several sections devoted most of their attention to supporting the *Saratoga, Lexington,* and *Langley.* Early in 1930 after the fleet completed two problems in the Caribbean it proceeded to Hampton Roads, which allowed Towers to observe flight operations. Admiral Moffett, who wanted more "flattops," was successful in getting only one new one approved, the 13,800-ton *Ranger* (CV-4), but the deepening Depression prevented it from being laid down.[28]

Towers often appeared before the General Board, alone or with Admiral Moffett or other BuAer officers. The board's members, including Admirals Jackson, Reeves, and Butler, sought his advice on virtually every aspect of aviation within the fleet. Towers educated them about torpedo design, aircraft construction, dive bombing tactics, bombing-plane characteristics, aeronautical intelligence-gathering abroad, the need for shipboard antiaircraft guns, and much else of a technical nature. He was not in the least bit reticent about volunteering information, making suggestions, or disagreeing, which earned him their respect.[29]

During one lengthy appearance in May 1931, Towers participated in the discussion over formulating the new naval policy. The board wanted to build up to full treaty strength, making the U.S. Navy second to none and on a par with Britain. Certain congressmen favored decommissioning some battleships and carriers as economy measures, in which case, Towers suggested, the naval policy should state that battleships would go first. This evoked an alarmed reaction from Admiral M. Meigs Taylor of the war plans division:

TOWERS: Don't you think though that in view of the fact that aircraft carriers are the newest type of vessels in the Fleet that they should be continued?

TAYLOR: At the expense of other ships?

TOWERS: Yes, sir.

TAYLOR: I wouldn't say so. . . . That is a statement that the most important development of the Fleet is aviation.

TOWERS: I don't think it is quite that.

TAYLOR: Pretty nearly.

TOWERS: It is an important element to have experience with at the present time because there is less history behind it.

TAYLOR: It means you are going to sacrifice other elements of the Fleet . . . I don't believe in tying myself down to it.[30]

While Moffett was in London, Towers and Ingalls headed a delegation of BuAer officers testifying before the House appropriations subcommittee.[31] Jack did his homework and made certain that his brother officers were equally well-prepared before appearing. As soon as the questioning began on the morning of 3 February 1930, Towers detected distinct hostility on the part of several subcommittee members who wanted increased competition for aircraft contracts. This problem, specifically with regard to spare parts, was a matter the bureau had been laboring to improve, and as the hearings progressed the members grew friendlier. The congressmen also opposed construction of the dirigible *Macon* and of a base for it at Sunnyvale in northern California, as well as the purchase of helium. But Towers used his experts to such effect that by the end of the hearings on the sixth he was happy with the outcome. In particular, "Mr. Ingalls was a tremendous help. . . . His personality seemed to make a most favorable impression upon the Committee."[32]

Indeed, the team scored such an important victory for continuation of current funding that two of the participants immediately wrote to Moffett about it. One, John C. Pugh, budget expert and assistant clerk of the committee, congratulated the admiral on his selection of officers: "They functioned like a well drilled team. . . . Commander Towers handled himself as if he had been appearing before Congressional Committees all his life. I have seen many officers in my time up here [on Capitol Hill], both Army and Navy, and I have yet to see one to handle himself better."[33]

Moffett was exceedingly pleased and showed Pugh's letter to Secretary Adams and Admiral Pratt, who agreed. He had been able to leave the country, Moffett wrote one officer, "knowing that Towers, assisted by all of you, would leave nothing undone." And he wrote to Jack, "I know that you are enjoying being Chief of Bureau, and let me say that there is no one who could perform the duties better than yourself." Towers did enjoy it, anticipating the day he might succeed to the throne.[34]

Towers helped Moffett prepare BuAer's book of aviation data for the American delegation to the London arms control conference, the admiral advising him to deal directly with Assistant Secretaries Ernest Lee Jahncke and Ingalls in assisting the delegation's work. The conferees refused to allow more carrier tonnage, since the United States still had 69,000 tons of unused allotment from the Washington Treaty of 1922. Towers followed the conference closely in the daily press and from Moffett's letters, often making comments in reply. Reflecting Moffett's discouragement, early in February he lamented to Pierre, "Have they given away all our Navy in London?" The admiral complained to Jack about "some of the greatest minds of the world giving their whole time and effort to submarines, battleships, and even cruisers that will be largely obsolete in a comparatively few years, and certainly will be after the next war, being all replaced by aircraft carriers."[35]

By April 1930, however, Towers learned that Moffett had succeeded in awakening the American delegation to the importance of carriers. Not only was the U.S. carrier tonnage of 135,000 tons not reduced, as the British were advocating, but Moffett had interjected the idea of putting a short flight deck on a new class of light cruiser for scouting and spotting planes. By the time Moffett returned to Washington in May, Towers was involved in lengthy hearings before the House Naval Affairs Committee. The London Treaty was signed and ratified, extending the Washington provisions limiting battleships to the end of 1936, and Moffett had three alternate designs worked up by his staff for the "flying-deck cruiser." Towers liked the compromise ship and spent a great deal of time promoting the idea, especially before the General

Board, but it never carried. He and the admiral were more successful in finally initiating construction of the new carrier *Ranger*. It was begun in September 1931.[36]

Given Towers' performance during his first two years at the bureau, as well as over the ten years before that, Admiral Moffett had no hesitation recommending his promotion to the rank of captain. The timing for Towers' promotion was ripe, in spite of a mild speeding ticket that made the papers early in 1930. Not only was he naval aviator no. 3, but as a newly instituted monthly flight time system revealed, his cumulative flying record was impressive: 2,385 hours by the end of the year. And on 23 May, at a ceremony on the White House lawn, President Hoover pinned the NC gold medal on his uniform.[37]

On 6 June 1930, the navy announced that Towers was one of fourteen commanders selected by the president for promotion to captain. Things were certainly looking up for Jack: he and Pierre decided to tie the knot that August, the reason, according to Pierre, being that their long-distance phone calls had gotten too expensive! Furthermore, old friend Glenn Curtiss asked Jack to participate in the annual New York State "air tour" set for mid-July. Towers, who had recently sent Curtiss photographs of their early days together, was anxious to help out. The summer of 1930 was going to be a hectic one.[38]

When Towers flew to New York, where he and Dick Richardson were among the pilots flying forty-five planes across the state, Curtiss had been hospitalized for an appendectomy. Sadly, his condition worsened and he passed away on 30 June. Jack hurriedly had orders cut to be the official navy representative and an honorary pallbearer at the funeral, along with Richardson and Lanny Callan, now a reserve commander. On 25 July, as Jack watched ten planes fly over and drop flowers on the grave site, he remembered "the memory of a June day twenty years ago" when "Glenn flew over Keuka in the first Navy seaplane. I heard again the hum of that now archaic engine when the ship rose in a wake of foam. Recalling it I realized with a deep pride that as the planes of tomorrow roar down eternal airpaths, the gleam of their wings in sunlight, the sound of their motors at night will forever remain the symbols of that man's greatness."[39]

Aviation had its own history at this point, one in which Jack Towers had figured prominently alongside the quiet genius of Hammondsport. But now the future beckoned, and three days after the funeral Towers received his ad interim appointment as captain. The regular commission would come in January.[40]

Jack and Pierre journeyed to the home of Reggie Gillmor on the shores of Lake George for the wedding. Gillmor, '07 but long since out of the navy and married into wealth, would be best man. By a great coincidence, Stephen H. P. Pell, owner of historic Fort Ticonderoga on Lake Champlain, had been a friend of Pierre's father before the war; the mother having appointed him to be Pierre's guardian, he gave her away at the wedding. It took place on a sunny 9 August in the sumptuous garden of Pell's estate near the fort, with Lanny Callan and a group of BuAer officers as groomsmen. After a week-long honeymoon at Lake George, the newlyweds were joined there by Marjorie and Chas, who would stay for the rest of the summer.[41]

At long last, the forty-five-year-old was happily married to his French lady of twenty-eight. Pierre would become a second mother to the children when they were not in New York City with Lily. The new bride loathed Jack's passion, bridge, but could make a fourth if necessary. Like the children, she was expected to join Jack in his daily swim before breakfast if they happened to be living near water. She shared her husband's deep love of dogs, tennis, entertaining, and dancing. Jack now began to cherish his home life. As in his professional work, patience and perseverence had finally paid off.[42]

Navy and Washington society quickly embraced this charming, talented, and vivacious woman, who proved to be the perfect foil for her reserved captain. "She's tall and distinctively handsome," a society columnist would write in 1939. "Life to her is a vibrant adventure to a degree that infuses even her more lethargic friends with enthusiasm." Like her husband, she had integrity and no pretense, and when Towers received his transfer orders early in 1931 the news of their leaving, said one newspaper, was "received with much regret in official circles in the Capital, where they have enjoyed great popularity."[43]

After they settled into a Washington home rented from one of Jack's classmates, then in China, Towers accompanied Dave Ingalls on a flying inspection of the two key naval air facilities in the secretary's new VIP Curtiss Helldiver. First they flew to Pensacola, then pressed on cross-country, through New Orleans, San Antonio, El Paso, and finally on 7 November to San Diego, where they were greeted by Admiral Reeves.[44]

Towers remained at North Island analyzing recommended alterations to the facility while Ingalls flew north to inspect Sunnyvale, the LTA site finally selected for the fleet's new dirigibles. Ingalls returned with a passenger, the humorist Will Rogers, a unique and effective advocate of naval aviation. "Just think," Rogers reported in his column, "a man in charge of aviation that can fly! It's almost like a general fighting his own war." Though Ernie King's

Natty as ever in bowler, cane, and spats, Towers poses in the high company of humorist and aviation enthusiast Will Rogers, *center,* at NAS Anacostia, 21 January 1931. The others are, *left to right,* aviation promoter Casey Jones; Commander Hugh Douglas, station commander; and pilot Frank Hawkes. They stand before Assistant Secretary Ingalls' Curtiss F8C Helldiver, loaned to Rogers and Hawkes to fly to the flood-stricken Mississippi Valley for charity shows to aid the victims. Note the enclosed, heated cockpit behind Douglas. (National Archives)

Lexington and Frank McCrary's *Saratoga* were anchored off Long Beach, their planes operated out of San Diego, giving aerial demonstrations for Ingalls, Rogers, and Towers, representing Admiral Moffett. Reflected the Oklahoma wit, "In spite of our diplomats and their social sinking conference, we've got a lot of Navy left, in fact about enough for two more conferences."[45]

Watching flight operations aboard the *Langley* one day, Towers and the VIPs saw the immense form of the *Lexington* approaching. Ere long, a *Lex* signal light blinked out a message addressed to Towers: "JACK, WHERE ARE YOU GOING IN THAT COVERED WAGON? KING." Towers immediately dictated a reply for his hard-driving former BuAer colleague: "WE'RE GOING TO JAMAICA HIC ERNIE HIC WHERE ARE YOU UNDERLINED HIC GOING? TOWERS." Upon receipt of this little riposte, according to Ensign Robert Heinlein of the *Lex,* "King gave a wry smile and told the signalman, 'No answer.'" The exchange was a mark of mutual respect, not of close friendship, as future science fiction writer Heinlein thought.[46]

It also reflected the seagoing navy's contempt for prohibition, normally violated during rest periods in the rum-rich Caribbean and in Mexico. One night Ingalls threw a small party at the gambling and racing resort in Agua Caliente, a Mexican border town. The only anxious moment came when customs officials caught and held the secretary while he was crawling back through the barbed wire to his car; the U.S.-Mexican border had closed at midnight. Towers nevertheless had him back on the plane after sunup on the nineteenth for the return cross-country flight to Washington.[47]

Towers accompanied Moffett and Ingalls to more appropriations hearings over the winter. The admiral did most of the talking to insure completion of the carrier *Ranger* and of the dirigible *Macon*. Though naval aviation received no growth in funding from 1929 to 1932, the overall annual BuAer budget remained about $31 million. Severe cuts would not begin until 1933, and in April 1931 Jack could still paint a rosy future for aviation in an address to a convention of the Daughters of the American Revolution: "In the tomorrow of Aviation airplanes can and will be flown by children. . . . Instead of wondering if the children of tomorrow are at the local country club or baseball game on a sunny afternoon, their parents will be wondering whether they are in the Adirondacks or at Pinehurst, and if they will be home in time for dinner." His prophetic abilities had not improved since those bad guesses back in 1919.[48]

Towers learned in January 1931 that he would return to sea as chief of staff to commander, Aircraft Squadrons, trading jobs with Captain Arthur B. Cook. Rear Admiral Harry E. Yarnell, chief of BuEng, would relieve Bull Reeves as air commander. Towers was detached on 6 June. Moffett held a farewell dinner for him and Hugh Douglas, en route to become exec of the *Saratoga,* Yarnell's flagship. Moffett praised Towers, proclaiming that "no one has done more for aviation than yourself, and I hope, some day, that you will get the complete recognition that you deserve." Jack, "rather overcome" by these remarks, mumbled an inadequate reply. Later in a letter to Moffett, he was more coherent: "I cannot begin to tell you how I appreciate it and how I hope that it may all come true. My tour of duty at the Bureau under you was, by far, the most interesting and instructive that I have ever had. As you know, I began it with extreme reluctance and finished it with equal regret."[49]

Moffett soon found that Towers' departure left an immense void. A. B. Cook simply lacked Jack's political savvy. Towers was not able to brief Cook completely on the duties of the assistant chief before leaving, and in the first crisis after Jack's departure the admiral had to fend for himself. Moffett would correspond heavily with Jack, on one occasion even summoning him back to Washington to help. Indeed, the admiral urged Towers to write him "whenever you have the time and inclination. . . . Again let me beg you to help us all you can by criticism and suggestions, and don't be afraid of hurting our feelings."[50]

Towers departed from the bureau guardedly expecting to come back in two years as chief. Moffett would retire at the mandatory age of sixty-four in 1933, and he wanted Towers to succeed him. It was a heady prospect, for the post automatically carried the rank of rear admiral. The fact that Towers would be a captain for only three years and a flag officer at the age of forty-eight meant his appointment was bound to be met with considerable opposition. Much depended on his continued superior performance with the fleet.

For the cross-country journey to the West Coast, Admiral Yarnell and Towers elected to drive separate cars, rendezvousing at points along the 3,000-mile route. Guided no doubt by the Navy Department's informal motoring manual, "Across the Continent by Automobile," they and their wives set out with some trepidation on 7 June 1931. Admiral Yarnell—who became Harry during the trip—and his wife Emily took Jack's naive young French bride under their wing along the way. When they rolled into Indianapolis Pierre wondered where the Indians were, figuring that city was their capital! Alas, Indians were not encountered until Santa Fe, and they were not at all the wild savages Pierre expected. Because of the predictably bad western roads the eleven-day odyssey proved exhausting, and Jack whisked his bride off to Mexico for a week of much-needed rest. Then they rented a nice house at Coronado, the second of what would be fourteen residences in the ten years between their marriage and the outbreak of World War II.[51]

Yarnell, a naval aviation observer, had surely consulted with Towers on selecting his other staff officers, among them Lieutenant Commanders Arthur Radford, flag secretary; Forrest Sherman, navigator; Ralph Davison, operations officer; and Lieutenant A. P. "Putt" Storrs, flag lieutenant. Yarnell relieved Bull Reeves on 27 June 1931, and within less than a month Towers could announce, "The Staff officers know their jobs so well that there is really very little for the Admiral or me to do."[52]

Headquarters of Aircraft Squadrons Battle Force (formerly Battle Fleet) was located at North Island, still the focal point of fleet aviation. All carrier squadrons—and the *Langley,* when she returned from Atlantic duty—were based there. The air station, commanded by Rip Paunack, was still over-crowded, and the Army Air Corps finally agreed that autumn to move most of its planes inland to March Field.[53]

From the very first, Harry Yarnell and Jack Towers got along together famously. Both short, quiet men, they shared a dedication to the advancement of aviation. What Yarnell himself did not know, he found out by asking Towers, the pilots, and the mechanics. Yarnell "seldom raised his voice above a conversational tone," remembered Arthur Radford, "but he could be as hard as steel if the occasion demanded. . . . He [Towers] and Admiral Yarnell were a good team." In addition, no friction existed between the staff and the ship's officers, a situation rare in flagships.[54]

The *Saratoga* had become the fleet's carrier showpiece, a premier ship brought into commission by Yarnell and now commanded by Frank Mc-

Rear Admirals Harry E. Yarnell and Bull Reeves on board the *Saratoga* in 1931, probably during the change of command on 27 June. Towers stands at left; Ralph Davison is behind and between them. (Towers collection)

Crary, with Hugh Douglas as the new exec. Air officer Win Spencer ran a smart 888-foot flight deck, having planes towed around and respotted with the aid of a 1922 Maxwell motorcar. The *Sara* operated seventy-two planes: two fighting, dive bombing squadrons of F8C Curtiss Helldivers and Boeing F4Bs; one scouting squadron of Vought Corsairs; one torpedo squadron of Great Lakes TG-1 versions of the Martin T4M; and a couple of OL-8 Loening amphibians for utility work. Three of the squadron commanders were future wartime luminaries Jerry Bogan, Matthias B. Gardner, and John J. Ballentine.[55]

The *Saratoga*'s sister ship *Lexington* naturally competed with the flagship but had rarely outshown her until the arrival of Captain Ernie King in mid-1930. A tough, exacting skipper, King was served by two successive and equally somber execs, "Genial John" Hoover and Vic Herbster, "a small fussy officer with no visible talent" in one officer's opinion. King dominated the taut *Lex,* and the easier-going officers of the *Saratoga* enjoyed needling him. Whenever the *Lex* "did err," recalled Radford, the *Sara*'s flag staff "took more than routine pleasure in preparing critical dispatches and letters to her [the *Lex*'s] commanding officer."[56]

Over the summer and fall of 1931 routine operations and fleet drills were observed by VIPs and visitors from BuAer intent on improving the carriers. Spig Wead called upon the *Sara*'s fighter pilots to do some stunts as stand-ins for actors Clark Gable and Wallace Beery in the filming of Wead's newest movie, "Hell Divers." And, late in the year, each of the large carriers was assigned a Marine Corps scout-observation squadron, an experiment destined to last only three years.[57]

A major task of Yarnell and Towers was keeping Admiral Moffett and Assistant Secretary Ingalls apprised of their needs, especially as BuNav continued to thwart BuAer on key personnel assignments. In November Towers learned that Ingalls intended to resign the following summer to run for the governership of Ohio. "You will lose a very strong and valuable friend at court," Bob Molten warned Jack. As Ingalls' aide, Molten advised Towers to solicit "all of the influential friends you have both in and out of the Navy, particularly on the Hill and those in high places in the commercial and scientific aeronautical circles" to support Jack's cause to be the next chief of bureau. "I believe," Molten explained, that "Admiral Moffett will always stick by you as his choice, but he is and will continue to be the lone wolf."[58]

Towers lost the direct support not only of Dave Ingalls, but also of Trubee Davison, the army's assistant secretary for air, who would himself resign to run for office. Herbert Hoover allowed both posts to fall dormant as an economy measure. When Ingalls and Davison were later crushed in the Democratic landslide of Franklin Roosevelt, neither post would be revived.

Training operations took on a more urgent aura after Japan unexpectedly annexed Manchuria in the autumn of 1931. Building on war games of the preceding three years that had demonstrated the need for increased carrier mobility, Grand Joint Exercise No. 4 offered fresh possibilities. Recalled Radford, "Admiral Yarnell, Captain Towers, and the staff appreciated what an opportunity this exercise was to dramatize the fleet's carrier air power" on the offensive. The *Saratoga* and the *Lexington* would be used to launch a sneak attack on the army's defenses in Hawaii, then to cover landings by the marines. To Towers as chief of staff went the responsibility of directing the planning and staging of this operation. He began by putting all the fighters on the *Saratoga,* all the torpedo-bombers and scouts on the *Lexington.* And he welcomed aboard old friend Grover Loening as technical observer.[59]

Departing Coronado Roads at the end of January 1932, the fleet and its carriers headed toward Hawaii. On 5 February Yarnell broke away from the main body, forming a separate task force with the "Lady Lex," "Sister Sara," and destroyers. Planning to strike Pearl Harbor and army installations on Oahu at dawn on Sunday the seventh, the force made a high-speed, twenty-five-knot run-in, placing it 400 miles from the target on Saturday. Working to the launch position 100 miles north of Oahu during the night, the carriers were buffeted by rain squalls and heavy seas. Force radio listeners, however, had intercepted messages from the islands showing the defenders to be completely unaware of the approach. Admiral Yarnell therefore elected to launch his planes, although it meant slowing down the carriers to minimize their rolling. This doubled the time required for the planes to take off, and pitch darkness compounded the problem.

Using the big battery of searchlights at Kahuku Point as a beacon, the planes headed toward Oahu. Just as dawn broke over Pearl Harbor that Sunday morning, the attacking carrier planes swept over the slumbering bases. They bore down in simulated attacks on the army's three airfields, ammunition depots, railheads, hangars, and barracks. Although the fields were destroyed in theory, the umpires allowed the Air Corps planes to take off. Unable to find the attacking planes' line of retirement to the carriers, the army planes landed about 0700—whereupon the second carrier-plane wave struck. Towers and the staff had calculated the moment perfectly. This time, however, a few army planes reached the carriers, along with a defending submarine, and scored some hits.

The army minimized the extent of the damage in the sneak attack, claimed its planes had critically damaged the carriers, and protested the legality of attacking on a Sunday(!). When the umpires and admirals agreed with the minimal damage estimate to Pearl Harbor, Towers protested violently, so much so that he was reprimanded. Still, the message was clear enough for those who cared to read it. In an essay Grover Loening lauded the "great speed" of the carriers, which "gave them a mobility as a base that would be a priceless asset in war," and noted two lessons: that planes could launch undetected in predawn darkness, and that heavy seas were a negligible factor because of the big carriers' inherent stability.

The fact that Japan nearly duplicated this attack on Pearl on Sunday morning, 7 December 1941, was no accident. Early in the 1950s Towers dined in Tokyo with a Japanese vice admiral who had participated in the planning. "He told me they simply took a page out of our own book! Too bad our high command did not keep that page open before them." But the rules of the exercise were too rigid to allow the umpires, the Air Corps, and the battleship admirals to accept reality.

Carrier planes raided the islands on successive days, then laid down a smokescreen to cover marines hitting the beach from the battleships. But the air aspects of the amphibious phase had to be cut short because, as Radford put it, "some of the dogfights were getting too realistic."[60]

Fleet Problem XIII immediately followed the Pearl Harbor attack. A Blue Fleet from the western Pacific and Hawaii supported an expeditionary force against three supposedly unfortified atolls along the U.S. West Coast, defended by the Black Fleet. Admiral Reddy Leigh commanded Blue and the battle line, with Admiral Yarnell in charge of its air component, the *Saratoga* and planes based in Hawaii. The scouting force cruisers arrived from the Atlantic to comprise Black, which included King's *Lexington,* Jake Fitch's *Langley,* and tender-based patrol planes.

As far as the carriermen were concerned, their first task was to neutralize the enemy's air power. When Blue left Lahaina Roads near Maui in mid-March, the *Saratoga's* scouts took off and "sank" a prowling Black submarine, getting two more subs on each the next two days as the carrier screened the advancing convoy. Towers had personally instructed strike leader John Ballentine not to hit the *Lex* until her planes were manned and away, when she would be defenseless. Not finding the *Lex,* however, Ballentine and his TG bombers surprised a Black cruiser, which they neutralized, and pressed on toward the *Lexington,* sixty miles beyond. They ran into a *Lex* strike group as well as antiaircraft fire, through which they pressed home a dive bombing attack. Both carriers then launched strikes against the other, after which the umpires assigned 38 percent damage to the *Lex* and 25 percent to the *Sara*.

The ever-competitive Ernie King, hating to lose at anything, obtained permission from his immediate senior, Admiral William H. Standley, to operate independently. So he kept the *Lex* well out of the *Saratoga*'s range until just the right moment. Ballantine's bombers disposed of two more Black cruisers, neutralized a third, and sank another sub that day. But just as the last planes were coming aboard the *Sara* late in the afternoon, four dozen *Lexington* planes swept in to inflict 49 percent more damage, effectively disabling the *Sara*. Next day Captain Bill Halsey's destroyers further damaged the *Sara* with torpedoes, and the *Lex*'s planes crippled the battleship *Pennsylvania,* flagship of U.S. Fleet commander Frank H. Schofield. The two fleets then moved toward the West Coast. When they lost contact with each other, Schofield terminated the exercise.[61]

In response to Admiral Schofield's praise of the *Lexington*'s attack on the *Saratoga,* Yarnell and Towers recommended that the navy utilize between six and eight such carriers for operations across the Pacific. With overwhelming force, a fleet of carriers could proceed to the enemy's coast and force a fleet action. Fleet Problem XIII, Towers wrote to Admiral Moffett, was "the most valuable fleet exercise carried out in recent years. In my opinion it made an irrefutable case for . . . more carriers and flying-deck cruisers," especially to support overseas convoys. Moffett was glad to hear this, not only from Towers but "from all sides." Unfortunately, Congress had no intention of expending funds on new construction.[62]

Worse, the navy had decided to keep the *Lexington* with the scouting force when it returned to the Atlantic during the summer. Admiral Yarnell protested loudly, pointing out that the development of carrier tactics would be delayed for years if the two big carriers were divided between oceans. He recommended that the *Langley* rather than the *Lex* be moved to the Atlantic. Not only was this alternative rejected, but the *Langley* was earmarked to go to the Asiatic Fleet, where it would be exposed should war break out with Japan.[63]

Before the transfer occurred, both large carriers required an overhaul. With the *Saratoga*'s departure to Bremerton, Yarnell shifted his flag to the *Lexington* for an exercise en route, during the spring. Throughout the cruise, according to Radford, "Captain King and Captain Towers—both ambitious, both meticulous as to detail, and both very energetic—drew sparks from each other on almost every contact. There was rather frigid politeness evident whenever they had occasion to do business together. The staff, loyal to a man, supported Captain Towers in the feeling that Captain King was difficult to get along with."[64]

While Towers labored afloat, three related matters commanded his attention. One was Admiral Moffett's battle in Congress to thwart a fresh attempt to create a separate air force under a unified department of national defense. Economy was the official reason behind the move, as Congress—with BuNav approval—now cut overall military funding for flight pay. Just when Moffett convinced one committee to reject unification, another came out favoring it. This problem was complicated when Dave Ingalls, in his last days as assistant secretary, threatened to support the proposed bill. Moffett fumbled his efforts to influence Ingalls; Towers would have to bail him out.

The second problem was the question of Moffett's successor; since Moffett wanted Jack, the latter needed to protect his position against Moffett's and his own enemies. Moreover, before Towers could become chief of BuAer, he would have to have a major carrier command. He intended to get the *Lexington*. The third problem was that Jack's enemies planned to stop his bid for chief by focusing on his eye problems. Towers' 1932 physical had revealed the vision in his right eye to be deteriorating rapidly.[65]

On 7 May 1932 Admiral Yarnell received a frantic cable from Moffett requesting Towers' presence in Washington. Moffett lied to his counterpart in BuNav, Brooks Upham, saying that Towers' expertise was needed for a decision on the purchase of a new navy aircraft. In reality, Moffett believed that only Jack could dissuade Ingalls from supporting unification, muster key congressional support, and then represent BuAer in committee hearings. Towers was only too happy to oblige, for he could also use the opportunity to defend himself against his opponents in Washington.[66]

Arriving by rail on the fifteenth, Towers went to see Moffett immediately and spent most of that and succeeding days with him. He straightened out Moffett's platform, appeared on Capitol Hill, and garnered the support of key congressmen, notably his old friend Georgia Senator John S. Cohen and Representative Carl Vinson. Jack conferred closely with Dave Ingalls, helping to persuade him against unification before he left office. "The great thing," Towers was able to write Pierre on the nineteenth, "is I have forced W.A.M. [Moffett] to come out of his little corner. Mrs. M. is most enthusiastic. She also says I have 'saved his life' by coming. She says she was not sleeping and was worrying and that all has changed since I got here." With Moffett's confidence restored, the admiral, Towers, and their colleagues were able to counter the latest bid for a separate air force.[67]

At one meeting, Carl Vinson asked Towers if he thought Admiral Moffett might agree to a seven-month extension as chief of bureau, beyond March 1933 until his retirement at the end of October. Such a temporary measure was perfectly acceptable to Towers, but when he broached the idea to Moffett the admiral passed it off with the remark that he had had "enough of it." Senator Cohen supported Jack's candidacy and promised "to do anything he could."[68]

Towers fully appreciated the professional risks he ran by engaging in such political maneuvering, namely, supporting Moffett against BuNav and advancing his own career. "The old guard probably will hear of things soon and will be after my scalp, but I believe they will be too late," he told Pierre. His detractors already were after him, using the Bureau of Medicine and Surgery (BuMed) as their hatchet. Although Towers had passed his annual physical with the usual waivers in January, because of his eye trouble the new chief of BuMed and surgeon general of the navy, Rear Admiral Perceval S. Rossiter, now required that he take an informal eye exam. In questioning Towers' visual acuity, however, Rossiter admitted that his examiners had always assumed Jack wore "trick glasses" when he flew. By denying this, Jack threw BuMed on the defensive, and he was safe for the time being.[69]

Before his next physical, Towers expected to be in command of the *Lexington* and already earmarked as Moffett's relief. Ernie King had just turned over the carrier to Captain Charles A. Blakely for the immediate future, leaving Towers to try for the next rotation. Jack made the rounds at the Navy Department and learned that Captain Jerry Land of the CNO's staff was about to take over C&R in the rank of rear admiral after considerable opposition. Towers abstained from drinking on his visit until Ernie King, in town for hearings, insisted they imbibe together.[70]

On 26 May, his political position with Moffett and the bureau strengthened, Towers finally boarded the train for San Diego. Though he left without assurances that he would get the *Lexington,* he was prospective successor to Moffett as chief of bureau and thus went away greatly encouraged.

Indeed, Towers had stirred up considerable activity in the halls of the Navy Department over the Moffett succession, alerting other contenders, notably Captain Ernie King. Admiral Yarnell was being mentioned as a possible candidate, Jack told him, whereupon Yarnell penned a handwritten letter to Moffett rejecting the idea. Yarnell wished Moffett could stay another four years, but, knowing that unlikely, he recommended Towers: "I feel that by reason of experience and ability he is the best fitted of any one on the Navy list for the promotion, and that under him naval aviation would continue to maintain its supremacy over the other Navies of the world."[71]

Early in July, forced to act on the matter, CNO Pratt called in Moffett for a private conversation. This was followed by one with both Moffett and Upham. Pratt "spoke very highly of you," Moffett reported to Towers, "but said you were too far down the list." Moffett argued that "seniority should apply to seniority in aviation, not in the whole Navy," but they did not agree. After considering other candidates, Pratt and Upham asked Moffett if he would agree to remain as chief the additional seven months until his retirement in October 1933—Carl Vinson's suggestion. This meant being appointed for an abbreviated fourth term, during which time the matter of his ultimate successor could be resolved. By then the presidential succession would be settled and Admiral Pratt's as well; all rumors pointed to William H. Standley as the next CNO.[72]

Moffett agreed, reluctantly, and only if need be. "I had no intention of remaining after March 13 but will now," he informed Jack. He advised Towers to complete two years as a captain; then he would be reassigned to the bureau preparatory to becoming chief. The admiral enjoined Towers to share this plan with no one except Yarnell. Towers, who had just informed Moffett he was "not worrying" about the succession, replied that since A. B. Cook wanted to relieve Captain Bill Steele on the *Sara* the following June, he would be pleased to replace Cook as assistant chief "for the period from June until your retirement, with the hope of stepping in." Moffett, however, confided to Yarnell that Jack would still "have to leave nothing undone to get it."[73]

The entire debate took a dramatic turn in August, when Captain Steele, Pratt's candidate, ran the *Saratoga* aground, the traditional death knell for a naval career. Pratt and Upham offered Moffett's post to Yarnell, who declined, as did John Halligan, both men preferring to remain at sea. Although Secretary Adams opposed the retention of Moffett beyond March, Pratt and Upham saw no real alternative, and by early September his extension had been approved.[74]

Meanwhile, the summer concentration enabled Air Squadrons to train with the rest of the fleet, which was rewriting its tactical doctrine, drawing the criticism of Yarnell and Towers for being too defensive and exclusively concerned with a battle line action. They recommended that fleet tactics "follow the conditions to be used in the progress of a trans-oceanic campaign." Instead of defensive cruising screens, Yarnell called for offensive operations against the enemy's fleet, scouting forces, ports or bases, convoys, commerce, and industry, especially with air raids. Towers agreed completely, though the high command did not. Towers at least had a friend in the new battle force commander, Luke McNamee, now a four-star admiral.[75]

The growing menace of Japan plagued fleet planning, a problem accentuated by the visit of a two-ship Japanese training squadron to San Pedro during April. Yarnell and his staff acclaimed the decision of the Navy Department in June to keep the *Langley* at San Diego instead of going to the Asiatic Fleet, and they worked mightily to prevent the *Lexington* and the rest of the scouting force from returning to the Atlantic. They believed that these units, the *Saratoga,* and the still-building *Ranger* should be concentrated in the Pacific. Finally, although the *Lex* did leave for the East Coast in July, the admirals decided to return her to the fleet over the winter and thereafter keep her on the West Coast.[76]

The summer and ensuing months also brought the normal personnel turnovers, notably Commander Kelly Turner replacing Hugh Douglas as exec of the *Saratoga.* Turner, a tough but thorough individual who performed exceptionally well in the post, insisted that pilots stand OOD or department watches, a philosophy long advocated by Towers.[77]

With the cream of naval aviation centered in the San Diego area, Jack Towers enjoyed the local social scene to the full with his new bride. Pierre fitted into the fraternity nicely, even using her skills to make the wedding dress for fighter pilot Stanhope C. Ring's fiancée. Every Sunday, Jack, Pierre, and a gang of flyers and wives would motor fifteen miles across the Mexican border to Rosarita Beach for beer parties. The Towers maintained a small apartment in Long Beach, where the *Saratoga* was normally anchored.[78]

Pierre learned to handle Captain Ernie King, next to whom all the wives dreaded to sit at dinner. King liked to meet attractive girls, and at one party she innocently informed him in her thick French accent that she had "just met a charming girl. I'm going to bring her over here." When she did, King froze up and announced coldly, "We've already met. It's my daughter!"

On Saturday afternoons when Jack played bridge with friends, Pierre stole away for private flying lessons at a small airfield at nearby Chula Vista. Saving her housekeeping money to pay for the lessons, she learned quickly, passing her first test after only eight hours of instruction. Having put down Jack as her next-of-kin on the lesson application form, she finally decided to tell him. "Well, I'll be damned," he retorted, "I don't know whether to switch you or to kiss you!" Amused that she had learned so quickly, he asked her,

"Why did you *do* it?" Replied Pierre, "I just had to know what you were talking about with all the boys!" He was immensely pleased, and Pierre continued to fly as often as she could afford the gasoline.[79]

The major event for the navy in the fall of 1932 was the landslide presidential victory of pro-navy Franklin D. Roosevelt. This sharpened the debate over the next chief of BuAer. Moffett suspected that CNO Pratt was

Greeting Admiral Moffett on a visit to NAS San Diego, 15 September 1932. Standing before a Loening OL amphibian are, *left to right,* Rear Admirals Harry Yarnell, Thomas J. Senn, Moffett, and John Halligan, and Captains Towers and John H. Hoover. (Navy Department)

leaning toward King, now a student at the Naval War College. King himself wrote Moffett a long and friendly letter requesting his support, to which Moffett replied that Towers was still his first choice; he told Carl Vinson, "I think all of Aviation wants to see Towers here." Selected for rear admiral in December, King kept up his campaign.[80]

Between November and January Moffett and Towers discussed the succession in several letters. Moffett advised Jack to write everyone of influence, which he did, maintaining the support of the Georgia delegation to Congress, including Cohen and Vinson. He received the active endorsement of his old NC compatriot Dick Byrd, now in the permanent rank of rear admiral, retired. As for the aircraft manufacturers, Moffett suggested that soliciting their support might incur Towers' debt to them. But several came forward anyway. Moffett urged Jack also to court Admiral Standley, anticipated to become the next CNO. To outgoing Secretary Adams, Moffett said he was supporting Towers because "there is a great battle coming"—namely, the reorganization of the Navy Department and "the old question of a united air service"—"and . . . it is essential for the Navy's interests, if for no other reason, that the head of this Bureau be an aviator and a real one."[81]

Indeed, the struggle over the replacement of the giant who had been BuAer's first and only chief for twelve years had implications for the entire navy. For Towers was known to be every bit the political fighter that Moffett was, and the Depression threatened the navy's needs for long-range flying boats as well as planes and personnel for the carrier *Ranger,* now nearing completion.

The fight for aviation's prominence could best be demonstrated in the annual war games. Given the Japanese threat, Fleet Problem XIV was designed to simulate a war in the Pacific, one initiated by carrier operations. Anticipating that Japan would attack before formally declaring war (as she had done against Russia in 1904), the scenario envisioned the sortie of the Japanese fleet eastward across the Pacific. This fleet, its sinister designation Black, had ominously prescient orders: "To inflict maximum damage on the PEARL HARBOR NAVAL BASE in order to destroy or reduce its effectiveness." Black would then undertake carrier raids against Puget Sound, San Francisco, and the San Pedro–San Diego area.[82]

The Black Fleet, commanded by Vice Admiral Frank H. Clark (a nonaviator), comprised the two big carriers plus escorting cruisers and destroyers. Partly because the army and its planes lacked sufficient funds to participate in the defense of Hawaii, Black bypassed Hawaii in favor of the West Coast targets. Admiral Clark formed three groups. The Northern

Carrier Group, under Vice Admiral Standley (another nonaviator), was organized around Charles Blakely's *Lexington* and proceeded toward San Francisco. The Support Group of cruisers formed a "fake" screen. The Southern Carrier Group, Rear Admiral Yarnell, was centered around the *Saratoga* and earmarked to hit San Pedro—the type of independent operation Towers preferred.

The defending American fleet, designated Blue, was ordered to concentrate its East and West Coast units to defend the expeditionary forces forming at the three bases to relieve Hawaii. Under Admiral Luke McNamee, Blue comprised most of his Battle Fleet and submarines. Knowing Black was heading east, he was authorized to consider it hostile once it passed Midway Island in the Hawaiian group. Expecting simultaneous attacks on San Francisco and San Pedro–San Diego, McNamee formed two groups to defend each place, ignoring Puget Sound. There were patrol seaplanes and landplanes at both places, and Pat Bellinger's *Langley* was at San Francisco.[83]

The operation commenced on 10 February 1933. Admiral Clark of Black decided to send the *Saratoga* against San Pedro before Blue's East Coast units arrived. This attack was planned for the sixteenth, the day the *Lexington* would strike San Francisco. The following day both carriers would swing north, the *Lex* against Puget Sound and the *Sara* for a follow-up strike on San Francisco. However, on the fifteenth a *Lexington* plane spotted smoke from a Blue submarine, leading Clark to form his cruisers into a battle column for a possible surface action. This stripped the *Lex* of her screen, and as she was preparing for her dawn launch against San Pedro next day, two Blue battleships suddenly loomed up within 4,500 yards of both sides of the carrier. The umpire, none other than Admiral Bull Reeves, ruled her put out of action; she had failed to launch a single plane.

Yarnell and Towers had the *Saratoga* launch strikes and defensive fighters from Santa Barbara Channel after sunup on the sixteenth. The bombers struck oil refineries and docks in the Long Beach area, losing three of their number to defending fighters, while Black cruisers sank a Blue cruiser and two submarine support ships. Shortly after recovering her fighters, however, the *Saratoga* was hit by eight dive bombers from the beach. This claimed twenty planes on her deck, which was ruled put out of commission for two hours. Yarnell took his Japanese group north during the night for dawn strikes on the bay area the seventeenth. That day, however, the *Sara* was attacked and put out of commission by all twenty-one planes from the *Langley* and by seaplanes and cruiser scouts. Half of *Sara*'s planes survived to damage the San Francisco dock areas and airfield and the *Langley*.

Fleet Problem XIV ended with the critique at Long Beach on 3 March. Admiral Clark's entire plan of operating the big carriers was "most severely criticized," Towers informed Moffett; once mentioned for command of the U.S. Fleet, Clark was shunted off to the General Board instead. Yarnell and Towers believed—and Admiral Leigh concurred—that the carriers had been misused by attacking shore installations before neutralizing the enemy fleet; winning command of the sea should take priority. The same choice would confront both American and Japanese commanders in the Pacific war (just as it had the French and Spanish navies in the Age of Sail). Yarnell and Towers felt Fleet Problem XIV had not been nearly as instructive as XIII the year before. Yarnell also wanted the functions of bombing and torpedo-dropping divided between specialized planes, a recommendation that would be adopted. But both the torpedo-bombers and the flying boats, too old and slow, needed to be replaced.[84]

Yarnell and the staff headed by Towers urged that the more heavily gunned and sturdier cruisers rather than the destroyers be used as plane guards, and Yarnell begged for three more 18,000-ton carriers, as allowed by the Washington and London treaties. He believed that a minimum of six was needed for fighting Japan. Happily, President Roosevelt and Congressman Vinson concurred; in June the Vinson-Trammell Act authorized two 19,800-ton carriers—the *Yorktown* (CV-5) and *Enterprise* (CV-6), to be followed by a 1934 authorization for the smaller *Wasp* (CV-7).[85]

Returning with the fleet to Long Beach, Yarnell and Towers settled back into the weekday routine of offshore exercises. Late in the afternoon of 10 March, Jack and Pierre returned to their apartment in the Riviera Hotel, where staff operations officer Ralph Davison joined them to go over the following week's ops orders. Suddenly the room shook violently, and, in Jack's words, "the building began to rock to such an extent that we all thought it would topple right over into the street." The earthquake knocked out the electricity, "and the trip down the dark stairs was nothing to laugh about"— twelve floors! When they reached the street, they saw that the entire front of the three-story apartment house opposite had fallen. Harry and Emily Yarnell were near the Riviera; Emily, thrown to the ground by the initial jolt, had suffered a severe leg injury.

Fortunately, the fleet was in port, and landing parties immediately restored order throughout the panic-stricken city. Jack and Pierre hastened to the home of Hugh Douglas, inspector of naval aircraft at Santa Monica. Finding the building intact, they returned to the Riviera, where they discovered a piece of the ceiling had fallen smack onto Jack's pillow. Towers went aboard the *Saratoga;* the quake had traveled up her anchor chains and rattled the entire ship. Severe aftershocks continued throughout the night and all next day, and that afternoon Jack brought his wife aboard. Already hundreds of refugees had arrived, stringing diapers between the guns. And the people did not want to leave. The Towers followed the Yarnells to Coronado on Sunday. That evening Pierre developed a severe case of shock that lasted several days.[86]

The quake also upset telegraphic, telephone, and even mail communications, so that Towers had difficulty staying in touch with Moffett over the crucial events in Washington. Rumors of Moffett's short-term reappointment from March through October were received "to the joy of all aviation out here," Towers informed him. But Moffett told Jack that "the situation here is very much confused," especially when he discovered that his term would expire not on 13 March as expected but on 22 April, on which date four years before he had been confirmed by the Senate. For all Moffett knew, FDR might decide "to give me a gunboat commission." Both the president and the new secretary of the navy, Claude A. Swanson, wanted Moffett to stay on, but both were opposed to the six-month renewal of what was normally a four-year term. Still, there was plenty of time till 22 April, Moffett told Towers, "and I am not worrying about it."[87]

Moffett was glad to learn that Towers, who had flown to Sunnyvale after Fleet Problem XIV, "was most favorably impressed with the location and lay-out." For the airship program remained one of the admiral's pet projects. He personally commissioned the new dirigible *Macon* at Akron on 11 March and continued to show off her sister, the year-old *Akron,* operating out of NAS Lakehurst, New Jersey. He even invited former Secretary Josephus Daniels and Commander Pete Mitscher to take a ride in it with him on 4 April. A last-minute meeting with FDR caused Daniels to beg off, and work kept Mitscher at the bureau. Both men were lucky, for the *Akron* encountered a violent electrical storm and crashed into the sea. Moffett perished with her in the line of duty.[88]

The news stunned the nation, the navy, and the naval aviation community, not least Jack Towers. More than Jack's political supporter, the admiral had been his friend, mentor, and confidant, almost a father. Moffett had not been called the Father of Naval Aviation for nothing. Now, abruptly, he was gone, along with seventy-three of the seventy-six men aboard. The rigid airship program virtually died with him. Sunnyvale opened a week later and was renamed Moffett Field in June. The *Macon,* operating out of there the following February, also went down in an offshore storm.

And so, the problem of Moffett's successor became urgent. No one realized this more than Harry Yarnell, who fired off a letter to CNO Pratt on the day of Moffett's death. Fearing the independent air force zealots would seize on the *Akron*'s demise to promote their cause, he urged Towers' prompt appointment as chief of bureau. Arthur Cook became acting chief while the battle raged over the next three weeks. Senator Cohen spoke for Towers, as did Secretary Swanson, who sent a memo to that effect to the president on 15 April. Grover Loening also wrote to the president supporting his old friend.[89]

Towers learned later that King had an important champion in the new assistant secretary of the navy, Henry Latrobe Roosevelt. A distant cousin of the president, he had also been an academy classmate of King's before resigning to enter the Marine Corps. Towers had met Roosevelt in 1914 when they crossed the Atlantic together in the *Tennessee,* but their paths had not crossed since.[90]

Among the uniformed cadre, CNO Pratt and BuNav chief Upham held the upper hand. Ascertaining that neither Bull Reeves, Harry Yarnell, nor John Halligan wanted the job, Admiral Pratt turned to King, suggesting that he make a formal request asking consideration for the post. King complied on 13 April, pointing out he had already been selected for rear admiral in December, which gave him seniority over the younger Towers. Pratt favorably endorsed King's letter next day and forwarded it to Secretary Swanson. Though Swanson favored Towers, he and the president could not ignore the sentiment of the high command. And King's record was impressive. On 19 April Swanson formally nominated him. FDR approved, as did the Senate, and King cut short his tour at the Naval War College to assume the post on 3 May.[91]

Towers was in Long Beach when he heard the news. Vice Admiral William Standley, fleet cruiser commander but already tapped to be next CNO, remarked to him, "Better luck next time." Towers had lost the biggest battle of his career. In a letter of 28 April to Major General Benny Foulois, chief of the Air Corps, lamenting a new proposed cut in flight pay for both services, Towers remarked, "The Old Guard of the Navy lost no time in taking advantage of Admiral Moffett's death and have strengthened their position by selecting a successor which [*sic*] is one of their crowd. The main opposition to me was that I was not one of their own crowd and would not fall in line with their policies. What KING will do I do not know as he is utterly lacking in any political support."[92]

Foulois, long an opponent of service conservatism and now embarking on another struggle for aviation within the War Department, could sympathize. The common goal of army and navy aviators toward salvaging flight pay remained at the forefront. On the eve of congressional hearings on the matter Foulois replied, "Hope that I shall be able to save something out of the fire which your non-flying admirals have gotten us into."[93]

Assuming that Towers' career would progress normally, that he would continue to advance on the merits of superior performance, and that the victor would not retaliate against Towers, the appointment of King was fair and sound. He had an impressive background in battleships, submarines, aviation, and strategic thinking at the Naval War College. In some ways, King was also a compromise candidate, for in claiming the leadership of naval aviation as a qualified pilot for a four-year term, he effectively eliminated the older naval observers and JCLs from any chance of ever achieving the post.[94]

It was true, however, that King lacked political support. Unlike Moffett and Towers, he had little experience in courting congressional or industrial aircraft leaders to win appropriations, though the accession of a pro-navy man to the presidency made up for this. Neither did King have a following within the navy. In contrast to Towers, who collected around him such talent as Radford, Sherman, Davison, Ramsey, Bogan, and Jock Clark, King was a lone wolf. Most of the men who served as his key subordinates in aviation commands and/or who became his drinking buddies were comparatively lackluster, as events were to prove before and during the war. In all likelihood, King resented Towers having his own team and would keep a wary eye out for this rival. But King was neither jealous nor spiteful.[95]

Towers, in any case, had lost his direct pipeline to the front office of BuAer, and Harry Yarnell would not be able to help him much. For Yarnell had been selected to take command of the Pearl Harbor Navy Yard and Fourteenth Naval District. On 8 May in one of King's first acts as chief of bureau, he recommended Towers be assigned as a senior course student at the Naval War College. Towers had no complaint, wanting to get this duty behind him before trying again for a major billet. He received his orders on the sixteenth.[96]

The simultaneous departures of Yarnell and Towers from the carriers was an additional blow to the aviation community, coming as it did in the wake of Moffett's passing. Rear Admiral John Halligan and Commander Ernest D. McWhorter, an observer and a latecomer respectively, relieved them. As Captain Rufus Zogbaum of the *Saratoga* put it, "The new Staff did not measure up to Yarnell's high standard and there developed some of that usual friction that the captain of a flag-ship dreads," a frustration shared by his exec, Kelly Turner.[97]

Whether Towers would ever return to carriers, or even stay in the navy, remained problematic. The steadily deteriorating vision in his right eye, diagnosed as 10/20 during an annual physical in January, raised doubts about his future. His civilian eye specialist decided that a cataract was forming. In May Admiral Rossiter, navy surgeon general, reminded BuNav chief Upham that Towers was still fit to pilot aircraft but that his defective eye should again be examined over the summer. In fact, by May the loss of vision in the right eye was nearly total.[98]

The threat of a medical discharge thus came in the wake of Towers' defeat over the BuAer succession. Detached from the fleet on 10 June, he departed with Pierre by automobile for Newport, Rhode Island. He officially reported on 29 June and was joined by Marjorie and Chas, now sixteen and thirteen respectively. While settling into the war college routine, and keeping the family in trim with early morning dips in the brisk New England waters, Towers faced up to the dreaded physical.[99]

The news was bad. On 9 August the examining doctors confirmed the formation of a cataract and sent Towers to appear before a board of medical survey in Washington. Arriving there early, he pleaded his case to Secretary Swanson, the new CNO Admiral Standley, the chiefs of BuAer (King), BuNav (William D. Leahy), and BuMed (Rossiter), and others. On 21 August he was admitted to the navy hospital, where doctors found the vision in his right eye down to 20/200. They diagnosed the cataract as insufficiently developed for surgical removal. Conclusion: "vision will become less acute until it is lost."

The examining board ruled that Towers was unfit for service and recommended "that he be ordered to appear before the U.S. Naval Retiring Board." End of the line![100]

But Towers refused to give up. His civilian eye specialists had told him that the cataract could be removed surgically once it was fully developed, which they believed would be about two years hence. Confronting Admiral Rossiter in person, Towers argued that since he expected to occupy shore billets for three years, any action on his retirement ought to be postponed until the end of that time. Meanwhile, he could have the cataract removed in an operation. Rossiter retorted that he would never change his mind, despite the results of any operation. Rossiter's eye specialist, Lieutenant Commander Ross T. McIntire, also White House physician, advised Towers against such an operation; it would mean Jack would have to wear glasses, possibly leading to double vision. This opinion was contrary to those of the civilian specialists Jack had consulted.[101]

To Admiral Leahy, chief of BuNav, Towers' arguments seemed reasonable. "The Bureau of Navigation does not consider that an officer with useful vision in only one eye should be permitted to operate or command a ship of the Navy," wrote Leahy in his endorsement of the survey's findings on 25 August.

> However, in consideration of the long service . . . of Captain Towers in connection with Naval Aviation, the probable future value of his experience in the continued development of that essential branch of the Naval Service, and the fact that revocation of his aviation's qualification would, under existing law . . . , prevent his employment in command of a naval air station, for which duty he is believed to be fully qualified; it is recommended that he be retained for the present in his active duty status and not ordered before a retiring board at this time.

Secretary Swanson concurred the same day.[102]

So it was not the end of the line—yet. The fair-minded professionalism of Leahy, Standley, and King in sending him to the Naval War College no doubt saved Towers from being summarily retired at this time. He was valuable; the navy badly needed talent. Like Frank McCrary and Rufus Zogbaum, who were both passed over for flag rank but who successively commanded NAS Pensacola from 1933 to 1936, Towers could be put to good use as an air station commander before being retired. But Leahy had also ruled out half-blind aviators from commanding carriers. More fierce battles loomed as Jack prepared to fight the medicos and BuNav for his professional survival.

10

CARRIER STRATEGIST
1933–38

Japan's absorption of Manchuria and growing militancy erased any doubts in the U.S. Navy about Japanese designs for hegemony in the Pacific and Far East. The Naval War College embodied official navy thinking, and Towers utilized his year there as a senior course student to sharpen his own strategic thinking, particularly over the potential use of the aircraft carrier against Japan. He hoped to return to the fleet to apply what he had learned.

During the autumn of 1933, Towers heard retired Captain Dudley W. Knox present an incisive lecture entitled "National Strategy." Knox envisioned the United States as the "world island" whose task was to promote peaceful maritime commerce around the globe. Building on the prewar visions of the great Mahan, he argued for American economic internationalism, with the navy as the principal formulator and agent of national strategy. The "strategic blunders" of American foreign policy after the world war, notably the government's refusal to build up the navy to treaty limits, had made "our whole national strategy revolving around the Open Door [in China] and naval limitation . . . a dismal failure." Inasmuch as "the world will profit most from a strong America," Knox proclaimed (and Towers agreed), the navy should educate the American people about maritime and strategic realities. This view had first been espoused by retired admiral William S. Sims and his key wartime overseas advisers, Knox, Harry Yarnell, and Luke McNamee.[1]

"Admiral Mac" was the new president of the Naval War College, much to the delight of "Captain Jack." Towers was one of five captains and thirty-four commanders of the line in the senior course, the only other one of subsequent note being J. O. Richardson. With the junior class, the student body totaled eighty-eight, mostly navy and Marine Corps officers. The small fraternity shared their social lives as well as ideas in the classroom. Rental housing was fairly spartan, and the only reason that no one had taken the place leased by Jack and Pierre when they arrived was that it lacked a garage. Jack persuaded the owner to add one. Although prohibition ended in December 1933, Towers still had to keep up appearances whenever he and Pierre motored down to Connecticut for visits with his teetotaler brother Fullton, still vice president of Ford, Bacon, and Davis. When they arrived for Christmas Eve dinner, recalled a cousin, Fullton "ran out to their car and snatched a leather gladstone bag which he took to the front door and dropped on the slate door sill. In a half a minute the bag leaked Scotch and probably gin and bourbon." Jack wanted his martinis, even if in the privacy of the guest room. Fullton thought it was "terribly funny."[2]

The year of quiet home life enabled Towers to give his full attention to the mission of the college—thinking about fighting the next war. Traditional policy called for the battle force of the U.S. Fleet, built around the dozen newest battleships, to advance inexorably westward against Orange, the Japanese empire and fleet. The students tested this doctrine in the operations department, which included strategy and tactics; intelligence; and research. The broader theoretical philosophy of war was gleaned from reading the classics of historical strategy by Karl von Clausewitz, Sir Julian Corbett, Alfred Thayer Mahan, and Admiral Sir Herbert Richmond, along with translations of recent German and French theorists. And special attention was given to the grand strategy, command, and tactical examples of World War I, notably the Battle of Jutland.[3]

In college war games as in fleet problems, Pacific wars had traditionally focused on the big battle à la Trafalgar, Tsushima, or Jutland. But the simple naval strategy of winning command of the sea in one decisive engagement had begun to yield to the probability of a longer, more complicated struggle. Either way, the role of aviation took on new importance. In a freshly revised college booklet entitled "The Naval Battle," Towers read, no doubt with satisfaction, that the few American carriers should operate well away from the battle line for their own safety. Or they could cruise at the center of a tactical formation that included gunships. Carrier planes would have to launch early attacks on the enemy's carriers to win command of the air over both fleets. Then these planes could bomb and torpedo other enemy ships. "Aircraft are the *eyes* of the fleet in battle," announced the booklet; as such they should scout enemy ships and submarines. In October Towers listened to a lecture by Commander Hugh Douglas, the only aviator on the faculty, who maintained that carrier planes would achieve tactical concentration through their maneuverability and volume of fire. Aircraft, however, could not alone win the battle or command of the sea.[4]

The point of departure was always the war game, with battle doctrine embodied in the highly formalized "Estimate of the Situation," the forty-two-page bible of fleet planning, instructions, and orders. Any estimate was based on one's own mission, the strength of the enemy, the enemy's probable intentions, one's own tactical options, and finally the decision itself. Not only was this decision-making process rigid, it was vague. Worse, guessing an enemy's *intentions* could be exceedingly dangerous; Admiral McNamee's successors revised this to meet an enemy's *capabilities*.[5]

The preceding college class, '33, with much the same directing staff, had established many of the prerequisites for the Blue U.S. Fleet fighting Orange Japan. That class included three prominent aviator captains—King, McCrary, and Whiting—as well as Bill Halsey, who, however, had not yet entered aviation. Following the navy's Orange Plan to drive across the Pacific, the Class of '33 had decided that the fleet must aim for an economic blockade of the Japanese home islands. The forward base that Blue would need was Truk in the Caroline islands of the central Pacific. Ernie King had insisted that the next objective be the Marianas (Guam, Saipan, and Tinian). The final target was Okinawa in the Ryukyu chain, which if captured would seal off Japan from her overseas trade. And significantly, the fleet's carriers might even begin bombing strategic targets inside Japan. Such an air-sea blockade would presumably force Japan's surrender, for no real thought was given to invasion.[6]

Towers and his classmates of '34 built on this scenario. In the summer of 1933, during the demonstration exercise and initial tactical problem, Towers commanded first Orange then Blue heavy gun forces, directing movements of the small leaden ship models between squares on the game board that covered the floor of the large gaming hall. Tactical Problem II, in September, was more interesting. Blue, using the new carrier *Ranger,* had to protect a convoy out of Truk against the attacking Orange fleet, which had the *Lexington.* A big battle resulted northeast of Truk during which extensive air operations and a naval gunnery duel destroyed the flight decks of both carriers. In Tactical Problem III that autumn, Blue tried to gain control of the western Pacific; both sides were equipped with a *Saratoga*-type carrier. The ensuing four problems tested similar situations as well as the traditional yet by now fanciful battle with Red (the British fleet) in the western Atlantic. Particularly unusual was Tactical Problem VI in which Soviet Russia was allied with the United States against Japan. And the Battle of Jutland was analyzed.[7]

In addition to war games, readings, and lectures, there was the thesis. Or rather the theses, because for the first time the Department of Intelligence required two of each senior student. Topics could be selected from two of three areas: the relationship between national policy and war strategy at a particular time in history; the relationship between wartime strategy, tactics, and command; and/or a topic of the student's own choosing, with departmental approval. Theses, which were usually drawn from the same sources and tended to sound alike, were not normally preserved by the college. Not so Towers'. The library archives retained both of his, along with only six others from the Class of '34. The first he submitted on 1 February, the second on 7 May 1934; Pierre typed them both.[8]

Perhaps the fact that she was French influenced the topic he selected for his first thesis, "The Relationship between French Policy and Strategy in the War of the Coalition, 1777–1783, and Its Lessons to Us." Drawing on his own wide reading of history, Towers used Mahan and Corbett plus nineteen standard histories and biographies to trace the role of France and her navy in helping America win her War of Independence. Familiar with the long uncertain history of strategy in France, Towers observed how rare it was that any nation actually recognized its own policy sufficiently to carry it "through to a conclusion." In the few instances where a nation did, success was due "rather to the singleness of purpose and the tenacity of the [military] commanders-in-chief than to the higher [political] authorities."[9]

Towers concluded that eighteenth-century France provided twentieth-century America with a good example of a faulty grand strategy. French war aims in the American Revolution had been based purely on revenge, that is, the crippling of British power. Yet the French navy, forced into a defensive strategy, was never allowed to "secure command of the sea," that "object of naval warfare" articulated by the late Corbett. Thus even when it had superior strength the French navy could not attack British naval and colonial power decisively. Towers demonstrated this with an analysis based heavily on French naval operations. "War, as an instrument of national policy," he argued, "should never be embarked upon unless it is supported by the national strategy."[10]

Towers drew a parallel between the French example and the indecisive national policy of his own country: "While we may not have a policy of war against Japan, our official actions have been such as to lead that country to believe that such is our policy, and it may be forced upon us. We should either abandon a policy which appears warlike, and may provoke war, or, if we adhere to that policy, we should adjust our national strategy to support it." The national policy and the navy's mission should be complementary, he believed, their objectives clearly defined even if limited in scope. Towers was reflecting navy frustration over an understrength fleet. In his second thesis he declared flatly that the U.S. Navy was not strong enough to support American national policy.[11]

Towers left no doubt that he believed in America's global reach. Isolationism was no longer viable—"our interests extend throughout the world." He urged that the United States seek "open friendships" with nations "whose interests parallel ours," friendships that would develop into alliances during war. By inference, he meant Britain and France in Europe and China in Asia. In other words, America could not stand alone, as she had tried to do by not ratifying the Versailles Treaty and not joining the League of Nations; relying unilaterally on arms limitations treaties would not insure peace. In particular, he believed America should shore up the Open Door policy, conducting peaceful commerce with China to counter Japanese strength. These were the national policies sought by most of his peers at Newport and many but not all admirals, some of whom rejected the idea of American involvement in the Far East.[12]

The lack of strategic direction of which Towers wrote would continue until and into World War II. No coherent political-military strategy for the Pacific would develop except through what Towers in his thesis called "the singleness of purpose and the tenacity of the commander-in-chief" of the U.S. Navy. In World War II that person would be Admiral Ernest J. King. Towers and King were among the few articulate individuals, political or military, who foresaw the need for a new global order of sea power based on American naval supremacy.[13]

Towers' second thesis was a topic of his own choosing, approved by the Department of Intelligence and not yet examined by anybody, anywhere— "The Influence of Aircraft on Naval Strategy and Tactics," a title borrowed from the example of Mahan. The airplane, he wrote, had to be "silhouetted against the . . . curtain of History" to determine whether and how such a "new species" of technological development was significantly different from others. For instance, the much-vaunted torpedo had failed to revolutionize naval warfare. Not even the submarine had lived up to expectations (Towers thought, wrongly as it turned out, that the armed merchantman would prove the demise of the sub). In any case, since new weapons had always stimulated counterweapons, he refused to regard the airplane as revolutionary.[14]

In point of fact, Towers admitted, the development of the airplane and its use with navies had not yet "reached a point from which the future trend can be predicted with confidence." Nevertheless, the navy was obliged "to anticipate the future insofar as practicable," which was the aim of his thesis. Looking primarily at the Pacific, Towers envisioned naval aviation being utilized both in battles at sea and against shore-based aircraft. The aircraft carrier must continue to support the battle line in a naval engagement but while operating well beyond sight of opposing battleships and their spotting planes. Its greatest defense against enemy bombers and guns, in Towers' view, was evasion through high speed and by attacking opposing carriers. The carrier could also be used to protect convoys and on antisubmarine patrol.[15]

Since the carrier was untested in war, and because the navy still had only two front-line carriers in commission, Towers had to rely on his own knowledge and experience in fleet problems to examine carrier tactics. In so doing, he anticipated the choices that would confront tacticians in the Pacific war. Though torpedo planes were vulnerable to antiaircraft fire and defensive fighters when lining up for their drops, dive bombers had proved extremely difficult to stop during high-speed, high-angle dives. So carriers could either be concentrated together defensively, which would make them more susceptible "to wholesale bombing," or be widely separated, thereby increasing the difficulties of mutual logistic and operational support. (The latter tactic would be followed before 1943, the former afterward.) Towers believed that the rules imposed in fleet problems and in college war games tended to "overemphasize the vulnerability of carriers to bombing attack, in comparison with other vessels." The carrier's great offensive power was its strength, he said, first through scouting, then attacking, and always supported defensively by heavy cruisers. Since both ship types had to train together, "type organization should give way to task organization," as indeed it would in World War II.[16]

The role of large shore-based aircraft concerned Towers because the range of some patrol bombers in the world had already reached 700 miles and promised to increase. When an attacking fleet attempting to impose a blockade came within range of large numbers of such bombers on islands or in countries—by inference Japan and the mandated islands—that fleet faced "considerable risk of loss or heavy damage." Furthermore, attacking carrier planes would have great difficulty destroying land-based air forces. In fact, that could only be accomplished with "an overwhelming superiority in carriers," which did not exist in 1934 (but would ten years later). As for raiding the enemy's coast or "some outlying base . . . surprise can be effected by remaining beyond the probable scouting range from shore, until darkness, then by dashing in at full speed and launching the aircraft in time to reach their objective by daylight." Towers had done just that with Yarnell's carriers against Pearl Harbor in 1932; the Japanese would repeat it in 1941. Or, carriers could strike in late afternoon and retire under cover of darkness, a tactic also destined to be used in the Pacific war.[17]

Towers also made some wrong guesses, by reason of changing technology. He thought that aerial smoke-laying had "more value defensively" to the battle line than a squadron of fighters did. As for the airship, large or small, he concluded that, "at present, it exercises no influence on Naval Strategy and Tactics." He admitted, however, that "future developments may change this," as indeed they would, namely, the small antisub nonrigid blimp. Looking for a quick, inexpensive substitute for more carriers, Towers continued to advocate the flight-deck cruiser, but that was a dead issue. Also, certain minor aspects of aircraft tactics that he extolled would prove erroneous because of newer and better planes. Technological progress being inevitable, "history has shown us that Naval Strategy and Tactics are never in a static state."[18]

What kind of a tactical commander would Towers be in battle? By the end of his war college duty, all signs pointed to him as a potentially aggressive leader. He had shown it at sea while in command of the *Langley* and on board the *Saratoga* as chief of staff to Harry Yarnell. As a student of history, he had read widely on the great captains of old and had the memory of his father's service with the great Forrest in the Civil War. In his first war college thesis, he followed Mahan in criticizing British admiral Rodney for failing to pursue the defeated deGrasse after the Battle of the Saints in 1782, thus missing "the opportunity to practically annihilate the disorganized French Fleet." And from his service in wartime London, he knew how Jellicoe's urging of his admirals to be independent and take the initiative had failed at Jutland. On the subject of naval battles, Towers proclaimed in his second thesis, "[T]he doctrine of aircraft attacks should be: 'as early as possible, and as often as possible. . . .'" Towers was clearly a proponent of the aggressive use of carriers.[19]

He lauded Britain's accomplishments as a seagoing nation, underscored American progress in the air, and made a curious reference to Japan without naming her: "The American nation is rapidly becoming an air-going nation, excelling in building and in flying aircraft. Furthermore, aircraft warfare is individualistic, no other part of the Fleet is broken down into such small units. Blind obedience and fatalism, characteristic of certain foreign peoples, while possibly elements of strength in mass warfare on land or on sea[,] have no place in the air." This allusion to the fanaticism of the Japanese probably emanated from conversations with his college classmate Ellis M. Zacharias, who in his own thesis on Japanese conduct in the war against Russia warned of their "contempt for death."[20]

Towers concluded his second thesis by wedding the advancement of naval aviation to Mahan's view of Anglo-American individualism: "It would seem that the American people by their national characteristics are particularly adapted to air warfare, and that the more we can carry naval warfare into the air, the greater the advantage to us. Should we not, therefore, shape our plans towards these ends?"[21]

The Naval War College accomplished its purpose in enhancing the education and thinking of Jack Towers. At the graduation exercise held in the just-opened Pringle Hall on 25 May 1934, he easily identified with the remarks of the keynote speaker, Admiral William D. Leahy, chief of BuNav: "To survive at sea, study and knowledge of history are helpful—plans for the future are necessary—and with these, with which you are now well provided, you should more easily acquire that facility of meeting unanticipated changes in conditions which is the final essential to success at sea. My closing advice is that you should assiduously cultivate this facility. . . ."[22]

That facility Towers would develop, assuming that normal vision could be restored to his right eye. His annual physical in December 1933 had confirmed near-blindness in his eye. Surgeon General Perceval Rossiter refused to approve Towers "for aviation duty involving actual control of aircraft," still wanting to retire him, but Admiral King saved Jack by again convincing BuNav chief Leahy of his value to aviation. Leahy continued the waiver, stipulating that Jack fly only with a copilot.[23]

In fact, King did not even wait for Rossiter's verdict before recommending in January 1934 that Towers be given command of NAS San Diego, home of the fleet's air operations. Leahy agreed and issued the orders on 10 March. Immensely pleased, Jack arranged passage for himself, Pierre, and son Chas in the commercial liner *Pennsylvania* cruising via the Panama Canal to the West Coast. On 8 June they left Newport and arrived at San Diego on the twenty-ninth. Jack relieved Johnny Hoover the next day.[24]

Command of North Island was important, though not nearly as important as a carrier command would have been. Still, Towers' administrative talents would be essential when the *Ranger* (CV-4), commissioned on 4 June, arrived with her planes and the first reserve pilot trainees in a new aviation cadet program. He worked with an old *Michigan* shipmate now commanding the Eleventh Naval District, the congenial Rear Admiral William T. Tarrant, who soon developed a great admiration for Towers' abilities. They and their spouses enjoyed a close social relationship, though Tarrant was a strict teetotaler. Daughter Marjorie joined the family at San Diego, and Pierre quickly adapted to the role of raising the teenagers, for Jack as usual remained engrossed in his work. Marge had blossomed into a pretty eighteen-year-old, while Chas was a serious lad of fourteen. Jack acquired a Scottie for Marge called Cinders. Cinders sired Mr. MacTavish, who became Jack's pet; Jack always put a bow tie on him during parties.[25]

Towers had an excellent staff at his disposal, notably his exec, Commander Wadleigh Capehart, an aviator since 1915, and the head of the assembly and repair department, Lieutenant Commander F. W. "Horse" or "Gee Gee" Pennoyer, Jr., a flying member of the Construction Corps. Their airmen conducted experiments for lightweight flight suits, controllable-pitch propellers, and new cockpit instruments and radios. The physical plant was enlarged with new buildings, hangars, and paved landing areas. The fleet's return in November 1934 gave San Diego responsibility for all twenty-two battle force squadrons, four squadrons of the base force, and two of the Marine Corps, plus the station's own planes. The arrival of the *Ranger* the following April brought the fleet's aircraft strength there to over one thousand planes, but they were of so many different models that Towers and Pennoyer had their hands full keeping them all in operating trim under the handicap of mounting Depression-era budgetary constraints.[26]

Flying so many plane types was pure joy for the navy's senior aviator. North Island received one of only five Douglas R2D (DC-2) monoplane transports to replace its big aging Ford Trimotor. Towers loved the Douglas. Recalled station test pilot Lieutenant George van Deurs, for whom Towers was "a mythical figure," "several times he thought up excuses to go places in it, flying as my second pilot. For instance, he filled it with doctors from the Naval Hospital for an overnight trip to Reno."

Van Deurs' admiration for his boss grew quickly. In spite of the eye problem, Towers "could fly just as well as he could when he was a kid, and he loved flying. He used to call up the test line. If we had a new fighter up there that he hadn't seen, he wanted to try it, and he could do a beautiful job with it—cataract or no." Because of the BuNav requirement for a safety pilot, van Deurs fulfilled that role during 1934–35. But "I never touched the controls.

The man was a perfectly good pilot. He could easily take a plane up, feel it out, something he'd never been in before, and ease it back on the field just like it was a breeze."

The more they flew together, the better van Deurs got to understand Towers. "People who didn't like him said he was a stuffed shirt, that he was very hard to know, and rather snooty. During the time I was there I discovered that it was not that at all. . . . He was a very smart man, but he was also very shy, and the shyness was what gave people the idea that he was stuck up. . . . He was a very friendly bird, and when he was convinced that you knew what you were doing, he could be very friendly."[27]

Van Deurs was a good example of the kind of superior aviator and officer that Towers tried to help out. When van Deurs was passed over for promotion to lieutenant in 1935 for the third time, partly because of Depression promotion decelerations, Towers let him use a plane to fly to Washington to plead his case with Admiral King. The BuAer chief was sympathetic, but it was Towers who actually insured his promotion two years later.[28]

Towers kept better informed about aviation logistics than any other senior officer in the operating fleet after discovering Lieutenant (jg) James W. Boundy, an NROTC Supply Corps product who had teamed up with the chief aviation supply clerk to learn the ropes of aviation logistics firsthand. Jack made Boundy the air station mess manager and worked closely with him to insure comfortable living conditions for the pilots. According to Boundy, Towers believed "that a flyer should be in good shape—know his job—do it well—and then be able to relax in proper surroundings and get a good night's sleep." Long unhappy with the bachelor officers' quarters, Jack set out to make it "the best damned mess—ashore or afloat." He did it by arranging for the El Cortez and Coronado hotel chefs to give his navy cooks on-the-spot classes.[29]

The navy's 567 acres of the 1,340-acre North Island, always crowded, had by now become so congested that safety and efficiency were dangerously compromised. The army still refused to give up its adjacent Rockwell Field, and Towers and Admiral King campaigned vigorously for the transfer of the property to the navy. Not until late 1935 did the army agree to trade Rockwell Field for certain other navy properties. On 2 October of that year President Roosevelt and Admiral King inspected North Island to see what the navy was getting, which was a newly built circular landing field as well as the army's older layout, now South Field. Towers had many old wartime buildings razed, occupied sixty-one brand new ones, and welcomed additional acreage created by harbor dredges that widened the anchorage for easier use by the *Saratoga* and *Lexington*. The smaller *Ranger* could use the same dock as the *Langley*.[30]

As career patterns went, Towers at forty-nine was still in the pipeline for one of the coveted big carriers, although the competition for them increased as more JCLs earned their wings—"using aviation duty as a stepladder," in Towers' words. Of all the influential senior officers, the one who concerned Towers most was JCL King. Jack was apparently ignorant of the admiral's key role in saving him from premature retirement at the hands of the surgeon general. On one of King's inspection trips to North Island, he, Jack, and Pierre dined with Admiral Tarrant, after which Towers invited King for a highball at his house across the street. The two men sat in front of the fireplace drinking Scotch and discussing and arguing over virtually everything. The marathon lasted several hours. Pierre retired after the third round of drinks.[31]

Towers' feelings about King bordered on paranoia. During a party at the Hotel Del Coronado, the two found themselves alone in the men's room. King had been his usual social self, flirting with the ladies and talking too loudly to suit the reserved Towers. Both men had been drinking, and they began to argue about King's conduct. Jack accused Ernie of being a "penny whistle"—a noisemaker. For the rest of his life Towers brooded over the incident, calling it the "one great mistake in my life." He believed his relations with King were never the same again. Inasmuch as King tended to discount social insults, of which he had aplenty, in all likelihood this reaction was largely of Towers' own making.[32]

In 1950, after both men had retired, King learned of some negative remarks Towers had made about him at a party. A mutual friend stopped Jack with the question, "Who helped you out when you had trouble with your eyes?" Whereupon Towers was given the facts about King's role. Indeed, after Jack's annual physical in November 1934 had again found him unqualified to fly, King interceded for the second time, saving Towers by recommending disapproval of the medical report. Supplied with these facts in 1950, Jack was finally able to admit he had been wrong about King, at least in the matter of his salvaged career.[33] Still, King in his memoirs revealed his displeasure over "those who seemingly felt that if one were to fly one had to be born with wings. . . ."[34]

Towers' concern over King's refusal to support his candidacy to be next chief of BuAer, of course, was entirely accurate. In March 1935 he learned from his contacts at the Navy Department that King would relieve Henry V. Butler as carrier admiral during the summer or fall, a post that now carried

Towers greets President Franklin D. Roosevelt on the latter's visit to San Diego, October 1935. Next to FDR is Rear Admiral William T. Tarrant, commandant of the Eleventh Naval District. (Towers collection)

three stars. Worse, he was informed by Captain A. B. Cook of the *Lexington* that King's departure "is being kept secret while K is trying to fix it up" for Cook to succeed him. Cook assured Jack and others that he would not campaign for the post, but that he wouldn't reject it if offered. Again, it seemed, Towers would have to campaign to become chief. He wrote three long letters at the end of the month. From the CNO, Admiral Standley, he asked for support. From Rear Admiral Joe Richardson, war college classmate and now budget officer of the navy, he sought advice. And from Congressman Carl Vinson he hoped for covert political backing; Vinson told Jack's brother-in-law Ed Maddox that he, Vinson, would at least discuss the matter with Secretary of the Navy Swanson.[35]

"You know K.," Jack told Richardson, "he is unforgiving and ruthless when it comes to getting his own way. He knows I am qualified for the job, and entitled to it, but I feel sure he will do his utmost to keep me out." Jack's record had "no spots," and "those who are against me probably will repeat the old legend that I am a Radical." Only a moderate could have helped suppress the movement for a naval air corps. As for his "relative juniority," Towers cited the case of his '06 classmate Norman M. Smith, now a rear admiral and chief of BuDocks. On the matter of Towers' one bad eye, there was the example of the one-eyed civilian pilot Wiley Post, "the only man who had flown around the world *alone;* as regards other naval duties Admiral Lord Nelson had but one eye."[36]

From Towers' point of view, the "most dangerous" competitor for chief of BuAer was Arthur Cook, "an excellent officer" and "a good personal friend" of Jack's. Of the latecomers to aviation, Cook had the reputation as "one of the finest. . . . I think, in the final analysis, King will back him as being the only hope of defeating me."[37]

Final say in the matter belonged not to King but to CNO Standley on the advice of King and the incoming BuNav chief, Rear Admiral Adolphus Andrews, a friend of Towers' since their earliest days in the navy. The CNO told Towers quite frankly that he could not support Jack's candidacy because of "your status under the medical survey and the fact that this has precluded your close contact with fleet matters. . . ." Since Towers had been ashore for only two years, Standley's stance may be explained simply by his desire to thwart Jack's political maneuverings in recent years.[38]

So there it was. Towers lost again in his bid to become chief of BuAer. Standley forced King to remain in that post for another year, during which King never wavered in his support of Cook, whom he regarded as "steady as a rock and always ready to learn" whatever he lacked in knowledge. Cook would relieve King as chief of bureau in June 1936. Though King had saved Towers' career, he had also blocked his rise to the top job in aviation.[39]

Jack decided that his only hope lay in correcting his eye problem and returning to the fleet, thereby countering the CNO's objections to his advancement. During the autumn of 1935 he visited one navy and three civilian eye specialists. All agreed that the cataract had reached maturity and ought to be removed surgically. On their advice, in September he arranged a trip to San Francisco to consult Dr. Otto Barkan, leading eye surgeon on the West Coast and equal to any in the country. Barkan confirmed that the eye was ready for surgery. Although it would be an expensive, painful, and "delicate and dangerous operation," the surgeon believed that, if successful, it would result in the complete restoration of peripheral vision unaided by glasses. This convinced Towers, who promptly took leave from the navy to have the operation performed.[40]

Dr. Barkan removed the cataract from Towers' right eye on 29 October 1935. Because of the proximity of the cataract to the lens, the lens was also removed and replaced by a contact lens, at the time an almost unknown corrective device. Within weeks Barkan found that, with the contact lens,

Towers' vision was again 20/20 in both eyes. Even before the operation, the ophthalmologist had been amazed to find that in the left eye Towers enjoyed extremely fine depth perception. This was because the left eye had compensated for the deterioration of vision in the right. In other words, Towers' depth perception had become even more acute than that of a normal person. He proved this to himself by shooting a forty-three on his first nine holes of golf after the operation. Barkan concluded that his patient would be "a good risk" in the cockpit, either alone or with passengers.[41]

This diagnosis was confirmed by Towers' annual and flight physicals on 6 January 1936. Since Admiral Rossiter was absent from Washington, the acting chief of BuMed approved the exam, though he still insisted on a copilot for Towers. Word spread throughout the naval aviation community, beginning with Admiral King, who promptly recommended that Towers relieve A. B. Cook in command of the *Lexington.* By the end of January, Towers' future seemed to be back on course.[42]

But Towers had not reckoned with the formidable Perceval Rossiter, who upon his return to Washington became enraged at Towers for having circumvented the system. Rossiter had Andrews order Towers back to Washington for a more thorough examination, to be undertaken on the advice of President Roosevelt's private physician Ross McIntire of the Navy Medical Corps. As the navy's senior ophthalmologist, McIntire took a dim view of Towers' rejecting his advice of 1933 against such an operation by a civilian. For five days in early February Towers underwent an intensive examination by a board of doctors and again passed with flying colors. Its recommendation for his return to duty was endorsed by BuNav.[43]

This was too much for Rossiter, who promptly disapproved the board's recommendations on 21 February: "Under present day operating conditions in the Fleet, an officer is in need of all his special senses and this Bureau is of [the] opinion that the placing of an officer with Captain Towers' visual defects in command of a ship, or as a pilot of an airplane, constitutes an unwarranted jeopardy to himself, to the crew, and to the ship." Given this dictum, Andrews saw no recourse but to cancel Towers' orders to the *Lexington.*

Shocked by the rejection, Towers visited Rossiter and meticulously explained Barkan's findings, that he did not require the "corrective lens" except in an emergency, and that in twenty-five hours of post-operation flying in California he had made dozens of good landings without his copilot's assistance. So on 5 March the surgeon general ordered a third examination, after which Jack thought he had them convinced. But he was wrong. Next day Rossiter recommended he be presented to a retiring board.[44]

Towers felt naked. Secretary Swanson was bedridden from an accidental fall, and CNO Standley was attending an abortive arms limitation conference in London, leaving BuNav chief Andrews as acting secretary. Since Towers had already appealed to Andrews, he could only turn to Andrews' assistant, acting chief of BuNav Captain Chester Nimitz. Nimitz agreed that Towers might get an impartial medical officer to explain the technical aspects of the case, but none could be found to buck the surgeon general. King and other bureau chiefs sympathized with Towers, as did Admiral Bull Reeves, now commander in chief, U.S. Fleet. In a long letter to Reeves, Jack concluded in frustration, "As it now stands, the only court of high appeal is the President, and he has constantly at his elbow the Surgeon General's henchman, Dr. McIntire."[45]

Reeves, having discussed Towers' case with the medical examiners at San Diego, wrote a strong personal letter to Andrews in which he made no attempt to question the medical findings: "The point at issue is can he perform his duties? I know the answer to that—there is not the slightest doubt that he can perform all his duties ashore and afloat. . . . I am willing to stake my reputation that Towers is fully qualified to take command of the LEXINGTON." An even more powerful ally was Carl Vinson, surely the congressman who threatened to "tear the hide off the Navy Department on the floor of the House" if Towers was retired.[46]

Ernie King stepped in with a compromise solution, again rescuing Towers. On 9 March King and Andrews agreed that Jake Fitch would be given the *Lexington,* but that Towers would be immediately ordered to sea as chief of staff to Vice Admiral Butler, the carrier commander. Jack's orders were issued that very day—to report to the flagship *Saratoga* in less than a month. The haste may have been designed to get the matter settled before CNO Standley returned to Washington and King was detached. Arguing that Towers' eyes could be tested under operating conditions at sea, King and Andrews got Admiral Rossiter to agree, "provided that such an assignment did not involve his personally handling a ship or Fleet from the bridge, or piloting of aircraft."[47]

It was only a small victory, for Towers would be stepping back into the same job he had had under Harry Yarnell three years before. Still, back on board the *Saratoga,* he could again circumvent Rossiter's restriction to prove his worth. In fact, Andrews was so concerned about this that he got King to insist that Towers indoctrinate his copilot fully. Andrews also required Jack to keep his contact lens handy, so Pierre made a small leather pouch for it which Jack would hang around his neck. He received his orders on 11 March.[48]

Not to be forgotten is the fact that all the while Towers remained reserved. His cool professionalism, dignified manner, and unparalleled ability continued to command the respect of all with whom he served and the loyalty of the aviation community of career pilots. This view was shared enthusiastically by Admiral Tarrant, who in his fitness report rated Towers as "fully qualified in all respects for a capital ship command."[49]

Towers relinquished command of North Island on 4 April 1936 and relieved his classmate Jake Fitch on Butler's staff the next day. Henry Varnum Butler, not highly regarded by any officers of his staff, was headed toward retirement. Butler and his staff did not dictate air policy; this was done by the commander in chief, U.S. Fleet, Admiral Bull Reeves, and his staff aviation officer Commander Frank Wagner. They used the same aggressive aerial doctrines earlier practiced on the *Langley*. And now they had four flattops: Halsey's *Sara*, Arthur Cook's *Lex*, Arthur L. Bristol's *Ranger*, and Johnny Hoover's *Langley*, though the Covered Wagon was earmarked for conversion into a seaplane tender.[50]

The fleet sortied late in April 1936 for Fleet Problem XVII in Central American waters, the ships concentrating on tactical, screening, and flight exercises rather than war games. Admiral Butler allowed Towers to direct the division of four carriers and their plane guards in all operational and tactical situations, openly defying the surgeon general's order forbidding it. On 9 June, three days after the ships returned to their home ports, Butler turned over the carrier command to Frederick J. Horne and wrote a glowing fitness report of Towers that concluded, "Qualified for promotion and recommended for selection." Although the regular flag selection process was not supposed to tap the Class of '06 for another two years, the endorsement could only enhance Towers' ultimate candidacy.[51]

Vice Admiral Freddie Horne, an aviation observer and former skipper of the *Saratoga*, was pleased to have the navy's foremost aviator as his chief of staff, they being of like mind and temperament. In fact, the Horne-Towers team proved to be "a wonderful combination," in the words of navigator Wu Duncan of the staff, a staff that included Alfred E. Montgomery and then Arthur Radford as operations officer and John Ostrander as gunnery officer.[52]

The annual summer rotation in the high command worked to the carriermen's advantage, for the new commander in chief, U.S. Fleet, Admiral Arthur J. Hepburn, was a battleship man who let Horne and Towers run air operations. Jack worked closely with Hepburn's aviation officer, Commander Bob Molten, during daily exercises off the southern California coast. Horne allowed Towers to handle the carrier formations and rewarded him with accolades in fitness reports, recommending him for a carrier command and eventual promotion to rear admiral.[53]

Jack continued to influence all facets of naval aviation. He examined and approved Jerry Bogan's new syllabus for instrument flying at Pensacola. He was one of three naval aviators (with King and Cook) named to the Honorary Advisory Committee of the Society of Automotive Engineers, whose national aircraft production meeting he attended in Los Angeles in October. And he convinced Horne and the staff to reject Hepburn's idea to reduce the angle and speed of dive and to lower the bomb-release point of dive bombers in the interest of safety, since this would nullify the advantages of dive bombing. Lacking dive flaps and other "speed inhibiters," existing planes could simply not slow down during their dives. This resulted in the development of a plane incorporating such features, the Douglas SBD Dauntless.[54]

In mid-December 1936 Towers took his annual physical at San Diego and received the usual waivers for flying with a copilot. One month later Admiral Horne wrote a lengthy endorsement, saying that he had "observed him on inspections and drills of aircraft carriers and found his vision keen in noting defects that would probably escape most observers." It didn't matter. Surgeon General Rossiter, noting that the 20/200 vision in Towers' right eye (that is, without the lens) had not changed, rejected the report of the examiners. He insisted that Towers not solo in an airplane; BuAer and BuNav chiefs Cook and Andrews agreed, and while allowing the waiver to continue, Andrews would not give Towers command of a carrier. Learning this, in mid-March 1937 Towers drew up a twelve-page "Appeal for Redress of Wrong" to the secretary of the navy setting forth the facts of his case. In it he argued that his eyesight was being judged more severely than that of his peers; Captain Bill Halsey, two years older than Jack, had required a corrective lens in the cockpit while earning his wings in 1934–35.[55]

A. B. Cook, now chief of BuAer, wrote to Secretary Swanson urging that Towers be appointed to a carrier command. Reflecting the frustration of many aviators now being passed over, Cook touched on an increasingly sensitive matter: "Failure to command a carrier at this time may result in his not being selected to the rank of Rear Admiral. . . . The Aeronautic Organization is already considerably handicapped by the lack of officers of flag rank of the requisite experience and service. Captain Towers' retirement as a Captain will seriously augment this condition."[56]

Jack must have noted the irony in a feature story about him in the *Los Angeles Times Sunday Magazine* that February when it concluded, "Capt. Towers has travelled the uncharted skyways which led from the primitive to the modern, and he can still feel some of the bumps!"[57]

Supported by a contingent of high-ranking officers headed by Admiral Reeves, and probably including the new CNO, Admiral Leahy, Towers was ordered to Washington for a special medical survey in April. This time the weighty evidence of Dr. Barkan and the several admirals prevailed, and Towers passed. Surgeon General Rossiter agreed to rate him as "physically qualified to perform all his duties at sea and ashore," but only "WHILE WEARING THE SPECIFIED CORRECTING APPLIANCE" and with a copilot in the cockpit. That same day Admiral Cook recommended to Admiral Andrews that Towers be given command of the *Saratoga* in the forthcoming June rotation; the appropriate orders soon followed. Over the summer Andrews would threaten to retire Jack unless he promised to use the contact lens whenever operating the ship or an airplane. Jack agreed, reluctantly.[58]

Towers returned from Washington just in time to participate in Fleet Problem XVIII. Leaving their West Coast ports on 16 April, the fleet's ships exercised en route to Hawaii and then with army and navy units in and around the islands. Horne kept the flag aboard Pat Bellinger's *Ranger,* which comprised part of the White Fleet assigned the defense of the Hawaiian islands against the attacking Black Fleet. This left Black's carrier force of the *Saratoga*, the *Lexington,* and their escorts, plus seaplanes tended by the *Langley,* to cover a successful amphibious assault on Midway.[59]

Admiral Horne moved Towers and the staff back to the *Saratoga* for a Black attack on Pearl Harbor, defended by the *Ranger* and patrol planes under base force air commander Ernie King. Horne and Towers believed that the staff tactical officer, Wu Duncan, should get into the air during such exercises; Duncan complied and once took along Towers as an observer. Foul weather initially inhibited the extensive three-day air operations of early May, and a White submarine sank the *Langley.* The *Ranger's* planes attacked and damaged the *Saratoga,* and White's cruisers struck the *Lex* before Black's bombers put all four defending cruisers out of commission. Heavy aircraft losses were sustained by both sides. A tragedy occurred when the skipper of the *Saratoga's* Scouting Squadron 2 crashed into the sea, killing him and his

Towers dazzled observers when he wore his medals, especially those awarded as a result of the NC flight. The Portuguese Order of Tower and Sword is around his neck, as well as the badge. The NC medal and Navy Cross are first and second in the row of ribbons, and the RAF Cross is last in the row. (Towers collection)

rearseat gunner. The *Lexington* was ruled further crippled by battleship fire and a submarine torpedo hit, and the *Ranger* sustained aerial torpedo hits. The problem ended with Black's landing forces taking Lahaina under cover of Horne's carrier planes.[60]

Fleet Problem XVIII had revealed a serious flaw in the strategic use of carriers. The battle force commander, Admiral Claude C. Bloch, contended that the carriers should be kept in formation with the battle line, protected by antiaircraft guns on the battleships and cruisers. The airmen could not have disagreed more. Admiral Horne and his staff of Towers, Radford, and Duncan said that command of the air should be achieved before surface ships engaged. Furthermore, they insisted, "once an enemy carrier is within striking distance of our fleet no security remains until it—its squadrons—or both are destroyed. . . ." The carriers, they concluded, should be released to operate independently of the main body. Even though this represented a risk for the latter, the fleet was "playing for high stakes." Admiral King of the patrol bombers was similarly disappointed. Admiral Bloch, however, remained adamant, and when Horne circulated a treatise of his own authorship calling for independent carrier operations Bloch ordered him to recall all copies. Enraged, Horne had them all burned.[61]

The crucial question was whether or not to tie carriers to the battle line and/or to an amphibious mission before winning command of the air. If the latter took priority, Horne, Towers, and *Saratoga*'s Halsey were of one mind that the carriers should exploit their mobility as an independent task force. Fleet Problem XVIII had not only failed to resolve the question, it had further polarized the differences between Gun Club battleship men like Bloch and the aviation community. Still, fleet commander Hepburn appreciated the seriousness of the dilemma and agreed that carriers could operate independently; in case of danger, the gunships might be moved over to cover them rather than the reverse—a doctrinal step in the right direction. When the new carriers *Yorktown* and *Enterprise* arrived, the fleet would have five carriers. A possible compromise might then be to assign the smaller, lightly armed *Ranger* to the battle line to protect and augment its spotting planes. For the time being, as Bob Molten of Hepburn's staff noted, "the reaction seems to be to keep [all the carriers] under the protection of the antiaircraft batteries of the battle line and screen."[62]

Horne and Towers could not agree more with Hepburn's final recommendation that future fleet problems should concentrate on working out a proper carrier tactical doctrine. Indeed, the events of the Pacific war would expose this very question in both opposing navies. The Japanese fleet would be repulsed at the battles of the Coral Sea and Midway for dividing its mission between the amphibious task and the carrier battle, while the Americans would win only incomplete victories at the battles of the Philippine Sea and Leyte Gulf for similar reasons. Effective aerial tactics were also essential in a naval battle; Hepburn and his Towers-led staff were displeased at the "ragged manner" in which dive bombing attacks had been executed by the squadrons of the *Lexington*. This was particularly distressing to the men of that ship, whose performance in recent years had surpassed that of the *Saratoga*.[63]

On 9 June 1937, soon after the fleet returned from Hawaii, Towers relieved Halsey in command of the *Sara* at Long Beach. The two men had become friends, sharing ideas on carrier doctrine and operations, and Halsey bequeathed to Jack a happy ship. And by remaining on the *Saratoga,* Jack's close relationship with Admiral Horne and his staff remained unbroken. Old friend Pat Bellinger filled Towers' shoes as chief of staff, while Wu Duncan fleeted up to head operations and Lieutenant Commander Cato D. Glover became tactical officer. As for ship's officers, Commander George D. Murray reported aboard as exec, with Knefler "Soc" McGinnis as first lieutenant and George van Deurs as air operations officer.[64]

Nine years had passed since Towers had left the *Langley,* his last ship command, and the *Saratoga* was the realization of every naval officer's dream, a major ship command. From his tours of duty on the staffs of Yarnell and Horne, Towers knew the *Sara* well and would have no trouble handling her. She was a top fighting ship.

After a three-month overhaul at Puget Sound the *Sara* operated out of Long Beach, where Jack and Pierre entertained ship and squadron officers in dances on board and at Sunday night dinners in their new home ashore. Jack's daughter Marge, now twenty-one—"one of the most beautiful young women on the entire West Coast," remembered pilot Ben Scott Custer—joined Pierre in the cockpit after earning her private flyer's license at the Ryan School of Aeronautics in San Diego. Brother Chas, seventeen, divided his time between California and his mother Lily in New York. Towers' health remained good through daily workouts and walks with his Scottie, Mr. MacTavish. His annual physical in December gave him a clean bill of health, which Surgeon General Rossiter even approved. It was the last time Towers would have to deal with this gentleman, soon to retire.[65]

By December 1937 Towers had logged a phenomenal 2,965.5 hours in the air since that first flight in July 1911, and he continued to operate naval aircraft regularly as part of his normal routine. His safety pilot, Lieutenant John G. Crommelin, marveled at Towers' skill in the cockpit, Crommelin finding his own presence superfluous. The eighteen-plane squadrons of the *Saratoga* consisted of Fighting 3's Grumman F3F fighters and Scouting 3's Curtiss SBC scout bombers. Bombing 3 and Torpedo 3 began trading in their old biplanes for the navy's first monoplanes, the Vought SB2U Vindicator and Douglas TBD Devastator respectively (the nicknames were assigned later). During the changeover ashore, the *Saratoga* drilled the *Ranger's* bombers. Five utility planes and three for the flag rounded out the regular air complement of eighty-one planes. On 26 January 1938, a TBD landed on the *Saratoga,* the first landing by a TBD on a carrier.[66]

Then, three days later, an unprecedented midcycle command reshuffling took place, with conservative battleship tactician Bloch relieving Hepburn in

A Douglas TBD Devastator torpedo-bomber, the most modern carrier monoplane of its day, makes the first TBD carrier landing as it is waved aboard the *Saratoga,* 26 January 1938. It was obsolete four years later, when TBD squadrons were annihilated at the Battle of Midway. (National Archives)

command of the U.S. Fleet and Ernie King replacing Horne as carrier commander. Hoisting his flag in the *Saratoga,* King now inherited Jack as flagship captain and Pat Bellinger as chief of staff. Simultaneously, BuAer chief Cook recommended that Towers be appointed assistant chief of BuAer the following summer. No one at the Navy Department disagreed, and Towers' orders were issued on 17 February, effective 2 July. One newspaper's headlines declared, "Trio Who Commanded Planes in 1919 Transatlantic Flight Will Change Duties," while other papers singled out Towers for separate stories. Jack of the NC-3 would switch jobs with NC-4's Putty Read, the incumbent assistant chief of BuAer, with Bellinger of the NC-1 to command NAS Norfolk. The NC adventure was still news.[67]

Having obtained his command of a large carrier, Towers would then be returned to the same post he had held under Admiral Moffett from 1929 to 1931, and for the same reason—to be in line to relieve Cook as chief of BuAer. And in the fall the Class of '06 would come up before the flag selection board. Once selected for rear admiral Towers could become chief in the summer of 1939, finally accomplishing his goal as undisputed head of American naval aviation. The fact that he had spent his career in aviation billets was, however, risky when reviewed by admirals of the Gun Club who valued "normal" line assignments: battleships and cruisers. For this reason Captain Richmond Kelly Turner made the momentous decision to get out of aviation after ten continuous years in it.[68]

Towers faced an immediate challenge with the presence of Ernie King on board the *Sara* as admiral. In maneuvers off the southern California coast with the battleships during February, however, King consciously avoided interfering with the flagship's operations and made a concerted effort to be cooperative and pleasant. Towers personally whipped his ship into operating trim, tightening up the more lax routine of the Halsey regime. Although squadron pilots had to stand top watch on the bridge, Towers did not trust them all and made certain he or navigator Ben H. Wyatt was present when they had the conn. Towers was determined to restore the *Sara*'s primacy over the *Lex*.[69]

King kept all the carriermen jumping, never letting anyone anticipate his moves, which forced his officers to think for themselves. In tactical maneuvers, conducted about ten days per month, each pilot was required to carry with him a mimeographed sheet containing relevant operating instructions, signed by the ship's captain and air ops officer—in *Saratoga*'s case Towers and van Deurs. With King keeping everyone guessing until a half-hour before dawn, the two men agonized with chief of staff Bellinger over his intentions. Van Deurs devised an ingenious system of making up several op plans, each covering a possible contingency, plus a blank one in case King fooled them all. After a few hours' sleep, Van would climb the four decks up to the captain's sea cabin with perhaps five stencils. "I would find Towers sitting up in his bunk reading a book about two-thirty in the morning. We'd talk about the plans . . . then Jack Towers would sign all of them. . . . King was always up. I don't know when he slept." When the order came from the flag, van Deurs would fill in the blanks and have the plans quickly run off and placed in the hands of the pilots before they launched minutes later. The system usually succeeded.[70]

Despite the attempts at pleasantness, King was rough on everyone. He brought on the disdain of the airmen when he had the carrier planes take off and land in total darkness. According to van Deurs, "There wasn't any love lost between the flag and the navigating bridge at all. . . . I was kind of in the middle of the sandwich that year in the *Saratoga*." King, a great innovator in carrier tactics, liked to experiment. Towers let out his frustrations only to his own officers. "They didn't see eye to eye on many things," flag ops officer Duncan recalled, adding, however, that Towers managed the relationship "very well." Only once did Duncan observe King upset with Towers. Returning to port, Towers allowed a cruiser division on a crossing course to have the right of way when in fact it belonged to the *Saratoga*. Remarked King to Duncan, "Towers should mind his sea manners."[71]

King had every intention of correcting the misuse of carriers in Fleet Problem XVIII during Problem XIX. The *Saratoga* sent her Fighting Squadron 3 ashore with its F3F-1 fighters and replaced them with Marine Fighting Squadron 2, flying the higher-performance F3F-2. Bombing 3 and Scouting 3 retained their older Curtiss BFC and SBC dive bombers, and Torpedo 3 introduced the new TBD into fleet operations.[72]

The fleet left port on 14 March 1938, divided into Black and White fleets, with the *Saratoga* assigned to Black. Black, further split into two parts, was to establish a base on the (imaginary) coast of White by first concentrating to destroy the White Fleet. King protested having to divide his two carriers *Sara* and *Lex* and to cruise with two battleship groups, but he had to comply with the Gun Club scenario. White was comprised of a heavy gun force, the *Ranger,* and two PBY patrol-bombing squadrons at San Diego. On the afternoon of the seventeenth, the *Ranger*'s planes attacked and damaged the *Lex* with 100-pound bombs. But that evening, six hundred miles off the coast, no fewer than three dozen PBYs located and attacked the *Lex* for two hours with 500- and 1000-pound bombs, putting her out of commission and dropping flares that exposed Black's ships to the main batteries of White. Then the PBYs flew six hundred miles back to base. King, separated on the distant *Saratoga,* could not have Towers launch search strikes until the following morning, but then the launch was too slow to allow an attack before dark, when the planes had to be back on board. The inability of carriers to operate independently had again led to failure, although the patrol bombers had dramatically demonstrated their worth.[73]

Proceeding to Hawaii, the fleet reconcentrated in new designations to test army and navy defenses there against invasion. The Blue Fleet was to land marine amphibious forces at Lahaina and French Frigate Shoals for their utilization as advance air bases before the Red Fleet arrived. Red's air defenses in the islands consisted only of Army Air Corps planes and navy PBYs. King was allowed to devise his own tactics for a surprise raid to cripple Red's defenses. After excusing the *Lexington,* whose crew had been suddenly stricken with a tonsillitis epidemic, King assigned John S. McCain's *Ranger* to cover the landing at French Frigate Shoals; the *Saratoga*'s planes would attack Pearl Harbor and the defenses of Oahu. In many ways, Blue's goals closely resembled those the Japanese would employ during the Midway operation of 1942—trying to seize islands within bombing range of Pearl Harbor, which could then be neutralized at leisure by planes operating from those islands. As at Midway, it had to be done before the defending fleet arrived.

But the closest parallel would be with the Pearl Harbor attack in December 1941. King had Towers take *Sara* northwest to launch a predawn attack on the morning of 29 March. Luckily, when she reached a position some eight hundred miles north of Oahu, the carrier and her escorting destroyers encountered a thick weatherfront of clouds, fog, rain, and low visibility heading south. The ever-cagey King ordered Towers to move the *Sara* into the front and stay in it all the way to Oahu. The big carrier usually rode steadily in any kind of sea, but as Jack ordered the turn south, just before dinnertime, freak sea conditions suddenly caused her to roll abruptly 35 degrees to one side and 40 to the other. During the previous overhaul, workers had neglected to secure the steel tables to the deck. Now the heavy tables slid, crushing wooden chairs, sending crockery crashing, and tossing food off the galley stoves. File drawers even emptied out. All hands ate "cold canned Willy" that night.[74]

Otherwise the operation proceeded without a hitch, and on the two-day run south in the murk Blue radios intercepted messages between navy PBYs of the Red Fleet, cruising safely outside the edges of the front. Neither they nor army air patrols could locate the task force. The ruse was a complete success.

At 0450, 29 March, a hundred miles north of Oahu, Towers sent off two groups of planes, one to strike Pearl, the other to reconnoiter and photograph the target beach at Lahaina. The *Sara*'s marine fighters and navy bombing planes surprised and struck NAS Pearl Harbor, the army airfields of Hickam and Wheeler, and a radio station. In the meantime, King had Towers run the *Sara* at high speed to the east, closing the distance to the planes, all of which returned around 0835. Pearl Harbor was again proved vulnerable to carrier air attack. An hour later, a second strike took off to work over the defenses of Lahaina. But Towers also put up thirty fighters—marine F3Fs and Curtiss BFCs—just in time to absorb three waves of counterattacking patrol bombers. The umpires ruled that the *Saratoga* had lost forty-five of her seventy-two planes during the course of the day. The *Ranger,* after successfully supporting the marines' seizure of French Frigate Shoals, rejoined the *Sara* during the night.[75]

At dawn the next day Towers and McCain launched strikes from the *Sara* and *Ranger* to support the assault on Lahaina. Red army and navy planes attacked the transports and bombardment battleships, but the *Saratoga*'s fighters shot down thirty PBYs and two army bombers. In the afternoon Towers sent off strikes that again hit the army and navy airfields at Pearl Harbor, but a PBY strike inflicted 80 percent damage on the *Ranger*. The weather had already taxed the crews of the defending PBYs of Rear Admiral Charles Blakely and Captain Ken Whiting; thirteen-hour searches the day before had been followed by minimal rest. A predawn launch, which encountered an even worse storm and zero visibility, ended in tragedy as one patrol plane slammed into the surf of Oahu and another simply disappeared; other PBYs were damaged trying to take off, and some were forced down. Admiral Bloch canceled the operation so that all the ships could carry out a search. Eleven men had perished. Bitterness over these and earlier fatalities reached all the way to the White House.[76]

Anchoring at Pearl, the fleet critiqued the impressive offensive carrier tactics employed by King and then conducted more maneuvers before undertaking the last phase of Fleet Problem XIX. The *Saratoga* sent VB-3 over to

The *Saratoga*, commanded by Captain Towers, steams off Hawaii, 8 April 1938, displaying her full aircraft complement: Grumman F3Fs of Marine Corps Fighting Squadron 2 parked forward; Curtiss BFCs of Bombing 3; Torpedo 3's new TBD monoplanes; Curtiss SBCs of Scouting 3 spotted aft; and assorted other types—O3Us, SBUs, OSUs, and J2Fs. Note the 8-inch guns bracketing the island superstructure. (National Archives)

the *Ranger* in exchange for the latter's VS-42 of Vought SBUs. King was now allowed to form an independent carrier striking force as the Purple Fleet approached Green—the enemy base at San Francisco and an expeditionary force forming there. Leaving the *Ranger* with the main body, King broke away with the *Saratoga* and the *Lexington* on the morning of 24 April. Four Purple destroyers fatally damaged the *Ranger* with torpedoes the next night, but the following dawn, before sinking, she got off strikes that put all four of her assailants out of action.

Towers' *Saratoga* and Leigh Noyes' *Lexington* sped toward San Francisco at twenty-five knots throughout the twenty-fifth, following King's idea of masking their approach by not operating planes until the day of attack. Low clouds helped, especially when some PBYs made feeble attacks late in the day and early the next. Many were shot down, though the *Lex* sustained 25 percent damage. Working to within thirty miles of the coast, King had 140 planes launched at 1400 on the twenty-sixth, keeping them at 15,000 feet until they reached the target. The planes used 500-pound bombs to hit Mare Island Navy Yard and damage the seaplane tender *Wright* at Alameda. When the attackers returned to their carriers, all hands were chagrined to see a real Japanese oil tanker heave into view and observe them.

Turning to sea at twenty-seven knots for an attack on the Green Fleet defending San Pedro, King's carriers rendezvoused with Purple's main body at daylight on 27 April. Defending PBYs attacked the *Saratoga,* which sustained some damage, but Towers' defending fighters plus flak shot down seventeen of them. King's scouts located Green's main body of heavy cruisers, destroyers, and submarines, which *Sara* and *Lex* planes attacked at 1600. An hour later, Admiral Bloch terminated the problem and the ships and planes returned to base.[77]

Fleet Problem XIX demonstrated how difficult a carrier attack on the Japanese homeland would be. In their critique, the admirals decided that the carrier attack on San Francisco's coastal targets had been a success, but that it would have been more successful with all three instead of two carriers. Defending the coast against a large fleet with carriers would be extremely difficult; the defenders would have to stop the fleet before it could launch. Barring that, an enemy like Japan would surely try to inflict maximum damage to make carrier attacks unprofitable. Which was exactly what Japan would do with her land-based bombers and suicide kamikazes in 1944–45.[78]

As for Jack Towers, he had performed admirably in the fleet problem, and Ernie King gave him high marks in his fitness reports. King was also responsible for keeping Towers' record unblemished. One week after Jack

The U.S. Fleet at anchor in Pearl Harbor, 8 April 1938, following the carrier plane attack on that base. At the left of Battleship Row is the Ford Island carrier pier and Towers' old ship, the *Langley,* since converted into a seaplane tender. The scene would look much the same prior to the Japanese carrier attack on 7 December 1941. (National Archives)

turned over command of the *Saratoga,* an inspecting board gave an unfavorable and unfair official report on the ship's condition. Towers lost no time presenting the facts to Vice Admiral King, who agreed immediately: "You will recognize the fact that I am deeply concerned—and, consequently, that every effort will be made to clear up this matter as soon as may be." Thanks to King, the report never saw the light of day.[79]

The *Saratoga*'s officers and crew gave their skipper high marks for restoring the ship's reputation. Disciplinarian though Towers was, they respected his skills. Pierre Towers discovered this to her surprise one day when a gas station attendant, a former crewman, remarked to her, "Your husband is a hard man, Ma'am, but he's fair!"[80]

Towers was able to inform Admiral Harry Yarnell, now commanding the Asiatic Fleet, "I had a most successful year in every respect and, for the first time in many years, the *Saratoga* was conceded to be the superior of the *Lexington*."[81]

During May and June 1938 Towers took the *Sara* out of Long Beach for her usual exercises as his enjoyable tour drew to a close. On the morning of 16 June the crew mustered at quarters on the flight deck for the change-of-command ceremony. Towers and Putty Read read their orders and Jack departed. Having played a key role in helping the fleet to prepare its air arm for the Japanese enemy, Towers now headed for Washington to put his experiences to good use at BuAer.[82]

I I

MOBILIZING AVIATION
FOR DEMOCRACY
1938–40

By the time Towers reported as assistant chief of BuAer on 2 July 1938, Japan had been at war in China for a year and Nazi Germany threatened to engulf all Europe. Although new Carl Vinson–sponsored legislation now raised the navy's aircraft inventory from two thousand to three thousand planes and authorized another carrier, there seemed to be no sense of urgency in peacetime Washington, except perhaps in the person of Rear Admiral A. B. Cook, Towers' new boss. An able if unexceptional chief of bureau, Cook surprised Jack by appearing "highly nervous" and "developing a thorough case of the jitters." One day he required Towers' presence for three and a half hours in four separate sessions that, in Jack's opinion, deserved but ten minutes each. Maybe the sustained heat was a factor; because of it, the government closed down early three days in a row. "At the moment," wrote Jack in a letter on 23 August, "things around [the] Bureau are—well—inexcusably or unnecessarily strenuous because of his nervous state. I think all hands will sigh with relief when he shoves off [on leave]. I know I will." Cook left three days later.[1]

Towers had personal concerns too. Pierre was in Paris at the height of the Munich crisis, and he had to pack Chas and Marjorie off on vacation trips. Twenty-two now, Marge appeared in a *Look* magazine article that featured her

Daughter Marjorie Towers, age twenty-one, in
front of the Ryan ST trainer in which she learned
to fly at San Diego, 1938. (Courtesy Lynne L.
Riley)

flying skills and she made her debut. On a blind date she met and fell in love
with a dashing thirty-three-year-old divorced naval aviator, Lieutenant Herbert D. Riley, so accomplished in the cockpit that he had become VIP transport and test pilot at Anacostia and occasional White House aide. Ere long the
two became engaged, whereupon father and fiancé agreed that they would
never work near one another in order that Jack not influence his son-in-law's
career. Jack would give Marjorie's hand in marriage to Riley on 11 June 1940.
Because of Riley's association with the White House, Marge soon became "a
good friend of the Roosevelt family" and stayed with the president's family at
Hyde Park.[2]

When Pierre returned from Europe, she and Jack rented a place in
Washington and soon became, according to one magazine, "notable capital
hosts." Every Sunday they held open house for up to thirty people, mostly
aviators. Reporters found Towers "affable, jovial, and with a pleasing smile,"
full of "twinkles" and wonderful stories. "He's no stuffed shirt. He loves his

home and enjoys his friends." His fair skin, graying blondish hair, and direct blue eyes gave only a hint of his fifty-three years. His shyness always impressed observers, while the charming Pierre remained his social foil. And since peacetime military dress in Washington was civilian, Jack stayed ever stylish, with custom-made suits, a cane, and a straw hat in the summer. His financial situation was at last secure.[3]

Socially and professionally Towers renewed many contacts, in particular with Rear Admiral Joe Richardson, chief of BuNav and champion bridge player. Jack's counterpart as BuNav assistant chief was his classmate Captain Frank Jack Fletcher, who, having failed a physical to enter flight training in 1928, persistently denigrated naval aviation during cocktail chatter. Reticent about Fletcher, who would eventually command carriers in battle, Jack once counseled Pierre, "He doesn't know what he's talking about. It's no use discussing it." Another classmate was the genial, brilliant Captain Robert Lee Ghormley, director of the war plans division in the Office of the Chief of Naval Operations. Smart as he was, however, Ghormley appeared not to be well physically and seemed to have difficulty making decisions.[4]

Towers looked forward to stepping into Cook's shoes and being promoted to rear admiral, a subject that generated much discussion within the naval hierarchy and especially among aviators, for the annual flag selection board was scheduled to convene in November. The general feeling was that he would be easily selected. Only four qualified aviators held flag rank at the time—King, Cook, Blakely, and, since March, Halsey—but all were JCLs. The aviators who had spent their careers in the air looked to Towers' promotion as a signal for their own advancement.

A new law in June not only raised the number of admirals from fifty-eight to seventy but permitted the flag selection board to reach back to the previous Navy Academy class for captains already passed over. So the nine vacancies in 1938 could come from '05, not just '06. Six affirmative votes were required from the nine admirals on the board. One news story commented, "Selection of Jack Towers would mean having to drop some loyal officer of all-around ability on surface vessels," highly dubious given the makeup of the 1938 board—eight Gun Club mainliners and naval observer Frederick Horne. And the board's president was none other than Admiral Claude C. Bloch, the highly esteemed commander in chief of the U.S. Fleet and dyed-in-the-wool big-gun battleship man. Towers could count on the support of his old boss, Horne, as well as Bill Tarrant, who had admired his work at San Diego. Of the rest, he reflected later, "strangely enough, only two others . . . knew me at all well."[5]

The board of admirals convened on 15 November 1938 and deliberated for more than a week, then delayed an announcement because of President Roosevelt's absence from Washington. Towers simply went about his business and waited for the outcome; he had never been passed over before—although he had been turned down for a ship command in 1921—and saw little reason to believe he would be now. CNO Leahy and Joe Richardson had practically assured him of his selection. The day of the announced selections Towers was at home and Pierre out, attending a matinee play with a group of navy wives. She telephoned him during intermission. "Well," he told her in his casual way, "I've been passed over."

"You haven't!" Pierre exclaimed. "I don't *believe* it!"

"Yes. It's all right. There's nothing to be done or said about it."

"I'll come home."

"No, don't. I'll take Mr. MacTavish for his walk and I'll see you later on."

Pierre hurried home and they talked. The nonaviator black shoes had finally stopped him.

Then several aviators, disconsolate over the news, began to drop in. One of them, Lieutenant P. D. Stroop of the BuAer plans division, was in such a terrible state that he actually chewed on his hat: "Captain, Captain, what's happened?"

"I'm sorry," Towers replied, "just have a drink. I don't know what's

Marjorie and Pierre with Scotties Cinders and Mr. MacTavish. (Towers collection)

happened." More people arrived, and before long an impromptu cocktail party developed that lasted into the night.[6]

The board's first choice had been from the Class of '05, the rest from '06. John M. Smeallie, scouting force chief of staff, had stood seventh from the bottom of '05 and was already near the end of his career. Of Towers' classmates, two selectees were JCLs, Leigh Noyes and Arthur Bristol. The others were Lee Ghormley, Bill Calhoun, Russell Willson, Bill Glassford, Frank Jack Fletcher, and Milo Draemel.[7]

Details of the highly secret balloting may only be surmised. Horne and Tarrant surely gave Towers high marks, but the others were probably swayed by Admiral Bloch's arguments to select only Gun Clubbers. Physical disability was probably a factor as well, although Towers informed Harry Yarnell, "I can state definitely that the physical aspect had nothing whatever to do with it." His informant about the discussion was in all likelihood Horne. Tarrant, thoroughly embarrassed by the outcome, henceforth acted awkwardly toward Towers.[8]

"Pierre was very badly broken up," Jack told Yarnell, but Towers kept up his own spirits. "[T]here are reasonably good grounds for believing that I will be nominated in the next spring [command rotations] to succeed Admiral Cook next summer," which assignment would automatically carry the rank of rear admiral. The reaction around BuAer and in aviation circles was especially acute. Outrage was expressed most vigorously in the aviation-conscious national press. The navy editor of the San Diego *Tribune Sun* sneered, "The continued services of Capt. Towers apparently were not desired or needed by the Navy in a day when supremacy in the air holds the key to war or peace."[9] In a perceptive analysis, *U.S. Air Services* proclaimed that Towers' "capabilities make him welcome where the best minds consider design, construction, and operational phases of all kinds of airplanes and naval vessels. In fact, it is difficult to conceive of a more well-rounded, balanced, and versatile officer in the entire U.S. Navy. . . . We have . . . been here and there in the Capital striving to understand many strange situations during the last twenty years. We have never run across anything equal to this."[10]

Another disgusted observer, and the most important one, was the commander in chief of the navy, Franklin Delano Roosevelt. When the president had appointed Joe Richardson chief of BuNav in March, he warned him "about the White haired boys which you and I know all about." Towers' rejection was proof positive of this admonition. Within days of the outcome, FDR summoned Jack to the White House. "Well, Towers," he said, "so they nicked you. What the hell happened? Couldn't you beat the gang?"

"I guess not, sir."

"Well," the president chuckled, "we'll fix *that*. I'm going to appoint you Chief of the Bureau, which automatically gives you the big stripe. Let them look at that!"[11]

FDR, in the words of Richardson, "loved to tinker with the assignment of the senior officer personnel" and made no official announcement of his decision on Towers until he sounded out trusted Rear Admiral Jerry Land, now head of the U.S. Maritime Commission. Land, a long-time friend and admirer of Towers, helped convince Roosevelt to place Towers' name at the top of the list for BuAer, followed by two latecomers to air: newly selected Arthur Bristol and Jake Fitch, also passed over. Neither Secretary Claude Swanson, Assistant Secretary Charles Edison, nor any senior officer in the Navy Department objected, and by the middle of December Towers was able to tell his old compatriot, General Hap Arnold, that the department would nominate him to relieve Cook.[12] In January the story leaked out to the press, and Arnold sent Jack "heartiest congratulations" on his selection as Chief of BuAer. Startled by the "premature and inaccurate" story, Towers thanked Arnold but cautioned that the department had yet to nominate him to the President.[13]

Towers apparently had his reassurances by the end of January 1939, for on 1 February he initiated a major if unobtrusive measure to assist in the transition to chief of bureau. He began a diary recounting major conversations and meetings, dictated at the end of the day to a secretary. This "Memoranda for Files" enabled him to keep on top of airplane procurement, carrier design, personnel assignments, and the reasoning behind all major policy decisions. The diary quickly became an invaluable managerial tool that he shared with others whenever necessary for the business of the bureau.[14]

Roosevelt preferred to make no formal announcement until he had returned from witnessing Fleet Problem XX in the Caribbean. In the meantime, Assistant Secretary Edison worked up the slate of new bureau chiefs for the president on 7 March. He recommended Towers for BuAer and Rear Admiral Chester Nimitz, then in command of a battleship division, for BuNav. Roosevelt approved, and the announcement was made on the fifteenth, along with the statement that Towers would hold the rank of rear admiral. The appointment was for four years.[15]

Among many publications, the *Army-Navy Journal* observed that the appointment of Towers "will put heart into the old-timers in naval aviation, for he is the first of that category to reach flag rank and first to head the bureau." "The Navy's No. One aviator" had made it. Reporters remarked that both Towers and Nimitz were relative youngsters, at fifty-four, to get the posts, especially Nimitz in the powerful BuNav. He relieved Joe Richardson, slated to command the battle force and whose Washington townhouse it was that Jack and Pierre were renting.[16]

The flood of congratulations included one from Vice Admiral Ernie King, for which Jack thanked him, admitting, "I realize I am stepping into a very difficult job, and one which has been filled most capably since its creation." This was a nice gesture to King, whose own future now seemed destined for an inglorious finish. For instead of being elevated to CNO or commander in chief, U.S. Fleet, as he had hoped, King had been ignored by Roosevelt and ordered to the General Board, which also meant reverting to his permanent rank of rear admiral. At sixty King could not expect to return to sea. Still, his latest tactical innovations with the carriers in the Caribbean

Captain Towers poses for a newspaper photo following his announced promotion to chief of bureau and rear admiral, 17 March 1939. The model is a Curtiss SBC-3 Helldiver scout-bomber, which first entered the fleet with Scouting Squadron 5 in mid-1937 and operated with Towers on the *Saratoga*. Though he would make the SBC-4 version available to the French in 1940, this last American combat biplane was obsolete by the time the United States entered World War II. (AP/Wide World Photos)

had been impressive, and Towers added a generous postscript: "From all I can hear, the operations of Aircraft, Battle Force, during [the] recent [fleet] problem were so extraordinarily successful as to bring forth high praise from everyone in the Fleet."[17]

Towers' orders were to assume the post of chief of bureau on 1 June 1939, his date of temporary commission as rear admiral being 23 May. The next flag board officially selected him as its first choice. Towers received his formal commission of rear admiral, lower half, in February 1940, to date from 29 December 1939. His eventual elevation to the upper half would be dated 30 June 1942.[18] The press took note immediately of his new situation. Noting that Towers hated "just sitting," *Newsweek* reported he rejected his flat desk by adding a chest-high drafting table "from which he worked standing. Even then, he gave the impression of being poised for flight."[19]

Towers' rise to bureau chief placed him in the company of the top national strategy decision-makers on the eve of World War II. When the infirm Secretary Swanson died in July, Assistant Edison became acting secretary and relied most heavily on the new CNO, Admiral Harold R. Stark; the director of the war plans division; and the chiefs of the three major bureaus, navigation, ordnance, and aeronautics—Nimitz, William R. Furlong, and Towers respectively. Nimitz and Towers soon proved to be the most effective of the chiefs on Capitol Hill.

A major imbroglio between C&R and BuEng over responsibilities for new ships and aircraft led the powerful Carl Vinson to try to centralize navy logistics in June with a new office of naval material. Also, a director of naval aviation would be established in the Office of the Chief of Naval Operations to coordinate all operational responsibilities of fleet aviation. Towers had not been party to the proposed reorganization, which he opposed. In Jack's view, too much would be lost if the chief of BuAer gave up his hard-won prerogatives and powers to a material chief after two decades of administrative struggle. Towers momentarily convinced Vinson with a formal statement to that effect in September.[20]

Secretary Edison pressed ahead for the office of naval material, but realizing Towers' influence on Vinson he called Jack in for a long discussion at the end of February 1940. Jack recommended against reorganization. He especially feared that "a new overlord of all the bureaus" would short-circuit the bureau chiefs' direct access to the secretary and either become "a rubber stamp" for the chiefs or require a huge staff with in fact less technical expertise than the chiefs themselves.

The secretary asked Towers for "any alternative which might accomplish his purpose." Towers thought that another assistant secretary might be appointed; in fact, the assistant secretaryship for aeronautics, dormant since 1932, could be resurrected. But Edison decided to solve the most immediate problem of friction between BuEng and C&R by merging them into one Bureau of Ships (BuShips), a measure that worked to BuAer's advantage in that new carrier construction could now proceed more efficiently.[21]

Towers had to cooperate with the Army Air Corps and Hap Arnold in mobilizing the nation's military aviation. The intimate friendship between Jack and Hap led to visits between offices and telephone calls to circumvent many a potential interservice problem. "Of course, they fought like hawks," remembered Robert A. Lovett, "but were very close personal friends. . . . In spite of all the interservice rivalries and jealousies, I know there was great respect on both sides and I think a wider sense of the ultimate purpose of an Army and Navy than existed in the minds of some of their subordinates."

"I have often heard Hap Arnold referred to as an impatient man," Towers wrote after Arnold's passing in 1950. "That is perfectly true, but his was the kind of impatience which bore fruit. He was impatient of unessential but required procedures, of delayed decisions upon matters which appeared obvious, of anything which impeded the build-up of the air power which he so rightly considered necessary to the winning of the war." Devoted to the cause of strategic bombing, however, Arnold and the Army Air Corps again resurrected the specter of a separate air force.[22]

A long-festering army-navy dispute over defense of the American coasts was heightened by the debut of the Air Corps' B-17 Flying Fortress and the navy's newest-model PBY-5 and PBM amphibian patrol bombers. And just when the Air Corps had better bombers on the drawing boards, the navy was authorizing new patrol bombers. Towers, however, when queried by the president in July 1939 "as to the sizes seaplanes might reach within the next years," replied that the flying boat had almost reached its limit with two new four-engine models, Consolidated's 60,000-ton 1,500-mile-range PB2Y Coronado and Martin's behemoth PB2M Mars of twice that size and range. Their great cost as well as the difficulties handling them in restricted areas and "getting them out of the water" onto tenders for servicing were serious handicaps. More than that, Towers told FDR, "I saw no reason from a Naval scouting point of view to go into tremendous sizes to get further increase in [cruising radius]," especially since the twin-engine PBY Catalina and PBM Mariner could match the range of the Coronado.[23]

Guided by the conviction that more efficient planes were better than simply bigger ones, Towers presented BuAer's specific recommendations to the General Board as the best bargain. Numbers were the key, in order that the navy's five patrol wings (of four squadrons each) could adequately cover all approaches to American territory and overseas bases. He defeated an obsolete war plans division recommendation for a large intermediate VPJ-type coastal patrol plane, a purely defensive aircraft for antisub work but unable to defend itself. As for tenders, Towers rejected another war plans idea of a seaplane carrier for transporting both VPJs and Marine Corps attack planes. And he wanted tenders small enough to navigate the lagoons of Pacific atolls. A new *Curtiss* (AV-4)–type pure tender was the answer.[24]

Every airplane was a compromise, Towers often observed, but its primary function had to dominate the design. The same was true of ships, lest their performance and efficiency be weakened with the incorporation of too many missions. A case in point was a General Board scheme to convert ten old *Omaha*-class light cruisers into antiaircraft cruisers but to retain the basic features of conventional cruisers, which included two on-board spotting planes. Towers informed the board that the need for planes on such an antiaircraft vessel would only be secondary; they ought to be removed, which would also save sixty tons, the planes, catapults, gas, and men. Admiral King acidly remarked, "The Bureau of Aeronautics then can't be put to the trouble of acquiring planes?" Towers said only a couple of dozen planes would be involved. The ten *Omaha*s were not converted, nor were destroyers for the same reason. Carriers and escorts alike would simply have to carry more antiaircraft barrels.[25]

In addition to flying boats, LTA continued to be considered as a possibility for the supplementation of coastal patrols. The numerous crashes of rigid dirigibles effectively sealed their fate as far as the navy was concerned, but Congress and the president toyed with the idea until Towers and the bureau presented evidence that finally killed it. Still, by keeping a few nonrigid blimps active, the navy remained the only military service in the world with any airship program at all.[26]

In any case, the navy was not preparing for a war along the American coastlines. Like the Army Air Corps, with its Europe-oriented strategic bombers, the navy and its air arm beefed up continental defenses while planning for an offensive transoceanic war. As far as Towers and other aviators were concerned, the primary element of the fleet was the fast aircraft carrier, embodied in Bill Halsey's Carrier Division 1 of the *Saratoga* and *Lexington,* Charles Blakely's Carrier Division 2 of the newly completed *Yorktown* and *Enterprise,* the *Ranger* in the Atlantic, and the authorized *Wasp,* *Hornet,* and *Essex.* Towers not only believed these were inadequate, he adhered to the view that instead of being relegated to the status of auxiliary to the battleship, the carrier should operate in independent task forces. "I am convinced," he told the General Board in July 1939, "that carriers must be considered, not as individual vessels, but as part of a striking force" and that the design of the new carriers

> must be directed toward the most effective offense of this force as a unit. My idea of such a force would include two carriers, four heavy cruisers and four destroyers. Such a force incorporates a high degree of maneuverability, good defensive qualities and an offensive power which, together with its speed, should enable it to engage most opposing combinations under favorable conditions, or to avoid engagement when advisable. I believe acceptance of the carrier as an integral part of some such force, is an essential to a practicable solution of the design problem.[27]

Each new carrier, Towers believed, must combine high speed, a large enough air group of the most modern planes, sufficient armor to absorb bomb and torpedo hits, and adequate protection from its own guns and those of its escorts. In several appearances before the board in 1939 and early 1940 Towers played a major role in the design of the new carriers by insisting on the characteristics embodied in the *Yorktown* and the *Enterprise*. The *Essex*, prototype of a ten-year carrier building program, offered the best hope, and the only reason he would tolerate expenditures on improving existing carriers was expediency: Japan was on the move and might wage war before the new carriers could be produced.[28]

The General Board agreed with Towers that any new carrier must displace at least 20,000 tons, as would the *Yorktown*, *Enterprise*, and *Hornet*, still under construction. Their 32.5-knot speed was close to the 33 knots Towers desired, and their ability to operate four eighteen-plane squadrons (one VF, two VSBs, one VTB) called for the minimum seventy-two-plane air group he considered imperative. A fifth squadron of nine fighters might be assigned "in emergencies." Optimum flight-deck length should be 830 feet, 20 more than the *Yorktown*'s, and the flight deck should include two catapults. An increased fuel capacity of 200,000 gallons, Towers believed, was essential to give the new carriers a cruising radius slightly longer than the *Yorktown*'s. This should be augmented by underway replenishment, just being introduced to the fleet.[29]

As for defense, said Towers, "the carrier must depend largely on its attached aircraft, its speed, and the gun power of attending craft for protection against bombing." Deck armor was necessary to protect machinery, which meant armoring the hangar deck, and in July he applauded a decision to reject an armored flight deck. Since at least half of the carrier's planes remained spotted on the flight deck, any bomb detonation there would surely destroy them, thereby eliminating the ship's striking and main defensive power. Bombs penetrating the wooden flight deck to detonate in the hangar, on the other hand, would cause damage that could be repaired without injury to most of the planes. Side armor, however, he believed necessary to deflect gunfire from enemy cruisers. Also, the hangar should be kept open to allow free ventilation during engine warmups and for use of an athwartship catapult there.[30]

Towers' views prevailed, and by January 1940 design teams had hammered out the basic plans for the *Essex.* Towers endorsed design number CV-9F, one of seven proposed for consideration, "because of the greater protection which it incorporates, at rather minor and acceptable compromises in other characteristics." The design especially pleased him in that it allowed for the new and larger aircraft BuAer anticipated. And though he thought seventy-two planes would be the regular air group, the new ships would accommodate ninety. Towers had admired the 8-inch guns of the *Lexington* but yielded to the omission of 8- or even 6-inchers from the *Essex;* escorting cruisers were supposed to take up the slack. The largest gun on the *Essex* would be the dual-purpose 5-inch/38 caliber, primarily used for antiaircraft fire. Considerations of gasoline storage, a longer flight deck, the elevator arrangement, and anti-torpedo blisters raised the *Essex* from 20,000 to 27,000 tons, but the desired top speed of thirty-three knots was assured.

The design favored by Towers and BuAer was approved by the secretary a month later, although owing to the ship's complexity it would be another full year before the keel of the prototype was laid down. All in all, the *Essex* class would spearhead the wartime task forces envisioned by Towers, whose contribution to its adoption had been a major one.[31]

In the midst of the *Essex* discussions, the war plans division resurrected an earlier idea of a small, 10,000-ton scouting carrier, now championed by Admiral Lee Ghormley and Captain John McCain of the *Ranger.* Towers would have none of it, as he told the board in November 1939: "In my opinion, there is no such thing as a good small carrier," due to a lack of both flight deck takeoff length and protective battery. He said the same about the flight deck cruiser, the hybrid he and Admiral Moffett had pushed so vigorously in 1930. The fact was that until the United States actually got into a war, no one could be certain about actual carrier needs. The day of the armored deck and small carrier had not yet come, and plans for both were filed away.[32]

The aviation shore establishment badly needed to be expanded, so concluded a board under Admiral Hepburn at the end of 1938. Congress approved most of the fifteen sites for new or expanded air stations that it recommended, including a new facility at Jacksonville, Florida, but it omitted Corpus Christi, Texas. Unfortunately the program meant starting virtually from scratch. Towers worked closely with Rear Admiral Ben Moreell, chief of BuDocks, in drawing up the necessary plans. In June 1939 both men had to face Carl Vinson, who insisted that the development of Corpus Christi as a training base go forward. Towers opposed this on the grounds that the base would be an expensive duplication of Pensacola. Vinson, however, convinced that war lay in the offing, ordered CNO Leahy to provide specifications, which Towers and Moreell did. Vinson opposed giving Florida more business after the Pensacola and Jacksonville expansions. Even the president pestered Towers and Moreell about construction plans for Jacksonville.[33]

BuAer's internal affairs were administered in the eighth and ninth wings of the main navy building on Constitution Avenue. The 66 naval officers and 171 civilians on duty there in mid-1939 continued to operate in much the same way they had since the bureau's creation in 1921. Towers' small staff consisted of an assistant chief, a chief clerk in charge of civilian employees, a junior administrative officer, and a general information (intelligence) officer. His own successor in the post of assistant chief was Captain Pete Mitscher, a virtual executive officer who advised his boss on overall policy and directly supervised the twelve divisions of the bureau.[34]

To coordinate bureau funding, Towers depended heavily on the head of the financial division, Captain Elwood A. Cobey, Supply Corps, generally recognized as the brains behind all aviation logistics. Cobey accompanied Towers to hearings before congressional committees, notably the House and Senate Naval Affairs Committees. As in the days of Admiral Moffett, Towers insisted on complete and correct financial data, which Cobey ably provided. Jack usually began his testimony with a prepared statement. Sometimes he had with him only the lieutenant from plans in charge of long-range aircraft procurement, first P. D. Stroop, then George W. Anderson, Jr.[35]

The handling of aviation personnel continued to be coordinated between BuAer and BuNav, except that the growing number of pilots led to inevitable disagreements between chiefs Towers and Nimitz. Towers admired the BuNav chief, but as Jack once told Pierre, he was "very Dutch, very thick-headed and hard to convince. But when you did have him convinced, he stayed that way." As for Nimitz, recalled a confidential aide, "he just didn't care much for Admiral Towers," especially his methods. The thing that most impressed Pierre about Nimitz was his passion for walking. Nimitz, she remembered, "I saw regularly when I drove down to pick up Jack at the Department in the late afternoon: Nimitz was always *walking* home, in the broiling summer, in his shirt sleeves, refusing a lift."[36]

The newly authorized total strength of three thousand regular navy aviators and a minimum strength of six thousand in the naval reserve was an imperfect scheme that led to Admiral Horne's appointment to study the navy's aviation personnel needs. Towers admired new aviation cadets for their civilian college training in engineering, and he told the Horne board that cadets and reserve pilots should be employed on active duty. But he believed that only regulars should be retained long enough to fill "senior brackets" in the aeronautical organization. His idea was counterproductive, since non-regulars, with no hope of advancement, would have no impetus to remain in the service; indeed, in 1939–40 a BuAer recruiting campaign failed to generate the desired numbers of new pilots. Lack of urgency prevented Towers and his planners from giving up peacetime recruiting practices centered on Annapolis graduates.[37]

Early in 1939, however, an unexpected potential source of pilots suddenly presented itself. Robert H. Hinckley of the new Civil Aeronautics Authority (CAA) conceived the idea of a civilian training program to produce twenty thousand college-age pilots. FDR actively supported the idea of providing a reservoir of pilots from which the military could draw in wartime. In hearings before a Senate commerce subcommittee in April 1939, Towers endorsed the proposed legislation, which would "provide an immediate source of partially trained personnel, and thus reduce materially the time required to develop them into competent naval pilots." Congress passed the law in June and the program got under way in October, headed by Hinckley.[38]

As for personnel assignments, Towers handled requests from all sides. He agreed with CNO Stark and Nimitz to have Halsey relieve a sickly Charles Blakely in the carrier command. And on the sudden death of the skipper of the *Saratoga*'s VF-3, Jack accepted Halsey's recommendation that the squadron exec be fleeted up to command it. This was Lieutenant J. S. Thach, at that very time developing the Thach weave, a basic defensive-fighter tactic that would become standard during World War II. Towers welcomed eager managers from the business sector to assist him, notably W. A. "Gus" Read, a Wall Street banker who had worked in Towers' wartime office, and the brilliant petroleum engineer and pilot-inventor Luis de Florez, who earned his wings at age fifty by completing the grueling eleven-month course at Pensacola in a record six weeks.[39]

Towers' longtime interest in scientific applications to aeronautical technology deepened in May 1939 as he resumed his membership on NACA for the third time. NACA decided to use the prestige of three of its members in winning congressional approval for a new research laboratory at Sunnyvale, California. Those members were Charles Lindbergh, Hap Arnold, and Towers, all appointed in June to the Special Survey Committee on Aeronautical Research Facilities, chaired by Lindbergh and soon joined by Robert Hinckley of the CAA. The four men had great success; Congress approved funds for a new NACA lab in August and selected Sunnyvale.[40]

That November Towers expressed his dedication to scientific research in his first annual report, which requested increased funding to institute "a well-considered and comprehensive experimental program" for naval aircraft and to standardize materials, processes, and equipment used by BuAer and the Air Corps. NACA endorsed a recommendation by the Lindbergh committee for yet a third lab (after the Langley and Sunnyvale facilities), this one to concentrate on airplane engines. The following June Congress approved this proposal for development of a site near the Cleveland airport. As for Lindbergh, "I know him well," Jack wrote to his brother Will in 1940, "and have a great admiration for him in many respects, but when he gets on the subject of international affairs"—as a dedicated isolationist—"he's getting out far beyond the field of his ability."[41]

Towers remained with NACA throughout his tenure as chief of BuAer. That his contributions to it were immense was recognized by Jerry Hunsaker, who became NACA chairman in 1941. In a note to President Roosevelt the next year, Hunsaker complimented Towers for being "farsighted" in having supported scientific research in aerodynamics and for being constructive and helpful in urging and accelerating improved military aircraft. Towers' presence on NACA also strengthened his communications with the Air Corps and CAA.[42]

One of Towers' greatest assets was his long and intimate association with the select founders of the aeronautical industry, among them Grover Loening, who in May 1939 gave a dinner in New York in honor of him and all the aviation officers of the Atlantic Squadron. Ten days after that Towers dedicated the naval aviation exhibit at the New York World's Fair, part of Pan American World Airways' inaugural transatlantic commercial air service— twenty years to the week after the NCs had shown the way. In June Pierre christened the PBY-4 American Export Airlines survey plane *Transatlantic* at the Battery, trying eight times before she could break the ceremonial champagne bottle. Such doings kept Towers in the public eye, as did speeches he delivered around the country, articles carrying his byline (usually ghost-written by Joy Bright Hancock), and photographs in aviation journals.[43]

The biggest news during the summer of 1939 was the inexorable drift of the European powers toward war. Ever since the Munich crisis one year before, Britain, France, and the Netherlands had been frantically ordering warplanes and engines from American companies, and Towers and Arnold had to approve the resulting disruption of their own production schedules to permit it. During an inspection trip to Pensacola in mid-July, Jack was called back to Washington to attend a special conference with the president and Admirals Leahy and Moreell on air base construction. Time was running out for Europe, and the American military had to prepare for possible war in the face of public apathy and opposition.[44]

During August, as the cataclysm approached, Jack and his family squeezed in a two-week vacation at Hammondsport. On 21 August CNO Stark convened a meeting of bureau chiefs and department heads to discuss the general state of the navy. When the Canadian air force requested the purchase of American military aircraft, the U.S. government allowed foreign purchases to be made directly from the manufacturer. Though the Air Corps agreed to supply some bombers, Towers cautioned Secretary Edison on the thirtieth that it was of "utmost importance" that Canada be regarded as a neutral. And he recommended against slowing down the navy's PBY acquisitions in favor of Canadian purchases. FDR and Assistant Secretary of War Louis Johnson concurred. The Americans could not be certain whether Canada, a dominion of the British Commonwealth, would automatically become a belligerent should Britain go to war. If she did, the problem of continental defense would be compounded. No one had to wait long to find out.[45]

On 1 September 1939 Hitler's armies invaded Poland, and the Commonwealth rallied behind the British (and French) declaration of war two days later. World War II had begun, and Towers reacted as promptly as he had upon the outbreak of the first war, in 1914, when he had instantly requested duty abroad. The very day of the German attack, 1 September, he went directly to Admiral Stark in hopes of strengthening America's East Coast air defenses. To the CNO he proposed that the maximum possible number of PBY planes be ordered immediately. It would take a long time to produce them, but he would solicit Congress for a diversion of funds from other airplanes already allocated.[46]

While Stark awaited the president's reaction to events in Europe, Towers chanced to encounter the irrepressible Reuben H. Fleet, president of Consolidated Aircraft, builder of the PBY. After lunch together, Towers took Fleet to his office and asked him flatly, "What would you propose that the Navy buy from you in case we get into this war? How long would it take you to build 500 patrol bombers?"

"Well, Jack," said Fleet, "the twin-engine PBY has been flying long enough now . . . that it has most of our ideas in it, and it's a damn good ship. You ought to buy it. But I don't think the four-engine PB2Y is worth a damn," because it was a conglomeration of too many ideas, many from BuAer engineers. Jack agreed and asked for a price tag and timetable for 500 PBYs. Fleet could only promise 200 planes at $100,000 apiece, or $20 million, over

Upon learning of the British and French declarations of war, Sunday, 3 September 1939, American policymakers meet at the State Department. *Left:* Secretary of State Cordell Hull. *Right:* Acting Secretary of the Navy Charles Edison. The chief spokesmen for military aviation are Towers of the navy and, *second from right,* Assistant Secretary of War Louis Johnson for the army. Johnson would gain notoriety in the postwar unification dispute as secretary of defense. (AP/Wide World Photos)

two years. The size of the factory would have to be doubled, a cost the navy must bear. Towers offered to give Fleet the order right then and there.

"No," Fleet demurred, "I can't take it, Jack. The government has never awarded a $20 million order for aircraft without calling for bids. I don't think you or I should be parties to such a thing." Doubting whether another company would bid and pointing out that time was of the essence, Towers got Fleet to settle on a gentleman's agreement: Consolidated would begin work immediately on 200 PBY-5s while the navy paid to double the size of the factory. Meanwhile Towers would call for bids; if another company got the contract, the navy would pay Consolidated for the work already done.[47]

In boldness Towers was matched by President Roosevelt: on 5 September the president ordered the navy to form a neutrality patrol from the Atlantic Squadron. Next day Admiral Stark approved Towers' agreement with Fleet for the 200 PBYs, "such an order to carry an option of not less than 100 additional." The measure was unorthodox in the extreme. Bids would be advertised a month later, and tax laws would jeopardize the program, but by his initiative Towers had taken the first major step in the mobilization of the aircraft industry for a wartime navy. When no competitive bids came forward, he completed the formal agreement with Fleet on 25 October—the largest single order for navy planes since World War I.[48]

To further bolster the nation's defenses, FDR declared a limited national emergency on 8 September, which meant extending air and ship neutrality patrols into the Caribbean and from the Philippines. Stark and Towers immediately transferred three PBY squadrons, one from Norfolk to Puerto Rico, a second from Panama's Coco Solo to Cuba's Guantanamo Bay, and a third from Pearl Harbor to the Philippines, which would island-hop via Midway, Wake, and Guam. The *Langley* followed the latter unit as its tender. The U.S. Fleet and its carriers remained concentrated on the West Coast, except for the *Ranger,* which joined the neutrality patrol in the Atlantic, and Towers hastily assigned spare spotting planes to three planeless Atlantic battleships. In November the president pushed through Congress a new neutrality act allowing private industry to sell weapons to Allied belligerents on a cash-and-carry basis. And the United States joined her Latin American neighbors in the Declaration of Panama, proclaiming a hemispheric "safety belt" reaching between three hundred and a thousand miles beyond the coasts.[49]

The limited emergency put life into BuAer's sluggish training program. Towers agreed to double the monthly number of new aviation cadets from 50 to 100 and to cut the eleven-month training syllabus to six and a half months.

In October he urged the creation of long-range plans to raise the quota to 150 cadets per month. Admiral Nimitz's BuNav planners expressed concern over training pilots in excess of the fleet's requirements for the 3,000-plane inventory authorized by Carl Vinson's legislation, but Congress quickly authorized the increase.

For additional training fields, Vinson remained convinced that Corpus Christi should be developed and in November had Towers accompany a naval affairs subcommittee to inspect two prospective sites. But when Towers recommended the next month that an air station be established at Corpus Christi, the subcommittee stood unanimously *against* it. Towers told Stark that many local Texas citizens opposed having such a station in their midst and that the Florida delegation feared it would draw away activity from Pensacola. Seeing as Congress was generally bent on economizing, Jack recommended against seeking funding for Corpus in the next session. That he was correct was borne out in January when the legislators refused a navy request to double its airplane ceiling to 6,000. All that BuAer and the Navy Department could do was request supplemental funding for Corpus and other installations.[50]

The mood of Congress did not change over the winter. Members grew suspicious of the navy's preparedness campaign under the guise of Roosevelt's policy of neutrality. So in April 1940 Towers was challenged in hearings for wanting to build temporary hangars at New York, Key West, and elsewhere to support the neutrality patrol. He nevertheless stoutly defended the legality of these measures as essential to national defense.[51] His singularity of purpose in preparing naval aviation for possible war soon made him "a thorn in the side of Congressional committees, planning sections, [and] all the inner circles of the Navy High Command," according to a feature story on him five years later. "He had never been an apple polisher, giving way to his superiors out of mere deference to their higher rank. Indeed there were many officers in the service . . . who disliked him intensely. He made then, and makes now, no secret of returning the compliment."[52]

Towers' new eminence[53] led to a subtle change in him that was discernible to his followers in the naval aviation community. Never one of the swashbuckling reformers, he had always been regarded as an outspoken champion of their cause. Since becoming chief of bureau, he appeared to many to be surprisingly careful, even compromising, especially since he steadfastly refused to endorse a separate naval air corps for the navy like that of the army. On a personal level, individual pilots no longer found him as accessible when they wanted to discuss their problems. The time for such opportunities was simply circumscribed, as were opportunities for relaxing or getting in flight time. Towers had to settle for routine "pay hops" in older planes instead of qualifying in the newer ones as they came out.

"Naval airmen soon realized," in the words of *Time* magazine, "that Admiral Towers and Captain Towers were two different birds. Fighting Jack had become a diplomat." The article quoted a congressman who questioned him during a hearing: "I'd like this answer from Captain Jack Towers and not from Admiral Towers who is taking orders from too many line admirals." *Time* thought this a "cruel judgment, which overlooked the realities that a Navy Chief of Aeronautics had to face," namely that naval aviation "is still subordinate, existing on sufferance." Even Towers' brother Will, remarking on a speech Jack gave in Georgia, reported that some of their fellow Romans "thought that you, because you were part of it yourself, failed to give aviation quite the credit to which it was due."[54]

In fact, Towers' fundamental ideas had not changed since his earliest days in the cockpit, nor had his sense of balance about the realities of modern conflict and the need for tact in gaining for naval aviation the role it deserved. "I am an aviation enthusiast," *Flying* magazine quoted him as saying, "but I hope I do not allow my enthusiasm to get the better of my judgment. Air is no panacea. . . . Do not be misled either by aviation enthusiasts who have not bothered to study the history of warfare, or by students of warfare who have not bothered to study aviation. There is much wishful thinking behind their extravagant statements." Also, he cautioned, "Do not think of disposing of the battleship or the foot soldier."[55]

He was not equivocating. From his vast reading of history, his studies at the Naval War College, and his perceptions of the modern world, Towers had a full understanding of the task that lay before the United States. Like Woodrow Wilson in World War I and now Franklin Roosevelt, he knew that his country would have to arm to save the democracies of Europe and thereby guarantee its own survival in a hostile world. The freedom-loving nations on both sides of the Atlantic first and foremost needed modern aircraft to carry on the fight, and to this end he devoted a major share of his energies as chief of BuAer.

The U.S. Navy came first, however, and though Towers convinced Congress to allocate 518 more scouts and trainers, he failed to obtain funding for a five-year research program, especially in the revolutionary field of jet propulsion, now being explored in Europe. His forthright actions were perhaps too aggressive to suit the CNO, Admiral Stark, who elected not to involve the chief of BuAer in deliberations over the general expansion of naval aviation. In response to Congressman Vinson's request for navy estimates to meet the emergency, the General Board recommended to the CNO that naval aviation be increased 25 percent. During a meeting with Towers on 1 November 1939 Vinson learned that Jack had not been consulted on this crucial policy matter. Two days later Towers received a copy of Stark's memo to Vinson requesting 2,395 new and replacement planes.

Towers was appalled that he had not been a party to the recommendations and said so in a long memo to Stark. The recommendations ignored the need for training planes for new pilots, made no provisions for certain types of patrol planes or additional squadrons, and underestimated costs for replacement planes and new types requested by the General Board. Also, by checking with Admiral Moreell of BuDocks, Towers found that the request for increased aviation facilities ashore had overlooked an additional $100 million price tag. The plain fact was that the CNO could not expand the navy without including his chief of BuAer in the intimate details of aviation planning. Ironing out these inconsistencies consumed much of the navy's planning throughout the fall and winter.[56]

Of vital importance was streamlining the navy's aircraft procurement policy, this in the face of congressional distrust of manufacturers' greed. The Vinson-Trammell legislation of 1934 had required that at least 10 percent of the navy's airplanes and engines be constructed at the Naval Aircraft Factory in Philadelphia "to safeguard the Government's interest relative to costs and time of construction, and to stabilize the labor turnover." So Towers let the factory specialize in N3N trainers. Even more restrictive was a provision in that law limiting profits of manufacturers of navy planes and ships to 10 percent. Such attempts to police profits enraged the manufacturers, doubly so now that foreign orders were to be subjected to the same tax laws enforced by the Internal Revenue Service. Towers therefore had to work closely with Secretary of the Treasury Henry Morgenthau to insure that fiscal controls did not inhibit production.[57]

The American aircraft industry was still relatively small in 1938–39, and the prospect of wartime orders demanded plant expansion and hard choices in some equipment. One choice the navy made was to adhere to the air-cooled radial engine because of "its lighter weight, greater reliability, and lower vulnerability to enemy gunfire." The Army Air Corps, by contrast, preferred the lower-performance, liquid-cooled in-line engine and threatened to force the entire industry to adopt it. Towers would have none of this; he insisted on the air-cooled radial, paraphrasing the words of his papa's commander Nathan Bedford Forrest: Jack wanted "to get there fastest with the most horses"—horsepower, that is. And so the air-cooled radial would prevail in the navy and appeal to many foreign buyers.[58]

Towers' reputation among the founding kingpins of the aviation industry greatly enhanced their production of first-line navy aircraft. The United Aircraft Corporation (United Technologies many years later) headed the list as the largest conglomerate. In May 1940 Gene Wilson, Bull Reeves' former chief of staff, became president of United's four companies: Chance Vought, Sikorsky, Pratt and Whitney, and Hamilton-Standard. The dynamic new general manager at Vought was C. J. McCarthy, former coworker with Towers on the NC project. The other companies were run by men who, in Wilson's words, "compressed into brief business careers the whole history of aviation"—Roy Grumman, Donald Douglas, Reuben Fleet, and "the Old Master," Glenn Martin. They, and the Curtiss-Wright and Brewster companies, were the navy's prime contractors. Pioneer aviator Jack Towers had their respect as well as their friendship.[59]

Towers monitored development and production by giving each contractor personal attention. Company engineers and presidents would fly to Washington to discuss the new planes with Towers or his specialists. No industry head was more persistent in salesmanship than Consolidated's Reuben Fleet, who loved to bend Towers' ear. Once, trying to prevent him from staying too long, Jack had all the chairs taken out of his office before Fleet arrived. Undaunted, this character, known affectionately as the Major for his former Army Air Service rank, simply pulled out a desk drawer and sat on that. He then held forth for two hours. Another time, eager to make a sale, Fleet reputedly followed Jack around the office on his knees. "At times," Towers recalled, "he's ruthless and rude but he's a loveable old son-of-a-bitch."[60]

Though Towers coordinated production of new aircraft as rapidly as possible, it was not fast enough to suit the impatient fleet carrier commander, Admiral Bill Halsey. In mid-1940, ignorant of the progress of Grumman's new F4F Wildcat fighter, Halsey proclaimed the existing Brewster F2A Buffalo "the best airplane that has ever been delivered to the Navy" and begged that its production be accelerated. Towers assured him that the F4F airplane was one of the best all-around fighters in the world and well worth waiting for. Grumman also had a unique twin-engine fighter under development, the XF5F Skyrocket. But Gene Wilson of United had the ultimate solution in a sturdy, 400-mph fighter that could double as a bombing plane, the Vought F4U Corsair. It held great promise, and Towers lamented that production lay at least a year away.[61]

The carriers' antiship punch lay in the two-seat scout dive bomber, but progress was so slow in new models that Towers had to continually calm Halsey. The first year of production saw so few of the new Douglas SBD Dauntlesses that by July 1940 Halsey was suggesting that the Douglas company be forced to divert production from the DC-3 commercial airliner to the SBD. Even were this possible, the 1,200-hp Dauntless was already earmarked for replacement by either the powerful 2,000-hp Curtiss SB2C Helldiver or perhaps the Brewster SB2A Buccaneer. Realizing the urgent need for replacements, Towers told Halsey the navy was proceeding with the procurement of 115 SB2Cs or SB2As (or both) without waiting for prototype tests. The decision was a fateful one, for the prototype Helldiver crashed at the end of the year and required time-consuming modifications.[62]

The situation was little better in torpedo planes and catapult scout planes. To replace the slow and already obsolete Douglas TBD Devastators, BuAer contracted with Grumman and Vought respectively for TBF Avenger and TBU Sea Wolf torpedo bombers. But the former would not be ready for service until 1942, and the latter would be eliminated by the superior TBF. Towers regarded TBDs as so inferior that he even contemplated replacing some of them with dive bombers on carriers. As for floatplane scouts, the new Vought OS2U Kingfisher deployed in mid-1940 and would have to be retained when its supposed successor, the Curtiss SO3C Seamew, failed to measure up.[63]

Towers also maintained BuAer's interest in advancing commercial aviation, whose progress had always benefited naval aeronautics. Of particular immediacy was the breakthrough by Pan American World Airways into transoceanic passenger service with Clipper flying boats, although several crashes had led the industry to begin advocating landplanes with comparable ranges. Juan Trippe, the dynamic founder of Pan Am, would telephone Towers to work out the Clippers' use of navy seaplane anchorages in both oceans. After the war began in Europe, Trippe would gain Towers' support to insure that neutrality legislation would enable his amphibians to call at British islands in the Atlantic and Pacific.

Understandably, Trippe wanted to monopolize the transatlantic passenger route and attendant government mail subsidies, which led him to oppose the CAA when it granted a rival license to American Export Airlines in December 1939. Admiral Stark solicited Towers' views, which became those of the navy: greater competition in flying boat design and use would stimulate progress and supply more trained personnel in the field, which would aid the navy in an emergency. The license was granted the following July.[64]

The greatest stimulus to the aircraft industry during Towers' first year as chief of bureau, however, was the foreign market. While the U.S. economy continued its peacetime operation, the European economies geared for war. Whatever the several American companies could not sell to the Army Air Corps and navy could be marketed abroad. For example, in mid-1939 Towers and Hap Arnold had to approve the sale of a projected Douglas four-engine DC-4 to Japan because it was a commerical airliner; the Air Corps had been content with its twin-engine DC-3 (or C-47). Such aeronautical hardware, even if not directly imitated, provided invaluable know-how to a potential enemy.[65]

Towers had to make certain that navy contracts not be jeopardized by such foreign orders. Thus before the outbreak of war in Europe he was perfectly willing to permit Consolidated to sell PBY-4s to the British and Dutch as permitted by law. But he warned the company against offering its experimental types, which "might shortly come within the direct purview of the Navy." The same held true with the Martin XPBM flying boat, unless President Roosevelt authorized it. The French simultaneously contracted with Pratt and Whitney and the Wright companies for four thousand engines and agreed to pay for plant expansion; the order virtually saved the former from going under for lack of new U.S. orders.[66]

The war not only accelerated Allied airplane contracts but also led the president to accuse the aircraft industry of making "an inordinate profit" from foreign orders. On 8 November 1939 Assistant Secretary of War Louis Johnson convened a meeting to discuss the matter with General Hap Arnold, CNO Stark, Towers, and BuOrd chief Furlong. Arnold revealed that the large French order prevented the British from ordering engines, though Towers and the navy pointed out that as long as the British funded the cost of plant expansion, enough engines could be produced for them *and* "increase the capacity to meet our needs in an emergency," that is, American entry into the war. This represented the view of FDR, who wanted the aircraft industry expanded so that on short notice it could produce thirty thousand planes a year.[67]

The conferees agreed that some method had to be devised allowing the manufacturers to write off the cost of plant expansion at foreign expense "and thus avoid heavy taxation for excess profits" gained thereby. Such taxation reflected the public distaste for American munitions manufacturers accused (by the Nye investigation in Congress during the 1930s) of being "merchants of death" whose search for profits had contributed to the coming of World War I. And Treasury Secretary Morgenthau did not want the airplane producers to exploit the Allies, whose cause he supported.

Roosevelt's solution in December was the creation of the Interdepartmental Committee for Coordination of Foreign and Domestic Military Purchases, or the President's Liaison Committee. Morgenthau dominated it, playing watchdog over the industry, much to the chagrin of top company executives whose expansion was inhibited by the taxation. But this committee in no way satisfied the need for centralized munitions-production planning by the U.S. government. At least the anxious British and French got together to create the Allied Consolidated Purchasing Mission, headed by Sir Henry Self, formerly of the Air Ministry, and René Plevin.[68]

In November 1939, after Nazi Germany and Soviet Russia carved up Poland, the Russians invaded Finland, whereupon Roosevelt forced Towers to divert the first-production Brewster F2A Buffalos to that country. Jack objected strenuously to the fact that these fighters had been earmarked to replace obsolescent fighters on the *Saratoga* and the *Lexington;* the older planes in turn were badly needed as trainers at Pensacola. Towers turned over the project to Captain Sidney Kraus, the bureau's head of material who coordinated the transfer of the planes by ship to neutral Sweden, whence the Buffalos were flown to Finland. Once ordered to make more planes available, Towers obeyed, in contrast to Hap Arnold, who resisted giving up planes earmarked for the army. In a meeting with the two men in March 1940, Secretary Morgenthau, recorded Towers, "expressed appreciation of what the Navy had done and stated politely that he thought it was the Army's turn to make some gesture." It was a moot point, however, for Finland surrendered to the Russians before the end of the month.[69]

In the midst of helping the Allies and Finland, Towers had to sell his proposed $35 million fiscal 1940 supplementary aircraft budget of October 1939 to Congress. At the end of November he convinced Clifton A. Woodrum's House appropriations deficiency subcommittee and the Bureau of the Budget to agree to his request. It then went to Carl Vinson's Naval Affairs Committee, which was attempting to create a new naval expansion bill and to which Towers presented his budget early in the new year. The navy's case looked good.[70]

Towers' effectiveness in dealing with the politicians naturally caused concern in the Army Air Corps, for it wanted similar funding. General Arnold remained in close touch with Towers informally and on the six-member Army-Navy Aeronautical Board. But they lacked coordination of effort, and so in December Arnold got Towers to agree to the development of a joint "long-range procurement planning program involving studies by the principal aircraft and engine manufacturers covering all phases of expansion necessary to meet a wartime program." What especially alarmed Arnold was the rising cost of airplanes, due in part, he felt, to the sudden foreign demand. With increased prices, Air Corps and navy competition for funds could only increase. Towers disagreed fundamentally with Arnold. In Jack's view, the rising costs were not abnormal.[71]

Arnold took another step that very month by asking Dr. Vannevar Bush and the National Academy of Sciences to investigate aircraft costs, whereupon Bush sent one Leonard S. Horner to interview Arnold and Towers. Towers flatly rejected such an investigation as fruitless, especially since the rapid expansion of the aircraft industry would quickly make any report obsolete. He reiterated these views to Horner two months later. Specifically, in regard to two of Horner's ideas, Towers stated "that I regarded measures toward quantity orders with cheaper materials and curtailment of development as being more dangerous than beneficial under present circumstances." He refused to provide naval officers for a nebulous study committee, and when Horner announced he would tour West Coast factories on behalf of the army and navy, Towers observed

> that the original request had come from the Army and that the Navy was not a party to it, and warned him that representations to the manufacturers had better be accurate. This appeared to anger him very much and some of his subsequent remarks contained veiled threats. . . . It appears to me that Mr. Horner is endeavoring to get a group of people to do a considerable amount of work for him for which I believe he is receiving a fee, and I am very doubtful as to his qualifications for the job.

Actually, as Towers would soon learn, Horner had been chief of staff for the army's aircraft production under Arnold during World War I and had once headed a similar study. Part of Arnold's problem was the encroachment of foreign orders on the American aviation market, and he particularly resented what he regarded as meddling by Treasury Secretary Morgenthau. This became obvious in January when Morgenthau gained FDR's approval to divert twenty-five of the army's first eighty-one P-40 Warhawk fighters to the French.[72]

The war for which Towers and the navy were preparing was an oceanic one—the Americas would be defended in both oceans. Thus, he argued, naval aviation should take priority over the Air Corps, whose long-range strategic bombers were clearly designed for service in Europe. The Air Corps continued to resent the navy's expensive coastal defense purchases, claiming they encroached on army missions. Towers said to Admiral Stark that increases in B-17 and B-24 strategic bomber production "for overseas work will result in corresponding decreases in Navy planes for that purpose, a situation which I believe we should view with grave concern."[73]

Fresh Allied proposals to procure as many as 8,500 of the latest American fighters and bombers and some 14,000 engines by September 1941 caused such apprehension in the administration that the president convened a special meeting to discuss it on 17 January 1940. Present were Morgenthau and Henry E. Collins from treasury, Generals Barton K. Yount and George H. Brett from the Air Corps, and Towers, Kraus, and paymaster-general Rear Admiral Ray Spear. Towers discerned that Morgenthau "was anxious to see the munitions business given a wider geographical spread," which Roosevelt suggested be done by relocating existing plants or building new ones in the interior, away from coastal points exposed to enemy attack. This attitude reflected further the administration's desire to prevent blatant war profiteering by the major manufacturers, as well as to ease the persistent unemployment that FDR's New Deal programs had failed to eradicate. Towers, forced to adopt a more pragmatic position, pointed out that centralized location on the coasts would best hasten production, and "that from the Allied point of view quick delivery is all important. . . ."

Roosevelt agreed with this analysis and was pleased to learn that the major aircraft companies were subcontracting out their work as much as possible. Concerned, however, with the deferred deliveries of planes from the Air Corps and navy to the Allies, the president asked the services to help manufacturers meet the foreign orders and announced he would hold future meetings to monitor their progress. Clearly, FDR, Morgenthau, and the army and navy leaders realized that if the Allies fell, the United States would stand alone. But only Towers and the navy were systematically supplying planes to the Allies; the Air Corps steadfastly opposed the practice.[74]

Partly through Morgenthau's influence, FDR was anxious to distribute the wealth emanating from foreign and American orders. Shortly he initiated a memo to Towers: "On our next 500 planes can we give a large part of engine orders to the smaller companies and not to the three big ones? This to spread the load." Towers shot back immediately "that the big companies are big because they have developed and produced satisfactory engines of the large horsepowers required for most of the current military types, and the small companies are small because they have not." Thus BuAer had stuck with Pratt and Whitney, Wright, and Allison-General Motors, though Towers was encouraging the Ranger engine division of the Fairchild airplane company to produce additional engines. He told the president that the bureau had done "everything within reason" to get the smaller companies to experiment with large engines. But such "experimental development takes a long time," and Towers saw "little prospect of pulling the small companies into big business on big engines for at least two years." Time was running out; 1942 would be too late. FDR, for the time being, yielded to Towers' reasoning.[75]

As Towers promoted production, the Senate dealt his proposed $35 million emergency supplemental request a blow. It cut over $6 million for 81 additional scout-bomber seaplanes of the 518 total aircraft requested. Towers considered these scouts essential for "inner or intermediate patrol" over neutral American waters. This left BuAer with a final supplement of over $28 million or a total of over $111 million for fiscal 1940—twice the amount of any previous BuAer annual appropriation. Still it wasn't enough.[76]

This setback occurred on the eve of Towers' testimony before the House Naval Affairs Committee on 24 January 1940. Carl Vinson was introducing a new naval expansion bill for fiscal 1941 that included a total strength of 6,000 "useful" naval aircraft and 36 nonrigid airships. This would double the number of planes authorized by the act of May 1938 and almost triple the number then in service. In fact, Vinson was boldly looking to wartime preparedness, for Towers and his planners had called for only 4,900 planes for fiscal 1941. Glad to have the lesser figure from Towers, the committee now agreed to it. Towers could not support the need for three dozen blimps in peacetime either, although he thought them "extremely useful in time of war for patrol of the sea lanes, outside the harbors and along the coast." He therefore compromised with Vinson: the bill should include an authorization of four blimps per year.

Given the healthy supplement for fiscal 1940, the isolationist House members prevailed by cutting $33 million for 224 more navy planes and experimental programs from BuAer's $131 million request. The cuts included $10 million for the 111 new planes Towers and the bureau had earmarked for the new carrier *Hornet,* due for commissioning late in 1941. In mid-February 1940 this alarming omission led Admirals Stark and Towers and all the bureau chiefs to meet with their key supporters on the Vinson committee to map out a strategy for restoring the *Hornet* planes. The committee got the powerful John Taber of New York to agree to support restoration of the *Hornet* cuts, but the House Appropriations Committee turned out to be uncooperative.[77]

The only recourse was to approach the next link in the political pipeline, the Senate appropriations subcommittee, chaired by sympathetic James F. Byrnes of South Carolina. Byrnes invited Towers to testify at his subcommittee's hearings in the near future. The matter was tied in to the general public debate over America's growing involvement in the European war, the desire of the Roosevelt administration to assist the Allies, and the Air Corps' lack of enthusiasm in helping to meet the crisis. Indeed, the Air Corps was continuing to press for complete independence from the army, since the General Staff was not sympathetic to all its professed needs.[78]

Like FDR, Carl Vinson placed his confidence in the navy's air arm. During the late January hearings Towers testified that, in the current war, the RAF and Royal Navy had not been cooperating; the U.S. Navy's anticipation of such a shortcoming was "one reason the Navy has so consistently opposed a separate air force." Vinson commented, "I am glad to hear what the Admiral has said, and I think it should stop for all time the idea of an independent air force." This was only wishful thinking, as events were to prove.[79]

With Towers' appearance before the Byrnes committee pending, FDR and Morgenthau sought an update on the military aircraft aid situation. Morgenthau, lunching with Towers, Arnold, and procurement director Collins on 6 March, casually reminded Arnold of his published testimony on the fifth before the House Appropriations Committee. In it, the general had complained about the rising costs of aircraft. The price tag for the Air Corps' 2,100 new planes had already jumped $20 million beyond the original estimate. Arnold laid the primary blame on companies giving first priority to foreign orders, an indirect slap at the president and Morgenthau, who had established the policy. Arnold naively thought he had made his testimony in secret, but the press had told all.[80]

Morgenthau called upon Towers, who repeated his firm belief that the president's policy of foreign purchases was stimulating the American aviation industry. He "pointed out that . . . aircraft were increasing in size and complexity year by year and that these facts naturally caused an increase in cost of newer types over that of older types. General Arnold did not entirely agree and I explained to Mr. Morgenthau that this had been a controversial matter between us for the past several months."[81]

Franklin Roosevelt became furious at Arnold for his criticism of administration policy and for refusing to release new engine designs to the Allies. In contrast, he wholly admired Towers for executing the policy in spite of initial disagreement. The president called a special conference one week later, 13 March. The secretaries and assistant secretaries of war and the navy were there, along with Morgenthau and Collins from treasury, Towers, Arnold, and navy paymaster-general Spear.

The president, recorded Towers, expressed displeasure over the "current criticism at the Capitol and in the press regarding aviation matters. [T]oo much loose talk . . . had been emanating from the War Department and particularly from the headquarters of the Air Corps. He was very caustic in his criticisms and pointedly stated more than once that they did not apply to the Navy as he had observed nothing to criticize on the part of the Navy." FDR stressed that the Army Air Corps was "not acting in accordance" with his policy on foreign aircraft orders and—words that made an indelible impression on Arnold—that officers who could not "play ball" could always be transferred to a place called Guam! Towers' star could not have been higher, nor Arnold's lower; Hap was virtually banned from the White House for months thereafter and he remained fearful of being replaced. In addition to helping the Allies, foreign orders meant prosperity for the country and a Democratic victory at the polls in November.[82]

The higher costs of aircraft weren't all that bothered Arnold. The release of new American equipment to foreign powers was another concern, one which Towers shared. Before entering the White House for the stormy conference on 13 March, Assistant Secretary of War Louis Johnson had held a press conference in which he announced that his department's policy "is not to release aircraft, aircraft engines and other items of aeronautical equipment until such time as a similar type, or types, of superior performance is under contract for the United States Government." Reporters stopped Towers after the meeting and obtained a similar statement with regard to naval aircraft. Johnson and Towers revealed that one army and four navy planes were being delivered to the Allies—the Curtiss P-40 fighter, PBY, F4F, F2A, and SB2U—but "stripped of secret equipment such as bomb sights."[83]

To ascertain the Allies' needs, the president had Harry Collins invite members of the Allied Purchasing Mission to meet next day with officers handling the sales, a meeting at which Towers and General Brett represented the services. The Allied spokesmen complained about the slow output of American aircraft engines. Also, they wanted the newest engines and planes so that their equipment would not be obsolete by the time it was delivered. The British and French wished to know of even newer types that might suit their needs; the present release policy—the very thing Arnold wanted to enforce—had prevented their access to such information. Roosevelt and Morgenthau agreed in principle with the Allied request.[84]

After the meeting adjourned, Towers hurried back to the department to discuss a navy response. He talked with the assistant CNO, his old classmate Rear Admiral Lee Ghormley. In light of the president's displeasure with the Air Corps, but not wanting to give the Allies complete access to the newest American equipment, Towers recommended that he "be authorized to inform Mr. Collins that representatives of the Mission would be permitted to examine the performance characteristics data of such of our experimental aircraft as appeared to me as being of possible interest to the Mission for procurement and as might be sufficiently far along in development to be produced in quantity by next year."[85]

Ghormley, though in relative accord, thought the matter too important for him to rule on and had Towers telephone Stark at home. The CNO readily concurred with Towers, as did the administration soon thereafter. By his hasty initiative, Towers was able to maintain control over how much technical data the Allied representatives would be allowed to see. Shown data on the navy's newest aircraft, French Colonel Paul Jacquin of the mission expressed particular interest in the XF5F Skyrocket fighter, the dive bombing XSB2A Buccaneer, and the XSB2C Helldiver, types potentially useful against the German Luftwaffe and army. Because Pratt and Whitney was falling behind in its enormous orders for foreign engines, Jacquin wanted to purchase both the F5F and F4F Wildcat fighters, but only if they were powered by Wright engines, because these were currently available. Grumman quickly complied. By mid-April the Allies had concluded contracts totaling $1 billion for more planes.[86]

Towers finally appeared before Senator Byrnes' appropriations subcommittee on 20 March and argued forcibly for the restoration of the $10 million cut for the *Hornet*'s planes. The subcommittee moved slowly on the request. In asking for the restoration of $2 million for experimental aircraft Towers made an error, admitting that the navy had profited by delaying its F2A Buffalo contract in order that first-production models go to Finland; improvement to the plane had then been possible. So Byrnes and his colleagues demurred from funding "expansion aircraft" in favor of purchasing only current types.[87]

The senators brought up the matter of foreign purchases, the effect of these on costs, and the government's release policy of equipment to the Allies. Towers, off the record, stated that his views in this case were his own and not those of the navy or government, but in fact he reinforced the administration's position on helping the Allies.

Senator David Walsh, an avowed isolationist, "endeavored to get me to admit that I was advocating a policy little short of open governmental support of the allied nations." Of course, Towers was doing just that, as was FDR, but Towers "refused to make any such admission, and pointed out that I was favoring permitting our aviation industry to carry on the foreign commercial business of a legitimate nature, which business would not only help the country financially but should be of direct benefit to the national defense. . . ."[88]

The touchy matter of releasing the latest equipment to the Allies prompted the Army Air Corps to take the next step. On 25 March General Brett invited Captain Kraus to the War Department to look at a newly proposed and more liberal release policy that Kraus understood to be for the Air Corps only. But Brett refused to let Kraus take back a copy for Towers to see. Next morning, Towers was surprised to receive a phone call from Hap Arnold asking "if the Navy Department approved of the new release policy for aircraft." Jack admitted his ignorance of it and noted Brett's refusal to share the Air Corps proposal with him. So Arnold had Brett and two majors hand-deliver it to Towers a few minutes later.

Towers noted immediately that the proposal, "Government Policy on Aircraft Foreign Sales," contained no mention of the navy. He also found it "unduly restrictive" in not allowing engine manufacturers to sell to any foreign country. Brett explained that this provision had been inserted to prevent a repetition of the big French engine order that had greatly slowed army aircraft output. When Brett revealed the president had adopted the policy, Towers wondered how it "could have been so definitely set up without any reference to the Navy."

Just then Admiral Ghormley called up and asked Towers to come over and see the very same document, just received by the CNO from the White House. When Towers arrived, Ghormley asked him what should be done about it. Jack "told him that it appeared to be finished business and that it should be forwarded to the interested bureaus and offices of the Navy Department for compliance."[89] As it turned out, Towers supported the generally liberalized release policy, which stated that "no military developments should be divulged or released to any foreign purchaser, unless or until a superior plane was actually in the process of manufacture for the U.S. War Department. No delivery delays were to be tolerated in our operating requirements." This followed the outline in the Air Corps proposal Towers had seen, except that FDR had made some changes, notably switching the phrase "War Department" in the title to "Government." FDR's swift decision almost backfired, for the proposal was still too vague to be workable.[90]

This became obvious the very next day when the chief executives of the major aircraft companies were assembled in Collins' office at the Treasury Department to be briefed on the new release policy. Collins admitted that the release policy was tentative. And since, recorded Towers, "the interpretation was very sketchy and rather badly phrased the manufacturers immediately began to ask questions." When General Brett backed off from answering, "Captain Kraus and I . . . explained the basic intent, pointed out that it represented a real liberalization, and called attention to the fact that in order to make the policy stand up before the critics it had to . . . show clearly the interests of the Government were being served." After a two-hour discussion, Collins asked Towers to write a press release explaining the policy.[91]

So Towers had bailed the Air Corps out of an awkward situation. But both the services and the industry now faced potentially dangerous delays in setting up the procedures for implementing the new release policy. On 1 April Towers convinced the Army-Navy Aeronautical Board to assign its permanent working committee to develop a draft. Next day Towers gave a copy of it to Captain Collins, who "realized the Navy Department was going ahead and acting in accordance with the new policy, . . . but such was not the case regarding the War Department."[92]

The dispute reflected the almost ad hoc nature of American military procurement as the nation tried to decide its foreign policy with respect to the warring powers. The Air Corps was understandably anxious that its multi-engine bombers, such as the B-17 and B-24, and plans for the experimental B-29 not be given over to foreign nations, whereas the only twin-engine navy plane at issue was the Grumman XF5F. In April hearings the Senate Appropriations Committee insisted that aircraft funds allocated for fiscal 1941 not be used for foreign planes, with which Towers agreed. But he did protest that all future policies should be made in full consultation with the navy. The Roosevelt-Morgenthau program of foreign aircraft sales could be implemented with planes already allocated.[93]

On 9 April 1940 the administration was shocked out of its inaction regarding the centralization of munitions production when Germany attacked Denmark and Norway. The German blitzkrieg—army columns spearheaded by panzer tanks and dive bombers—overran the Danes, captured Oslo, and stood poised to envelop the Low Countries and France. Britain rushed an army to the continent to shore up the defenses of her allies. The "phony war" was over. World War II began to engulf all Europe, encouraging Mussolini's Italy and Hirohito's Japan to join in the spoils.

Towers, like most of his peers in the military as well as FDR, believed the United States must keep the Allies in the fight while preparing to participate in the war against fascism. By now, Jack had developed an inner circle of procurement planners to develop the navy's air program—Captain Mitscher,

Commanders Ramsey and Laurance B. Richardson, and Lieutenant George Anderson. Their planning now went into high gear.

Towers spent much of April 1940 before the Senate Naval Affairs Committee vigorously defending Carl Vinson's naval expansion bill for fiscal 1941; already having passed the House, it called for an 11 percent increase of the fleet. The isolationist members of the committee tried to get him to admit that the new government policy of releasing aircraft to the Allies would cause greater delays in deliveries to the navy and Army Air Corps, and they insisted that all new monies allocated for new aircraft be used for American rather than foreign orders. Towers assured them that, except for the naval planes going to Finland, only the Air Corps had been affected by deferred orders—the navy had no intention of using BuAer fiscal 1941 appropriations for anything but U.S. Navy planes.

Nonetheless, at a dinner given by Senator Peter G. Gerry of the committee, the guests expressed their growing concerns to Towers. "After the dinner I was questioned for over two hours as to my views regarding effectiveness of bombs against various types of men-of-war, methods and accuracy of bombing, the situation in Norway, aircraft release policy, the effect of [a possible] Italian entrance into the war, and the Far Eastern situation, the last named with specific regard to what we can do in case of war with Japan." Such concerns were shared by the president. After Fleet Problem XXI, he ordered the new commander in chief of the U.S. Fleet, Admiral Joe Richardson, to keep the fleet in Hawaii as a deterrent to Japanese aggression instead of returning it to the West Coast.[94]

The country needed two or three years in which to rearm, and the buildup was in such an early stage that BuAer's flight training program already suffered from a lack of instructor pilots. Desperate, Jack had written a letter to Hap Arnold in March asking the Air Corps to lend five hundred such instructors to the navy in order to produce a backlog. Without them, he feared, "there will be nothing in front but a thin red line of heroes." Arnold could not spare the pilots; Towers would have to get them from the naval reserve, Marine Corps, and commercial airlines. Until these sources could be tapped, Jack kept close watch over training by personally inspecting his air stations.

In late April he and Captain A. E. "Monty" Montgomery, head of BuAer's flight division, departed on a cross-country junket to San Diego. With Herb Riley (soon to become Jack's son-in-law) at the controls, they flew to NAS Seattle to discuss its expansion with the commanding officer, Arthur W. Radford, and to dine with Captain Baldy Pownall in the *Enterprise*. Riley deftly handled the bureau's temperamental Lockheed XR40-1, the only one ever built for the navy, in a tense flight to Oakland, after which the party proceeded to San Diego for a four-day inspection.[95]

Returning to Washington just as the British were vainly contesting the German invasion of Norway, Towers found that Vinson had obtained and endorsed a hasty BuAer estimate for fifteen thousand trained naval aviators in case of war. What Towers did not know was that the astronomical figure fit into the congressman's vision for a two-ocean navy. On 10 May, the day Germany attacked Belgium and the Netherlands, Vinson called Towers into his office to discuss his proposal. When given the details, Towers observed that "he was taking hold of the wrong end of the stick; that three major factors are involved in [the] building up of Naval Aviation: First, adequate bases from which to operate, whether they be ships or shore bases. Second, aircraft equipment. Third, pilots and other personnel." Towers explained that pilots could be trained as fast as planes could be procured, but that bases and equipment would take longer. In any case, all the factors should be considered together and in the light of strategic needs. Vinson nevertheless directed him to prepare an estimate of the additional training facilities needed "to triple the present output of pilots."[96]

The strategic needs of which Towers spoke were the crux of the problem, for although the administration wanted to strengthen America's defenses, Congress and public opinion remained divided over the huge outlays being suggested. But what the president could not do, Carl Vinson could with his vision of a navy strong in both oceans, especially in aircraft carriers. Vinson's program would give FDR the tools for his strategy, though the two men operated independently of each other. And increased numbers of carriers and pilots formed the cornerstone of his thinking.[97]

On 11 May, the day after this discussion, Vinson met with Secretary Edison, Towers, and the chiefs of BuEng and C&R, Rear Admirals S. R. "Mike" Robinson and A. H. Van Keuren, to announce his next move. According to Towers, Vinson said he wanted "to put through as quickly as possible necessary legislation to expedite [the] shipbuilding program and to greatly expand [the] Naval Aviation program." After a lengthy discussion of ship construction, Towers presented to Secretary Edison the navy's needs for pilot training, repeating his observations of the day before to Vinson. Vinson concluded the meeting by announcing he intended to initiate hearings on aviation expansion, at which Towers should be prepared to explain the views of the Navy Department. So Towers' thinking on aviation now became that of the navy, a navy heavily weighted to its air arm. Strategic necessity was breeding a naval revolution, with Vinson as political catalyst and Towers professional guiding hand.[98]

On 13 May, at a general conference between the CNO and the bureau chiefs, Towers asked for 105 planes for the *Hornet* earlier deleted from the fiscal 41 appropriations, or $22 million. They would be newer models than those originally anticipated. Taking stock of recent innovations in aeronautical technology, he also solicited funds "to modernize planes for greater protection"—namely, for self-sealing gas tanks and armor plating behind the pilot's seat. Stark took these requests to the White House, then reconvened his admirals later in the day to tell them what FDR had approved. The total navy request came to $285 million. The *Hornet*'s planes again deleted, the CNO prepared a supplemental list that included those planes in the amount of an additional $175 million.[99]

Roosevelt was rushing ahead. Next morning, the fourteenth, the day Holland surrendered, he sought decisions on the needs of the army and the navy. After the War Department presented the president with a figure of $750 million for total army expansion, he convened all his military planners, including Towers. FDR said he would turn over $100 million of the $750 million to Morgenthau for the expansion of aircraft plants. But when he saw the navy's list of items, according to Towers, "he threw up his hands and stated that the ceiling was in the neighborhood of $1 billion and that $250 million was all that he would allow for the Navy"—that is, a $35 million reduction from the navy's requests. He ordered the navy to revise its estimates in the neighborhood of $250 million for cash items and other essentials to be handled by contract authorizations paid for with later supplemental funding.

None of this satisfied Towers, whose BuAer estimates for the implementation of Vinson's 15,000-pilot proposal stood firmly at $155 million. He informed Vinson, whereupon the latter went straight to the White House to parlay with FDR. The president now acceded to Vinson's arguments that $100 million of the $250 million allowed the navy for fiscal 1941 "would go towards the aviation expansion program." Roosevelt also assured Vinson he would not oppose the expansion bill. Vinson directed Towers to draw up the proposed bill and have it in his hands by the time of the planned press release. All of this Towers dutifully reported to CNO Stark.[100]

At this point FDR seized the initiative. On 16 May, as Belgium fell, the president announced, on the advice of Congress, his proposed defense budget of over $1 billion for fiscal 1941, a fourth of which would go to the navy. The most dramatic aspect of the announcement was his call for 50,000 military airplanes a year, a figure at which he and his advisers had arrived arbitrarily but that underscored America's intention to arm to the teeth in the face of fascist aggression. The absence of strategic direction prevented useful figures; the administration simply divided the 50,000 figure to give two-thirds, or 36,500 planes, to the Air Corps, and one-third, or 13,500, to the navy.[101]

Of the $100 million to be allocated for naval aviation, nearly $44 million would go to BuAer, $38 million for training planes, and the balance to other bureaus providing aircraft equipment and support. Towers, his planners, and Vinson agreed that training facilities should be expanded at Pensacola and still-uncompleted Jacksonville and Miami and that Corpus Christi should be developed as a duplicate of Pensacola. Eventually, these four air stations should accept a total of 800 students per month, a fivefold increase. The total ceiling of useful navy planes should be increased from 4,500 to 10,000; additional training planes would require another $100 million. All these and other plans were accepted on 20 May when Towers met with Vinson, Senator Walsh, and Admiral Stark.[102]

Next day, fortified by news that the German army had reached the English Channel, Towers asked the Senate appropriations subcommittee on emergency naval supplements for an additional $21 million for 113 more planes. Then, at noon, he joined Vinson, Walsh, Stark, and Admiral Moreell of BuDocks at the White House. FDR, convinced by Towers' arguments, supported the $100 million for additional training planes and $99 million for air base expansion, Jack assuring him that industry and the Naval Aircraft Factory could deliver the trainers. Walsh obtained the president's authority to raise the inventory ceiling of navy aircraft to 10,000, of which the navy hoped to base 4,500 at sea and 5,500 on land for the defense of seaports—the first time the navy had ever considered a land-based need. Also, the number of navy pilots was raised to 16,000.[103]

In the hearings before the Vinson committee on 22 May, Towers' projection of a four-year buildup to train sixteen thousand pilots failed to satisfy the congressmen now alarmed over events in Europe. Just how alarmed became apparent when Towers witnessed the spectacle of Vinson and Melvin Maas demanding accelerated output of pilots. Vinson ordered that each member of the committee be given a copy of the "magnificent" Horne report on aviation personnel. He further ordered Towers to draft legislation "immediately" to extend to new pilots the hope of regular navy commissions. Declared Vinson, "[Y]ou may have no doubt but that this committee will go along with you. . . . We want you to have all these aviators."[104]

Towers, caught off guard by Vinson's zeal, pointed out that although BuAer had often recommended such legislation, it was "not the function of the Bureau either to draft or submit to your committee personnel legislation." To which Congressman Maas replied, "If Navigation does it, we will get nothing"—a blatant slap at BuNav chief Nimitz and the staid Gun Club. But Towers believed that Nimitz was responsible and asked Vinson to seek the draft from BuNav. Vinson agreed.[105]

The alacrity with which Vinson moved was nothing short of phenomenal, for he was creating not only a mammoth wartime navy but a postwar fleet with reserve air stations around the country in peacetime. "Let the Judge Advocate General," he said, "prepare an amendment [to the proposed bill for base expansion] . . . , because after we turn [the newly trained aviators] over we do not want them to grow stale." Whereupon Maas, a marine reserve aviator, demanded that the number of Marine Corps pilots and planes be increased in spite of the fact that the Marine Corps high command wanted no more than the 558 pilots allotted in the 16,000-pilot program. Marine air was crucial to holding captured island bases, he said. Towers agreed.[106]

It is no exaggeration to say that more was done toward creating the modern air-centered wartime and postwar U.S. Navy on this twenty-second of May 1940 than had been in years of struggling by BuAer and the fleet's aviators, Towers foremost among them. Vinson, with no small help from Maas, had set the pace; the Walsh naval affairs committee in the Senate merely had to follow it and BuAer to work out the details in concert with the other bureaus. On the morning of the twenty-third Towers informed the Walsh committee that under the new authorizations the navy expected to have a total supply of 3,850 pilots in 1941, 6,800 in 1942, 12,100 in 1943, and 18,500 in 1944.[107]

That all lay in the future. When Towers revealed that the navy had only 1,367 modern combat planes on hand and just 2,250 projected for 1941, some senators wondered if such a gloomy picture ought to be kept from the press and the world. Maryland's Millard E. Tydings thought not: [T]here is nothing that Admiral Towers is telling here that every government does not pretty well know. We might as well have the truth out in the open and arouse this country . . . and give the Navy and the Army what they ought to have. . . ."[108]

What Towers found difficult to accept was the sudden determination of many legislators to spend lavishly on military preparedness. This came out in a dialogue with Senator Harry Byrd of the Walsh committee on 24 May. When Byrd told him to forget about money and concentrate on the navy's real needs, Towers replied, "That depends on the national policy. . . . The Congress makes the policy. . . . We [the navy] make recommendations about measures to support or to implement that policy—a fleet of a certain strength."

Said Byrd, "I am asking you . . . whether this program is one you recommend in view of the crisis that confronts this country, regardless of the amount of money involved?" When Towers countered that he had to consider funding, Senator Walsh broke in to rescue him: "Let me add, in fairness to Admiral Towers, . . . that if it was not for his persistency and his determination and his fighting qualities this bill would not be before this committee."

Senator Scott Lucas agreed: "Instead of anyone being condemned here we ought to be congratulated for the position that we are in under all of the circumstances." He found it surprising that a peace-loving nation such as the United States was "as adequately prepared and concerned, as we are at the present time." Towers responded that his predecessors (Moffett, King, and Cook) deserved credit for what was "far and away the finest naval air service in the world."

"I hope the boys will print that!" said Lucas. They did.[109]

Towers deserved much of the credit too. And he had no problem taking his message to the public. On 26 May, on a radio program during the National Aviation Forum, he proclaimed, "Our aviation, in naval parlance, is in A-1 condition—meaning that it is ready to fight." Such reassurance added a modicum of comfort to an aroused America, for the news from Europe was all bad, with the British army pinned against the sea at Dunkirk.[110]

To insure a coherent 50,000-plane program, Roosevelt appointed a joint army-navy special aviation board headed by Admiral Horne. Towers and Hap Arnold were the key members, assisted by representatives from the respective war plans divisions, notably the brilliant naval aviator Commander Forrest Sherman. When the board first met in Towers' office on 27 May, the army airmen admitted they had no well-developed expansion program and agreed with Horne's suggestion that they develop one, based on the same assumptions as the navy's. Arnold was given a copy of the navy study.[111]

What was clearly needed was a centralized aircraft production body to coordinate the needs of both services. The president took the first step on 28 May by creating the National Defense Advisory Council (NDAC) under his own general direction. To handle industrial production, particularly of aircraft, FDR appointed the dynamic president of General Motors, William S. Knudsen. Equally significant, Roosevelt decided to replace his secretaries of war and navy, Harry Woodring and Charles Edison, with avowed Republican interventionists Henry L. Stimson and Frank W. Knox, to give him a coalition war cabinet. And to the new Executive Office of the President he appointed knowledgeable administrative assistants from the private sector, notably James V. Forrestal, president of Dillon, Read investment firm and World War I aviator in Towers' office. Forrestal's genius as a manager soon became apparent to Knox, who selected him to become the first undersecretary of the navy in August. Of similar build and personality as Towers, Jim Forrestal was described as "five feet nine inches of reticence."[112]

Until aircraft production moved into high gear, hard choices had to be made, a problem confronted at a meeting on 31 May between Stark, Ghormley, Towers, and FDR's naval aide, Captain Daniel J. Callaghan. At it, Towers informed Stark that the crucial need for training planes meant delays in getting combat aircraft to the enlarged fleet—specifically delays in "the creation of some new patrol plane squadrons and the establishment of the inner patrol units." Stark accepted the necessity of the changes, which Towers said he would try to minimize. But this and similar decisions for long-term advantages would require potentially dangerous short-term sacrifices. Indeed, reality would set in when the numbers of PBYs available were insufficient to detect the Japanese Pearl Harbor striking force in December 1941 and to patrol the entire Atlantic seaboard during the deadly German U-boat offensive of early 1942.[113]

Because of such deficiencies Roosevelt sent another message to Congress the same day, 31 May, urging more supplemental legislation, especially for the additional naval, marine, and reserve air stations recommended by the Hepburn Board. At the same time, Towers provided BuNav chief Nimitz with BuAer's expansion plans, the first priority being to train the maximum number of students as soon as possible at existing and new training stations. The CNO approved and ordered all naval activities involved to lend maximum possible support.[114]

Early on 5 June, amidst grim news that the British had completed the evacuation of their beaten army from Dunkirk and the Germans were throwing everything at the French, Towers had his first meeting with NDAC production chief Knudsen. He assured Knudsen that the navy's carefully laid plans required no change, unlike the army's, still mired in confusion. Air Corps problems surfaced at a forenoon meeting of Horne's special aviation board, at which Hap Arnold took exception to plans for navy fighters to defend overseas naval installations, an army mission. Admiral Horne explained that he had included them since the Air Corps had not and that he would withdraw them from the navy program as soon as the Air Corps made such provision, an amicable solution.

At 1145 Towers proceeded to Secretary Morgenthau's office in response to an urgent request by the president to provide dive bombers to the faltering French. Towers immediately came up with fifty old Curtiss SBC-4 reserve biplanes, idle at the time because their pilots had been rushed to Pensacola as instructors. Ironically, this irritated the Air Corps, only recently awakened to the efficacy of dive bombing by the German blitz and wanting these reserve scout bombers from the navy. "Nuts on the Army!" retorted Morgenthau, who then asked Towers if he could provide spare parts from Curtiss for the SBCs.

"Of course," observed Jack, "you realize we are subject to attack on the Hill."

"So are we all. Look what I went through a year ago," replied Morgenthau, recalling criticism of the first Allied purchases.

After luncheon at the Australian embassy, where he listened to Australian appeals for American planes, and afternoon meetings on aircraft production, Towers and Stark attended a conference at Morgenthau's home. There the secretary informed the British and French ambassadors of the president's approving immediate delivery of the SBCs to France's only carrier, the *Béarn,* at Halifax, Nova Scotia. At 2030 Towers convened Mitscher, Ramsey, Kraus, and George Anderson at his own home to make plans for the transfer. After they had worked out the details, Towers telephoned the CNO with "a proposed dispatch to start things moving." Stark approved it, whereupon Towers' typically busy day ended.[115]

This pragmatic solution to the SBC problem was immediately ruled illegal by the navy's judge advocate general, Rear Admiral Walter B. Woodson. Towers therefore had to spend several hours on 7 June discussing the matter with Stark, Woodson, and paymaster-general Spear, at the end of which he recommended that the transfer be made through the army under an existing law. Towers, Stark, and Woodson then called on outgoing Secretary of War Woodring, who refused to agree unless the attorney general approved. Towers and Woodson journeyed to see him, only to learn that Woodring had changed his mind. Whereupon Attorney General Robert H. Jackson approved, and Towers arranged the details of the transfer to the army. Such personal action by Towers was necessary to counteract the sluggishness of some of FDR's officials, whom the president was determined to replace.[116]

On 10 June, the day Mussolini's Italy attacked France, Towers testified on the proposed naval aviation personnel bill before the Vinson committee. After Chester Nimitz presented BuNav's draft of the bill, Towers challenged a provision prohibiting any increase in the numbers of naval aviators beyond the rank of lieutenant commander, the selection boards being bound by law to select sufficient numbers of all ranks "in accordance with the needs of the service." More reserve pilots and aviation units would create the need for aviators to command them as commanders, captains, and rear admirals. Nimitz disagreed, fearing that additional promotions would simply swell the higher ranks. The committee supported Towers completely, rejecting Nimitz's restriction.

The bill, passed in August, gave the secretary of the navy power to commission as many reserve navy and Marine Corps aviators as necessary. For inducement, each aviation cadet was to be given an annual bonus of $500 during his four years' active duty and the option of thereafter transferring into the regular navy. In June 1940 only 16 percent of the officers in the navy were in aviation. But the 16,000 new pilots would be triple the number of existing nonflying line officers, 6,600. By sheer size, aviation would dominate the navy. And the way was now clear for more air admirals. Each time he won such a battle, Towers strengthened aviation but gained enemies for himself, in this case Nimitz.[117]

The biggest boost to naval aviation came in the form of the two bills authorizing expansion of the navy's air strength, to be completed in 1944. The passage of the fiscal 1941 budget on 14 June raised the ceiling of navy aircraft from 3,000 to 4,500 and authorized three more carriers of the *Essex* class. And the very next day the third Vinson bill was passed, increasing the navy by 11 percent; it raised the aircraft ceiling to 10,000, created an upper limit of forty-eight blimps, and provided training facilities for 16,000 pilots. Supplemental bills would fund the program as specific needs arose. The two laws came none too soon, for the Germans marched into Paris on the fifteenth and France surrendered a week later. Britain stood alone.[118]

The fall of France acted as a catalyst for the American government and aviation industry. To the president's projected 50,000 airplanes were added 14,000 for the British, who now took over French contracts, promising to make the aircraft industry into the largest business in America. And Carl Vinson drafted yet another bill, for a two-ocean navy that included seven more *Essex*-class carriers. This fourth Vinson bill, passively cosponsored by Senator Walsh, would increase the navy by 70 percent and to the tune of $4 billion. Vinson sold the White House on it in mid-June.[119]

To minimize the risk of war profiteering by manufacturers Congress and the administration agreed that profits should be held down, as those for airplanes had been (at 12 percent) since 1939. Towers had no quarrel with such a ceiling, but FDR thought 12 or even 10 percent too high for the expected boom and at the end of May decided to push for a special tax on excess profits. In the meantime, Congress wrote into the new bill emergency provisos lowering the profits limitations on negotiated shipping contracts from 10 to 7 percent and those of competitive aircraft contracts from 12 to a pitifully low 8 percent. Though sound politically, the new limits threatened defense contracting altogether.[120]

Towers first learned of the proposed new ceilings on 18 June, and when he queried Morgenthau, the latter professed no part in the scheme. But next day, at Senate Naval Affairs Committee hearings over a separate bill to expedite shipbuilding, Towers discovered that the Treasury Department had indeed helped to draft the provisos. Called to testify were members of Knudsen's NDAC, now charged with coordinating industrial production. Captain Kraus and Fred Eaton opposed the 8 percent profit limitation on aircraft, and when they started to explain why, Walsh and two other senators, in Towers' words, "showed immediate and violent hostility." Later that day Towers and Admiral Robinson of BuShips testified, taking a stance against the limitation because they feared it would delay passage of the two-ocean navy bill and thus the necessary construction and procurement of ships and planes. Towers said the earlier 10 rather than the recent 12 percent limit on aircraft had always been sufficient. But the congressmen were not swayed, and the 8 percent figure stood when the profits limitation bill became law on 28 June.[121]

Carl Vinson called Towers before the House Naval Affairs Committee on 20 June to testify on the two-ocean navy bill. Towers stated flatly that for the proposed navy, with seven more carriers, the 10,000-plane limit just authorized would be way too low. He wanted it raised to 15,000 and with latitude to plan above that, should the national defense require it. Vinson instantly agreed and ordered Towers to draft such an amendment to the bill.[122]

Vinson's committee had no further need of Towers, except to report occasionally on the progress of the various new programs. Thus did Towers complete his crucial role in the authorization of the two-ocean navy. His amendment was incorporated into the fourth Vinson bill, enacted into law on 19 July. In addition to the 15,000 planes, it authorized the seven additional *Essex*-class carriers (making a total of eleven to be built) along with the conversion of nine uncompleted cruiser hulls into 11,000-ton light carriers. Although Towers had steadfastly opposed smaller carriers, carrier planes then under development would be able to operate from such relatively inexpensive and quickly converted carriers.[123]

The two-ocean navy was formidable enough on paper, and appropriations bills would make the money readily available, but little could be done to implement construction of the ships and planes until the manufacturers were willing. The *Essex* herself had yet to be laid down and would not be until the problem of the profit ceiling could be solved, along with certain design alterations. As for aircraft, Towers soon began to see the unhappiness of their builders. With his new profit limitations FDR had completely alienated the aircraft industry, which recoiled at his implicit distrust of their patriotism and apparent desire for exorbitant profits. At least he turned over the review of airplane and engine contracts to William Knudsen, whose managerial skills both services now enlisted for a coherent program of aircraft production.

Knudsen, Towers, Hap Arnold, and their staffs set to work to clear away the difficulties of placing contracts for new aircraft, difficulties Towers believed were due not only to the 8 percent limitation but even more importantly to the services' "inability to arrange with the Treasury various principles and details." For example, on 5 July 1940, while attending Bureau of the Budget hearings on the next appropriations bill, Towers learned that the administration had cut the figure for expanding aircraft manufacturing plants from $45 to $35 million. He told Lewis Compton, acting secretary until Frank Knox was sworn in a week later, "that our aircraft procurement program is being held up because of [the] reluctance of manufacturers to enter into contracts unless and until they know where they stand with regard to financing of plant expansion and cost accounting [required] under the [1934] Vinson-Trammell Act." Such accounting to the Treasury Department was supervised by naval officer inspectors assigned to each company.[124]

Worse, the president slashed another $56 million from BuAer's supplemental request as part of an overall $300 million navy reduction, leaving $500 million for new naval aircraft authorizations. This was the bare minimum that Towers and his planners believed necessary for 4,028 new planes to be delivered over the next two years but not nearly enough either for aircraft maintenance or to cover plant expansion. Knudsen's anticipated two-year program for both air arms required $45 million more for the naval aircraft plant expansion, which need Towers conveyed to Secretary Knox on 18 July and to Admiral Stark on the nineteenth. Supported by Knudsen, he presented these figures before the House appropriations subcommittee on the twenty-third, which duly impressed the entire House with the need.[125]

Part of the confusion stemmed from the division of responsibility between Knudsen for aircraft production and Morgenthau for supplying the British. All agreed that the situation was urgent, for German bombers were now striking British seaports and the Japanese were moving into Indochina, leading FDR on 25 July to halt certain war material exports to Japan. On the twenty-third a fresh British request for more planes prompted Morgenthau, Knudsen, Towers, and Arnold to hammer out a two-year overall aircraft production schedule: 14,440 planes for the British, 12,200 for the Air Corps, and 6,200 for the navy. As in the past, production of engines was tightest, for the British needed 35,000 of them, though Towers was willing to deter certain navy orders, thereby releasing 3,200 more engines to the British. He could do this, whereas Arnold and the overburdened Air Corps could not. For, aside from PBYs being provided by Consolidated, all British aircraft requests were for Air Corps planes.[126]

All these schedules depended upon resolution of the profit limitations dilemma. Actually, the outcry of the aircraft manufacturers had led the president to agree to drop the profit limitations and to grant a favorable plant amortization policy, but the companies refused to act until Congress wrote such changes into law. Towers conveyed this fact to the House deficiency subcommittee on the twenty-sixth. Plant expansion would mean unknown costs that the companies could not anticipate, even with volume sales. Accelerated wartime production left no room for the normal peacetime amortization of new facilities over sixteen to twenty years. Companies needed protection from high costs and taxes once the war ended. Neither could they subcontract for parts with confidence. Towers disclosed that since the passage of the limitation law on 28 June he had been able to obtain but one contract, with Stearman for training planes. He had done that only by making a gentlemen's agreement with its president that part of the cost of one piece of the plane's equipment be used toward the necessary plant expansion associated with that part, and by promising to "do everything within my power to get Treasury approval of that item when the time arrived."

The House subcommittee was suitably alarmed, especially when General Brett of the Air Corps and Edward R. Stettinius of the Knudsen committee strongly supported Towers. After the meeting Towers suggested to John Pugh, senior clerk of the House Appropriations Committee, that new legislation restore the airplane profit limitation from 8 to 12 percent. He then got Vinson to agree not only to introduce such legislation but also to try to repeal the amended Vinson-Trammell Act of 8 percent profits altogether, since its strictures seriously inhibited aircraft production. Vinson asked Towers to draft a memo outlining the problems of procurement as the basis for new legislation.[127]

While Towers took the initiative to resolve the profit ceiling crisis, Morgenthau introduced the administration's own solution, an excess profits tax. FDR could support repeal of the amended Vinson-Trammell law but not until passage of this excess profits legislation, which lay weeks or even months in the future because of the need for hearings and all that they entailed. When Towers informed Secretary Knox of his discussions with Vinson, Knox agreed that repeal of the amended 1934 act made sense from a business standpoint but that any attempt to repeal it would probably be unwise politically. The entire month of July was wasted while Congress and the administration tried to come up with an equitable excess profits tax law.[128]

To help educate the new secretary about aviation, Towers arranged an inspection trip to Pensacola. On 30 July, taking along his new special assistant, Lieutenant Commander Gus Read, Towers picked up Knox at Norfolk and flew south in the temperamental Lockheed R4O. A sudden storm off the gulf forced them to fly through heavy showers to the Mobile city airport. Though they were all dressed in civilian suits, the press spotted and interviewed the secretary as he waited for a car to take the party on to Pensacola. At length, as Read recalled the incident, up drove an undertaker's Cadillac, "of somewhat ancient vintage, with a highly nervous driver at the wheel." A lady in the gathering crowd handed the hungry Knox a large ham sandwich and a quart of milk as he sat down in the front seat. He thanked her, then boomed, "Well, driver, let's go!" As Knox put the milk to his lips, the driver raced the engine and let out the clutch with a bang; the car lurched forward, catapulting the milk all over the secretary's three-piece double-breasted suit. Knox sat in glum silence all the way to Pensacola, then delayed the welcoming honors until he could change clothes. But he enjoyed the visit immensely and laughed about the incident all the way back to Washington.[129]

Waiting for Towers on 1 August with ominous news were three representatives of the aircraft industry. C. J. McCarthy of Vought-Sikorsky, Burdette Wright of Curtiss, and Guy Vaughan, president of Curtiss-Wright, aired their grievances over contractual problems with navy aircraft. They were chagrined that FDR and Morgenthau, still hoping to spread the wealth and alleviate unemployment, now wanted the industry to license the government to build aircraft engines at government-owned factories. Vaughan confided to Towers that eight companies planned to issue a joint press release in a rare expression of unanimity, announcing the industy's position vis-à-vis the national defense program. They could do the job themselves with sufficient government support. Matters were reaching a crisis, even as British and German fighters were slugging it out in the furious Battle of Britain. Towers had drawn up his proposed draft to repeal the profit ceilings but delayed giving it to Vinson until he could learn what Morgenthau and Knudsen planned to do. Impatient, Vinson set about drawing up his own draft.[130]

Finally, on the fifth, Towers learned that Morgenthau, Knudsen, and the new secretary of war Henry L. Stimson had drafted an excess profit tax bill. It would purportedly regulate profits, repeal the amended Vinson-Trammell 8 percent ceiling, and allow the depreciation of expanded munitions plants (including shipyards and airplane shops) at an annual rate of 20 percent per year over five years instead of the usual twenty years. In discussing the situation with Knox next morning, Towers was given permission to provide his own draft to Vinson as promised but to remind Vinson that the president did not want any other bills introduced on the matter. When Towers confronted Vinson after leaving Knox, he found the congressman miffed at FDR and determined to introduce his own bill anyway. Towers could not dissuade him from taking that action but pointed out that Vinson's draft for repeal lacked the necessary plant depreciation measure. Jack suggested that Vinson have John Pugh of the House Appropriations Committee redraft it, which was done.

Towers was caught in a tug-of-war between the several interested parties. FDR and Morgenthau wanted the tax to restrict war profiteering. The industry did not want it; as Gene Wilson of United Aircraft observed, it was "political in character, uneconomic in principle" and would in the long run cause aircraft costs to soar through padded expense accounts and general waste. Towers and Vinson wanted airplanes, and fast, thought the tax bill would consume months of debate that could not be spared, and sided with the industry in advocating a bill only to repeal the profits ceiling and to establish the five-year plant amortization. So when John Pugh telephoned Towers later that day to read his revision of Vinson's proposed draft, Towers found it satisfactory. But he "also explained to him [Pugh] my rather delicate position in regard to this matter and he assured me that my participation would be kept secret."[131]

Gus Read, officially on ninety-day reserve duty leave from his Wall Street banking vice presidency, counseled Towers to deal with the aircraft manufacturers on a case-by-case basis, no matter which legislation was enacted. This was not difficult. With the exception of Reuben Fleet's Consolidated company, the industry tended to speak with one voice. On 7 August Towers accordingly met with the chairman of the board and the president of United Aircraft, Frederick Rentschler and Gene Wilson, to discuss the problem of twelve thousand engines to be produced by their subsidiary, Pratt and Whitney. Rentschler revealed that the necessary plant expansion would run between $15 and $18 million, but that United was not interested in government financing, lease, and engine construction. Pratt and Whitney, said Rentschler, could expand its plants by itself if it could be assured of the anticipated depreciation schedule and use the customary practice of dividing "the cost of the expansion by the number of engines to be manufactured and add this figure on the quoted price of the engines." Though sympathetic, Towers had to agree with them that none of this could be guaranteed until a new depreciation law and/or profits tax law was enacted.[132]

Next day, at a meeting of the material bureau chiefs, Towers responded to Assistant Secretary Compton's request for advice on the dilemma: raise the profit limitations on aircraft from 8 to 12 percent; repeal the amended Vinson-Trammell profit ceilings altogether; and insist on rapid depreciation of expanded plant facilities. The other chiefs present supported him. Towers then learned that Vinson's entreaties to the president to restore cuts to aviation plant expansion had borne fruit. FDR suddenly authorized the additional $45 million Towers had needed (along with $90 million for plants serving the Air Corps). And when Towers took his case to the Senate appropriations subcommittee on the thirteenth, it gave blanket approval and added $10 million more for Link trainers, machine tools, and other aviation equipment needed by BuAer. Senator Jimmy Byrnes confidentially told Towers afterward that the estimates would go forward "practically as submitted." They did and became law on 9 September, a total funding package of $155 million for naval aviation's expansion program. Yet, in spite of the monies, plant expansion could not proceed until the profits imbroglio was resolved.[133]

At this impasse James Vincent Forrestal made his timely appearance. During one of Secretary Knox's conferences on 22 August Forrestal was sworn in as undersecretary of the navy and immediately heard Towers report that BuAer's procurement program "was pretty thoroughly bogged down." While Forrestal lent his considerable management expertise to studying the problem from the navy standpoint, the same thing was happening in the War Department in the person of the new assistant secretary of war, Robert P. Patterson, who had just replaced Louis Johnson. The prominent lawyer and former U.S. Circuit Court of Appeals judge would become the first undersecretary of war in December. The new look of civilian management, guided by Secretaries Stimson and Knox, gave fresh vigor to the administration's preparedness program.[134]

This became immediately apparent when, on 27 August, Rentschler and Wilson of United again met with Towers and offered to expand their engine plant facilities. Pratt and Whitney would put up $2.5 million for the actual buildings at its own expense if the government would allow the $11 million for machine tools and test stands to be written in as an item of engine cost in the two-year contract. Furthermore, they wanted the 12,000 engines contracted to be procured by the navy, representing the army as well and using transferred army funds. Towers especially liked the latter idea and proposed that engine production be split between Pratt and Whitney for the navy and Wright Aeronautical for the Army Air Corps. The scheme was refined so that the navy would actually retain title to the engines produced by Pratt and Whitney, thus avoiding any criticism of the government trying to operate munitions factories.

Secretary Knox balked at Towers' urging that all engine production be split between the two services, fearing it would be illegal. But when the Judge Advocate General, Admiral "Sal" Woodson, reassured him, he approved. Next day Towers sold General Brett on the idea and Knox did the same with Secretary Stimson. And a week later Forrestal and Towers negotiated the first airplane contract with United under this arrangement—for 1,006 SB2U Kingfishers by the Vought subsidiary.

Now all the aircraft companies except Consolidated came forward to negotiate their own contracts. The firms were also gladdened by the completion and final passage of the excess profits tax law on 8 October as part of the Internal Revenue Act of 1940. The law repealed the profit ceilings on ships and planes, set the five-year plant amortization schedule, and established a complicated tax structure that would in fact give the biggest companies unfair tax advantages. Though imperfect, it assured financing for the war effort in general and enabled the president's 50,000-airplane program to proceed without further delay.[135]

The major problem regarding Consolidated Aircraft stemmed from the navy's failure to pay for the two hundred PBYs and the attendant plant expansion agreed on between Towers and Reuben Fleet the previous year.

When Fleet confronted Forrestal over the matter during a meeting of the ten major aircraft companies in September, the new undersecretary had a check for nearly $2 million drawn up immediately. Meeting with Knudsen, Forrestal, and Towers on the eleventh, however, Fleet tried to outsmart the three men by writing into the cost of each new airplane a 3 percent increase to help finance his next plant expansion. But he underestimated the fiscal acumen of the chief of BuAer.[136]

Towers pointed out that the additional 3 percent would bring Fleet over $5 million, $1.2 million more than was actually needed to expand Consolidated's physical facilities. When Fleet replied that he was including the cost of his current expansion, Towers put him down: "I pointed out that this had been handled under our current contract for 200 PBY5's and could not be collected twice." When Towers added that Fleet wanted to recoup his expansion costs over two years instead of the five-year amortization set forth in the pending legislation, Fleet changed the subject. He finally agreed to a separate contract covering expansion along the lines of the other companies; the government's Reconstruction Finance Corporation would extend the credit. Towers appreciated Fleet's zeal and his airplanes; the chief of BuAer also knew how to handle the "lovable old s.o.b."[137]

For all their difficulties with the navy, the aircraft manufacturers knew they could trust the man they had known since the birth of their industry. Loyal though he was to FDR, Towers regarded Henry Morgenthau's persistent efforts to check excess profits and disperse lucrative contracts as dangerous to the expeditious production of aircraft. Hap Arnold shared this point of view. Needless to say, therefore, Towers was alarmed when early in September Carl Vinson read aloud to him a proposed amendment to a new conscription bill authorizing the first peacetime draft; the amendment empowered the secretaries of war and the navy to commandeer any factory not cooperating on contract negotiations or munitions deliveries. Towers objected to such legislation, claiming that naval aviation's problems had been indirect or stemmed from government competition "for equipment not subject to profit limitations," by which he meant planes produced by the Naval Aircraft Factory. From his experience in aircraft procurement during and since World War I, Towers believed that government control was inferior to private enterprise. Reliance on the latter gave the democracies an inherent advantage over their authoritarian enemies. The provision was nevertheless included in the Selective Service Act in mid-September.[138]

A kindred spirit was James Forrestal, who in a meeting of the material bureau chiefs on 12 September recognized that the contract problems facing aviation were more difficult and complex than those facing ships and shore installations. Forrestal believed that part of the difficulty lay in expediting contracts, that "there was an inadequacy of legal talent in the Navy Department as a whole," with which Towers agreed. Asked "why lawyers experienced in contract matters could not be placed in the different bureaus," Jack answered that over the years judge advocate generals had resisted this. But Forrestal had already gotten the current judge advocate general Woodson's agreement, and now Admirals Towers, Robinson, and Moreell welcomed the idea. Forrestal asked each to assign an officer from his bureau to explain the contracts to him. Thus began the navy's policy of bringing in top civilian legal talent to expedite naval preparedness; BuAer became the first bureau to streamline contracting procedures.[139]

Over the tumultuous summer of 1940 relations between Towers and the Air Corps remained cordial on a day-to-day basis but less so in high-level planning. The two aeronautical branches shared technical data and worked out common standards for pilot selection and training. Eventually, early in 1941, Towers and Arnold made a verbal agreement that neither service would extend its field of officer procurement "without first advising the other Service, and coming to an equitable understanding." This became policy.[140]

Towers and Arnold met often as members of the informal Army-Navy-CAA Board. The greatest issue between the CAA and military aviation concerned Robert Hinckley's brainchild, the five-year Civilian Pilot Training Program, enacted into law in June 1939 to the tune of $37 million. After the program had produced more than ten thousand pilots the first year, Hinckley announced in June 1940 that he would increase the number fivefold over the ensuing year. Towers and the Air Corps cautioned him not to allow his program to interfere with their military programs. Towers and Arnold agreed that all civilian trainees should now be required to meet service mental and physical requirements. But by the end of August Towers had decided that the civilian program was too competitive for instructors and equipment, especially since the CAA had no four-year service obligation. Presenting his reasons before the Civil Aeronautics Board, he asked that the program be drastically reduced. Arnold concurred. In spite of the CAA program's strong political backing, its funding was now reduced by Congress, and Towers and Arnold continued to battle with Hinckley throughout 1941 until the average number of CAA graduates enrolled in navy flight programs comprised only 11 percent of the total.[141]

Where Towers alienated the army's airmen was over the latter's recurrent demands for service autonomy. "Towers Condemns Separate Air

Force," announced a New York *World-Telegram* headline on 2 August 1940. "I think a separate air force is the worst possible thing that could happen to national defense as a whole and to the Navy in particular," he was quoted as saying. Using the analogy of football, he saw aviation as "the forward pass of warfare—the quick open play with the element of surprise. But you've got to have line play or you can't get away with forward passes." He regarded the naval aviator as "part of a team. If he doesn't practice with the team he can't do his share; he doesn't know the signals or the plays. Airplanes today are as much a part of the navy as its guns." Airmen from a separate air force would lack sufficient knowledge to identify target ship types, to distinguish them from friendlies, to comprehend the meaning of ship movements, and to know how to bomb enemy ships. A naval aviator learned all that, said Towers, by living and operating with the fleet. Some duplication of effort between navy and army air existed, he admitted, "but it could well be called competition . . . , and a little competition is healthy," since it led to better equipment and techniques, like the navy's development of the air-cooled engine and of dive bombing.[142]

Hap Arnold and the Air Corps were almost frantic over the lack of progress in aircraft procurement as they learned of Hitler's seven thousand front-line combat planes on the eve of the Battle of Britain. By 20 August, one hundred days of negotiations had yielded contracts for only 343 new Air Corps planes, a mere pittance when thousands were required, not to mention those for the British. On 5 September, Towers learned that Air Corps estimates for plant expansion under the next deficiency appropriations bill far exceeded the requirements submitted by manufacturers and programmed by the Knudsen committee. Such a discrepancy so alarmed Towers that five days later he had a long conversation with army chief of staff General George C. Marshall "regarding [the] aviation program in general and [the] enormous Air Corps expansion in particular. It was very evident that General Marshall felt that the Air Corps was getting completely out of hand. I let him infer that I had the same feeling and he requested further conversation some time in the near future."[143]

Senior Bureau of the Budget officials met on 11 September with Knudsen, Towers, Arnold, Brett, and their advisers to address this huge discrepancy. The Air Corps was sharply criticized for the request, which Arnold could not justify on any grounds other than the general "uncertainties of the situation." Under the Air Corps formula, Towers figured that the navy would rate a total of $108 million for plant expansion. On the contrary, he pointed out, the navy had concluded it needed only $15 million to supplement the $45 million appropriated for plant expansion on the ninth; a total of $60 million was considerably less than $108 million. Towers did not necessarily oppose the needs of the Air Corps, but he did oppose its nebulous planning, since that adversely affected the navy's. Knudsen, Brett, and navy Captain William W. Webster were delegated to work out the correct needs for plant expansion. Only then did the Air Corps get what it wanted.[144]

When Towers testified before the Woodrum House appropriations subcommittee on the thirteenth to ask for the navy's additional $15 million, he was surprised that the hearing was "suddenly concluded" after he mentioned the bloated estimates for the Air Corps. The navy's request was accepted and would be enacted into law early in October. On 16 September Admiral Horne met with Towers and Forrest Sherman to discuss the army's minutes of their 5 June meeting of Horne's joint aviation board, at which the Air Corps had complained about navy defensive fighters being assigned to naval bases. These minutes, noted Towers, "set forth in detail and in quotations various alleged agreements concerning the general policy, missions, etc. Admiral Horne, Sherman, and I all agreed that none of these quoted items had been discussed in any manner whatsoever, and a check of my diary substantiated this." They had Sherman draw up a letter describing this revelation to General Arnold, with a copy for Admiral Stark, who might use it to show General Marshall if necessary. Clearly, the Air Corps was bending the rules to get its way, but rarely did it put something past Towers and his colleagues.[145]

By early October 1940, coinciding with the RAF victory over the Luftwaffe in the Battle of Britain, the big hurdles for aircraft production on a massive scale were out of the way. Through the guidance of Knudsen's NDAC, with its Air Corps and navy representatives, Congress had appropriated the funds for American and British aircraft output. Contracts could now be let, with the obstacles of excess profits and plant amortization finally removed by the passage of the excess profits law. Though Towers remained suspicious of Henry Morgenthau's plant dispersion plans, the creation of new aircraft factories in Oklahoma, Texas, Georgia, Ohio, and elsewhere became essential to national defense as the prospect of war for America loomed larger with each passing day. Towers' great chagrin was that the excess profits imbroglio over the summer had cost the nation many months of production, the cause of which—government inaction—he candidly reiterated before congressional committees over ensuing months. Resulting shortages would prove nearly fatal when the Pearl Harbor attack came.[146]

With the wheels of the aeronautical industry now in motion, Towers had but to insure that they kept running. Thus early in October he accompanied Knudsen in a navy plane on inspections of the rapidly growing factories in the New York–New Jersey–Connecticut area: Brewster, Curtiss-Wright, Grumman, and the United complex of Pratt and Whitney, Hamilton Standard, and Vought-Sikorsky. At Vought, Towers lauded the new F4U Corsair fighter as "the fastest in the world." All the factories were moving into high gear. The chief of BuAer cited the following production statistics in his diary: airplanes—Vought 17 a week, Brewster 18, Grumman 30 to 40; engines—Wright 600, Pratt and Whitney 800; and propellers—Curtiss 800, Hamilton Standard 1,200.[147]

Towers had played a major role in placing the American aviation industry on a wartime footing and helping to make the United States into what Franklin Roosevelt in December 1940 called "the arsenal of democracy." Secretary Knox gave Towers the highest possible mark, "outstanding," in his fitness report for the critical period of 25 June to 30 September 1940 and rated him "one of [the] best informed officers in American aviation. Highest technical knowledge coupled with sound judgment. Aggressive type of naval officer."[148]

12

ARCHITECT OF
NAVAL AIR POWER
1940–41

"Great Britain—and China, too—believe in and are fighting for the same things we are for," Admiral Towers remarked before the Young Men's Board of Trade at Longchamps Restaurant in New York City on 25 October 1940. "I believe we ought to let them have anything in the way of planes we can spare over our absolute needs for maintaining and training our forces. It would be a tragedy for us to hoard fighting planes now."[1]

Though Towers spoke only of aircraft, his sentiments reflected the basic strategic realities then confronting American military planners. A few days later, the army endorsed a navy recommendation to defeat Germany before Japan if and when the United States had to fight a two-ocean war. At the same time, Admiral Joe Richardson was informed he would be prematurely relieved as commander in chief of the U.S. Fleet for criticizing FDR's policy of keeping an exposed and unprepared U.S. Fleet in Hawaii. This meant personal inconvenience for Towers, who would have to vacate Richardson's home early in 1941 for another rented house, the third Jack and Pierre occupied in as many years.[2]

Roosevelt's reelection in November 1940 gave the president what he regarded as a mandate to proceed with his mobilization program, which included all-out assistance short of war to Britain and China while trying to buy time for America's military buildup. To orchestrate his strategy, FDR relied on Knox and Forrestal in the navy secretariat and Stimson and Robert Patterson in the War Department. Also, in April 1941 he would appoint Robert A. Lovett—naval aviator no. 66, First Yale Unit, and wing commander in the 1918 Northern Bombing Group—to the long-vacant post of assistant secretary of war for air. Needless to say, Jack Towers welcomed the presence of Lovett in the military hierarchy, and the two men became great friends on the social scene. Furthermore, the following September the dormant position of assistant secretary of the navy for air would be filled by Artemus L. Gates, naval aviator no. 65 and also First Yale Unit alumnus and combat veteran.[3] Lovett and Gates were both skilled Wall Street bankers.

The uniformed architects of navy and army air power remained Towers and Arnold. Towers, ever committed to keeping naval aviation within the administrative fabric of the line, joined a chorus of senior nonflying admirals in rejecting arguments for a separate naval air corps set forth by Congressman Maas and the Horne aviation board in November 1940. Jack's equal opposition to an independent air force was more difficult, inasmuch as the expansion of the Army Air Corps to two-thirds above the size of naval aviation, and oriented to the doctrine of strategic bombing separate from army operations, gave credence to the case for its greater autonomy. Consequently, in October 1940 chief of the Air Corps Arnold was given a second hat as deputy chief of staff of the army. Next spring the Air Corps was upgraded to U.S. Army Air Forces (AAF), still under Arnold.[4]

Though Arnold and Towers cooperated informally and on NACA and the Aeronautical Board, their access to the highest-level interservice planning body, the Army-Navy Joint Board, was indirect. In addition to CNO Stark, army chief of staff General Marshall, and their assistants, the six-man Joint Board included the directors of war plans for each service—for the navy, Rear Admiral Richmond Kelly Turner. Over time, the need for senior aviation representation became acute, with the result that, finally, on 10 July 1941 Arnold and Towers would be added to the Joint Board. By the end of the year the administrative machinery had been created for what would evolve into the wartime Joint Chiefs of Staff (JCS).[5]

As the American strategy of Europe-first developed, so did the administrative outlines of the two-ocean navy. In November 1940 the Atlantic Squadron became the Patrol Force under Rear Admiral Ernie King and included the carriers *Ranger* and *Wasp*, A. B. Cook commanding. Halsey kept the *Lexington*, *Saratoga*, *Yorktown*, and *Enterprise* in the Pacific. To enhance hemispheric and base defense, two patrol commands were upgraded to flag billets, Pat Bellinger's Patrol Wing (Patwing) 2 in Hawaii and Ernest D. McWhorter's patwing Patrol Force at Norfolk. On 1 February 1941 the major reorganization took place, the entire fleet being divided into the Atlantic, Pacific, and Asiatic fleets. Admiral Husband E. Kimmel got the largest as both commander in chief Pacific Fleet (CINCPAC) and commander in chief U.S. Fleet, and King received four stars as commander in chief Atlantic Fleet. The tiny Asiatic Fleet continued as before, with only one patrol wing.[6]

In aviation the choice seagoing job to which all airmen aspired, Towers among them, was the three-star Commander Aircraft Battle Force. This was still commonly known as the carrier command, in which Towers had served twice as chief of staff and which was now occupied by Halsey.[7] With the mounting threat of war, the post assumed crucial importance. At the end of February 1941 chief of BuNav Nimitz wrote to Kimmel that "in the ordinary course of events," that is, the midyear rotation, Cook should relieve Halsey. Nimitz could not decide what to do with Halsey and even considered transferring him to command of the Norfolk Navy Yard after his two years at sea were up in mid-1942.[8]

Towers coveted the job, especially if America got into the fighting. When Captain Johnny Hoover stopped in to see him in June 1941, prior to taking command of naval activities in the Caribbean, Towers asked after Halsey.

"Oh, he's fine," Hoover said. "He's having a little trouble with his eyes."

"He ought to retire," grumbled Jack.

As for Hoover, he and Towers had never been mutual admirers. Recalled Hoover, "I don't believe he wound up with many friends. He was all for himself." Hoover, of course, was not known in the navy as Genial John for nothing. His brusque manner had not endeared him to Towers when they had been neighbors at San Diego in the mid 1930s. Now Towers infuriated Hoover by refusing both to assign him a transport plane for Caribbean governors and to award him flight pay, since his Puerto Rico billet was not in aviation; in fact, Hoover relieved his good friend and black shoe there, Rear Admiral Ray Spruance.[9]

Whatever happened in the Pacific, Towers and the navy remained most concerned about Britain's stand against Hitler. In August 1940 the Anglophile Towers had attended a dinner at the British embassy at which a plan was discussed for the United States to obtain ninety-nine-year leases on British bases in the Caribbean in return for fifty World War I–vintage destroyers for strengthening Britain's Atlantic convoys. The deal was consummated on 2

September 1940, whereupon the British threw in Bermuda and Argentia, Newfoundland, as bonuses. Within ten weeks U.S. Navy PBYs were flying neutrality patrols out of Bermuda.

Also in August 1940 a British scientific mission led by Sir Henry Tizard, permanent secretary of scientific and industrial research, had arrived in Washington, and at a luncheon he impressed Towers by warning against the United States repeating Britain's mistake of delaying weapons design and development. That evening at the British embassy Tizard's staff showed a film on "aircraft detection by radio waves," a new technology that had been crucial in the Battle of Britain. The British were giving the Americans everything they had on this "radar," which was revolutionizing naval and air warfare. Small wonder then that two days later, at a high-level navy meeting considering the exchange of information with the British, Towers said that BuAer "was willing to release information on anything under its cognizance."[10]

In September 1940 a means for systematically allocating American-built aircraft to the army, navy, and British was realized with the establishment of the Army-Navy-British Purchasing Commission, Joint Aircraft Committee (JAC). It consisted of two army members, notably General Brett; two navy members, Towers and Captain Webster; two representatives of Sir Henry Self's British purchasing commission, especially aircraft manufacturer C. R. Fairey; and one member from Morganthau's Presidential Liaison Committee. JAC's charge was to collaborate so closely with William Knudsen's NDAC that the latter body, according to the directive, "can proceed to establish a firm schedule of deliveries, take full advantage of potential deliveries, and plan for future productive capacity." Each representative of the army, navy, and British on JAC was "authorized to act for and oblige the agency it represents."

In other words, Brett, Towers, and Fairey had to provide precise information on their respective needs through the committee to Knudsen. It was an imperfect arrangement, since it tended to duplicate much of Morgenthau's and Knudsen's work, but it was a major step toward centralized planning. At the first meeting, in Towers' office on 20 September, the committee decided, in the interest of expanding deliveries, to standardize only planes in the prototype stage rather than planes already in production. And it appointed two subcommittees, one for standardization and one for allocation. To the latter Towers assigned Captain Duke Ramsey, his head of plans, and Lieutenant George Anderson, in charge of BuAer's programs and allocations section.[11]

JAC had begun debating even the day before its official first meeting. Knudsen disagreed with everyone else by refusing to grant the British more than the 40 percent of the total engine production agreed upon, although the British had paid for the plant expansion to provide Pratt and Whitney engines for the training planes they desperately needed. As for new antisub-patrol PBYs, Towers was willing to let Consolidated move its British models to the head of the production lines. But to standardize the PBY-5, he argued, the British would have to adopt American bombs and bomb racks, which were larger than the British preferred.

This critical decision could only be settled at the highest level, namely, by Knox, Forrestal, and Stark of the navy and Patterson and Marshall of the army. Towers and Brett convinced them of their logic on 7 October. The following February JAC would establish a subcommittee, with Forrest Sherman the senior navy member, to standardize bombs. The big problem was the top-secret Norden bombsight, tied in to the American Sperry automatic pilot system needed by the British; the Americans refused to share the Norden for fear it would be captured by the Germans. This problem was ultimately solved when Sperry company technicians modified army and navy planes destined for the British so that they could use the automatic pilot without the bombsight.[12]

Towers' views on assisting Britain bore directly on the question of allocating aircraft. In his address to the Young Men's Board of Trade on 25 October, he declared that the United States should allow the British to purchase the Air Corps' principal bomber, the B-17 Flying Fortress. Since America was not yet at war and would not be able to deploy such bombers for a long time after entering the war, the country would be "putting the bombers to the purpose for which they were intended [strategic bombing]." In the first public discussion of the Norden bombsight by a senior official, Towers rejected the idea of letting the British have that device along with the plane. Developed by the navy originally as a precision antiship device, it did not work at night unless the target was lighted. Because the RAF was generally inaccurate in nighttime area bombing of German factories, it would have little use of the sight. Also, the British lacked bombers with the range to reach Berlin carrying an adequate bombload. The B-17 would help them greatly.[13]

More than that, however, Towers could see that JAC, though relatively successful in setting priorities between government and industry, "had neither authority nor talent to determine priorities" between the army's and navy's air arms. At a meeting of Secretary Knox's "council" of senior advisers and admirals on the last day of October, Jack pointed out "that due to the fact that the Army Air Corps started its expansion about a year ahead of ours we are unable to get deliveries on certain articles, particularly aircraft engines of certain types, because large Army contracts antedated ours." Admiral Robinson of BuShips agreed, explaining that shipbuilding was similarly hampered by late starts. The carrier *Hornet* would not be launched until mid-December, and the keel of the *Essex,* first of her class, was still months away from being laid down. Satisfied that the joint committee could not solve the problem, Knox agreed to convene a special conference to discuss it.[14]

Robinson, Towers, and Furlong (BuOrd) then worked up a plan to set priorities for service needs: emergencies first, then repairs and replacements, next the 11 percent increase of the navy, and finally all other navy and army expansion. When they met again with Knox on 4 November, the secretary observed that the army would insist on higher priority for some of its present equipment. On the seventh Towers learned from Morgenthau that FDR wanted every other major army-type bomber being produced, including the B-17, to be given to the British. And he insisted that the Norden bombsight be included. Stimson refused to agree to any of this, although the British were allowed to use the Sperry automatic pilot. Then there were apparent shortages in machine tools, aluminum supplies, and aviation gas that had to be addressed.[15]

Clearly, something had to be done to streamline military aircraft priorities. The Knudsen advisory committee, JAC, the British Purchasing Commission, Morgenthau's liaison committee, the Army Air Corps, and BuAer were all working toward the same end—an effective policy of allocation. But they disagreed over major items and lacked centralized coordination, largely, it seemed, because of the sluggishness of Knudsen's committee.

An additional wrinkle occurred in the form of agitation by organized labor. It began with Reuben Fleet of Consolidated trying to set wage scales and determine living conditions for his workers, as he had in the past, a potentially dangerous initiative. Undersecretary Forrestal asked Towers whether or not the government ought to take over Consolidated. Then the workers at Brewster and Vultee struck. When the latter company gave in to its workers' demands late in November, Towers met with Knudsen and key leaders in the War and Navy Departments and industry. The government, Jack argued, should announce that this settlement set no precedent and that the navy would not underwrite wage increases beyond the terms set forth in contracts. Forrestal agreed. Nevertheless, Fleet settled with the "extremely patriotic" union at Consolidated; he wrote Towers in December that Consolidated had given workers sufficient wages for a two-shift, fifty-hour work week so that they could "live in decency and comfort."[16]

Just before Christmas, President Roosevelt took action to improve the coordination of production and allocation not only of aircraft but of all munitions. He decided to eliminate NDAC in favor of the new Office of Production Management (OPM), effective 7 January 1941. As before, FDR made himself the head, appointing two subheads: Knudsen as director general to continue coordinating production and union leader Sidney Hillman to handle labor problems. Secretaries Stimson and Knox were the other members. Merrill C. "Babe" Meigs, publisher of the Chicago *Herald American* and a prominent amateur aviator, was brought in to head the aircraft division of OPM (with Fullton Towers as assistant director of priorities). The new organization had more power than NDAC but still not enough authority to direct procurement agencies or to control expenditures. But any such agency, in Towers' opinion, was better than none.

On 23 December Towers was called to a meeting at the State Department to discuss supplying new army P-40 Curtiss Warhawk fighters to the Chinese. It was decided that, as part of a new British order for more P-40s, a certain number would be earmarked for China. On 30 January, because of such demands from nations other than those belonging to the Commonwealth, the Army-Navy-British JAC simply became JAC. Under the chairmanship of General Arnold, it began to meet weekly; whenever Arnold was absent, Towers presided. Under the urging of Babe Meigs, however, it was soon restructured and given real authority in controlling aircraft output.[17]

Concurrent with his decision to create OPM, the president announced a program he had worked out with his close adviser Harry Hopkins to lend or lease war materials to Great Britain on a massive scale. Early in the new year he also initiated informal "American-British conversations" (ABC) for contingency strategic planning in Washington to affirm America's Europe-first decision, known as Rainbow 5. Towers got his first inkling of it the day after Christmas when ordered to provide estimates for U.S. naval air operations out of Iceland and Scotland should the United States enter the European war on 1 April 1941. It was more than coincidence that, on 30 December, all the navy's aircraft were ordered repainted from peacetime silver and chrome yellow to wartime blue and gray.

On 2 January Towers and his fellow bureau chiefs were briefed in person by Knox, who warned them to "assume that the real emergency will occur not later than 1 April 1941." The U.S. Navy had to be ready by then to escort transatlantic Lend-Lease convoys to Britain. Next day, Towers relayed the news to his heads of divisions in BuAer. The new Atlantic Fleet would be reinforced by more units from the Pacific and a special support force established in March under Rear Admiral Arthur Bristol, Towers' academy classmate. It included four twelve-plane patrol squadrons of PBYs and PBMs. Lend-Lease was FDR's signal that war with the Axis powers appeared not only inevitable but imminent, and Towers stopped worrying about inadequate funding.[18]

His considerable public image increased apace. In the autumn of 1940 he attended the commissioning of NAS Jacksonville and of the seaplane tender *Curtiss* at Philadelphia. On 5 December he released his annual report

BuAer and BuNav chiefs Towers and Chester W. Nimitz, *right,* look on as President Roosevelt presents the Herbert Schiff Trophy to Lieutenant Commander H. B. Miller at the White House, 5 February 1941. Miller's patrol squadron, VP-33, won the prize for its superior performance during fiscal 1940. The ceremony is also witnessed by Secretary of the Navy Frank Knox, CNO Harold B. Stark, and William Schiff, donor of the trophy. (Navy Department)

as chief of BuAer summarizing progress in naval aviation over 1940 and noting that its annual appropriations had risen from $48 million in 1939 to almost $111.5 million in 1940. The general tone was optimistic, except for his warning "that lack of emphasis on development and experimentation may leave us with aircraft inferior" to the newest planes being developed abroad. He wanted—and would get—the increased funding.[19]

On 7 January 1941 Towers appeared as the first witness before an all-day hearing of the House Naval Affairs Committee, seeking an update on the preparedness program. He made front-page headlines with his revelations about delays in aircraft engine production. He blamed several factors—the late start in plant expansion; shortages in machine tools, aluminum castings, and skilled supervisors; and the former restrictions on profits imposed by Congress. Since Congress was altering the tax laws based on navy recommendations, however, he believed that more contractors and subcontractors would enter the industry and help provide sufficient engines and essential spare parts by mid-1942. With more powerful air-cooled radial engines, self-sealing gas tanks, and armor-plated cockpits, Towers asserted, eighteen months hence the United States would have more and better naval aircraft than any foreign power, including Japan.

Alarmed questioners Vinson, Maas, and Warren Magnuson could elicit no remedy from Towers for hastening engine production, although auto makers Studebaker, Buick, and Ford were beginning to retool for airplane engines. Jack highly praised the aircraft companies for being cooperative, saying that to nationalize any of them would be nothing short of "a national calamity." Although the navy's airplane inventory had made a net gain of only 445 new planes in 1940, there would be an output of some 3,700 more in 1941, making headway toward the two-year anticipated goal of 15,000.[20]

Immediately after the hearings Towers boarded the train for Detroit. Following an address to the Society of Automotive Engineers next day, he conferred with attendees from the Ranger division of Fairchild, producing engines for the Curtiss SO3C scout but threatened with a CIO strike at its Long Island plant. Upon ascertaining the positions of management and labor, Towers agreed with the former "that the best interests of the country would be served by letting the strike take place"; the navy should not force a settlement. This position was accepted by Undersecretary Forrestal upon Towers' return to Washington next day.

Reappearing that morning before the Vinson committee, Towers shared its outrage over such threatened walkouts; he believed a strike at the Ranger plant would seriously hamper national defense. Vinson said that FDR would probably have the government seize companies whose patriotism took second place to the issue of wages and hours. This stand surely influenced the disputing parties at Ranger, for they reached a settlement two days later. But organized labor was not easily intimidated, and strikes would plague the aircraft industry throughout the year.[21]

The major progress that Towers reported to the Vinson committee on the ninth and tenth of January lay in personnel training and base construction. Although the navy and Marine Corps had only 3,639 pilots, one year hence nearly 6,000 would be in service, plus another 4,200 undergoing training. The ultimate goal was 17,000 pilots. Along with Pensacola and Miami, Jacksonville had admitted its first aviation cadets two weeks before, as would Corpus Christi in the spring. The last of the naval reserve pilots, two hundred employed by the commercial airlines, would not be called up until the summer, giving the airlines time to adjust. The thirteen existing naval reserve air stations would be expanded and eight new ones built to conduct primary training, and the training of enlisted aviation personnel was under way. When asked about British bases obtained through Lend-Lease, Towers refused to comment; such information was no longer to be given out in public now that the country was moving toward war.[22]

Towers' relations with Congress remained generally amicable throughout 1941. He often testified on progress as well as on fiscal 1942 and 1943 and deficiency appropriations, the latter also requiring his presence at Bureau of the Budget hearings. Money was no longer a serious object; total naval aviation funding for fiscal 1941 would exceed $452 million, quadrupling that of 1940.[23]

He did clash with two lawmakers trying to win pork-barrel support for their home states. Senator Charles L. McNary of Oregon, the only state to produce fiber flax in quantity, personally visited Towers to protest against the Southern cotton lobby, which he claimed had caused BuAer to adopt cotton thread instead of flax for its parachute webbing. When Towers explained that cotton thread was less than half the cost of flax, McNary stomped out of the office. The chairman of the House appropriations naval subcommittee, former governor of Nevada James G. Scrugham, tried to force the navy to develop "a small air station" in Boulder City near Las Vegas. But in hearings Towers declared that "a waste of government money," whereupon Scrugham "became very indignant, and a rather acrimonious discussion followed." Scrugham tried to get even by leaking a story to the press that Towers was opposed to the revival of the post of assistant secretary of the navy for air, whereas in fact he opposed it only if it was to be a political appointment.

Towers could not be bought. He also helped Carl Vinson thwart fellow Georgians from obtaining an exorbitant price in leasing Atlanta's county airport for a new naval air station.[24]

Meanwhile, in spite of their house moves and busy schedules, Jack and Pierre led comfortable lives. They employed a couple who did the cooking and butler chores for their entertaining; the man also acted as chauffeur in the family Oldsmobile when they attended unofficial functions. For official activities, Jack had a very reliable navy driver in A. Joseph Draghi.[25] The energetic Pierre was involved in war relief work, the Red Cross, and South American cultural relations. Jack still tried to take his customary pre-breakfast swim at the Chevy Chase Country Club, but the press of business prevented him from playing golf or bridge. Daughter Marjorie, married in June 1940 and now twenty-four, lost a baby by premature birth early in 1941; she lived in Coronado where husband Herb Riley served as an aide to Admiral Bristol and then Admiral McCain. Son Chas, who turned twenty-one in January, got a job with Grumman Aircraft as "a grease monkey," his father kidded. And through careful planning, Towers was able to get Pierre out of the wintry capital for a week's leave in sunny Palm Beach, where they celebrated his fifty-sixth birthday.[26]

After his return on 5 February, Towers found the secret ABC discussions under way as well as the planning for Lend-Lease. The air planners, who formed a separate subcommittee, were Air Vice Marshal John C. Slessor of the RAF, Captain Duke Ramsey of BuAer, and Colonel Joseph T. McNarney of the Army Air Corps. The ABC-1 report, developed over two months of deliberations, confirmed the Rainbow 5 decision of defeating Hitler before taking on Japan. ABC-2 dealt separately with the allocation of military aircraft once America entered the war. Towers, wrote Slessor in his memoirs, was "friendly and cooperative," in contrast to the irascible Rear Admiral Kelly Turner of war plans, who continually played down the importance of air planning in the overall conversations.[27]

Towers' role in the ABC deliberations was fairly passive; his charge would be to implement final decisions regarding naval aircraft. There were exceptions. At a meeting at the White House on 28 February Towers agreed with Forrestal, Harry Hopkins, and several fellow admirals that precise planning was premature until Lend-Lease could be finalized and a definite national policy articulated. Nevertheless, on 9 March Towers warned Hopkins in a private meeting that fulfilling Lend-Lease orders "would interfere seriously with our own program" of aircraft allotments. Soon after Lend-Lease became law on 11 March, the Slessor Agreement of the ABC-2 report was reached, according to which the British, less concerned with the Pacific, had to yield to the U.S. Navy's insistence that its 15,000-plane, two-ocean program continue. However, all new American-built planes would be available to the British until the United States entered the war; thereafter they would be divided between the two powers or as required on the fighting fronts.[28]

Lend-Lease allowed all aircraft allocation to be placed under a greatly strengthened JAC in April. Arnold would still act as chairman, Towers taking that role in his absence. Also, in May Towers created a defense aid division in BuAer under Commander Gus Read to handle all Lend-Lease matters pertaining to naval aviation. The subsequent success of the reconstituted committee was due in no small measure to the chief of BuAer.

Reminiscing many years later, Sir Henry Self volunteered a handsome tribute:

> I have not mentioned Admiral Towers, and I have not seen general recognition of the part he played in supply for the American navy. He had a cool, incisive way with him. He always brought the discussion down to earth if it got at all high-falutin. It always had to be related to the basic plan or policy, with a direct approach to the objectives in a way which reflected his mind—clear-cut in its approach. He did a most effective job on the part of the Navy. He was very good indeed in this joint administration. . . . I should very much like to see Admiral Towers' name recalled. I have a great admiration for him.[29]

The first test of the new set-up came with the call for more Grumman F4F fighters and more patrol bombers—Martin PBM Mariners and Consolidated PBY Catalinas and PB2Y Coronados. Reuben Fleet of Consolidated wanted to charge a higher fixed fee to raise wages above what the navy believed necessary, but Towers held firm. Finally, Towers requested $10 million to expand the plants at Grumman, Martin, and Consolidated for an additional 150 F4Fs, 50 PBMs, 150 PBYs, and 50 PB2Ys. He flew to San Diego in late April 1941 for more discussions with Fleet and found flying boat output slowing down because of work on the army's XB-32 bomber. This problem he rectified, upon his return, through the assistant secretary of war for air, Bob Lovett. The money was approved before the end of the month, though the settling of final contracts consumed more precious time. Expansion of the Pratt and Whitney engine plant came next, followed by other factory expansions as more British orders flowed in. Streamlining BuAer's administrative machinery for delivery of the new production took the rest of the year.[30]

Towers remained actively involved in the details of airplane production, inspecting all the major factories. In management, he rallied to the aid of

J. Carlton Ward, president of Fairchild, who was being forced by the army to move to Republic; Bob Lovett stepped in on Towers' behalf. Jack became embroiled in disagreements over priorities for commercial airliner production but was anxious to have three Sikorsky VS-44A commercial flying boats completed for American Export Airlines, which planned to use them on its new transatlantic route. And, on Forrest Sherman's advice, Towers rejected Juan Trippe's request for the navy to take over Pan Am in some nebulous shared-management arrangement. That company's commercial B-314 Clippers were useful for naval personnel hops, especially via Lisbon and the Azores. As for critical raw materials, in April OPM reported an apparent shortage in magnesium for use in British incendiary bombing. In a meeting Towers informed Knudsen's managers that magnesium shipments could be reduced if Britain substituted thermite and because she had just received a huge shipment of magnesium from Japan. His recommendations were adopted.[31]

In addition to allocating and scheduling aircraft, Towers continued to hammer out differences with the British over standardizing airplanes. In January he hosted an Anglo-American conference with Air Marshal Hugh Dowding for the production of British airplane turrets and in February insisted that PBMs ordered by the British follow American design specifications for optimum interchangeability of parts. In June, visiting Air Marshal Arthur T. Harris raved to him that one of the RAF's new 4,000-pound blockbuster bombs had "destroyed half of Berlin." Towers promptly called in Commander Paul Pihl, just back from attaché duty there. Pihl said he had seen the big crater from the bomb in Berlin's central park; aside from the hole, all it had done was to knock out a lot of windows. This infuriated "Bomber" Harris. He told Towers, "You've got to get rid of that guy. He's been converted. He's a Nazi!" But Jack knew better of the man he had selected to head the bureau's aircraft production section. The blockbuster's effect had simply been overrated. This event notwithstanding, Harris admired Towers greatly and they became close friends.

At Secretary Knox's order, Towers worked out a plan with Air Marshal Slessor to assign up to fifty U.S. naval aviation officers to England to observe air operations and assist with Lend-Lease. Harry Hopkins wanted Towers and Brett to go to London themselves to discuss Lend-Lease with the British. Much as he wanted to go, Jack told Hopkins that neither he nor Brett could be spared. So Forrestal and Hap Arnold went instead, along with W. Averell Harriman, FDR's special representative. Before his departure Harriman consulted at length with Towers.[32]

Given the fact that in 1940–41 the British and U.S. navies lacked enough aircraft carriers to combat the U-boat, both looked for shortcuts to put more aircraft at sea quickly. The British were catapulting single fighters from merchant ships in the desperate Battle of the Atlantic, a technique that in October 1940 had impressed President Roosevelt enough to solicit plans for a rapidly converted merchantman. Towers had just the solution. Early in his tour as chief of bureau, he had been visited by retired Admiral Hutch I. Cone, chairman of the board of the Moore-McCormack passenger steamship line. Cone had wanted Towers' advice on adding short flight decks to several liners on the company's West Indies–South America run; on-board planes could fly passengers ashore, eliminating the need for port stops. The project was feasible, and although Moore-McCormack did not pursue the idea BuAer did. So when FDR, impatient over and doubtful about the program for large *Essex*-class carriers, called for conversion plans Towers was ready with the Moore-McCormack liners. Two were selected, the *Mormacmail* and the *Mormacland*. Newport News Shipbuilding would place a 360-foot flight deck on the former to create the auxiliary aircraft carrier USS *Long Island;* the latter was to be converted into a similar vessel for the British, HMS *Audacity*.[33]

Both navies warmed up to this idea of what would eventually come to be known as the escort carrier (CVE), and in March the ninety-day conversion of the *Long Island* began. BuShips gave the project top priority, but prospective captain Wu Duncan had difficulty making necessary changes in the design. He went straight to Towers, who saw that they were approved by Captain Edward L. Cochrane, head of BuShips' preliminary design branch. On 3 May, limited by the number of available catapults and arresting gear units, Towers recommended only three more U.S. conversions; three days later Stark informed him that the British wanted twelve in all. The final American program, agreed upon a week later, added four more conversions to Towers' proposed three. This was only the beginning of what would grow into a mammoth program of dozens of escort carriers for both navies. Meanwhile, many fundamental design changes to the *Long Island* would be necessary after she was commissioned on 2 June.[34]

This expediency was a brilliant one, for the construction of the new front-line *Essex*-class carriers had been excruciatingly slow in getting under way. The keel of the *Essex* was finally laid in April, but her completion was not due for perhaps two more years. Early combat lessons had to be incorporated into her design, and in May Towers flew to Norfolk to inspect the British carrier *Illustrious,* under repair from bomb damage sustained in the fighting for control of the Mediterranean sea lanes. Between May and November keels were laid for two more *Essexes* and the first four of the nine converted *Independence*-class light carriers.[35]

"Carriers," reported *Time* in June, "are much on Jack Towers' mind nowadays," because there were not enough of them. The reason, explained the news weekly, was that "the Navy had ceased to think in terms of concentrated battle lines" and therefore "plans instead for dispersed 'task forces'—units of battleships, carriers, cruisers, and destroyers on special missions. This conception requires more carriers than the Navy has in service and in sight." This was pro-air exaggeration, for although task forces did employ carriers, the battle line still dominated official tactical doctrine. On the qualitative side, Towers had to admit to the General Board in April, "In the light of present standards of landplanes operating in the active theater of war in Europe, the majority of naval aircraft now assigned [to] squadrons of the fleet and Marine Corps are at the present time ineffective for combatant missions. With respect to probable opposition of naval aircraft of potential enemies in the Pacific the aviation component is considered to be reasonably effective." He believed that once delivered, however, the newer models would be vastly superior.[36]

"This show," Towers wrote of the war to his brother Will on 8 May 1941, "will last for *years*." The very next day JAC received a request from China for no fewer than 1,463 aircraft by the end of the year, during which time the committee had planned to provide only 6. The administration quickly decided to increase aid to China and to impose more stringent economic sanctions against Japan. By contrast, anti-German measures had been accelerating with air base construction at newly leased Argentia, Newfoundland, for a PBY squadron and for Admiral Bristol's support force. On 20 May Towers and Bristol flew to Argentia in a PBM to inspect the progress. They returned the next day, just as the American merchantman *Robin Moor* was being sunk by a U-boat in the South Atlantic. The German battleship *Bismarck* broke out into the North Atlantic to attack British shipping, and the Argentia PBYs joined in the search for her. On the twenty-seventh, President Roosevelt declared an "unlimited national emergency." The *Bismarck* succumbed to British carrier aircraft and heavy guns the next day, and the U.S. Atlantic Fleet soon initiated convoys as far as Iceland. One month later Hitler invaded Russia.[37]

Of immediate concern to the British was getting the many newly completed Consolidated PBYs across the Atlantic. Their contract provided that Consolidated's pilots ferry the planes as far as Bermuda, where British pilots would pick them up for the final hop. Consolidated was doing so well that the British could not take them away fast enough, due largely to a dearth of British pilots—an unsatisfactory situation, in Towers' view. Harry Hopkins summoned him late in May to see if the navy might help; this was followed by a decree from FDR that the navy should fly the planes to Bermuda. The RAF found this solution unpalatable, as did Towers, since it would cost BuAer valuable flying personnel.

Towers had an alternative solution: let the U.S. Navy train the "big boat" crews in the States, so they could assume the entire ferry role. Furthermore, by retaining certain single-engine planes ordered by the British, the navy could also train British carrier pilots for service in Lend-Lease American combat planes. The RAF, which had already accepted a similar invitation from the AAF, greatly appreciated the offer, and when Towers presented his proposal at a conference with FDR and his top advisers on 16 June, the president approved. Towers immediately worked out the details with Air Marshal Harris. The training program, which the Royal Navy dubbed the Towers Scheme, also enabled Hap Arnold to yield some SNJ (AT-6) trainers to the navy, which Towers had begged from him. Eventually, the Scheme would provide more than one-third of the British navy's pilots and enable British naval squadrons to work up in America.[38]

At this moment, mid-June, *Time* magazine carried Towers' portrait on the cover and ran a long account of his key role in naval air preparedness over exactly thirty years of naval flying.[39] Towers' star was continuing to rise, especially in the eyes of the president and the secretary of the navy. On the twenty-fifth Knox took Jack and two British admirals on a dinner cruise down the Potomac in the secretary's yacht *Sequoia*. For the months of April through September Knox would give Jack's fitness report a resounding 4.0.[40]

The *Time* article addressed the persistent frustration of aviators, army and navy, over the lack of centralized planning, which still failed to include them. JAC, the technical Army-Navy Aeronautical Board, and NACA provided the only high-level formal contacts between army and navy air, and late in May FDR placed NACA directly under the Aeronautical Board. NACA's most far-reaching work developed from a decision earlier in the year when NACA head Vannevar Bush, Arnold, and Towers had agreed to expand research into jet propulsion. The work was directed by eighty-two-year-old Dr. William F. Durand, Towers' former Morrow Board associate. Towers also stayed in contact over progress in jet engines with the father of American rocketry, Robert H. Goddard.[41]

The point of dispute between the two air arms remained the setting of

Admiral John H. Towers as Chief of the Bureau of Aeronautics, 1941. (U.S. Navy)

priorities, although a major improvement occurred in June when Under-secretaries Forrestal and Patterson were appointed to the Army-Navy Munitions Board and its restructuring was undertaken by Forrestal's former law partner Ferdinand Eberstadt. These changes came none too soon, for the dispute reached its climax when FDR, impressed with the requirement for strategic bombing against Hitler's Germany, expressed a desire to speed up heavy bomber production to five hundred B-17s and B-24s per month, plus development of the very-long-range B-29 Superfortress. Because such a change would give the AAF priority over the navy for critical materials, Towers and his navy peers steadfastly opposed it as a matter of policy.

The basis for FDR's stance was aircraft report 8-E, issued on 16 May by JAC to give A-1-b priority to big-bomber production. Towers joined the army and British in approving the report but changed his mind when he realized that navy aircraft production might be seriously hampered. He wanted to restrict priorities being placed on prime contractors and not simply on the subcontractors for machine tooling. The showdown came over a directive from the White House on 23 June that the AAF interpreted as an order to initiate large-bomber program expansion.[42]

Alarmed that the directive threatened adequate machine tool output for both air arms, Towers prevailed upon Forrestal to call a meeting at which Jack hoped to withdraw the navy's approval of report 8-E. The meeting convened in Forrestal's office on 27 June. Present for the navy were Stark, Towers, Admiral Mike Robinson, Eberstadt, and assorted lesser-ranking experts. Knudsen and one aide represented OPM. The only person present from the War Department was Assistant Secretary for Air Lovett, an advocate of strategic bombing who, however, had labored for six months developing machine tool and engine production and who had given priority to training over combat planes in the AAF. Ex-naval aviator Lovett was also sympathetic to the navy's aviation needs.[43]

When Knudsen argued that the bomber program would not interfere with the navy's machine tools, he was disputed by all the navy representatives. Knudsen promised that there would be no interference, in which case, everyone agreed, "the only part of the Navy program which might be jeopardized was Navy aircraft." Towers' meticulous notes of the crucial discussion are such a complete record that they deserve to be quoted:

> I insisted that if the huge Army bomber program was given a priority above all Naval aircraft, inevitably there would be serious interference, largely because of shortages of materials, accessories and equipment. I pointed out shortages were already affecting the aircraft program as a whole. . . .

Mr. Lovett stated that the Army is proposing to put the $400,000,000 into facilities to expand the production of materials, especially aluminum and magnesium, but agreed with me that there would be critical shortages for some time to come. [He referred] . . . to a cable from London in March urging increased production of bombers over twenty tons in size. He then read the two letters from the President dated 4 May and a letter a few days later from Secretary Stimson to the President, in which the Secretary made the point that a productive rate of 500 a month by 30 June 1943 could not be achieved without an A-1-b priority for the facilities and the bombers and an A-1-a priority for machine tools for machine tool makers.

I interrupted . . . to point out that there was no evidence that the President had ever approved these recommendations. He next read a letter from Mr. Stettinius [director of priorities for OPM] to the Army and Navy Munitions Board, which stated that in accordance with the desire of OPM the Board was requested to give A-1-a priority for machine tools for the program and A-1-b priority for the bombers, and followed this with the Army and Navy Munitions Board letter signed by Brigadier General [Charles] Hines [secretary of that board], setting up such a priority.

Mr. Forrestal interrupted at this point to state . . . that actually the matter had *not* been referred to the Secretary of the Navy or any other responsible officer of the Navy Department and that it had not been referred to him although he was the Navy member of the Board. When Mr. Lovett tried to make the point that, after all, it was the priority set up by a Presidential directive, Admiral Stark stated that the President informed him he had given no such directive, had no intention of conveying such an idea, and that he, Admiral Stark, was authorized to say so.

A very heated discussion lasting nearly two hours followed, Admiral Stark insisting that the matter was a military one and that the bomber program should be fitted into the whole defense scheme. He asked Mr. Lovett if he would recommend to Secretary Stimson that the Joint Board make a study and recommend priority. Mr. Lovett refused and countered with the proposition that the Joint Aircraft Committee make a study to determine if the bomber priority would affect the Navy program. I denied this, informed him that I had refused to even consider placing it in top priority when so recommended by a subcommittee, and that it was not until after it had been given the high priority by the Munitions Board that it had been so scheduled by the Committee.

Mr. Knudsen then suggested that representatives of the Bureau of Aeronautics get together with the Aircraft Production Section of OPM [headed by Babe Meigs] to determine whether or not the bomber program as scheduled in Report 8E appeared likely to interfere with the Naval aircraft program as scheduled in the same report. I agreed to this but pointed out that I was worrying about the future more than the present, that past schedules had not been met, and that I had grave doubts of anything definite coming out of the conference. Admiral Stark then said that if a common understanding could not be reached between the Army, Navy, and OPM, the only solution appeared to be to take the matter up with the President, and that he proposed to do so.[44]

Over the ensuing week Towers and Forrestal tried several different tacks to convince Lovett to modify his stance on the bomber priority, but Lovett would not yield, preferring to let FDR decide. Towers accepted defeat, for Patterson of the War Department, Knudsen of OPM, and Hines of the Munitions Board also remained hostile to his scheme. "It became evident," Towers informed Forrestal on 3 July, that attempting to get Navy machine tools placed on the top priority list "could not be accomplished without placing the Navy in the position of deliberately holding up the whole program." He reminded Forrestal of Knudsen's promise not to allow the bomber program to interfere with navy machine tool requirements, then recommended the matter be dropped for the time being, which it was. The real culprit, in Lovett's view, was the inefficiency of the OPM in meeting the needs of the military.[45] Centralized planning needed to be improved, toward which end a major step was made on 10 July when both General Arnold and Towers were appointed, finally, as official members of the Army-Navy Joint Board. Aviation now had full representation at the highest level of strategic planning, where cooperation was essential.[46]

Since the decision on aircraft priorities fit into the Europe-first strategy, the navy had no choice but to take second place to the big-bomber program. The AAF now placed its goal at 26,000 combat planes and 37,000 trainers by 1944, plus 17,000 in all for the British, followed by the navy's 15,000. No one had wanted to drag the president into the debate, which would only have caused further delays and probably not affected the outcome anyway. In mid-August FDR journeyed to Argentia, where he met with Prime Minister Winston Churchill to affirm the goals for victory in the Atlantic Charter of the democracies against fascism. When he returned, he invited Jack and Pierre to the White House for dinner on 25 August. The new aircraft schedule was finalized by the Joint Board and made part of the overall "Victory Program" in September.[47]

A concurrent problem affecting aircraft production was initiated by a North American labor strike that resulted in a two-year contract guaranteeing no further strikes on defense production. From the airplane and air equipment manufacturers, Jack learned that, in spite of the contract, organized labor still resented the failure of wages to keep pace with inflation, also the existence of closed shops. The situation intensified after the German invasion of Russia on 22 June, with the ensuing demand for faster production.[48]

On 9 July Sidney Hillman of OPM called a meeting in his office of aircraft manufacturers to discuss the regional stabilization of labor wages in the aircraft industry. Towers acted as spokesman for the government. At this meeting the army and navy agreed to consider wage stabilization adjustments on a case-by-case basis "to insure stabilized and continuous production of military aircraft over an extended period of time." The West Coast representatives took this formula as the basis for all regional wage adjustment procedures, and in less than a month Donald Douglas won OPM approval to set minimum wages in the booming Los Angeles–San Diego region. Though the crisis seemed to be averted, labor discontent festered.[49]

The sudden mushrooming of the navy's air arm put a strain on BuAer, specifically on Towers and assistant chief Captain Pete Mitscher, after July 1941 Duke Ramsey. By peacetime standards, the two individuals were supposed to manage bureau operations directly. But whereas BuAer's annual budget in the 1930s had averaged $36 million, the projection for fiscal 1942 alone was over $1 billion, a thirty-fold increase. The need for executive talent at headquarters grew apace as the staff swelled from 100 officers and 192 civilians in mid-1940 to 176 and 518 respectively in mid-1941.[50]

BuAer's administrative problems were part of the navy's difficulties in general. In March Secretary Knox ordered a management survey of each bureau to pinpoint weaknesses and recommend remedial action. Hired to conduct the survey was the New York–Chicago consultant firm of Booz, Fry, Allen and Hamilton. Though its office-by-office examination of the facilities and procedures of BuAer alone would consume no fewer than six months, glaring deficiencies were reported immediately to Towers.

At the outset, the most serious was found to be in procurement and supply coordination for the many new and expanded naval air stations. To address the problem Towers created the progress division in April, charging it to work closely with BuShips and BuOrd in obtaining materials. He appointed as its head Captain Irving M. McQuiston, a World War I aviator on active duty since 1930 administering the reserve aviation program. McQuiston immediately confirmed the consultant's findings and in May got Towers to centralize all aircraft and base equipment coordination under his, McQuiston's, control. To improve coordination between procurement and production, Towers also strengthened the production division.[51]

The Booz study of BuAer, formally submitted as a 209-page report on 16 August 1941, faulted the bureau for "too much individualism" at the top and in the several divisions, which reflected peacetime attitudes, "the false assumption that every officer is competent to handle whatever is assigned to him. Little effort is being made to recruit trained executives for these positions requiring business training rather than naval background." The report made no fewer than 133 recommendations, on which Secretary Knox ordered Towers to act. Towers did not agree with many of the specifics but did accept a general criticism of "lack of internal balance," and he set about devising a reorganization plan.[52]

At the top, the report recommended that an experienced business executive be appointed to the rejuvenated post of assistant secretary for air. This was done with the arrival of Artemus Gates on 5 September.[53] Then, on 7 October, Towers ordered the complete reorganization of the bureau, adding, "I desire it to be thoroughly understood that the new organization represents my views, and I depend upon the full support of all personnel in putting it into effect as quickly and as smoothly as possible." He wanted no grumbling about outside experts having dictated the changes.[54]

Instead of twelve major divisions, the bureau was now centralized into five: planning, material, maintenance, flight, and one for personnel and training. The Marine Corps aviation division remained separate. To relieve the administrative workload on Towers and Ramsey, many of their responsibilities were delegated to the five division heads, while Ramsey took direct charge of the administrative, financial, and progress organizations. Towers joined Admirals Stark, Robinson, and Spear in rejecting the recommendation from another independent study to conduct all navy material inspection from one office. Towers also added three special assistants, reservists from the business sector, to work respectively on contracts, production, and labor; finances and legislation; and civilian personnel and bureau routine.[55]

Although directly commissioned civilian talent proved a boon to Towers, it also created tensions with the regulars. Take the unorthodox, irrepressible Commander Luis de Florez, brought in to shorten the training syllabus so that pilots could graduate faster. He told Towers, "Besides being taught merely to fly airplanes, these young men ought to be given a trump card, some means for making them more ready than the enemy for a fight." "That will be your baby," said Jack. "Find a way to show them what they'll be up against." De Florez convinced Towers and Forrestal to commission Dr. Donald L. Hibbard, president of Parsons College in Iowa, to be his assistant. Devoted to developing "synthetic" training devices, the jovial de Florez conceived all manner of inventions and could be seen dashing down the corridors of the Navy Department to implement his ideas. Impetuously pragmatic, for example, he flew his own plane to New York to interview Jockey Club officials for jockeys to man bubble turrets that had been designed too small. This earned the wrath of BuNav and BuMed officers, and de Florez had to be rescued by Towers.[56]

The admirals puzzled over this unknown character's bulky, detailed reports for improved Link trainers, gunnery simulators, and gadgets by the score. Lacking funding, de Florez and Hibbard could do little until April 1941, when Towers created the special devices desk in the engineering division. The engineers, however, failed to appreciate their work, so de Florez asked the head of the division, Commander John Ostrander, for a transfer. "Why," the genial Ostrander retorted, "I'll bet you ten dollars in gold we couldn't get rid of you if we tried!" Luis went straight to Towers, delivered one of his typically "eloquent harangues," and in June was moved to the training section, much in need of funds. Before leaving engineering, he gathered a large group of officers to witness his retrieval of ten dollars in gold from Ostrander.[57]

In the training section de Florez's work took off, as he, Hibbard, and engineers from MIT produced hundreds of special devices for training and operations. During the fall of 1941 he journeyed to England, bypassed everyone there to observe British synthetic training, and wrote such an exhaustive report on it that the British adopted it as their own manual. Back home, he saw his budget rise from $50,000 to $1.5 million as he set about revolutionizing aviation training with safer and cheaper devices that did not tie up or risk valuable airplanes or pilots. Before another year passed, the AAF would also adopt his devices, and his budget would soar to $10 million. One of Towers' greatest coups, de Florez would win the Collier Trophy in 1944 for his contributions to aviation and earn a promotion to rear admiral.[58]

Responsibility for aviation personnel continued to be shared by BuAer and BuNav, and Towers and Mitscher preferred to keep it that way. Still, Towers and Rear Admiral Nimitz, chief of BuNav, disagreed over many items, all revolving around the acute need for personnel. Commander Artie Doyle of BuAer marveled at Nimitz's great patience at joint meetings. "The amazing thing was that he was not more anti-aviation: all they [BuNav] heard all day was that same kind of [pro-aviation] talk, all day long!" Doyle would play doubles in tennis with Nimitz at the Army-Navy Club, after which their wives would join them for beer, paid for by the losers. On one of these occasions Mrs. Nimitz gave Doyle a rare insight into her husband's frustration with the brown shoes. After emptying their pitcher of beer, they "sent for another one, and I [Doyle] reached for the check. But Nimitz sort of insisted, and Mrs. Nimitz piped, 'Isn't it typical! Only an aviator would compete with an admiral in trying to pay for drinks!' "[59]

So the two bureau chiefs battled over manpower. Towers lost out to Nimitz in a bid to draw large numbers of trained enlisted personnel from the fleet to help man aviation training stations. On the other hand, he resisted Nimitz's desire to employ nonaviators as captains, executive officers, navigators, and air officers of carriers and seaplane tenders. And though Nimitz refused to support Towers' idea for an advertising campaign to recruit aviators, both men agreed on the need for more enlisted pilots. Nimitz did not like Towers' influence with the Vinson committee, his intimate relations with civilian superiors like Forrestal, or his support of women in uniform. Towers' large staff of female clerks and yeomanettes had been indispensable to him during World War I. One of these veterans, the bubbly, efficient Joy Bright Hancock, now served as Towers' civilian speechwriter and editor of BuAer's newsletter. Over the years, Towers had admired many female aviators, and when the famous aviatrix Jacquelyn Cochran proposed a women's air corps in 1940, Towers announced publicly that women "would undoubtedly be of valuable service in noncombat activities," citing the example of female ferry pilots in Britain. But Nimitz would have none of it.[60]

An order by Admiral Stark in July 1941 for Towers to improve coordination of BuAer training and personnel led to a heated controversy over whether the existing shared system with BuNav should be continued. On 3 October, though willing to maintain the status quo, Towers recommended that all matters relating to aviation training be centralized under BuAer. But under the BuAer reorganization order four days later, the association with BuNav was continued. For the time being it worked, often through subterfuges. For example, whenever Lieutenant Commander John Crommelin wanted something changed in the training curriculum, he would cross the hall to BuNav, take some letterhead stationery, write up the order and process it through BuNav, "which never knew what the hell 'those aviators' were doing," as Crommelin put it.[61]

Such antics, ill-suited for wartime mobilization, led to increased tension. When Artie Doyle returned from an inspection trip of the aviation training program in England, he reported to Towers, "The RAF is so far ahead of us there is no competition"; the training system should be changed completely, with its own division status under a captain. Towers concurred and eventually accepted a compromise, drafted by Forrest Sherman and agreed upon by Nimitz, that required the head of the new division to wear three hats instead of one: director of training in BuAer, assistant for aviation training in the Office of the Chief of Naval Operations, and assistant director of aviation training in BuNav. Towers decided to bring in Commander Arthur Radford, then establishing an air station in Trinidad, to occupy the three posts. On 21 November, Towers separated personnel and training and had Radford promoted to captain.[62]

The question of LTA posed special problems as new nonrigid blimps entered service. The navy's Mr. Dirigible, Captain Charles Rosendahl, attached to the CNO's office, continued to clash with Towers, who had lost the enthusiasm he had once had for airships. Although Congress had authorized forty-eight of them, neither FDR nor Towers pressed production until Rosendahl convinced CNO Stark to direct construction of the still unstarted twenty-one blimps. Towers complied and dutifully defended the program against many critics and before the House appropriations subcommittee during the summer. He also tried to develop competition between builders, but Goodyear was the sole company producing them; only ten had been completed by December.[63]

Towers continued to play an active role in many specific aspects of aviation mobilization. After some reticence, he approved the creation of the new specialty of air combat intelligence. He initiated the centralization of aircraft testing at a new facility that eventually became NAS Patuxent River in Maryland. He approved the conversion of one hundred obsolete torpedo planes into experimental radio-controlled air-to-surface "assault-drone" missiles. Accepting the advice of Commander Jim Boundy, his former mess manager at San Diego, he endorsed the creation of an aviation section within the Bureau of Supplies and Accounts to improve the efficiency of aviation logistics. And he battled fiery New York City mayor Fiorello LaGuardia to take complete control of Floyd Bennett Field, then the city's only municipal airport. In April 1941 Towers personally obtained the lease from LaGuardia, and the city's airliners shifted to the new airport that bore the mayor's name. On 2 June Towers and Forrestal attended the formal commissioning of NAS New York, which became the eastern terminus of the navy's ferry command.[64]

Much of June and July were devoted to personal inspections of key naval air installations. Accompanied by Nimitz, Towers visited the training stations at Jacksonville, Miami, Pensacola, and Corpus Christi and was gratified to find the program progressing ahead of schedule. He flew west with Forrestal to inspect NAS Alameda and spent four days in Hawaii, where he saw Admiral Pat Bellinger's patrol squadrons and Admiral Bill Halsey's carrier maneuvers from the *Enterprise*.[65] Back in Washington, Towers accompanied William Knudsen on inspections of the aircraft plants of Grumman, Ranger, Brewster, Curtiss Propeller, United, and Martin. Although he and Pierre managed a short vacation at Hammondsport, Jack kept in close touch with his office as the mobilization rushed forward.[66]

In September, Towers was visited by one Victor Emanuel, president of the Aircraft Corporation (AVCO), who made a proposal to acquire control of Consolidated Aircraft by buying out Reuben Fleet. The tenuous labor situation and excess profits tax had discouraged Fleet, and he was rushing AVCO to consummate the deal. But Towers refused to be pushed, informing Emanuel that "our primary interest is in . . . economy and efficiency." Jack wanted assurances that any changeover would guarantee that. He listened to more details over ensuing days and conferred with his superiors. Fleet did not press the matter, which if carried out might result in dangerous production delays. At the end of the month, accompanied by Assistant Secretary Di Gates, Towers made an extensive inspection tour of the air bases in the Caribbean, including Miami, Guantanamo, Puerto Rico, the Virgin islands, and British Trinidad.[67]

During their absence the labor situation flared up again, with Consolidated's twenty-four thousand workers demanding the same blanket ten-cents-an-hour wage hike just granted aircraft workers at Lockheed. Fleet refused to agree and rushed to Washington, where on 1 October he asked Forrestal, with Gates and Towers present, to have the government absorb the $82 million price tag of a new pay hike. Forrestal refused, leaving Fleet fed up with the lack of government support and continual investigations by the Vinson committee over possible profiteering. On the seventh Vinson introduced a bill to further limit munitions profits, but when he solicited Towers' advice Jack counseled him against pushing the bill, believing it would force manufacturers into fixed-fee contracts. These would remove any brake on wages, since the unions could threaten to demand raises whenever costs rose, leaving the government with the bill. Vinson finally agreed not to push the legislation.[68]

Again, the culprit was lack of centralized government management for handling munitions contracts between OPM, the army, the navy, and industry. The outcome of the Consolidated dispute would determine the stance of the entire aircraft industry. The navy had worked out its most recent $22 million fixed-price contract for PBYs and PB2Ys with Consolidated to absorb predicted increases in wage scales, with which Fleet had no quarrel. But the army's $340 million worth of fixed-price contracts for B-24s had carried no such adjustments. Thus, although Fleet's quarrel was with the War Department, he lumped all government contracts together in his demands. At his insistence, OPM labor boss Sidney Hillman flew out to San Diego, only to find himself berated by Fleet at a luncheon attended by local business and civic leaders. Hillman agreed to government cooperation, but Fleet refused to sign a new labor contract until he had telegrams from OPM, the army, and the navy guaranteeing that the government would absorb increased costs. Since no one agency could speak for Uncle Sam, Fleet shrewdly determined to go to all three principal agencies. But no telegrams were forthcoming.[69]

Matters were thus highly charged when on the evening of 16 October Towers answered the telephone at his home. It was Reuben Fleet. In the presence of his board of directors, and apparently with a phone hookup to an adjacent room where the union leaders could listen in, Fleet warned Towers that labor was meeting to vote on whether to call a strike. Without government guarantees, Fleet could not meet their demands. Towers did not hesitate to speak for the navy. He outlined its cooperation to date, which Fleet conceded, noting that the War Department was the only real roadblock.

Playing on the patriotism of the labor leaders, Towers said he "felt the union would be putting itself in a very bad light if they struck without allowing the Government time to study the matter. . . . I stated . . . that while I recognized the rights of unions I felt they were constantly being exceeded nowadays and the matter would inevitably end in the unions' downfall if they did not discontinue their highhanded methods." Towers' tough talk did the trick, for after further discussion of wages and contract prices, Fleet announced that the union had voted overwhelmingly to forgo a strike until the government had studied the matter.[70]

Undersecretary Forrestal convened a meeting next morning with Gates, Towers, and their legal experts to discuss the Consolidated situation. All agreed that the navy could not take a position until the War Department had made its decision. That afternoon Assistant Secretary of War for Air Lovett convened Forrestal and Undersecretary of War Patterson to telephone Fleet. When Lovett suggested to Fleet that the government take over Consolidated, Fleet said the government would still have to come up with the $82 million. Lovett backed down, and all three—he, Forrestal, and Patterson— immediately hastened telegrams to Fleet pledging that the government would absorb costs. Fleet then negotiated a new one-year contract with the union. While the costs of wartime mobilization grew apace, Towers had been instrumental in preventing a potentially disastrous strike.[71]

Time was running out. Even as the dispute with Fleet ended, Towers responded to an urgent British request by having Grumman divert twenty-nine new F4F Wildcat fighters from the navy over the next two months. Next day, 18 October, he and Gates departed by air for San Diego and took along

The dedication of "Consair's" new parts factory at San Diego, 20 October 1941. *Right:* "Major" Reuben H. Fleet, president of Consolidated Aircraft, host. (*Left to right*) Rear Admiral A. L. Lyster, fifth sea lord of the British Admiralty, Towers, and Assistant Secretary (air) Artemus L. Gates. (Ticor collection, San Diego Historical Society)

Rear Admiral A. L. Lyster, Fifth Sea Lord, chief of Naval Air Services, and a celebrated carrier leader in the Mediterranean. Because of Britain's orders with Consolidated, Lyster advised Towers and Gates to ensure the navy's control of its own air arm, which they intended to do. After dedicating Consolidated's new parts factory, they returned to Washington. Towers recommended that Lyster inform his government that no increases could be made in naval plane production for Britain; the situation in the Pacific was getting too critical. On the twenty-fifth, Towers took Lyster on inspection visits of the United and Grumman factories.[72]

Although Reuben Fleet had played the proud host at the dedication of his new plant, he informed Towers by phone on 31 October that he still planned to sell his controlling interest in Consolidated. Instead of AVCO or its Vultee subsidiary taking over the company, Fleet preferred to sound out Fred Rentschler and Gene Wilson of United, since he hoped to continue as president of the company. But he said he would take no action until Forrestal, Gates, and Towers advised him of their preference.

Towers and Gates met with Vultee officials on 3 November and heard AVCO's proposal to buy out Fleet, remove him from active participation, and "refrain from any drastic measures which might result in disorganization or upset of production." Gates called Rentschler, who said United executives would rather not take over Consolidated unless absolutely necessary, whereupon the navy got War Department approval to support the AVCO takeover. But when Towers informed Fleet by phone that AVCO would retain him only in an advisory capacity, Fleet began to reconsider his plans. On the seventh he called Towers to say that instead he might "sell only a small part of his stock and remain in active charge of the company." AVCO demurred, and two weeks later Fleet agreed to sell out and remain with the company only as a consultant. Consolidated and Vultee then merged, eventually to become known as Convair.[73]

Even as Towers dealt with Consolidated, the directors of American Export Airlines protested to him over the navy's threatened requisitioning of three huge Sikorsky flying boats it had on order. Though Towers sympathized with the company's desires to compete with Pan Am in the commercial transatlantic market, German U-boat successes in the Atlantic had increased the need for unfettered military air transport service to beleaguered Britain. In the end, however, the navy did not commandeer the Sikorskys, preferring instead to contract five of Pan Am's B-314 Clippers.[74]

Yet another crisis unfolded simultaneously, over threatened shortages in machine tools for aircraft engine production. Early in October FDR ruled that the navy could contract for machine tooling as well as for ship and airplane construction and repair without competitive bidding. But later in the month the War Department announced it intended to more than triple tank production by the following spring. Towers and his fellow bureau chiefs protested that this would greatly hamper the aircraft program, for tanks used airplane engines. Towers recommended the navy only reduce machine tooling for its engine production if the AAF did the same for its bombers, which led to much debate throughout November as OPM and the Munitions Board tried to juggle priorities. Towers convinced Forrestal of the urgency of defending the priority status of machine tooling for the navy's fighter and torpedo plane programs ahead of the AAF's big bombers. On 2 December Hap Arnold challenged most of Towers' arguments in a heated debate with the priorities subcommittee of the Munitions Board. The result was a compromise, which Towers reluctantly accepted, giving priority to machine tooling for the bombers, with the bomber program itself split into increments alongside the navy's combat planes. Such compromises, however, further betrayed OPM's shortcomings in centralized munitions production.[75]

Towers' struggle to keep up combat plane production was the result of his original decision to emphasize training planes first. He had since had to make compromises as needs arose, for instance in November when BuAer, with OPM approval, requested 2,020 planes specifically for new escort carriers, advanced training, and transport to fleet and advanced bases in the Pacific. On 17 November Towers informed the House appropriations subcommittee that the navy's 15,000-plane program would not be completed, nor that of the two-ocean navy, for another five years.[76]

Admiral Stark believed that the navy's island bases were stationary aircraft carriers and that Marine Corps squadrons defending these bases should be assigned twin-engine medium bombers. In a stormy meeting in Stark's office on Thanksgiving Day, 27 November, this attitude was challenged by the men who recognized the essential need for attack planes to be mobile: Towers, Atlantic Fleet commander King, war plans director Turner, and marine Major General Commandant Thomas C. Holcomb. The issue was not settled. Towers was carefully orchestrating the employment of navy planes where he believed they would do the most good. And though he regarded medium bombers as wasted on the islands, defensive fighters and scouts were another matter. For at this very moment, the *Enterprise* and the *Lexington* were embarking Marine Corps scouts and fighters at Pearl Harbor for delivery to Wake and Midway.[77]

The navy and its air arm were not ready for war, through no fault of theirs. The American public had been aroused too late to the necessity for mobilization, and isolationist sentiment remained intense. Yet, in spite of the late hour, Jack Towers had worked hard to design the navy's air program for global war, and like any architect he doggedly defended and explained it to all interested parties.

On 1 December he welcomed the laying down of the fourth and fifth *Essex*-class carriers at Newport News. He was in Columbus on the fourth to speak at the dedication of a new Curtiss plant, and on the fifth he informed Forrestal of his acceptance of the new priorities list for machine tooling. Next day the Senate began hearings on supplemental aircraft funding for fiscal 1942.[78]

Towers' quiet Sunday, the seventh, was interrupted the same way it was for all Americans. At about 1430 he heard the announcement of the Japanese carrier attack on Pearl Harbor. After telephoning Ralph Davison, head of plans, he proceeded to the Navy Department immediately, where he established a continuous duty officer watch as all personnel reported in. Everyone seemed dumbstruck. In the words of then–Lieutenant Commander Roy L. Johnson of planning, "I've never seen people who looked so helpless. There was nothing you could do in the face of this disaster we'd just suffered."

Someone said, "Break out the war plan," which appeared pretty useless once the news came in.

Japanese carrier planes had caught the entire battle line, moored alongside Ford Island, by surprise. The lack of enough PBY patrol planes had enabled the enemy to approach undetected and sink or seriously damage virtually every battleship as well as destroy most aircraft. The fleet would not be heading west according to the Orange Plan for a very long time to come. Towers remarked to his officers, "Well, let's get busy and size up the situation here, what we've got, and make sure what we have left of the carriers." That part of the news was good. The *Lexington* and the *Enterprise,* en route to Wake and Midway to deliver Marine Corps planes, had missed the attack and survived. Towers stayed in Admiral Stark's office late into the night, helping prepare dispatches and furnishing information about the distribution of army and navy aircraft.[79]

Next day, for the first time in years, all hands reported to the Navy Department in uniform. While Towers hastened to the Capitol with his fellow admirals and Secretary Knox, twenty-five of his senior officers gathered in his large corner office to listen to FDR's radio war message to Congress. A reporter witnessed the scene:

> Gray and white-haired four-stripers were very much in evidence; there were very few commanders, and very few of lesser rank. . . . [T]hey listened to the President in absolute silence.
>
> As the President finished, there followed the bars of *The Star Spangled Banner.*
>
> An unidentified officer said one word: "Gentlemen."
>
> Twenty-five officers came to their feet in rigid attention.
>
> As the last words died away there was a very short pause.
>
> "Gentlemen, we have work to do." The officers filed out.[80]

13

AIR CHIEF OF THE
WARTIME NAVY
1941–42

The blows delivered by the Japanese at Pearl Harbor—and in the Philippines and Southeast Asia—thrust Towers into the role for which he was most eminently suited: directing the air arm of a navy now officially at war. While his planners feverishly reworked the fleet's aircraft needs, Towers attended a special meeting of the Army-Navy Joint Board on 8 December 1941 to consider defense plans. He assigned Lieutenant Commander George Anderson to provide aircraft figures to a shaken CNO Stark; Anderson observed that General Marshall was calm, Towers "relatively unruffled." The board, fearing a renewed Japanese attack on Hawaii, considered recalling the *Lexington* or the *Enterprise* to California to pick up army and Marine Corps planes for reinforcing Pearl. With the battleships neutralized, however, no carrier could be spared to make the run.[1]

Next day, the ninth, with invasion hysteria mounting on the West Coast, the Joint Board wondered why the Consolidated factory at San Diego was not being blacked out at night. Towers took full responsibility, having reasoned that that would greatly hamper aircraft production. The board agreed that all such decisions should henceforth be centralized and that "anti-light windows" be installed at all West Coast plants. Hap Arnold and Towers accordingly drew up a joint message advising West Coast commanders of this and other antiair defensive measures to be instituted.

How both men felt immediately about the Pearl Harbor disaster came out as driver Joe Draghi was chauffeuring them through downtown Washington, and Towers remarked, "We won't live to see it, but if Draghi here lives his normal span of life, he will live to see Roosevelt's name go down as the blackest in history."

"No question about it, Jack," replied Arnold. "I agree with you."

Though no invasion came, the Japanese were overrunning most of the Pacific west of Hawaii as well as British Malaya and the Dutch East Indies, and on the eleventh Germany and Italy declared war on the United States, leading to public alarm over the security of the eastern seaboard. Even six weeks later Towers had to calm congressional inquisitors fearful of a massive air raid against the Atlantic coast. Such a "stunt" could be executed by very few planes at most.[2]

Towers and his BuAer planners carefully calculated their needs for more aircraft and on 10 December decided to ask an additional $500 million for 3,076 more planes as well as advance base equipment, maintenance, plant expansion, training devices, and experiments. Next day Admiral Stark summoned bureau chiefs and representatives to discuss the navy's financial needs for the next several months. Towers being the only one present prepared with a firm estimate, all agreed with his suggestion to insert the half-billion dollar figure into contract authorizations of title V for fiscal 1942, about to be reported out of Senate subcommittee. Acting Secretary Forrestal gained subcommittee approval over the phone, hearings were conducted a few hours later, and the funding was approved without question on the fifteenth. The total title V supplement for naval aviation came to over $949 million.[3]

At these hearings, incidentally, Towers was the first navy officer to appear before congressmen who were anxious for news and critical of the military. According to George Anderson, one of them remarked, "Now, Admiral, what do you mean about this backbone of the fleet having been sunk at Pearl Harbor?"

Retorted Jack, "You're in error, because the backbone of the fleet is in the aircraft carriers and that was at sea."

In fact Towers was appalled at the utter lack of aggressiveness on the part of the Pacific Fleet. On 11 December, though Marine Corps troops repulsed a landing force at Wake and Admiral Kimmel, commander in chief, Pacific Fleet, was assembling a relief force, Towers concluded nothing substantial was being done to reinforce Wake. The normally feisty head of war plans,

Kelly Turner, informed Stark on the twelfth that he expected a Japanese carrier raid on Puget Sound or Mare Island, San Francisco, that very day. In the midst of defeat and confusion, Secretary Knox left Washington for Hawaii to inspect damage to the fleet.[4]

A few days later, according to then–Commander John Crommelin of BuAer's flight division, Towers summoned him to his office. "Sit down," said the admiral. "Well, what do you think?"

"Admiral," answered Crommelin, "I think we're in deep trouble."

"The carriers sure showed them what they could do, didn't they?"

"They certainly did show us."

"You know, they called me in today and offered me the job of commander in chief of the fleet."

Surprised, Crommelin said, "Admiral, did you take it?"

"No."

"Why not?"

"I told them that I could serve my country better in this job, that it's going to be a long war, that we have to broaden the base of our training program, that we have to get the material, and that really I think it should be a young man in command of the fleet, some man like Radford. I turned it down."[5]

No other record exists of the offer. Towers made no mention of it in his diary or to Pierre, who many years later—when she learned of this conversation—doubted it had been made. In any case, Jack rarely discussed such matters with her. She suggested that Jim Forrestal, a fervent admirer of her husband, might have said something to him about his possibly replacing Kimmel. For during Secretary Knox's week-long absence, Forrestal served as acting navy secretary. Perhaps Knox did informally discuss the possibility with Towers upon his return to the department on the fifteenth.

Towers did record in his diary that on this date he had a "long discussion" on the subject of changes in the high command with Atlantic Fleet commander King but gave no details. That same evening Knox conferred with President Roosevelt about command changes, and surely Towers' name came up. But it was probably eliminated from a list of possible fleet commanders because of Towers' reputation as a crusader and because of his primary identification with only one arm of the fleet. Also, his talents in helping mobilize the navy had become essential.[6]

On its own merits, however, Crommelin's account has credibility. Though Towers no doubt would have liked to be commander in chief of the Pacific Fleet, crippled though it was, he did have the example of Admiral

Moffett, who had repeatedly turned down tempting seagoing commands to battle for aviation. The forces of unification Moffett had fought were now stronger than ever, and as the acknowledged leader of naval aviation Towers was indispensable to its wartime development as the navy's principal striking element. In the overall hierarchy, he had also been the steady counterbalance to the Gun Club and Chester Nimitz's powerful BuNav. And he may well have considered himself to be the logical wartime successor to Stark as CNO, the most coveted job of all. So Towers' thinking, as recalled by Crommelin, was entirely plausible. The possible flaw in it—if Crommelin's memory was correct—was that aviators like Radford, only now about to be promoted to captain, were simply too junior to be elevated to fleet command, just as Towers as a new captain had been too junior to succeed Moffett as chief of BuAer in 1933.

As far as Towers' suitability for the job of fleet commander in the Pacific, there was no doubt about his aggressiveness and knowledge of the proper use of carriers, the only capital ships left to carry out the fight. On 16 December he recorded, "I urged Assistant Secretary Gates to use his influence with the Secretary in an effort to break the present defensive attitude in the Pacific Fleet, which attitude definitely has the support of Admiral Turner of War Plans, and to recommend most strongly that a heavy force, including at least one carrier, preferably two, be sent to relieve Wake, the carrier to fly off a squadron of fighters and some dive bombers to land on Wake and assist in its defense. Mr. Gates stated he approved highly of the recommendation and would try to put it over."[7]

That evening at the Navy Department Gates advised him of new changes in the high command just put forth by Knox and FDR. Stark would remain CNO and Kimmel would be relieved as commander in chief of the U.S. Fleet. But the latter post—COMINCH—would be moved from the Pacific to Washington and given to Ernest J. King. In accepting the post, Towers' old nemesis demanded that he rather than the secretary be given direct administrative control over the bureau chiefs, a proviso surely aimed at Towers more than anyone else. But FDR demurred, agreeing only that he would replace uncooperative chiefs. Kimmel's relief as CINCPAC was BuNav chief Nimitz. If Towers indeed believed a younger man should have gotten the post, he was disappointed, for Nimitz was his own age and one year ahead of him at the Naval Academy. Nimitz now wore four stars.[8]

In succeeding days and weeks the wartime commands were reshuffled. Overlapping between the offices of COMINCH and CNO would prove so unwieldy that in March 1942 they would be combined under King alone as COMINCH-CNO, though he kept two distinct staffs. As COMINCH he directed the operating forces, and as CNO he gave the fleet logistic support. Assistant CNO Royal Ingersoll took over the Atlantic Fleet and was replaced by Frederick Horne, soon upgraded to vice CNO in the rank of vice admiral and given a virtual free hand by King to handle the duties of CNO. This elevation of Towers' old carrier commander boss Horne thus gave Jack an informal pipeline to the top. Nimitz's replacement as chief of BuNav was Rear Admiral Randall Jacobs, and the bureau now carried the more accurate title Bureau of Naval Personnel (BuPers). King would exercise direct authority over all flag assignments. Of the academy graduates of '06 Towers remained the only bureau chief.[9]

Now that carriers comprised the only surface striking force in the Pacific, Towers was naturally anxious to have the best available men command the task forces built around them. The retention of Vice Admiral Bill Halsey in the carrier command, its flagship the *Enterprise,* was fine, but Towers was chagrined to learn that Kimmel's interim successor, Vice Admiral William S. Pye, now assigned the *Lexington* and the *Saratoga* task forces to nonaviators Wilson Brown and Frank Jack Fletcher respectively. Then the relief expedition for Wake was botched, and that island fell to a Japanese assault on 23 December before the carriers could be employed. Towers took the position that the appointment of nonaviators to command of carrier task forces was in direct violation of the law, namely, the Morrow legislation of 1926 that he had helped to write. When visited by retired Admiral Harry Yarnell in late January, he was glad to hear his former boss echo his views about the lack of an offensive attitude in the Pacific. As carrier raids and battles occurred throughout 1942 and carriers were lost, his criticisms became persistent, to the great annoyance of Secretary Knox.[10]

The way to insure that the carrier experts would lead the carrier war was to have the best of them promoted to flag rank. Towers and his planners calculated that the navy would require thirty-one air admirals by 1943, and BuPers concurred. But late in January 1942 when the House Appropriations Committee tried to restrict the number of aviation flag officers to nine, BuPers chief Jacobs urged Towers to do what he could "to have the limitation removed." Jack then testified before the Senate naval subcommittee recommending the figure be raised to thirty-one, won its approval, and personally arranged with the House committee to concur.[11]

The flag selection board, meeting concurrently, picked Pete Mitscher and Baldy Pownall, to Towers' great joy. Latecomer Alva Bernhard was also picked. Neither Mitscher nor Pownall would pin on their stars until flag billet vacancies opened up several months hence.[12]

Prime Minister Churchill and several senior British military officers arrived in Washington on 22 December 1941 to develop strategic planning with the Americans. Admiral Stark was selected to preside over what was loosely designated the U.S. Chiefs of Staff Council, which included King, Assistant CNO Horne, General Marshall, and Marshall's AAF deputy Hap Arnold. To represent the Navy Department on the council Stark designated three other officers: Towers of BuAer, Turner of war plans, and Walton R. Sexton of the General Board. Meeting daily from 24 December through 14 January, the Anglo-American planners hammered out details for defeating Hitler first, while supplying Russia against Germany, China against Japan, and trying in vain to hold the line in Southeast Asia. Since the chiefs did most of the talking, Towers and his fellow service representatives only provided technical information. The Allied conferees soon formalized their organization as the Combined Chiefs of Staff (CCS), with the senior American representatives designated the Joint Chiefs of Staff (JCS).[13]

Immediately apparent to the CCS was the major role of the AAF, not only for the strategic bombing of Germany but also for the supply of China and for transatlantic aerial communications. Like Towers, RAF Chief Marshal Sir Charles Portal believed that America's carriers should be the primary instrument for eventually bombing Japan, whenever enough carriers were available—a view shared by the U.S. Army's new director of war plans, Brigadier General Dwight D. Eisenhower, who urged carrier over battleship construction. On 19 December the British had asked Towers to step up the production of Grumman F4F fighters for Britain without upsetting the strategic bomber program. Towers could offer no encouragement, given the four-engine-bomber priority, a view he reiterated at the first meeting of the CCS on Christmas Eve. The call for B-17s and B-24s would hamper navy aircraft production for at least eight months, he announced; material diversions had already slowed plant work weeks to forty hours a week.[14]

U.S. naval aviation thereby assumed a role subordinate to that of the AAF in overall strategic planning, while the AAF became an independent service in practice if not administrative fact. Hap Arnold was promoted to lieutenant general in mid-month, giving him clear seniority in rank over his navy counterpart, Towers, and during January he was the only American aviator to participate in the highest-level strategy meetings between FDR and Churchill. At the end of the month Admiral King urged that the JCS absorb the functions of the Army-Navy Joint Board to avoid redundancy and stream-line strategic planning. General Marshall agreed but suggested that Arnold and Towers of the Joint Board be retained on the JCS as the representatives of military and naval aviation. King agreed on Arnold, given the AAF's enlarged role, but he saw no need for Towers' membership since BuAer was such an integral part of the navy. So early in February when the JCS first met formally, its members were Marshall, Arnold, King, and Stark—two army, two navy. By excluding Towers, King was able to keep him in a subordinate position; the old rivalry continued.

With the amalgamation of the offices of COMINCH and CNO in the person of Admiral King, the Joint Board rarely met again. Its demise ended the coequal administrative status of prewar army and navy aviation, although King wore navy wings. Towers and Arnold still belonged to the Aeronautical Board, JAC, and NACA, and Towers continued to attend most meetings of the JCS and those with the British representatives of the CCS, though in an advisory capacity. And Jack and Hap maintained their usual informal working relationship even as they clashed on matters of aircraft allocation and overall air policy. With Admiral Stark's departure in March, however, the army had a two-to-one advantage on the JCS, which left King at something of a disadvantage. And the executive order amalgamating COMINCH-CNO excluded the chief of BuAer, Towers, from the highest level of navy planning.[15]

Ernie King, a superb strategist and military thinker, was nonetheless a blunt and tactless administrator who insisted on unity of command. He resented the traditional arrangement whereby the chiefs of bureau reported directly to the secretary, who initiated weekly conferences with them at which Towers was particularly influential. King disliked Undersecretary Forrestal's low-keyed intellectual approach to problems, and he resented Towers' close relationship with Forrestal and Assistant Secretary for Air Di Gates. King grew almost obsessive in his desire to reorganize the department to strengthen his own authority. He could go to petty lengths, for example when he appropriated Towers' new R5O Lodestar to be his own private plane.[16]

Centralized industrial mobilization now became mandatory. In January FDR replaced William Knudsen's Office of Production Management with the War Production Board (WPB) under Donald Nelson, while Forrestal upgraded navy procurement under his direct authority and with a czar of his own. Towers, whose BuAer boasted the most effective procurement program in the navy, learned about it on 22 January when Gus Read brought him a memorandum from Assistant Secretary Ralph A. Bard ordering the bureau to vacate several offices by midnight. The reason, recorded Towers, was to create space for a chief of material. Assuming that such a post would go to the chief of BuShips, Rear Admiral Mike Robinson, Towers telephoned Robinson, who explained he did not want the job and didn't care which spaces he would occupy. The chief of this new Office of Procurement and Material (OP&M, not to be confused with the defunct OPM), Robinson, would carry the rank of vice admiral, senior to the bureau chiefs, who would report to him.

Towers was incensed, both at Forrestal's not having consulted with bureau chiefs and at the arbitrary order to vacate office spaces. When he confronted Forrestal the latter equivocated, leaving Towers with the impression that the decision had been hasty. It had not; Forrestal had organized the new office with help from management experts Ferdinand Eberstadt and Edwin G. Booz. Next day Towers convinced Booz, Di Gates, and Ralph Bard that the plan to give a chief of material the power to formulate and execute procurement programs was a mistake, at least for aviation. Gates promised to try to get BuAer "taken out from under the proposed office." He wrote a letter to that effect and with Forrestal and Bard presented it to Secretary Knox on 24 January. It stated that BuAer's procurement policy to date had "been highly satisfactory and better than any other bureau's." Knox, aware of criticism of all the material bureaus, agreed to compromise; OP&M's authority would "extend no further than coordination and general supervision as directed by the Secretary." Robinson took office under those terms on the thirtieth.[17]

OP&M became the navy's crucial liaison agency for obtaining vital war materials from the WPB and the Munitions Board. Towers had protected BuAer's actual control over aircraft procurement and allocation, but it was another instance of his compelling the secretary to give aviation special treatment. Indeed, Towers' forthrightness could be irritating to his civilian superiors. After his earlier attempt, through Gates, to expedite the relief of Wake Island, he had been told to stick to material matters and leave operations to the proper commanders and officers. A loyal officer, he obeyed when he was told to, but until then he acted on his own initiative to establish workable policies.[18]

The divorce between BuAer and operational policy may have frustrated Towers, but it was a good decision because it forced him to concentrate his considerable managerial talents on developing wartime aviation material policy. The five-year, 15,000-plane goal of 1940 had been rendered inadequate by America's untimely and forced entry into the war. In addition to new planes for the seven fast carriers in commission, aircraft would be needed for the eleven *Essex*-class units under authorization, the two approved by new legislation on 23 December, and the nine converted light carriers of the *Independence* class. Construction of the latter and of the first few auxiliary escort carriers had only just begun. Beyond carrier planes, the new wartime fleet would require many more land-based and amphibian patrol planes, Marine Corps aircraft, battleship and cruiser catapult scouts, trainers, utility and miscellaneous planes, and cargo-passenger transports for the new Naval Air Transportation Service (NATS), established on 12 December.[19]

Making airplane projections for the duration—the "numbers racket," as it was known—was difficult. Towers' planners spent December working feverishly with CNO and General Board representatives to develop a new navy aircraft program. Its real architect, however, was Lieutenant Commander George Anderson, head of BuAer's programs and allocations section. Towers presented the finished report to Secretary Knox on 2 January. It proposed 27,500 aircraft, "envisioning the requirements of naval aircraft in the current war." Including replacements for planes lost both in combat and through attrition from other causes, the bureau set productive capacity at 18,000 navy planes per year. The study was based on the rough operating force plan, which included twenty-four fleet carriers. These figures were far lower than those of President Roosevelt, who next day informed the armed services that total aircraft strength should be 45,000 combat planes and 15,000 trainers for 1942 and 100,000 and 25,000 respectively for 1943. Like his grandiose 50,000-plane figure of eighteen months before, FDR had apparently picked these numbers out of the air, for they were not based on army and navy projections. The president presented the new program in his annual message before Congress on 6 January.

On the eighth, shocked by the president's huge figures, the lame-duck OPM called a meeting of all interested parties. At it Gates, Bob Lovett, Towers, and Babe Meigs all agreed that FDR's program would be impossible to accomplish. OPM's figures were 44,416 total aircraft for 1942 and 66,769 for 1943. OPM now offered a compromise, which Towers opposed because it included the "unsound" stipulation that all the nation's available aluminum be committed to aircraft alone. The conferees decided to urge FDR to scale down his figures; to accelerate production further would upset the numbers of planes that the manufacturers could realistically deliver.

In conversations with Forrestal, Gates, and Towers that day and the next, Knox agreed that the original OPM figures should be kept but warned against taking "the matter up with the President at any time in the near future. . . ." And so the WPB (which superseded OPM a week later), army, and navy would pay lip service to the president's enormous goal while following their own realistic schedule. FDR would not learn the truth until the summer, and when he did he would not be pleased. As a start, however, he approved Towers' 27,500-plane proposal for the navy.[20]

With BuAer's aircraft goals thus set for the next eighteen months, the bureau immediately stepped up procurement, training, and base expansion. Towers appeared before the usual congressional committees over the first nine months of 1942 to obtain funding. He generally got what he needed from a Congress now unified behind the goal of victory. Additional supplements brought naval aviation's total fiscal 1942 appropriation to nearly $7 billion and fiscal 1943's to almost $4 billion.[21]

Towers continued to maintain his working relationships with the captains of the aircraft industry.[22] He welcomed the appointment of Tom M. Girdler as chairman of the board of newly merged Consolidated-Vultee (Convair), who soon proposed an expansion plan for an accelerated output of PBYs, PB2Y Coronados, and AAF B-24 Liberators. Both WPB's Donald Nelson and Towers endorsed it enthusiastically, though Di Gates thought too much money was being pumped into Convair. The company was delivering the goods, however, and Girdler later visited Towers to further increase production by arranging to lease adjacent plant facilities from Ryan Aircraft.[23]

The Grumman success story had continued unbroken since the founding of the company in 1929, and Towers kept writing letters of congratulations for its relentless output of quality F4F Wildcats and TBF Avengers. "The success of our operations in the Pacific," Towers informed Roy Grumman in July, after the Battle of Midway, "can be directly attributed to the production from your plant." Unfortunately, though, the need for planes was so great that the production of adequate spare parts suffered. Towers had to insist to Grumman that this be corrected. He then appointed a special board to develop a spare-parts schedule for all navy contractors. With his help, Grumman was able to accelerate production of the TBF and to keep up the output of Wildcats. Though impressive in the hands of top pilots, the F4F-4 did not prove superior to the Japanese Zero fighter; this was partly because of modifications to standardize the wings of the Martlet version for the British.

Grumman had the solution in an improved design, the XF6F Hellcat (bypassing the less promising XF5F). When it first flew in June 1942, the prototype lacked sufficient power using the Wright R-2600 engine Towers' engineers had assigned it. George Anderson figured that more power could be provided by the Pratt and Whitney R-2800 Double Wasp engine just entering production for the first Vought F4U Corsairs. The difference in performance was phenomenal, and when Grumman sent the figures to Anderson he took them straight to Towers. Jack ordered the change without hesitation and urged haste in production. Tireless Grumman workers would have the first-production F6F-3 in the navy's hands by October. It would become the fighter to beat the Japanese Zero.[24]

A similar success story eluded the Brewster Company, whose existing planes were no match against the Japanese and whose management problems grew steadily worse when a pending takeover by U.S. Rubber failed to materialize. In spite of Towers' concern about the company needing to line up subcontractors, Di Gates would not sign a letter of intent for Brewster fighters until its management got better organized. Neither Admiral Robinson of OP&M nor the BuAer production division could help Brewster solve its complex problems, and so FDR authorized the navy to seize control of the company late in April. Captain Conrad Westervelt, long retired but now recalled to active duty, took charge of Brewster.

In May Towers and Gates summoned Reuben Fleet to Washington to help correct the Brewster dilemma, and Jack even brought his brother Fullton to Washington for advice. Now president of the Ford, Bacon, and Davis engineering firm, Fullton made several recommendations but said his company could not become involved because Jack was his brother. Gates and Towers finally arranged to have Fleet and his Convair colleague C. A. Van Dusen reorganize Brewster's management with Van Dusen as president and chairman of the board. Even under Van Dusen the company continued to have troubles. In July, however, it was given a contract to build fifteen hundred copies of a proven plane, the Vought F4U Corsair, as the F3A. Under a similar arrangement, Goodyear undertook additional Corsair production as the FG.[25]

That Towers enjoyed such broad material and procurement power continued to rankle Admiral King, as did the fact that he had no direct access to Towers on personnel matters like aviation captain assignments. On 18 March, for example, King sent his chief of staff to Jack for recommendations of specific individuals, such an awkward system of organization that King planned to place the material chiefs directly under his authority. On 1 May King called in Towers to discuss his reorganization scheme. He planned to create three assistant CNOs, for air, personnel, and material, their duties to be performed by the actual chiefs, Towers, Jacobs, and Robinson respectively. As assistant CNO (air), Towers would be responsible to the vice CNO, Vice Admiral Horne, but also of course to King. On the other hand, regarding the membership of the JCS, King indicated to Towers that he was "in the same echelon as General Arnold." Perhaps King was only baiting Towers to gain his support by intimating that Jack should be added to the JCS as a counterweight to Arnold. When the press learned of King's plans, it assumed Towers would be promoted to vice admiral. On 15 May, leaving these possibilities aside, King ordered the establishment of assistant CNO (air). At the same time, Towers and Gates recommended that all aviation personnel and training be concentrated in BuAer under a new assistant chief for personnel and training. Like Nimitz before him, BuPers chief Jacobs resented any such idea.

King's elaborate scheme immediately miscarried when FDR learned of it. Undersecretary Forrestal objected as well, advising Knox that procurement should remain under civilian control—his own. Incredibly, King flaunted FDR's wishes by ordering the creation of assistant CNOs for personnel and material on 28 May. Then on 3 June Admiral Horne rejected the Towers-Gates recommendation and, in accordance with King's wishes, ordered that all personnel, including aviation's, be transferred to the authority of Jacobs as assistant CNO (personnel).

FDR and Towers moved simultaneously against these plans. On 9 June the president called King and Knox to the White House to reject the overall reorganization, while Towers testified before the Vinson committee against the order transferring BuAer training and personnel to BuPers. Next day, Vinson summoned Towers to his office to discuss Horne's order of transfer. "As I was talking with him," Towers recorded, "a memorandum from Admiral Horne was brought in which stated that Admiral King had directed cancellation of the subject order."[27]

By aligning himself with his civilian superiors Roosevelt, Forrestal, and Gates, Towers was being both loyal to them and true to his own convictions. But by his action he also probably killed any remote possibility of King's ever supporting him for elevation to the JCS. For FDR now ordered King to cancel all his reorganization plans, though the aviation division remained in Horne's office. King's control over Towers therefore remained indirect. As for the president, he decided to appoint a personal chief of staff to be his liaison with the JCS and especially to act as a buffer against Ernie King. Former CNO Admiral Leahy was recalled to active duty in July to fill this post and to act as presiding chairman of the JCS, now settled into its membership for the duration: Leahy, King, Marshall, and Arnold—again, two army, two navy.

Central to the entire naval air effort, and caught up in the above imbroglio, was the immense training expansion demanded by the new 27,500-plane program. "The training organization to make such a program possible," in the words of then–Commander Herb Riley, "was built by the foresight of Admiral Jack Towers . . . a very long-range thinker and a great planner" who had brought in Captain Arthur Radford to implement it. The projected 7,200-pilots-per-year goal of the prewar program was suddenly inadequate, and less than a week after the Pearl Harbor attack Radford and his staff worked out and got approved a new program for 30,000 navy and marine pilots a year.[28]

Initially, Towers and Radford figured that the number of naval air training stations set for the 15,000-plane program would be sufficient for the wartime expansion. But by the end of February the need was apparent for additional training fields. Working with Admiral Moreell of BuDocks, Towers concluded that twelve new intermediate training bases must augment Corpus Christi, Pensacola, Key West, Jacksonville, Miami, and Banana River. Since all but the first of these existing ones were located in Florida, where the AAF was also establishing fields, Towers worked out a gentlemen's agreement with Hap Arnold for mutual cooperation in base site selection and expansion in that state. A "Stratemeyer-Towers Line" devised with Arnold's chief of staff, Major General George E. Stratemeyer, divided the state between the navy on the east coast and the AAF on the west coast and in central Florida. Disagreements had to be negotiated and were often solved by Towers and Arnold agreeing to share facilities. Towers also spent a great deal of time fending off pork-barrel efforts by several states to erect naval air facilities.[29]

As vast numbers of college men began to arrive for flight training, Towers realized that jurisdiction over the widely scattered training stations should be shifted from naval districts to a centralized system. Before Pearl Harbor, Captain Putty Read had recommended that in the event of war all flight training be placed under his authority as commanding officer at Pensacola. Towers regarded such a scheme as unwieldy until February 1942, when he recommended to King that aviation training be administratively centralized in four commands, each under an admiral directly responsible to Radford's office of training. His proposal was quickly approved, and on 30 April the first one, the Air Operational Training Command, was established with headquarters at Jacksonville. A dispute with BuPers delayed the creation of the other three—the Air Technical Training Command for specialist officers and enlisted mechanics, the Air Primary Training Command, and the Air Intermediate Training Command—until September.[30]

After initial resistance from BuPers chief Randall Jacobs, BuAer was allowed to undertake "a somewhat flexible program" to commission bright Wall Street lawyers and brokers and to procure and train additional reserve officers for air combat intelligence (ACI) work. Towers decided the ACI officers (ACIOs) should be a minimum age of twenty-eight and experienced in the professions of business, law, banking, and engineering in order to learn to brief and debrief pilots and assimilate lessons from their combat experiences. In mid-December 1941 he charged his senior special assistant, Commander Gus Read, to arrange for the establishment of an eight-week ACIO course at NAS Quonset Point, Rhode Island. Graduates between the ages of twenty-eight and thirty-three would be commissioned as lieutenants (jg), over thirty-three as lieutenants. Towers personally ruled on anyone forty-two years or older, starting with forty-three-year-old Lieutenant Commander John Jay Schieffelin, World War I naval aviator, whom he appointed officer in charge of the ACIO school.

Gus Read wisely avoided going through Congress, a time-consuming process, particularly because he believed thousands of ACIOs might eventually be needed to serve the many new squadrons and carriers. When he said so to Towers and Captain Van Hubert Ragsdale, head of the bureau's personnel division, Ragsdale remarked to Towers with a smile, "He's certainly entitled to his opinion."

"Well, Rags, you lose," replied Towers. "You never have come anywhere close to estimating the eventual size of this thing, and I'm going to make it a thousand men to start with, two classes at five hundred each!" Towers personally presented diplomas to the first fifty-six graduates on 10 April. When the eight-week-wonders began to report to aviation units, Pensacola men derisively labeled them "those ground-swells from Quonset Point," but they quickly proved their worth in the fleet.[31]

Towers had the 1917–18 experience in mind when once again he actively promoted the return of women to navy uniform. The army had led the way late in 1941. But when Radford queried BuPers on the prospect of admitting women shortly after Pearl Harbor, BuPers replied in the negative. Towers had BuAer initiate legislation before a generally receptive Congress, and when BuPers refused to push it, Captain Irving McQuiston, head of BuAer's progress office, sought out Margaret Chung. This San Francisco lady had entertained so many army and navy aviators over the years that the recipients of her hospitality regarded themselves as "the sons of Mom Chung." She approached Congressman Melvin Maas, like McQuiston one of her sons, and he got the Vinson House committee to endorse the bill.

Then David Walsh and several fellow senators complained that the navy was no place for women. A relative of George Anderson's happened to be Walsh's chief assistant, and Towers had Anderson ply both men with Scotch one night a week at Anderson's home. George worked on Senator Walsh until one evening he agreed: "All right, I'll withdraw my opposition on the assurance that the morals of these girls will be protected, and never will anybody propose that they be sent to ships." Finally in June, with a gentle nudge from Eleanor Roosevelt, FDR agreed, and on 30 July a bill passed creating the WAVES (Women Accepted for Volunteer Emergency Service). The president of Wellesley College, Mildred McAfee, was made director in the reserve rank of lieutenant commander.

The reluctant BuPers did not know how many women the navy would need or exactly what to do with them. After several weeks passed, Admiral Jacobs suggested that Commander McAfee interview the bureau chiefs for suggestions. In September, when she got to Towers, she "was perfectly astonished at the violence with which he spoke." "Where have you been all this time?" he barked. "We've been clamoring for these WAVES and nobody's ever listened to us. . . ." He revealed that BuAer had just asked for 20,326—the largest single request by any bureau and over twice the number of women BuPers had planned for the entire navy. Towers' planners had generated the program that would eventually grow to 12,000 WAVE officers and 75,000 enlisted women. When Joy Hancock applied, BuPers turned her down for being thirty-three pounds underweight, but her friends in BuAer let the flight surgeons give her a passing exam, enabling her to be commissioned a lieutenant. McAfee immediately made Hancock the BuPers women's representative at BuAer, where she helped assign WAVES to duties involving training, communications, planning, personnel, clerical work, and eventually more technical activities at some fifty naval air facilities.[32]

Another area of dispute between Towers and the black-shoe navy involved publicity. Inasmuch as the public relations office had no aviator on its staff, Towers insisted that all stories regarding aviation first be cleared through BuAer. And because he and his fellow brown-shoes felt aviation was not getting the attention it deserved in the press, he used the bureau's training literature section as "a sub-rosa publicity department" to sell naval aviation to the public. Also brought in to Radford's training division was the eminent photographer Edward Steichen, who produced naval air photographs to outclass the recruiting posters of the AAF. And when Joy Hancock transferred to the WAVES, she made certain that advertising executive Lieutenant (jg) John Monsarrat replaced her as Towers' speechwriter and editorial censor. Finally, Towers managed to get a former aviator assigned to the navy's public relations office. No matter that Lieutenant Ben Hoy had lost a leg in an accident.[33]

Towers reserved a special role for Spig Wead, a genius at turning out aviation film scripts ever since his crippling accident in 1927. Towers recalled his old *Langley* shipmate to active duty in the rank of lieutenant commander, assigned him to head the strategic air information section in planning, and gave him an office with a big board on which to plot aircraft strengths. Spig's activity was top secret and off limits to most personnel.[34]

As for aviation hardware, Towers only occasionally played a direct role in the decisions of his experts to adapt new ordnance to existing and projected aircraft. As early as 7 January he directed that powerful 20mm cannon be installed in place of machine guns on the newest dive bombers and fighters, primarily the SB2C Helldiver. He encouraged experimental designs of new plane types, like the Vought XF5U circular-wing fighter and a single-seat version of the three-place Grumman TBF torpedo bomber. But as the industry tooled up for mass production of planes already in the program, these innovations had to be either scrapped or left to postwar development. Needed changes would be made on existing types; BuAer ordnance experts operated on a crash basis, instituting modifications to navy planes throughout 1942.[35]

Hard-pressed for the new planes, Towers was lukewarm to diverting funds, personnel, and precious time to unproved concepts. He endorsed television-guided assault drones after successful tests during the spring, although he objected to the appointment of a nonaviator, Captain Oscar Smith, to head Project Option when Admiral King formally established it in May. The next month, when Smith called for one thousand of these "guided missiles," requiring thirteen hundred naval aviators and eighteen squadrons, Towers demanded that the program be reduced to five hundred assault drones. Vice Admiral Horne, handling the program on behalf of King, concurred. But in July Smith sidestepped Towers by trying to institute the expansion, forcing Jack to have Horne reject it until the experimental concept was proved in combat. Henceforth, Towers viewed Smith with suspicion.[36]

Another thorn in Towers' side was Captain Charles Rosendahl, head of LTA projects in the Office of the Chief of Naval Operations and long antagonistic to Towers. Towers realized that blimps provided a quick, efficient means to patrol coasts and offshore convoys, especially in the Caribbean, and he guardedly accepted legislation in June to increase the 48 authorized blimps to 200. Admiral King wanted Rosendahl moved into BuAer as Towers' special assistant for LTA until the blimp program matured, but Jack quickly informed the zealous Rosendahl that he would have no administrative authority whatsoever. When Rosendahl tried to campaign for a new LTA division at the bureau, Towers elicited King's agreement that Di Gates would insure the viable administration of the blimp program under the existing system. Rosendahl rejected the King-Gates arrangement, complained to Carl Vinson, and became so obnoxious that in late July he was ordered to sea to command a heavy cruiser. In a heated exchange with Towers, he threatened to undertake a letter-writing campaign, which Towers advised against, in Rosendahl's own interests. Rosendahl went to sea.[37]

Towers' confidence in the navy winning command of the sea lay in the fast aircraft carrier, proved in combat by the British in the Atlantic and Mediterranean and by the Japanese at Pearl Harbor. Five days after the attack, in a memorandum to the CNO, Towers confirmed his preference for the projected 27,000-ton large *Essex*-class carrier over any small carrier, but he conceded that emergency construction was essential. In a meeting in Secretary Knox's office on 20 December 1941, Towers therefore agreed with Stark, King, and his fellow bureau chiefs that the conversion of four *Cimarron*-type fleet tankers into additional auxiliary (escort) carriers be undertaken as soon as possible. An impatient FDR advised Secretary of War Henry L. Stimson that he wanted to get more carriers into the Southwest Pacific to challenge the Japanese, and on 14 January 1942 Stimson called in Towers for his views. Towers, who believed that only large fast carriers would be useful in that theater, tried to convince Stimson that to use slower and more vulnerable conversions in those waters would be unsound.[38]

The submarine torpedoing of the *Saratoga* south of Hawaii three days before forced her to retire for major repairs and heightened a festering debate over the protection of her and her sister *Lexington*. Towers wanted their 8-inch guns retained, but King ruled with the majority of his advisers that the large guns be removed as superfluous, which was done immediately. The *Yorktown* was being returned from the Atlantic to the Pacific and would soon be followed by the *Hornet* and the *Wasp*. Whether the new escort carriers would be useful there was still uncertain. But war experience had already convinced the General Board to propose a new and even larger 45,000-ton carrier with an armored flight deck for maximum protection against bomb hits. In a hearing before the board on 6 March Towers testified strongly in favor of such a vessel, arguing that a full air group of larger and heavier planes would require a greater flight-deck area as well.

"In my opinion," declared Towers, "it is perfectly obvious that the spearhead of any offensive in the Pacific must be the carriers." Their survivability against enemy planes based in the Japanese islands and homeland would be best guaranteed by big carriers with armored decks, a lesson the British had learned from German land-based air attacks. As carrier battles over the spring proved the wisdom of these observations, the navy decided to abandon a new 58,000-ton class of battleships in favor of no fewer than ten *Essexes* over the thirteen already authorized, along with four of the new 45,000-tonners, which would become the *Midway*-class battle carrier (CVB). Towers testified for this program in executive session before the Vinson committee in mid-June, and Congress passed it in July.[39]

Though prevented from becoming directly involved in the combat operations of naval aviation, Towers played a major role in assigning carrier captains. It was no secret that he had definite views about which admirals should command carrier operations. He was particularly disturbed when Admiral Nimitz assigned nonaviators to lead some of the first carrier raids in the Pacific. On 1 February the *Enterprise* and the *Yorktown* struck Japanese positions in the Marshall and Gilbert islands in the central Pacific. Though aviator Halsey had the former task force, Rear Admiral Frank Jack Fletcher—Jack's classmate who had disparaged aviation before the war—had the latter. Three weeks later, Vice Admiral Wilson Brown, another black shoe, led the *Lexington* force in a foray toward Rabaul in the South Pacific. When the uneven results of these first air actions were made known, Towers felt his views confirmed and early in March expressed them to Forrestal. Sharing the general desire to hold the line to Australia as the Japanese overran the Philippines, British Malaya, and the Dutch East Indies, Towers agreed that all available naval aviators and aerial torpedoes in Australia should be made available to the army in its desperate defense. But the tiny Asiatic Fleet was obliterated. Jack's old command, the *Langley,* was sunk by Japanese planes while ferrying army fighters to Java. Such reverses cemented his conviction that only experienced aviators should command the surviving American striking forces—the carriers—and that these should be used offensively.[40]

In the matter of promotions Admiral King, not well acquainted with many aviator captains and rear admirals, sought the advice of Admiral Harry Yarnell, who in turn referred to his old chief of staff, Towers, for recommendations. Jack devised two lists, one of flag officers, the other of captains from the academy classes of '11 to '18. He decided that the selectees must exemplify four traits: established professional ability, aggressiveness, physical stamina, and "modernized conceptions," meaning the use of aviation. He then had Captains Duke Ramsey, Ralph Davison, Arthur Radford, and Forrest Sherman collaborate with him. Although they disagreed somewhat, he was struck by their "astonishing unanimity of views."

The two lists were handed to Yarnell on 2 March. Towers had made certain that one-third of the names on each list were aviators. The thirteen airmen of the thirty-nine admirals or admiral-selectees he and his collaborators picked were aviation pioneers Towers, Bellinger, Baldy Pownall, Pete Mitscher, Charlie Mason, and Ramsey, and JCLs King, Arthur Bristol, Jake Fitch, John McCain, Johnny Hoover, Alva Bernhard, and J. W. "Black Jack" Reeves, Jr. Nonaviator Frank Jack Fletcher was also on the list. JCLs Cook, Ernest McWhorter, and Leigh Noyes were not, a bit of a slap at the man who sponsored them, King. The thirteen aviators of the thirty-eight captains recommended were all career pilots: Rosendahl, Henry M. Mullinix, Davison, Jerry Bogan, Radford, Cy Ginder, John Dale Price, Wu Duncan, Harold B. Sallada, Forrest Sherman, and Jock Clark. That virtually every one of the thirty-six aviators Towers listed (except Bristol, who died that April) attained major commands during the war attests to their ability and to Towers' judgment and support of them.[41]

Although King did not consult Towers on flag commands, leaving that to Pacific and Atlantic Fleet commanders Nimitz and Ingersoll, King held long discussions with Towers on 14 April and 1 May over the assignment of aviator captains. Towers was now able to get his own men into key carrier jobs, from which they would surely progress to flag rank and commands. Among others, Ramsey was already earmarked for flag after a tour of duty commanding the *Saratoga*. Davison moved up from head of BuAer planning to succeed Ramsey as assistant chief of BuAer. In May Forrest Sherman relieved Reeves in command of the *Wasp* on the eve of her transfer from Norfolk to the Pacific. And when Rear Admiral Dick Byrd begged to be returned to aviation duty, Towers got him assigned as a special assistant to help establish naval air bases overseas.[42]

In their meeting on 1 May Towers offered King an innovative proposal, "that there be created in the Pacific Fleet a pool of flag officer potential task group commanders and carrier group commanders. . . . With such an arrangement, plans for subsequent operations could be made while task forces were at sea, matters of leave and recreation could be taken care of," and other advantages gained. King agreed to study the unique idea and would in fact adopt it in a matter of weeks.[43]

The Pacific was on both their minds as Admiral Nimitz dispatched the *Yorktown* and the *Lexington* to the Southwest Pacific to intercept a Japanese expeditionary force reportedly moving on southern New Guinea and the southern Solomon islands. In early May, under Admirals Fletcher and Fitch, the two carriers repulsed the Japanese invasion fleet in the Battle of the Coral Sea—the first naval battle in history in which opposing ships had not sighted each other. SBD dive bombers sank an enemy light carrier and damaged two large carriers, but at the cost of the *Lexington* and a badly damaged *Yorktown*. Thus American carrier strength in the Pacific was dangerously weakened. The carrier-versus-carrier action had shown the flattop to be the primary weapon in this war, as Towers never failed to point out.[44]

Another story altogether was the North Atlantic, where PBY and PBM patrols fought the cold weather as well as Hitler's U-boats. Franklin Roosevelt and his military chiefs hoped to mount an amphibious assault against the coast of Nazi-occupied France as soon as possible, spearheaded by a strategic bombing offensive by the RAF and AAF. Unfortunately, until wartime production reached its projected peak in mid-1943, there just were not enough planes to go around. Realizing from the experience of the RAF's Coastal Command that land-based patrol bombers were better suited to all-weather operations over the North Atlantic, Towers included in his January 1942 navy-plane request 1,300 army landplanes—400 four-engine heavy B-24s (navy PB4Ys) and 900 twin-engine medium B-25s (navy PBJs). In midmonth, therefore, he requested Hap Arnold to transfer these from army to navy production, so that the navy could undertake land-based antisubmarine warfare air operations. In response to an AAF query for details, Towers reiterated his request and was backed by a strong endorsement from Admiral King.

Since the army had always been charged with continental landplane defense, Arnold refused to turn over any bombers to navy control. King sent a memo to Towers and Di Gates on 26 February: "The time has come for a show-down on the 'antiquated' premise *revived* in" Arnold's refusal; the peacetime struggle over coast defense had resurfaced. Though reluctant to shift bombers to ASW operations, Arnold and his planners finally followed the example of the RAF and on 9 March offered to create their own AAF antisub force. King did not respond—army pilots were not skilled in overwater navigation and antiship attacks. Meanwhile Towers and his planners continued to urge the AAF to transfer the planes to the navy.

Then, at the end of March, the British offered some advice unwelcome to U.S. Navy ears. Air Marshal Douglas C. S. Evill of the British CCS mission in Washington observed that since Royal Navy torpedo squadrons operated under the RAF's Coastal Command through "close liaison and cooperation," the United States armed forces might do the same with their own antisubmarine air effort. Evill had himself been a naval aviator during World War I before transferring to the RAF. When Secretary of War Stimson relayed this information to Secretary Knox, Knox gave it to Towers for comment, remarking that he intended to take the matter of army landplane transfers directly to the president.

"If Air Marshal Evill," responded Towers strongly on 4 April, "is endeavoring to convince Mr. Stimson that the R.A.F. Coastal Command is an activity which should have its counterpart in the Army Air Forces, his recall should be requested." Echoing the sentiments of King, Towers insisted that " 'liaison and cooperation' are not satisfactory in a fast-moving and coordinated game like anti-submarine warfare. Direct command, authority and responsibility are the only effective means of controlling the diverse elements, aircraft, escort vessels, fleet units, convoys, etc. that comprise our offense and defense against submarines. This is the Navy's job and we ought vigorously to combat any attempt by the Army to encroach on this ground. . . ." This was the U.S. Navy's position, and a sound one, except it ignored the fact that the British navy and air force, after more than two years of fighting the Axis, had indeed learned to cooperate. Such cooperation did not seem possible between American admirals and air generals, and Stimson would not agree with Knox to take the matter to FDR.

Meanwhile, however, U-boats were sinking merchantmen, making interservice compromise essential, which is what Ralph Davison's BuAer planning division recommended to Gates on 23 April. For the navy's part, it suggested that PBY production at Convair be cut back in favor of B-24s and PB2Y Coronados; that Boeing's projected twin-engine PBB Sea Ranger be eliminated so that Boeing could concentrate on army B-17s and B-29s; and that the navy request for B-25s be modified in favor of Lockheed Vega twin-engine PV Ventura landplanes. Bob Lovett agreed on behalf of the army. In late March the AAF had granted vague operational control of antisubmarine warfare to the navy until it established its own related command in early June. At that time the War Department finally conceded landplanes to the navy along the lines proposed by Towers' planners, which led to a formal agreement on 7 July. The solution was far from perfect, but it enabled both air services to face the U-boat threat squarely over the critical year of mid-1942 to mid-1943. At the end of that time, King would have his way by creating the Tenth Fleet and absorbing all AAF antisubmarine functions, which was the ideal solution.[45]

Unfortunately for Hap Arnold, he lacked the planes to support FDR's desired cross-channel assault on occupied France in 1942 unless the British allocation was reduced. In April, therefore, the CCS charged its three key air leaders—Arnold, Towers, and Air Marshal Evill—with the task of reexamining aircraft allocations. In so doing, Towers was surprised to learn that Arnold seemed to have CCS support in cutting transport planes promised to Soviet Russia. Accordingly he wrote a memo to King on the twentieth warning against the political ramifications of such a plan and criticizing Arnold for thinking only of the AAF. King, impressed by Towers' reasoning, forwarded the memo to General Marshall. Marshall replied that Towers, "not fully informed" about the cross-channel plans, was ignorant of the critical need for paratroop-carrying and glider-towing transports for that operation. This was true, Towers not being privy to the highest-level planning of the JCS. So Russia did not get the transports, though it did receive an Anglo-American promise to open the second or Western Front before the end of the year. At the same time the British wanted more American-built planes with which to shore up their defenses in the Middle East.[46]

With these strategic matters before it, the so-called Arnold-Evill-Towers Board deliberated over the respective needs of the AAF, Great Britain, and U.S. naval aviation. When on 6 May Evill objected outright to American demands to cut back allocations to Britain by five thousand planes, Arnold wanted to dump the whole matter back into the lap of the CCS. But he agreed with Towers first to allow Evill a chance to study and discuss the situation with his superiors. Evill had received no reply from Air Marshal Portal in London when the three men met again on 8 and 15 May. Instead, FDR received a message from Winston Churchill on the twelfth asking for two hundred transport planes along with two hundred F4F Martlets (Wildcats) to reinforce British carriers in the Indian Ocean. On the advice of his counsellors, Roosevelt decided that Arnold, Towers, and Evill should fly to London to work out a new allocation policy with Portal and the Royal Navy, then bring Portal back with them "for the final discussion."[47]

On 20 May FDR and Harry Hopkins summoned Marshall, King, Arnold, and Towers to the White House to discuss the American position that the two aviation leaders would take to Britain. FDR wanted all American-built planes in Britain and the Middle East (Syria) to be manned by American personnel, which, however, Marshall opposed as impracticable. Towers observed that American pilots could hardly be expected to man U.S.-built British naval aircraft in the fleet air arm or the RAF's Coastal Command, with which FDR agreed.

Towers then held forth on the general aircraft situation, namely, that the navy had asked for very few modifications to the existing allocations schedule, a position the Admiralty found entirely just. Inasmuch as AAF and RAF expansion plans were based on the same production planes, Towers noted, "British Lend-Lease aircraft were being counted twice." Something had to be done, but Towers, seconded by FDR and King, doubted whether the British would "agree to accept any modifications of real magnitude." The conferees decided that Arnold and Towers should insist that American-built planes be utilized to develop and train U.S. crews for the cross-channel attack, except for PBYs and Coastal Command planes. For British operations defending Egypt, the British could operate U.S.-supplied planes. The conferees also agreed with Towers' suggestion for a compromise, if necessary, to strengthen RAF units in the Middle East. And the Russians would continue to man American-built planes.[48]

FDR kept Towers after the meeting to instruct him to sound out the British on a scheme of his. Like Churchill, the president liked to dabble in operational ideas. He believed the German battleship *Tirpitz,* though helpless at anchor in a Norwegian fjord, ought to be attacked by carrier-based dive bombers for propaganda purposes. Since no U.S. carrier was available, FDR thought that an American SBD squadron might be loaned to the British for the mission. Towers made a quick study and decided the best means for success would be for a British carrier to retire at high speed after launching its fighters and bombers. Following the attack, they could fly west and land in the Orkney and Shetland islands. Towers, however, would find the British opposed to risking one of their carriers for such an uncertain adventure, which they had already tried.[49]

Towers reported before dawn of 23 May to Washington's Bolling Field, accompanied by George Anderson. Hap Arnold and Colonel Hoyt S. Vandenberg were there from the AAF, as well as Air Marshal Evill and army Major Generals Dwight Eisenhower and Mark W. Clark. They boarded an AAF four-engine C-54 transport and took off. After being forced by foul weather to lay over one night at Gander, Newfoundland, they reached Prestwick, Scotland, late on the twenty-fourth. The party boarded the train to

London, where it was met by Ambassador John G. Winant and various British officials. Towers and Anderson were given rooms at the Dorchester Hotel as guests of the Royal Navy. Then, at 1100 on the twenty-fifth, the British and American officers and Lend-Lease representative Averell Harriman gathered at No. 10 Downing Street to begin negotiations with Churchill and his air commanders.[50]

Churchill wondered why the Americans, with a 60,000-plane program, were quibbling over a mere 5,000 to be allocated to the British. Arnold cautioned that current allocations were inadequate for defending Anglo-American territory in the Pacific and Indian oceans. When the prime minister called on Towers he, Arnold recorded, "said his problem was simple and could be ironed out without difficulty. [The] Navy needed only torpedo planes, dive bombers, and fighters for carriers, with patrol bombers." Arnold asked if the navy "did not also need heavy land-based bomber support." "Why certainly," Jack responded, but Arnold had caught him short for overlooking the festering antisubmarine controversy at home.[51]

The British seemed generally amenable to adjusting aircraft allocations, wanting only to maintain current fighter levels on all fronts. The rapt attention the London press paid to Arnold and Towers fed speculation about the forthcoming American bomber offensive and future Allied plans, and the spirit of cooperation was repeated in the rounds of official receptions and inspections.

The Admiralty and Coastal Command wanted 150 PBYs over the summer and to trade 85 U.S. Navy land-based Venturas for an equal number of PBY Catalina amphibians then in production. Towers agreed to this and to the Coastal Command's request for 244 antisubmarine B-17s over the remainder of the year. But Arnold did not, citing basic differences over strategic priorities: "I told them that the number looked excessive and that the whole question had to be decided upon as to which use was the more important—using heavy bombers to carry bombs into Germany, or to go hunting for submarines."[52]

In their long association, Towers and Arnold had no sharper disagreement than this one over projected allocations of B-17s. They clashed openly in a meeting with Air Ministry officials on 28 May. Arnold stated flatly that he could not accept the requested B-17 allocations and, according to Towers, "made various accusations against the British representatives regarding concealment of figures, etc. I took issue with Arnold on a number of matters." First, when Arnold asked if navy patrol squadrons could be sent over to help the Coastal Command, Towers said none could be spared.

Second, Towers said that more transport planes could be had by converting one B-17 factory to cargo plane production. Asked what the navy could convert, Towers replied that nothing the navy had in production could help; again, multi-engine supporters failed to appreciate the months required to convert a plant from production of single-engine planes or flying boats to production of large landplanes. And third, when final statistics were called for, Towers wanted another day to work up the navy's. With that the meeting broke up, nothing definite having been decided.[53]

Jack actually wanted the delay to resolve his differences with Arnold. Supported by Stark, he persuaded Arnold to see Portal again. Arnold did, the following morning, and while he refused to give up any B-17s he did suggest B-24 Liberators in their stead and offered to turn over a large quantity of light twin-engine bombers. George Anderson worked out the details for the navy part of the agreement, which primarily involved PBYs. On 30 May, Air Marshal Slessor and Admiral Lyster agreed to it on behalf of the British.[54]

It is a tribute to Hap Arnold's honesty and generosity that in 1949 when he recounted these events in his otherwise candid memoirs he did not mention Towers by name, only the generic "our Naval officers." "It looked to me, at that time," recalled Arnold, "as if we were travelling a one-way street. The Army Air Forces was expected to give everything to everybody, and nobody was going to help the Army Air Forces. Naturally, from then on, I had to take a much more hard-boiled attitude."[55]

The final decision of course rested with the higher-ups, and it was agreed that when Arnold and Towers returned home they would be accompanied by Air Marshal Slessor as Portal's representative and by Vice Admiral Louis Mountbatten of the Royal Navy. In spite of their differences over allocations, Arnold and Towers had developed a sound basis for hammering out a final solution.

Before leaving Britain they had a weekend fling with other guests of Churchill at the opulent Chequers, the country estate of prime ministers. After a tasteless dinner on 30 May, the guests were treated to a movie. When it started Towers noticed in Churchill's possession a full decanter of brandy with a straw, and during the movie he heard slurping sounds coming from the prime minister. When the lights came back on the bottle was empty, yet Churchill showed no effects whatsoever. He wanted to talk more and kept his guests up till the wee hours. "There was considerable excitement all during the evening," Towers recorded, "due to the bombing raid on Cologne," the RAF's largest such raid to date, "and news coming in from the Libyan campaign" as the British army battled Rommel's Afrika Corps.[56]

On Sunday morning Towers and Arnold breakfasted together in the large dining room, after which they both visited the john. The impish Arnold turned the key in the lock to Jack's stall and he couldn't get it open. Jack, recalled Arnold, "called to me in great consternation to come and help him. Thirty-odd years before, he had contributed to the invention of aviation's first safety-belt, but it couldn't aid him now." No help was available because all the carpenters were in town, it being Sunday, and Arnold left Towers to his fate to go for a stroll in the garden with Churchill's wife Clementine. Suddenly, "to our surprise," he wrote, "we saw first the feet, then the blue uniform trousers, and finally the full uniform of an American admiral climbing out of a window on the first floor of Chequers Castle [and down a drainpipe]. Mrs. Churchill said, 'My what an extraordinary way to leave the house!' " According to Arnold's aide, Colonel Eugene Beebe, everyone gave Towers "quite the razz on account of that little incident."[57]

"England is the place to win the war," Arnold jotted in his log. "Get planes and troops over as soon as possible." But intelligence from the Pacific revealed ominous moves by the Japanese, and as the C-54 winged the conferees back to Washington Arnold spent an hour with Averell Harriman. Harriman shared Arnold's fears: "We are so afraid of a Japanese raid that we are apt to postpone our main objectives."[58]

On 4 June, as Arnold and Towers reported on their London visit before the JCS and then met with the CCS, the epic Battle of Midway raged in the Central Pacific. When it ended, four Japanese carriers had been sunk by planes from the *Enterprise, Yorktown,* and *Hornet,* under the command of nonaviators Spruance and Fletcher. This victory came at the cost of the *Yorktown* and most of the obsolescent TBD torpedo planes and their crews. Meanwhile the Allied situation on the other war fronts of the world looked bleak, with Hitler's Wehrmacht hammering away at Soviet Russia and the Suez Canal, threatening vital British Middle Eastern oil fields and the lifeline to India.

American aircraft production being a key element for turning the tide, Towers and Arnold conferred with Air Marshals Slessor and Evill on 20 June and finalized what now came to be known as the Arnold-Towers-Portal Agreement, which all parties accepted by 2 July. Aircraft allocations to the British would be cut by nearly 4,000 planes, 718 of which were naval, though American-built planes lost through attrition would be replaced. Monthly schedules of deliveries were established, along with dates for assigning American air units to the secondary theaters of war. The agreement also committed the United States to supplying aircraft to Australia and New Zealand. It took effect in August, to last through the following April.[59]

With the Pacific Fleet down to four carriers—the *Saratoga, Enterprise, Wasp,* and *Hornet*—Towers looked to the future, the new *Essexes*, but the European theater always crowded to the fore. On 10 July he attended a special meeting of the JCS to consider a new strategic proposal just received from the British. Given the fact that Soviet Russia might succumb to the German offensive, Churchill and the British chiefs wanted to abandon the 1942 cross-channel invasion, staging instead an Allied landing in North Africa to ease the pressure on Suez. General Marshall reacted adversely to such an expensive sideshow, with which King heartily agreed, and Towers added his objection to the transfer of carriers from the Pacific to support a North African operation. Impatient with the British, Marshall proposed that instead of North Africa or a cross-channel operation, an all-out effort be launched in the Pacific—entirely to the navy's liking. Four days went by before FDR agreed with Churchill; a landing in Axis-held Morocco would at least be a step toward the primary goal of defeating Germany. Subsequent deliberations set the North Africa assault for November, but rather than employing carriers from the Pacific to support it, the Atlantic Fleet would use the *Ranger* and the four newly converted *Cimarron* escort carriers.[60]

The global character of World War II demanded transport planes to move key personnel, critical materials, and light cargo rapidly between bases and theaters and across continents and oceans. After Pearl Harbor the army, in charge of cargo plane production, had ordered cutbacks in favor of more bombers. Towers continually urged more four-engine DC-4s (C-54s) for both services, but the War Department refused to listen. In desperation, therefore, he arranged contracts with two newcomers for such aircraft, inferior though the designs were. In March, using a BuAer-Vought-Sikorsky design, the Nash-Kelvinator corporation received a navy order for one hundred JRK four-engine transoceanic flying boats. Then Towers resurrected a three-year-old proposal by the Edwin G. Budd Manufacturing Company—a railroad firm!—to build a transport plane from stainless steel rather than desperately needed aluminum. In April he signed a contract for no fewer than eight hundred of these twin-engine cargo landplanes. Only two hundred were for navy use as RB Conestogas; the rest were reserved for the AAF as C-93s.[61]

As in the matter of antisubmarine warfare, the War Department could not ignore such navy initiatives, and it reversed itself with a vengeance to produce cargo planes. Not only did the AAF decide to establish its own air transport command and refuse the new transport plane production, but Towers learned on 18 May, while renegotiating the navy's existing Pan Am transport contract, that the AAF intended to "gain complete control of all commercial air lines, domestic and overseas, and have sole control over any transport lines established by the Government." Towers had already turned down a proposal in March for the navy to take over Pan Am, and he alerted Forrestal and Horne to the AAF's scheme.[62]

The very next day, reasoning that the best defense against an AAF takeover was a strengthened NATS, Towers suggested to Horne that it be placed in his, Towers', proposed new office of assistant CNO (air) and headed by an experienced aviator. Captain Frank Wagner got the nod, and though the reorganization proved to be short-lived, NATS emerged as a separate office under the CNO. The move did not discourage the War Department, however, from trying to dictate cargo plane policy in order to emphasize its strategic bombers. On the Army-Navy Munitions Board and before congressional committees, the case for bombers over transports was pressed by Undersecretary of War Patterson, "who," wrote Towers in 1947, "rather blindly accepted the Air Force views rather than giving the matter any serious personal study," a criticism shared by WPB, Morgenthau, and the British. "Actually Arnold and Company were wishfully thinking that the Army could win the war with bombs: that such an outcome would add inestimable prestige to the Army Air Force, and therefore it must be followed regardless."[63]

The controversy heated up in late July when Patterson gained JCS approval to reject the WPB schedule for more cargo planes, including Towers' two emergency aircraft, the JRK and the RB. Towers convinced Forrestal and Horne to oppose the army's moves, though Ferdinand Eberstadt of the Munitions Board tried to work out a solution. Meanwhile, the heavy U-boat sinkings of merchant ships in the Atlantic made Congress, the public, and even the military receptive to fresh ideas.

Onto the stage stepped industrialist Henry J. Kaiser, a peerless manager whose personal dedication to winning the Battle of the Atlantic had caught the public's fancy, notably his mass production of merchant ships. To take navy air power directly to Hitler's U-boat wolf packs, Kaiser convinced the government in June to let him turn out no fewer than fifty of a new class of escort carriers. Now, in July, he announced in the press that the ultimate solution was to transport cargo *over* the subs, in huge flying boats. He offered to turn out five thousand of Martin's big 72-ton four-engine PB2M Mars flying boats as transports. In addition, he wanted to design and develop a giant

200-ton "flying cargo ship"—in effect a bulk cargo carrier with a 150-ton payload and a range of 3,700 miles, making it immune to U-boat attack.[64]

Towers, respect him though he did, could not get Kaiser to provide definite detailed proposals for the two projects. This he reported on 5 August to a special Senate committee taken in by the industrialist's naive notion that cargo planes in any number could compete with ships in bulk tonnage carrying capacity. In private meetings at his office and in Kaiser's hotel room, Jack found the man's cost estimates to be unrealistically low and his requirements for machine tooling unavailable from industry.

Kaiser obviously lacked knowledge of aircraft manufacturing, and an industry already committed to its own contracts was in no position to help him, nor did it really care to. Towers summoned Reuben Fleet from San Diego for counsel and, with Babe Meigs and T. P. Wright of the WPB, drew up letters of intent to support Kaiser's plans as long as they did not interfere with existing war production and strategic materials. Kaiser resented such restrictions, also Forrestal's suggestion that he take ninety days' leave from other activities to come to Washington and solve the problems with his cargo plane scheme.[65]

The WPB's Donald Nelson, under political and public pressure, felt he had to give Kaiser *some* kind of contract, even as Towers and the navy took a long look at their cargo plane needs. Towers invited Glenn Martin to produce a potential cargo version of the Mars but said the navy would not need a huge fleet of them. Too much material and too many facilities would be required, Towers advised Congress, to produce in quantity a plane already "obsolete as far as performance is concerned." This killed Kaiser's bid to build five hundred more Mars boats, although Martin's company would eventually turn out a few of them in the JRM transport configuration.

Kaiser did conclude a partnership with the brilliant airplane engineer and manufacturer Howard Hughes to develop the 200-tonner. When the Kaiser-Hughes group offered to design and build such a flying boat of "duramold or some other non-metallic material" not critical to other production, Nelson had his solution. He obtained the approval of Towers and Bob Lovett of the War Department for both services to underwrite the construction of three experimental big boats within two years. Kaiser subsequently let Hughes take over the whole project, which Towers would examine when he visited Hughes' plant early in 1944. It had partially completed one eight-engine seaplane, already a white elephant, eventually nicknamed the Spruce Goose. Jack admired it but thought its production a waste of talent; the government cancelled the contract that February. Hughes continued with his own resources, but the Spruce Goose flew only once, and then just skimming the water.[66]

Meanwhile, the War Department continued to consolidate its control over transport aviation. On 6 August it canceled Pan Am's contract for the South American ferry route. NATS, however, maintained its contracts with Pan Am and American Export Air and drew several hundred landplanes from the army, notably the DC-3 or C-47 (navy R4D) and the DC-4 or C-54 (navy R5D).[67]

As for the Battle of the Atlantic, army and navy antisubmarine forces— land-based, seaplane, blimp, and convoy—faced a long and difficult autumn, winter, and spring. Not until the escort carriers appeared in hunter-killer groups would the tide begin to turn against the U-boat. Quantity production of these antisub weapons and of merchantmen would then erase the memory of the briefly considered miracle cargo planes.

No one in the high command—neither FDR, Knox, Marshall, King, nor Arnold—could deny that Admiral Towers was ably representing the navy and its aviation in high-level conferences at home and abroad. But Towers continued to be rankled by the fact that he was not accorded the rank, vice admiral, to match that of his counterpart in the army, Lieutenant General Arnold. Nor were the carrier forces in the Pacific being led by the men most qualified—aviators. In spite of Fletcher's and Spruance's victories at Coral Sea and Midway, the *Lexington* and the *Yorktown* had been lost. Thus Towers continued to press for his own promotion and for carrier task forces led by aviation admirals.[68]

At the beginning of July, Carl Vinson wrote a letter to the president urging that the post of chief of BuAer carry the rank of vice admiral for the duration. His reasons included the fact that Towers was outranked by all other officers when he attended JCS and JAC meetings, that he had the same rank as most other admirals in aviation, and that another officer, Halsey, held an aviation command in the rank of vice admiral. FDR liked the idea but revised it. When he brought it up with Secretary Knox the latter agreed immediately, namely, that Towers relinquish his post as BuAer chief and become a member of King's staff in the rank of vice admiral.[69]

Whether or not King or Towers wanted such an arrangement is not known—probably neither one did. FDR and Knox had certainly twisted Vinson's intent. Under King, Towers would no longer enjoy the relative freedom he had exercised by reporting directly to the secretary. This was borne out on 8 July when he had a long discussion with William C. Bullitt, a veteran diplomat whom Knox had just appointed as his special assistant. Towers revealed that morale among naval aviators was low because their own seniors were not being given carrier force commands. Criticism of the navy over this neglect was mounting in the press, and Towers believed that unless Knox took drastic action he would surely become the target of that criticism. Bullitt agreed to discuss the matter with Knox that very evening.[70]

The secretary did not appreciate such forthrightness. "Knox, ever since Pearl Harbor," one news analyst would write in September, "has become increasingly touchy, and now is extremely hard for independent-minded admirals to deal with"; Towers "wouldn't 'yes' Secretary Knox on demand." In April, for example, Knox had retained King, Horne, and Towers after his regular morning conference to state, in Towers' words, "that he felt he was not being consulted sufficiently with regard to such matters" as approving funding for training bases in Florida. He rejected Towers' explanation that the bases had been approved through normal channels until Towers was able to produce documents proving that Assistant Secretary Bard had signed them as acting secretary when Knox was away. It was just such assertiveness from his admirals that annoyed Knox.[71]

Perhaps that is why Knox welcomed FDR's suggestion to transfer Towers to King's custody. Knox did not sign or even rate Towers' fitness report for the period October to March. Undersecretary Jim Forrestal was Towers' champion in the front office, and it was he as acting secretary rather than Knox who would give Towers 4.0 marks on the subsequent fitness report in October 1942. Yet even Forrestal would mark Towers down with respect to cooperation; in this alone, Towers was not "exceptionally successful." On an inspection trip of several bases in Florida late in July, Towers shared his frustrations with Captain Jerry Bogan, commanding at Miami. "Admiral," said his old shipmate, "shouldn't you walk soft, maybe, for a while? You are bucking some strong people even if you are right!" "They can't touch me," retorted Jack. "They wouldn't dare!"[72]

On 15 July Towers received three vaccinations, for cowpox, typhoid, and tetanus, an indication that he expected to be transferred to the Pacific, either by the intimation of his superiors or because of wishful thinking.[73] That very morning an editorial appeared in the *Washington Post* announcing the need for air admirals in the fleet. It prompted reporter John Norris of the same paper to seek an interview with Towers. In the meantime, *Time* magazine also advocated the case of aviators. Towers, though he disliked appearing in press conferences, decided to hold one, and so on 18 July Norris and his colleagues of the press gathered in BuAer's boardroom. In walked the admiral, quiet but assured. "The aircraft carrier will spearhead this war," he remarked. "Successful action . . . will be accomplished by naval aviation operating from aircraft carriers fighting as the Number One naval strength. The battleship is no longer the spearhead."

This was old hat within BuAer and among members of the General Board, both forward-looking organizations. The Gun Club had heard the idea and didn't like it. To the press, however, it was revolutionary. "Silence . . . fell like a thick blanket" over the boardroom, Joy Hancock recalled. Then John Norris spoke up. "Will you repeat that, Admiral?"

"The aircraft carrier will spearhead the action in this war," replied Towers quietly.[74]

The journalistic shock waves generated by this remark reverberated throughout Washington and the land. On the front page of next day's *Washington Post* Norris' double-column story carried the headline "Flying Men Have Little Say in Navy's Councils." Because King's staff had few air officers, and Towers had not been promoted to vice admiral or retained as assistant CNO (air), "the naval airmen are not getting a fair deal. More important, neither is the Nation." Norris pointed out that the army now required half of its officers on the General Staff to be aviators, in marked contrast to the navy. Navy aviators, moreover, resented the disparity between their own ranks and those of hastily promoted AAF officers. The story quoted a sign posted in a navy officers' club: "No drinks served to lieutenant colonels of the Air Force under 21 years of age who are not accompanied by their parents." As for the matter of nonairmen commanding carrier forces at sea, naval aviators grumbled that an even greater victory could have been won at Midway if the retreating enemy fleet had been aggressively pursued.

An editorial in the *New York Times* the same day called for reform in the Navy: "Surely the huge and growing importance of our power at sea, as well as on land, would justify far greater emphasis on assignment and elevation in rank of trained air officers in the naval arm, not only abroad but especially in Washington." Similar sentiments were expressed by other newspapers in the ensuing week, and Towers was interviewed by several reporters seeking details.[75]

The most adverse reaction came from Secretary Knox, who the next day discussed the matter with Towers, Assistant Secretary Di Gates, and Admiral Russell Willson, King's chief of staff. During the discussion Knox "asked what measures could be taken to counteract the effects of the *Post* article. I told him the most effective measures would be to make those changes about which the Department is in agreement should be made, primarily to cease assigning as Task Force commanders of groups built up around a carrier or carriers flag officers who are not qualified aviators and therefore who necessarily are lacking the experience regarding carrier operations."[76]

Towers' carefully worded reference to the Navy Department referred to plans already initiated to bring more air admirals into task force commands. Still, although Admiral King dominated flag promotions, he avoided imposing tactical commanders on Nimitz, whose judgment in such matters he trusted. The most King or Towers could do was provide the men; Nimitz selected the ones he wanted. King continued to rely heavily on Towers' advice for the right people, particularly in light of the controversy. On 23 and 24 July Towers personally delivered to King's personnel chief his recommendations regarding promotions to rear admiral, captain, and commander. In two separate meetings in August he went over these lists with Knox, King, Horne, and key BuPers officers.[77]

But Nimitz had already assigned his carrier flag officers for the Marine Corps landing at Guadalcanal to thwart a fresh Japanese advance into the South Pacific. The carrier covering force was under the command of Fletcher in the *Saratoga,* with Thomas C. Kinkaid in the *Enterprise* and Leigh Noyes in the *Wasp*—two cruiser men and a JCL. The *Hornet* was still in Hawaii training pilots. The landings on 7 August went unopposed, except that Fletcher decided to abandon Admiral Kelly Turner's amphibious forces for fear of a possible counterattack by five Japanese carriers at Rabaul. On the ninth, when a Japanese cruiser force made a surprise night attack in the Battle of Savo Island, it sank four cruisers. All that Towers could say about Fletcher was, "He ran away!" Two weeks later, in the Battle of the Eastern Solomons, Fletcher erratically fought his three carriers against three of Japan's, sinking one. The *Enterprise* was forced to withdraw after receiving heavy bomb damage. And on the thirty-first the poor old *Saratoga* was torpedoed by a Japanese submarine for the second time in the war and had to pull out.[78]

Fletcher was relieved for rest and recuperation after a fairly unimpressive display of command. To his credit, however, he penned a long letter to Nimitz that repeated what Towers had been saying: "The experiences of this war so far have shown that command of the air is the decisive factor in naval engagements, and fleets must be built around the carrier rather than the battleship." But he concluded his six-page discussion of carrier tactics with a statement that epitomized the defensive attitude: "A carrier task force should turn and as soon as possible run away at high speed from an impending air attack." As Towers said, he ran away.[79]

In spite of Secretary Knox's disaffection with Towers over his earlier pronouncements to the press, Jack was clearly the recognized spokesman for the navy in all aspects of aviation. In fact, the director of public relations at the Navy Department, Captain Leland P. Lovette, and a civilian aide, Frank Mason, wanted Towers to give another interview to the press in order to calm the criticism. And several individuals urged him to take a more aggressive stance in open forum. But Towers had had more than enough of publicity, and he knew that another press conference would only be detrimental to the navy.[80]

In the midst of all the hoopla President Roosevelt discovered that, in spite of his oft-repeated statements for the country to build up to 45,000 combat planes and 15,000 trainers in 1942, the goal would not be met—nor would the projection of 100,000 and 25,000 more during 1943. Late in August he demanded explanations from the navy in the persons of King and Towers. The latter maintained that the new demands for antisubmarine warfare, changing needs in the Pacific, forthcoming carriers, Allied requirements, and other factors made the WPB 1943 goal of 107,000, with the navy's part to be 23,500, a more realistic one. King, realizing this lower figure would not satisfy the president, called for a "theoretical" 1943 navy goal of 45,500 of the total 125,000 planes FDR wanted. In particular King differed with Towers in wanting to cut back seaplane production in favor of more antisubmarine landplanes. Hap Arnold called for 131,000 planes in 1943, leading an appalled Bob Lovett to bypass him and tell Forrestal and King to settle for 107,000. Lovett used the same tactic with Harry Hopkins, who finally got FDR to accept it as well. The groundwork laid during 1942 enabled the aircraft industry to shift into high gear in 1943, although in fact it would only be able to turn out 86,000 planes that year.[81]

Though down the years King maintained his professional respect for Towers, he shared the disdain of many officers for what they viewed as "the Towers gang," that growing clique of career aviators who followed the lead of the senior pioneer. And King was among those who resented Towers' strong political support from the likes of Carl Vinson. The emergence of so many ACIOs from Towers' Quonset Point program generated much criticism, reflected in columnist Drew Pearson's jibe that "a lot of Admiral Towers' sociable friends somehow or other fell into cellophane [i.e., transparent] commissions." These and other well-heeled aviation talents regarded the advocates of "trade school" (Annapolis) thinking with equal disdain. They reflected Towers' feelings but, lacking his tact, only exacerbated their leader's difficulties. King could also do without Towers' growing power and independence at the Navy Department. And Knox would eliminate it. The secretary wanted Towers transferred.[82]

King and Towers could agree on one thing: the need for aggressive commanders in the fleet and sound administrators in the vital training commands. On 2 September Jack recommended to King the immediate promotion to flag rank of seven aviator captains—Putty Read, Elliott Buckmaster, Duke Ramsey, Charlie Mason, Alfred Montgomery, Arthur C. Davis, and Frank Wagner, all career airmen save JCL Buckmaster. Towers then recommended men as first chiefs of the new training commands: Read, the technical command; Buckmaster, the primary command; and George Murray, the Naval Air Training Center at Pensacola. It may be said that Towers regarded these three individuals as better managers than combat commanders. King approved all the recommendations without reservation, and the navy immediately announced that it was accelerating aviators more quickly to fill important posts. The press lauded the seven new "flying admirals."[83]

Events in the Pacific were moving at a rapid pace, requiring even greater administrative streamlining. The pool of task force commanders that Towers had recommended enabled the various admirals to take carriers to sea when needed, whether or not they happened to be naval aviators. Since all type commanders should be shore-based at Pearl, on 1 September Nimitz combined the carrier and patrol wing type commands under one commander Air Force Pacific Fleet (ComAirPac) and appointed Rear Admiral Jake Fitch to the post. Undersecretary Forrestal, on an inspection tour in the South Pacific, saw that the theater and land-based air commanders, Vice Admiral Lee Ghormley and Rear Admiral John McCain, were exhausted.[84]

Admirals King and Nimitz had this information when they conferred at San Francisco on 7–8 September. King wanted Towers for the job of ComAirPac; he also wanted to grant Towers a third star. Nimitz could not refuse, for he owed King a favor after the latter transferred a meddlesome Admiral Claude Bloch from Hawaii as Fourteenth Naval District commander. McCain, a King man, could then relieve Towers as chief of BuAer. Halsey, returning to sea, would report administratively to Towers and operationally as senior carrier task force commander to Ghormley. Nimitz, no doubt reluctant to accept the man with whom he had clashed over personnel policies, could not, however, deny Towers' expertise.[85]

On the morning of 12 September Secretary Knox called Towers in to give him the news. Apparently not surprised to learn of his projected transfer to the Pacific, Jack was, however, shocked at the selection of McCain to relieve him. He told Knox that while he was delighted at his own assignment to Pearl Harbor, Admiral McCain was not qualified for duty at BuAer since he lacked any experience in procurement. Jack suggested that "he give this matter very careful consideration, as I was fearful of the prospective situation and particularly fearful that he would be subjected to criticism for nominating as Chief of Bureau an officer not qualified. He stated laughingly that he was quite accustomed to criticism and tried to dismiss the matter. I told him that there were a number of officers whom I did consider qualified, and named Ramsey, Davison, and Radford. He appeared unconcerned." Knox would be glad to have Towers out of his hair.[86]

Towers' concern about McCain was genuine. As Drew Pearson noted in his syndicated column, McCain "is a tough fighting flier, who can boast both the vices and virtues of Ulysses S. Grant." Personally he was a fine fellow whom everyone liked. The fact that he rolled his own Bull Durham cigarettes and let the tobacco dribble all over his uniform placed him in marked contrast to the spit-and-polish Towers. Though able, McCain preferred to delegate administrative responsibilities, and in the future the men of the Towers team—Radford, McQuiston, Kraus, and especially Ralph Davison—would run BuAer for him.[87]

When the news circulated, Hap Arnold wrote Towers a letter of congratulations and sympathy. Replied Jack: "I, too, feel that you and I working together under extreme difficulties and much pressure through these past several years, have managed to coordinate our respective organizations in a manner which left little to be desired, and it is my sincere hope that my successor, surrounded as he will be with officers who know my views and understand your problems as well as ours, will slip right into the groove."[88]

While Towers would be headquartered in Hawaii, Halsey was to have the carriers—if any were left. By September only the *Wasp* and the *Hornet,* flying the flags of Leigh Noyes and George Murray respectively, were operational; the *Saratoga* and the *Enterprise* were out of service for repairs. Then, on the fifteenth, a Japanese submarine torpedoed the *Wasp* while she was escorting a Guadalcanal convoy, and Captain Forrest Sherman had no choice but to order her scuttled. At least the debacle released the superb Sherman for duty elsewhere; Towers immediately obtained Nimitz's permission to take him on as Jack's chief of staff. Meanwhile Halsey concentrated on preparing the *Enterprise* for sea.[87]

To the announcement that Towers' new job was "the most important air command afloat," that is, away from Washington, the press reacted in mixed ways, depending on journalists' knowledge of the facts. *Collier's* magazine thought the move a "silly" way to get Towers promoted. A particularly caustic *Time* magazine, under the kicker "Battle Lost," rated the change "a demotion for the Navy's air arm." For, in spite of McCain's brief tenure in aviation and his being "a good officer," he was really "a battleship admiral with pay-and-a-half and a flying suit." This left "no airman in a position to participate in the strategic thinking of the Navy." The *New York Times* reported "unconcealed disappointment" among naval aviators at McCain's appointment and in an editorial lauded Towers' "fine qualities of leadership," hoping his new appointment meant a change in navy command policy. The editors of the *Washington Post* adopted a wait-and-see attitude about Towers' new role. But most papers, like the Charlotte *News,* hoped that Towers' new post meant a more aggressive attitude in the Pacific. "[T]here is nowhere in the world," it gushed, "another man so suited for the job."[90]

Needless to say, Frank Knox did not share this opinion, nor did he care for the criticism in the press. Returning from a long trip in mid-October, the secretary wrote to Nimitz about "the considerable newspaper comment, aroused, I think, by unwise and ill-informed friends of Towers. Consequently, McCain will have to break down some unfriendliness . . . in certain quarters, which I feel sure he can do. I feel certain, in addition, that the Bureau itself will gain by the change. Towers, while able, is not a good administrator or coordinator. I think McCain is both." Knox was plainly wrong about Towers' lack of ability; he was simply *too* good for the secretary's taste. The letter must have come as no comfort to Nimitz, Towers' new boss.[91]

Towers' promotion made him the first pioneer aviator to attain the rank of vice admiral; for this and the new position expressions of praise were in order. "I want to congratulate you," wrote Treasury Secretary Henry Morgenthau, "upon this recognition of the brilliant and loyal service you have rendered, and I know that the country is also to be congratulated upon having a man of your caliber in this important post." In thanking him, Towers expressed honest regret at leaving Washington with so many tasks unaccomplished.[92]

Jack would have to leave Pierre behind, as navy wives were forbidden to live in the Hawaiian war zone. Daughter Marjorie, again pregnant, had come back to Washington with her husband, now on duty at BuAer. Son Chas, who had already earned his private pilot's license while working at Grumman, had enlisted in the navy and at twenty-two began his flight training as an aviation cadet.

Pierre looked forward to at least one pleasant task in the immediate future. In March, because of her French origins, she had been invited by Knox to christen the second of the *Essex*-class carriers, the *Bon Homme Richard* (CV-10), named for the French-built frigate commanded by John Paul Jones during the American Revolution. However, in September when the navy finally announced the sinking of the *Yorktown* (CV-5) in June, it decided to change the name of CV-10 to *Yorktown* in honor of the first one. Knox now wanted Eleanor Roosevelt to christen the CV-10, since she had also launched the predecessor. Admiral Jacobs had the unpleasant duty of informing Jack of the switch. Jim Forrestal wrote a disappointed Pierre the formal letter, to which she replied gracefully but not without a barb: *"Qui donne qui reprend va en enfer,"* meaning "He who gives and takes back goes to hell"—an Indian-giver. Forrestal said she could later christen another carrier to be named *Bon Homme Richard* (CV-31).[93]

The morning of 2 October "Slew" McCain arrived at the bureau, and Towers immediately turned over the reins to him. From his BuAer staff Jack had selected Commander Gus Read to be his flag secretary, Lieutenant (jg) A. Lee Loomis his flag lieutenant. Bidding their wives farewell at Anacostia on the eighth, they flew to San Diego, then Alameda, where Towers received his vice admiral's commission on the twelfth. On the thirteenth, they boarded the Pan Am–operated navy Clipper flying boat for Hawaii. Little did Jack know that he would remain there, in the Pacific, for four and a half years.[94]

As Gus Read observed many years later, Towers "was the kind of man who wouldn't take any credit for anything he did, and I never noticed that he got particular credit anyway for a lot of things that he did," but his contribution to the Allies' ultimate victory was "incalculable." Or, as the editors of the Charlotte *News* had observed in September: "The U.S. can thank him today for the finest naval aviation in existence." Towers' three years as chief of BuAer had been an unqualified success.[95]

There is no more poignant expression of this judgment than a letter Jack received from Babe Meigs, chief of the WPB's aircraft branch.

> When I reached the office this morning I was conscious of a sense of depression. Analysis of the reason brought forth the fact that this is the day you are leaving the Bureau. I can't tell you how much I am going to miss you, not only from a personal standpoint but from a professional one as well. We here in the Aircraft Division always felt perfectly free to bring any of our troubles to you with the utmost frankness, knowing that you would review every situation and give an unprejudiced decision.

In Meigs' two-year association with Towers, "I have said to many people that you are one of the most efficient, reliable executives with whom I have come in contact. . . . To an intimate friend or two I have left out the 'one of the most' and changed it to 'the most,' which is the honest to God way I feel about it." Meigs concluded by mentioning his son, "someplace in the Pacific. He's a lieutenant (jg), in charge of mine laying and the gun crew. I get some small comfort in your going because I feel that he will be a lot better protected with you in close proximity."[96]

14

AIR CHIEF AGAINST JAPAN

1942-43

The Boeing B-314 Clipper flying boat whisked Vice Admiral Jack Towers into the Pacific theater of war, where American naval fortunes were ebbing daily. It carried only Towers, his aides Gus Read and Lee Loomis, and Commander Robert B. Pirie, a top navy pilot assigned to his staff. Approaching Hawaii early on 14 October 1942, the navy-chartered plane had to orbit off Oahu while a barrage balloon drill was carried out. Ignoring strict security regulations and the Pan Am pilot's protests, Towers kept the window curtains open to see "his" installations as the Clipper flew along the coast to Waikiki and finally put down in the seaplane area near Panama City. The barrage balloons, designed to deter low-altitude dive bombing, seemed to Towers entirely too passive a defensive device; he would soon have them removed.[1]

Towers and his three staff officers were immediately struck by the shock lingering at Pearl Harbor from the memory of 7 December. Worse, three carriers had been lost in the battles of the preceding five months, and the remaining three continued to suffer in the desperate bid to resupply the marines at Guadalcanal, where air, sea, and land battles were being fought daily and nightly. Pearl Harbor even seemed vulnerable to another carrier attack, leading to antiaircraft drills each day and partial blackouts and curfews at night. Only a small staff was on hand at Towers' new headquarters. At least with each sunken carrier, more good men were made available to him.[2]

If anybody could help retrieve American naval fortunes, it was aggressive operational commanders. Shore-based as ComAirPac, Towers was prevented from becoming one of these, but the return of Halsey to the war zone was universally applauded by airmen, especially when, four days after Towers arrived, Halsey suddenly relieved Vice Admiral Lee Ghormley as commander South Pacific Force. This left the *Enterprise* force under black-shoe Kinkaid and the *Hornet* force under early aviator George Murray. Admiral Nimitz, however, remembering his disputes with Towers over control of personnel when they were bureau chiefs, had no intention of involving Towers in flag command selections in the Pacific Fleet. "Dear Chester," Towers had addressed a letter to Nimitz when first notified of his new job, "I am sure there is no need of my telling you that I am delighted to have the opportunity to serve under you." He signed it "Jack." The attempt at familiarity, a carryover from their days as fellow bureau chiefs, was forced.

Never one to criticize fellow officers openly, Nimitz had merely written an understated letter to his wife, "I am to have a new air adviser. Never mind. We will get along fine." Nimitz's flag secretary, Captain P. V. Mercer, recalled, "I felt that he just didn't like Towers' methods. He didn't go into it in any detail, but I just sensed this thing from the very few things that he said." By the same token, Towers' staff only surmised their admiral's frustration with Nimitz and, according to Pirie, "never heard him discourse on his feeling toward Nimitz or Spruance." The two men were too professional to air criticism and kept their relationship strictly formal; the mutual form of address was simply "Admiral."[3]

The first step in the offensive was to be the capture of the advanced Japanese base at Rabaul on New Britain. Forces of the Southwest Pacific theater under General Douglas MacArthur would advance along the New Guinea coast, and those of the South Pacific, now under Halsey, would move up the Solomon island chain. Halsey's theater belonged to Nimitz's administrative control as CINCPAC, while all ship movements throughout the Pacific theaters—South, Southwest, Central, and North—came under Nimitz's jurisdiction in his dual role as commander in chief Pacific Ocean Areas (CINCPOA). Nimitz's deputy CINCPAC-CINCPOA was Rear Admiral Spruance.

Towers had never served with Spruance, who had become Nimitz's alter ego. A brilliant officer, with three separate tours of duty at the Naval War College and a career in the Gun Club, Spruance was a careful, methodical planner, much like Towers. They even had similar personalities, Spruance having been "a shy young thing," according to his Annapolis classmates of '07, "with a rather sober, earnest face and the innocent disposition of an ingenue."[4]

Nimitz surrounded himself with nonaviators. Among the type commanders at Pearl, only three were vice admirals—Bill Calhoun of the service force, H. Fairfax Leary of the battleships, and now Towers of air. But for additional counsel Nimitz would soon bring back the erudite Lee Ghormley as commander of the Fourteenth Naval District and Hawaiian Sea Frontier. None of these men, save for Spruance in his brief but superb performance at Midway, had any real experience in aviation—a vacuum Towers intended to fill.

In accord with the defensive mentality in Hawaii, many PBYs were being kept for advanced training at NAS Kaneohe. Despite the desire of their commander, Rear Admiral Pete Mitscher, to send them to the war zone, and of frantic appeals for them from Rear Admiral Jake Fitch in the South Pacific, Mitscher's staff did not want to cut short the training syllabus. When Towers discovered this, he issued a mandate ordering their immediate deployment, after which they performed immediate and invaluable service.[5]

Before Towers could begin to solve the almost overwhelming problem of strengthening his air forces in the south, the Japanese struck again, their four carriers sinking the *Hornet* and seriously damaging the *Enterprise* in the Battle of the Santa Cruz Islands, 26–27 October. Significantly, for Towers, it was the carrier under nonaviator Kinkaid that had been lost. The "Big E" limped back to Halsey's base at Nouméa, New Caledonia, for repairs, leaving the Pacific Fleet without any carrier at all. Taking stock of Japanese aircraft losses—caused by Wildcat carrier fighters and antiaircraft fire from the battleship *South Dakota*—and damage to two Japanese carriers, Towers sized up the situation in a memo to Nimitz and Spruance on the twenty-eighth: "Present situation in South Pacific indicates to me probability of more extensive use by Japanese of heavy surface forces. Our position in that respect is weak. Temporary disablement of one of our BBs by torpedo might render it critical." He recommended that one division of battleships be transferred from Pearl to Halsey. "Danger to them from aircraft attack certainly would be much less than heretofore." The three men discussed the idea, but Nimitz took no action.[6]

When Nimitz had Kinkaid shift his flag to the *Enterprise* in the face of a new Japanese threat, Towers reacted strongly. As far as he was concerned, Kinkaid was to blame for the loss of the *Hornet,* and on 9 November he recommended to Nimitz that Mitscher relieve Kinkaid. Before Nimitz could react, the Japanese struck again. As Towers had predicted, they threw a large force at the Guadalcanal beachhead in what came to be known as the Naval Battle of Guadalcanal, 12–15 November. Kinkaid put to sea with the partially repaired *Enterprise,* whose planes helped repulse the Japanese attack, though top honors went to the battleships *South Dakota* and *Washington* under Rear Admiral W. A. Lee. Two Japanese battleships and seven troop transports were sunk, a major triumph for the U.S. Navy and particularly for Halsey, who was immediately promoted to full admiral, a reward richly deserved.[7]

Although the Japanese had been badly hurt by this defeat—sufficiently, as it turned out, to give up altogether their designs on Guadalcanal—Nimitz and Halsey dared not expose what was left of their meager carrier strength until the new *Essex*-class carriers began arriving many months later. At the very least, however, Towers insisted that the use of nonaviator admirals like Fletcher and Kinkaid to lead carrier forces be stopped because it violated the Morrow laws. Though Nimitz did not accept Towers' arguments in principle, he now reassigned Kinkaid to command of a large cruiser force, only to have Admiral King tap Kinkaid to head the North Pacific force in the Aleutians.

When Nimitz met with King in San Francisco early in December, they agreed that the commander of a task force to which a carrier belonged need not be an aviator and that Towers was out of line to insist upon it. And early in the new year, Nimitz cautioned Halsey after the latter gave Rear Admiral Charlie Mason tactical command over a task force that already had a more senior nonaviation admiral: "Nothing would be more harmful to the morale of our senior officers than to create the impression that only aviators may command task forces which have carriers included." One may infer that chief of staff Spruance strongly endorsed this view. Although this was to be the official policy, rarely again would a black-shoe admiral exercise tactical command over carriers; seniority became expendable in the quest for victory.[8]

The fact was that the newly selected air rear admirals recommended by Towers gave Nimitz a reservoir of excellent men. Duke Ramsey now hoisted his flag in Jerry Bogan's repaired *Saratoga,* while latecomer Rear Admiral Frederick C. "Ted" Sherman, a JCL, did the same in Osborne B. Hardison's *Enterprise.* But Halsey would no longer allow these carriers to operate within range of Japanese land-based air; the risk of losing either one was simply too great. Towers and his staff debated the possibilities of using the first slow, 18-knot escort carriers to help fill the gap and finally recommended three of the converted *Cimarrons.* Having just successfully covered the North African landings, the *Sangamon, Suwannee,* and *Chenango* were ordered to hasten from the Atlantic to provide air cover for Halsey's convoys and amphibious forces.[9]

In the meantime, over the winter of 1942–43 and into the spring,

Towers collected information and comments from aviators on the proper use of carriers in battle, while Ramsey and Ted Sherman tested different tactical formations at sea. All agreed that mobility and flexibility were essential whenever carriers operated in confined waters. "It is fundamental in carrier operations," Towers advised Nimitz in January and April 1943, "that their attack power . . . be developed by use on offensive tasks, and that between tasks they should make use of their high strategic mobility to withdraw from areas of exposure to enemy action," notably land-based air forces. Carriers should "be employed to move forward, strike the enemy and withdraw." Two schools of thought developed on cruising dispositions: Ramsey, Halsey, and Bogan believed carriers should disperse under air attack, while Ted Sherman led a chorus of Mitscher, Kinkaid, Buckmaster, and Noyes insisting that three or four carriers should be kept concentrated for mutual protection. Until the new *Essexes* arrived, Towers only recommended general flexibility.[10]

The air war shifted to land-based air on both sides, the campaign toward which the office of ComAirPac now turned its full attention. Although Jake Fitch coordinated all of Halsey's South Pacific air forces, an aggressive local commander was needed to concentrate on the aerial defense of Guadalcanal against Japanese planes coming down from Rabaul. Towers immediately recommended that Mitscher join Halsey as commander Fleet Air Nouméa. Halsey heartily concurred, Nimitz agreed, and Mitscher was on his way by the end of December.[11]

Keeping the fleet's vital aircraft, flying personnel, and aviation supplies flowing to and from the forward areas was the major task of ComAirPac. Towers controlled three new fleet air commands headed by rear admirals—those at Seattle, Alameda, and San Diego (West Coast)—which provided the Pacific air force with planes and squadrons. Towers' office then arranged for repair and upkeep, predeployment training, tactical doctrine, and overall combat readiness of all navy and marine squadrons, carriers, and seaplane tenders. Operational control by ComAirPac was not possible unless authorized by CINCPAC, but it would never be. In effect, ComAirPac was to act as a forward BuAer.

Towers' headquarters and living spaces were located on Ford Island in the middle of Pearl Harbor, physically removed from Nimitz's offices, housed across the harbor at Makalapa. Though Nimitz held daily morning conferences with his principal advisers, Towers as a type commander was not included. Except for the one aviation officer on Nimitz's staff, Captain Ralph Ofstie, the black shoes and brown shoes remained in separate domains, not conducive to cooperation and understanding. Chief of staff Forrest Sherman dubbed Towers the owner of Quarters K, whose occupants and brown-shoe guests referred to the black shoes as buffalo hunters because of their Indian-fighting, meaning old-fashioned, mentality. The admirals of Makalapa became known sarcastically as uncles since they made everyone else "say uncle" to their way of thinking. CINCPAC Nimitz became Uncle Zink instead of Zinc Pac.[12]

Meanwhile Towers refused to truckle to Nimitz. The latter enjoyed long walks and threw horseshoes for relaxation. Towers did not play horseshoes, and because of the ankle injury from his first plane ride in 1911 he tired easily during long walks. So, of necessity, their contacts were restricted to the official levels. In time, Forrest Sherman began to ingratiate himself to Nimitz and, like Spruance, elected to take the demanding five-mile hikes. Once asked about this by Pierre, Towers gave a wry laugh. "I couldn't walk, and I'm glad I couldn't walk."[13]

Nimitz's professional esteem for Towers came out in the first fitness report, covering Jack's initial six months on the job: 4.0 across the board. "Vice Admiral Towers is an officer of the highest personal and military character, who has most satisfactorily performed his duties as Commander Air Force, Pacific Fleet. His long and varied aviation experience particularly fit him for the duties he is now performing." Of course, in so saying, Nimitz was also declaring that Towers should remain in this job rather than have an operational command.[14]

Jack resumed his swimming routine the very first morning at Quarters K. He rousted his aides out of bed an hour before breakfast for a swim in the cold Ford Island pool. Forrest Sherman soon had all hands swimming more often than that. After his traumatic experience abandoning the stricken *Wasp,* Sherman believed that any "ship-dweller" should learn endurance swimming underwater to avoid burning oil and develop speed on the surface. Bob Pirie recalled himself as the only commander or captain on the staff "who hadn't swum away from a sunken aircraft carrier." The officers worked at it, and within a few weeks all had developed muscles, stamina, and hearty appetites.[15]

Towers soon brought in the *Hornet's* former exec, Captain Apollo Soucek, and the recent air group commander of the *Wasp,* Commander Wallace M. Beakley, to be assistant chief of staff for operations and operations officer respectively. Both were extremely able men. Towers also obtained aeronautical engineer Captain Horse Pennoyer from BuAer to be assistant chief of staff for material and Captain George D. Thompson to be force medical officer. Thompson had been one of the flight surgeons who had passed Jack on many of his earlier controversial physical exams.[16]

Rounding up a complete staff took many weeks, for upon his arrival Towers had inherited the skeleton remnant of Pat Bellinger's former patrol wing staff, most of whom proved unequal to the job. Two key men he obtained were Commanders L. W. "Slim" Johnson from the sunken *Wasp* to handle personnel and H. B. "Hebe" Jones of the Civil Engineer Corps to coordinate airfield construction with the Seabees, naval construction battalions.

Another *Wasp* survivor was brought in on the advice of Forrest Sherman—his able ACIO, Lieutenant G. Willing "Wing" Pepper. Pepper established a small staff intelligence unit that evolved into the operational intelligence section. It maintained a war room and a situation room with twenty-four-hour watches, where ship locations were plotted, action reports were summarized, and the fleet was provided with monthly analyses of aircraft operations. Pepper and his officers briefed Towers and Sherman each morning on the war situation. Admiral King, incidentally, criticized Nimitz for decentralizing his intelligence operations by assigning so many intelligence officers to Towers' office, but Nimitz did not change the policy.

Towers continued bringing in his own men to tackle specific problems that others could not, especially in aviation logistics. He had to fire more than one officer before acquiring Commander Jimmy Boundy, who demonstrated again that he was the best aviation logistician in the navy. The sorry state of NATS in the Pacific—in terms of both cargo plane numbers and the lack of air cargo control—led Towers to recall Commander Dave Ingalls, his old boss, to active duty to coordinate NATS activities in the forward areas. Reporting in November 1942, Ingalls impressed all hands as an extraordinarily unstuffy patrician; he never let on that he was the navy's only World War I ace. Ingalls' eventual recommendations for NATS supply routes were integrated verbatim into the existing Pan Am system the following spring.

The talent Towers amassed at his headquarters defied peacetime navy practices, as had been the case at BuAer. Many young and prosperous Wall Street executives had joined up to help win the war and had no interest in pay, promotions, or protocol. Among them were Lieutenant (jg) August Belmont, who masterminded the fleet's advanced air base system, and three civilian insurance actuaries whom Captain Pennoyer put to work compiling vital statistics to establish exact airplane needs. Recalled Pennoyer, "They lacked computers, but from a huge mass of action reports and other data they developed formulae with long strings of variables that enabled them to

Towers and his ComAirPac chief of staff, Captain Forrest Sherman, *left,* confer with two unidentified officers on a warship in the Pacific. (Naval Historical Center)

predict the precise requirements by way of aircraft for any given operation or objective. They never missed."[17]

Towers' staff grew to some one hundred officers in the first five months. At its head stood Forrest Sherman, whose brilliance and overall ability Towers had admired for twenty years. This respect was reciprocated, especially since Towers had saved Sherman from possible career oblivion after he lost the *Wasp.* "He rarely talked," recalled Gus Read, but everyone looked to Sherman for guidance after his combat experiences.[18]

No better source of knowledge about the naval air war existed than men such as Sherman—the carrier admirals, captains, and aviators fresh from combat. Whenever a damaged carrier or seaplane tender returned to Pearl from combat, Towers had a navy band playing on the dock. When senior aviation officers flew in, he met them at the seaplane base and invited them to his mess, where the food was renowned. There were the potent martinis that had become a Towers trademark and bridge in the evenings for guests at Quarters K. All this attention was new to the aviation community in Hawaii, and it caused morale to soar.

Towers milked these men for all their knowledge and impressions and inspected their ships to see the effect of enemy action. One of the first visitors was Captain Andrew C. McFall, whose information on the loss of the *Hornet* led to improvements in damage control techniques. Towers saw the battle-scarred *Enterprise* docked alongside ComAirPac's administration building. The most heart-rending sight he witnessed was Charles Rosendahl bringing in his cruiser *Minneapolis,* crippled by torpedoes near Guadalcanal in late November; when water was pumped out of the dry dock, the shattered skeletons of crewmen were revealed trapped in the wreckage. And when the damaged seaplane tender-destroyer *McFarland* returned after delivering aviation gas to beleaguered Guadalcanal, Towers entertained the crew and presented them with the Presidential Unit Citation.[19]

The impression combat-hardened visitors had of Towers during these stopovers was most favorable. He was perceived as a gentleman, firm but not authoritarian.[20] His ire rose, however, if aviators were mistreated by the Gun Club. When the *Enterprise* put in to rotate air groups during the spring of 1943, Lieutenant J. D. "Jig Dog" Ramage of the air group approached him with a problem. Ramage related how a certain Captain Robertson of the naval district refused to allow him to buy a ticket for his wife, a native of Honolulu, for passage to the West Coast.

Grumbling about those "black shoe sons of bitches," Towers put in a call to the captain. "Robertson," he said, "I have one of my aviators in the office who says that you won't let him buy a ticket for his wife to return to the mainland." When the captain started to explain, Towers cut him off: "While you have been sitting on your ass here in Pearl Harbor this young man has been in the South Pacific fighting the Japs. Here is what I want you to do. Not only will she be allowed to go to the mainland, but I want her to accompany her husband on the transport with the air group." The task was accomplished forthwith.[21]

Important as personnel were, however, they were only as good as the fleet's logistics allowed them to be. The Guadalcanal campaign had been planned by battleship men who thought in the customary terms of only ship's fuel and ammunition. Aviation logistics, of which they were ignorant, was vastly more complicated. Without a steady flow of spare parts, any damaged plane was a total loss; it simply could not fly again. From the first, Towers was deluged with pleas for more aircraft and spare parts for the carriers and land-based units on Guadalcanal. The NATS pipeline of a few PBM Mariners was not supplying the needed parts. Since few new planes would be available until production could deliver them many months hence, control over air cargo had to be established, quickly. As Bob Pirie put it, ComAirPac's overall logistical situation "was catastrophic."

In November 1942, therefore, Towers dispatched Horse Pennoyer and Pirie to the South Pacific to see what could be done. Upon their arrival at Guadalcanal in the midst of air raids and Japanese ship bombardments, Pennoyer was stunned to see the so-called Bone Pile, "a huge 3–4 story stack of the carcasses of aircraft cannibalized for spare parts. The Marine F4Fs and SBDs had been flown into Henderson Field with practically no logistic preparations except for fuel and ammunition. Even they were on a shoe-string. The defense was down to a handful of operational aircraft with the Jap air force on their backs. One squadron had only one airplane on the line." The required spare parts were supposed to be there, and no one knew why they weren't. Pennoyer and Pirie could only advise the defenders to cannibalize more efficiently until parts could be found.

Proceeding to Nouméa, Pirie followed Towers' instructions to check the NATS terminal to see what it was carrying in the way of spare parts. What Pirie found were large crates of mimeograph paper! On inquiring, he was told by a disheveled and disinterested lieutenant (jg) that Admiral Turner, the amphibious commander, needed it for distributing his operations orders. "When I got back to Pearl Harbor and told Admiral Towers this," recalled Pirie, "he almost went crazy."

Frantic dispatches to Washington producing no satisfactory answers, Towers allowed Pennoyer to fly back to the States "as a self-appointed trouble-shooter" to locate the spare parts. It wasn't easy, but by persistent searching he found them—in boxcars on a railroad siding between Salt Lake City and Ogden, Utah. "They were stalled behind miles of freight cars laden with general stores ranging from brass polish to deck swabs. Furthermore, freight trains were arriving daily at an accelerating rate much faster than they could be unloaded by the supply depot."

The furor that followed gave Towers all the clout he needed to demand that the aviation logistics pipeline be streamlined for future operations. But it would not happen overnight, and as late as May 1943 Towers, supported by Halsey, begged his BuAer successor McCain to expedite delivery of plane parts to the South Pacific. At Towers' insistence, no campaign would be planned, no aviation units committed to battle, without all squadrons at full combat strength and with complete logistical backup. ComAirPac would thus become a major supply command alongside Bill Calhoun's service force.[22]

Towers always kept the big picture in mind as he labored to strengthen Halsey's South Pacific force and to anticipate aviation needs for the eventual offensive. He and his planners were amazed that CINCPAC had initiated no plans to increase docking facilities for carriers beyond the one adjacent to ComAirPac's administration building. Early in 1943 Jack therefore recommended the addition of three new carrier berths at Ford Island for the expected *Essex*- and *Independence*-class carriers. Getting no action, he informed Di Gates of the fact three months later, pointing out that six months would be required to build them and that "the need prior to that time will be critical." In less than a week, Vice CNO Horne authorized their construction. Towers also wanted to centralize naval aviation activities in Hawaii by creating a naval air center, but King overruled him, saying that their jurisdiction belonged to the Hawaiian Sea Frontier. A year later, however, King saw the sense in the proposal and approved the new center.

Towers caused less germane projects to be halted, such as that for one hundred F4F-7 reconnaissance seaplanes—there was a desperate need for landplane F4F Wildcat fighters. Conversely, he promoted projects whose need was revealed by combat experience; his endorsement of the experimental MAD/retro-rocket system for attacking submerged submarines early in 1943 led to its deployment—and ultimate success—in the Atlantic. And when he realized that marine pilots were still being trained for carrier flying even though the Corps "didn't want carriers," he had them eliminated from such training.[23]

On 26 December—after a Christmas of light snow on a Hawaiian mountainside[24]—Towers departed for the South Pacific in his flag plane, a specially equipped XPB2Y-1 Coronado, "which is both the most comfortable and the fastest transport in the whole Pacific." Accompanied by Beakley, Ingalls, and Loomis, he wanted to inspect the aircraft situation for himself and in the process see the islands, which had "always fascinated" him. He inspected the base at Espiritu Santo in the New Hebrides and dropped in on the NATS terminal at Nouméa, already infamous for its mimeograph paper. He encountered the same "dirty little j.g." whom Bob Pirie had crossexamined two months before. After upbraiding the man for his appearance, Towers said, "What are in those crates?"

"Condoms," answered the jg.

Taken aback, Towers exploded, "Who the h--- are they going to f--- down here?!"

Apparently the aviators had requested the rubbers to waterproof their cigarettes and matches if they went down at sea. Tied to a string around the neck, the cigarettes could be smoked during lonely hours in a life raft while a flyer awaited rescue.

That one incident led Towers to assign Commander Pirie the task of monitoring all NATS cargo as it went through Pearl. This brought the first semblance of control to air supply in the Pacific.[25]

Talking not only with Admirals Halsey and Fitch but pilots at Guadalcanal and Nouméa, Towers found them pleased with their F4F Wildcats but anxiously anticipating the new F6F Hellcat. The F4U Corsair, already en route to the marines in the South Pacific, would enter combat in February. After discussions with New Zealand Air Commodore R. V. Goddard, Towers urged the greater use of that country's planes; Halsey strongly concurred. "Our naval and Marine air are Hot," Jack later wrote his brother Will, although "Army air suffers from poor equipment and inadequate training but will come up. It doesn't suffer any from under advertising!" While at Nouméa Towers witnessed the arrival of the *Suwannee,* first of Rear Admiral Andy McFall's three *Cimarron* escort carriers to reach the South Pacific direct from Norfolk. Glad to leave embattled Guadal "untouched either by bombs, bullets, malaria or dysentery," Towers flew on to Samoa and then back to Hawaii.[26]

The presence of VIPs in the forward areas hinted at the turning tide of battle. At Nouméa Towers had conferred with Admiral John McCain and Lieutenant Commander George Anderson, both out from BuAer to assess theater air needs. Jack was pleased to learn from Anderson that the first pilots "who have flown the Hellcat are most enthusiastic." One plane, however, proved less than perfect: the Vought OS2U-3 Kingfisher. Heavier than the two earlier versions because of more armor and extra wing tanks, the -3 included forward wing slats to give it better lift at low speeds. This worked well enough from land fields, but, remembered Pirie, "they were a menace on water." He and Beakley had the plane restricted to land operations. This disturbed Towers, who had been bureau chief when the contract was let for the plane. Realizing this, Pirie and Beakley decided to have some fun with their boss by ordering a couple of these "turkeys" parked under Towers' bedroom window. He was not amused. "Get those damned things out of my sight!" he yelled.

Towers provided Admiral Nimitz with his own Coronado for a trip with Secretary Frank Knox to the South Pacific, but when it took off on 14 January two of its engines quit and the pilot had to set it down in the harbor. The PB2Y landed so hard that the hull was punctured and it sank. Rescue boats retrieved the occupants, whereupon Towers gave them another plane. The fact that Nimitz had cut his head and required stitches did nothing to relieve his distaste for flying.[27]

Towers and his entourage take a barge out to their plane, the specially equipped PB2Y-1 Coronado staff flying boat, for the return to Hawaii in January 1943 as local commanders at Samoa see them off. *Left to right:* a Commander Green; Air Commodore R. V. Goddard, Royal New Zealand Air Force; Towers; Commander E. G. Konrad; Commander Wallace M. Beakley; flag lieutenant Lee Loomis; Commander W. F. Boone; Brigadier General L. G. Saunders, AAF; and Lieutenant Commander David Ingalls. (Towers collection)

At Nouméa Towers had learned firsthand of the overall supply backup there. As more supply ships crowded into its harbor during the spring, Towers came up with a subterfuge to speed the unloading of aviation equipment. When the new escort carrier *Barnes* arrived at Pearl Harbor, en route south ferrying landplanes, Jack told her skipper, Captain Cato D. Glover, that "a hundred ships" would be ahead of him waiting to unload at Nouméa. He presented Glover with a case of Scotch whiskey with which to bribe his way to the head of the line, knowing that Scotch had become a rare commodity in those parts. The liquor did the trick, and the *Barnes* was unloaded her first night in port.[28]

Planning the forward movement of squadrons and equipment from the West Coast, Towers flew to California in early February to confer with his three fleet air commanders—and to see the ladies in his life, now increased to three. At twenty-six, Marjorie was mother of a two-month-old baby girl, making Jack a grandfather. Pierre had moved to San Diego to participate in war work, hardly knowing which end of a screwdriver to use. Asked for her Social Security number, she produced the Social Register of Washington! Tired of doing menial chores, she took the initiative to form a corporation of navy wives because Convair had rejected them individually for being quali- fied "only to play bridge." The women won a contract to sort rivets in a "feeder shop" devised by Pierre, who also took charge of recruiting. She rented an empty store near the plant where tons of rivets were deposited each day for sorting in four-hour shifts. "Result—," Jack told his brother Will, "women contributing to war effort instead of playing bridge. Consolidated being helped. No transportation except truck load of rivets per day. Rather smart idea." Chas, now twenty-three, had entered the navy's flight instructor school at NAS New Orleans in October and would graduate to become a primary flight instructor at Glenview (near Chicago) in September 1943.[29]

The Japanese suddenly evacuated Guadalcanal in February, enabling the next stage of the Solomons campaign to commence. Admiral Fitch's South Pacific air forces attacked New Georgia, preparatory to the assault on that island planned for the summer.[30] Japan now shifted to the strategic defensive in the south, buying time for the critically depleted American carrier force. By March the Pacific Fleet was down to the *Saratoga* and the *Enterprise,* with the latter badly in need of overhaul. McFall's converted carriers continued to escort convoys to and from the Solomons, where their fighters received the brunt of Japanese air attacks. Admiral King therefore prevailed upon the British to loan a carrier in place of the Big E. HMS *Victorious* pulled into Pearl on the cold, windy night of 4 March, her chilled officers clad only in tropical white shorts and stockings. Towers hosted the skipper, Captain L. D. Macin- tosh, and his officers at dinner that evening. Macintosh, who was a naval aviation observer, had an RAF flight officer to handle air operations. Towers and Macintosh spent the evening discussing the American and British sys- tems.[31]

Towers enjoyed renewing his contacts with the Fleet Air Arm. This time he was the teacher rather than the student. The *Victorious* needed ten weeks to learn American procedures before she could replace the *Enterprise* in the South Pacific. Meanwhile, a British observer arrived in the genial person of Rear Admiral Denis W. Boyd, about to become Fifth Sea Lord and chief of naval air equipment. Towers profited from these direct contacts with the ally for which he entertained such great respect. He arranged to have Com- mander Richard M. Smeeton assigned as a regular British observer on his staff. Smeeton had earlier served in this capacity at BuAer.[32]

The growing importance of aviation was being felt in every theater, accelerating the demands by its advocates for a greater voice in running the war. The crusade heated up for an independent air force built around the strategic bombers now pounding Nazi Germany, and AAF chief Hap Arnold was promoted to four-star general. Admiral King again tried to reorganize the Navy Department with four deputy CNOs but was turned down by the president—except in the matter of a deputy CNO for aviation. On Secretary Knox's advice, FDR approved the creation of this post to handle all matters relating to aviation readiness and logistics; the chief of BuAer would continue to handle everything else. So King decided that in mid-August 1943 John McCain was to be promoted to vice admiral and made deputy CNO (air). He would be replaced as chief of BuAer by Rear Admiral Duke Ramsey.[33]

As far as Towers and the aviation community were concerned, the change was little better than a compromise, as Towers explained in a letter to Di Gates in late May. "A real reorganization is what is needed. Patching may keep the old ship from sinking but it doesn't give it any more speed or fighting power. The Army has shown the way [with its AAF]. The Navy would do well to follow, deviating in minor ways as necessary. Congress would support a real reorganization. They have been screaming for it for years." Specifically, Towers thought King's dual COMINCH-CNO role should be consolidated under one title, one staff, one officer—the CNO—with his top deputy a naval aviator.[34]

Towers and his fellow aviation flag officers were particularly concerned that the newly constructed fleet about to gather at Pearl Harbor for the great transpacific offensive be directed by qualified airmen. King was an aviator, to be sure, and more aviators were being added to his staff, but it was not nearly enough, given the comparative growing strength of aviation within the army. The new deputy CNO (air) post would at least place aviation directly under the cognizance of the vice CNO, Vice Admiral Horne.

At the end of June Towers wrote his old boss Horne a long letter of frustration in which he set forth his views in detail. "I wonder if you and the others of the high command in Washington realize the . . . threat of a separate Air Force," Towers began. Alluding to the exorbitant and completely false claims by the AAF that its B-17s had been a major factor in the victory at Midway, he declared,

> The gain in our position by the Battle of Midway (and it was not as much as it should have been because of Army publicity, never fully rebutted) has been more than lost in the recent past. The Army Air Force has become very strong. . . . I believe it is safe to say they are about ready to drive for a separate Air Force. The resistant position of the Navy is weaker. . . . [T]he general

impression is growing outside the Navy that best use is not being made by the Navy of its most potent weapon.

The commentators in the press "seem to feel that this is partially because of ultra conservatism and partially because of jealousy. . . . [I]n many cases they are reflecting the views of naval aviators with whom they have made contacts. There is great discontent within aviation out here. . . ." Towers listed five reasons for this discontent. First was "the Midway publicity"— AAF claims when navy torpedo squadrons had sustained heavy losses in helping to sink the four Japanese carriers. Second was the slowness in awarding navy decorations. Third was "the extreme tardiness" of BuPers in making spot promotions to deserving officers, a policy that hurt morale. Fourth was the failure to promote deserving lieutenant commanders to higher grades on a par with AAF officers elevated to colonel and brigadier general. Last was "the general belief" that senior aviators were not being given "a real voice in strategic plans."

Towers cited his battles on the Morrow Board in 1925 and in helping Admiral Moffett in the early 1930s to discourage a separate air force and a separate naval air corps. "Many seniors," he reminded Horne, "have become so discouraged," particularly over lack of a voice in strategic planning, "that they are becoming resigned to the prospect of a separate Air Force. . . . I do not agree, but I feel you ought to know what is going on in the minds of some of our best officers. . . . Incidentally, but not too incidentally, they do not repose trust and confidence in [the] current Chief of Bureau. (I do not want the job back, even if such were considered, which is unlikely.) Is there any possibility of McCain's wish to be relieved being granted?"[35]

Though Towers did not yet know of McCain's prospective elevation to be deputy CNO (air), his appeal to Horne struck a responsive chord. Surely with King's approval, Horne charged Admiral Harry Yarnell, Towers' other prewar carrier boss, to make a survey of the situation. Because of his seniority Yarnell would step on relatively few toes. His specific tasks were to poll the naval aviation community for its views, to examine the question of unification of the armed forces with a separate air arm, and to study the question of the size and composition of the postwar navy—all interrelated matters.[36]

The true worth of naval aviation would be revealed by its performance in a war that promised to be long and difficult. While in Nouméa at the first of the year, Towers had found Bill Halsey disturbed over something he had been quoted as saying the day before, namely, that the war with Japan would be over before the end of the current year, 1943. In two letters to his brother

Will, in March and April, Jack reflected on Halsey's remark, uttered merely to uplift morale:

> You will note he has not be[en] *requoted* along these lines. It is going to be a long hard pull. There are no short cuts. I fear the Japs will have to be largely exterminated and I mean just that. It can be done but will take time.
>
> . . . Shipping is and will continue to be the key item for us and for Japan. . . . Fortunately [the] Jap submarine force has not shown any great efficiency, in fact it appears well below (no pun intended) [the] rest of their Navy. Our subs are showing up well. . . . Japan's Empire will collapse because . . . of loss of shipping, and the lack of materials and building facilities to replace it. They gradually will be forced to draw back under pressure *and* to shorten their shipping lines.
>
> They probably will continue to fight to the last, which may of necessity be destruction of all their cities and of large numbers of their peoples who have not already starved. All this will take TIME. You can see I am not an optimist. I am too realistic for that.[37]

Aside from the submarine campaign against Japanese shipping, exactly what offensive strategy would be used to defeat Japan? Of all the Allied and American high commanders, Admiral Ernie King alone had a clear vision of that. As Towers had observed in his first war college thesis, only a great commander in chief could formulate and persist in realizing a singular grand strategic design. And King was, in the later words of historian Samuel Eliot Morison, "undoubtedly the best naval strategist and organizer in our history." Japan would be defeated, believed King, by a strategy of concentration: Allied power and Chinese armies would be massed against the main Japanese armies on the continent of Asia, while concurrent offensives would be undertaken by American naval, ground, and air forces driving across the Pacific to the Chinese coast. Japan's merchant marine, fleet, and air forces would be destroyed in the process, her island outposts captured and converted into naval and air bases. Admiral King reasoned that the Japanese home islands would be blockaded by air and naval forces, starved and bombarded into submission without the need for a direct invasion.[38]

King would steadfastly adhere to this strategy as the navy member of the JCS, although specific details over particular operations and priorities would lead to variations in his program. MacArthur's projected drive up the New Guinea coast would tie down many Japanese forces in the Southwest Pacific, while Halsey pressed up the Solomons toward Rabaul in the South Pacific. King tapped Admiral Tom Kinkaid to retake two islands in the Aleutians and force Japan to look to her North Pacific defenses. But the main thrust would be in the Central Pacific, where Nimitz's newly built and trained fleet would realize the time-honored Orange Plan: to drive westward to Truk, the Marianas, and the Philippines, then to China and up the Chinese coast to Japan. Hap Arnold's strategic bombers would be able to operate out of Chinese and Western Pacific airfields and join the new carriers in attacking the Japanese homeland itself.

As strategy maker for the Pacific, King began to press Nimitz for offensive actions as early as December 1942. Impatient over the war of attrition around Guadalcanal, he asked Nimitz why he couldn't just bypass the Solomons and Rabaul altogether by seizing the Admiralty islands off the north coast of New Guinea. Nimitz and Halsey talked him out of this premature idea; they lacked the forces to hold the new conquests and to keep the bypassed areas neutralized. Towers was alerted to the same radical idea of bypassing certain islands during his stopover at Samoa in January 1943. In a long conversation the defense commander at Samoa, Marine Major General Charles F. B. Price, related to Jack and Wallace Beakley his belief that the defeat of Japan could be hastened by "island hopping" certain outposts and thus outflanking them. A brilliant thinker, Price had been shunted to backwaters from which he never escaped. Towers agreed with his concept and upon returning to Pearl shared it with Forrest Sherman. Henceforth, because bypassed islands could be kept neutralized by air forces, island hopping was absorbed into ComAirPac's strategic thinking. In fact, Jack Towers became the principal proponent of the revolutionary idea.[39]

In February King met with Nimitz in San Francisco to implore him to initiate offensive action, possibly by taking the Gilbert islands in the Central Pacific to prevent a Japanese southeastern thrust. Again Nimitz demurred, for lack of resources and for fear of another Japanese carrier attack on Pearl Harbor. He even wanted to recall some of Halsey's forces to help protect Hawaii. In this view he was supported by his deputy, Spruance, and by the army commander in Hawaii, overly cautious Lieutenant General Delos C. Emmons, who wanted more land-based bombers to help defend the islands. And that very month Vice Admiral Lee Ghormley returned as commander of the Hawaiian Sea Frontier and of the Fourteenth Naval District. Relieved in the South Pacific four months before for his pessimistic leadership, Ghormley lost no time laying plans to build bomb shelters in Hawaii.

Towers held his tongue until May, when Ghormley "forced down the throat" of NAS Pearl Harbor the necessity of surrendering valuable space and of building one of the shelters to the tune of $400,000 over a six-month period. "Admitting that it is not directly my business," Towers finally scolded his classmate, "I cannot but cry out against this costly project. I often wonder if Hitler's secret weapon isn't our defensive attitude. . . . With so much to be done in the combat areas, the waste of men, money, materials, and shipping on such projects at this time makes me shudder."[40]

Such defensive extravagance aside, Nimitz thought the best solution was indeed to seize the Gilberts and Marshalls. If some of Halsey's forces could be recalled to the defense of Hawaii, they could then be used to raid or mount an assault on these forward Japanese-held island groups. Nimitz sent Spruance to Washington in mid-March to argue his case before the JCS. King used these arguments to convince the JCS to endorse his Central Pacific offensive instead of diverting major forces to MacArthur in the Southwest Pacific. As the JCS deliberated on the Pacific timetable and specific targets, Nimitz, fully appreciating the need for overwhelming carrier and land-based air power, decided to solicit the views of Towers for the contemplated Central Pacific campaign. In particular, he asked him to prepare a brief plan for raiding Japanese bases in the Marshalls.[41]

Given limited resources in land-based air, shipping, and amphibious troops, Towers counseled Nimitz in a long memo on 28 April that the fleet could only launch one offensive during 1943. Moreover, the shifting of forces and of "supporting base developments" from the South to the Central Pacific "would be impossible." Towers therefore recommended that the fleet's effort continue to focus on Rabaul in the South Pacific. Once Rabaul was taken—and he believed it could be—the fleet could move against the enemy's advanced fleet anchorage at Truk, or against his communications in southeast Asian waters. To support this reasoning, Towers presented Nimitz with a study of the Japanese air base network in the Pacific. It showed that the Solomons would remain the major area of dispute because of the proximity of shore-based air for both sides. Thus, "in this area will be found the opportunities to bring [Japan's] naval forces to action at sea, which we desire"—another major battle that could destroy the Japanese fleet.

Towers also gave Nimitz the requested air plan for striking the Marshalls. He argued, however, against exposing the new carriers and battleships to "mutually supporting" enemy land-based air there and in the northern Gilberts unless such operations were sustained and enemy air strength materially weakened, requiring the Japanese to divert forces from the South Pacific. Towers did not want the new ships used merely to "cover our essential positions in the Central Pacific," the Hawaiian group. To do so would "constitute a complete reversion to the strategic defensive." These strong words were obviously designed to convince Nimitz to employ his new fleet aggressively.[42]

Two days later Towers gave a copy of this memo to Captain Miles Browning, Halsey's visiting chief of staff. Browning, finding it "encouraging evidence of sound viewpoint in Airpac," sent it on to Halsey. On 1 May Browning met with Spruance and Nimitz's war plans staff to go over the projected plans for Halsey and MacArthur's simultaneous advances during the summer. Browning later assured Halsey, "No question regarding the re-deployment of the fleet was mentioned." Towers' arguments had clearly lent weight to the notion that weakening Halsey to reinforce Hawaii and raid the Marshalls was undesirable.[43]

What Nimitz, Spruance, Halsey, Towers, and the other Pacific planners still failed to grasp was that the overwhelming power of America's new ships, planes, and trained troops would enable all *three* offensives—South, Southwest, and Central Pacific—to proceed almost simultaneously. King, however, did understand this, and during May he had his strategy confirmed by the JCS and CCS and conveyed to Nimitz: MacArthur would rely on land-based AAF air power; Halsey on the multiservice air forces of the Solomons, plus a carrier or two; and Nimitz on a new Central Pacific force of new carriers, battleships, and support ships for the drive across the Central Pacific. The first element of the new fleet appeared on 30 May when Captain Wu Duncan brought the *Essex* into Pearl Harbor, although the Central Pacific force would not be ready to advance until the autumn. In the meantime, MacArthur and Halsey began their respective advances up the coast of New Guinea and up the ladder of the Solomons toward Rabaul. For strategic backup, Halsey had Duke Ramsey's two-carrier force of the *Saratoga* and HMS *Victorious,* plus Andy McFall's three escort carriers. As Towers had surmised, the Japanese concentrated their available naval and air strength in the south.[44]

King initiated the directive for the new Central Pacific force to undertake the conquest of the Marshalls in November, less than six months away. Suddenly Nimitz began to solicit both Towers and chief of staff Forrest Sherman for their advice on the optimum employment of the fleet's air forces. Jack happily reported to Admiral Horne the "sudden change of heart out here. Sherman and I are now given a chance to find out what is going on and [to] express views." Though the two aviation experts might have disagreed with Nimitz, he nevertheless added their counsel to that of his nonair advisers. In fact, Nimitz became so impressed with Sherman's erudition that at the end of July he personally told King he wanted Sherman to stay on as chief of staff to Towers as long as possible.[45]

But it was Nimitz's deputy Spruance who really had his ear. No sooner had the JCS directive for the Marshalls invasion been received by Nimitz in mid-June than Spruance began arguing for the seizure of the Gilberts ahead of the Marshalls. Although he hoped the Japanese fleet would sortie from Truk to defend the Marshalls, Spruance entertained doubts about the inexperienced Pacific Fleet units and amphibious forces plunging into the Marshalls and fighting a fleet engagement straightaway. More importantly, he wanted land-based air forces to reconnoiter the Marshalls targets, as they had done targets in the South and Southwest Pacific, then to join the carriers in supporting the landings. But since no U.S. bases were within land-based B-24 bomber range of the Marshalls, Spruance wanted to take the Gilberts for these forward air bases. Neither Towers nor anyone else at fleet headquarters supported this position, but during late June and early July Spruance was so persistent in arguing his case that Nimitz finally agreed.

One reason was that Nimitz had decided to assign command of the Central Pacific Force to Spruance; accordingly, Spruance should control the operational plan. Nimitz had him elevated to vice admiral at the end of May and shortly thereafter ordered him to prospective command of the new force. On 20 July Nimitz recommended the Gilberts operation to the JCS and won formal approval. The new timetable called for Operation Galvanic—the assault on the Gilbert islands of Tarawa and Nauru—to take place in mid-November. This would be followed by Flintlock, the invasion of the Marshalls, on New Year's Day 1944. Towers, kept out of these deliberations, still opposed the Gilberts operations as a waste of time, resources, and lives. If the Central Pacific Force was to launch a major offensive, Towers believed, the new carriers ought to punch through the Gilberts directly to the Marshalls with aerial reconnaissance, close air support for assault troops, and an attack on the enemy fleet at or near Truk. Unlike Spruance, Towers did not believe the new fleet needed the Gilberts operations to gain experience.[46]

Towers' opposition was compounded by the news of Spruance's appointment to command the new fleet. During the prewar fleet problems, Towers had maintained that the fast carriers should operate as an independent task force. It was no secret that he still held this view and that he wanted to be the one to command such a force. On 10 June his office issued PAC 10, setting forth the carrier tactical doctrine of defensive concentration and offensive flexibility. But Nimitz had no intention of allowing Towers to go to sea. And Spruance, who had grown to dislike Towers for the criticism of his, Spruance's, defensive thinking, surely rejected any thought of the fleet's forthright air boss serving under his tactical command. So although Towers established carrier doctrine, it was nonaviator Spruance who would exercise operational command of the carriers in the forthcoming operations.[47]

Yet, Spruance had no immediate idea of his exact role in leading the new Central Pacific Force. For all he knew he would be shore-based in Hawaii, directing his task forces much as Nimitz had done during Midway and Halsey had done in the south. "Radio and aircraft have brought about a lot of changes in naval warfare these days," he confided to his wife on 4 July, "and things have to be run from places wherein communications are good." This observation showed Spruance to be a meticulous tactician who expected solid information in running an operation. It also revealed his battleship training: he would seek out the classic gunnery duel à la Jutland—although in that battle, lack of intelligence had hindered Jellicoe. Task forces, battleship and/or carrier, would be sent out as before. Whether or not Spruance went with them, his carrier task force commanders would be men he liked and trusted. One such individual being considered for carrier division command was his old chum Johnny Hoover.[48]

But Nimitz expected Spruance to go to sea as the head of task forces consisting of various mixes of new ship types. Unlike the existing task force organization of one or two carriers, each with its own admiral, the new fleet would soon have a dozen carriers and half as many new battleships. As far as Spruance was concerned, the latter would comprise the battle line for engaging its Japanese counterpart. Though Spruance wanted to lead that engagement, as overall force commander he would need a tactical battleship commander. In mid-July the man who had led the battleships so effectively at Guadalcanal, Rear Admiral W. A. "Ching" Lee, was therefore appointed commander Battleships Pacific. As a type commander, Lee would ordinarily have remained shore-based at Pearl; instead, he was earmarked to lead the battleships at sea. If the type commander for battleships was to take them into combat, why shouldn't ComAirPac similarly direct the carriers afloat? Again, because King, Nimitz, and Spruance did not want Towers there.

Towers at least hoped that Spruance would assign a senior aviator to his staff to advise him on carrier doctrine. In this Jack was sorely disappointed. For his key advisers Spruance selected two of his prewar war college associates, Rear Admiral Kelly Turner to lead the amphibious forces and Captain Charles J. Moore to be chief of staff. Spruance accepted the nonair staff Moore arranged. For his one air officer Spruance got Commander Robert W. Morse, "a very fine officer but not a very strong officer," in the view of then-Commander Truman J. Hedding, exec of the *Essex*. That was the kind of staff Spruance preferred, mild-mannered individuals with personalities close to his own. In addition, remembered Hedding, "Admiral Towers was quite concerned that Admiral Spruance's staff did not have anyone that really represented modern carrier thinking." And Morse was so junior that he would rarely be consulted by Spruance during his year on the staff.[49]

As for carrier division commanders, however, Towers could exert tremendous influence, and Nimitz apparently relied completely on his advice about which aviators to employ in key combat positions. One logical choice for a carrier division was Rear Admiral Pete Mitscher, whom Halsey wanted kept in the Solomons to lead a carrier task force should more carriers be assigned there. But Mitscher's combat experience had left him exhausted and he transferred to the West Coast as commander, Fleet Air, relieving Baldy Pownall. Halsey thought Mitscher's talents would be wasted at San Diego, and Towers bemoaned the "wreckage" caused by Mitscher's relief.[50]

On 7 June Rear Admiral Ted Sherman reported to Pearl, Sherman thought, to become Spruance's senior carrier leader. He hoisted his flag on the *Essex* for joint training exercises with the veteran *Enterprise,* while Towers rode the *Essex* as an observer. These operations were successful enough, but apparently the bombastic latecomer Sherman impressed neither Towers nor Nimitz sufficiently to be retained in the Central Pacific. Also, Genial John Hoover and Pownall, both senior to Sherman, were now ordered to Hawaii for carrier duty. So in mid-July Sherman was suddenly ordered south to replace Ramsey—recalled to be BuAer chief—as Halsey's carrier commander, which suited Halsey fine. Nimitz told Sherman, the latter recorded in his diary, that "he had not recommended me to go down."[51]

Towers, not Nimitz, was responsible for Sherman's move south. Never an admirer of the man's overbearing style of leadership, Jack had recommended that Sherman be sent to Halsey and that the first Central Pacific Force division commanders of the new *Essex*-class carriers be Hoover, Pownall, and Alfred Montgomery. To command the first division of the new *Independence*-class light carriers, Towers wanted Captain Arthur Radford. Rare in the navy's annals, Radford was being promoted to flag rank without ever having commanded a ship, so great had been his success as director of aviation training. After touring the South Pacific with Assistant Secretary Gates, Radford had reported to Pearl in May and worked on tactics with Sherman before hoisting his flag on the *Independence*. To relieve Andy McFall in command of the existing escort carrier division, Towers pushed for Van Hubert Ragsdale. Nimitz accepted all these recommendations.[52]

As the new carriers began arriving in Hawaii, Towers orchestrated the assignment of carrier division commanders. In mid-July the *Enterprise* left Hawaii for overhaul and was replaced by the new *Yorktown,* which arrived on the twenty-fourth under Captain Jocko Clark. Towers recommended that the skippers of the *Saratoga* and *Enterprise,* Henry Mullinix and Samuel P. "Cy" Ginder respectively, be made available to command carrier divisions. And at the end of the month, Secretary Knox asked FDR to approve seven more aviator captains for advancement to rear admiral. All were carrier airmen high on Towers' list: Wu Duncan; Harold B. "Slats" Sallada; Forrest Sherman; Thomas L. Sprague, who was bringing out the new *Intrepid;* John Ballentine of the new *Bunker Hill;* Jocko Clark; and H. S. Kendall.[53]

Nimitz's only serious reservation, which Towers probably shared, was about Genial John Hoover. Nimitz had accepted Hoover only after putting off the entreaties of King, pressured by Spruance, to do so for more than a year. Spruance had been a close friend of Hoover since their days at the Naval Academy. But Hoover's dour manner pleased neither Nimitz nor Towers, and before Hoover even arrived Nimitz reassigned him to command land-based air forces in the Central Pacific Force. This was at the direct instigation of Spruance, who, according to Hoover, wanted "someone he knew up front."[54]

Towers and Spruance were diametrically opposed in their selection of commanders.[55] On 5 August Spruance formally assumed command of the Central Pacific Force and next day simply accepted the senior carrier division commander, Pownall, as his fast carrier leader. According to his operations officer, then–Commander E. P. Forrestel, Spruance "had no preference for that assignment." Such a lackadaisical attitude toward command of what Towers regarded as the primary striking force of the fleet was too much for Jack.

On the eighth Towers confronted Nimitz in person and then wrote a memo regarding the task force commander assignment. Nimitz and Towers had worked out a plan for a special operation in the near future: on attack on remote Marcus Island in the north Pacific; the *Essex, Yorktown,* and *Independence* would conduct a carrier raid to test tactical doctrine and new equipment, gain battle experience for the crews, and initiate the Grumman F6F Hellcat fighter. In point of experience and knowledge of the units and personalities involved, Towers argued his own qualifications for command of the operation. He would leave Forrest Sherman as acting ComAirPac, embark on the *Yorktown* with Captain Beakley as senior staff officer, "and make fullest possible use of the experienced personnel of the ship"—skipper Jocko Clark, navigator George Anderson, and air group commander J. H. "Jimmy" Flatley, Jr. Of course, leading the first combat raid of the new carriers would also strengthen his case to go to sea as Spruance's carrier commander for the entire Central Pacific Force.[56]

Because of Towers' seniority among the air admirals, Nimitz decided to pass the request along to King, even as he directed Towers, on 11 August, to develop "a new concept in planning and development" for the carriers in the forthcoming offensive. Five days later Towers, his key advisers, four carrier admirals, and seven carrier captains hammered out carrier division and air group composition. The heavy and light carriers should be integrated administratively in two-, three-, and four-carrier divisions and operationally in task groups, a force of unprecedented size. King would not accept the new carrier division organization until it could be tested in combat, but Towers had laid the groundwork. He then began to work up the formal paper on carrier doctrine that Nimitz wanted.[57]

Meanwhile, in a letter to Nimitz Admiral King erupted: he refused to permit Towers to lead the Marcus or any other operation. Without mentioning him by name, King observed that the air type commander should not absent himself from fleet headquarters. "If the Chief of Staff [Sherman] can conduct affairs, what is the need of having a Principal? Where is the task force staff to come from? The absence would involve not only physical absence [during] the period of the 'excursion,' but 'mental absence' during the period of organization, preparation, and training!" If Towers wanted to see "active service," said King, he could always trade jobs with Jake Fitch in the South Pacific. As for Towers' relative seniority, King dismissed it as "of no moment."[58]

On 16 August Nimitz informed Towers that he would not be permitted to lead the Marcus operation. Nimitz revealed that he had "exchanged views" with Admiral King and that "his views coincide with mine." He said he would gladly consider any request Towers might make "for other duty in the air organization of the Pacific Fleet which might involve combat operations." This was the hint that Jack could always relieve Fitch in the south, thus getting him out of Pearl Harbor and away from the main event in the Central Pacific.[59]

Two days after this joint rebuff Towers replied to a note in which Undersecretary Forrestal said, "Don't give up the battle on Naval Air. It may seem slow from out there but I think we are making progress." Replied Jack: "I must confess that those of us out here who are in a position to have a reasonably good idea of not only what is going on, but also of what is planned, have a feeling approaching utter hopelessness, and when I say this I am referring to major plans and major policies." He believed that naval aviation would be cut up into "small pieces" to prevent it from ever having "any effective voice in court" and thus to allow the creation of a separate air force. This observation inferred that the new carrier divisions would not be centralized under his own operational command.[60]

Three days later, Towers presented the formal ComAirPac statement on the employment of carriers to Nimitz. It read like the carrier admirals' critique from a prewar fleet problem. The carriers, said Towers, were the fleet's principal offensive means of attacking the Japanese on land and sea, which included direct support of amphibious operations. They should be tactically concentrated to achieve command of the air over the fleet. Carriers and land-based air should therefore hit Truk, then spearhead the offensive through the Marianas to the Philippines and Malaya. All attacks on Japanese shore bases and positions should be devised "to bring important enemy fleet units to action on terms favorable to us"—for another Midway.

Only "officers thoroughly trained" in carrier air operations should command them, to insure "skill and imagination" in their use. "To be 'air-minded' is no substitute for long aviation experience." Inasmuch as "operations and logistics cannot be divorced," command of the "major carrier striking force, when assembled, should be exercised by Commander Air Force [himself] who would have a Deputy commander to carry on his administration duties during his absence at sea." Thus he was demanding that role for which he had just been turned down. In addition, the commanding officers of large naval forces or their senior staff officers should be aviators, meaning that either Spruance or Carl Moore should be replaced by a senior aviator. For that matter, so should Nimitz's own chief of staff, black shoe Rear Admiral Charles H. McMorris.[61]

This outright criticism of the Pacific Fleet command structure and Towers' relentless effort to gain command of the carriers reached Nimitz on the heels of Admiral Harry Yarnell's form questionnaire soliciting the views of naval aviators, senior lieutenants and above, about the status and treatment of aviation in the navy. Though Yarnell had sent covering letters to both Towers and Nimitz, the latter regarded the survey as a breach of the chain of command and suggested that the air flag officers reply through him to Yarnell. Nimitz received his letter first and gave a copy to Towers, the mails taking over three weeks from Washington. Because these flag officers were about to embark on the Marcus and other operations, Towers drew up a quick memo for Nimitz so that the latter could compare Towers' views with those of the other air admirals before they deployed.[62]

On 23 August, Towers personally presented his memo to Nimitz. In it, Jack reiterated the views he had presented in his long letter to Admiral Horne in June: the separate air force movement was gaining momentum partly because of the navy's refusal to grant naval aviation a greater role in directing policy. Aviator morale, he stated, had seriously deteriorated since the Battle of Midway, and the chief of BuAer's influence had been weakened by the creation of a deputy CNO for air. Citing General Marshall's strengthening of the AAF, he believed the navy should do the same, allowing aviators to direct aviation policy and play a greater role in the high command. Nimitz challenged what Towers regarded as facts, as Jack later reported to Yarnell: his "rather violent reaction . . . was to the effect that I did not know what I was talking about." When Towers asked whether he should reply to Yarnell's questionnaire, Nimitz directed him to go ahead. "Based on my experience out here," Jack informed Yarnell, "I am inclined to believe that the official Fleet recommendation [on the status of naval aviation in the key commands] will be to hold fast to the status quo."[63]

Spruance took no part in these discussions, for he had departed on an inspection trip of the South Pacific in Towers' Coronado flying boat. On 22 August, as the plane brought the party back, the pilot radioed ahead that he could not lower the port pontoon. Alerted to the crisis, Towers sped out into the bay in his gig, loaded down with life preservers, and stood by anxiously as the PB2Y made its approach. Just as it touched down, several passengers ran through the hatch to weight down the starboard wing, preventing the plane from tipping to port. Jack was justly relieved.[64]

With Spruance back, planning for Galvanic—the Gilberts operation—began in earnest, the most immediate concern being its vast logistical requirements. Admiral Nimitz yielded to army pressure for a Pacific area army-navy joint staff, established on 6 September, in order to improve logistics by using better developed army practices. As always, however, aviation logistics required its own specialized organization, headed by ComAirPac's experts, Captain Horse Pennoyer and Commander Jim Boundy. So Towers was included in a major logistics conference called by Nimitz on 26 August. Supported strongly by amphibious commander Kelly Turner, Towers argued that aviation logistics had to be carried out at "a speed far greater than is normally accepted for logistic support as a whole." The preparation of advance base "Acorn" aircraft repair units was immediately stepped up.[65]

That Nimitz's logistical system was inadequate to meet the demands of the offensive became evident with the visit in mid-September of Lieutenant General Brehon B. Somervell, the army's overall logistics commander. Admiral Calhoun had command of Nimitz's service force, but no organizational scheme existed for supplying Spruance's new fleet and its army and Marine Corps components. Somervell and Towers found themselves in close agreement, namely, that while at sea Spruance should have a deputy air commander to handle all forward administrative and logistical matters. Johnny Hoover got the nod. Also, Towers urged the use of mobile supply ships and forward anchorages, as did Somervell. Most immediately, the offensive supply pipeline had to start in the Southeast Pacific and move from Samoa and the Ellice islands toward the Gilberts. The anchorages and bases along this line needed fighters for defense and seaplanes for antisub patrols, needs which Towers assessed in mid-September during an inspection trip to Canton and Funafuti.[66]

Nimitz decided to appoint Admiral Pownall commander Carriers Central Pacific Force, perhaps to justify his going to sea as a type commander. Pownall and Towers first learned of this upon the return of Pownall's task force from the successful Marcus raid on 8 September. Jack told Pownall he thought the title superfluous as long as the carriers were dispersed among several task forces, though there can be little doubt that Towers regarded the move as but another measure to thwart his own ambitions. In any case, he was charged with providing staff officers for both Pownall and Hoover, a task made difficult by the nebulous nature of both commands.[67]

The Marcus strike itself immediately gave rise to questions about carrier commanders, notably the captain of the *Independence,* George R. Fairlamb, Jr., who had become completely distraught under the pressure of combat and would have to be relieved. It was a ticklish matter; Towers had to use senior flight surgeons Frederick Ceres and George Thompson to force Fairlamb to relinquish command of his ship. More ominous was criticism of Pownall himself, whose lack of resolve in the heat of battle was reported to Towers by flagship navigator George Anderson and Wallace Beakley, whom Jack had loaned to Pownall for the raid. On 18 September, needing more experience, Pownall hoisted his flag in the new *Lexington* for a raid on Tarawa in the Gilberts, only to behave erratically again in the eyes of Beakley and others. At least one man waited anxiously in the wings should Pownall prove unequal to the task. "Dear Jack," said a letter from Pete Mitscher on the West Coast, "I am feeling great now. When do I get out of here [?]"[68]

The preparations for these first operations of the Central Pacific offensive further emphasized the differences between Spruance and Towers. Spruance avoided direct involvement in logistics, whereas Towers immersed himself in the subject. In tactical training, Spruance lost no time putting the new fast battleships through maneuvers designed for the traditional gunnery drill, anathema to Towers. When Nimitz called a special conference on 19 September to consider mounting a carrier raid on Wake Island, Towers "urged as large a carrier force as possible," particularly since the expected battleships would not be available. Though not familiar with Spruance's plans for training, he argued that he "could think of no better training for carriers and the escort forces than the operation proposed. After some discussion Spruance agreed."

No fewer than six carriers were assigned—three heavies and three lights, the largest carrier force since the Japanese attack on Pearl Harbor. Commanded by the tough, hard-driving Rear Admiral Monty Montgomery, their planes worked over Wake for two days, 5–6 October, and for the first time Hellcats shot down Japanese Zero fighters. Thus while Spruance trained for a battle line duel that might never happen, Towers had the carriers exercised in battle to make certain they would never let that duel occur.[69]

"I am terribly busy nowadays," Jack wrote to his brother Will on 21 September,

> and my part of the Fleet has grown enormously. For example, I have more men under me than the whole Navy had a very few years ago. Shortly you may expect to hear of things really happening. The training job is about over—for the first team, anyway. . . . I fear I am doomed to sit here and tell others what to do and how, rather than get in much on the real thing. There is no desire on the part of some "exalted personages" [King and Nimitz] for me to be recalled to public attention, and I'll have to admit this is a huge job that I can do well.[70]

As for the timetable for victory, "We have quite a pool bet on it here in my staff, which incidentally now numbers 130 officers, and all *busy*." He put his money on December 1944 for the defeat of Germany, 1946 for Japan.[71]

Indeed, the work was mounting so rapidly that Towers felt the need to further streamline his organization. King wanted Towers' planning officer Beakley for his own staff, so Jack arranged to have him relieved in November by George Anderson, then in the new *Yorktown*. Plans was to be upgraded to division status, and Towers brought in his old compatriot and paraplegic Commander Spig Wead to help Anderson run it. But Towers was so chagrined to learn of orders transferring Gus Read to command of NAS Barbers Point at Pearl Harbor that he delayed Read's orders indefinitely to keep the able administrator in charge of advanced air bases. Like Spruance, Towers preferred to have his own team advising him.[72]

In the midst of the vast preparations for the offensive, Commodore Oscar Smith arrived at Pearl Harbor in November to promote Project Option, the use of air-to-surface assault drones in the Pacific. As chief of BuAer Towers had opposed the deployment of these untried guided missiles, and now he did so again, advising Nimitz and Smith that aviation logistics was so strained there was "no room for anything of doubtful usefulness." Furthermore, he saw "two great defects" in the missile: it was "a one-strike weapon" and too slow to work into carrier operations successfully. Nimitz finally ruled "that he did not want any part of the drone project moved out here until his principal aviation advisers assured him it would be useful." Smith would persevere, however, until he demonstrated the drones on bypassed targets in the South Pacific one year later. But independent studies at the CNO's office confirmed their lack of readiness for use aboard carriers, and major progress with such guided missiles had to await the postwar period.[73]

The debate over the target drones showed Nimitz beginning to develop an appreciation for the considerable talents of both Towers and Forrest Sherman. He had added Jack to the daily morning conferences at his Makalapa headquarters, Sherman appearing whenever Towers was absent and then with him as the planning intensified. Towers' top staff officers worked so closely with Nimitz's that Nimitz would transfer some of Jack's to his own staff. But CINCPAC remained wary of his ComAirPac.

There is evidence, as Wing Pepper observed, that Towers had a quicker mind than Nimitz—a prodigious memory, an ordered way of thinking, and an ability to sort out information and make quick, incisive, usually correct recommendations.[74] Towers' resentment at Nimitz's unquestioned faith in Spruance and at being rejected for higher command made his directness appear more than a little threatening. Forrest Sherman, every bit as ambitious as Towers, was smoother, certainly more brilliant than any other senior officer at Pearl Harbor, and thus more persuasive. Soc McMorris usually absorbed all points of view before advising Nimitz with clear precision, and he gradually came to share Towers' thinking on many key issues. The methodical, erudite Spruance was a superb orchestrator of the many facets of his new Central Pacific command, while cantankerous Kelly Turner focused on the needs of his amphibious forces during the Pacific planning conferences.

By mid-September 1943 the planners were conferring daily on the optimum use of their new fleet, while Halsey was advancing toward Bougainville in the northern Solomons and MacArthur up the coast of New Guinea. Planning for the Central Pacific offensive Towers found too slow and conservative, particularly as regarded the use of carriers. He took issue with Nimitz's plans officer, Captain J. M. Steele, who believed that every island in the Pacific needed to be captured, starting with Nauru. "Why Nauru?" Towers asked Steele at one conference. Steele replied that it had an airfield. "So what?" said Towers. Nauru lay 380 miles from Tarawa, the other target island in the Gilberts, and Towers believed Nauru could be bombarded and by-passed. This sentiment, for additional reasons, was shared by Spruance, Turner, and Major General Holland M. "Howlin' Mad" Smith, Turner's fiery Marine Corps assault commander. They recommended to Nimitz that Nauru be replaced by Makin in the northern Gilberts, closer to the Marshalls. Towers disagreed; he thought Makin was also unnecessary.[75]

Steele's lack of imagination was a telling example of Towers' frustration with the "battleship gang," as he often referred to the black shoes. His caustic treatment of them during these debates annoyed a lot of people. Recalled George Anderson: Towers "was somewhat supercilious and critical of other people, and that word would get around." Among his own staff Jack rather inappropriately referred to Steele as Boob Steele.

Particularly galling to Towers was the lack of aviators participating in Galvanic planning. Spruance wanted to lure the Japanese fleet into battle but opted first to cover the assault forces. Three task groups totaling eleven carriers—under Pownall, Radford, Montgomery, and Ted Sherman—were to cruise in assigned sectors off Tarawa and Nauru or Makin, absorbing attacks by Japanese planes coming down from the Marshalls to hit Turner's amphibious ships. These fast carriers, along with escort carrier groups, would also provide close air support for the army and marines going ashore on 19 November. Hoover's long-range bombers would lend a hand from bases in the south. If the enemy fleet appeared, Spruance planned to meet it with Lee's battleships in the traditional gunnery duel. Spruance seemed oblivious to the fact that carriers deprived of their strategic mobility were extremely vulnerable. Towers still opposed the Gilberts operation altogether, believing the island group should be bypassed in favor of the Marshalls; at the very least, a large-scale carrier attack should be delivered against Truk as soon after the Gilberts operations as possible. He formally recommended this to Nimitz on 21 September.[76]

After hosting Eleanor Roosevelt on the twenty-second and a visiting Senate committee the next day, Nimitz, Towers, and the other admirals received Admiral King and a large entourage on the twenty-fifth, followed by Admiral Halsey and his new chief of staff, Rear Admiral Robert B. Carney. The Pacific admirals quickly gained King's and JCS approval to substitute Makin for Nauru and made the basic decisions for the Marshalls operation. Command and logistical arrangements between the South and Central Pacific were worked out and personnel changes agreed upon. Towers convinced

King to authorize the construction of a fifth carrier pier at Pearl Harbor. He failed to win him over to the idea of a separate system of "floating aviation supply vessels that can move in and out of areas," although mobile service squadrons with fuel oil and aviation gas would soon become part of the service force.

When Halsey stressed the need for air reinforcements for his Bougainville landings, scheduled to take place 1 November, all agreed that the *Bunker Hill*'s new F4U Corsair fighter squadron should be replaced by an F6F Hellcat squadron and moved to airstrips in the Solomons for additional fighter cover. This change eliminated the Corsair from the carriers, for the F6F handled better in shipboard landings. The SBD was eliminated from the light carriers altogether and the SB2C Helldiver introduced as its eventual replacement in the heavies. King was especially anxious about night training for carrier pilots, because Japanese night air attacks, introduced at Guadalcanal, promised to intensify in the future. Towers assured King that he was working on it. Nimitz had wanted one night fighter squadron per carrier division, but Towers urged proceeding slowly, utilizing practices learned in Europe. No night fighters were assigned to the carriers yet.[77]

In a special meeting on 29 September, after King had departed, Towers, Halsey, and Carney "took strong exception" to Spruance's argument that he needed all eleven carriers kept together for the Gilberts assaults. Towers argued that the light carrier *Monterey* should be sent south to reinforce the *Saratoga* and that both of these under Ted Sherman should support Halsey at Bougainville. To keep the Japanese at Nauru occupied, Towers recommended that the two carriers be augmented by battleships to bombard that island before Operation Galvanic. He reminded Nimitz of his recommendation that the carriers strike Truk after Galvanic, and he introduced the idea that Japanese air bases in the Marshalls be hit before the Gilberts landings to minimize danger to the carriers. Finally, as he noted in his diary, "In polite language I protested the over-stressing of the training for the CLASSIC fleet engagement, pointing out that although the proponents apparently were overlooking the fact that we had overwhelming carrier strength, we could be assured the Japs were not overlooking that fact."[78]

Nimitz continued this vital discussion over strategy the next day. Halsey set the overall tone by insisting that since the South and Central Pacific operations would be running concurrently, Nimitz should "exercise overall strategic control." All hands agreed. Then Halsey outlined his plan to take Bougainville, Spruance his to take the Gilberts. Spruance, noted Towers, "continued to emphasize the necessity of training for Fleet action, and this was criticized by both Halsey and me." Towers also challenged Spruance's assigning of carrier groups to defensive cruising sectors, reiterating the advantages of his plan for the carriers to strike Nauru and the Marshalls first. Nimitz ruled that at least the *Saratoga* and the *Monterey* would be assigned to Halsey and not considered available for Galvanic.[79]

Towers won his case, for during discussions over the next two days Nimitz accepted his proposals and directed that details be worked out. Both carrier operations were to be undertaken at the end of October. First, Sherman's two carriers from the south and two carriers plus battleships from Spruance's force would attack Nauru. Then Montgomery would use more carriers to strike at enemy airfields in the Marshalls. With Japanese air power thus neutralized, the carriers could cover the landings at Bougainville and Tarawa-Makin in relative safety. Towers justified the Marshalls operations primarily, however, on the grounds that oblique photographs of their landing beaches could be concurrently obtained. Nimitz assigned plans officer Captain Steele to work out details. This black shoe failed to assign any light cruisers or sufficient destroyers as escorts for the Marshalls raid. When Towers objected, Nimitz agreed and ordered that the maximum number of light cruisers and destroyers be assigned. Steele was simply not the informed planner CINCPAC needed, and Nimitz decided to replace him. The use of offensive air before putting troops ashore was surely impressed upon Towers by Rear Admiral Alan G. Kirk, who spent the evening of 1 October describing the successful Allied assault on Sicily that July.

Towers' advocacy of fast carriers for offensive strategic flexibility was sound, though it flew in the face of Spruance's plans for the complex amphibious assaults of 19 November and for a battleship engagement. Spruance therefore developed a counterargument and obtained Nimitz's approval to present it in a special meeting after the regular morning conference on 5 October. The debate brought to a head the divergent tactical philosophies of Spruance's Gun Club conservatism and Towers' carrier-centered aggressiveness.

Spruance argued that the pre-Galvanic carrier operations would interfere with his tactical training and the upkeep of carriers for the ensuing operation. Also, he and Turner had agreed that vertical photographs of the targets provided by long-range bombers were adequate, making carrier strikes for the obliques unnecessary. Spruance recommended the Marshalls strikes be canceled. And he wanted the Nauru bombardment delayed until after the Gilberts landings; otherwise it would be too far in advance of the landings to divert Japanese attention and would interfere with the tactical exercises of his battleships, aimed at a possible fleet action. Even if delayed, he said, the Nauru operation should be conducted only with South Pacific carriers and light cruisers. Turner supported Spruance by insisting that "all possible carriers" be employed protecting troop convoys and providing "close fighter coverage" at the Gilberts beaches.

Nimitz was taken aback by Spruance's presentation, believing that everyone had agreed on at least the Nauru raid. Spruance, who hated open arguments, had not challenged the earlier discussions but had instead marshaled the evidence for this formal presentation. He brought in his chief of staff, Carl Moore, to hammer home many of his points. They "differed in some respects from anything we had heard before," observed Towers. For instance, Moore felt that the proposed strikes would strain the number of destroyers available for the landings.

All this was too much for Towers. When Nimitz called upon him for comment, Jack stated flatly that "too much caution was being exercised, too large forces being employed against secondary objectives . . . it appeared we were using elephant guns against rabbits." Galvanic was not justified and ought to be abandoned in favor of immediate landings in the Marshalls. Their seizure would render the Gilberts useless to the enemy—as Towers had told Nimitz in the spring. Nimitz replied that because Galvanic had been ordered by the JCS it had to be carried out. "I did not remind him that Galvanic had been drastically modified since first ordered"—Makin substituted for Nauru —"nor did I remind him that it had been recommended by him" to the JCS.

Too many carriers were being allotted to Galvanic, said Towers, thus making the Nauru and Marshalls raids entirely possible. Indeed, that very day Montgomery's six carriers were clobbering Wake. Unless they were kept active, Pearl Harbor would become hopelessly congested with stagnant shipping. Towers challenged Spruance's contention about carrier upkeep being jeopardized by the proposed strikes; that was Jack's responsibility as air type commander, and he had no such fears. Towers was surprised as Baldy Pownall rallied to Spruance's side, talking about the immediate need for two weeks of night fighter training. Jack countered this new idea with the observation that no carrier fighters were yet equipped for it. He got Turner to admit that the need for photos should not be a determining factor. But then Towers and Forrest Sherman argued with Turner over the value of hitting Marshalls airfields as "indirect support" for the Gilberts landings. Turner denied the value of such strikes.

Nimitz wanted to reexamine the whole issue in detail, especially since Soc McMorris supported both of Towers' proposed raids. Though a great manager and compromiser, Nimitz was caught in the middle of a major strategic dilemma. He wanted to let the trusted Spruance run the forthcoming operations without interference, but he could not deny the merit of the carrier strikes advocated by Towers and Sherman.[80]

Towers then made two errors of timing. The first was his decision, finally, to submit his reply to the Yarnell questionnaire via Nimitz in the midst of these discussions. Nimitz knew the general tenor of the aviators' replies to be critical of fleet policy regarding aviation. Towers crowned the criticism by bringing up three matters: the sentiment within the navy for a separate naval air force (which he opposed), the resentment between non-aviators and aviators, and the makeshift nature of the deputy CNO (air) arrangement. Towers recommended better centralization under a five-star CNO or chief of naval staff and a four-star deputy chief, one or the other to be an aviator. Five assistant chiefs should be vice admirals. Similarly, each fleet commander in chief or his deputy should be an aviator, and fleet operational and planning staffs should be "reinforced" with naval aviators. These were the same arguments Nimitz had challenged in August, and here Towers was implying that he, Towers, should be either CINCPAC himself or at least Nimitz's deputy. Towers' second mistake was flying to San Diego the night of 5–6 October to preside over a long-planned four-day conference with Mitscher to discuss vital logistical and training activities. His absence enabled Spruance to marshal arguments against Towers' proposed pre-Galvanic carrier raids on Nauru and the Marshalls.[81]

Forrest Sherman acted as a stand-in during Towers' brief, fateful absence. Though only a captain, he had been selected for rear admiral. What was more, he enjoyed the complete respect of Nimitz. The latter had been favorably impressed with Sherman's reply to Yarnell's questionnaire one month before; he had said much the same thing as Towers but in a toned-down manner. For four days Sherman carried on the debate with Spruance, carefully recording it in Towers' diary. But in the end Spruance and Turner convinced Nimitz to cancel the pre-Galvanic Marshalls raid and eliminate battleships from the Nauru bombardment. Sherman engaged in a particularly heated exchange with Turner, who insisted that all the carriers be tied down off the target beaches; Sherman said enemy air ought to be eliminated at its source, the Marshalls. But the only change was minor; the light carrier *Princeton* went south to replace the *Monterey*, in need of maintenance.[82]

Nimitz was in a quandary. His habit of accepting bad advice and compromising in the interest of harmony were traits that led King to regard him merely as a "fixer." Nimitz now opted for the Spruance-Turner plan to tie down the carriers off the Gilberts, although he allowed Towers to speak his mind on his return on 11 October. Towers repeated his arguments, including the recommendation to bypass the Gilberts in favor of the Marshalls. This time Soc McMorris thought it desirable but impracticable, and Towers had strong support only from Johnny Hoover, Captain Ralph Ofstie, and two other Nimitz planners.

At this point, quite possibly at Spruance's instigation, Nimitz decided to try and remove Towers as the source of irritation. That evening Nimitz had hand-delivered to Towers' quarters a memo: "With reference to your memorandum of 8 August . . . for assignment as task force commander . . . would you like to be considered as the relief of Vice Admiral Fitch as ComAirSoPac, if and when Fitch is relieved?" This would also remove Fitch, who during a recent visit had castigated Nimitz for the "damned aviator" attitude prevailing in the fleet.[83]

Much of Nimitz's difficulty stemmed from the poor advice he had been receiving from his plans officer, Captain Steele, over the use of the carriers. So Nimitz probably half welcomed a dispatch from Admiral King on 11 October instructing him to appoint an aviator to replace Steele, the very thing Towers and the other aviators had been advocating. Next morning Nimitz asked Towers to make recommendations. Towers listed three men: in order of seniority, Radford, Forrest Sherman, and Wu Duncan. Nimitz pressed Towers to arrange them by preference, and Jack reluctantly placed Sherman first. Hating to lose his able chief of staff, Towers requested that in the interest of fairness he be allowed to replace Sherman with either Radford or Duncan. Nimitz agreed, and before the day ended Sherman had been selected to become Nimitz's plans officer and Radford as Towers' chief of staff. After the change occurred, Steele would be given command of the battleship *Indiana* (only to lose that job after his ship collided with another battleship).[84]

Towers lost no time taking advantage of King's coincidental decision to support his contention for more aviators in key staff positions. Next day he replied to Nimitz's offer to have him relieve Fitch in the south by declining it; as he had told Nimitz before, that job would be "of diminishing importance, whereas mine inevitably would increase in importance as we gained carrier strength." Furthermore, Towers defended his letter of 4 October to Yarnell: "Nothing in it was intended as a complaint about my personal situation." Indeed, its intent "was along the lines of what is about to occur in your staff. I haven't the slightest idea as to what caused Admiral King to send that despatch, but apparently I was thinking along the same general lines he is." As soon as Sherman joined Nimitz's staff, Towers concluded, "I venture to predict that within a short time you will feel your position is stronger and your path easier."[85] Sherman would not move over until Radford was available to Towers after the completion of Galvanic, in which "Raddy" would command a fast carrier task group. When he did move, Sherman exerted enormous influence over Nimitz. As Wing Pepper, who would join Nimitz's staff a year later, recalled, "Forrest Sherman . . . really directed the War in the Pacific from the moment . . . he transferred from COMAIRPAC to CINCPAC as Head of the Plans Division. Both Admiral Nimitz and Admiral McMorris relied on him and they almost blindly followed his brilliant leadership."[86]

The most impressive case for naval air was made by the forces returning from the 5–6 October Wake strike. They brought with them dramatic combat movie footage, action reports, and testimony by leaders from the six participating carriers and land-based navy PB4Y Liberators. Thus it was with incredulity that returning Admirals Pownall and Radford studied Spruance's detailed op plan for Galvanic on the fourteenth. Spruance planned to station their two task groups of three carriers each off Makin, the northernmost objective, closest to the Marshalls and Truk, there to absorb incoming enemy air strikes and to engage the Japanese fleet should it appear. The five available fast battleships would cruise in the screens of these two groups and form Lee's battle line if and when the Japanese fleet appeared. As little more than sitting ducks for the enemy's planes, submarines, and now fleet, Pownall and Radford would be unable to exploit their carriers' maneuverability.

The two men complained to Towers that this plan was downright dangerous. They wanted to operate separately from the landing forces, with plenty of sea room. Towers, not privy to the detailed op plans but aware of the general outline, could only agree. Since Nimitz and Spruance already knew his views, he suggested to Pownall and Radford that they, together with Montgomery, visit Spruance with their suggestion. They did so immediately, to no avail.[87]

Nimitz could not provide a final court of appeal because he had landed in the hospital for a week with a prostate malady. As Spruance, Turner, and Moore proceeded to finalize their op plan, they met another protest from an unexpected quarter on 17 October. Lieutenant General Robert C. Richardson, the new army commander in Hawaii, protested that his troops, once they seized Makin, would be exposed to Japanese air strikes from the

Marshalls until they could build an airfield there. He wanted carriers kept off Makin indefinitely to provide combat air patrols, which both Towers and Spruance agreed would be an improper use of the ships. Turner added that the carriers' fighters could not be spared from protecting the unloading of his transports. Towers and Sherman disagreed "with Turner's ideas that the best defense was purely local defense" and still advocated striking the Marshalls. For the moment, all the navy could guarantee the army was one squadron of Hellcats. These would be flown ashore from two escort carriers to operate out of the airfield on Tarawa, once the marines captured it.[88]

As the final preparations gathered momentum, Towers dealt with fresh problems and found time to welcome Rear Admiral Henry Mullinix and the *Liscome Bay,* first of the new *Casablanca*-class escort carriers to reach the Pacific. The first acrimony between the AAF and the navy developed when Major General Willis A. Hale protested being subordinated to Admiral Hoover's land-based control, but the navy prevailed. And Admiral Ghormley's nervousness suddenly resurfaced when Japanese submarines were reported southwest of Hawaii. Ghormley asked for an escort carrier and destroyers to look for them, but Towers had the request denied; the search surely would have been futile.[89]

On 23 October, the day after Nimitz returned to duty from the hospital, Vice Admiral John McCain arrived in Hawaii. Escaping from Washington, he had come out to promote an extravagant scheme of his conceived in August —a carrier operation against the Japanese home islands. Because of the sheer logistical complexity, Spruance and logistics boss Calhoun refused to take the idea seriously. In a special meeting of senior planners, the aviation officers, including Towers, Pownall, Sherman, and Hoover, thought the operation "attractive and desirable at some future date" but unrealistic for the time that McCain suggested, June 1944, or "at least until the use of Truk is denied to the enemy." McCain's brainstorm did not help the credibility of the air admirals in the eyes of their critics. Aggressive and popular though he was, McCain failed to match his peers in intellectual ability, which is why Towers had opposed his appointment as chief of BuAer and then deputy CNO (air).[90]

The key was Truk, and, before that, the Marshalls, scheduled to be assaulted on 1 January 1944, though the JCS and Nimitz were still debating exactly which Marshall islands to capture. The shipping that would be required, however, led to the postponement of Flintlock—the Marshalls assault—to mid-January. In a conference on 23 October Spruance thought the optimum tidal conditions for getting the landing boats over the coral reefs would occur on 1 February. Towers, McMorris, and two of Nimitz's planners thought an earlier date preferable. Nimitz settled on 21 January. Either way, Towers had recommended in late September that "a large-scale carrier air attack" be made against Truk shortly after the Gilberts were secured. Admiral King liked this idea and on 21 October instructed Nimitz to study the possibility of such an operation in the sixty days between Galvanic and Flintlock. The lack of a forward anchorage at Truk, however, presented a problem, since the Gilberts had none. Nimitz deferred the discussion.[91]

On 29 October Spruance issued his final op plan for Galvanic. During the landings on 19 November Montgomery's three fast carriers and Ragsdale's three *Cimarron*-type escort carriers would support the Marine Corps assault on Tarawa in the southern Gilberts. Radford's three fast carriers and Henry Mullinix's three *Casablanca*-class escort carriers would cover the army assault at Makin in the north. Pownall's three fast carriers would comprise the "carrier interceptor group" off Makin to prevent Japanese planes in the Marshalls from interfering with the operation. Prior to the landings Pownall would be permitted to strike Milli and Jaluit in the southern Marshalls but not the larger airdromes at Kwajalein and Maloelap in the north. Ted Sherman was to remain in the Solomons with the *Saratoga* and the *Princeton* supporting Halsey's conquest of Bougainville, to begin just three days hence.[92]

Although Spruance had had his way with the defensive cruising sectors, Towers sought to minimize the danger to his carriers by pressing Nimitz for immediate post-Galvanic strikes. On 30 October Nimitz shared King's memo for a Truk strike with his admirals, and two days later Towers responded with a long memorandum of his own. Barring heavy losses in Galvanic, the fast carriers and fast battleships could leave the Gilberts about 1 December, replenish at Efate in the south, hit Truk at midmonth, then return to Pearl by the thirtieth. This, however, would replace the planned pre-Flintlock strikes against the Marshalls, designed to include the necessary aerial photo-intelligence reconnaissance of those islands. If Flintlock was delayed, Truk could be hit, then the Marshalls, both for the photos. Since Towers did not favor a long delay for Flintlock, he recommended strong carrier strikes against the Marshalls immediately after Galvanic, with an alternate plan to move against Truk, depending on developments. But one or the other should be executed as soon after Galvanic as possible.[93]

This sort of strategic flexibility was the sort of thing that the meticulous Spruance tried to avoid, particularly since a complicated amphibious operation was involved. But it was what Towers—and Halsey—regarded as essential to exploiting opportunities. This became evident immediately. For after the *Saratoga* and the *Princeton* supported Halsey's landings at Bougainville on 1–2 November, the Japanese rushed most of their carrier planes and seven cruisers south from Truk to Rabaul to contest the landing forces. Halsey took a desperate gamble. On the morning of the fifth he had Ted Sherman launch all ninety-seven available planes from the *Saratoga* and the *Princeton* to attack the cruisers at Rabaul, depending upon his shore-based air to cover the two exposed flattops. The scheme worked masterfully. The SBDs and TBFs heavily damaged four Japanese heavy cruisers and struck two lights at a cost of only eight planes lost to Zeros and flak. The Japanese surface fleet was suddenly crippled.[94]

Electrified by the news, Towers recommended to Nimitz that Montgomery's task group "be made available to Halsey for use in conjunction with Sherman's task group in a heavy strike against all ships in and near the Rabaul area." Nimitz called a special meeting with Spruance, McMorris, Sherman, and new joint staff head Vice Admiral John Henry Newton so Towers could present his case. Jack noted the obvious weakness of Japanese air strength in the Solomons-Bismarcks area and thought that another blow would be decisive. They all agreed, as did Halsey when informed. Next day Nimitz cautioned that Montgomery's three carriers might be delayed in the south and prevented from covering the Tarawa landings. Spruance and Turner protested. Nimitz suggested that the Makin assault be delayed. Towers, who thought it ought to be eliminated altogether, now suggested postponing Galvanic for two weeks. Nimitz refused to alter the carefully laid Galvanic plans. He did, however, direct Montgomery to join Ted Sherman for another crack at Rabaul.[95]

That evening Kelly Turner spoke at length with Towers. Turner believed that Truk should be assaulted and captured, then the Central Pacific force utilized in the South and Southwest Pacific for the general drive westward. Towers urged him to present these views to Nimitz. Turner did so, but it generated no response. The JCS, Nimitz said, wanted Central Pacific operations to proceed "as rapidly as possible." On the second the JCS had agreed to postpone Flintlock to 31 January, in accordance with Spruance's wishes, but they hoped for an earlier date, at midmonth.[96]

Events began to move rapidly. At the time of his decision to release Montgomery with the *Essex, Bunker Hill,* and *Independence* to Halsey, Nimitz moved the Gilberts assault back one day, to 20 November. After Montgomery's force and Ted Sherman's *Saratoga* and *Princeton* struck Rabaul, both groups would proceed to Tarawa to support the landings there. Spruance was set to sortie with the Central Pacific Force on 10 November. Pownall would be in the *Yorktown* and would have the new *Lexington* and *Cowpens* as well in his interceptor group. Radford would be in the overhauled *Enterprise,* along with the light carriers *Belleau Wood* and *Monterey.* On 8 October Towers urged Nimitz to give him at least tentative plans for post-Galvanic operations before the fleet sailed so that he could provide for replacement pilots, planes, and equipment. That afternoon Nimitz announced that King wanted Galvanic "executed with as much despatch as possible" so as not to hinder future operations. Nimitz decided Flintlock should commence on 17 January, despite the latitude of the JCS, which said it could be delayed two more weeks.

Pownall now presented his own plan for post-Galvanic carrier operations: all available carriers should strike the three northern Marshall islands earmarked for seizure during Flintlock—Kwajalein, Maloelap, and Wotje. Towers urged that the fast battleships accompany the carriers, making use of their numerous antiaircraft barrels, but Spruance would have none of it. Preoccupied with his classic gunnery duel, he insisted the battlewagons remain in the vicinity of the Gilberts "to afford protection against enemy heavy units," the Japanese battle line. Nimitz ruled that all such details would be decided after Galvanic.[97]

Looking ahead, Towers exerted powerful influence on Deputy CNO (Air) McCain in the assignment of carrier admirals and captains for the offensive. In a meeting on 24 October Jack stressed that talent should override seniority. For the divisions of fast carriers, both men agreed on the best possibilities: Montgomery, Black Jack Reeves, W. K. Harrill, Arthur Davis, Frank Wagner, Alva Bernard, Cy Ginder, and Jerry Bogan. Ted Sherman was earmarked for a rest with fleet air in California. For escort carrier divisions Towers wanted to retain Mullinix and Ragsdale; Cal Durgin was a good prospect. Though Spruance wanted Ernest Gunther with the carriers, Towers had Gunther replace Osborne Hardison as commander Fleet Air South Pacific; Hardison had been a thorn in the side of both Towers and Jake Fitch, greatly exacerbating command relationships in the south. Nimitz approved Towers' recommendation to have Hardison transferred to a training command. Towers' big concern was Baldy Pownall, senior carrier division commander. He felt Pownall should be relieved "either at the conclusion of Galvanic or the conclusion of Flintlock."[98]

The striking power of fast carriers was again demonstrated on 11 November, when Montgomery's three carriers struck Rabaul from the south and Ted Sherman's two hit from the north. They sank two destroyers and damaged other vessels, while Montgomery's defensive fighters and guns drove off a determined attack on his task formation by over a hundred Japanese planes. The Curtiss SB2C Helldiver was baptized in the operation, though top honors went again to the Grumman Hellcat. Meanwhile, Montgomery and Sherman joined Pownall and Radford in the north, there to begin prelanding strikes against Tarawa, Makin, Nauru, and the southern Marshalls.[99]

In the week between the second Rabaul raid and the Gilberts landings, Towers fought another battle over the fleet's doctrinal inflexibility. This time a proposal was made for "pooling all Pacific Ocean Areas shipping and establishing rather rigid rules regarding priorities. I pointed out that mobility was one of the principal values of aviation and that very value made it difficult to predict needs far in advance," especially by dictates from Washington. He proposed his own plan allowing for flexibility in the assignment of shipping, and Nimitz adopted it verbatim. Towers also played a leading role in helping the Marine Corps establish a logistical organization for its Pacific ground forces along the general lines of ComAirPac.[100]

By now Admiral Nimitz had come to value Towers' judgment so highly that he also solicited Jack's views on overall Pacific strategy. When Nimitz's staff considered the idea of attacking Japan via the Kurile islands and Hokkaido from the north, Towers reminded Nimitz that he had consistently opposed any such campaign. Towers supported the southern approach to Japan and discussed with his staff details of an eventual landing on the coast of China. He agreed that Amoy would offer the best fleet anchorage on the Chinese coast but that Formosa had first to be reduced. Unfortunately, the topography and defenses of Formosa "would make seizure an operation of the first magnitude."[101]

Towers elected to spend the morning of 20 November, D-Day in the Gilberts, flying instead of attending the morning conference. Throughout the day reports came in of successful landings at Makin and Tarawa, although at the latter atoll unfavorable tidal conditions hung up landing craft on the reefs and stiff resistance resulted in heavy marine casualties. Enemy air opposition was light until dusk, when some fifteen long-range torpedo bombers from the northern Marshalls attacked Montgomery's task group. Most were shot down, but not before one had planted a torpedo in the engine room of the *Independence*. She limped away to the south at fifteen knots; repairs would take her out of the war for six months.[102]

Towers' worst fears had been realized the very first day of the invasion. What lay in store for the carriers over the following days could only be surmised. Livid with Spruance for his tactics of immobilizing the carriers offshore, Towers demanded a special conference on the morning of the twenty-first. Nimitz readily agreed and included only Admirals McMorris and Sherman and Captain Steele.

Towers immediately

> recommended that Spruance be directed to modify existing orders which restrict operations of all three carrier task groups to very limited areas between Tarawa and Milli. I reminded Nimitz that I had strongly objected to this plan and . . . that the three task group commanders (Pownall, Montgomery and Radford) had gone in a body to Spruance and protested the plan. He asked why Spruance insisted on the plan, and I told him that he had been influenced by Turner . . . but that primarily . . . he was anticipating the probability of the Jap fleet coming out of Truk with carriers towards [the] Gilberts and had set up his plan in a way to maintain a concentration of the main strength of the fleet, including its carriers, in order to be prepared to fight the fleet engagement. McMorris concurred with me in this statement.
>
> I recommended that Spruance be directed to send the carrier task groups against the air bases in the Marshalls instead of maintaining a defensive position with the extreme likelihood of great damage from submarine and aircraft attack, particularly aircraft torpedo attacks around dusk. Nimitz finally instructed McMorris to get together with Sherman and draft a despatch of instructions to Spruance on this matter.

When Sherman and Steele withdrew, Towers convinced Nimitz to have Sherman relieve Steele "as soon as possible in order that he could have control of the planning for prospective operations." On Nimitz's instructions, Towers issued orders to Sherman to report for duty as CINCPAC plans officer three days hence.[103]

The despatch to Spruance had not been worked out by predawn of 24 November when a Japanese submarine attacked and sank the *Liscome Bay* off Makin. The lightly constructed escort carrier went down so fast that 644 of her 860 crewmen perished, many in burning oil on the water. Among the casualties was the excellent Admiral Henry Mullinix. When the news reached Hawaii Nimitz had Towers, McMorris, and Sherman send Spruance his new orders. He was to release the carriers, Pownall's and Montgomery's six, "with necessary cruiser and destroyer support, to deliver an air attack on [the] Marshalls as soon as practicable, primary objective Kwajalein." Ted Sherman's two carriers would cover the five fast battleships in the bombardment of Nauru.[104]

Although Tarawa and Makin were generally secured after three days of fighting, Japanese night air attacks from the northern Marshalls continued, demonstrating the immediate need for night fighters on the carriers. Admiral

Radford had developed a makeshift night team on the *Enterprise* and obtained Spruance's permission to launch it. For, after the sinking of the *Liscome Bay,* remembered Radford, Spruance "practically let us write our own ticket." Unfortunately, the scheme misfired when the night pilots became confused and shot down their own leader, the popular ace "Butch" O'Hare. Towers decided to immediately train special teams of F4Us and F6Fs equipped with airborne radar and put them aboard the big carriers for Flintlock.[105]

Pownall's and Montgomery's six-carrier raid on Kwajalein was designed to eliminate the major Japanese air opposition at the Gilberts. On 4 December the planes shot up enemy air strength at Kwajalein but missed one field loaded with unscathed torpedo bombers. When four of them attacked the task force and missed, Pownall decided to run for home without finishing the job. His destroyers could not keep up with the carriers in the high-running seas, and he had no choice but to slow down. That night the force was subjected to a continuous seven-hour torpedo plane attack. The *Lexington* was hit in the rudder by a torpedo and only saved from further damage by the antiaircraft guns of the force driving off the attackers. Captain Jocko Clark of the flagship *Yorktown* drew up a white paper for Towers' eyes condemning Pownall's lack of aggressiveness, and he even sent one of his officers home to gain the ear of the president, to whom the man's family was close. Pownall had to go.[106]

Another command problem surfaced as relations deteriorated between John Hoover and AAF General Willis Hale over land-based air supporting Spruance's fleet and occupation forces. Army General Richardson complained to Towers about small and widely dispersed air raids Hoover was sending into the Marshalls, unnecessarily jeopardizing the air crews. Towers tended to blame Spruance and his chief of staff Carl Moore, neither of whom was experienced in directing operations of shore-based aircraft. For his part, Spruance disliked Towers issuing Hoover certain orders involving planes and personnel, though Nimitz and McMorris ruled that Towers was in the right. Furthermore, Hoover wanted an aviator rear admiral assigned as his deputy to coordinate base and air activities on the captured atolls. When Spruance advocated a nonaviator for the job, Forrest Sherman reacted vehemently and with Towers convinced Nimitz to reject the idea as unconducive to army-navy cooperation. Towers had been fending off army attempts to take over navy airfields in Hawaii for months and did not want to exacerbate interservice tensions in the forward areas.[107]

Nimitz thought the best solution was for Towers to pay a visit to Hoover's Ellice and Gilbert island bases to investigate the matter for himself.

On 9 December, with several captains and commanders in the flag Coronado, Towers flew to Canton, then to Funafuti, where he was weatherbound for three days. He flew on to Tarawa—an "unbelievably horrible" place with rotting corpses—and Makin, inspecting everything and talking with Hoover and Hale before returning to Pearl. At Tarawa he learned from Admiral Mick Carney, Halsey's visiting chief of staff, that the South Pacific commanders intended to delay the mid-January target date for Flintlock. This view was shared by many Central Pacific officers stunned by their losses and the laborious task of sustaining the momentum of the campaign. Nimitz, upon learning this, was upset that others were attempting to influence his timetable. Towers reported on the strained relations between Hoover and Hale and supported the idea that a command center be established at Kwajalein once it was taken. Nimitz finally decided to assign Rear Admiral Alva Bernhard to the post, thus giving Hoover the air deputy he wanted.[108]

Towers had gained Nimitz's ear on all aviation matters, much to the chagrin of Spruance. The Rabaul and Gilberts operations had proved the correctness of Towers' thinking on the strategic use of carriers—and Spruance's misuse of them. Towers had conflicted with Spruance's old chum Hoover and criticized Pownall, for whom Spruance had developed a certain fondness. Now, on 23 December, in a meeting with only Nimitz, McMorris, and Sherman, Towers "strongly recommended changes to bring about more aggressive use of carrier forces and specifically recommended that Mitscher be made senior division commander and that Pownall relieve Mitscher" as commander Fleet Air West Coast. Sherman supported the recommendation, and the four men agreed that plans be made for Mitscher to be brought out for Flintlock, assuming that Admiral King concurred. When Nimitz discussed the proposal with Spruance, however, Spruance defended Pownall.[109]

This was the state of affairs as Towers and his small official family spent their second business-as-usual Christmas at Quarters K, joined by Rear Admiral Ralph Davison who had just arrived from the coast. Though Christmas trees were rare in wartime Hawaii, the staff managed to have one flown over from a mountainside forest on the island of Kauai. In the morning the four admirals discussed Pete Mitscher and later in the day attended a Yule luncheon at the home of Walter Dillingham.

Christmas Day was cause for special celebration for Towers and the entire naval aviation community. For that day Nimitz wrote a memo to Jack soliciting his overall views on "the characteristics and abilities of aviation flag officers" in the Pacific Fleet—clear recognition that aviation was to be given an enhanced position in the fleet in the form of more combat admirals.

Nimitz, about to meet with King again, wanted Towers to be candid in his appraisals. The successful prosecution of the carrier-spearheaded offensive would depend on having the very best.[110]

Two days later Towers drew up a long memo in which he assessed each man. As events were to prove, most, though not all, of his judgments were sound. In every case, though, it was the hand of Jack Towers and not of Chester Nimitz or Raymond Spruance that singled out the major admirals for the new carrier war.

"Quiet, hardworking" Pete Mitscher headed Towers' list, "tops for carrier task force command . . . tough and aggressive." The man Mitscher should relieve, Baldy Pownall, received Towers' lengthiest comments. It was painful for Jack to reject a friend and colleague he had admired for many years, especially as an administrator. Nonetheless, according to responsible officers, Pownall "worries intensely before and during operations. . . . This worry bears down on him mentally and physically," leading to a "lack of aggressiveness" that was "deplored," even "strongly resented, by practically all subordinate flag and commanding officers. . . . [N]ational interests better would be served by replacing him" with the aggressive Mitscher.

Of the two land-based senior air admirals, Towers rated Jake Fitch a fine leader but Johnny Hoover "rather an enigma," unpopular "probably because of his standoffish nature." Hoover had "a difficult job" commanding land-based Central Pacific air and one "which I fear has not been accomplished too well so far."

The best brains among Pacific aviators in Towers' opinion were Forrest Sherman, Arthur Radford, Ralph Davison, and Slats Sallada, whom Towers would be pleased to have as his chief of staff given a vacancy. All four would go on to play key roles in administrative as well as combat capacities.

Towers qualified his high marks for Monty Montgomery and Ted Sherman, already fast carrier admirals. Highly respected by all, Montgomery was "in no way brilliant, but energetic, courageous and determined." By contrast, Sherman had compromised his successes by a self-serving "intolerance towards views of other," making him so unpopular as to undermine the loyalty of his subordinates. Nevertheless, both men would remain in key combat roles to the finish.

As for John Henry Newton, just elevated to be Nimitz's new deputy, Towers said he lacked understanding of ComAirPac's logistical responsibilities with advanced base units and other necessities of fleet aviation, shortcomings of which Nimitz had already become aware. Some change had to be made.[111]

Nimitz accepted Towers' and Sherman's advice over the objections of Spruance. At sea Mitscher should replace Pownall, a change Halsey heartily endorsed. On the morning of 27 December, therefore, Nimitz held a special meeting of Towers, Newton, Spruance, Sherman, Pownall, and Soc McMorris. Using the evidence of Jocko Clark's report, he criticized Pownall for being too cautious in the Kwajalein raid, pointing out that carriers "were always risked" when used to inflict maximum damage. Although he noted that Spruance had praised Pownall for his performance during Galvanic, Nimitz pointedly instructed Spruance and Pownall to submit their air plans early enough so that the CINCPAC staff, including Towers and Sherman, could study them.

Pownall, stunned by the criticism, tried to defend himself. After the meeting he met privately with Nimitz to answer additional charges, part of Clark's paper, that he had refused to rescue a TBF crew after the Marcus raid so as to expedite his hasty withdrawal from the target area. He then spent an hour with Towers discussing it. The search off Marcus had finally been made after a boisterous confrontation with Clark, but the crew was not found (in fact they were picked up by the Japanese and imprisoned).[112]

Nimitz made no announcement of his final decision, for it had to be confirmed by King during their next meeting at San Francisco. There on 3–4 January 1944 King agreed, whereupon Mitscher flew out to Pearl and relieved Pownall. He moved in with Towers temporarily at Quarters K.

No one was more shocked by this sudden change than Spruance. Although loath to criticize fellow officers, Spruance laid the blame on Towers and on Undersecretary Forrestal as the power behind him. As Spruance wrote years later, "Forrestal had served under Towers . . . during World War I, and he had a very high opinion of Towers. If you were not an admirer of Towers and did not play on his team, your path was not made smooth if he could help it. . . ." Spruance was sure Towers disliked him. According to Spruance's chief of staff, Carl Moore, "Spruance told me many times that Towers . . . was doing everything he could to hurt him . . . [Spruance] was very suspicious of him and extremely careful in his dealings with him. I tried to reassure him, 'I know Admiral Towers is certainly not going to take advantage of anybody. . . .' He said, 'Yes, he would.'"

Towers, by exposing Spruance's faulty carrier tactics and poor judgment over Pownall, had undermined Nimitz's faith in him. As for Spruance, by focusing on Forrestal as a culprit, he incorrectly underestimated the power and influence of the man who orchestrated all major command changes, Ernie King. King, though he disliked Towers for his political connections, could not deny the aviation community's criticism, especially when carriers were being lost and crippled and men unnecessarily killed.

The Yarnell report, submitted in early November, had been sweeping in its criticisms and recommendations. Among other things it urged that the Pacific commander in chief be an aviator. King rejected that but not the repeated suggestion that all major nonaviator commanders have aviators as chiefs of staff, and vice versa. And at San Francisco Nimitz told King that he wanted to replace the ineffective Newton with Towers as deputy CINCPAC-CINCPOA, with Newton going south to become Halsey's deputy.[113]

At the San Francisco meeting King wanted to discuss the "Newton-Towers shift" with Forrest Sherman, whom Nimitz had brought with him to San Francisco, before approving it. As Wing Pepper observed, at these high-level meetings King "listened to Forrest Sherman and . . . wasn't listening much of the time when others were talking." Sherman supported the shift, whereupon King concurred, though it had to wait until the conclusion of Flintlock. In addition, all matters involving aviation policy would come under Towers as Nimitz's deputy; henceforth commander Air Fleet Pacific, would be concerned primarily with logistics. That post would go to Pownall. The appointment of Towers would serve to quiet Forrestal and other critics at the Navy Department.

Nimitz had carried to San Francisco a memo from Soc McMorris recommending that Spruance be assigned a senior aviator as his deputy. This lent weight to the idea that aviators should be deputies or chiefs of staff to all nonair admirals, and vice versa. Finally, armed with Towers' memo on aviation flag officers, King and Nimitz agreed on several aviation command changes. The new arrangements marked a major victory for Towers and the aviators. From now on fleet air doctrine would play a dominant role not only in Pacific planning but also within the navy at large.[114]

As soon as Nimitz arrived back at Pearl on 6 January 1944 he called in Towers to inform him of his new job. Forrest Sherman and Captain Matt Gardner, skipper of the *Enterprise,* tried to talk Towers out of it—"on our knees, literally," recalled Gardner—and into a seagoing carrier command. But that was a two-star billet and one King and Nimitz would never assign to him.

In any case Jack was ecstatic. He wrote to his brother Will a week later,

I become in effect general manager of everything out here except MacArthur's show in [the] Southwest Pacific. It may or may not mean that I am being lined up to relieve Nimitz at some later date. I think *not* because although King gave me the new job, he still hates me. I suspect the Army (Marshall and Somervell) had something to do with my new assignment. I know they are unhappy about things out here and I know they rank me rather high. That makes three of us! . . . I will be busy and no fooling.[115]

Towers' elevation within the command structure at Pearl Harbor was less exciting as far as the public and press were concerned, though the home state Atlanta *Constitution* honored him with a laudatory editorial in December. Moreover, the aviators' clamoring for outright control of the war in the Pacific was not really satisfied. But more astute participants in the policy-making hierarchy such as James V. Forrestal appreciated the significance of the change. Unless Towers and/or Mitscher blundered, which seemed unlikely, there was no turning back. After they succeeded in defeating Japan at sea, as surely they must, naval aviation would at last gain control of the navy. Forrestal sent congratulations from the department. "Your friends back here are delighted about the news of your appointment. Beyond that I am confident it is a good thing for the Navy throughout the country. All your associates of the old days in Naval Aviation will be pulling for you. Good luck!"[116]

In the autumn of 1943 Jack Towers had been the man of the hour at Pacific Fleet headquarters. No other individual in the navy combined the administrative skill, genius for aviation logistics, determination, and tactical knowledge to force King, Nimitz, and Spruance to reshape Pacific strategy around the new fast carrier forces. A lesser man would not have been equal to the task, at least not in the short time frame of a few weeks. Thus, Towers saved lives, ships, planes, and invaluable time—for only he fully appreciated how best to sustain the momentum of the Pacific offensive with the new fleet of carriers.

15

STRATEGIST-ADMINISTRATOR

OF THE PACIFIC OFFENSIVE

1944

Nimitz's six senior admirals, including Towers and Spruance, learned of the long-range strategic plan for the defeat of Japan at a special meeting on 19 December 1943. Rear Admiral Charles M. "Savvy" Cooke, Ernie King's chief of staff, flew in from Allied conferences at Cairo and Teheran to outline the strategy of concentration designed by King: MacArthur's and Halsey's forces from the Southwest and South Pacific and Nimitz's from the Central Pacific would converge on the region of Luzon, Formosa (Taiwan), and the Chinese coast near Amoy for a major assault during the spring of 1945. An air-sea blockade of the Japanese homeland would then be instituted, the vast Chinese army assisted against the enemy's major ground forces, and a direct invasion of Japan contemplated. The individual responsible for administering the entire Pacific Fleet and its air force would be Vice Admiral Jack Towers upon his appointment as Nimitz's deputy CINCPAC-CINCPOA in February 1944.[1]

At a luncheon and dinner on 20 December in honor of army chief of staff General George Marshall, who had accompanied Cooke from Cairo, Towers learned details of the JCS strategic plan. After capturing the Marshall islands in February, Spruance's Central Pacific forces would seize Ponape in May, while Halsey took Rabaul. Nimitz would then shift his Central Pacific force to the Southwest Pacific to support MacArthur's landings at Hollandia, New Guinea, in June. In late July Spruance's fleet would assault mighty Truk and in October follow that with landings in the Marianas (Guam and Saipan), where new long-range AAF B-29 Superfortresses would be based to bomb Japan. The diverse prongs of the offensive were designed to converge at the Luzon-Formosa-Amoy bottleneck the following spring.[2]

The JCS did not accept the idea of bypassing certain Japanese strongholds, though during 1943 it had been practiced on a minor scale in the North, South, and Southwest Pacific areas and at Nauru in the Central Pacific. Towers and Forrest Sherman had been discussing it ever since Towers' visit with General Charles Price at Samoa at the beginning of 1943. Now, early in December, Towers recommended to Nimitz that during Flintlock projected targets Wotje and Maloelap be bypassed in favor of Kwajalein. He also argued that Milli and Jaluit did not need to be captured. The four lesser islands, even though they encircled Kwajalein with airfields, could be kept neutralized "by blockade and air bombardment."[3] With Towers off inspecting the Gilberts, Sherman, now Nimitz's plans officer, advised his boss that the four islands, once cut off and neutralized, could be left to "wither on the vine." Spruance and assault commanders Kelly Turner and General Holland Smith, with their customary underestimation of air power, objected strenuously. But Nimitz and McMorris accepted the audacious plan, and Nimitz's decision was announced on 14 December. If these islands were successfully leapfrogged during Flintlock, why not bypass other, even bigger targets as well?[4]

This was precisely what Jack Towers asked himself as he pondered the new JCS Pacific timetable, writing his thoughts in a long memorandum to be given to Nimitz following the latter's return from the San Francisco meeting with King in early January 1944. Taking stock of heavy bomber losses being sustained at the hands of Japanese fighters, he reasoned that Hap Arnold's new B-29 Superforts should not be sent over Japan without fighter escort— the same lesson the AAF was learning over Germany. And since the Marianas–Japan run was beyond U.S. fighter range, the Marianas should not be captured. The B-29s should be based on mainland Asia, toward which the offensive was headed anyway. Unlike King, who had always believed the Marianas to be of capital importance, Towers thought them "a narrow, completely exposed salient thrusting toward Japan." They should be bypassed.

Towers recommended that the Pacific offensive be concentrated in the south. Following the Marshalls operation, Rabaul, other points in the Bismarck Archipelago, and the adjacent Admiralty islands should be taken. Not only were these places more strategically advanced, but from airfields there and in the northern Solomons planes could bomb Truk, six hundred miles to the north, day and night. The Japanese would be forced to withdraw their fleet from Truk and divert valuable forces to help defend it in fear of a landing. The strategic initiative and element of surprise, reasoned Towers, thus remained with the United States. For these reasons, he concluded, "the assault, capture, and development of Truk as a fleet base is unnecessary and undesirable." By eliminating Truk and the Marianas from the Pacific timetable, Towers believed the offensive could speed along the southern axis toward the Philippines, the *only* advantageous target to capture on the list. The fast carriers could make a diversionary raid against Truk in June, followed by capture of the Palau islands for advanced bases in July, then air attacks against the Japanese Philippines in August, and finally invasion of the southern Philippines in October.

Towers' thinking differed from King's only with respect to the route for getting to the final goal. King would advance simultaneously in MacArthur's Southwest Pacific and in Nimitz's Central Pacific via Truk and the Marianas; Towers would concentrate along MacArthur's front and advance to and through the Philippines. King would seize Luzon in the northern Philippines, whereas Towers would progress there via the southern Philippines. Both believed that air and submarine bases should be established somewhere in the Philippines to break Japan's sea lanes to the East Indies and to mount the invasion of China and possibly Formosa. Both agreed that Chinese ports were needed. Arnold's bombers and fighters, based in China, could then undertake the strategic bombing of the Japanese homeland.[5]

Chester Nimitz, no original strategic thinker, took Forrest Sherman with him to meet King at San Francisco on 4 January. There King reiterated his basic strategy. According to the minutes, he "stressed the point that all operations were aimed at a drive through the Pacific to China in order to exploit [the] Chinese geographical strategical position and manpower." The Marianas were "the key" to the Pacific, providing a forward base for the liberation of China and for Arnold's B-29s. Sherman, no doubt privy to Towers' plan, came up with a compromise: avoid the cost of assaulting Truk by going directly from the Marshalls to the Marianas. No decision was reached, except to stage a surprise carrier raid against Truk before the carriers shifted south to support MacArthur at Hollandia, New Guinea.[6]

The proposed strategies of King and Towers both had merit. Towers had more supporters, especially MacArthur, who resented the preeminence of the navy's Central Pacific over his own Southwest Pacific. Towers' memo was waiting for Nimitz when he returned from San Francisco on 7 January. In the ensuing days Jack argued persuasively for bypassing Truk and the Marianas in favor of the southern route and quickly won adherents to his strategy. Small wonder that Nimitz seemed apprehensive, caught as he was in the middle of the debate. He therefore decided to convene a conference with MacArthur's and Halsey's representatives later in the month to discuss subsequent operations.[7]

Meanwhile planning for Flintlock proceeded, with Towers and Spruance again disputing the proper use of the fast carriers, and Nimitz sandwiched between the two. The late-January invasion of Kwajalein was to be preceded by preliminary attacks on Wotje and Maloelap, lest the Japanese stage planes through them to contest the landings. Since neither of these islands was to be taken, the unoccupied atoll of Majuro, lying between Maloelap and Milli, would be seized for its vast natural lagoon. Majuro would become a forward anchorage for the fleet. Late in December Nimitz, Soc McMorris, and Sherman directed that the pre–D day attacks on Maloelap and Milli occur on D minus 10 and D minus 9, using the carriers and fast battleships. Spruance protested to Nimitz that the carriers might be lost or damaged if committed so early in the operation. Sherman in turn reacted against Spruance's objections. At this juncture in the debate, 27 December, Nimitz and Sherman departed to the West Coast for their meeting with King.

Towers, not privileged to see Spruance's op plan, got wind of it from Baldy Pownall during the latter's discussions of fueling requirements for the carriers he still assumed he would command. Towers learned that Spruance intended to defy Nimitz's directive by postponing the prelanding strikes a full week, to D minus 2, and that the fast battleships seemed to be excluded from the bombardment. On the thirtieth Towers pointed this out to McMorris and John Henry Newton, wanting to assure himself that Nimitz knew of the current plan. McMorris supported the original directive but also saw merit in Spruance's plan for constant air coverage of Kwajalein, Wotje, and Maloelap by the carriers and land-based air from the Ellices and Gilberts. Given recent losses of heavy bombers, Towers questioned their ability to give constant coverage during D minus 2 and D minus 1. He argued at length for the D minus 9 plan and got McMorris to write Nimitz immediately, outlining the discussion.[8]

Nimitz responded immediately with a dispatch on New Year's Day ordering Spruance to carry out his original directive to strike Wotje and Maloelap on D minus 10 and D minus 9. Spruance was unhappy about the order—he still feared losing carriers—and for lack of sufficient ammunition he "objected violently" to using fast battleships. He wanted to conserve his shells "for prospective use against light surface forces"—his hoped-for gunnery exchange with at least some elements of the Japanese fleet. Pownall sided with Spruance. Admiral Radford, now Towers' chief of staff, aligned himself with his boss. Finally, McMorris agreed with Towers, favoring the early strikes and battleship bombardment of Wotje and Maloelap. They decided to put the matter before Nimitz when he returned.[9]

On 5 January Admiral Pete Mitscher arrived from San Diego and relieved Pownall as ordered; he was followed by Nimitz the next day. After hearing out Spruance, Nimitz decided to let him write his own op plan, and Spruance eliminated the D minus 9 strikes in favor of the D minus 2. Furthermore, because Mitscher had never commanded a force of carriers, Nimitz directed that Pownall work with Mitscher until the latter no longer needed him. It was an awkward situation for the two classmates, for Mitscher did not need Pownall's advice; Pownall would ride on Spruance's flagship during Flintlock. Mitscher inherited Pownall's chief of staff, Captain Truman Hedding, whom he instructed to work closely with Spruance on the op plan because of the weakness of Spruance's staff in aviation planning. Mitscher lived with Towers at Quarters K for a week, enabling them to discuss the forthcoming operation.[10]

What no one realized was the weakness of Japanese air defenses in the Marshalls. The dual thrusts against Rabaul and the Gilberts had forced Japan to commit its available air strength to those places, where less experienced pilots had suffered heavily in combat against American fighters. Lessons learned there were being incorporated into the new op plan, and Towers sent a party under Rear Admiral John Dale Price to the Gilberts to rectify defects in aviation logistics. The big boon was the overwhelming strength of Spruance's newly designated Fifth Fleet, organized around Mitscher's Task Force 58; it consisted of four task groups of three carriers each. No fewer than eight fast battleships lent the heaviest weight to their escort, although Spruance still hoped for a gunnery duel. Three *Casablanca*-class escort carriers and three *Cimarrons* would provide much-improved close air support. Johnny Hoover was in charge of land-based air, but to soothe AAF sensitivities Towers and Sherman convinced Nimitz to appoint General Willis Hale as operational air commander at the tactical level under Hoover.[11]

While the Fifth Fleet made ready for a 22 January sortie, Nimitz and his admirals turned their attention to post-Flintlock operations, notably Towers' idea for a strike on Truk. On the thirteenth Nimitz had the necessary op plan drawn up and presented to the others by McMorris, Sherman, and Captain Cato Glover, Sherman's new assistant and an aviator. After Towers and Radford criticized the plan, Nimitz directed Glover to work with George Anderson of Towers' staff in making the necessary improvements. Following the seizure of Kwajalein, one carrier task group would cover landings at Eniwetok atoll in the northwestern Marshalls while the other three groups attacked Truk and with luck the Japanese fleet there. All agreed that speed was essential to trap the enemy fleet at Truk before it escaped.

Next day Nimitz expressed concern over the advisability of questioning directives from the CCS and JCS for future operations, as Towers was doing with the Pacific timetable. Towers argued that Flintlock had been modified as a result of lessons learned in Galvanic and that "it was our duty to criticize" the CCS and JCS directives "and recommend changes if we believe such changes would be an improvement." Nimitz agreed to keep an open mind about it and await the outcome of Flintlock.[12]

The biggest strategic issue involved Towers' memo recommending that all plans for the conquest of Truk and the Marianas be abandoned in favor of the southern line of advance. Both McMorris and Sherman endorsed the idea of neutralizing Truk by air attack, then bypassing it, but they thought some central Pacific base would be needed further west—if not the Marianas then Palau, as Towers had suggested. On 16 January, after considerable thought, Nimitz concurred with Towers' proposal to bypass Truk and with the endorsements of McMorris and Sherman forwarded the lot to King.[13]

The matter of long-range strategy was brought home the very next day when General Hale presented to Nimitz, Towers, McMorris, and Sherman a dispatch from Hap Arnold projecting the redeployment of forty-one AAF groups—fighters, bombers, and transports—from the European theater to the Pacific about 1 March 1945, by which time he reckoned Germany would be defeated. Arnold said that Pacific facilities and services ought to be ready for these groups two months before that date. Towers was incredulous. Far too many army and navy planes would be available by that time, and logistics, aircraft-ferrying ships, and viable basing areas presented "limiting features" for the employment of so many aircraft. "I expressed the opinion that we had hold of the wrong end of the stick"—a favorite simile of his—"that a firm campaign plan should be agreed upon and that *then* the aircraft requirements . . . should be determined." The others agreed "that if such a course is not followed, we would find ourselves swamped and lose flexibility of operations."

Especially sensitive to potential competition between the services over aircraft facilities in Hawaii, Towers recommended that a board be appointed to study the matter. Nimitz agreed and appointed Towers to head it after Hale concurred. Ten days later Hap Arnold instituted a similar study at the JCS level, and by February the Towers board found itself becoming involved with more immediate operations. For example, Towers proposed, and Nimitz agreed, that air base expansion should begin around immediate service needs until a grand strategic plan was forthcoming.[14]

The first step toward that goal was the purpose of the meeting of the South, Southwest, and Central Pacific staffs convened by Nimitz on 27–28 January. He distributed the agenda to his own people on the twenty-fourth, leading Towers to protest that two days was not enough time for discussion. Nimitz said more time could be used if necessary but doubted whether firm plans could be projected very far into the future without knowing the effect of the Marshalls-Truk operations. He was surely thinking of King's response to any plans that might be contrary to his, King's. Towers was unsympathetic: "I took the attitude that we must have a firm plan projected well into the future and with the superior air and naval forces available to us force the Japanese to react in a manner upon which the plan is predicated." General Robert Richardson agreed, adding that the JCS and CCS would surely accept any unanimous plan recommended by the conferees.[15]

The first guests having arrived early, Nimitz convened a special meeting on the morning of 25 January to initiate the discussions. In addition to seven of Nimitz's own admirals and General Richardson there were five representatives from the Southwest Pacific, including MacArthur's chief of staff Lieutenant General Richard K. Sutherland, his air commander Major General George C. Kenney, and Vice Admiral Kinkaid, commander Seventh Fleet. "The high point" of this preliminary meeting, in Towers' view, was an acerbic remark by Sutherland: he said Nimitz's opening briefing was the first time he had heard any definite statement by the navy on forthcoming operations—a not so subtle allusion to King's keeping MacArthur in the dark about the navy's Pacific strategy.[16]

Rear Admiral Mick Carney and Major General Millard F. Harmon, Halsey's chief of staff and army commander respectively, arrived with five other members of the South Pacific staff that afternoon. Towers put them all up at Quarters K. Late in the day Sutherland and Kenney asked Towers to pay them a visit. When he did, the three men held an hour's discussion on the "grand strategy of the Pacific campaign." Towers was pleased to learn that both men agreed with him about bypassing Truk and the Marianas in favor of the southern advance. "Towers and I," recalled Kenney, "were in complete accord strategically almost all through the war. . . ."

Assets should be pooled in the Southwest Pacific, Towers, Carney, Sutherland, and Kenney agreed, and they spent the twenty-sixth convincing others of the soundness of this strategy. Bill Calhoun thought that the single front would be easier for his logistical forces. Kinkaid and Forrest Sherman went along with it, and Sherman's support meant that Nimitz could probably be sold on it. The Southwest Pacific generals therefore drew up a new recommended timetable for bypassing all of the Central Pacific except Palau, which was necessary for covering the northern flank. The plan was identical to Towers' original recommendation to Nimitz.

For the formal meeting on the morning of 27 January Nimitz invited the best minds from all his agencies, including Towers, Radford, and Anderson. In what Kenney later described as "a regular love feast," the conferees to a man supported Sutherland's formal proposal for the southern advance. By the same token, Kenney and McMorris thought the Marianas unsuitable as B-29 bases. If they were not suitable, said Towers, there was no reason at all for capturing the Marianas. Kinkaid and Sherman thought them undesirable as bases of any kind. It was decided that Sutherland and Sherman would be sent to Washington to present their case to the JCS. Overall, recalled Kenney, "the meeting finished with everyone feeling good and ready to work together and get the war over."

Next morning the discussion centered on logistical requirements. Afterwards Nimitz and McMorris suddenly announced the proceedings had come to an end. According to Towers, their reasons were that "the conference was not for the purpose of making decisions, but merely [for] exchanging views. . . ." The premature ending of the session left Towers "with the distinct feeling that all the visitors were both disappointed and bewildered." Not Sutherland, though, who informed MacArthur that he had won over Nimitz.[17]

As for Nimitz, he surely had one misgiving: the anticipated reaction of Ernie King. Indeed, King reacted with fury to the minutes of the conference in a long letter to Nimitz. He singled out Towers as the major culprit for trying to reject the Marianas because of their lack of suitability as B-29 bases. King scolded Nimitz for allowing Towers' arguments "to go unrefuted," implying that Nimitz had again allowed himself to be swayed by questionable advice. The primary reason for taking the Marianas was not for the B-29s; that was to be a fringe benefit. King restated his strategy of concentration to

Nimitz: drive across the Central Pacific to China, taking and developing the Carolines, Marianas, and Palaus along the way. Luzon in the northern Philippines was "the key point for opening up sea routes to Ports in China" and for cutting Japan's sea lanes to the oil-rich Indies, not to the southern Philippines. China was the principal objective; King complimented Nimitz for at least appreciating that.[18]

As Towers had observed in his war college thesis on eighteenth-century French policy, only a great commander in chief could formulate and execute a grand strategy to achieve ultimate victory, and King was that person for the Pacific war. The dual advance by Nimitz and MacArthur would keep the Japanese off balance, but the most economic route, aimed at winning the war sooner, was Nimitz's direct drive to Luzon-Formosa-China. Japan's huge army on the continent had to be defeated before Japan would submit. By contrast, MacArthur wanted to fulfill a moral promise he had made in 1942 to free the Philippines; to achieve this goal his southern route was the more advantageous. Towers and the others were attracted to the economy of force represented by a single southern advance. But Towers also wanted to exploit maximum strategic air power against Japan, using fighter escorts for the B-29s; this was possible from China but not from the Marianas. The concentration of forces in the Southwest Pacific would have worked, to be sure, but the dual advance and spearhead in the Central Pacific would work better, as events were to prove. King was correct. MacArthur, Nimitz, Towers, Sherman, Halsey, Kinkaid, Calhoun, Carney, and a host of generals were not.

The immediate test of King's strategy was the Marshalls invasion and Truk raid. Mitscher's Task Force 58 struck the airfields in the Marshalls on schedule, 29–30 January, and found Japanese air defenses virtually nil. Furthermore, preceding bomber raids had severely damaged the target islands. On the thirty-first, assaulting army and marine troops, skillfully supported by carrier planes, found enemy opposition on Kwajalein comparatively light; within five days the atoll was secured.

Unable to affect the operation while it was in progress, Towers took a long-planned trip to the West Coast to discuss aviation logistics with Admiral Keen Harrill. Before departing, Towers made proposals regarding the follow-up carrier operations against Eniwetok and Truk, namely, an immediate attack on the latter. Nimitz and Sherman accepted this the next day, 2 February, except that Nimitz only "suggested" rather than directed that Spruance launch it.[19]

The speedy victory in the Marshalls made Towers' plan to strike Truk feasible at least, and haste was necessary if the Japanese fleet was to be caught at anchor there. Nimitz gave Spruance the go-ahead to have Mitscher with his three task groups hit Truk as early as possible, while the fourth covered the landings at Eniwetok. On 8 February, Nimitz was pleased to receive word from Spruance that Truk would be attacked on the fifteenth. Next morning, however, Nimitz "expressed surprise" to Towers, just back from California, that Spruance had ordered a two-day delay. He wanted to lead the expedition himself and to command the battle line should the Japanese fleet sortie for a gunnery duel. The loss of time while he hastened from Kwajalein to Majuro caused chagrin in Task Force 58, for it gave the enemy additional time to escape from Truk.[20]

In spite of Spruance's obsolete battleship fixation, no one could gainsay his achievement in taking and holding the Gilberts and Kwajalein—nor Kelly Turner's in leading the the amphibious forces. On 10 February President Roosevelt asked Congress to promote both men, Spruance to admiral, Turner to vice admiral. When Spruance put on his four stars eleven days later, he would outrank Towers.

One person greatly concerned about such changes was the deputy CNO (air) John McCain, a vice admiral and anxious to return to the fighting. King wanted McCain out of Washington because he was ineffective in his job. Towers met with him at San Diego on 2 February, and instead of discussing logistical matters all McCain would talk about was his scheme for sending carriers to attack Japan. McCain proceeded west to inspect air bases in the Gilberts, then met with Nimitz, Towers, McMorris, and Sherman at Pearl Harbor on the ninth. Contrary to their desires, he insisted that Arthur Radford return to the Navy Department to be his assistant CNO (air) and run the increasingly complicated business of aircraft logistics. He promised to keep Radford only six months. It seemed that McCain was maneuvering to return to sea at the end of that time. So Nimitz reluctantly let Radford go. Six months later, however, McCain decided to keep Radford longer. Being a King man, McCain would become a difficult factor in Towers' efforts to provide the fleet with superior carrier leaders.[21]

The logistical demands of the offensive were mushrooming at such a great rate that the very best managers were necessary to keep planes and spare parts flowing to the Pacific. While Radford undertook the work from the Washington end, Baldy Pownall as the new ComAirPac would be in charge at Pearl Harbor, assisted by Rear Admiral John Ballentine. Both Pownall and Ballentine would work directly under Towers when he became Nimitz's deputy. So too would Rear Admiral Johnny Hoover, who continued to wrangle with not only Hale and the AAF but Nimitz and Towers over a reorganized air command proposal in the captured atolls. Hoover even bent McCain's ear about it; when McCain echoed these criticisms to Nimitz the latter "told him to go down below and read it and write him a memo of comment." Nimitz appreciated Towers' directness and ability to keep schemers like McCain and Hoover in line.[22] But when Towers inspected the captured Marshall islands in mid-February, Hoover skillfully avoided him.[23]

On 16–17 February (east longitude date) the fast carriers attacked Truk. Most of the Japanese fleet units had already fled westward to safety in the Palaus, but Mitscher's carrier planes decimated the air forces and merchant shipping there, and Spruance was even able to use the guns of his battleships to help sink a cruiser and a destroyer trying to escape. Aircraft losses were relatively light, as F6F Hellcats and their well-trained pilots proved superior to anything Japan could put into the sky. The Americans, however, were again punished for the lack of an effective night doctrine: a night-flying torpedo plane hit the carrier *Intrepid* in the rudder, forcing her to withdraw for repairs. Despite this setback, Spruance could now release Mitscher with six carriers to head for strikes on the Mariana islands of Guam, Saipan, and Tinian. On 22 February, after refueling from tankers of the new mobile service squadrons, Task Force 58 planes repelled enemy air attacks and completely shattered Japanese air defenses on those islands.[24]

During these bold and successful attacks, the debate raged in the high command over whether these island bases should be captured. On 17 February Forrest Sherman showed Towers an eighteen-page memorandum MacArthur had sent to the JCS setting forth the reasons for bypassing the Central Pacific in favor of the Southwest Pacific and a rebuttal from King to General Marshall. Towers, predictably, found the principles behind MacArthur's thinking "perfectly sound." King would not waiver on the importance of taking the Marianas, but because of Task Force 58's success at Truk he was receptive to Towers' proposal to bypass that Japanese bastion. He informed Nimitz of his new viewpoint on Truk in a letter even as Task Force 58 was attacking the place. King wanted Nimitz to come to Washington soon to meet with the JCS. He warned Nimitz to be careful about leaving the fleet in the hands of the new deputy, Towers, suggesting that the latter might initiate some measure that could embarrass Nimitz.[25]

Nimitz had no such fears. Unlike King, he had learned to trust Towers implicitly and would leave him in charge during several trips over the spring. On the nineteenth he told Towers to "take over as soon as possible" as deputy, without waiting for the return of Pownall to become ComAirPac. Towers was ready to comply. Three days later he advised Nimitz to reject a sudden attempt by Spruance to have Pownall remain afloat or in the forward areas as an observer with him. When McMorris and Sherman supported Towers, Nimitz ordered Pownall to return to Pearl immediately. Spruance hated to release Pownall, who had "been of great assistance" during the recent operations, Spruance wrote to his wife on the twenty-third. Pownall "is a splendid officer, an excellent shipmate and a very fine character. He is going to relieve Towers, which pleases many persons."[26]

On 25 February Nimitz invited Towers to accompany him and Admiral Charles A. Lockwood while he presented awards to submarine officers, including Lockwood, on board the sub *Tullibee*. After the last award had been given, Nimitz surprised Towers by having him step forward to receive the Legion of Merit. Jack was cited as "an excellent officer who has performed most satisfactorily the highly important and complex duties of Comairpac during a period of great expansion." The citation, which may have been written by Sherman, was right on the mark:

> Displaying sound judgment and keen resourcefulness, Vice Admiral Towers promptly inaugurated an intensive program to improve and coordinate Naval air operation in the Pacific area. By his broad vision, initiative, and splendid administrative ability in handling the varied problems incident to training and logistic planning, Vice Admiral Towers was largely responsible for the effective organization and development of aviation components attached to carrier striking units operating with such conspicuous success against enemy forces in the Mandated Islands.[27]

At 0830 on 28 February Pownall relieved Towers as ComAirPac and at 1145 Towers in turn relieved John Henry Newton as deputy CINCPAC-CINCPOA. Towers had earned his advancement, and Nimitz had given him the necessary accolades—evidence of Nimitz's good sense in expediting the offensive.[28]

Not least among Towers' contributions was the strategy of bypassing major objectives. Though inspired by Charles Price of the marines, the idea of leapfrogging the Marshalls airdromes—and now Truk—can be mostly credited to Towers. His argument to avoid the Marianas continued, but in vain. On 23 February he had told McMorris that too much faith was being placed in an untried airplane, the B-29, earmarked to operate against Japan from China and the Marianas. On the twenty-ninth, the day after he became Nimitz's deputy, Towers listened to Forrest Sherman present the first detailed plans for Operation Forager, the projected landings in the Marianas. He in turn read to Nimitz, McMorris, and Sherman a paper by Spruance's chief of staff, Captain Carl Moore, forwarded to him by Pownall, recommending that in light of recent carrier raids Truk and the Marianas be bypassed. Sherman obtained a copy of it to take with him on Nimitz's impending trip to Washington, which the four men then discussed. They decided that the easy conquest of Kwajalein, Eniwetok, and Majuro, plus the destructive Truk-Marianas raids, meant that the next major Central Pacific landing, Truk or the Marianas, could be moved up to June from July or October respectively.[29]

On 2 March Nimitz and Sherman proceeded to Washington, where they presented their ideas to the JCS. On the twelfth the JCS ruled that Truk be bypassed and the Marianas assaulted, in mid-June. The compromise meant that both King and Towers in their respective positions had partially succeeded. Following recent gains in the Bismarcks and New Guinea, MacArthur would assault Hollandia in mid-April, supported by Task Force 58. Rabaul, finally encircled by Halsey and MacArthur, would be bypassed and kept neutralized by land-based air power, as would Truk. After much wrangling between MacArthur's and Nimitz's staffs, it was decided that newly taken Seeadler Harbor and Manus in the Admiralty islands would be shared by the forces of both theaters in their eventual thrust toward the Luzon-Formosa-China bottleneck.

The JCS envisioned both forces converging on China for landings now set for February 1945, MacArthur via the southern Philippines, Nimitz from the Marianas. Meanwhile the Nationalist Chinese armies of Chiang Kai-shek were proving ineffective as the major Allied weapon on the continent of Asia, and the JCS and MacArthur began seeking the entry of Soviet Russia into the Pacific war for the required manpower with which to defeat the Japanese army. King now ordered studies for supporting operations to Russia via the north Pacific.

The basic strategy for the great offensive of 1944–45 had been set. King remained architect of this strategy, Nimitz his agent in orchestrating the vast operation. Towers now became general manager—his own term—of the entire organization and responsible specifically for its aviation policy. Spruance commanded the Fifth Fleet, the tool with which to fight and defeat the Japanese at sea. His key tactical leaders were Mitscher of the fast carriers and Turner of the amphibs.[30]

Henceforth, for discussing matters of strategy at Pacific Fleet headquarters, Nimitz convened his three major advisers—Jack Towers, Soc McMorris, and Forrest Sherman. These "big four" worked well enough together, although

Vice Admiral John H. Towers, deputy CINCPAC-CINCPOA, in 1944. (Towers collection)

clashes were inevitable, especially as Sherman shifted his allegiance from Towers to Nimitz and often openly disagreed with his former boss. As George Anderson pointed out, "Towers was a strong supporter of Halsey and not an enthusiastic supporter of Spruance," Nimitz's favorite.

Towers insisted that as Nimitz's deputy he should move his office from Ford Island to Makalapa in the interests of administrative efficiency. No longer with a staff of his own, he was permitted to bring Anderson and Hebe Jones as assistants. Nimitz "did not like this particularly," Anderson recalled, but he nevertheless acquiesced. "Commander Jones and I were really hatchet men, you might say, because Towers insisted that we try to find out what was going wrong," which usually meant identifying which senior officers were failing to carry out their duties. This led to tension with key men on the staff. One was Captain Preston Mercer, Nimitz's flag secretary, whose inefficiency forced Towers to attend to many details himself. Another was Soc McMorris, whom Towers suspected of deliberately thwarting him, possibly because McMorris was reluctant to surrender prerogatives to the new deputy. Eventually, and rather than involve Nimitz, Towers confronted the chief of joint staff in person and "criticized him very sharply for his apparent lack of cooperation." McMorris disclaimed any intention of trying to undermine Towers and promised henceforth to cooperate all he could.[31]

Towers continued to look after the interests of aviators, at one point drawing the ire of Nimitz. Unlike the AAF, the navy was slow in issuing awards to veteran carrier air groups rotating home. As aviator morale sagged, Towers had George Anderson look into the matter. When Captain Mercer found out he informed Nimitz, who "hit the ceiling," as Anderson put it. Nimitz had a marine orderly summon Towers and Anderson to his office and gave them "the darndest bawling out." Said Nimitz, "Towers, I don't want you or any of your staff that you brought over here having anything to do with awards and decorations—or public relations!"[32]

Towers had stepped over the line, for Nimitz believed administration and logistics to be Jack's proper responsibilities. To speed up improvements in this area Jack got army Major General Edmond H. Leavey appointed head of the logistics section of Nimitz's joint staff. Some navy people, particularly in the service force, resented this move, but Leavey was particularly able. He had long talks with Towers over logistical matters and brought to the staff progressive navy logistical thinkers, notably Captain Henry E. Eccles. As Towers and Leavey streamlined logistical management, they began to uncover inadequacies in Admiral Bill Calhoun's service force, which they attempted to correct.

One flag officer on whom Nimitz and Towers could agree was John Hoover, administrator of the forward areas. Disgusted with Hoover's recalcitrance on several personnel matters, Nimitz sent Towers out to Kwajalein in April to set Hoover straight on fleet policy regarding the chain of command, not only relative to General Hale but to atoll commanders as well. Otherwise Hoover was doing his job, and Nimitz had his command upgraded to commander Forward Area Central Pacific, in the rank of vice admiral, leaving air operations specifically to Hale. But Hoover continued to exacerbate command relationships.[33]

Towers' biggest task as Nimitz's deputy was looking after the day-to-day administration of the fleet. With Nimitz he parried General Richardson's demands for the army to share overall command on an equal basis. The joint aviation board that Towers headed met regularly to establish air installations throughout the Pacific, which brought him into conflict with Richardson over the Keehi Lagoon and Barking Sands areas in Hawaii.

Towers also hosted visiting VIPs involved in aviation at home—during the spring Grover Loening, Gene Wilson, Luis de Florez, Charles Lindbergh, and executives from Grumman as well as British naval observers. He dealt extensively with civil affairs in Hawaii and in the newly liberated islands and looked after "rest homes" and USO clubs in Hawaii for battle-weary sailors and marines. He advised Nimitz on prisoner of war camps and on handling race riots in Seabee units. He took responsibility for storing vast quantities of beer for shore parties in the forward areas. At one point he even reversed a service force policy that had stripped Hawaii of Kotex sanitary napkins for the use of liberated native women! And he played a leading role in helping reorganize the Marine Corps in the fleet. In these and many other tasks, Towers was the ideal executive officer for Nimitz.[34]

During Nimitz's absence in March 1944 Towers, McMorris, Sherman, and Cato Glover carried out their chief's orders, sent by dispatch, for planning the next operation. Mitscher's Task Force 58 was to undertake another long-distance raid, all the way to Palau in the western Carolines, where it again hoped to trap the Japanese fleet. When Nimitz returned on 15 March, plans to strike Palau two weeks hence were finalized. After that the task force would support MacArthur's landings at Hollandia, New Guinea, set for 22 April. As in Flintlock, the air planners wanted to begin striking target beaches several days early, and again Spruance objected, not wanting to lose the element of surprise or suffer early risk to the carriers. In the end Spruance got his way: the carriers would attack one day before the initial assault. Given the fleet's overwhelming strength, however, surprise seemed less essential than before, as Spruance discovered when the enemy detected the carriers halfway en route to Palau. The Japanese fleet escaped, Spruance advanced his target date by two days, and on 30–31 March Task Force 58 mauled Japanese air at Palau. Spruance then returned to Hawaii to concentrate on planning for the Marianas operation, leaving Mitscher to lead the carriers at Hollandia.[35]

Increasingly important to all future operations in the vast Pacific were the AAF's long-range land-based bombers, whose effectiveness Towers continued to doubt. The bad memory of B-17s missing everything but the accolades at Midway had been compounded by heavy losses to unescorted B-24s in late 1943. Towers was generally correct when it came to shipping targets, but General Kenney's medium bombers proved so effective against shore targets prior to the Hollandia assault that practically nothing was left for Mitscher's carriers to strike during the easy conquest of that region in late

April. Still, the great distances involved gave Towers pause, and he continued to criticize the Marianas operation—often in spirited arguments with Forrest Sherman—because B-29s from there would have no fighter escort against what promised to be a furious aerial defense of the Japanese homeland. Towers was pleased, however, over the AAF's plans to base the first new very-long-range Superforts in China.[36]

Towers was not picking on the AAF, for he held similar views regarding navy planes, views that Nimitz supported. Although prewar amphibians had been regarded as patrol bombers, they had in fact performed more as reconnaissance than attack planes. Five bombing raids by Midway-based PB2Y Coronados against Wake in January and February 1944 did nothing to change Towers' mind. Admiral John McCain recommended putting squadrons of carrier-type dive and torpedo bombers on captured islands for defensive purposes. When Towers rejected the idea, McCain appealed directly to Nimitz. Replied Nimitz, "I believe you misunderstand Towers' views. . . . It is not that we question the inherent combat efficiency of 'shore based Navy striking groups' but that we find them ill adapted to offensive use over the distances which exist in the Central Pacific, and in the present strategic situation our offensive requirements outweigh defense considerations."[37]

That carrier planes belonged on carriers for optimum striking power was again amply demonstrated on 29–30 April, when Task Force 58 returned to Truk and completely neutralized it as an enemy airdrome. In addition, escort carriers provided effective close air support for MacArthur's assault forces on New Guinea. On 5 May Towers convened a meeting with Mitscher, McMorris, and selected advisers—Nimitz and Sherman being in San Francisco with King—to consider yet another carrier operation. Towers wanted a training exercise for the freshly overhauled *Essex,* the new *Wasp,* and the new light carrier *San Jacinto.* All agreed, whereupon Towers and McMorris obtained Nimitz's approval by dispatch. Two weeks later Monty Montgomery led the three carriers in successful raids against Marcus and Wake. Task Force 58 now had fifteen fast carriers—seven heavies, eight lights—for the invasion of the Marianas.[38]

With once-feared Rabaul and Truk out of the way, Admiral King could now reorganize the Pacific Fleet for the relentless drive to the coasts of China and Japan. Politically, he faced two irritants. Secretary Knox suddenly died in April and was succeeded by Forrestal, King's adversary, pushing for greater civilian control of the navy. Second, the old issue of unification of the armed forces and an independent air force resurfaced during the spring with a congressional study. Two high-level personnel matters also demanded attention. The successful neutralization of Rabaul had turned the South Pacific into a strategic backwater, leaving the popular Bill Halsey without a meaningful job. And Vice Admiral John McCain, still agitating to return to sea, made repeated visits to the Pacific, while relying on his assistant Radford to run the deputy CNO (air) office. All these matters bore directly on Towers, since he was a favorite of Forrestal's, an outspoken opponent of a separate air force, a supporter of Halsey, and no admirer of McCain.

In early May 1944, when King met in San Francisco with Nimitz and Sherman, he obtained their endorsement of a new system of command. Spruance and Halsey would henceforth rotate in command of the fleet. Under Spruance it would be called the Fifth Fleet, under Halsey the Third Fleet, and the task forces would be renumbered accordingly (58 to be 38 and so forth). While one four-star admiral led an operation, the other would be at Pearl planning the next. The question of a relief for Mitscher to lead the fast carriers under Halsey generated considerable discussion. Towers wanted the job, while Nimitz and Mitscher recommended it be given to Ted Sherman, now taking a breather stateside. King, however, thought this an excellent opportunity to get McCain out of Washington and back to sea; he therefore forced Nimitz to take McCain as commander of Task Force 38. Mitscher would come to Washington after the Marianas operation to help develop the navy's case against the proposed amalgamation of the services. Secretary Forrestal opposed the change, thinking McCain would probably not command the same respect as Mitscher in the fleet and that the latter was not articulate enough to represent naval aviation in the unification debate. But King prevailed. So McCain had wrangled his way back to sea, to the dismay of Towers, Nimitz, and just about everyone else who knew him.

Meanwhile ships, planes, men, and material were assembling at Pearl to be sent on to Majuro for the initial Marianas assault. In midafternoon of 21 May, while working in his office, Towers heard an explosion. He thought it was blasting for one of the public works projects, but soon Soc McMorris rushed in to say that an LST—an amphibious ship loaded with artillery for the assault—had blown up in West Loch. Within minutes Lee Ghormley telephoned to say that a number of LSTs had caught fire from the blast and some were drifting toward a ship loaded with 3,000 tons of high explosive shells at the ammunition depot. Nimitz being en route by gig from West Loch, Towers gave Ghormley permission to have a PT boat torpedo the LSTs if they could not be towed clear. As it turned out, the drifting derelicts ran aground; six LSTs were lost and five damaged. A worse conflagration could have forced the postponement of the Saipan landings. Next day it was decided to bring up replacement LSTs from the South Pacific.[39]

On the twenty-fourth McCain arrived and in a special conference immediately began to criticize the general campaign plan, lacking knowledge of it and failing to comprehend the logistical difficulties involved. As in the past, Nimitz told him to study the plan and write out his comments. Nimitz also rejected a request by McCain to go aboard the *Enterprise* for the Saipan landings; he would instead ride with Spruance in the cruiser *Indianapolis* and transfer to the *Lexington,* Mitscher's flagship, later in the operation. Adjourning to Towers' office with Pownall and Ballentine, McCain began to skim a rough copy of the op plan, then became abusive in his criticisms of it and said he would send it to Radford in Washington. When Towers pointed out this was not possible, since not even Nimitz had yet seen the draft, McCain argued at length. When he drew up his comments, though, he was pleased to find Towers in agreement with many of them. Two days later they both argued with Forrest Sherman that too many medium bombers instead of fighters were being allocated for newly conquered islands. Sherman finally agreed that both Marine Corps F4U Corsair fighters and SBD dive bombers could be utilized.[40]

While Spruance and Mitscher gathered their Marianas-bound armada at Majuro, Nimitz ordered Towers to Washington to confer with King and Forrestal about Pacific Fleet matters and to bring back recommendations.[41] At noon on 30 May, accompanied by George Anderson and aide Lee Loomis, Jack took off in an RY-1, the transport version of the four-engine PB4Y Liberator. The plane flew seventeen hours nonstop to Albuquerque, New Mexico, a total of 3,295 miles—some 300 miles beyond its designed range. After refueling, the big plane took off again and flew on to Washington, landing in the evening. The Liberator had flown a total of 4,945 miles in $26\frac{1}{2}$ hours, 25 of which had been in the air—record time for a Hawaii-to-Washington trip. Towers had seen the airplane come a long way since 1911.[42]

The exceedingly hectic visit commenced on 1 June. Over the next few days the air buildup for the Pacific offensive dominated Towers' many meetings, notably with Hap Arnold about the B-29 program. On the second Vice CNO Horne convened all the bureau chiefs and division heads to hear and discuss plans with Towers. He also discussed plans for the postwar navy with Admirals Harry Yarnell and Joe Richardson, the latter heading a JCS study committee, and with Forrestal and Assistant Secretaries Gates and Bard. He exchanged thoughts on the marines in the Pacific with their commandant,

General A. Archer Vandegrift, and went over miscellaneous administrative matters with a host of flag officers. Jack managed to spend one night with his daughter Marge, her husband Herb Riley, and eighteen-month-old granddaughter Lynne, whom he gave "a high mark in both looks and behavior."[43]

A cross-country flight on 6 June—D-day at Normandy for the liberation of Europe—brought Towers to San Diego for two days of inspections and a long-awaited visit with his wife. Pierre was so busy at Convair that she had had to turn down an offer from Rear Admiral Louis E. Denfeld, assistant chief of BuPers, to christen the new *Essex*-class carrier *Bon Homme Richard* on the East Coast. Jack urged Denfeld to keep after her, whereupon Denfeld offered to let her sponsor the second of the big *Midway*-class carriers the following spring. She accepted. Jack tried in vain to telephone Chas, now a lieutenant (jg) at NAS Glenview. Immensely pleased that Chas, Pierre, and Marge were all pilots, Jack told a reporter, "After we have won this war and I've gone home, the main quarrel in my home will be, 'Who's going to fly the family airplane today!' "[44]

Returning to Pearl on 9 June, Towers briefed Nimitz, McMorris, and Sherman on the general approval in Washington of their future plans and heard a brief presentation on Operation Forager, the Marianas landings. Task Force 58—15 carriers, 7 fast battleships, and 1,000 planes, plus escort ships—was scheduled to attack Saipan, Tinian, and Guam in the Marianas and Japanese airdromes at Chichi Jima and Iwo Jima for three days prior to the Saipan landings, set for the fifteenth. Supporting Kelly Turner's assault forces at the beaches would be no fewer than eight escort carriers, seven prewar battleships, eleven cruisers, and many destroyers. While neither Nimitz nor Spruance expected the Japanese fleet to contest the Fifth Fleet, Admiral King was less sure. Recent reported movements suggested to him that the enemy fleet might indeed sally forth from the southern Philippines. King worried that Spruance was ill-prepared for a naval battle.[45]

Towers shared King's concern. Everyone at Pacific Fleet headquarters closely followed the progress of the operations and intelligence reports on Japanese fleet movements. Mitscher elected to launch a powerful fighter sweep a day early, the afternoon of 11 June, which succeeded in easily destroying all Japanese aerial opposition in the target islands. But then reports indicated that the Japanese fleet was indeed going to intervene; it lay four days' cruising time from the Marianas. After the regular morning conference on the thirteenth, the "big four"—Nimitz, Towers, McMorris, and Sherman—had a long discussion about "measures to be taken dependent upon [the] Japanese reaction." Afterward, Towers mulled it over and decided that the Japanese fleet "might well proceed within 600 miles of [the] Marianas and from that point launch their aircraft with the intention of landing in the Marianas after an attack on our forces, thus keeping their ships out of range of our carrier aircraft." In other words, if Spruance kept Task Force 58 off Saipan, the 500-mile round-trip range of Mitscher's planes would prevent them from reaching the enemy fleet.

Towers hit exactly on what the Japanese planned. Late that afternoon, he summoned Forrest Sherman to his office to discuss his thoughts. Towers wanted to suggest to Nimitz that Spruance be advised of it and that Task Force 58 be released from the beaches to head west and attack the enemy fleet. Sherman demurred, and so Towers made the suggestion to Nimitz before the morning conference the next day, 14 June (the fifteenth, or D-day, at Saipan). This initiative provoked no immediate response from Nimitz. Intelligence confirmed the Japanese fleet's course, however, and the following day, after the regular morning conference, Nimitz kept Towers, McMorris, Sherman, and several others to discuss the situation.

Towers recorded the meeting in his diary: "Study of positions and sightings, courses, taken in conjunction with information in captured documents [on Japanese naval tactics] as to probable line of action and with predicted weather conditions indicated great likelihood of Japs launching [carrier] air attack tomorrow afternoon [the seventeenth, Saipan time] with plan to strike, then land somewhere in the Marianas. It was agreed Spruance should be informed promptly of the result of our studies." McMorris drew up the dispatch. It gave Spruance the information but no order for Task Force 58 to be released westward to attack the Japanese fleet. Nimitz did not want to act as fleet tactical commander from afar.[46]

Predictably, given his tactics during the Gilberts operation, the Fifth Fleet commander elected to concentrate Task Force 58 off the Marianas to await the Japanese carrier air attack. He believed this to be the surest way of protecting his amphibious forces. Moreover, the Nimitz staff's timing was off, for the Japanese fleet would not be in position to launch its planes until dawn of the nineteenth. The preceding night, Mitscher himself asked Spruance's permission to head west to intercept the Japanese carriers. Spruance refused, citing his fear of an "end run" by enemy fleet units, which might attack the assault shipping (which, however, had already withdrawn safely eastward). He simply did not comprehend the fact that ships could not outflank carriers and their planes. And he still had no senior aviator on his staff to so advise him. Consequently, Japanese carrier planes and others from the outlying islands struck throughout the nineteenth. Those that managed to land at Guam were destroyed there; the rest were shot down by Mitscher's F6F Hellcats in the great "Marianas Turkey Shoot"—some four hundred in all!

Mitscher sent out searches during the day, but as Towers had predicted, the enemy fleet was too far away. In the event, subs located and sank two of nine Japanese carriers; the surviving seven turned tail for home. According to General Edmond Leavey of Nimitz's joint staff, Towers was disgusted at Spruance for missing this chance to destroy the Japanese fleet. "I told them not to send him out there!" he said. By the time Mitscher was released that night, it was almost too late to catch the enemy. Task Force 58 pursued throughout the twentieth, hoping to make contact. When Towers learned of the pursuit he remarked to Leavey, "I was wrong. Spruance is a great man." The search planes finally overtook the enemy fleet, enabling Mitscher in late afternoon to get off a long-distance strike that managed to sink one carrier. The planes had to return to their carriers in the dark. Many dropped into the sea when they ran out of gas; most were picked up in a determined rescue effort. Six of the nine Japanese carriers had escaped destruction in the complex Battle of the Philippine Sea.[47]

Towers' alleged view of Spruance's greatness did not last beyond his realization that the Japanese fleet had escaped. On 21 June he wrote to his brother Will, "Am terribly disappointed about recent naval actions west of the Marianas. Believe there will be some changes in high commands." After the war he said that the chance to annihilate the Japanese fleet "at very slight risk was lost because of ultra-conservatism." Virtually every aviator roundly condemned Spruance for his missed opportunity—at Pearl, Towers and Halsey, and at sea, Mitscher and all of Task Force 58. Many nonaviators joined the chorus as well. For days after the battle, following each CINCPAC morning conference, critics gathered to pan the whole affair. Some thought Spruance should be replaced. Towers wanted the Fifth Fleet command for himself; barring that possibility he backed Halsey, who was at least in line to rotate with Spruance in August.[48]

Were the criticisms justified? Raymond Ames Spruance was a great fleet commander. His victory at Midway and his orchestration of the three major amphibious conquests of the Gilberts, Marshalls, and Marianas had proved that. Thus King and Nimitz, to quell the criticism, chose to downplay his decision in the Philippine Sea and retain him in command. But Spruance still had his blind spot, aviation. Although he accepted its importance, he could never bring himself to admit the carrier had replaced the battleship as the main striking arm of the fleet. Indeed, he had separated Admiral Lee's fast battleships from the carrier screens before the Turkey Shoot in hopes of a gunnery duel. In short, he had refused to think like an aggressive carrier tactician; to rely on the judgment of the best one available, Mitscher; or to add one to his own staff. Although aviator Art Davis would replace Carl Moore as his chief of staff in midsummer, Davis was even more mild-mannered than Moore. The last thing Spruance would ever do was accept the thinking of the man he loathed, Jack Towers.

Spruance had failed to realize that his amphibious forces at Saipan were never in danger from the Japanese fleet. A mobile Task Force 58 could cover the ocean out to 250 miles, making surprise or serious damage highly unlikely. As a tactician, like many naval commanders before him, Spruance was methodical, careful, and by the airmen's standards, conservative. Towers could make such a judgment of Spruance from his own close study of naval tactics going back to the age of sail. In his war college thesis on eighteenth-century French policy and strategy ten years before, Towers had echoed Mahan in criticizing the fleet admirals—the Briton Rodney and the Frenchman de Grasse—who had contested control of the Caribbean in early 1782:

> Fortune offered de Grasse a splendid opportunity to overwhelm a part of the English fleet, but he did not avail himself of it, and withdrew. The English pursued, and on 12 April, the decisive battle of the Saints was fought. Rodney broke the French lines, disorganized their fleet and captured five ships, including the flagship. Rodney failed to pursue, and lost the opportunity of practically annihilating the disorganized French Fleet. On the whole, de Grasse's West Indian campaign appears as a series of wasted opportunities. Had he possessed tenacity of purpose, the map of that area might present today an entirely different appearance.

The dogged interwar struggle between the Gun Club and the aviators reached its climax in the Battle of the Philippine Sea. The black shoes had dominated tactical thinking at the war college, Spruance having had three tours of duty there. Similarly, the battleship admirals had tried to dictate prewar tactical policy in the fleet problems held between California and Hawaii. But they had steadily lost credibility with the addition to the fleet of carriers and aggressive carrier commanders—foremost among them King, Towers, and Halsey. Based on their performances in the prewar exercises, any one of these three men would have made better use of Task Force 58 off Saipan. From this, one may infer that King, like Towers and Halsey, was highly displeased over Spruance's tactics. Save for one remark approving Spruance's conduct, King elected to remain silent on the matter.[49]

The controversy had immediate repercussions in that it adversely affected Towers' relations with Nimitz and Sherman. Sherman, having completely shifted his loyalty to Nimitz, took umbrage at Towers whenever the latter challenged him. The two men had several heated arguments over assorted matters during the summer. If Towers had always been ambitious, Sherman was even more so. And if Towers was respected for his brains, Sherman was admired for being a near genius.

On 26 June Towers recommended to Nimitz—in the absence of Sherman—that within three weeks Task Force 58 be sent further west to strike targets in Japan itself, taking advantage of enemy air weakness from the battles of the week before. Nimitz liked the idea, but Sherman later had it tabled. Soon Towers realized that he was being increasingly left out of major strategic discussions. He was ordered not to deal directly with MacArthur's headquarters, whose views on strategy he shared. He remained critical of Soc McMorris' inefficiency in running the staff, the truth of which Nimitz was forced to admit.[50]

The day-to-day meetings of the big four nevertheless forced them to work in concert. Each was talented in his own way, and their spirited interchange is precisely what made them into such an effective team, convincing King to treat their views with respect.

Towers' biggest personal frustration after the move from Ford Island to Makalapa was losing the use of the officers' pool for his daily swims. He began to badger Nimitz to have a pool built for senior officers in residence and in transit to and from combat. Nimitz, fearful of criticism in the press, resisted the idea, but Towers persevered until he got approval on 10 July.[51]

Work at Makalapa during June and July 1944 was dominated by two interrelated matters—the progress of the fighting in the Marianas and future strategy. Even as assault troops were encountering heavy resistance at Saipan, a dispatch arrived from General MacArthur recommending an accelerated timetable in the Pacific. MacArthur wanted to invade Mindanao in the southern Philippines in late October and Leyte in the central islands in mid-November, thereby liberating the islands from Japanese rule. In mid-January Nimitz's forces could land in northern Luzon and join up with MacArthur coming up through Mindoro; their combined forces could go ashore together at Lingayen Gulf, Luzon, for the drive to Manila in April 1945. Towers liked the general plan and said so to Nimitz.

478

The existing plan for the Central Pacific was to assault Palau in mid-September and then go on to Luzon and/or Formosa/China in February. Any acceleration seemed difficult, however, since the fighting on Saipan led Spruance to postpone the planned assault on Guam for at least fifteen days. Guam would not be invaded until 21 July, followed by Tinian three days later. MacArthur informed Nimitz he was sending General Sutherland to Hawaii to discuss the coordination of plans between the two theaters. King responded with a dispatch to Nimitz requesting an interim recommendation on changes in the strategic timetable.[52]

On 1 July, after Sutherland and two other officers arrived at Pearl, Nimitz instructed them to meet with McMorris and Sherman to discuss future strategy. He did not include Towers until the following day, when both staffs considered MacArthur's proposal together. Towers suggested that everything in the Pacific could be speeded up if the Marianas effort was reduced, possibly by eliminating the assault on Tinian for the immediate future. Sherman opposed him, and Nimitz concurred with Sherman. Next day the planners resumed the debate, this time with Halsey, the man who would command Nimitz's fleet in the upcoming operations.

The conferees agreed to recommend to King that Palau be taken in mid-September; the timetable, however, would be revised so that Halsey's Third Fleet could support MacArthur's proposed landings at Mindanao and Leyte in October and November. Nimitz refused to comment directly on the rest of MacArthur's proposal, stating that his charge was only to plan for the Formosa landings. Towers urged him at least to begin planning the proposed post-Leyte operations to expedite coordination with MacArthur. Nimitz did not include this in the recommendation to King, thereby leaving open the possible substitution of Luzon for Formosa, anathema to King. The dispatch was sent off to King.[53]

The huge task of assaulting Formosa had become increasingly apparent to the Pacific Fleet staff, though it dutifully went ahead with plans for the operation as ordered by King and the JCS. On 5 July Towers met with McMorris, Sherman, and Lieutenant General S. B. Buckner, commander of the Tenth Army, assigned to invade Formosa. They wanted to discuss with Towers the implementation of civil affairs activities during the occupation. The conversation, however, drifted to the operation itself, and Buckner "tacitly expressed doubt as to its feasibility." The proximity of Japanese airfields worried him. When Sherman remarked that MacArthur's conquests in the Philippines would result in new AAF fields to keep down Japan's air forces, Towers countered that the time between establishing those fields and the date of the Formosa assault, maybe two months, was too short to assure air superiority.[54]

The question of Pacific strategy was becoming critical, especially since a massive Japanese ground offensive in China was overrunning areas adjacent to the Chinese coast, which would make any assault at Amoy or Formosa extremely difficult. MacArthur continued to insist, moreover, that he be allowed to liberate the Philippines. Meanwhile President Roosevelt planned to visit the Pacific and wanted to meet with Nimitz and MacArthur to consider the course of the war. Given these events, and the need for changes in personnel and the carrier program, King decided the time was ripe for another visit with Nimitz, this time at Pearl Harbor. With Nimitz's staff behind him, King hoped to present a united navy front favoring Formosa over the Philippines. This was important, for he had not been invited to the meeting between FDR, Nimitz, and MacArthur.

The carrier program lay at the heart of the navy's contribution to the final offensive. Nimitz, Towers, and the staff accordingly recommended that carrier construction be accelerated. The Marianas Turkey Shoot and continuing carrier strikes on Japanese airdromes at Chichi and Iwo Jima convinced Towers and the air planners that more fighter planes were needed, which meant reducing the number of dive bombers and torpedo planes on each of the carriers. The Japanese emphasis on night attacks also led them to agree immediately to equip the light carrier *Independence* solely for night operations and to undertake night training without delay. The *Enterprise* and three *Cimarron*-class escort carriers should be similarly equipped by the end of the year. All these matters had to be discussed with King.

The question of carrier commands was equally crucial. Except in the case of McCain, appointed at King's insistence, Nimitz as usual deferred to Towers' judgment. They decided to retain Mitscher in command of the fast carriers under Halsey at least for the Palau operation, with McCain riding aboard as a possible alternate until he could learn the ropes.[55] For the pool of rear admirals to take up task group command, Towers drew up a list of the best and gained Nimitz's approval: Jocko Clark, Monty Montgomery, Ralph Davison, Gerry Bogan, Matt Gardner, and Ted Sherman. Nimitz and Towers agreed that Baldy Pownall had to go as ComAirPac; Pownall could trade jobs with George Murray at Pensacola. Though he had been absent from sea duty for two years, Murray would be promoted to vice admiral in December, which led Ted Sherman to gripe, "Friendship with Towers seems to be the only answer. . . . Polish up the handle of the big front door and never go to sea seems to be the answer." In fact, Murray was simply the latest of the type commanders to get his third star.[56]

The downright failure of several air admirals—Pownall, Ginder, and Harrill—to perform aggressively under the pressure of combat strengthened the argument of senior aviation planners to replace assignment practices with a more pragmatic policy. For instance, in August Forrest Sherman endorsed Towers' rejection of a carrier command for Rear Admiral Ralph Wood with this handwritten observation to Nimitz: "I differ basically with the whole approach to the question of command of carrier units at sea. In this as in other cases the question is not 'Does this officer deserve consideration?'—it is 'What officers will do the *best* job for their country?' " Nimitz concurred, and henceforth this philosophy dominated carrier flag assignments. Only the admirals best suited in Towers' view were given carrier commands. None of them failed to measure up.[57]

King arrived in Hawaii on 13 July, accompanied by assistant chief of staff Savvy Cooke, chief of BuPers Randall Jacobs, and assorted lesser advisers. On this day and the next King, Nimitz, and their respective staffs discussed personnel, future operations, and the carrier program. King "expressed reluctance" over Towers' desire to accelerate carrier construction. No fewer than twenty-two fast carriers and twenty-six escort carriers had been assigned to the Pacific Fleet, and more were on the way. "The Japs are taking an awful beating," Jack wrote to his brother Will, "particularly on shipping lanes, but on the other hand, their lines of communication and supply are getting shorter; therefore less shipping is required. What they will do is anybody's guess." He stuck to his prediction that Germany would quit by 1 December 1944 and Japan would not surrender before late autumn 1946. Carriers would be needed in abundance, and King finally seemed to agree with Towers' argument for stepping up production. Nimitz and his deputy had prevailed; twelve months hence, the Pacific Fleet would have no fewer than twenty-eight fast and sixty-three escort carriers, with many more under construction.[58]

In late July King and Nimitz hammered out their immediate plans. The two-platoon command arrangement of Spruance and Halsey was confirmed. The idea of bringing Mitscher back to Washington to fight unification was dropped in favor of his becoming part of a two-platoon carrier command rotation with McCain. In August the post of commander Fast Carrier Force Pacific Fleet would be split between commander Task Force 58 (Mitscher) and commander Task Force 38 (McCain). This omitted any possibility of Towers commanding either the fleet or the fast carriers, much to his chagrin.

Nimitz, tired of Jack's criticisms and repeated requests to go to sea, asked King to say something to him. As the two were driving across Oahu, King set Towers straight. "You have to do the job" of deputy CINCPAC, he said, "and you are the man to do it." That was that.

Among the personnel problems was finding McCain a chief of staff, who by King's fiat had to be a nonaviator, just as the reverse was now required of all senior nonair admirals. The job was offered as a fop to Carl Moore, who recalled that none of the top admirals had confidence in McCain. Furious, Moore turned them down, and Wilder Baker got the nod. After a discussion with Towers King approved the other aviation flag changes. What Chester Nimitz did not like was the Navy Department's decision to send WAVES to Hawaii; at least he didn't want them at Pacific Fleet headquarters. Towers, long an advocate of women in the navy, observed that two WAVES could do the work of three enlisted men. That was a battle Nimitz lost to Towers.[59]

As for Nimitz's recommendations about aviation policy, King agreed that fighters had to be increased at the expense of some dive and torpedo bombers on the carriers. He also endorsed the proposed night carrier group, although instead of slow escort carriers the *Enterprise* and the light carriers *Independence* and *Bataan* would be used. King got himself into a corner arguing relative airplane characteristics with Towers, leading Nimitz to interject that "the views of the older aviators regarding this question should be accepted because of their wider range of experience." Towers had the facts on aviation, not King, and Forrest Sherman agreed with Jack on most such matters.[60]

The major item was strategy. King listened to Towers and Carney criticize the projected Formosa operation; they were echoing what King had heard from Spruance and Turner when he visited Saipan. The main point that Towers pressed was the marginal suitability of the Marianas as a base for both the fleet and B-29s. That the Marianas lacked a decent anchorage was the weakest aspect of King's Central Pacific strategy. Towers admitted that Saipan and Guam could be developed as fleet supply bases and anchorages, but not if twelve B-29 groups were installed in the islands. After considerable discussion, King gave priority to the navy's facilities by cutting back the B-29 force to four groups. Knowing the AAF "would fight any change," Towers got King to guarantee his support before the JCS for the necessary changes in construction and shipping priorities. Towers then reviewed the Pacific base network and concluded it to be adequate for the Palau operation and MacArthur's proposed Mindanao-Leyte landings, especially after Ulithi atoll with its big lagoon was taken. But all these bases, he believed, were inadequate for the Formosa-Amoy operations, so San Pedro Bay in Leyte Gulf was discussed as a possible fleet anchorage.

King reported that Spruance and Turner wanted to occupy Luzon in order to use Manila as a forward fleet base, but since it lay on the west coast of the island it would be hard to reach. In any case, he would not consider going to Luzon before Formosa unless the Marianas proved inadequate for basing. Eniwetok in the Marshalls would be the backup. Towers thought Eniwetok was too far away, but "if timing were perfect" and fleet units there could be coordinated with those in the Marianas, it might work. He further observed that bases in the Amoy-Formosa area would become available only after considerable time was consumed developing them. But King would not yield; Formosa-Amoy was key to his Central Pacific strategy. The next anchorage after these, said Nimitz, should be further up the Chinese coast at Shanghai, and King advanced his idea to open a seaway to the Russian maritime provinces should the Soviet Union enter the fight.

During a luncheon Nimitz gave for King and some forty flag and general officers on 21 July, Towers sat next to King and tried to convince him to endorse his idea for carrier strikes on the Japanese homeland, which Sherman had had Nimitz table. The matter was taken up by the conferees. Given the timetable of fast carrier strikes between scheduled landings, they decided that strikes could not be made against Japan until late January. Dissatisfied with this explanation, King bought Towers' idea and ordered Nimitz to draw up plans for such an operation to take place, if possible, before the end of 1944.

"Since we have gone so far in our commitment" to base the B-29s in the Marianas, said Towers, turning to a related point, intermediate air bases should be taken—at Chichi Jima in the Bonins and Iwo Jima in the Volcanos—to provide fighter escort fields and additional bomber strips. Since Palau and Leyte were more important, however, Towers agreed that any assault on the Bonins or Volcanoes would have to wait until 1945. Though Sherman thought their seizure in the near future would make them into an exposed salient for Japanese air raids, Nimitz found this no hindrance: the Japanese would "feed their planes into this sink hole." King ordered Nimitz to make plans to invade the Bonins, but they should not be implemented until Formosa was secured and the invasion of Japan itself at hand.[61]

By the time he and his party departed for San Diego on 22 July, King believed he had lined up Nimitz's people behind the Formosa-Amoy operation, although questions over adequate bases had made the Philippines— Leyte and Luzon—look more inviting. General MacArthur could be expected to elaborate on the advantages of the latter when he met with President Roosevelt on the twenty-sixth. Nimitz ordered Towers to plan a massive army-navy aerial parade during FDR's visit. Jack was to greet MacArthur's plane and invite the general to stay at Nimitz's quarters.

When MacArthur's plane landed at 1400 on 26 July, Towers welcomed the southwest Pacific commander and extended Nimitz's invitation. "After considerable discussion," Towers learned that MacArthur had already accepted an invitation from General Richardson to stay at his quarters. MacArthur, it turned out, resented having to fly all the way from Australia to Hawaii for what he regarded as a showpiece for FDR in the latter's bid for a fourth term. So when Towers said they should proceed to the cruiser *Baltimore*, just then arriving with the president, the general remarked condescendingly, "I am going to my quarters! When the President wants me later, he may send for me." Taken aback, Towers hurried to the dock where he joined the host of high brass. Nimitz and Richardson had already gone aboard to greet the president, and Towers made sure he was the next flag officer to go aboard so that he could convey MacArthur's message. At this, an embarrassed Richardson hastened by car to fetch MacArthur, who ere long made a grand arrival. It was Towers' first encounter with the man whom the men of the fleet disdainfully called Dugout Doug for rarely mentioning the navy in his news releases.[62]

Neither Towers nor any other member of Nimitz's staff was party to the discussions between Roosevelt, Nimitz, and MacArthur. The latter worked his persuasive logic and rhetoric on FDR to win approval for landings first at Leyte and then Luzon, though the JCS had to make the final decision. On the twenty-eighth, MacArthur departed and the following day Towers attended a luncheon Nimitz gave in the president's honor. Over martinis, FDR renewed his long acquaintance with Jack, who used the occasion to promote his idea for the Makalapa swimming pool. FDR took him up on it, telling Nimitz, "What you need out here is a swimming pool for these young officers." Nimitz informed him that he had already approved the project; construction was to begin on 3 August. After the luncheon the *Baltimore* departed for home with the president.[63]

Meanwhile, Kelly Turner put his assault troops ashore at Guam on 21 July and at Tinian on the twenty-fourth. The fighting progressed well, though Towers labored daily at expediting the evacuation of wounded by air to hospitals in Hawaii. To prevent Japanese aerial interference and to obtain photographs of landing beaches for the next operation, Mitscher's carriers struck the Palaus and the Bonins. Organized enemy resistance ceased on

Tinian on 2 August, on Guam ten days later. Work began immediately on the construction of the naval bases and B-29 fields on Guam, Tinian, and Saipan, tasks skillfully and energetically coordinated by Towers.[64]

The offensive was now aimed at the enemy's inner defense line. Whichever route the JCS decided on for the final drive toward Japan, Nimitz wanted to be closer to the scene of operations in order to better direct them. Early in August he therefore charged Towers with the task of developing a forward headquarters for him at Guam as part of the new fleet base there. Towers drew up a plan that included moving the type commanders with Nimitz. Forrest Sherman, knowing Nimitz's preference for a small staff, argued forcibly with Towers and McMorris against moving them. Towers, seeing the difficulties of Nimitz trying to coordinate material needs from Guam with type and logistics commanders back at Pearl, opposed the plan to move the headquarters at all. The discussion dragged on through the autumn, with Sherman finally conceding Towers' point.

Nimitz, on the other hand, had complete confidence in Towers' ability to administer the fleet from Pearl, and he intended to leave him there after the move. A new assistant chief of staff for administration had just reported in the person of Captain Bernard L. "Count" Austin, who, working closely with Towers, greatly enhanced Pacific Fleet management. In fact, Towers had set up the best logistical operation in the Pacific while he was ComAirPac, and his supply system became the model for Marine Corps logistics in the Pacific.

For these reasons, and because the lack of precisely delineated responsibilities had circumscribed efficiency on the staff, in mid-September Nimitz revised the duties of deputy CINCPAC-CINCPOA. In addition to aviation policy, Towers now assumed jurisdiction over logistics, base development, and military government in Hawaii and the newly liberated islands. He performed these manifold duties "most satisfactorily," wrote Nimitz in Towers' next fitness report. The usual high marks continued for command ability, initiative and responsibility, and leadership, though Nimitz marked Jack down slightly on his conduct and work habits—not cooperating with others, inability to adapt to change, and not delegating responsibility effectively. In the interest of efficiency, Towers was indeed exacting and uncompromising.

The task of expediting construction of new fleet and air bases meant that Towers had to depend on service force commander Bill Calhoun to meet the complex logistical challenges of the accelerating drive westward. In a matter of weeks, Towers became aware of serious shortcomings in Calhoun's performance and organization, accentuated by mounting criticism of him by his own staff and others. Finally, early in November, Towers felt obliged to report to

Nimitz "that our advanced base development is bogging down and that . . . the principal cause for this situation is that Service Force is not properly organized or staffed for its functions." On Nimitz's instructions Towers repeated his allegations to Calhoun, who was shocked to learn of the criticism and most amenable to Towers' recommendations for reorganizing his command.[65]

As for military government, Towers was plagued by shortages of housing in Hawaii. Increased construction required civilian workers from the States as well as growing numbers of military personnel. Among other projects they were providing for the anticipated contingent of WAVES; Towers, Nimitz, and Ghormley—in dress whites, no less—greeted the advance planners, Lieutenant Commander Joy Bright Hancock and others, in October. Nimitz had finally accepted the WAVES, but he did not want them at his headquarters. Jurisdictional disputes arose between army and navy engineers, as for instance when army workers swiped paving materials from a navy project. Nimitz was content to let Towers handle the volatile General Richardson in these ticklish matters.

Jack flew out to the Marianas for a week in September, for "I am the boss of all those islands and it is quite a side show," he related to his brother Will. He was setting up "10,000 acres in truck gardens to feed the garrisons and the natives," which involved detailed planning for seed, fertilizer, farm implements, dairy cattle, and hogs. That the immense task took so long to get under way added to his misgivings about the projected conquest of Formosa. "Our show is rolling along rapidly," he wrote, "and very few people realize the enormous staff effort necessary to keep it going."[66]

The strategic bombing of Japan became Towers' direct concern as soon as B-29 base construction began in the Marianas. His point of contact was Lieutenant General Miff Harmon, who activated the Pacific ocean areas AAF headquarters there in August. From the outset, Towers and Harmon worked well together, agreeing that in spite of pressure from Hap Arnold fleet base construction took precedence over B-29 strips, and that the Superforts should not be sent forward until their fields were ready to receive them. Furthermore, the navy had final say on airfield design. Gradually, the number of B-29 units in the Marianas would increase from the initial four groups to five complete bomb wings. Admiral Hoover and General Hale moved into the islands for bombing, defensive, and reconnaissance purposes.

The friction over command authority between these two men continued unabated, and in September Towers rejected Hoover's request to leave his command for two weeks to be an observer with the fast carriers. Towers realized that once Nimitz moved his headquarters to the Marianas, "the importance of Hoover's job would be greatly lessened" and the tension no doubt reduced. Besides, the B-29s, adding an entirely new dimension to the war in the Pacific, would outshine Hoover. Though they began striking the Japanese homeland from bases in China during the summer, their deadly destructiveness would not be fully felt until they operated from the Marianas beginning in late November.[67]

Towers accepted the new strategic bombers and aided his AAF colleagues whenever possible, but he remained adamantly opposed to the growing political sentiment for postwar unification. The strategic bombing of Germany and Japan clearly demonstrated the virtual autonomy of the AAF, crowned in December when its chief, Hap Arnold, received his fifth star along with generals of the army Marshall, Eisenhower, MacArthur and the new fleet admirals Leahy, King, and Nimitz. What Towers continued to fear was that an independent air force would absorb naval aviation, an opinion he shared with the unification investigating board of Admiral Joe Richardson at Pearl in December. Towers would accept unification only if it meant a combined general staff and board with adequate naval aviation participation. Five months later Richardson's board reported favorably for unification and a separate air force, but Richardson himself wrote a minority report echoing Towers' views.[68]

As for the navy's air war in the Pacific, Towers remained in control. He continued to select carrier task group commanders and to make the final judgments on air weapons and air group composition. In August Generals Vandegrift and Field Harris, director of Marine Corps aviation, convinced Towers that they were now ready to put marines on carriers, specifically escort carriers to insure effective close air support during marine landings. The training program was initiated at once. During the fall the Japanese introduced kamikaze suicide plane tactics, requiring the immediate increase on fast carriers of defensive fighters to replace some dive and torpedo bombers. A makeshift solution was to use marine squadrons while navy air groups were reshuffled. To work out the details of all such deliberations on aviation Towers drew primarily on Forrest Sherman, George Murray, and George Anderson.[69]

New aircraft and armaments continued to be of vital interest to Towers. He had great hopes for the Tiny Tim aerial rocket and for airborne early-warning radar on TBMs, but neither of these innovations would mature before the end of the war. Assistant Secretary Di Gates arrived in late August with Admirals Ramsey and Radford to discuss aircraft production in relation to the needs of the fleet. The growing requirement for more fighters led Towers to urge cutbacks in SB2C dive bomber production in favor of new fighter aircraft. Grumman was bringing out two new models, the twin-engine F7F Tigercat and single-engine F8F Bearcat, and Ryan was producing the navy's first plane with an auxiliary jet engine, the FR Fireball. Towers urged that FM Wildcat production be reduced, since the F6F Hellcat was to replace the FM on the *Cimmaron*-type escort carriers. The smaller F8F could replace the F6F on the light carriers. But the F7F, he said, was too large for carriers and should be shore-based, as should the FR if it proved successful. All were important elements for the expanded air program in a war that Towers and his colleagues still assumed would last until the end of 1946.[70]

In spite of his immense workload, Towers managed to enjoy some diversions. Twice a month he got in a two-hour flight at the controls of an SON, the Naval Aircraft Factory version of the Curtiss Seagull scout. He participated in "We the People," a national radio broadcast over CBS in October. What he wanted most, however, was to resume his daily swimming. The Makalapa pool formally opened on 3 December. It was a big day for Jack. When the dedication plaque was unveiled it bore the title Towers

After much campaigning, Towers got the senior officers' swimming pool built at Makalapa. He was surprised when Nimitz dedicated it to him. Here Nimitz congratulates the SeaBee officer who superintended its construction, 3 December 1944. (Naval Historical Center)

Pool. Nimitz had paid him this small though sincere tribute. Lieutenant Bob Crosby's Marine Corps swing band and singer Dennis Day provided the music, and the first newly reported WAVE officers competed in swimming relays.[71]

All of Towers' work revolved around the progress of the fighting. In late August Halsey relieved Spruance in command of what now became the Third Fleet, and John McCain replaced Jocko Clark as a task group commander. Towers told McCain that the latter would replace Mitscher as commander Task Force 38 as soon as Nimitz and Halsey felt McCain was ready. McCain lost no time suggesting that he visit MacArthur's forces to coordinate planning, whereupon Forrest Sherman told him all that had already been done at higher levels. Nimitz concurred. McCain protested to Towers that he would not be allowed to inherit Mitscher's staff. Jack told his classmate to borrow some of Clark's people until his own staff was broken in. Furious that someone was trying to "cut his throat," McCain went to see Nimitz, who only supported Towers.

Mitscher wanted to extricate Clark as soon as possible so that Clark could return as leading task group commander when Mitscher resumed task force command after the Philippines campaign. Towers approved Mitscher's request for Clark's leave, but Sherman had Nimitz disapprove it; they just weren't sure about McCain. Suddenly, in early October, Halsey sent Clark and his staff home without Nimitz's approval. Towers had a lot of arguing and explaining to do to his irate boss, but Mitscher's wishes prevailed. McCain's uneven performance at sea would confirm the fears of many.[72]

Immediate objectives were the simultaneous seizures of Palau in the western Carolines and Morotai in the Southwest Pacific on 15 September. From these places land-based air and carriers would attack Mindanao in the southern Philippines, followed by the assault there on 15 November and then Leyte in the central Philippines. Beyond that, the decision had yet to be made for Luzon or Formosa early in the new year. In mid-August King again ordered Nimitz's staff to plan for Formosa, whereupon it heard General Buckner repeat his doubts over the Tenth Army's ability to take the big island. Nimitz dispatched Forrest Sherman to Washington to seek definite instructions. There Sherman learned that, with the exception of King, the JCS was beginning to regard Luzon as the easier target. It ruled, however, that the Leyte assault would occur on 20 December, after which the decision would be made for Luzon or Formosa on or about 1 March 1945. Much depended on whether Germany was defeated before the end of the year. By the time Sherman returned Towers and the staff had heard Rear Admiral

Arthur D. Struble discuss the difficulties of the assault in June on Normandy, like Formosa a large, tough beachhead.[73]

Between 31 August and 13 September Task Force 38 attacked Japanese airfields and interceptors in the Bonins, Yap, Wake, the Palaus, Mindanao, and the Visayas. "Thank Heavens Halsey and Mick Carney have slipped into the driver's seat," wrote Towers. The strikes, in preparation for the Palau-Morotai landings, revealed to an astounded Halsey the weakness of Japanese air defenses. In the boldest strategic move of his career, Halsey immediately recommended to the JCS that Palau, Morotai, Yap, and Mindanao be by-passed and that existing assault forces be pooled for an immediate landing at Leyte. Land-based air at Mindanao no longer seemed necessary for the Leyte assault; the fast carriers could cover MacArthur's forces there. MacArthur and Nimitz concurred, although they wanted to proceed with the Palau and Morotai operations. The JCS, then meeting with the British chiefs in Canada, approved without hesitation on 15 September, the day Towers returned to Hawaii from a week-long inspection of the Marianas (where he "got shot at twice while driving through [the] jungle on East side of Guam"). The assault date for Leyte was fixed at 20 October, two months ahead of schedule. Such mobile use of the carriers was entirely to Towers' liking, although the speed-up greatly complicated his logistical base requirements. The only dark spot in the hasty decision was the seizure of Palau, where fanatical Japanese resistance caused heavy loss of life.[74] The altered timetable meant that King and Nimitz had to parlay again about subsequent operations in the central Pacific. The meeting was set for San Francisco at the end of the month.

Towers felt pleased that his strategic thinking was having an impact just as it had had early in the year. "They are finally, and again, using my strategical concepts," he wrote Pierre on 21 September, "but I am sure I will not get any credit." Festering tension between him and Nimitz Jack laid to Forrest Sherman. "I hate to say it," but Jack's ambitious former chief of staff seemed to be "quietly . . . fomenting trouble" between Nimitz and Towers. With Sherman away in New Guinea, Jack therefore had a frank talk with Nimitz, which cleared the air between them. He also argued against Formosa and apparently convinced Nimitz to oppose the operation.

For on 23 September, the day after Sherman returned, the latter briefed the Pacific Fleet planners on a meeting he had just attended with MacArthur at Hollandia. MacArthur wanted to go on to Luzon in December, a desire that now seemed destined to be approved by the JCS. In the discussion Nimitz "continued to support" the Formosa alternative, recorded Towers, "although Sherman's presentation indicated that he [Nimitz] no longer considered it desirable. Nimitz stressed the necessity for large land masses from which to operate bombers against Japan." Towers seized the opportunity to push for his long-desired plan to use carriers against Japan. He thought the occupation of Formosa no longer necessary, "as . . . carrier attacks against their home land[,] air[,] and industry would make it impossible for them to wage any kind of an air campaign." This was a subtle suggestion that carriers rather than land-based bombers could fulfill the role of strategic bombing. He cited Halsey's recent successes over the Philippines and the fact "that our carrier force would be greatly augmented by early spring."

Nimitz made no decision but told Generals Buckner and Richardson to restudy the Formosa directive, while he and his three advisers contemplated what recommendation to make to King. Buckner had no doubts that he would lack the necessary forces to take Formosa and said so in a memo. Towers and General Miff Harmon of the AAF worked up a memo for Harmon's signature the night of 25 September, endorsing Towers' idea for carrier strikes on the Japanese homeland; the B-29s could be relied on to carry out their strategic bombing campaign of Japan exclusively from the Marianas rather than Formosa. Armed with these memos, Nimitz, Towers, McMorris, and Sherman decided to support the proposed landings on Luzon in December, followed by Iwo Jima and Okinawa in January and March respectively. Naval bases and airfields on all three islands would then be used for the final blockade and possible invasion of Japan. Formosa should be bypassed and kept neutralized by army and navy air. Nimitz took Sherman, Buckner, and Harmon with him to San Francisco, where they were joined by Spruance at the end of September. All succeeded in finally winning over a reluctant King to their point of view, and the JCS concurred.

Jack was elated at the news. "*My* strategical recommendations, which I have stuck to for these many months, went over the top!" He reiterated to Pierre that the credit, however, would go to others who "jumped on the band wagon when my predictions began to come true."[75]

The decision for Luzon in December made the stepped-up Leyte operation the crucial test of Japan's ability to defend the Philippines. Results were soon in coming. The seventeen carriers of Task Force 38 sortied from Ulithi and struck Okinawa, Luzon, and Formosa from 10 to 15 October. The Japanese reacted furiously, committing more than five hundred planes over Formosa in three days. Flown by grossly undertrained pilots, they were massacred by Halsey's Hellcats. In the midst of the action Halsey rushed off a dispatch to Nimitz requesting a great increase in fighters for the next operation. Towers and his planners accordingly met and decided to make the

Bunker Hill an all-fighter carrier (108 planes) for the moment and to build up the other fast carrier air groups from 36 to 54 fighters as rapidly as possible. Then intelligence reported Japanese fleet units to be on the move. On the fifteenth, "the imminence of a Fleet engagement absorbed the entire attention of everyone" at fleet headquarters.[76]

The brief sortie of three enemy cruisers from Japan proved premature, however, and Halsey shifted his fast carriers to targets in Luzon, including Manila, to secure MacArthur's northern flank during the Leyte assault on the twentieth. Admiral Kinkaid's Seventh Fleet carried out the landings as planned, under the cover of planes from no fewer than eighteen escort carriers. But now the Japanese fleet began to move in earnest to bring on the Battle of Leyte Gulf. In a masterful stroke, two Japanese battleship groups approached from separate directions through the Philippines toward the beachhead. The fast carriers (and submarines) worked over both forces as they approached, sinking the superbattleship *Musashi* and several cruisers, but a Japanese bombing attack succeeded in sinking the light carrier *Princeton*. Japan's "Center Force" withdrew, and that night at Leyte America's prewar battleships annihilated the "Southern Force" of gunships in the last major gunnery duel in history. Meanwhile, the enemy's "Northern Force" of four carriers was detected far to the north, and Halsey raced in that direction during the night to engage them.

Next day, the twenty-fourth (Hawaii time), Towers delivered the Navy Day address before the Honolulu Rotary Club at the Moana Hotel. In the course of it, he observed that a big naval battle might be in progress "right now. . . . We have every reason to believe the critical moment in our history is *this* moment." The moment was indeed critical, for the Battle of Leyte Gulf if not for the sweep of American history. For shortly after dawn, Halsey made contact with the four Japanese carriers and launched his strikes. Without planes to defend them they were sitting ducks. In fact, the planeless carriers were a Japanese ruse to lure Halsey away from the beaches, and it had succeeded. Just as Halsey was sinking the Northern Force carriers, the Center Force battleships and cruisers suddenly appeared in Leyte Gulf. Having again reversed course during the night, they now began striking Kinkaid's ships with their guns; the largest victim was the escort carrier *Gambier Bay*. Simultaneously, the Japanese initiated their first land-based kamikaze strikes, which sent the escort carrier *St. Lo* to the bottom. Heavier losses were averted when the Center Force broke off its attack and ran for home. The brilliant Japanese strategy failed to destroy Kinkaid's shipping only because of this sudden retirement.[77]

The complex Battle of Leyte Gulf was a victory in the sense that the Japanese fleet was repulsed and MacArthur's beachhead preserved, but it revealed many flaws at the command level. Towers blamed Kinkaid for not covering the northern approaches to the beachhead with air searches, the same sort of ineptitude Towers believed had cost Kinkaid the *Hornet* two years before. Halsey's aggressive run north surprised no one at Pacific Fleet headquarters; it was the sort of carrier tactics to which Towers himself subscribed. Halsey, however, could be blamed for not being meticulous in his planning or operations; he had never bothered to consult Mitscher, who with his staff had wanted to cover the northern approach to Leyte during the night. But the major culprit was interservice rivalry. Command of the operation had been divided. Kinkaid reported directly to Southwest Pacific commander MacArthur, Halsey to Pacific Fleet commander Nimitz, and neither communicated regularly with each other at the tactical level. This unfortunate army-navy dichotomy would continue to plague operations.[78]

The furious Japanese aerial counterattack did not end with the Battle of Leyte Gulf. Kamikaze attacks in particular intensified as American forces edged closer to the homeland. "I don't know when our war out here will be over," Towers admitted to his brother Will in November. "It depends on more than the mere military situation. The Japs are about licked now but when will they quit[?]"[79]

Indeed, the stout Japanese defense resulted in the eventual postponement of forthcoming operations: Mindoro to December; Lingayen Gulf and the drive to Manila, January; Iwo Jima, February; and Okinawa, April. Each operation increased the difficulty of logistics, but Towers proved equal to the challenge. The ultimate test of his skill would come with the biggest and final battle—for Japan itself.

16

THE INDISPENSABLE TOWERS

1944–45

Though the idea of invading Formosa had died, Admiral King and the navy did not deviate from their strategy of concentration for the final defeat of Japan. If the Nationalist Chinese could not defeat the main Japanese army on the continent of Asia, then the Soviet Union might accomplish the task, and over the fall and winter of 1944–45 King had Nimitz begin considering that eventuality. Both men, along with Towers, Spruance, Forrest Sherman, JCS chairman Leahy, and General MacArthur, believed, however, that Japan would be defeated by air-sea blockade alone. General Marshall nonetheless insisted on planning for the invasion of Japan—Operation Olympic—scheduled for the autumn of 1945.[1]

Whichever strategy prevailed, Towers' task as logistical manager of the Pacific Fleet and the Pacific ocean areas was greatly complicated as the momentum of the offensive increased. While the JCS wrangled over target objectives, he and his staff had to keep supplies and shipping moving westward to the advanced bases of Saipan-Guam, Manus, Palau, Ulithi, and Leyte-Samar. Furthermore, the systematic roll-up of old bases in the South Pacific commenced. Because of the different supply systems of the navy and army, and the increasingly close contact between these services as Southwest and Central Pacific forces began to converge in their operations, cooperation was essential. Towers had it in the persons of Generals Edmond Leavey and Miff Harmon of the army. But he had lost confidence in the ability of Admiral Bill Calhoun to run the fleet's service force. This view he apparently conveyed to Secretary Forrestal, for when King and Nimitz met in San Francisco in November 1944 King revealed Forrestal's desire to have Towers replace Calhoun. Nimitz wanted to keep Towers as his deputy, however, and so they decided to replace Calhoun with Vice Admiral W. W. "Poco" Smith, director of the Naval Transportation Service.[2]

In fact, some reorganization had to be undertaken if the navy's logistical system was to accommodate the needs of the massive land, sea, and air forces being concentrated for the final campaign against Japan. Early in October two of Towers' top aviation logistics planners, Captains Stanhope C. Ring and Jim Boundy, recommended the creation of a "supply assembly" in the United States to collect the material and train personnel to handle it. Towers endorsed the idea in principle. King had already decided he needed a very senior officer to coordinate all shipping from the West Coast and tapped his Atlantic Fleet commander, Admiral Royal Ingersoll, for the task. At the end of October Ingersoll flew to Hawaii and met with Towers and other key planners to work out his new duties, and the next month Ingersoll established his headquarters at San Francisco as commander Western Sea Frontier and deputy COMINCH-CNO.[3]

Because many details of fleet and air planning had to be resolved in Washington, Nimitz sent Towers there in December 1944. On the seventeenth he breakfasted at Secretary Forrestal's home, accompanied him to his office for discussions of policy, and lunched with old friends Dick Byrd and Grover Loening. He joined thirty others at a dinner party given by Forrestal for a preview of the film "The Fighting Lady," depicting life aboard the carriers, mostly the new *Yorktown;* it would win an Academy Award.[4]

Towers brought a realistic appraisal of the Pacific air war to the Navy Department. At a conference in the office of deputy CNO (air) Jake Fitch on the eighteenth, Towers explained the carrier war as being fought in three phases. The first was "the period during which we were largely engaging enemy vessels and their aircraft," and it ended with the Battle of Leyte Gulf. The second phase was in progress—"attacking enemy shore installations and combatting their very violent efforts to damage our carriers and other ships by attack with shore-based aircraft." The third phase, "yet to come, will be when enemy air resistance is largely broken and our efforts will be to destroy their sources of production." This meant the bombing of Japan, which might require a return to larger carrier bombing squadrons. At any rate, up to eight escort carriers were to be handed over to the Marine Corps so that marine squadrons could help support the final landings.[5]

During Towers' stay in Washington, the high command was shocked by a determined German counterattack on the Western Front, the Battle of the Bulge. To discuss this and to learn details of the progress in the Pacific, Congressman Carl Vinson summoned Towers to his office on the nineteenth. "He expressed the very strong view," recorded Towers, "that the war against Germany will not end for more than a year and that the country will not support an all-out land campaign against Japan. I admitted to him that I held similar views." The Bulge forced strategists to revise their expectations of a swift victory in Europe before July 1945 and therefore to plan their logistics more realistically. Meanwhile, potentially adverse public opinion increased the navy's determination to defeat Japan before an invasion was necessary.[6]

After more hurried meetings with King, Arnold, and others, Towers flew to California for logistical meetings and a Christmas holiday with Pierre. He had seen Marge in Washington but missed the marriage of Chas the month before. Towers "had tried to give him the idea of waiting until he is 30 but he broke down. He is going to Dallas to qualify in combat flying then probably will come out into the Fleet." Two months down the road Jack's relatives and old friends would be thrilled to read a feature story on him, "Naval Aviator No. 1," in *Liberty* magazine. Brother Will would complain, however, that the article gave the impression Jack was "hard-boiled." Boyhood friend Elmer Grant would be reminded of Captain Billy's remark upon seeing an encyclopedia entry that referred to Confederate General Forrest as illiterate: "The encyclopedia is wrong!" But of course Jack could be hard-boiled.[7]

Much happened in the Pacific during Towers' two-week absence. By the time a new flag R5D (C-54) Skymaster returned him to Pearl on 28 December, MacArthur's troops had assaulted Mindoro and Halsey had taken the Third Fleet into a disastrous typhoon, resulting in the loss of three destroyers and many lives. In January 1945 Halsey led his fleet into the South China Sea to sink shipping and cover the seaward flank of MacArthur's landing at Lingayen Gulf; two carriers were seriously damaged by attacking planes. The seventeen escort carriers at the beaches were now part of a new escort carrier force under Rear Admiral Cal Durgin. One was sunk and four others were stricken by kamikazes off Lingayen.

At this point a four-carrier British task force headed from the Indian Ocean into the Pacific to join Nimitz's fleet, against the wishes of King, who feared that British logistical requirements would place a burden on American facilities. In spite of FDR's mandate, King insisted they provide their own oil and aviation gas, but after Towers saw the folly in this he won Nimitz's approval to interpret King's policy liberally: "the total supporting vessels and bases should be considered as a pool and . . . any plan of segregation could only end in handicapping operations." But throughout the spring of 1945 Towers had to insure adequate U.S. logistic support of British air operations.[8]

Though logistics absorbed most of Towers' attention during January, questions over senior aviation commands demanded answers. Spruance, Mitscher, and Jocko Clark returned to Hawaii to relieve the Halsey-McCain team, whose performance throughout the Philippines campaign had been seriously flawed. However, both Halsey and McCain were scheduled to rotate back to command after the forthcoming Iwo Jima and Okinawa operations. In mid-January Assistant Secretary Gates and Admiral Fitch arrived to affirm aircraft production schedules, at which time Fitch lobbied to be reassigned to sea duty. Like McCain, he was a weak deputy CNO (air) who relied on Arthur Radford to administer the office. Now Radford resumed a task group command, along with Clark, Ralph Davison, Ted Sherman, and Matt Gardner.[9]

No one desired combat duty more than Towers, but his fate seemed to be sealed as Nimitz prepared to move to Guam. Jack used many arguments to prevent this change, which promised to divorce him from all but logistical matters. Nimitz would not be swayed, however, and King saw no reason to interfere. Finally at the end of January 1945 Nimitz, McMorris, and Forrest Sherman left for Guam. Commodore Count Austin tried to escape the tedium of Pearl Harbor, whereupon Towers confronted him in no uncertain terms: "I told Admiral Nimitz that you had to stay behind here, that I was not going to be left with all the administrative headaches without the assistant chief of staff of administration. . . ." Austin stayed.[10]

For all intents and purposes Nimitz's departure to Guam left Towers as CINCPOA, although his title remained deputy CINCPAC-CINCPOA. His task was to orchestrate the flow of supplies from rear areas to forward bases, the construction and government of which also came under his jurisdiction. This included redeployed units from the Atlantic as the naval war there wound down. Nimitz issued general directives from Guam, but it was Towers and the Pearl Harbor headquarters that had to cope with the complicated system.

As Towers had feared, the split headquarters hampered communications. Jack did not like it, and yet he deserved the lion's share of the credit for making the new arrangement work. Soc McMorris thanked him in a long letter six weeks later: "I hope you will continue to . . . express your views quite freely, and to be critical of what we may do here, with the full knowledge that they will be received in the spirit in which they are sent."[11]

Jack's advisers from the two services and two subservices were helpful. In addition to the daily morning conferences, Towers held weekly staff meetings of these men and the joint staff. Lieutenant General Harmon continued to coordinate B-29 deployment to the Marianas for the AAF until late February when, tragically, the plane carrying him from Kwajalein to Oahu was reported missing. Towers ordered the escort carrier *Corregidor* and patrol planes on a search that lasted two weeks, but Harmon was never found. General Hale assumed Harmon's duties. Admiral Mick Carney reported in to begin planning post-Okinawa operations for Halsey. That air logistical planners Horse Pennoyer and Stan Ring had become key men was recognized by their promotions to rear admiral. Although Vice Admiral Poco Smith relieved Calhoun as service force commander in March, Towers did not learn until several weeks had passed that Smith was an alcoholic, which greatly inhibited his performance. Towers confronted him with an ultimatum to get squared away or be exposed. He tried. By contrast, General Leavey provided superior leadership in joint logistics.[12]

At the end of January 1945 Spruance and Mitscher resumed command of Fifth Fleet and Task Force 58 for the Iwo Jima operation. It began with the attack long advocated by Towers and others, carrier strikes on Tokyo itself. The raid, on 16 February, further devastated Japanese air defenses but did not prevent kamikazes from sinking an escort carrier and heavily damaging the *Saratoga* off Iwo. Towers' old ship managed to limp back to Pearl, where Jack inspected her. Similarly, the marines suffered severe casualties in winning control of the island, which could now be added to the growing ring of airfields around Japan.[13]

With the Okinawa assault set for 1 April, planning activities at Pearl and Guam intensified, with Nimitz and Forrest Sherman arriving at Pearl on 1 March en route to Washington. Vice Admiral Savvy Cooke of the COMINCH staff flew in from the Yalta conference, while another plane brought Ambassador Patrick Hurley and Lieutenant General Albert C. Wedemeyer from China. Nimitz, Sherman, and Towers learned from these men that at Yalta the Russians had promised to declare war on Japan three months after the defeat of Germany; this would provide the manpower necessary to defeat the Japanese army on the continent.[14]

Jim Forrestal, after visiting Iwo Jima, expressed his desire that Towers attend the christening of the new *Midway*-class supercarrier *Coral Sea,* which

Towers and Vice Admiral Bill Calhoun see Secretary of the
Navy Forrestal, just back from Iwo Jima, off for
Washington, 2 March 1945. With Calhoun's transfer to the
South Pacific, Towers assumed more direct control over
Pacific Fleet logistics for the final campaign. (Navy
Department)

Pierre was scheduled to sponsor in New York City at the end of April. With
his heavy responsibilities Towers did not see how he could leave Hawaii.
"The next man on this Joint Staff [below] me in rank is a Major General of the
Army [Leavey], the next a Br. Gen. of Marines [J. F. Fellows]. They are
good," he confided to his brother Will, "but I can't see the Old Guard letting
them mess around with the Fleet. (They would do better than some Admirals
I know, however.)" Nimitz, however, gave Towers the go-ahead to make the
trip as part of a larger logistical mission; his duties could be handled by Vice
Admiral John Henry Newton, Nimitz's new deputy chief of staff.[15]

In early March a plethora of AAF generals visited Pearl for talks on
improving the strategic bombing campaign now beginning to ravage Japanese
cities with low-level fire bombing raids. Most pressing, however, was the
problem of slow advanced-base development in the Philippines and the
generally sluggish logistics of MacArthur's forces. Thus in late March Lieutenant General W. D. Styer, about to become MacArthur's logistics commander, arrived on a fact-finding mission. The eventual result of the army's

logistical confusion was MacArthur's insistence that General Leavey be transferred to his theater, thereby depriving Towers of Leavey's skills.[16]

The Okinawa operation began in mid-March when Mitscher's carriers attacked airfields in Kyushu, southernmost of Japan's home islands, only to be stricken by land-based bombers and kamikazes. The fast carrier *Franklin* was nearly sunk, and three other carriers were badly damaged by direct hits. In spite of the enemy's fierce response, Towers took a long look at American power and the Japanese defense and concluded that the end of the war was finally in sight. In fact, he made a "sizeable bet" at this time "that the fighting would be over within six months." That would mean before the end of September, a sage insight indeed.

On 1 April General Buckner's Tenth Army assaulted Okinawa with relative ease, but only because of an enemy ruse to wait until the Americans were ashore before furiously counterattacking with suicide tactics. The campaign would last three months before Okinawa could be secured. With such relentless attacks on the fleet, troops, and newly occupied airfields, Towers throughout the spring urged that Kikai Jima—the last Japanese home island before Kyushu—not be assaulted. Once occupied, it would be an exposed salient for kamikaze attacks and require protection from the carriers, which would best be released to strike kamikazes at their Kyushu bases. Also, Kikai was topographically difficult to develop as a fighter-bomber base and thus a logistical liability as the fleet's resources focused on Olympic, the projected invasion of Japan. Nimitz finally agreed to Towers' recommendation and canceled the Kikai operation on 1 June.[17]

On 6 April, just as the Okinawa fighting was intensifying, Towers received two highly classified dispatches from the JCS ordering the reorganization of the high command for the final operations against Japan. MacArthur was to command all army forces in the Pacific, Nimitz all navy forces, with the B-29s as a separate army air force responsible only to Hap Arnold in Washington. Coordination was essential, particularly in logistics, given the fact that the army's requirements were mushrooming as the invasion neared and the Pacific war promised to shift into a land campaign soon. The army and navy had always practiced different supply methods, and until a centralized agency was developed each service would continue on its own path. Nimitz and General Sutherland conferred at Guam on overall command and logistics during mid-month, but little agreement was reached.[18]

The two services therefore planned to convene the Army-Navy Shipping and Supply Conference in Washington on 1 May, and Nimitz surprised Towers by ordering him, as well as Poco Smith, to represent him. Before that took place, President Roosevelt suddenly died. Towers heard the news over Honolulu radio at 1230 on 12 April. Three mornings later Jack helped conduct a memorial service in Malakapa's junior officers' quarters. Vice President Harry Truman took the helm. Neither he nor the Allied CCS had much to say about the final campaign against Japan. The JCS was running it.

Secretary Forrestal announced that the second *Midway*-class carrier would be named *Franklin D. Roosevelt* instead of *Coral Sea,* as originally planned. Now that the vessel bore the name of FDR it seemed more appropriate that Eleanor Roosevelt, not Pierre, be the sponsor. The former First Lady having already preempted Pierre in the christening of the second *Yorktown,* however, she graciously conceded this honor to Mrs. Towers. Pierre begged "dear Jim" to provide her transportation via navy plane from San Diego to New York but was turned down for fear of setting a bad precedent. So she paid her own way as well as the expenses for "the big christening party" at the launching. Jack himself would arrive at the ceremonies prior to the logistics conference.[19]

To confer with Nimitz about that conference, Towers flew to Guam on 19 April, accompanied by George Anderson. After inspecting base development on Tinian and Saipan he met with Nimitz, Forrest Sherman, and Soc McMorris. Nimitz and Sherman, just back from Okinawa, were dismayed by the army's preference for constructing bomber fields ahead of fighter strips. Lacking adequate fighter coverage, the fleet was reeling from the kamikaze onslaught; the carriers *Hancock* and *Intrepid* had been seriously damaged. Nimitz had countermanded this bomber field priority and other items of army interference, but the interservice confusion at Okinawa strained his energies and patience. He needed a master logistician to deal with the army and to handle the immense supply system for Operation Olympic. That man was Jack Towers. Nimitz's respect for his deputy had grown so steadily that he was now addressing some of his letters "Dear Jack."[20]

Nimitz surprised Towers with a plan to appoint him to a new "super billet," namely commander Hawaiian Sea Frontier, "with additional duty as my Deputy for overall logistic coordination and for operational matters within the limits of the HawSeaFron," that is, shipping. He soon upgraded the recommended title to commander Mid-Pacific Area. Nimitz envisioned Towers being promoted to full admiral and operating on a par with Admiral Ingersoll, commander Western Sea Frontier and deputy COMINCH-CNO. Jack was pleased by the offer, though he still preferred sea duty. On 26 April, the day Towers departed Guam for Hawaii, Nimitz forwarded to King a recommendation that concluded, "In order to strengthen his position [vis-à-vis the army] and in recognition of his outstanding services to the country in naval aviation and more recently in the field of logistics I recommend that Towers be promoted to the rank of admiral. I believe that such action would have a desireable [*sic*] effect on naval aviation as a whole. . . . Towers . . . would prefer combat command at sea but like a good soldier will serve where higher authority considers [him] most needed."[21]

In general, King liked the idea, particularly the suggestion to reward Towers with a promotion to admiral. Nimitz had also recently informed King that Mitscher needed a "long rest" (probably from an unreported heart attack at sea). King brought up the idea of having Towers replace Mitscher as commander of Task Force 58. Both King and Nimitz, long antagonistic to Towers, had by now changed their opinion of him because of his brilliant performance. "Towers," Nimitz observed to King, "is probably better prepared to command a carrier task force than any flag officer available ashore. The best thing for the fleet would be for Towers to relieve McCain [as commander Task Force 38] and alternate with Mitscher." But Nimitz was also "agreeable to his relieving Mitscher. Although the matter is urgent, [I] recommend [the] decision be deferred until our next meeting unless you approve the original proposal which was based on Towers' specialized experience and ability." In other words, Nimitz wanted Towers in the super-billet if it was created.[22]

Ignorant of these exchanges, Towers spent one night at Pearl before departing for California on 27 April. From there he went to New York and joined Pierre for the christening of the *Franklin D. Roosevelt* on the twenty-ninth. Jim Forrestal spoke at the launching ceremony of the big 45,000-ton carrier, after which Jack and Pierre hosted the large reception at the Ambassador Hotel. Next morning they flew down to Washington, where Towers conferred with Admiral Ingersoll on matters to be discussed at the logistics conference. Jack was the guest of Forrestal at a luncheon for former navy secretaries and the members of the House and Senate naval affairs committees with whom Jack had worked over the years. He then called on Horne and King, who informed him of Nimitz's proposed super-billet.[23]

The Army and Navy Shipping and Supply Conference met from 1 to 5 May, chaired by Ingersoll, with General Styer, earmarked to be MacArthur's logistics commander, as senior army officer. For the final campaign against Japan the conferees succeeded in ironing out most logistical matters except control of shipping. Nimitz had instructed Towers to urge that a joint agency be created; if this were not done then the navy must insist on retaining its

CINCPOA joint staff system in order to supply navy forces. The conference could not agree on a joint shipping command, so Nimitz wired King on the fifth requesting that Towers be ordered to report to him for duty as commander Mid-Pacific Area and also as deputy CINCPAC-CINCPOA. Next day King met with Towers and Savvy Cooke to discuss the situation and decided that the best solution was to keep the existing logistics arrangement because the army was already satisfied with it. Nimitz therefore withdrew his recommendation for Towers' promotion and new job.[24]

This decision satisfied no one, least of all Nimitz, who had grave misgivings about the logistical demands of Operation Olympic. He ordered Towers to hasten to Guam and help him find a solution. On 7 May Towers flew from Washington to San Diego with Poco Smith, Stan Ring, and Pierre, whose travel in the R5D flag plane had been generously allowed by Forrestal. Next day they all celebrated the announcement that Germany had surrendered. Victory in Europe, however, portended a horrendous shipping problem, since men, material, and aircraft had to be redeployed from the Atlantic to the Pacific over the next fourteen months, the anticipated length of the final campaign against Japan. Jack visited briefly with Marjorie at Coronado, where she was living while husband Herb Riley commanded the escort carrier *Makassar Strait* off Okinawa.[25]

Several days later Towers flew to Guam to discuss reorganizing fleet logistics with Nimitz, McMorris, and Forrest Sherman. There Jack greeted Herb Riley, who brought in his ship and learned he had been promoted to captain three months before. Nimitz asked Towers to remain at Guam until he returned from meetings with MacArthur in Manila in a few days. But Towers demurred. Too much work had piled up during his absence from Pearl, he said. But he agreed to return to Guam if Nimitz needed him.

How right he was, for upon reaching Hawaii on 16 May he was inundated by a steady stream of visiting VIPs and Captain James S. Russell, relieving George Anderson as Towers' assistant.[26] Meanwhile, a restive King tired of Nimitz's ten-day silence over his logistical organization. Since Nimitz had withdrawn his recommendation for Towers' promotion, King thought it "appropriate to consider assigning him to a combat command" and for Nimitz to nominate another deputy for overall logistics. This surprised Nimitz, who thought King had rejected his plan for a supreme logistics commander. He replied that his withdrawal of the recommendation for Towers' promotion "makes no—repeat no—change whatsoever in Towers' status as my deputy for . . . overall logistics. These duties Towers has performed for me and is continuing to perform most satisfactorily with my complete confidence with the rank of vice admiral, which I consider ample and appropriate for the purpose."

Nimitz reviewed for King his desire to have Towers' responsibilities enlarged in the super-billet, giving direct logistical control to Towers rather than Nimitz's staff, which would also have been streamlined. Nimitz was trying to force King to accept his reorganization scheme by refusing to recommend Towers' promotion except under this arrangement. But King wanted to reward Towers with either a promotion under the existing system or combat command of the Fast Carrier Task Force, a vice admiral's billet. At this juncture Nimitz told King, "Our exchange of messages on this subject leads me to believe we did not understand each other. Because the status quo is satisfactory though susceptible of improvement I recommend nothing more be done until we can meet for thorough discussion. . . ."[27]

King was losing patience with Nimitz. He wanted the thorny question of logistical command and control for Olympic worked out before they met again several weeks hence. Some of Nimitz's staff officers recommended that the logistics command be moved forward to Guam, which Towers opposed, while King urged the JCS to create a joint army-navy agency. Early in June, while Towers and McMorris discussed reorganization of Pacific Fleet logistics at Pearl, Nimitz's and MacArthur's representatives met at Guam and agreed that at least for Olympic the services would run their own logistical shipping or favor the looser army system wherever they used a common port. All shipping would be regulated through Ulithi and Okinawa.

Confusion seemed to be the order of the day. Ingersoll's Western Sea Frontier was out of touch with the forward areas; shipping was already backing up at Guam and Okinawa because of poor planning by Poco Smith and a general lack of coordination between Guam and Pearl; and Towers thought MacArthur's Seventh Fleet logistical operations wholly inadequate for base development in the Philippines or Kyushu, once the home island was taken. In fact, Towers spent most of June trying to solve the congestion of shipping at Okinawa and flew to Guam in mid-month to work on the problem between swims and meals with Nimitz. It was finally decided to appoint a rear admiral as head of a logistics division at Guam but to leave the bulk of it at Pearl. Count Austin would move forward to Guam to help McMorris.[28]

The key figure in all of this was the deputy CINCPAC-CINCPOA. Quite simply, Towers would be a difficult man to replace, with or without reorganized logistics, especially where interservice cooperation was involved. Even now, in May and June, General Richardson was again harping about Nimitz's authority over him in Hawaii. After a meeting with Richardson, Towers informed Nimitz of the general's reluctance to obey navy directives. By contrast, relations with the AAF in Hawaii were downright amicable. General of the Army Hap Arnold flew in on 9 June and was met by Towers and the army generals. As the guest of Richardson—who he thought "talks too much"—Arnold heard out his complaints but was "glad to get [the] Navy side" by attending Towers' morning conference next day. After listening to the army generals complain about not getting fighters moved quickly to Iwo Jima and Okinawa, and hearing Jack's views, Arnold concluded in his diary, "It was AAF's own fault. . . . It is also clear that the Army has never had the long-range view for war or postwar that the Navy has."[29]

One matter on which Towers and Arnold did not agree was the continuing need for the fast carriers to provide close air support and combat air patrols at Okinawa. During May six American and several British carriers as well as many destroyers had been struck by Japanese suicide planes. Towers urged Nimitz to give greater priority to the construction of fighter over bomber strips at Okinawa; with land-based AAF fighters available, Task Force 58 could be released from the chore of providing air cover. And with restored mobility, the fast carriers could maneuver away from kamikazes. Nimitz was trying to change airfield priorities, but Arnold and the JCS wanted the B-29 strips pushed to completion.

On 1 June Pete Mitscher and his staff officers Arleigh Burke and Gus Read arrived, Spruance and Mitscher having just turned over the Fleet again to Halsey and McCain. Jack was adamant about giving Read "exact messages for oral delivery" to Secretary Forrestal. As Read recalled those messages, unless fighter strips were given priority on Okinawa promptly, Towers "would have no alternative except to offer his resignation as a naval officer!" Next day Read revealed this message to Mitscher, who agreed, and two days after that in Washington Read recited it to Forrestal, who had him repeat it to Di Gates.[30] Fortunately, the Japanese defense of Okinawa ended at almost the same time as Towers gave out his ultimatum. When Halsey broke away from Okinawa to attack Kyushu in early June, he took the fleet into another typhoon. He was tired, as was McCain, who like Mitscher probably suffered from a mild heart attack on this cruise. The fleet needed fresh blood for the final battle. On 5 June King sent Nimitz a proposed slate for his comments. Towers might replace Admiral Harold Stark as commander of U.S. naval forces in Europe, thus using his logistical skills for redeploying American military might to the Pacific. He would also rate promotion to full admiral. In this case, Johnny Hoover would relieve Towers as Nimitz's deputy, and Ted Sherman would replace Mitscher as commander Task Force 58—the latter move having been contemplated by King and Nimitz for several weeks.[31]

When this proposal brought no response, King goaded Nimitz three days later with another message recommending that Towers trade jobs with Admiral Jonas Ingram, commander in chief Atlantic Fleet. This way, Towers could still get his fourth star and coordinate the redeployment. Nimitz informed King he preferred that Hoover replace Towers, then sent a long message to King on 13 June: "It is of the utmost importance that my Deputy have a detailed knowledge of advanced base problems in the Pacific and a thorough grasp of the logistic problems of Pacific operations. Towers and Hoover have this knowledge, Ingram does not." After pouring out a tale of the sorry state of his "logistical personnel situation," Nimitz recommended that "Towers remain or be relieved by Hoover."[32]

King answered immediately, asking Nimitz if he was "agreeable to Towers replacing Mitscher," in which case Hoover would replace Towers. "If," however, "it is your view that Towers should remain your Deputy then he should have four stars," which would give him rank equal to Spruance, Halsey, Kinkaid, and Turner, the latter two newly promoted. Nimitz agreed that Towers should go to sea, but to relieve McCain as commander Task Force 38. Ted Sherman, promoted to vice admiral, would replace Mitscher, and Hoover would replace Towers, still as a vice admiral. No doubt Nimitz decided not to put Towers under Spruance because of their rocky relationship; Towers could serve under Halsey, for the two were of like mind. Though Halsey would continue to exercise tactical command over the carriers, at least Towers could prevent him from making any more blunders like running into typhoons.[33]

On 19 June, the day after Towers arrived at Guam to discuss fleet logistics, Nimitz informed him of the recommendation that he relieve McCain. But no orders would be issued until Nimitz met with King in San Francisco a few days hence to confirm everything. "I am going to sea very shortly," Jack wrote elatedly to his brother Will, "to command [the] Fast Carrier Task Force (practically the whole Fleet). It has been a long time coming because of jealousies. King himself has done this, strangely enough. Needless to say, I am delighted. It may lead to even bigger things." To King's lasting credit, he had been fair, finally.[34]

Jack Towers finally had his reward for loyal, effective, brilliant service, and what a command it was to be. Already intimately involved with the logistical planning for Olympic, the massive operation for the invasion of Kyushu, he now turned to the operational aspects. From mid-July until mid-August Halsey and McCain were to use four fast carrier task groups to strike airfields throughout Japan. Then they were to withdraw to Eniwetok to replenish, at which time Towers would relieve McCain as commander Second Fast Carrier Force Pacific (Task Force 38). His seventeen carriers would be spread among four task groups commanded by Rear Admirals Tommy Sprague, John Ballentine, C. A. F. Sprague, and Arthur Radford. Beginning in late August, Task Force 38 would resume its attacks on Tokyo and industrial targets east of Tokyo on Honshu and Hokkaido, while General Kenney's AAF planes would isolate Kyushu from the rest of Japan. B-29s from the Marianas and Okinawa would complement these strikes throughout Japan. As even more fast carriers arrived, they would join Towers' task formation.

Ten days prior to the scheduled 1 November assault on Kyushu, the fleet would be divided into the Third and Fifth Fleets for the first time during the war. Spruance's Fifth Fleet would carry out the landings of MacArthur's forces, Turner in amphibious command, supported by Ted Sherman's Task Force 58 and Cal Durgin's sixteen escort carriers. Halsey's Third Fleet was in fact to be all fast carriers and their escorts, that is, Towers' Task Force 38—three four-carrier task groups under Art Davis and the two Spragues— and Task Force 37, two British task groups. The Third Fleet was to strike air bases throughout the home islands of Honshu, Shikoku, and Hokkaido and the southern Kurile islands. It would also interdict Japanese lines of communication to Kyushu, destroy enemy naval forces and shipping, and keep open the sea lanes to Russia. Once airfields were seized by MacArthur's troops on Kyushu, land-based AAF and Marine Corps planes would be flown in there, releasing Task Force 58 to join the Third Fleet in ranging the length of Japan. If Japan continued to resist, which seemed unlikely, all this massive air power would support MacArthur's assault on Honshu and Tokyo in March 1946.[35]

Before Towers embarked on what promised to be a long and arduous campaign, he deserved leave in the States, having had no vacation in nearly three years. Nimitz instructed him to turn over his duties to Hoover as soon as Hoover arrived in Pearl, take a week's leave, and report back on or about 14 August to assume the carrier command. In the meantime, Towers spent late June and most of July hard at work, which included entertaining and conferring with a continuous stream of VIPs. On 13 July Towers received a large party, headed by Assistant Secretary Struve Hensel, to discuss logistics for Olympic. Jack must have enjoyed the irony of having as his overnight guest, along with Hensel, Vice Admiral Ross McIntire, the ophthalmologist who had tried so hard to have him retired before the war.[36]

"Needless to say," Jack reflected in a letter to Will on 23 July, "I am delighted to get out where I can play a more direct part in this war, and I am likewise very glad to get away from this duty which has been very difficult since Nimitz divided the staff between here and Guam." It was in fact a duty he had come to loathe, or so he once told Ernie King. But Nimitz had appreciated Towers' talents in the job. He gave him high marks in the latest fitness report, though he remained somewhat critical of Jack's inability to inspire more confidence in subordinates. Nimitz rewarded him with the Distinguished Service Medal for eighteen months of "keen foresight, indomitable determination and persevering efforts" as deputy CINCPAC-CINCPOA.[37]

Vice Admiral Hoover relieved Towers at noon on 26 July, whereupon Jack departed on a night flight to San Diego. Halsey's carriers had already been attacking targets in Japan for two weeks, and Towers had put in his requests for a top-notch group of staff officers. Because obtaining these men would take several days, he would delay his return until they could be transferred. As for poor Genial John Hoover, he did not last long as Nimitz's deputy. In early May Nimitz received instructions from Forrestal and King that the dour Hoover was not to be permitted to greet visitors. This was an impossible fiat to obey, given Hoover's new responsibilities. Sure enough, Hoover soon found himself entertaining Julius Ochs Adler, vice president of the *New York Times,* which had voiced some criticism of the navy. During a party at Hoover's quarters Poco Smith made slightly disparaging remarks about the *Times,* including a comment about its failure to print a comics section. Adler was offended, and Nimitz immediately replaced Hoover with John Henry Newton. Hoover had been on the job only twenty days, and the faux pas had not even been his fault. Towers' savoir faire was missed already.[38]

For his staff Towers had selected excellent men. The chief of staff had to be a nonaviator; Towers chose Captain John E. Gingrich, the man who had served four years as Forrestal's aide on Towers' recommendation and who had just brought the crippled cruiser *Pittsburgh* out of Halsey's second typhoon. For operations officer he picked Captain E. C. Ewen, former skipper of the *Independence* and recent liaison officer with the British carriers earmarked to operate with Task Force 38 in Olympic. Towers retained two commanders from McCain's staff, veteran fighter ace Noel A. M. Gayler, to be Ewen's assistant, and James H. Hean, to be tactical officer. Experienced in carrier staff work was Lieutenant Commander William N. Leonard, another assistant ops officer. For flag secretary Towers kept his aide of many months, Lieutenant Commander William W. Grant.[39]

Not all of these men were yet available to head west, so, in spite of the fact that he feared "the show [would] be over before I arrived," Towers decided to extend his leave. He and Pierre had spent a week at Coronado with Marjorie and Herb Riley and granddaughter Lynne, Riley being home on leave before reporting as Vice Admiral Ted Sherman's operations officer. Then, Jack took Pierre to Lake Arrowhead in the mountains above Los Angeles to stay with friends. There epic news reached him. On 7 August he learned that the atomic bomb had been dropped on Hiroshima in southwestern Honshu; apparently he had been only vaguely aware of its existence. Next day brought news of Russia's entry into the Pacific war. Jack returned to Coronado immediately. The Allied strategy was being fulfilled. While the Soviet army swept over the much-vaunted Japanese army in Manchuria with incredible speed, Halsey's carriers and the B-29s assailed the home islands in the air-sea blockade. On the ninth a second atomic bomb was dropped on Nagasaki. Japan reeled before the onslaught and sued for peace.[40]

Towers hastened to the fighting before it ended. Since Captain Gingrich was not yet available, Jack decided to retain McCain's chief of staff, Rear Admiral Wilder Baker. On the evening of 13 August, Towers and Herb Riley joined Ted Sherman on the R5D overnight flight to Hawaii. An hour after landing, they learned that Japan had agreed to surrender. Uncertain whether the truce would be honored, Nimitz decided to keep the Third Fleet on station rather than having it return to Eniwetok as planned. Towers flew via that island to Guam on the seventeenth, and on the nineteenth he conferred with Nimitz.

The Japanese seemed to be observing the cease-fire, but Nimitz wanted the change of command for Task Force 38 to proceed on schedule. McCain had not performed well during the second typhoon and was being ignominiously recalled home to finish his career as deputy administrator of the Veterans Administration. Towers, one of his severest critics, had been proved correct about McCain. He was understandably bitter about his pending relief, and to save Towers the embarrassment of relieving him Nimitz considered having Ted Sherman relieve McCain first for a few days. Unhappy and ill though McCain was, Halsey prevailed upon him to participate in the formal surrender ceremony. So Towers would relieve him directly.[41]

Towers was flown from Guam to Iwo Jima on 20 August; he inspected the island, then boarded the destroyer *Healy* for passage to the fleet. Two mornings later he transferred by high-line to the *Shangri-La,* McCain's flagship and one of the newest *Essex*-class carriers. The crew was at quarters, mustered in parade formation on the flight deck. Normal wartime patrols continued this day and the next, after which a peacetime routine began to be instituted, and the planes undertook aerial drops of supplies to prisoner-of-war camps. The war indeed seemed to be over, and Towers could collect the sizeable bet he had made in March that the fighting would end by September.

On the twenty-third Jack visited Halsey in his flagship, the battleship *Missouri,* and conveyed McCain's wish to be relieved and sent home immediately, but Halsey refused. When Nimitz got wind of this, he fired off an order to Halsey ordering McCain to relinquish command of Task Force 38 before the fleet entered Tokyo Bay to receive Japan's surrender. If Towers could not command his carriers in combat, he would at least have the honor of commanding them when the war officially ended. Jack Towers had been one of the major architects of the victory over Japan and richly deserved this honor. Next morning, 1 September, he relieved McCain and broke his flag on the

Towers spends time with his classmate Vice Admiral John Sidney McCain in a ready room on board the flagship *Shangri-La,* 31 August 1945, the day before Towers relieved McCain as commander Task Force 38. (National Archives)

Shangri-La as commander Task Force 38. Late that afternoon both men and their top staff officers boarded the destroyer *Wallace L. Lind* for passage to the *Missouri,* now anchored in Tokyo Bay.[42]

At 0645 on 2 September, after the *Lind* anchored alongside the *Missouri,* Towers and McCain transferred to the "Big Mo." They lined up in the front row to witness the Japanese surrender. Shoulder to shoulder stood Ted Sherman, Charles Lockwood of the subs, McCain, Towers, Turner, Halsey, and Mick Carney. Admiral Nimitz, with Forrest Sherman at his side, signed the instrument of surrender on behalf of the United States. General MacArthur signed for the Allies. After this, one thousand carrier planes roared over the ship in symbolic tribute to the triumph of carrier aviation—Towers' triumph. Operation Olympic had been unnecessary after all, thanks to the air-sea blockade and the Russian attack.

Following the ceremony Towers went aboard the battleship *South Dakota* to confer with Nimitz and Sherman. The Russians were moving across Manchuria and into northern Korea, while civil war threatened to erupt inside China. With the elimination of Japan as a Pacific power, the three men now had to face the problems of the postwar world.[43]

17

SHAPING THE NEW ORDER

OF AIR-SEA POWER

AFTER 1945

The defeat of the German-Japanese Axis ushered in a new age of sea power that historians would label the *Pax Americana,* a global peace enforced by American naval and air supremacy. Few American strategic leaders were as prepared as Admiral John H. Towers to participate in a command role, for Towers had maintained a prominent position in both the navy and aviation. He characterized himself as "a flier who always kept one foot wet."[1]

The dropping of atomic bombs on Hiroshima and Nagasaki and the almost immediate Japanese surrender cast doubt on the continuing efficacy of navies, although Towers believed the weapon had been little more than a "face-saving excuse" for Japan to capitulate.[2] In any case, "the bomb" greatly stimulated the movement Towers had steadfastly opposed for a separate air force oriented toward strategic bombing. When, on 16 September 1945, his flagship *Shangri-La* steamed into Tokyo Bay and dropped anchor, Towers went ashore at Yokosuka and inspected the officers club of the late Imperial Japanese Navy. After the fleet rode out the edge of a typhoon, he embarked in a PBM for a six-hour flight that took him over several Japanese cities, culminating with Hiroshima. He wanted to see for himself the effect of the A-bomb.[3]

The bomb's destruction appeared complete—"extremely interesting," was Towers' understatement. But the advent of atomic weapons, however revolutionary, did not alter the fact that the conventional aircraft carrier had replaced the battleship, and Towers correctly predicted that the United States would never again build another battlewagon. Looking to the future, he suggested the navy might one day design and construct ships that could minimize the effect of atomic bombs.[4] On 25 September, after motoring from Yokosuka to downtown Tokyo with Wu Duncan, he wrote to Will, "The devastation is indescribable. The Japs seem to be in a daze about it all. They are living in ditches, under culverts, in tin shacks, etc. It will be dreadful when winter sets in." That was the task of MacArthur and the army of occupation, to which the Navy could only render logistical support.[5]

Demobilization of the great Pacific Fleet and many of its exhausted leaders commenced at once. John McCain died just four days after the formal surrender. On the nineteenth Towers attended a farewell dinner for Halsey at the Yokosuka officers club, after which Spruance relieved Halsey as commander of naval forces in Japanese waters. A week later, Towers called on Spruance to warn him of critical shortages in the fleet. Spruance was not concerned. His job done, the great Fifth Fleet commander was ready for the beach, as was amphibious leader Kelly Turner. And, of course, Ernie King faced retirement; now approaching sixty-seven, he had been retained in his vital role as COMINCH-CNO three years beyond the mandatory retirement age.[6]

Jack Towers, by contrast, had no intention of stepping down. At sixty, he was full of vigor, with four years left to advance up the ladder. He hoped to become CNO (which office absorbed that of COMINCH early in October). Furthermore, he had waited too long to achieve a senior seagoing command to retire now. But he remained wary; an order arrived for him to take half of his force to California for an indeterminant stay. His "Magic Carpet" ships would be loaded with veterans earmarked for early discharge. "Just what will happen to me I don't know," he confided to Will at the end of September. "The Old Guard are doing their best to keep me out of a position of power, and it looks as though they will succeed, for they are thoroughly entrenched." The old guard included King, Nimitz, Spruance, and the new chief of BuPers, Vice Admiral Louis Denfeld. But the guard was changing, which Towers would soon discover.[7]

On 1 October, as Task Group 58.1, Towers' carrier force departed Tokyo for Okinawa, where it took on homeward-bound personnel and more ships for a direct voyage to the States. Since his staff lacked experience in day-to-day tactical maneuvering and underway replenishment, he borrowed

Radford's senior advisers for the cruise. On the sixth Towers departed Okinawa with the carriers *Shangri-La, Yorktown, Hancock,* and *Cowpens* plus escorts. Three days out they were joined by the *Bon Homme Richard* and the *Independence.* After a long week at sea the group began to break up, the ships steaming independently to ports in Washington, Oregon, and California. On 21 October Towers brought the *Shangri-La, Hancock,* and two destroyers into San Pedro Bay, their homeward-bound pennants held aloft by weather balloons. To the sirens and whistles of ships in the harbor and to the cheers of loved ones on the dock, the "Shang" tied up at Pier D, Long Beach. Pierre, on hand to greet Jack, joined him at a welcoming luncheon given by the city's elders. The victorious fleet was home, and its personnel paraded through the city.[8]

While at sea Towers had received a dispatch announcing his selection to relieve Spruance in command of the Fifth Fleet and in the rank of full admiral. Thus the old guard so feared by Towers continued the steady support it had given him throughout the year. Early in October Nimitz and King had agreed that Towers, still as vice admiral, should relieve Spruance and that the latter should replace Nimitz two weeks later. King wanted Nimitz to take over as CNO. They agreed that around April 1946 Towers should be promoted to full admiral and relieve Spruance as CINCPAC-CINCPOA. Spruance would assume the presidency of the Naval War College, finishing out his naval career there.

The change had been pushed by Secretary Forrestal, who intended to shake up the navy by bringing in top airmen to hold an equal share of the highest commands with nonaviators. And he planned to start with the most senior airman, Towers. Forrestal wrangled with King over several flag promotions, insisting, for example, that Towers rated four stars as Fifth Fleet commander. On 20 October Forrestal wrote to Jack of his elevation and promotion: "I know of no one that I would rather see elevated to this rank or to the Commander of the [Fifth] Fleet than you. . . ." Furthermore, he expressed the hope that "before many months are over, it will be possible to give you command of the Pacific Fleet."[9]

On 24 October, the day President Truman approved his appointment and promotion, Towers flew to Washington with Pierre. During a lunch with King he remarked, "If Spruance goes to Newport, why not make me CINCPAC at once?" that is, instead of waiting until April. King replied, "That's Nimitz's job. You talk to him." Nimitz could do nothing yet, for Forrestal did not want another strong-willed CNO to contend with; rather than Nimitz, he preferred the deputy commander in chief of the U.S. Fleet, Dick Edwards, or even Deputy CNO (Air) Pete Mitscher. Two weeks later Forrestal yielded to Nimitz's appointment but insisted that King step down as CNO in mid-December instead of January. In the event, Towers' pending appointment as Pacific commander in chief was moved up two months, to 1 February 1946. This suited Spruance, who wanted to get to Newport as soon as possible.[10]

Like their longtime boss, Towers' men would move into more key positions at the behest of Forrestal, who maintained that "the influence of air power upon the Navy will be an evolution, not a revolution. The actual fact is that the Navy is becoming an air Navy." In the reorganized Office of the Chief of Naval Operations, the vice CNO and two of the six deputies would be aviators, all vice admirals: Duke Ramsey (vice CNO), Forrest Sherman (operations), and Arthur Radford (air). The black shoes were Mick Carney (logistics), Louis Denfeld (personnel), and Richard L. Conolly (administration). In the Atlantic, Pete Mitscher as a full admiral would briefly command the new Eighth Fleet and then the Atlantic Fleet itself, while Towers got the Pacific Fleet. Jake Fitch had already taken over as the first aviator superintendent of the Naval Academy.[11]

When the news of this shakeup was made public in December, the press recalled Towers' travails and lauded his new appointment. *Time* magazine rejoiced in the knowledge that "to Birdman Towers came as much recognition and vindication as he could now expect." The appointment of Towers, Ramsey, and Mitscher meant, proclaimed the Dayton (Ohio) *Daily News,* that "the shackles of tradition have been cast off and we may expect the full utilization of the lessons that have been learned in the Pacific laboratory during the last four years." But Towers was the central figure: "His initiative and daring bespeak his restless intellect. There will be no sloth, no satisfaction with things as they are in Admiral Towers' command. It is pleasant to think that the naming of him and the other noted air officers indicates the policy which will prevail throughout the service." Jack was back in the news.[12]

By contrast, retiring Fleet Admiral Ernie King passed into history. King had indeed been Towers' wartime nemesis, owing in large measure to jealousy over his subordinate's political influence and popularity. But by the autumn of 1944 such fears had become irrelevant. This realization, coupled with Towers' loyal and impeccable performance, had led King to support his continued advancement, though Towers never fully appreciated the fact.[13]

Towers returned to Long Beach on 31 October to assume his short tenure at the helm of the Fifth Fleet. On board the *Shangri-La* he dissolved Task Force 38 and turned over the task group command to C. A. F. Sprague;

never again would he serve aboard his beloved carriers. Next he flew to Hawaii and from there took an R5D to Yokosuka, arriving 7 November. The following morning, at 1000 on the quarterdeck of the flagship *New Jersey*, Towers relieved Spruance, whose parting remarks were as generous as they were brief: "My successor Admiral Towers needs no introduction to you. The record of his long and distinguished naval career speaks for itself. I turn over the Fifth Fleet to him with great pride and assurance that I will follow his fortunes and wish for his success wherever I may be."[14]

In spite of the demobilization, the Pacific Fleet was still divided into three components that policed the vast waters between America and Asia. The Third Fleet had been downgraded to the West Coast element, shuffling Magic Carpet vessels to and fro. The Fifth Fleet was the naval element of the occupation forces of Japan. And the Seventh Fleet was in the "hot spot," participating in the liberation of Japanese-occupied China. Ominously, its ships and Marine Corps units were either being denied access ashore by the Chinese Communist army or getting caught in the middle of shooting incidents between the Communists and Nationalists as their long-festering civil war resumed. Should Mao Tse-tung depose Chiang Kai-shek in China, the continent of Asia would have its own new order—domination by Russian and Chinese communism. Towers shared MacArthur's concern about political conditions in China as well as in Japan, not to mention Southeast Asia, where native forces were challenging the return of European colonial rule.

Over the course of two months Towers met often with MacArthur and supervised fleet movements in and out of Japanese waters. He battled slovenliness in the performance of ships' companies and land-based air personnel, who resented being kept from going home. He assisted Ambassador-at-Large Edwin Pauley in obtaining war reparations and helped Rear Admiral Ralph Ofstie, conducting the U.S. Strategic Bombing Survey, interrogate Japanese leaders and analyze the effects of the air and sea war. After two weeks Rear Admiral Charles Wellborn, Jr., recent skipper of the battleship *Iowa*, replaced Duke Ramsey as Towers' chief of staff, and Captain P. D. Stroop reported as aviation officer.

Towers organized shore-based naval facilities in Japan but wanted to center fleet activities close to MacArthur's headquarters in Tokyo, whereas Spruance preferred splitting them between Tokyo and Yokosuka. Towers' pending relief of him led Spruance to yield. He also wanted to reduce the Pacific Fleet staff and base it in a flagship, an impractical whim that Towers strongly opposed in the interest of efficiency. Again Towers prevailed; his experience at fleet headquarters had been far greater than Spruance's.[15]

A JCS directive concerning the repatriation of Japanese troops from China and the general strife in that country brought Spruance to Japan early in December to confer with MacArthur, Towers, Seventh Fleet commander Vice Admiral Daniel E. Barbey, and General Albert Wedemeyer, commander of American troops in China. The pro-Nationalist Wedemeyer wanted to exceed the directive by recommending increased help to the Nationalists, either under the newly created United Nations or through the State Department. Spruance and Towers objected, agreeing with the JCS and the State Department about not increasing American involvement. MacArthur concurred, but the Truman administration could not decide.

All Towers was charged to do was keep the Fifth Fleet in operating trim, which task included maneuvers by the brand new *Essex*-class carriers now assigned to Duncan's Task Force 58, the *Antietam* and the *Boxer*. He spent a

CINCPAC Spruance confers with Fifth and Seventh Fleet commanders Towers and Vice Admiral Daniel E. Barbey at Atsugi Airfield, Tokyo, 6 December 1945, about the deteriorating political situation in China. Towers wears the aviator's "working green" uniform. (U.S. Army Signal Corps.)

lonely Christmas in the *New Jersey,* sending a big Christmas tree from Washington State to MacArthur, replete with decorations and gifts, for the general's wife and young son to enjoy. "Even they have practically nothing" in devastated Tokyo, Jack wrote Pierre.[16]

Early in January 1946 Towers made an inspection tour by air of navy and Marine Corps installations in the Chinese cities of Shanghai, Tientsin, Peiping, and Tsingtao. Satisfied that the harbor facilities of these cities were adequate for the repatriation of Japanese troops, Towers returned to Tokyo. Vice Admiral Ted Sherman arrived to relieve him on the seventeenth, the same day Towers received his final order as Fifth Fleet commander: Spruance directed him to deliver the only surviving Japanese battleship, the *Nagato,* and a cruiser to the Marshall islands for an atomic bomb test to be held there in the summer. Next day Sherman relieved Towers.[17]

Towers flew to Washington, picking up Duncan, his new Pacific Fleet chief of staff, at Pearl Harbor. Required to have a nonaviator deputy, Towers selected Vice Admiral Lynde D. McCormick, an experienced wartime planner, and he retained Admiral Charles Wellborn as deputy chief of staff for plans and Captain Stroop as fleet aviation officer. Towers and Duncan spent a week in Washington conferring with Forrestal and Nimitz and the several offices and bureaus concerned with the Pacific Fleet. Joined by Pierre, Jack flew up to New York to squeeze in a grand total of four hours with brother Fullton, son Chas—back at Grumman—and their wives. Chas and his wife had given Jack a grandson in October named John Carstairs Towers; John would eventually grow up to be a commercial airline pilot.[18]

At 1000 on 1 February 1946, Towers relieved Spruance as CINPAC-CINCPOA on the fast carrier *Bennington* at Pearl Harbor. The turnover was more than symbolic, as the distinct characters and styles of these wartime antagonists demonstrated. In Towers' fitness report Spruance had rated him excellent but, like Nimitz, marked him down slightly on "ability to work with others," "use [of] ideas and suggestions of others," and inspiring subordinates. Yet now, in his parting remarks, Spruance lauded Towers' experience: "My successor, Admiral Towers, is fortunate in bringing to his new duties a broad and intimate knowledge of the problems of the Pacific, acquired during the past 3½ years in the important commands which he has held in the Fleet." After the ceremony Spruance departed for the Naval War College to enlarge its curriculum for the study of future warfare. In fact, however, he would allow war games there to be dominated by surface tactics until Nimitz sent aviator Captain C. R. "Cat" Brown to put a stop to it.[19]

Towers now moved into Nimitz's wartime Makalapa quarters, a small frame house some one hundred yards from his offices. Heretofore a bachelor dwelling, its decor and equipment were suitable to wartime exigencies. Towers replaced most of the furnishings before Pierre joined him. In May, after completing several articles for women's magazines in New York, Pierre came out in the liner *Lurline* accompanied by their Scottie, Mr. MacTavish. She and Jack set to work discarding what was left of Nimitz's Victorian nik-naks, among them a stuffed seagull and, tucked away in a closet, the "enormous sex organ" of a walrus, three feet long, mounted with a lewd plaque; it had been sent by Frank Jack Fletcher as an expression of his distaste for duty in Alaska! [20]

Meanwhile, events in Eastern Europe and the Mediterranean catapulted the Soviet Union into the public eye as the new threat to world peace. With postwar Great Britain economically prostrate, the United States had little choice but to counter Russian moves on its own. The cold war had begun. Naval units were dispatched to the Mediterranean, and the bulk of American naval power shifted to the Atlantic in a return to the dominant Europe-first strategic orientation. By the end of the year, nine of America's fifteen carriers and three of her four active-duty battleships would be concentrated in the Atlantic. With the demobilized fleet in no position to give equal attention to east Asia, Towers was left in command of a secondary theater. [21]

Beyond remaining on the alert for hostilities in the Far East, Towers had no overall strategic policy to guide his actions as Pacific Fleet commander. The temporary wartime JCS—Fleet Admiral Leahy, General of the Army Dwight Eisenhower, Fleet Admiral Nimitz, and AAF General Carl Spaatz (Hap Arnold having just retired)—still handled strategy. Heavily influenced by Vice Admiral Forrest Sherman, the JCS practiced a vague "forward defense in depth" of the western hemisphere from a system of naval and air bases in the eastern Atlantic and western Pacific. These could be used not only to deter aggression in either ocean but to project American air power over the Eurasian landmass should the Soviet Union attempt to dominate it. For Towers, the strategy meant carrier air strikes launched from the Sea of Japan. But the JCS did not establish any specific force levels or operational plans. By September 1946 American foreign and defense policy and planning were decidedly anti-Russian, though the definite scheme of containing Soviet expansion would not be articulated until mid-1947. [22]

Towers therefore interpreted his mission in terms of "national policy"—giving permanence to the newly won bases, maintaining his reduced fleet as a viable police force against aggression, and keeping a close watch over developments in China. Of one thing he could be certain: the Pacific was a navy strategic preserve, and he had no intention of surrendering it to the army, namely, General MacArthur. By the same token, he continued to actively oppose the creation of a separate air force under a unified department of national defense. To police the vast Pacific the navy needed control of its own air forces, which had become the nucleus of the postwar navy.

As the Pacific commander on the Nimitz team, Towers made several trips to Washington during the year. Each time, he dined with Nimitz and King together, finding the retired COMINCH remarkably agreeable and supportive. Nonetheless Towers vigorously thwarted one of King's last measures, to reduce the number of rear admirals by downgrading a great many of them to the permanent rank of commodore, on the grounds that this would jeopardize the careers of many men who had proved themselves in combat. He also lent his weight to keeping a strong WAVE component in the postwar navy, a policy to which Nimitz finally adhered. And Jack's former BuAer helpmate, Captain Joy Bright Hancock, became director of the WAVES. But most of a visit in late February was devoted to ironing out problems of base housing, now that dependents were allowed to join the men in Hawaii, Japan, and the intermediate bases.[23]

The bulk of Towers' time as Pacific commander was spent administering the ocean areas from his headquarters at Pearl Harbor, among others assisted by deputy Charles Wellborn, chief of staff Wu Duncan, joint staff army commander Lieutenant General Robert Richardson, and Brigadier General Thomas D. White, commanding the Seventh Air Force.[24] The only "operation" conducted during Towers' tour of duty was Crossroads, the two atomic bomb tests at Bikini atoll in the Marshall islands. Vice Admiral W. H. P. Blandy commanded Joint Army-Navy Task Force 1 and met with Towers and his advisers in May, but Jack refused to be present for the actual tests. With the entire operation administered by the JCS, he believed that some critic might claim his presence would prevent a fair evaluation of damage to the target ships. But he hosted a throng of observers for the tests during the last week in June, as well as Marjorie, whose husband was now attached to Blandy's staff. The tests, conducted successfully during July, had ominous implications for the navy; Towers' old ship, the *Saratoga,* was sunk by one of the blasts. The atomic age had arrived, and the navy had best look to its defenses against enemy strategic bombers.[25]

The Pacific Fleet was centered on its six carriers. Personnel shortages threatened to compromise their effectiveness, especially the two operating with the Seventh Fleet in Chinese waters. Towers insisted that these two flattops not be jeopardized for want of full crews. The principal carrier planes were now the F4U Corsair fighter-bomber and SB2C Helldiver dive bomber, while the TBM-3 Avenger had been equipped with air-search radar for antisubmarine operations. Two new fighters, the Grumman F8F Bearcat piston-engine plane and Ryan FR prop-jet Fireball became operational, as did the new front-line attack bomber, the Douglas AD Skyraider. All shipping was coordinated with commander, Western Sea Frontier, Admiral Dick Edwards.[26]

Whatever the strength of the ships, Towers worked mightily to create an adequate base network that would preserve the Pacific as a strategic American lake. As early as May 1945 he had recommended that, in addition to Pearl

General of the Army Dwight D. Eisenhower, *left,* army chief of staff, inspects Pearl Harbor's facilities from the base signal tower with Rear Admiral E. W. Hanson, Towers, and Major General Howard McC. Snyder, medical adviser to Ike, 29 April 1946. (National Archives)

Harbor and the Philippines, three postwar strong points be developed: Guam, Truk, and Kwajalein or Eniwetok. Subsequent demobilization, however, had accelerated the general roll-up of Pacific bases and shipping. Amphibious LSTs were ubiquitous in moving equipment about, except that as men were demobilized many of these landing craft lacked sufficient crews. At each morning conference it was reported that more of the LSTs had been left immobile, leading Towers to complain that "he didn't want to hear any more about counting LSTs." Such craft, surplus equipment, and even small bases often had to be abandoned in the interest of "getting the boys home."[27]

On 29–30 April Towers hosted an inspection visit by General Eisenhower and in early June made a trip of his own to bases in Alaska, where he found "an attitude of defeatism and an extreme reluctance . . . to improve conditions." He reported this to Nimitz as part of an overall study to decide which installations to improve throughout the Pacific. It soon became evident that, between Hawaii and the Philippines, the keystone to the U.S. base network was the Marianas, notably Guam. Rear Admiral Baldy Pownall relieved George Murray as commander of the Marianas in February and labored against demobilization fever and personnel shortages to improve Guam's facilities.

In August Towers toured his western Pacific bases—Kwajalein, Truk, Guam, Palau, and Manila—to see for himself the extent of their deterioration. He decided to strengthen Pownall's position by having the latter establish his own logistics division, thereby thwarting repeated requests by Vice Admiral Oscar C. Badger, commander Service Force Pacific, to absorb that function. Towers also obtained Pownall's promotion to vice admiral in recognition of the latter's administrative accomplishments, which overrode his less successful wartime record. Finally, at the end of September, Towers and Pownall flew to Washington to affirm the primacy of the Marianas and to recommend other bases to Nimitz. Jack called for the development of Guam, with nearby Saipan, into a second or "little" Pearl Harbor; Guam's wartime breakwater had created an anchorage for four hundred vessels. On the northern flank Kodiak, Alaska, should be strengthened and, on the southern, Leyte-Samar abandoned in favor of Subic Bay and Sangley Point near Manila. Kwajalein and other hard-won islands could provide intermediate anchorages and landing fields, but all the temporarily constructed advanced wartime bases should be abandoned. Already dilapidated, they were too expensive to maintain. Nimitz and the deputy CNOs accepted Towers' recommendations and announced them in October.[28]

Towers continued his wartime role as head of the military government of the Pacific islands and worked toward integrating the newly liberated native peoples into the fabric of the American political system. Inasmuch as he and his local commanders made real progress in this endeavor, Towers took umbrage at former Secretary of the Interior Harold Ickes for publicly airing the view that Guam was being poorly administered by the navy. Jack personally voiced his objection to President Truman.[29]

America's new Pacific domain was also held together by an interlocking system of air lanes utilized by NATS and the AAF's Air Transport Command. NATS relied on its own R5D (DC-4) Skymaster landplane and its last flying boat, the big Martin JRM Mars, for transport service. As for commercial aviation, wartime relations with Pan American in the Pacific had deteriorated to the point where the company had tried to get out of its transport contract, but now it sought to regain navy cooperation on runs from Honolulu to the Admiralties and Australia. Instead of prewar flying boats, the company would use Lockheed Constellations and Douglas DC-4s. Towers maintained contact with Dave Ingalls, now vice president of operations for Pan Am, but would not lead the company to expect preferential treatment over competitors. The matter of servicing airliners along the way lay in the hands of the CAA, and Towers never did give Pan Am satisfaction that the navy would do it. Regarding land-based antisub patrols, the navy utilized the improved PB4Y Privateer but pinned its greatest hopes on the Lockheed P2V Neptune; one of these, the Truculent Turtle, flew some fifty-five hours nonstop, over eleven thousand miles, from Australia to Ohio. Transpacific flight had arrived, and the last patrol seaplanes, the PBY and PBM, were relegated to air-sea rescue duties.[30]

The only controversy over Pacific air bases developed when the AAF tried to establish a B-29 bombardment wing in Hawaii. On three separate trips to Washington Towers argued at length with King, Nimitz, and Forrest Sherman against the proposal, simply because he could see no strategic need for B-29s there. The Marianas airdromes were closer to potential targets on the Eurasian landmass. Despite Towers' urging to study the matter from a strategic standpoint Nimitz remained silent, having conceded the request to the AAF. But a joint army-navy board, headed by Vice Admiral Montgomery and influenced by Towers' arguments, forced the issue into the open in June. MacArthur and other generals agreed with Towers, and the matter was not resolved before Jack left the Pacific. His argument was basically sound: the B-29s were better suited closer to the possible enemy. Towers nonetheless allowed the Superforts to stage through the navy's fields in Hawaii.[31]

The whole question of America's Pacific defenses was enmeshed in the welter of issues confronting foreign and defense policymakers in 1946–47. In spite of the developing cold war, Towers did not believe war with the Soviet Union was likely in the near future; that nation had suffered too heavily in the struggle against Hitler. Although he was irritated by incidents between Russian and American planes and ships in the Far East, none of these was threatening. The best security, he was quoted as saying in October, "is to keep our monopoly of the atomic bomb until the world is more settled than it is at present." The communist menace hung most heavily over wartorn Europe, which had added fuel to the AAF's insistence on independent status. Demobilization and economy spurred the movement toward service unification that Towers opposed. Finally, the chaotic situation in China and Southeast Asia exacerbated army-navy command relationships. Along with general unification, a unified command structure for the Pacific seemed to make sense, and the debate over it raged throughout 1946.[32]

The interservice quarrel in the Pacific was a continuation of wartime differences. MacArthur, as occupation commander in Japan, wanted overall unity of command in order to fashion a viable defense posture, eliminate duplication, and economize on precious manpower and resources. On the other hand, the navy had traditionally controlled the nation's defenses in the Pacific, which by definition was a water-oriented theater. In January Admiral Nimitz recommended that the army-navy Pacific command system be replaced by a two-theater arrangement along the wartime lines of the Central and Southwest Pacific. That is, MacArthur would command the western Pacific, Towers the rest as CINCPAC. Each would have his own army, navy, and AAF components.

The proposal enraged MacArthur, who regarded it as an attempt "to secure permanent control by the Naval Command of the Ground and Air Forces within the Pacific Basin." One thing was certain: the existing system had to be replaced. The press likened it to the command structure that existed on 7 December 1941, when divided responsibility in Hawaii had contributed to the Pearl Harbor disaster. Immediately upon assuming command in February, Towers urged his superiors to settle the question, but they—Forrestal, Nimitz, Sherman—demurred until the overall unification issue was resolved. Jack therefore rejected General Richardson's view that the navy had no authority over the army in Hawaii. MacArthur was further aroused when he learned that General Eisenhower agreed with Nimitz's proposal for a divided command system, which Towers seconded at length during Eisenhower's visit to Hawaii at the end of April. MacArthur's position

Towers plays his favorite card game, bridge, on a long flight in the command plane, 1946. (Towers collection)

was weakened by the pending independence of the Philippines. This would further erode his command authority in the Far East.[33]

Towers, like all his contemporaries in the navy, regarded MacArthur with mixed respect and disbelief. The general once sent him an autographed photograph of himself with the inscription, "To my fighting comrade-in-arms, Jack Towers," which Towers merely laughed off. Late in June, on the eve of the Bikini tests, Jack had the old war correspondent Frederick Palmer and Major John J. Slocum of the AAF as houseguests. The latter, on Admiral Blandy's staff for the tests, was a nephew of Reggie Gillmor, who had hosted Jack's wedding to Pierre. One evening Towers remarked to Slocum, "John, that MacArthur out in Tokyo acts as if the Pacific is *his* ocean."

Slocum, taken aback, had the temerity to reply, "Admiral, whose ocean *is* it?"

525

Towers, eyeing the AAF officer as if he were a blithering idiot, replied, "Why, it's *my* ocean, of course."

From that time on, remembered Slocum, "I thought all senior Admirals probably had the same proprietary attitude toward oceans adjacent to their command." Which was the whole point—admirals command oceans and what travels on them.[34]

Many of MacArthur's and Towers' anxieties arose from the precarious state of affairs in China. The civil war between the Nationalists and Communists stood poised to break wide open should negotiations undertaken by General Marshall fail. Towers had two staff army intelligence officers brief him once a week on the military situation on the continent and personally interviewed every officer, diplomat, and reporter passing through Hawaii on his return from China. One of these was Captain H. H. Smith-Hutton, detached from occupation duty in Japan, who spent the night as Towers' guest. Jack's questions and observations about China, the occupation of Japan, and MacArthur gave Smith-Hutton the impression that Towers was "an intelligent and thoughtful man." Also, "Mrs. Towers took an active part in the discussion, and it was evident that both she and the Admiral were interested in Far Eastern affairs. I was sorry I had to leave early the next morning for Oakland and Washington."[35]

The navy was not only supplying the Nationalist Chinese with surplus materials from rolled-up bases but also helping train its small navy, providing famine relief, and planning to assign advisers, as was the army. The Nationalists seemed the stronger of the warring factions, but Towers learned from the several observers that Chiang Kai-shek's corrupt leaders had compromised their material superiority. Still, he did not agree with General Wedemeyer's recommendation in March to deactivate the U.S. Army command in China and withdraw the twenty thousand marines who were keeping mines and railroads open. And he defended to Wedemeyer the marines' refusal to withdraw until ordered to do so by higher authority. Wedemeyer wanted to get out of China and relinquish all responsibility to Admiral Savvy Cooke of the Seventh Fleet. Cooke, whom Towers admired for his actions in Chinese waters, was unabashedly pro-Nationalist. Late in May Towers learned from Marine Corps General Roy Geiger, just back from China, that should the Marshall negotiations fail the Communists would probably occupy all the major cities of north China, including Peiping, the capital. The situation was obviously deteriorating, making the proposed reorganization of Pacific commands essential.[36]

Much depended on resolving the old problem of unification. At the request of Secretary Forrestal, Ferdinand Eberstadt had made a detailed study of the unification question and come up with sweeping recommendations based on the wartime experiences of strategic planning. That is, he would centralize industrial management to avoid past mistakes and create a separate air force. But the three services would not be unified under a single department or secretary of national defense; the army, navy, and air force could simply cooperate as they had during the war. The army, however, counterattacked with a proposal favoring a centralized command structure, including a single chief of staff. This drew navy opposition. On a visit to Washington in March Towers met with Nimitz, Sherman, and Ramsey to comment on Eberstadt's draft of proposed legislation. At Towers' suggestion, a preamble was added stating that the navy opposed a separate department of air if a secretary of common defense was created over the army and navy. Towers continued to lobby before visiting generals and congressmen in Hawaii, even after President Truman imposed a "gag" rule on vocal navy opposition. Opinion polarized as new legislation recommended unification under the army scheme.[37]

Forrestal, who had long wanted Towers to testify before the Senate Naval Affairs committee on unification, finally summoned him to Washington to do so early in July. When he arrived on the seventh he was met by Rear Admiral W. G. "Red" Tomlinson and Captain George Anderson and whisked off to Rear Admiral Luis de Florez's apartment to discuss the hearings. This was followed by lunch with Sherman. Towers saw the navy in a precarious position, for in addition to the proposed unification and separate air force, President Truman had issued a statement indicating the plan had the approval of Forrestal and Nimitz. Towers learned otherwise from them—that in fact Truman and Forrestal disagreed fundamentally—and prepared his remarks accordingly. On the morning of the ninth, an hour before the hearings, Rear Admiral Dick Byrd unexpectedly reported that the hearings were to be open to the public. Jack had Byrd telephone his brother, Senator Harry Byrd, to have them closed. Then he delivered his prepared remarks before Senator David Walsh and the two other senators present. As in prewar days, Captains Anderson and Stroop were at his side.[38]

Towers pulled out all the stops. Harking back to the Morrow Board hearings of 1925, he declared that "as the recognized leader of Naval Aviators" he had preached and helped attain integration of aviation into the navy until aviation now comprised 40 percent of it. The AAF had done otherwise, insisting not only on independent status from the army but threatening as well to absorb naval aviation, especially its long-range land-based patrol arm.

527

Equally bad, the army seemed bent on decimating the Marine Corps. One overall secretary of defense, moreover, would prevent navy commanders from having direct access to Congress to protect the navy's missions, a privilege Towers had long exploited. The unification bill thus contained "certain glaring defects which, potentially at least, could wreck the Navy."[39]

Under questioning by Senator Walsh, off the record, Towers feared that the issue was lost. He was told the Senate backed the proposal. But many wartime comrades were also giving testimony—Spruance, Mitscher, Turner, Nimitz, Ramsey—and Undersecretary John L. Sullivan. Their combined voice of opposition succeeded in killing the bill. Unification would not become a reality until naval aviation and the marines were protected.[40]

While the merger of the services could be put off, army and navy chiefs Eisenhower and Nimitz believed that the Pacific command reorganization could not. In August the two men agreed that the theater should be split into two commands—the rimlands of the western Pacific under MacArthur and the Pacific Ocean under Towers. MacArthur rejected this. He insisted at the very least that the Marianas with their B-29 airdromes be placed under his jurisdiction. It was a sensitive point, inasmuch as Guam was being turned into

Towers speaks and Vice Admiral Forrest Sherman, deputy CNO (operations), listens at a press conference on the future of Pacific bases and occupied territories, Washington, 30 September 1946. The note by Towers' cigarette hand, apparently jotted down by Sherman, reads, "We do *return* all anchorages and anchorage rights"—that is, to Japan. (National Archives)

Uncle John accepts a kiss from niece Edith Towers
at his brother Will's home in Rome, Georgia, 30
September 1946. Immediately after a press
conference he had flown to his hometown for a
formal dinner, his first visit since before the war.
(Courtesy W. M. Towers III)

the navy's major base west of Hawaii. When Towers flew to Washington in
late September, he opposed a draft by Sherman to give MacArthur supreme
U.S. command in the Far East; that would be too heavy a burden on top of the
general's duties as supreme allied occupation commander. After more deliberations, Sherman rewrote the document for presentation to the president.
Towers then flew down to Rome to spend a weekend with his brother Will. It
was his first visit to his hometown since 1939.[41]

On 20 September Towers and Baldy Pownall accompanied Forrestal to
the White House to discuss Pacific reorganization with the chief executive.
Truman was most interested in the political status of the mandated islands and
Okinawa. After Towers expressed his belief that her possession of them after
World War I had encouraged Japan to go to war in 1941, the president

remarked that they should be retained—at least until the United Nations proved to be a viable organization and could possibly take over their administration. Forrestal observed that the UN mandate gave the United States the right to exercise its own mandate over the islands.

Then Forrestal brought up the matter of MacArthur's demand for supreme command of the Pacific. "The president," according to Towers, "interrupted to say that he considered this a political matter and was not prepared to express any views at present." Jack was unimpressed by Harry Truman and felt no reluctance about stating his views on MacArthur at the ensuing press conference. He praised the general for performing the "colossal job" of reconstructing Japan along democratic lines, but as for his desire to control the entire Pacific, "I can't for the life of me understand why he'd want to take on anything more."[42]

The same afternoon Towers and Wu Duncan commented to Ramsey and Sherman on a reorganization draft that the Pacific should either be split or MacArthur compelled by the JCS to "meet his responsibilities under [the] present arrangement." The JCS then adopted the navy proposal for a divided Pacific command and obtained the president's approval in December. Seven geographical theater commands were to be established on 1 January 1947, patterned after the wartime practice of each service reporting to the theater commander. MacArthur would head the Far East Command, that is, all American forces in Japan, Korea, the Philippines, Bonins (Jimas), and Ryukyus (Okinawa). Towers would lead the Pacific Command, which consisted of everything else, as CINCPAC. He would also retain command of all naval forces in the Pacific as CINCPACFLT. The dispute over the Marianas resulted in MacArthur obtaining immediate jurisdiction, though the islands were, it was promised, eventually to be transferred to the Pacific Command. Thus MacArthur did not gain control over the entire ocean, but neither did the navy. The new system had worked well enough during the war and would again for the next several decades.[43]

Towers personally devised a new joint staff for the Pacific Command patterned after "the best features" of the JCS. He believed this resulted in "a more complete joint command set-up than I think we ever had at this level." Whereas Nimitz had merely absorbed army and AAF officers into his navy wartime staff, Towers had on his new joint staff the commanding general Army Ground Forces Pacific (Lieutenant General John E. Hull), commanding general AAF Pacific (Brigadier General Donald F. Stace), and deputy CINCPAC (Vice Admiral Lynde McCormick). General Hull enthusiastically endorsed Towers' system. As during the war, Towers kept administrative and general operational control of the Seventh Fleet. And in the general navy reorganization the numbered fleets were abolished as of 1 January in favor of one "task fleet" in each ocean; the new Pacific Task Fleet was given to Vice Admiral Montgomery, replacing the Third and Fifth Fleet organizations. The Seventh Fleet became U.S. Naval Forces, Western Pacific.[44]

The new setup came none too soon, for the truce between the Nationalist and Communist Chinese collapsed in October 1946 when General Marshall failed to obtain a settlement between them. Towers continued to argue for the retention of marine forces in China to keep mines and railroads operating, even after Marshall and Admiral Cooke recommended their withdrawal in December. Towers believed their stabilizing presence necessary as long as it was American policy to support the Nationalists. The problem was that policy toward China was confused in the extreme.

On 10 January 1947, en route home to become secretary of state, Marshall had a long discussion with Towers at Pearl Harbor in which he voiced complete pessimism over the quagmire in China. Since the "more liberal elements" had no hope of replacing the "selfish, self-centered group" of Nationalist leaders, Marshall hoped to withdraw the marines and let the Chinese fight their civil war to a finish. A month later Towers and Savvy Cooke developed plans for the possible sealift of the marines out of China. Marshall was eventually proved correct; China would fall to the Communists, though not until late 1949.[45]

Towers' future in the cold war navy was uncertain. He turned sixty-one in January 1946, supposedly leaving him three years' active duty, but Admiral King had instituted one last reform designed to weed out older, hidebound officers regardless of their specialty. The legislation lowered the mandatory retirement age from sixty-four to sixty-two. This, plus the need to reduce the bloated numbers of wartime flag officers, led to the creation of the Involuntary Retirement Board, popularly known as the Plucking Board. Composed of Halsey, Spruance, Towers, and Kinkaid, it convened during Jack's visit to the capital in March 1946. The task consumed ten days, with Towers recommending retirements for the aviation community. Thus he was able to subtly set the course for the postwar navy by insuring that the very best aviators be retained in the promotion pipeline.[46]

For Towers himself, the new retirement age came as a personal blow. He would have to step aside in January 1947. Like all career officers, Towers aspired to the top job of CNO. By following Nimitz as Pacific commander in chief, and because of Forrestal's policy of promoting pioneer aviators to senior billets, he was certainly in line for it. But Forrestal could not change the new law. Furthermore, Nimitz's two-year tour as CNO was not due to expire until December 1947, by which time Towers would be almost sixty-three. Had the retirement age remained at sixty-four, Towers could conceivably have been appointed in December 1947 for a two-year term to expire on the eve of his sixty-fifth birthday.

Disappointed though he was, Towers seems not to have complained to intimates or peers. He had always obeyed the law, and he recognized the need for younger men to run the new air navy of which he had been a key architect. Still, on one occasion years later, Gus Read was "squawking" about something relating to promotions at his bank. Jack interrupted him, "Gus, how would you like it if you were going to become president of the bank and you found that somebody had had a law passed so that you were just too old to be eligible for the job?"

Said Read, "I wouldn't like that."

"Well, that's what happened to me. I thought you knew that."

"No, I didn't realize that."

"It did."[47]

When Towers visited Washington during July 1946 to testify against unification, his name was not among those considered for reassignment. Suddenly an elder statesman, he met with Deputy CNO (personnel) Louis Denfeld, Vice CNO Ramsey, and Deputy CNO (air) Radford to decide on new flag billets. They approved Pete Mitscher to command the Atlantic Fleet immediately and Savvy Cooke to relieve Towers as Pacific commander in chief early in the new year. Towers strongly endorsed both men. On 25 September, again in Washington, he read in the morning papers the announcement of his own pending retirement on 1 February. He also learned that he would be replaced by Louis Denfeld rather than Cooke. Over dinner at Forrestal's home that evening Jack expressed surprise that Denfeld had gotten the nod, though he "had no doubt of Denfeld's ability to do the job." On the other hand, he was astonished that Denfeld's relief as deputy CNO (personnel) was Vice Admiral William M. Fechteler, since it had been Forrestal's policy to advance aviators to such key jobs. The Gun Club still exerted its powerful influence. Whereas black-shoe Denfeld had been assistant chief of BuPers for most of the war, Fechteler, another battleship man, had served in BuPers during 1942–43 and replaced Denfeld there early in 1945.[48]

On the matter of a replacement for CNO Nimitz, Towers agonized for several weeks before replying to a request from Nimitz for his thoughts on the subject. Finally he decided that

> because of the importance of Aviation and further because of . . . the unjustified but constant criticism from Army Air Force officers, Congress and the Press that the Navy is dominated by officers who have not a full appreciation of the value of aviation . . . Radford definitely would be the best choice. He is intelligent, has a fine, strong personality, is possessed of a background of Fleet and Navy Department experience of the most qualifying type and from all I can learn is highly regarded both professionally and personally throughout the service. His Vice-Chief should be a non-aviator.[49]

No doubt Towers picked Radford because of his forceful pro-air stance in the unification struggle, as opposed to the increasingly compromising positions of Forrest Sherman and Duke Ramsey. Since Nimitz's successor need not be chosen for another year, the matter was not pressing. Yet, as it turned out, Louis Denfeld would be selected as the next CNO, and Fechteler would eventually hold the post as well. The struggle of aviators to gain control of the navy was not yet over.

Towers' impending retirement notwithstanding, Jim Forrestal had no intention of putting his talented old friend out to pasture. Jack's skills deserved to be exploited in the navy or in commercial aviation. Back in November 1943 Forrestal had elicited lengthy commentaries from Towers, assisted by Forrest Sherman, on the role of American civil airline carriers in postwar international air transportation. In his remarks, Towers had warned of drastic postwar reductions in civil aviation, a position Forrestal had conveyed to the leaders of the industry. As a result, Gene Wilson of United Aircraft had flown out to Hawaii early in 1944 to confer with Towers and Sherman over the industry's postwar conversion to a peacetime economy. Instead of leading to concerted action, their shared fears had been realized with the postwar slump in commercial aircraft production. Towers might now help the situation in a new post envisioned by Assistant Secretary of State Will Clayton—that of secretary of state for air. To Forrestal Towers expressed definite interest in holding such a post. The State Department, however, was not interested in pursuing the idea.[50]

Forrestal decided to try and retain Towers on active duty beyond his sixty-second birthday by appointing him chairman of the General Board. The wartime board, relegated mainly to ship design functions, was limping along in this role under Vice Admiral Frank Jack Fletcher when a controversy developed in mid-1946 over its duplicating the work of the Ship Characteristics Board, part of Mick Carney's office of deputy CNO (logistics). In May Forrestal asked Towers whether he thought the board should be continued or abolished. Contrary to Nimitz and the deputy CNOs who resented duplication, Forrestal told Towers he felt that a revitalized board could "initiate recommendations to the Secretary" on such matters as "the use of atomic energy for ship propulsion, Navy Department organization, etc." If so, it "should have on it people of vigor and intellectual capacity."

Towers concurred wholeheartedly, urging that the board actively advise the secretary rather than being a mere pool for unemployed flag officers or a "dumping ground for minor problems." Drawing on an unusual source, Towers said, "To use one of Admiral King's favorite expressions, there is always a need for 'checks and balances,' and I do not believe that you can always expect that from any one Staff," namely, Nimitz's. The General Board could be the secretary's counterweight to the CNO. Forrestal accepted Towers' reasoning and offered him the post when he returned to Washington in late November to sit on a flag selection board. Jack accepted immediately, whereupon Forrestal obtained the president's approval to retain him on active duty beyond the mandatory retirement age.[51]

Towers' November visit to Washington coincided with a sudden breakthrough in the logjam over unification. At President Truman's urging Forrestal had developed an acceptable compromise: the three services—army, navy, and air force—would be coordinated but not subordinated to a secretary of national defense within a vague national military establishment. A permanent JCS would be created and the roles and missions of naval aviation and the Marine Corps defined and thus protected. When Towers and other members of the flag selection board were briefed on this compromise in Louis Denfeld's office on the eighteenth, such division of opinion arose that the same admirals moved to Nimitz's office for a special conference. Opposing the compromise were Towers, Spruance, Mitscher, Blandy, Radford, and Dick Edwards, defending it, Nimitz, Ramsey, and Sherman. The latter three "appeared rather hostile" toward the dissenters, according to Towers' diary.[52]

Next day Forrestal reconvened his admirals to hear them out. Called upon first, Towers agreed with everything except a separate air force and wanted the JCS reconstituted with two members from both the army and the navy, one of each pair to be an aviator. He reiterated his long-held belief that an "impartial body" along the lines of the Morrow Board should study unification and hoped that the president could be prevailed upon to appoint one, although Truman had heretofore refused to do so. Edwards, Mitscher, and Radford generally concurred with Towers, and Nimitz agreed with his suggestion for an impartial board, but Ramsey and Sherman insisted that a separate air force was inevitable because of AAF, congressional, and public demands. Denfeld was noncommittal. Over succeeding days Towers met informally with Forrestal to promote his position.

On 27 November Towers restated his stance in a general meeting of Forrestal, Undersecretary Sullivan, Assistant Secretary W. John Kenney, Ferdinand Eberstadt, and all the senior admirals including King. The same dissenters wanted statutory guarantees for the missions of naval aviation; "it seemed to me," recorded Towers, "the Navy might as well decide to fight against the third Service." Eberstadt thought the president would not appoint an impartial board and feared that a single unified department would result if the separate air force was not accepted. When Towers departed for Hawaii the next day, the navy position had not been resolved. Sherman and AAF Major General Lauris Norstad continued to hammer out details of their compromise package and had it ready for congressional hearings early in the new year. When Towers saw the final draft he had Duncan draw up a paper opposing it; the new system did not protect naval aviation.[53]

Unification at the theater level worked perfectly well, as Towers demonstrated with the new Pacific Command, his tour of duty as its head being extended another month until the end of February 1947. His counterpart in the Atlantic, Pete Mitscher, was not as fortunate. On 3 February Towers learned of his old compatriot's death and the appointment of Admiral "Spike" Blandy as his successor. Thus, when Denfeld replaced Towers in the Pacific, nonaviators would hold the two major fleet commands. Radford, a critic of unification, was transferred out of Washington to command the Atlantic Task Fleet, with Wu Duncan replacing him as deputy CNO (air).

Towers spent his last two months as Pacific commander in chief strengthening Pownall's organization in the Marianas and trying, with uneven success, to perfect transpacific air routes and way stations for NATS, the air transport command, and commercial carriers, notably Pan Am. He continued a policy of granting interviews with reporters on request and was surprised when a group of eight visiting editors and publishers conferring with him in February asked no questions about China or Korea. The American public had no interest in active involvement on the continent of Asia, a reluctance that would persist for decades in spite of future limited American wars in Korea and Vietnam.[54]

Towers had performed well as the first real postwar CINCPAC and very first head of the Pacific Command. By deftly handling the fleet in the midst of demobilization, he earned the plaudits of Chester Nimitz, who for the first time gave him straight 4.0 marks on his fitness reports. At 0930 on 28 February 1947 Towers boarded the escort carrier *Bairoko,* commanded by Captain Jim Russell, and turned over the Pacific Command and fleet to Louis Denfeld in a fifteen-minute ceremony. Jack and Pierre—and Mr. MacTavish, their Scottie—then proceeded to the Matson Line dock where they boarded the liner *Matsonia* for passage home. She cast off at noon. Thus Jack Towers left the Pacific nearly four and a half years after reporting there as ComAirPac in October 1942.[55]

They crossed the country by rail to Washington, where on 10 March 1947 Towers reported in as chairman of the General Board. He spent several days outlining the membership and functions of the revitalized board and attended the weekly CNO conference, presided over by Admiral Frederick Horne. Following a pleasant week of leave with Grover Loening in Palm Beach, Jack and Pierre moved into nice quarters vacated by Horne at Fort McNair.[56]

Towers' appearance on the Washington scene proved timely, for the Truman administration now made the cold war a national policy. Forrest Sherman had developed top secret war plans calling for immediate offensive naval operations in the event of war, but such plans proved difficult to articulate because of growing defense cutbacks by Congress.[57] During the spring, Towers criticized the navy's uncertain wartime mobilization plans so often that they were revised and updated. As he had said incisively in the months before Pearl Harbor, the navy could not make realistic strategic plans without clear national policy guidelines from the executive branch of the government. Mick Carney opposed him, but Sherman concurred, which meant Forrestal and Nimitz agreed, for Sherman had become their principal adviser. Still, the nonair admirals had difficulty envisioning needs for the immediate future. In mid-June, for example, Towers, Nimitz, and Forrestal were appalled by a Naval War College fleet problem presentation; by ignoring aviation in war games, Spruance's Newport staff was simply not responding realistically to the challenges of the cold war world.[58]

Of one thing Towers could be certain, as he told Forrestal in May: "Aviation is bound to be the principal naval offensive weapon in any war which may come within the next ten years." He admitted that to try and restore all the cuts recommended by Congress would be "fatal," but he pressed to salvage pay and subsistence for personnel. Conceding that the aviation shore establishment was too big, he nonetheless helped resist an attempt by Congress to shut down NAS Corpus Christi as a training facility.

And, working closely with Radford, he was able to shift and consolidate units and overhaul facilities at fewer installations.[59]

Forrestal's justification for involving the chairman of the General Board in such high-level discussions of overall naval policy was that he wanted the board to undertake a major survey of the navy's shore establishment. Towers was instructed "to make a critical examination towards the end of bringing about a better balance between the operating forces and the shore establishment . . . , taking into consideration the prospective postwar and tentative mobilization requirement and at the same time . . . the prospective financial expectations." It was a tall order, requiring Towers' participation in most of the navy's affairs. The board conducted its studies throughout the spring, made tentative recommendations, then held hearings with each bureau and office during July.[60]

Forrestal gave Towers carte blanche in making his survey. If he encountered opposition, he was to call on Forrestal personally to intervene. And because Forrestal wanted the General Board revitalized, he gave Towers full authority to pick only top men for its membership. This was necessary because board duty was considered a career dead-end. Towers retained Vice Admiral Soc McMorris on the board and welcomed Vice Admiral Pat Bellinger as the one other flag officer. For the remaining three members he selected promising but more junior officers—Captains Truman J. Hedding and Arleigh Burke and Colonel Randolph M. Pate of the Marine Corps. Towers wielded his new authority with an iron hand, especially because the survey, which would mean closing certain facilities and eliminating jobs, was unpopular. For instance, he threatened to take over future planning for BuOrd's shore installations if bureau chief Vice Admiral George F. Hussey refused to accept cutbacks. Forrestal backed Towers completely.[61]

On Forrestal's orders the subordinate secretaries—Sullivan, Kenney, and John Nicholas Brown, the new assistant secretary (air)—gave Towers their full support, as did Forrestal's new administrative assistant, Wilfred J. McNeil, and the architects of the new Executive Office of the Secretary, C. DeM. Asbury and John H. Dillon. Towers met with McNeil, Asbury, and Dillon to urge that the duplication of logistics under the CNO and the bureaus be reduced. This brought him into conflict with Mick Carney, deputy CNO (logistics), who resented the General Board's interfering with shore establishment matters and the duties of the Ships Characteristics Board. Especially important were plans to modify several *Essex*-class carriers, beginning with the *Oriskany,* in order to accommodate heavier aircraft—the

The General Board in November 1947, after several changes in its original membership.
Left to right: Colonel Randolph McC. Pate, USMC, Rear Admiral W. F. Boone, Vice
Admiral Soc McMorris, chairman Towers, Rear Admiral Charles B. Momsen, Captain L. J.
Huffman, Commander J. M. Lee (*standing*), and Captain Arleigh A. Burke. (A. A. Burke
collection, Naval Historical Center)

Grumman F9F Panther jet fighter and the AD Skyraider attack plane. Towers
persevered with his survey and had it completed by 1 August.[62]

The fact was, however, that Forrestal's streamlining of departmental
administration made a revitalized General Board superfluous. Towers discussed the situation with Nimitz, and late in June Forrestal expressed his own
doubts to Jack. Prospects for the board's success looked bleak, especially as it
devoted considerable effort to tedious hearings on minor aspects of navy
regulations, the modernization of the Panama Canal, new destroyer designs,
and an imbroglio over dress uniforms. Towers came to realize that the board
had no major role in the cold war navy. Four years later its main functions
would be absorbed by the Ships Characteristics Board.[63]

Forrestal nevertheless utilized Towers fully in overall policy matters, not
least the unification issue. The basic compromise bill called for a secretary of
national defense without departmental status, charged with coordinating the
departments and service secretaries. Towers' only quarrel with the package,

he advised Forrestal in early April 1947, was that the roles and missions of naval aviation and the Marine Corps should be defined by law rather than by temporal executive order as recommended. And he argued in favor of giving the three service secretaries cabinet status for direct access to the president, a measure the compromise avoided.[64]

Congressional hearings over the spring accentuated navy fears about a domineering secretary of defense. Senator Harry Byrd particularly opposed the lack of statutory guarantees for naval air and the marines and with several colleagues sought Towers' testimony to present this argument. Jack was reluctant, since his views were already well known. At least he learned from Nimitz and Sherman why they had acceded to the army refusal of statutory guarantees: the executive order, they felt, was the only workable compromise. On 24 April Jack attended a dinner at the British embassy in honor of the great savant of RAF strategic bombing, Air Marshal Sir Hugh Trenchard. There he discovered from Air Vice Marshal Goddard that General Tooey Spaatz, AAF chief, had brought Trenchard to Washington to testify for unification but that Goddard had dissuaded Spaatz for fear of hostile reaction to a foreigner's testimony.[65]

A week later, at Forrestal's request, Towers summarized the navy feeling about the bill. He declared that "the officer personnel were overwhelmingly against it" owing to 1) fear of the merger of naval aviation and the new air force; 2) army statements "to the effect that naval aviation will soon be washed out and the Marine Corps reduced to a police force"; and 3) a feeling "that in the negotiations with the Army they had been sold down the river by the Navy negotiator, Vice Admiral Sherman," a hard truth about uniformed opinion of Jack's longtime colleague. Towers confided in his diary, "I reached the opinion that Forrestal, supporting the Bill, is weakening, . . . that he fears that if some measure of unification is not approved during the current session of Congress, the Navy will receive the whole blame."[66]

When several navy men publicly denounced the unification bill in June, Forrestal yielded to pressure from Congressman W. Sterling Cole and others by inviting any naval officers who opposed it to testify before the House committee on expenditures in the executive departments. Many responded, but not Towers, until specifically requested by the committee chairman Clare E. Hoffman. Early on the twenty-eighth, before appearing, Towers was visited by Sherman and agreed to oppose an amendment calling for a fourth military service to handle procurement. He answered questions at the hearing but without major impact; Radford was now leading the fight, arguing that carriers could get in closer than projected long-range air force bombers to deliver air attacks against enemy targets. Without such a role in strategic bombing, the navy believed it would lose out completely to the new air service.[67]

The navy's complaints failed to delay the inevitable, especially since President Truman had agreed to appoint Forrestal as the first secretary of defense. On 16 July the Hoffman committee produced a clean unification bill incorporating guarantees for naval aviation and the Marine Corps. Congressman Cole met with Towers, assistant CNO (air) Rear Admiral Jocko Clark, and CNO planner Captain George Anderson to work out an amendment to preserve the navy's land-based patrol aviation. It passed. But their attempt to weaken the secretary of defense's control of service missions did not. On the nineteenth Sherman proposed methods of implementing the inevitable act, most of which Towers accepted.

When Jack and Pierre dined on the *Sequoia* as guests of the Forrestals three nights later, Jack told his host that as secretary of defense he would be too insulated from the transition and suggested that the General Board oversee it. Forrestal agreed in general. As it happened, his successor as secretary of the navy, John Sullivan, would not engage the board. On 24 July the compromise bill was finally accepted, and two days later the president signed it into law, issued the anticipated executive order defining service missions, and, pending Senate approval, appointed Forrestal secretary of defense.[68]

The National Security Act of 1947 had serious flaws because of the compromises necessary to secure its passage. Secretary of Defense Forrestal had no department of his own or real unity of command. The three service secretaries retained direct access to the president, which sowed the seeds of Forrestal's downfall and led to the creation of the Department of Defense two years later. Towers' most immediate concern was possible reprisals against aviators who had vociferously opposed unification, notably Radford, and he urged restraint on his superiors. Over the long term he worried about the lowered morale of junior aviators whose careers depended on the ability of naval aviation to thrive under unification. The battle was not yet over.[69]

One Towers recommendation did, however, bear some fruit. Although Truman had originally rejected Towers' scheme for a new Morrow-type board to examine aviation, the president changed his mind after months of heated hearings by two of Senator Owen Brewster's committees, the war investigation committee and the subcommittee on commercial aviation. Brewster tried to support Juan Trippe's attempt to merge Howard Hughes' TWA and his own Pan Am, which, like all the airlines, was suffering from a postwar slump. One way to do this was to embarrass Hughes by exposing his wartime Spruce Goose flying boat scheme. Towers had spent several months explaining the navy's reluctant role in that abortive venture and in thwarting Trippe from monopolizing American international air carriers under Pan Am leadership. These matters came to a head during the final unification debate when Howard Hughes thoroughly discredited Brewster by implicating him with Trippe. On the scandal of the Spruce Goose, Towers testified against the utility of Hughes' abortive behemoth by using pertinent diary entries and correspondence to keep the navy clean.[70]

The confusion over military and commercial aviation led Truman to appoint a presidential air policy committee for investigating the aviation industry; it was headed by Thomas K. Finletter, who on 25 July solicited the advice of Admirals Ramsey, Duncan, and Mel Pride. A month later Towers told Grover Loening, a consultant for the Finletter committee, that an "impartial body" like brother Fullton's engineering firm ought to investigate the industry. On 25 September Senator Brewster, acting on a recommendation from Forrestal, asked Towers to serve on a temporary advisory council for Brewster's Joint Congressional Aviation Policy Board. Meeting over several succeeding days, the board—which included manufacturers, airline heads, and Babe Meigs—organized along lines suggested by Towers. It broke into four subcommittees: manufacturing, combatant aviation, governmental organization and legislation, and air transportation. Towers found himself appointed to the first three. The entire board heard formal presentations by spokesmen for the navy, air force, and commerce departments.[71]

The combatant subcommittee convened early in November under the chairmanship of Congressman Carl Hinshaw to discuss air force requirements. In a late-night session on the third, Towers took six air force generals to task for the lack of coherent planning between the Air Transport Command, air force headquarters, and army ground forces. His exposure of their confusion was reminiscent of the prewar confrontations with General Hap Arnold, who happened to be present in retired status at this meeting. The Air Transport Command—soon to be merged with NATS to form the Military Air Transport Service—argued vaguely for five hundred C-54-type cargo planes as the navy contribution for airlifting men and material at the outbreak of war, along with a thousand air force C-54s carrying army troops to blunt the enemy's offensive efforts quickly. Towers forced the generals to admit that their plans had not been based on JCS or army estimated needs; he reminded them that the unification law guaranteed the navy control of its own land-based airlift. The absence of coherent presentations by the air force led

Chairman Hinshaw to order that service to study the "clear and understandable . . . Navy presentation and submit its own in the same form." The air force representative begrudgingly agreed to do so. The incident was reminiscent of Towers' upstaging the army's airmen in 1940.

Before the adjournment after midnight Towers delivered a last broadside that has relevance down to present-day strategic planning: "I expressed myself quite freely on . . . the rather fantastic plans of the Air Force for the movement overseas of the various military forces and their supplies. Among other things, I pointed out that airplanes to lift the load carried by one Liberty ship [10,800 deadweight tons] would cost somewhere between 300 and 500 billion dollars, and that airplanes to lift the troops carried by the *Queen Mary* [fifteen thousand men] would cost some 60 million dollars . . . [T]he time saved, if any, would not justify any such extravagances." Although Towers would not meet again with the board, Hinshaw later thanked him profusely for "your sincere and public-spirited efforts for the national well being," which "stand out as a fine example for all citizens to follow. These are trying times, when extreme demands are being made for just that sort of leadership and when, unfortunately, it is all too rare."[72]

Having lent his organizational talents to the Brewster advisory board, Towers now had to step aside. Several of his suggestions to the Finletter committee had been predicated on the model of the impartial Morrow Board of 1925, but, alas, the new body quickly assumed a pro–air force character and the next year would convince Congress to emphasize land-based strategic bombers against Forrestal's advice for a more balanced military establishment. That the new order of air-sea power was already taking a turn away from the Forrestal-Towers approach was revealed to Jack in October 1947 when he learned of a proposal "that one third of the annual graduates of the Naval Academy be assigned to the Air Force." Needless to say, he recommended rejection, as did the navy in general; a compromise was set at 7 percent of graduates. Animosities already engendered by the fight over the unification act thus mounted during its implementation.[73]

For the future of the navy, much depended on the man who would replace Chester Nimitz as CNO, which Towers and Forrestal discussed in June. Towers wanted an aviator, namely his heir apparent as the recognized and outspoken leader of naval aviation, Arthur Radford, then commanding the Atlantic Task Fleet. Nimitz and Sherman also favored a flyer—incumbent Vice CNO Duke Ramsey, who had supported unification. The Gun Clubbers were promoting Atlantic Fleet commander Spike Blandy. But Harry Truman wanted a mediator, someone who had not opposed unification. The logical choice, the man Truman finally selected, was CINCPAC Louis Denfeld, like Nimitz long a power in BuNav/BuPers. Being a nonaviator, Denfeld would require an airman as his vice CNO. Towers and Denfeld spent the evening of 1 November in Washington discussing the future. Towers promoted Radford as vice CNO and warned Secretaries Forrestal, Sullivan, and Brown about repercussions throughout the navy if Radford did not get it because he had opposed unification. On the day Denfeld relieved Nimitz, 15 December, Denfeld demanded Radford's appointment as vice CNO, and it was made.[74]

As for Towers, he had become the complete elder statesman, no longer eligible for CNO but too valuable to be released from government service. In June he was deprived of his flying status—hardly surprising at age sixty-two though surely a disappointment. Jim Forrestal, in his final official day on the job, 17 September, praised Towers in one more fitness report: "In signing the report, the last which I will make for him in my present capacity as Secretary of the Navy, I commend him for his many years of splendid service and the present excellent discharge of his duties in a position of high trust." Next day Forrestal became the nation's first secretary of defense and passed the navy secretaryship to John Sullivan, who continued as before drawing on Towers' counsel.[75]

Towers attended several briefings during the summer and fall on atomic energy and the general strategic situation, notably the Marshall Plan for European economic recovery and the Greek civil war. Jocko Clark proposed to him that the General Board endorse an original idea by the late Pete Mitscher to build one supercarrier capable of launching planes carrying atomic bombs. BuShips had been studying the idea, while BuAer had ordered a twin-engine carrier bomber—the North American AJ Savage—capable of delivering A-bombs from such a carrier to targets inside Russia. Towers agreed and obtained Sullivan's and Forrestal's approval, only to be ignored when the projected 69,200-ton flattop was discussed at a planning conference on 14 November. Nevertheless, work went forward on the design of what would be named the *United States,* the navy's answer to the air force on strategic bombing.

At a similar meeting five days later Sherman asked Towers to prepare a presentation of the General Board's view on the projected naval operating force plan through 1955. Though Towers complained the board lacked time and information, with typical zeal he assigned the task to Captain Arleigh Burke and helped Burke complete it in less than a week. It was in fact "so far superior to anything else," in Sherman's opinion, "that it would be adopted as the Navy Department position on this matter." Towers' impact on naval policy was reaching into the future.[76]

Small wonder, then, that Towers' superiors were loath to release him from government service. A key architect of the new order of American air and sea power, he might be retained in a retired capacity. Alarming to Forrestal and Sullivan was the sad state of the wartime merchant fleet, the ships of which were being mothballed or virtually given away to countries like Greece in need of ships to restore their devastated economies. They recommended that Towers replace Vice Admiral Poco Smith as head of the Maritime Commission. President Truman concurred. In mid-November Towers wrote to his brother Will of the merchant marine, "It's in a mess, and they think I could straighten it out." From a personal standpoint he would earn only $12,000 a year and have to give up his retirement pay. "Both Forrestal and Sullivan put a great deal of pressure on me to take the position but the more I examined it the worse it looked. . . ." He politely declined, and Smith stayed on.[77]

In fact, Towers was receiving business offers as he neared retirement, the most inviting one to be head of a newly formed private organization known as the Pacific War Memorial. Based in New York, it was a scientific body devoted to the preservation of the physical environment of the newly won islands in the central Pacific and the creation of a national shrine in Hawaii. Gus Read, treasurer of the organization, had first brought it to Towers' attention one year before, and now one of the directors, financier Laurence S. Rockfeller, guaranteed Jack an annual salary of $15,000 in addition to his retirement pay. On 5 November the board of directors unanimously elected him president, subject to his acceptance. He would run the memorial as a policymaker rather than mere titular head. Jack agreed and on 20 November submitted his formal request to retire from the navy. It was accepted.[78]

The day after Thanksgiving, the twenty-eighth, Towers made farewell calls on Sullivan, Kenney, and Chester Nimitz, who would follow him into retirement in two weeks. Next day he and Pierre journeyed to Philadelphia, along with the president, Forrestal, the service secretaries, and the JCS, for the Army-Navy game. Army won, 21–0. Finally, on Monday, 1 December 1947, he "closed out all matters in the Navy Department" and retired.[79]

That evening at the Carlton Hotel Forrestal gave a cocktail party for Jack attended by high officials and navy officers, all in formal evening dress. The atmosphere was strained as they waited for the host to arrive. One reason

Secretary of Defense Jim Forrestal, host of Towers' retirement party at the Ritz Carlton Hotel in Washington, 1 December 1947, draws a laugh from Towers, Admiral D. C. Ramsey, and John Nicholas Brown, assistant secretary of the navy (air). (Towers collection)

Louis Denfeld had beaten out Duke Ramsey as next CNO was that Captain John Crommelin had leaked to the press the fact that Ramsey had been a member of the illegal Green Bowl Society at the Naval Academy. Now both Ramsey and Crommelin were present to honor their old boss. But when Jim Forrestal walked in wearing a casual tweed coat and bow tie, it broke the ice. He recounted his World War I experiences in naval aviation, including an incident when the marines in Boston had put him in the brig because they were unable to identify his new marine-style aviator uniform. When his stories were over Forrestal said, "Well, I see here's Duke Ramsey and Johnny Crommelin, so guess everything's all right!" Everyone laughed and enjoyed this last official evening with the legendary Jack Towers, who relaxed, as usual, with his customary martinis.[80]

Towers' retirement went unnoticed in the national press for several days and then appeared only as a small item. Jim Forrestal, however, could not let it pass without a formal letter of appreciation on 7 December. He praised "the many and valuable contributions you have made to our national security. I have personal knowledge, starting in the Summer of 1940, of the judgment and foresight which you exercised in preparing for the expansion of Naval Aviation. The power of our carrier task forces in the Pacific, the quality of our equipment and the efficiency of our pilots was due in very great measure to your long-range planning." And all Towers' subsequent work "was marked by both diligence and intelligence. Well done! Best wishes for the future." No more handsome or appropriate tribute could have been paid.[81]

The honors to Towers, particularly for his achievements as chief of BuAer, included his "Honorary Appointment as a Knight Commander of the British Empire" by the Admiralty. Specifically, this was given in appreciation of the "Towers Scheme" of training more than one-third of the Royal Navy's pilots in the States, and for assisting the British navy in the Pacific War "to the end that both Navies might develop the maximum weight and efficiency against the enemy." The appointment had been made in December 1945, but a shortage of handcrafted porcelain insignia had postponed the formal presentation until July 1948, when Towers headed the list of sixty-five Americans whom the British decorated in Washington. He was also given the Order of Leopold by Belgium.[82]

Several patriotic organizations had proffered Towers honorary memberships, most of which he rejected at least while still on active duty. He was no "joiner," as he put it, and thus avoided veterans' groups. Some reputable organizations did, however, attract his attention. One was an association of his fellow alumni of the Class of '06. Interest had been growing ever since its thirtieth anniversary in 1936, and Towers now began to attend reunions. His former roommate, Captain Tommy Lew Atkins, was elected secretary, and with class historian Vice Admiral Sandy Sharp they prepared a class history book. Towers was one of three men who provided the funds for its publication in 1954.[83]

Towers' move from Washington to New York to head the Pacific War Memorial put him and Pierre close to Chas and his family on Long Island, where Chas worked for Grumman. Marjorie, who had never enjoyed being a navy wife or mother, divorced Herb Riley and married a civilian in Pensacola. Towers' presence in Manhattan also kept him close to key figures in the corporate business world with whom he had worked and served over the years, especially Juan Trippe and Dave Ingalls, president and vice president respectively of Pan Am. Only a few weeks passed before Jack's commitment to aviation led him back to the fold. When Trippe offered him a position as his assistant, Jack accepted. He tendered his resignation as president of the

Pacific War Memorial at the end of March 1948, having accomplished little in the job.[84]

Only sixty-three years of age and at the height of his intellectual powers, Towers stood ready to play a continuing role in implementing the new order of American air-sea power. He had a unique global view of the *Pax Americana,* both a maritime and an aeronautical perspective, which he revealed in a speech on television in March 1948. Noting the chaotic conditions prevailing throughout the world, especially in the Pacific and Asia, he declared that the United States must retain its hard-won islands to preserve the peace. "Certainly it is reasonable to have policemen around when mob violence threatens," he said, alluding specifically to upheavals and the communist presence in Indochina, the East Indies, the Philippines, China, and North Korea. "This postwar burden of policing in an unsettled world rests heavily upon the shoulders of the United States. We must maintain an Army, a Navy and an Air Force adequate to fulfill our obligations, and adequate also to insure our security and the integrity of our position in world affairs." Military power alone was inadequate, he believed; mutual trust and understanding counted as well. In any case, "it will take a long time to bring about a peaceful, decent world." The United States would have to "face the situation with patience, with strength and with the courage to see it through."[85]

With the realization in mind that the United States could not maintain global order without a stable system of international aviation and an efficient, balanced American defense organization, Towers took up his duties at Pan Am on 29 March 1948. Juan Trippe wanted Jack to use his navy connections to resolve the transpacific air traffic dilemma by obtaining landing rights for the Constellation and DC-4 airliners now beginning to girdle the globe. Though Towers had formerly opposed Trippe's attempts to monopolize such routes, he believed an accommodation could be reached between Pan Am, the other airlines, and the government that would bring order to the airlines industry. He journeyed often to Washington to enlist the navy's cooperation, meeting with Vice CNO Radford, Deputy CNO (air) John Dale Price, BuAer chief Mel Pride, Dick Byrd, George Anderson, and other former members of his team. A Pacific air-base agreement was gradually worked out over the ensuing two years, during which time Towers made inspection trips across the globe to observe Pan Am's operations. He also lobbied for congressional airline subsidies but without success.[86]

Ever alert to the problems facing the American defense establishment, Towers kept himself apprised of sagging navy morale as the air force garnered the lion's share of the defense budget. He welcomed an opportunity to play a role soon after the creation of a twelve-man study group known as the Commission on the Organization of the Executive Branch of the Government, headed by former President Herbert Hoover and including Forrestal. The Hoover commission set up a series of "task forces," among them Ferdinand Eberstadt's National Security Organization Task Force, to examine particular problems. On 10 May 1948 Towers received an urgent phone call from Eberstadt saying that Hoover had specifically requested he serve part-time on the advisory council of Eberstadt's task force. Jack accepted.[87]

On 23 May Forrestal breakfasted with Towers and Radford to discuss the possible reorganization of the National Military Establishment in the interest of achieving greater balance between the three services under a more centralized system. Although Towers trusted Forrestal to be fair, he was aware that future defense secretaries might be anti-navy and thus did not want the office to have too much power. For the same reason he continued to oppose a permanent chairman of the JCS, a view he presented to the Hoover commission on 29 June. Forrestal accepted the idea of air force supremacy in strategic bombing and the use of atomic weapons, and he did not believe the navy should develop "a new fleet of supercarriers" with a nuclear-delivery capability. But he did believe the navy should be allowed to develop its one supercarrier, the *United States,* to launch planes laden with atomic bombs against naval targets. He suggested that Towers and General Tooey Spaatz be recalled to active duty to resolve the conflict between the two services over the sharing of atomic weapons.[88]

The issue took on immediacy when, in June, the Soviet Union clamped a blockade on all American, British, and French overland traffic into Berlin. The prompt American response was to airlift supplies into the Allied zones of Berlin using C-47s and C-54s. The Soviets did not contest this undertaking, but the Americans had to prepare for a possible showdown. In mid-July, for example, Towers recommended to Dave Ingalls that Pan Am develop a contingency plan for alternative air routes to Europe should the situation become critical. This would mean suspending Pan Am's Atlantic air service and diverting global traffic to the Far East via Cairo, as during the war. Meanwhile the Mediterranean flank, and the support of the Greeks against communist guerrillas, assumed such importance that the navy established the Sixth Task Fleet there under Vice Admiral Forrest Sherman.[89]

On 4 August Forrestal brought Towers to Washington in a navy transport for a dinner meeting with Tooey Spaatz and General Omar Bradley, army chief of staff. After a lengthy discussion of the Berlin blockade and defense organization, recorded Towers, "Forrestal requested Spaatz and me to . . . reduce to its simplest terms the situation which has brought about the conflict between Air Force and Navy. We agreed. . . .'' Towers conferred with Admirals Denfeld, Radford, Price, Captain Herb Riley, and other key planners to clarify the navy position. Over the ensuing two weeks he met frequently with Spaatz, and they submitted their final report to Forrestal on the eighteenth. They achieved remarkable unanimity, agreeing that the air force should indeed have primary control of atomic weapons but that, since "no sharp line can be drawn between strategic bombing and tactical bombing," the navy also needed to utilize atomic weapons. Their only disagreement was over operational control, Spaatz arguing the air force should have it, Towers that the navy should, at least for its own forces.[90]

Two days after receiving the report, Forrestal was able to discuss it in a special conference on atomic weapons with the JCS at the Naval War College. The conferees agreed that the air force should have temporary exclusive control of atomic weapons until a permanent arrangement could be worked out, but that it must allow the navy to proceed with construction of the *United States* and its own nuclear capability. Towers learned the outcome personally from Forrestal on 1 September when he returned to Washington for the Hoover commission and Eberstadt task force hearings. He traveled frequently between New York and Washington over the next several weeks for these hearings, to discuss the international situation with his navy contacts, and to dissuade the air force from recalling certain commercial planes on loan to the airlines for use in the Berlin airlift. The Eberstadt report of 15 November recommended some increased authority for the secretary of defense but completely rejected the idea of a centralized Department of Defense or a single chairman of the JCS, reflecting the long-held positions of Towers. The Hoover commission did not agree and would recommend both in the new year.[91]

Meanwhile, the deteriorating position of the democratic powers extended to the Pacific as the Chinese Communists now drove the Nationalists from the mainland of Asia. General MacArthur wanted to help strengthen Japan by establishing an intra-Japan airline, a plan Towers helped formulate on behalf of Pan Am beginning in the summer of 1948. Juan Trippe tried to salvage the company's involvement in Chinese commercial aviation, but the Communist victory thwarted his plans. Instead, Pan Am had to assist the Nationalists in evacuating their last mainland cities to the island of Taiwan (Formosa). Towers flew to Washington at the end of November to discuss evacuation plans and the worldwide situation with CNO Denfeld, visiting CINCPAC Duke Ramsey, and Herb Riley, now naval assistant to Forrestal.[92]

The United States had no choice but to accept the challenge of the worldwide communist threat, and it did so by establishing its first peacetime alliance, the North Atlantic Treaty Organization (NATO), in April 1949. The Soviets soon terminated their blockade of Berlin. The American strategic policy of containment now also embraced the Pacific, on which theater Towers henceforth focused his attention, strengthening Pan Am routes and bases as General MacArthur rebuilt Japan and the Pacific Fleet policed western waters. Over the turbulent winter of 1948–49 he maintained his personal contacts with Forrestal.

In November Harry Truman was elected to a second term. The Democratic victory returned Carl Vinson to the chairmanship of the renamed House Armed Services Committee. Jack was pleased to renew his association with Vinson in several meetings. No one, least of all Forrestal, realized that Truman had decided to replace the first secretary of defense, who, exhausted, was losing his touch as a military manager. His abrupt firing came in March 1949, while Towers was on an inspection tour of Pacific bases and airfields. With Forrestal's removal, Jack lost his intimate role as a major adviser to the defense establishment.[93]

The new appointee was Louis Johnson, the very same prewar assistant secretary of war with whom Towers had battled over aircraft allocations. As in 1940, Johnson was still an outspoken advocate of land-based strategic bombing. Further, Truman wanted Johnson to reduce defense spending by eliminating duplication wherever possible. In April, a week after the keel of the supercarrier *United States* was finally laid, Johnson abruptly canceled its construction. Secretary of the Navy Sullivan immediately resigned in protest, and navy morale, shored up months before as a consequence of the Spaatz-Towers compromise, plummeted again. Towers was in no position to intervene.[94]

If more depressing news was possible, it came on 22 May when a broken Jim Forrestal committed suicide at Bethesda Naval Hospital in Washington. On the twenty-fifth Jack attended the funeral of his great friend and colleague. That day he tore out and saved Joseph Alsop's syndicated column: "It was not only the burden of his responsibility; it was also the pettiness and injustice and ingratitude for a . . . job well done that killed Forrestal. Those who knew him well, and remembered the vigor with which he attacked his task in the dark days of 1940 could see his strength waning through the last difficult years. . . . The truth is," wrote Alsop, using words that Towers understood all too well from his own career, "that the kind of public service Jim Forrestal sought to give—disinterested, professional, imaginative, and in

scale with this nation's great role—is made as unrewarding as possible."
Forrestal and Towers had been cut from the same mold and had endured
similar hardships. Whereas Towers survived the system, Forrestal—seven
years at or near the top of it—did not.[95]

Perhaps Forrestal should have quit government service earlier for an-
other career in business, as Towers had done. For on 7 June Jack succeeded
Dave Ingalls as a vice president at Pan Am, enlarging his responsibilities
immensely. Now he oversaw numerous company policies on the traditional
Atlantic, Pacific, and Latin American routes as well as routes to the Middle
East and the intra-Japan airline scheme.[96]

Overall, Forrestal's death acted as a catalyst to strengthen the office of
the secretary of defense. In August Congress replaced the vague National
Military Establishment with the Department of Defense and appointed a
permanent chairman of the JCS, General Bradley of the army. Towers opposed these measures, as did Radford, who in September and October 1949
rent the new Defense Department by leading a "revolt of the admirals"
against the air force's strategic bomber program. Navy morale reached its
nadir on 2 November when President Truman, on the advice of Fleet Admiral Nimitz, appointed Forrest Sherman as CNO, at fifty-three the youngest
officer yet to hold the post. Sherman had long been distrusted by most of the
navy, including Towers, for his overweening ambition and his role in shaping
the unification act. But Jack had known Sherman longer and better than had
any other officer, including Nimitz, and he was sincere in congratulating him:
"Based upon my very extensive and close associations with you over the
years, I feel confident of your ability to cope with [this] most disturbing and
distressing situation." Sherman replied, "As you know, I have always set my
sights high, but had no wish to be assigned to duty in Washington at this
time." Nevertheless, he would "turn to . . . promote stability and harmony"
among senior naval officers, and "help all hands to get on with the numerous
tasks which confront us. You, better than anyone else, can comprehend the
complexities which confront me."[97]

Thus was Towers' influence with the high command restored. Furthermore, Sherman's nonaviator vice CNO was Admiral Lynde McCormick,
Jack's former deputy CINCPAC. On 23 November Towers and Sherman
met in the latter's office, Sherman soliciting Towers' advice on a number of
navy matters, Towers obtaining Sherman's approval for Pan Am to operate
through Guam. On this visit to Washington Jack also saw Herb Riley, now
a student at the new unified National War College, to ascertain "who is
handling what nowadays in Secretary Johnson's office." Though divorce had

ended Riley's status as Jack's son-in-law, the two men remained close personal friends, and Riley acted as Jack's "spy" in the Defense Department until mid-1950. Towers renewed his discussions with Sherman in January 1950, at which time he also served as honorary pallbearer at the funeral of his old compatriot and sometime antagonist, General of the Air Force Hap Arnold.[98]

While Sherman set about restoring navy morale throughout the first half of 1950, Towers concentrated on strengthening Pan Am's service across the Pacific as an additional bulwark against the new Sino-Soviet communist bloc on the Asian mainland. Along with Jerry Land's Air Transport Association, Towers opposed air force attempts to take control of the airlines in times of emergency mobilization and alerted Sherman and the navy to the danger, recalling that the airlines had provided essential wartime services under contract. Towers spent most of June in negotiations for an internal Japan airline. In the midst of these, on the twenty-fifth, North Korea's Communist army crossed the 38th parallel into American-supported South Korea, starting the Korean War.[99]

Within four days Towers had organized ten Pan Am DC-4s to airlift military cargo and personnel across the Pacific to Tokyo in support of the "present limited emergency." He assumed personal direction of the airlift, which by mid-August comprised no fewer than twenty-seven airliners, a larger operation than Pan Am's regular commercial service. So Towers was a cold warrior again, "wearing a business suit instead of gold braid" according to one reporter, as America's understrength defense establishment labored to contain the Russian-inspired aggression in Korea. In March 1951 Towers flew to Hawaii to confer with CINCPAC Radford, then proceeded to Tokyo to discuss commercial aviation with the Japanese. He performed his tasks for the remaining two years of the Korean conflict.[100]

Towers agreed with Truman's decision to go to the aid of South Korea and disagreed with certain elements of the press who feared possible Russian involvement in the conflict. With the U.S. policy of standing firm in Korea, Towers told a Connecticut naval reserve unit late in 1950, he was confident that the president had deterred probable Soviet-inspired aggression in such global trouble spots as Indochina, Iran, Yugoslavia, and Germany. Drawing on his knowledge of Russian history, he had come to believe that the Soviet Union would not precipitate a war with the United States; the Soviet lacked steel production and their overland lines of communication were too long for an advance into western Europe. "The best thing a citizen can do," he

Towers, wearing a lei, is greeted by Admiral Radford at the Honolulu International Airport, 2 March 1951. Towers was en route to the Far East to administer Pan Am's military airlift service for the Korean war effort. The plane is the 70-ton, 112-seat Boeing 377 Strato Clipper, which established the standard for long-range airliners of the day. "Romance the Skies" reads the motto by the door. (National Archives)

declared, "is to keep his feet on the ground, eyes open, and not become hysterical," a reference to Senator Joseph McCarthy's anti-communist scare then sweeping the country.[101]

One thing of which Towers could be certain was the effectiveness of American leadership, especially in naval aviation. "I cannot but be proud of its present leaders, for after all I played a large part in their upbringing," he told an audience in 1952. "They are intelligent, they are able, and, most important, they are real leaders." CNO Forrest Sherman, once his chief of staff and the shining example of this group, succumbed to a heart attack in July 1951, having worked himself to death. Towers loyally supported Sherman's successor, Admiral Fechteler, and was pleased to see Wu Duncan succeed Lynde McCormick as vice CNO. Jack's other wartime chief of staff, Radford, remained at the Pacific Command, and Vice Admiral Jocko Clark finally headed the Seventh Fleet off Korea.[102]

No aviator would hold the post of CNO again until 1961 when George Anderson was appointed to it. The crowning achievement for naval aviation came early in 1953 with the selection of Radford as chairman of the JCS (Anderson was his principal staff officer). "I consider it a spendid choice," Jack replied to a query from his brother Will, "although there is sure to be considerable friction in his dealing with the Air Force." Since Sherman's passing, the JCS needed more "intelligent control and I feel sure he will exercise it in an indirect manner. I have known Raddy since he first came to Pensacola in 1921 for flight training and have picked him three times to serve on my staff which should be sufficient evidence of my belief in him."[103]

The overall leadership of the Department of Defense changed dramatically with mobilization. In September 1950 President Truman fired Secretary of Defense Louis Johnson in favor of George Marshall and then Bob Lovett. The newly unified department came under severe criticism after reverses in Korea, criticism that Towers, occasionally recalled to active duty to advise the Departments of Defense and Commerce, did not share. The unified National Security Council of the executive branch and the JCS were simply "snowed under" with a multitude of minor problems and tasks, he told a group of General Electric managers in February 1953. He believed the system should be given a chance to work. He found Vannevar Bush's idea for appointing "elder statesmen" of the three services like himself on the JCS and provide an objective viewpoint "very intriguing, but it has what seems to me to be the fatal defect of authority without responsibility."

The inauguration of Dwight Eisenhower that January gave Towers great hope. "Perhaps at the risk of appearing to venture into the political field, I

Jack and Pierre visit with Captain George W. Anderson, Jr.,
captain of the carrier *Franklin D. Roosevelt* (which Pierre had
christened), in late 1952 or early 1953. An intimate adviser
to Towers from 1940 to 1945, Anderson assumed the
mantle of leadership in naval aviation when he became CNO
in 1961 and ran the Cuban missile blockade the following
year. (Towers collection)

want to say, with deep conviction based upon intimate personal knowledge:
We now have a President who has shown throughout his career a genius for
organization" and who would restore order to American military administration. It was Ike who selected Radford to chair the JCS.[104]

Congress, as it had done in 1940–41, dropped all barriers in the race to
rearm, giving equal attention to the three services to fight in Korea and deter
the Soviet threat. "Despite the lessons of history," however, Towers observed at a reunion of the Princeton Class of '26, many people still believed
"there is a short cut to victory." He chided those who held that viewpoint:
"Just have a nice pile of atom bombs and a flock of long-range bombers ready,
then when the time comes lay them neatly upon all the important military and
industrial centers, and the show will be over. . . . It just isn't that simple. . . ."

The atomic bomb was important and necessary, he said, for both carriers
and the air force, but it was "far from a substitute" for other weapons. Indeed,
he was gratified that in March 1951 Congress authorized another super-

carrier, very much along the lines of the aborted *United States*. Towers had contributed much to this decision, always insisting, as had Forrestal, that such a ship be developed with an atomic-delivery capability. Particularly gratifying was the news that the new attack carrier (CVA-59) was to be named *Forrestal,* a supreme compliment to a great champion of naval aviation. More than that, the ship would be the prototype of an entire new class of carriers. Designed at 56,000 tons, the behemoth was to carry jet fighters (Vought F8U Crusaders) and attack bombers (Douglas A3D Skywarriors). The keel was laid in July 1952.

What concerned Towers, he informed the Princeton alums, was the possibility of American leaders overreacting to the Soviet threat. "I believe it was in 1946 that [Joseph] Stalin told [Harold] Stassen [that] Russia did not expect to have to fight the United States, because in our fear that he might start a war we would ruin ourselves economically by our feverish preparations for war, and his purposes would be accomplished without fighting." Towers believed in preparedness, to preserve America as well as "the security of free Europe and free peoples everywhere. My concept of preparedness is military readiness to check the enemy while building up an establishment of a military industrial base upon which we can build rapidly." In this remark, he anticipated Eisenhower's phrase "military-industrial complex" by several years.

In a warning germane for decades to come, Towers explained,

> I fear our original objective [containment of the Soviet Union] has been submerged by what appears now to be an all-out effort on the part of the military to become equipped and manned, and to so remain indefinitely, in readiness to fight an all-out offensive war from the very start. There has resulted an ascending spiral of expenditures which if not checked may well lead to economic collapse without any war—precisely the Stalin objective. . . . [W]e must take the calculated risk of what the Russians could do if we stop short of full readiness, in the interest of preserving our economy, and they decide to try their luck.

Towers doubted the Russians of 1952 could conquer western Europe or even win an atomic war. "Russia knows her weaknesses. We are inclined to look only at her strength. Personally, I believe Russia is just as anxious to avoid war as we are," a view shared by a growing number of informed Americans. The worst recourse was to allow America's fear of Russia to "become a political football," another reference to the McCarthy hysteria as well as to general partisan politics. "It may be vanity on my part," Towers concluded, "but I believe, if he were here today, that far seeing man, my very close friend and your fellow Princetonian, James Forrestal, would echo my views."[105]

The coming of Eisenhower brought permanence to the Department of Defense and the *Pax Americana*. In 1953 the new president succeeded in ending the Korean War with a truce roughly along the lines of the antebellum status quo. Although the lack of clear-cut victory left the military with a distaste for limited wars, all three services emerged from the conflict restored to fighting strength. To reduce costs of defense so dangerous to the well-being of the American economy, Ike relied on nuclear weapons to deter Russian aggression. They would be delivered by carrier as well as air force planes. Towers was pleased to see mothballed *Essex*-class carriers modernized and recommissioned; he personally inspected the second *Hornet* in October 1953. Especially encouraging was the construction of the *Forrestal*. And the keels for the new *Saratoga* (CVA-60) and *Ranger* (CVA-61) were laid in December 1952 and August 1954 respectively.

At sixty-eight, Towers finally decided to retire. In September 1953, two months after the Korean armistice, he resigned his vice presidency of Pan Am and accepted the less demanding role of president of the Flight Safety Foundation in New York, a nonprofit organization supported by aircraft manufacturers and airlines. Aviation safety had been a subject dear to his heart ever since his crash in the B-2 with Billingsley in 1913. Jack could now devote more attention to his family. He toyed with the idea of writing an autobiographical history of naval aviation, though he never got around to it.[106]

On 11 December 1954, a reporter present at Newport News Shipbuilding observed, "an item of quiet drama attended the official christening of the super aircraft carrier *Forrestal* here today. Standing among the hundreds of guests to the rites was a retired Navy admiral, who was back in his four-starred uniform for the ceremonies. But he went almost unnoticed by the milling throngs" and took no part in the ceremonies. "It was Adm. J. H. Towers," whose contribution to the birth of the new carrier the reporter then described. "It is a beautiful ship, isn't it?" Jack remarked as the *Forrestal* slid down the ways. Her prospective commanding officer was a former BuAer planner of his, Captain Roy L. Johnson, destined to command the Pacific Fleet during the Vietnam war. The new carrier and her sisters symbolized the final victory of everything for which Towers had worked in the forty-three years since he had first gone aloft in the Lizzie and the A-1 at Hammondsport. His career was now complete.[107]

Otherwise, Towers was not feeling well. During a September visit to Marge in Pensacola he had developed what he thought was a bad case of indigestion. Presenting himself at Bethesda Naval Hospital for a checkup, he discovered the examining doctor to be none other than Commander Bruce L.

Canaga, Jr., son of his fellow gunfire spotter on the old *Michigan*. Young Canaga could find nothing seriously wrong. Severe blockage in the intestines brought Jack back to Bethesda on the eve of his seventieth birthday, in late January 1955. An exploratory operation, performed "when I was more dead than alive," he reported to Marge, found a malignant tumor of the pancreas. Cancer had killed his father and would take his sister Nanie a year later. He was flown back to New York to spend a few days at the St. Albans Naval Hospital, then was moved to New York Memorial Hospital for chemotherapy treatment.[108]

Grover Loening and Grumman's Jake Swirbul invited Jack to come rest at their Florida homes as soon as the treatment allowed. But hope soon faded. Towers' condition worsened, and late in March he was moved back to St. Albans to await the end. Rapidly deteriorating, he refused to allow his grandchildren to visit him, wanting them to remember him as he was before the illness. Among his night nurses was a large black woman who reminded him of Big Sue, the person who had plied him with pones and wet hash as a boy in Georgia. Pierre helped care for him and spent the last weeks listening to him reminisce about his early days, jotting down his memories of Annapolis, the Great White Fleet, the *Michigan,* Curtiss, Ellyson, Mexico, wartime London, the NCs. Towers died peacefully in his sleep on the forenoon of 30 April 1955, exactly seventy years and three months of age, punctual to the last.[109]

In a tribute reserved for only its greatest heroes, the navy ordered all ships and shore installations to fly their colors at half-mast from midmorning until sunset the day of the funeral. A navy plane flew the body from New York to Washington for interment at Arlington National Cemetery. The funeral was conducted on 3 May at the Fort McNair chapel, attended by brothers Fullton and Will, sisters Jessie and Nanie, Pierre, Towers' children, and a host of senior navy officials and representatives of the aircraft industry. He was laid to rest with full military honors at Arlington. The pallbearers bespoke the esteem in which he was held: Arthur Radford, chairman of the JCS; Vice Admiral Matt Gardner, deputy CNO (plans and policy); Pat Bellinger; Gus Read; Dave Ingalls; Jake Fitch; Tommy Lew Atkins, his academy roommate; Grover Loening; Burdette Wright of Curtiss-Wright; and Harold M. Bixby of Pan Am. Fleet Admiral Bill Halsey was also present.[110]

The Father of Naval Aviation is what many people had been calling Towers in recent years, although Admiral Moffett was usually accorded that epithet. " 'Jack' Towers," observed the editors of the *New York Times,* "believed in, and loved, the Navy. His talent, his firm belief in naval aviation and his moral courage earned for him the respect of the Navy, even the respect of those who opposed his determined efforts to build the wings of the fleet. Admiral Towers met his last lingering illness . . . with the same courage, reserve, and objectivity he had met other crises in his long and distinguished career." But the navy was only half the story, as the *Times* and other newspapers pointed out. "His name will always be associated, not only with the Navy, whose uniform he wore, but with the history of American aviation, to whose development he contributed so much." The great carrier fleet he had been so instrumental in developing was his crowning achievement, proclaimed the Norfolk *Pilot:* "His monument encircles the globe today." Said the Norfolk *Despatch-Ledger,* "He was the kind of man to win the admiration of associates in a profession in which extraordinary courage, and extraordinary achievement, are commonplace. The Navy, and his country, are deeply in his debt."[111]

To perpetuate his memory, the navy named a guided-missile destroyer for him. Vice Admiral Monty Montgomery spoke at the launching of the *Towers* (DDG-9) in 1959; Marjorie sponsored her. In 1960 the airfield at NAS Jacksonville was renamed Towers Field. In 1966 Towers was enshrined in the National Aviation Hall of Fame at Dayton, Ohio, and in 1981 in the Naval Aviation Hall of Honor at Pensacola and in the Carrier Aviation Hall of Fame at Patriots Point, South Carolina. The navy created the Admiral John H. Towers Flight Safety Award, and the Apollo 17 lunar astronauts unofficially named a crater on the moon for him.[112]

Although Jack Towers had made headlines throughout much of his career, postwar historians virtually ignored his immense contributions to the navy and to the victory in the Pacific. Samuel Eliot Morison, for example, completely failed to give voice to his accomplishments. The fact is that Towers' career was a major success story, marred only by his having been kept from combat command during World War II and from the top post of CNO afterward. He had fought the good fight—for naval aviation, the navy, and his country—and he had won on all counts.[113]

Towers was, and will always be, the ultimate air admiral.

NOTES

CHAPTER 1. TO MAKE AN ADMIRAL, to 1909

1. Towers family records, compiled by Pierrette Anne Towers and including the Reuben S. Norton diary, courtesy of Robert Norton.

2. Typescript of William M. Towers wartime reminiscences, Mar 1900, 8–11, Towers papers. For a fuller account of Forrest by Billy Towers, see Reynolds, *Civil War,* 266–67.

3. Clipping, probably Rome *Courier,* 15 Sep 1904. Admiral Towers' Civil War roots are the subject of Reynolds, "Confederate Romans." See also Reynolds, *Civil War,* 396–97. Early examples of the "cavalry of the sky" were given in 1918 by "Contact" (Captain Alan Bott), *Cavalry of the Clouds,* and by the Italian theorist General Giulio Douhet, who in 1924 argued for "a cavalry of the air" in *Command of the Air,* 44. A close student of Civil War armies and contemporary of Towers was Ernest J. King (Buell, *King,* 34). William F. Halsey, Jr., applied Forrest's dictum to World War II carrier operations (Potter, *Halsey,* 37).

4. Rome *Tribune* special industrial edition, Oct 1902, 9–10; Aycock, 448; Grant, 6–7; Towers' navy medical records, 1902 to 1943, Towers papers; Towers' address to the Aviation Commandery of New York, 24 Oct 1952.

5. Unless otherwise noted, all stories regarding Towers' childhood are from family recollections. Towers' familial ranking and that of his leading contemporaries in the Pacific war reveal that only or firstborn children achieved the highest posts: Chester W. Nimitz and Raymond A. Spruance grew up virtually as only children, while King was the first of five. Marc A. Mitscher was second of three and Richmond Kelly Turner seventh of eight, in this most closely resembling Towers. Naval aviator no. 1, T. G. Ellyson, was third of seven.

6. *Atlanta Journal Magazine,* 7 Sep 1919; Aycock, 312; Battey, 291; Norton diary, 21 Sep 1888–June 1895. Towers, in a letter to his mother, 13 Dec 1908, spoke of his dogs Prince, Tronie, and Laddie.

7. *Atlanta Journal,* 7 Sep 1919; John Riley, 24 Feb 1946; Grant, 6, 16; I. F. Towers to H. H. Hicks, 21 Nov 1946. In letters to his mother, 16 Mar 1908; brother Fullton, 30 Mar 1908; and father, 2 Apr 1908, Towers wrote enthusiastically of hunting while the Great White Fleet was at Magdalena Bay, but he admitted being glad when he had missed hitting a deer. In a letter to his father, 8 Jan 1910, he boasted of his marksmanship in hitting clay pigeons.

8. Harris quote in *Atlantic Journal,* 7 Sep 1919, which also quoted brother Reuben Towers: "John was always smart in his studies and usually stood first in his classes."

9. *Atlanta Journal,* 7 Sep 1919; Towers to mother, 24 Jan 1909.

10. Rough statistics show that while some of the midshipmen obtained their congressional appointments by seeking vacancies in other states and a few may have had some experience with the sea, the interior states produced most of the leading midshipmen in the first decade of the twentieth century. The hinterland states of the Ohio and Mississippi valleys, the Great Lakes, and the Great Plains, including Texas and Tennessee, produced 88 of the 192 flag officers who graduated from the Naval Academy between 1902 and 1910. The 13 in Towers' class included Robert Lee Ghormley (Idaho), Russell Willson (Wyoming), William A. Glassford, Jr. (New Mexico), Frank Jack Fletcher (Iowa), Isaac Kidd (Ohio), Aubrey W. Fitch (Michigan), and the top man of the class, Allan J. Chantry, Jr. (Iowa).

The southeast and Gulf states—North Carolina to Louisiana—were more rural than maritime in character and turned out 29 admirals in that first decade; 2 of the 5 southeastern classmates of Towers were William L. Calhoun (Florida) and John S. McCain (Mississippi). The northeast, Virginia to Maine, produced 58 in those years. The Pacific states had 11. A half-dozen at-large appointments to flag rank included Alexander Sharp, Jr., of Towers' class.

"Tombstone" advancements upon retirement aside, most of the World War II–era (1940–46) five- and four-star admirals of these (and two earlier) classes came out of the heartland: William D. Leahy (Wisconsin) '97, Ernest J. King (Ohio) '01, J. O. Richardson (Texas) '02, Husband E. Kimmel (Kentucky) '04, Royal E. Ingersoll (Indiana) '05, Nimitz (Texas) '05, Towers (Georgia) '06, Spruance (Indiana) '07, Turner (California) '08, Charles M. Cooke (Arkansas) '10, and Mitscher (Oklahoma) '10. The others were Harold R. Stark (Pennsylvania) '03, William F. Halsey, Jr. (at large) '04, H. Kent Hewitt (New Jersey) '07, Richard S. Edwards (Pennsylvania) '08, and Thomas C. Kinkaid (at large) '08. Halsey and Kinkaid were navy juniors.

11. Towers' address to Princeton Class of '26 reunion, probably in 1952.

12. Ibid.; Georgia School of Technology transcript. His course grades were algebra (87), inorganic chemistry (79, 81), drawing (72, 70), U.S. history (77), basic geometry (75), solid geometry (75), shop (43, 65), and rhetoric (67). He began the third term in chemistry, geometry, drawing, trigonometry, shop, and rhetoric. His average was 71 in the first term, 72 in the second.

13. *Atlanta Journal*, 24 Feb 1946, 7 Sep 1919.

14. Atlanta *Constitution*, 13 Feb 1906; Aug 1902 clipping from an unidentified newspaper.

15. C. B. Hart, 190; Cummings, 131–39; *Class of 1906*, 2; physical record of Naval Cadet Towers, 1902; oath of allegiance, USNA, 30 Aug 1902. For a charming visual presentation of Annapolis during Towers' midshipman days, see Warren and Warren.

16. *Lucky Bag, 1906,* 48, 150.

17. Van Deurs, *Ellyson*, 13–14, 16, 19; *Lucky Bag, 1905*, 46, 53, 92; Towers' conduct record, noting Ellyson putting Towers on report, 17 Dec 1902. Another future aviator in '05 was Arthur B. Cook.

18. *Lucky Bag, 1903*, 54; "The Rodgers Family" in Reynolds, *Admirals*, 279–80.

19. Towers' conduct record. He was caught playing cards by Lieutenant (later Captain) George E. Gelm on 1 Mar 1905.

20. *Lucky Bag, 1906,* 61, 82, 89, 107, 113, and passim.

21. USNA academic records, National Archives RG 405; *Lucky Bag, 1904,* 114–20.

22. Towers' physical record, 1902; Surgeon general of the U.S. Navy, 3d endorsement, 9 May, to "Report of Special Medical Board, Naval Academy, 3 May 1904 in the case of Midshipman J. H. Towers, third class," and related documents; C. B. Hart, 203; *Class of 1906*, 35.

23. *Lucky Bag, 1906,* 150.

24. Towers to brother William, 25 Mar, 15 Dec 1908; Towers to brother Fullton, 30 Mar 1908.

25. C. B. Hart, 207–8; *Lucky Bag, 1905,* 109, 111.

26. Surgeon general of the U.S. Navy, endorsement, 28 Apr 1905, to Report of Special Medical Board, 5 May 1905, and surgeon general, 3d endorsement, 9 May 1905.

27. C. B. Hart, 216–18; *Lucky Bag, 1906,* 177–83.

28. Towers to mother, 29 Oct 1905.

29. Towers to mother, 29 Oct 1905.

30. Interviews of Fitch and Noyes by Pierre Towers about 1960; Naval Academy log book, Nov 1905–Feb 1906; *New York Times*, 7, 8 Nov 1905; Sweetman, *Naval Academy*, 154–55.

31. *Lucky Bag, 1906,* 150. No record of Towers' final physical examination survives. Allen Chantry would fail his precommissioning eye test two years later but by pulling strings in Washington be able to remain in the Construction Corps (*Class of 1906,* 35). Towers to mother, [21] Jan 1906).

32. Towers to mother [21] Jan 1906. Atkins issued three demerits to Towers for having "no insignia of rank on blouse" on 22 Dec 1905 and one for coming to breakfast formation late on 14 Jan 1906 (Towers' conduct record).

33. Towers to mother, [21] Jan 1906.

34. *Class of 1906,* 45–46.

35. Annapolis *Evening Capital,* 12 Feb 1906. The lyrics were written by Midshipman Alfred H. "Monk" Miles '07 and first sung at a football game in the fall of 1907. The tune was adopted by the Class of '07 as its march (*Lucky Bag, 1907,* 89, 266).

36. Small, 1403.

37. *Kentucky* log, Mar 1906. The classmates who reported aboard with Towers were Stephen Doherty, Reuben L. Walker, and George B. Wright, all of whom eventually attained the rank of captain.

38. *The Kentucky Budget* (ship's newspaper), vol. 2, no. 20, 6 Jan 1907, Towers papers; Baldridge to secretary of the navy, "Origins of the Navy 'E'," 1943, courtesy of Robert J. Cressman. The torpedo crews were also allowed to compete for the "E." Baldridge had recommended an "N" to match Naval Academy lettermen, but BuNav chief Rear Admiral George A. Converse had decided on "E."

39. Towers' fitness reports, 31 Mar, 30 June, 30 Sep, 31 Dec 1906 and 31 Mar, 30 Sep, 1 Nov 1907.

40. Medical Survey Examination Board No. 2122, U.S. Naval Hospital, Washington, 21 Aug 1933, and other medical documents; Towers to secretary of the navy, "Appeal for Redress" [Mar 1937]; Towers reminiscences. Unless otherwise noted, all Towers quotations are from speeches and reminiscences he gave or dictated in 1931 and the early 1950s. Three of his classmates survived the 13 Apr 1906 *Kearsarge* explosion—John Connor, W. Alden Hall, and H. Gard Knox.

41. Towers' fitness report, 31 Dec 1907. Captain Barry, though promoted to rear admiral and given command of the Pacific Fleet, ended his career in disgrace over a morals scandal (San Diego *Union,* 13, 16 Jan 1911).

42. E. F. Johnson, 21–22; *Lucky Bag, 1905,* 37, for Atkins.

43. Towers to mother, [late 1907].

44. Towers orders of 22 Oct, 19 Nov 1907; Towers to mother, 11 Jan 1908; *Lucky Bag, 1907,* 27. His assistant was George H. Bowdey, who had stood sixth in the Class of '07 and eventually attained the rank of commodore.

45. Towers to brother William, 7 Jan 1908; Towers' talk before the Institute of Aeronautical Sciences, 26 Jan 1954.

46. Towers to mother, 25 Nov 1906 and 21 June 1908. The Mahans had invited Towers to many social functions.

47. Towers to mother, 29 Dec 1907 and 1, 4 Jan 1908; Towers to brother William, 7 Jan 1908; the *Kentucky* equator-crossing program, 6 Jan 1908, Towers papers. Davy Jones' real name was J. H. Darley.

48. Towers to mother, 19, 26 Jan 1908; Towers to sister Mary ("Nanie"), 26 Jan 1908. The foreign cruisers were the *Puglia* and the *Bremen.*

49. Towers to mother, 26 Jan 1908; *Kentucky Budget,* 6 Jan 1907. Towers' appraisal of the four Argentine cruisers steaming in column was shared by Admiral Evans, who found them "admirably handled, and . . . trim and very businesslike" (Evans, 432–33).

50. Towers to sister Mary, 26 Jan 1908; Towers to mother, 26, 31 Jan and 2, 7, 9 Feb 1908; Towers to brother Fullton, 16 Feb 1908.

51. Towers to brother Fullton, 16 Feb 1908; Towers to mother, 15 Feb, 16 Mar 1908.

52. Towers to brother William, 25 Mar 1908; Towers to mother, [late 1907], 29 Feb, 7 Mar 1908. Towers' score of 9.23 hits per gun per minute beat Baldridge's score of 8.07 with the starboard batteries in 1905. The wardroom mess was adorned with the head of the Winged Victory

Lady of the General Sherman monument in New York's Central Park, executed by the late giant of American sculpture, Augustus St.-Gaudens. Towers would "liberate" the head when the ship was decommissioned and later, in 1943, donate it to the Naval Academy Museum (Baldridge, then director of the Naval Academy Museum, to Towers, 1 Feb 1943; Towers to Baldridge, 24 Feb 1943; Baldridge to Jessie Towers Maddox, 4 June 1943). The head was given to the *Kentucky* in 1905 by St.-Gaudens' son Homer as thanks for hosting him while he gathered material for a book.

53. Towers to brother William, 25 Mar 1908; Alden, 206, 217; E. F. Johnson, 22, 33; Towers to brother Fullton, 16 Feb, 30 Mar 1908; Towers to mother, 16, 23 Mar, 4 Apr 1908; BuNav chief to Baldridge, 11 July 1908, Baldridge papers; Towers to father, 2 Apr 1908.

54. Towers to father, 2 Apr 1908; Towers to mother, 26 Apr, 21 June 1908.

55. Towers to mother, 26 July and 2, 9, 30 Aug 1908; Towers to brother William, 15 Dec 1908; "Official Programme: Visit of the American Fleet to New Zealand, Auckland, August 1908," Towers papers; *Missouri* cruise book, Hewitt papers.

56. Continental C & G Rubber Co., "Souvenir of the American Fleet, Melbourne, August 29, 1908," Towers papers.

57. Towers to mother, 14, 20, 27 Sep 1908.

58. R. A. Hart, 218; Towers to mother, 19 Oct 1908; Wiley, 149; *Missouri* cruise book.

59. Towers to mother, 19 Oct 1908.

60. Ibid., 25 Oct 1908.

61. Craven to his wife, 23 Oct 1908, Craven papers.

62. Towers to mother, 25 Oct 1908.

63. Towers reminiscences; Towers obituary in the *New York Times,* 1 May 1955.

64. Craven to wife, 23 Oct 1908; Towers speech, "Early Days of Naval Aviation," early 1950s; Towers to mother, 25 Oct and 6, 8 Nov 1908; R. A. Hart, 227–28, 268; "Souvenir Program of the Reception Tendered the United States Battleship Fleet at Amoy, 1908," Craven papers; *Missouri* cruise book.

65. Towers to mother, 6, 8, 15 Nov 1908; *Missouri* cruise book; van Deurs, *Ellyson,* 28–37. He swapped with Ensign W. L. Friedel '05, who went on to retire as rear admiral. Towers' classmate Ensign Francis M. Robinson transferred from the portside 5-inch batteries to be executive officer of a gunboat; he retired as commander. Two of Towers' classmates now reported aboard the *Kentucky,* Ensigns and future Captains Conant Taylor and Edwin A. Wolleson.

66. Towers to mother, 8, 15, 22 Nov, 6 Dec 1908; Towers to brother William, 15 Dec 1908; Baldridge orders of 17 Nov 1908 (detached on the thirtieth), Baldridge papers. Baldridge attained the rank of rear admiral.

67. Towers to mother, 15 Dec 1908; Towers to brother William, 15 Dec 1908.

68. Coontz (executive officer of the *Nebraska*), 291–92.

69. Towers to brother William, 4 Jan 1909; Towers to mother, 10, 24 Jan 1909; Towers to sister Mary, 15 Jan 1909; R. A. Hart, 278. Claude Suydam, "a good-looking man," and the former Grace Denny, "extremely pretty," both of Seattle, had been "knocking around Europe," to which they returned from Algiers in the liner *Lusitania.*

70. Towers to mother, 10 Jan 1909; R. A. Hart, 307 and passim; *Kentucky* log, Feb 1909.

CHAPTER 2. TO MAKE AN AVIATOR, 1909–12

1. Sweet interview at the Navy Department, 9 May 1945; "Sweet Report: Memorandum for the Secretary of the Navy," 2 Dec 1908, signed by the chief of equipment, Rear Admiral William S. Cowles.

2. Towers to brother William, from Colombo, Ceylon, 15 Dec 1908.

3. Towers, en route to Tripoli, to mother, 10 Jan 1909.

4. Towers' orders of 18 Mar, 8, 22 June, 12, 17 July, 4 Aug 1909; Towers to BuNav, 12 July 1909.

5. Towers orders of 3, 8, 18 Sep 1909; Towers to mother, 5 Sep 1909; *Fleet Admiral King,* 40,

63–64. Usher had already commanded the torpedo boat *Ericsson* at the Battle of Santiago in 1898 and taken the cruiser *St. Louis* round the Horn to the Pacific in 1907.

6. Towers to mother, 5 Sep, 18 Oct 1909.

7. Canaga to Pierre Towers, 16 Mar [1959].

8. Ibid., 4 Nov 1958.

9. Ibid.

10. Ibid.; Towers to brother William, 25 May 1910.

11. Turnbull and Lord, 6; *New York World,* 30 June, 1 July 1910.

12. Sweet interview, 4 May 1945; secretary of the navy to Chambers, 13 Mar 1911, including order of 11 Feb 1911 establishing the office (all Chambers documents cited hereafter are from the Chambers papers); Towers' talk before Institute of Aeronautical Sciences, New York, 26 Jan 1954; Washington *Star* feature on Towers, 1 Mar 1942.

13. *Michigan* log, 1910; BuNav to Towers, 28 Nov 1910. The foregoing account is from Towers' dictated reminiscences in 1955.

14. BuNav to Towers, 28 Nov 1910, signed by Lieutenant Commander W. K. Harrison; Canaga to Pierre Towers, 16 Mar [1959].

15. R. A. Hart, 308–9; Canaga to Pierre Towers, 4 Nov 1958.

16. Canaga to Pierre Towers, 4 Nov 1958.

17. Van Deurs, *Ellyson,* 52–56; Halsey, 51.

18. Lord, 36–37, 44; Miller, 85, 93.

19. Chambers to Ellyson, 8 Feb 1911; Ellyson to Chambers, 14 Feb, 5 Mar 1911; Ellyson to the secretary of the navy, 31 Mar 1911; Curtiss to the secretary of the navy, 12 Apr 1911, Chambers papers; Towers' speech, "Early Days of Naval Aviation"; John R. Scanlan, a retired life insurance manager, to Towers, about 1955.

20. Canaga to Pierre Towers, 4 Nov 1958; Baldridge, "Origin of the Navy 'E' "; Blakeslee, 3.

21. Ellyson to Chambers, 2, 6 June 1911; Ellyson to BuNav, 14 June 1911; Towers' medical history. The rifle experts were Lieutenants William S. McClintic and Joseph V. Ogan, both of whom had stood high in the Class of '05.

22. Quoted in the *Atlanta Journal,* 7 Sep 1919.

23. *Michigan* log, June 1911; Blakeslee, 3.

24. Unless otherwise noted, all quoted passages are from Towers' talks in 1931 and the early 1950s and from his reminiscences of 1954–55, which differ only in minor wording.

25. All the key documents affirm that Towers reached Hammondsport on 27 June 1911, contrary to the date he mentioned in a medical report of 13 Jan 1913, in a letter to Captain Mark L. Bristol, 9 Feb 1914, and in later reminiscences; he recalled he had a full day of nonflying before his first flight, which he believed had been on the twenty-eighth, hence his reporting date, the twenty-sixth. That it was the twenty-seventh is confirmed in Ellyson to Chambers, 28 June 1911; Aviation log Curtiss hydroaeroplane navy no. A-1, entry (by Ellyson) of 27 June 1911; and Pers-3270-ghb of 16 June 1944, noting orders of 20 June 1911 detaching him from the *Michigan,* citing the twenty-sixth as the date of his detachment, and citing the twenty-seventh as the date of his reporting at Hammondsport; also Ellyson endorsement, 27 June 1911, of Towers' orders of 20 June 1911.

26. Studer, 308; *Hammondsport Herald,* 28 June 1911; Ellyson to Chambers, 28 June 1911; conversation with W. E. "Tony" Doherty III of Hammondsport in 1985.

27. Towers' medical report, 13 Jan 1913.

28. Casey, 60, 73, 84, 94, 96, 99, 100; "Curtiss Aeroplane" (1912 company catalogue), 11; A-1 log; "Aeronautics in the Navy," *The Navy* (Oct 1911): 11.

29. Ellyson to Chambers, 28 June 1911; A-1 log, 27 June–1 July 1911.

30. Chambers to the chief of BuNav, 1 May 1911.

31. A-1 log, 1, 2, 6 July 1911; van Deurs, *Ellyson,* 91–92; *Hammondsport Herald,* 5 July 1911; Ellyson to Chambers, 8, 10, 11 July 1911. When Ellyson hurt his leg, Towers advised him to "remain on crutches a long time. My ankle, which was not damaged so badly, still gives me a lot of trouble, and I think might have been all right now if I had been a little more careful in the beginning" (Towers to Ellyson, 28 Jan 1913, Chambers papers). Towers orders of 8 July 1911 were noted by Ellyson in A-1 log, 10 July 1911.

32. Ellyson to Chambers, 11 July 1911.

33. A-1 log, 12, 14 July 1911; Ellyson to Chambers, 17 July 1911.

34. Van Deurs, *Ellyson*, 96; A-2 log, 13, 18, 19 July 1911; Ellyson to BuNav, 13 July 1911, with BuNav endorsement, 17 July, and BuEng endorsement, 20 July 1911, and related documents appended to the reprinted log of the A-1.

35. Conversation with W. E. Doherty, Gink's son, in 1985; photographs of Towers, Curtiss Museum collection; *Hammondsport Herald*, 23 Aug 1911.

36. Kleckler to Pierre Towers, and Beckwith Havens to Pierre Towers, both about 1960.

37. Kleckler to Pierre Towers, about 1960; Ellyson to Chambers, 5, 19 Aug 1911.

38. *Aero* (26 Aug 1911): 453; van Deurs, *Ellyson*, 97; Towers to Chambers, 1 Sep 1912.

39. Towers, "My Friend Hap," 8–9; van Deurs, *Ellyson*, 105; *Aero* (26 Aug 1911): 454–59. Coffyn was fired two months later, though probably not for this incident alone.

40. Ellyson to Chambers, 23 Aug 1911; A-1 log, 30 Aug 1911; van Deurs, *Ellyson*, 99.

41. Studer, 291–92, which is slightly inaccurate; *Aero and Hydro* (7 Sep 1912): 496, "Roster of American Aviation Pilots" (19 Apr 1913): 38–40. Towers' judge may have been Aero Club secretary Augustus Post, but no record exists.

42. A-2 log, 10, 11, 13 Sep 1911; *Aero* (23 Sep 1911): 534.

43. Ellyson to Chambers, 3, 7, 13 Sep 1911; Aero Club 1911 list of 20 Jan 1912; *Aero* (23 Sep 1911): cover and 534. Ellyson's was no. 28, John Rodgers 48. Glenn Curtiss was no. 1, Orville and Wilbur Wright 4 and 5 respectively.

44. A-2 log, 16, 17 Sep 1911; van Deurs, *Ellyson*, 100; Hoaglund, 58.

45. See Janowicz, 7–12, 21, 38–39, 61, 131, 151ff, 168, 233ff.

46. Towers to Chambers, 28 Sep 1911; van Deurs, *Ellyson*, 104.

47. Towers to Chambers, 28 Sep 1911; van Deurs, *Ellyson*, 103; Towers, "My Friend Hap," 9; caption in Arnold photo album ("Hattie Towers in Army hydro at Washington barracks Sept. 1912"), Arnold papers. Other army flyers at the time were Benjamin D. Foulois, Frank P. Lahm, Roy C. Kirtland, and Charles deF. Chandler.

48. A-1 log, 30 Sep, 3 Oct 1911; Kinkaid to Chambers, 4 Oct 1911.

49. A-1 log, 10, 11 Oct 1911; *Michigan* log, 15 Apr 1911; Howeth, 190n.

50. The account of this trip is taken from Towers' reminiscences; A-1 log, 25–31 Oct and 2, 3 Nov 1911; Ellyson to BuNav, 6 Nov 1911.

51. Clipping probably from the *Navy Times*, Apr 1953.

52. Chambers to Curtiss, 17 Oct, 31 Dec 1911; Chambers to Frank H. Russell (manager of the Burgess Company), 27 Nov 1911.

53. Herbster to the navy secretary, 30 Dec 1910; *Lucky Bag, 1908*, 80, which noted also how Herbster steadfastly refuted the evolutionary theories of Charles Darwin—he *was* obstinate.

54. Rodgers report to Kinkaid, 18 Nov 1911; A-1 log, 15–18 Nov 1911; Towers' medical history; Towers to Chambers, 19 Nov 1911.

55. Ellyson to Chambers, 13 Dec 1911; Chambers to the BuNav chief, 18 Dec 1911; BuNav to Ellyson and Towers, 28 Dec 1911; Chambers to Curtiss, 31 Dec 1911; Curtiss to Chambers, 3 Jan 1912.

56. A. L. Johnson, 186–87; van Deurs, *Wings*, 64; Ellyson to Chambers, 13, 14, 29 Dec 1911; Chambers to Curtiss, 31 Dec 1911; Ellyson report to Kinkaid, 23 Dec 1911; A-1 log (with incomplete data), 18, 19, 20 Dec 1911. Towers' orders to San Diego were dated 29 Dec 1911.

57. Towers to Chambers, 18 Jan [1912]; Chambers to Curtiss, 10 Jan 1912; *New York Times*, 14 Jan 1912.

58. Bonnalie, 11.

59. Chambers to Curtiss, 3 Jan 1912.

60. Chambers to Curtiss, 31 Dec 1911, 3 Jan 1912.

61. Ellyson to Chambers, 14 Dec 1911, 3 Feb 1912; Casey, 108–10; Studer, 273; A-1 log, Jan–Feb 1912.

62. Studer, 293–94.

63. A-1 log, 30, 31 Jan and all of Feb 1912; B-1 log, Feb 1912; Towers to Chambers, 17 Feb

1912. See Casey, 79, 81. Pilot Lincoln Beachey had also removed the front elevator from his Curtiss-built planes.

64. Towers' report to Chambers, 1 Feb 1913. The Richardson flight log reveals that he learned his "grasscutting" in a Curtiss plane named Julia and was a passenger with Rodgers in the B-1 throughout Mar 1912.

65. A-2 log, 14 Mar 1912.

66. Towers to Chambers, 15 Mar 1912; van Deurs, *Ellyson*, 118–24.

67. B-1 log, 16, 19–22 Mar 1912.

68. A-1 log, 25, 26, 28 Mar and all of Apr 1912; Towers to Chambers, 5 Apr 1912. Richardson's notes on the behavior of pontoons, Mar–Apr 1912, confirm Towers' reminiscences (Richardson papers). Richardson made twenty landings with Towers aboard the A-1 between 28 Mar and 11 Apr 1912 (Richardson log). Towers also flew some mail in the Triad during an air meet in San Diego, the first person after Paul Beck to do so.

69. *New York Times*, 4 Apr 1912; *Aeronautics* (Apr 1912): 139; Towers to Chambers, 5 Apr 1912; Ellyson to Chambers, 8 Apr 1912.

CHAPTER 3. SENIOR AVIATOR, 1912–14

1. Towers to Clifford L. Lord, 9 Feb 1946, in Lord, preface. Foulois got the same treatment in the army (Foulois, 5).

2. Rodgers to Chambers, 3, 10 Apr 1912; BuNav telegrams to John Rodgers and to Rear Admiral J. A. Rodgers, 4 Apr 1912; Chambers to Ellyson, 4 Oct, [n.d.] Dec 1912.

3. Towers' Aviation Commandery speech, 24 Oct 1952. The first weekly report signed by Towers was on 10 Aug 1912.

4. A-1 log, 6, 7, 22, 28 June 1912; A-2 log, 21 July 1912; van Deurs, *Wings*, 63; Ellyson to Chambers, 24 June 1912; Blakeslee, 4.

5. Ellyson to Chambers, 31 Aug 1912; Chambers to Ellyson, 4 Oct 1912.

6. Chambers, "Report on Aviation," 21 Sep 1912, 155–70. Ellyson had totaled 40 hours 30 minutes and carried 111 passengers, while Towers had totaled 37 hours 2 minutes and carried 100 passengers. In the Wright planes, Rodgers had accumulated 132 flights over 33 hours 54 minutes by the time he left. Herbster had 59 flights in 14 hours 54 minutes. Towers blamed the open-air seats of the hydros for giving him the flu (Towers to Chambers, 1 Sep 1912).

7. Towers to Chambers, 1, 16 Sep 1912.

8. Ibid.

9. Ibid.; van Deurs, *Wings*, 66, 76.

10. Towers' report to Kinkaid, 8 Oct 1912, Chambers papers; A-2 log, 6 Oct 1912; *Aero and Hydro* (12 Oct 1912); van Deurs, *Wings*, 77; Blakeslee, 3–4. The aneroid barometer required a correction by the observer to ascertain the actual altitude. His hydro endurance record would be broken by army Lieutenant B. Q. Jones on 15 Jan 1915: eight hours fifty-three minutes.

11. A-2 log, 11, 23 Oct 1912; *Fleet Admiral King*, 86; Buell, *King*, 41.

12. Towers' reports to Chambers of 2, 16, 23 Nov 1912, Chambers papers; A-2 log, Oct–Nov 1912; B-2 log, Oct–Nov 1912; Towers to the navy secretary, 18 Dec 1912; Bellinger, "Gooney Bird," 14–18; Bureau of Medicine and Surgery, circular letter 125221, 8 Oct 1912; A-2 and B-2 logs, Oct–Dec 1912; Towers' reports to Chambers, 2, 7 Dec 1912. Towers recorded that Bellinger reported on 26 November, Billingsley on 2 December.

13. Van Deurs, *Ellyson*, 143–49, 177; van Deurs, *Wings*, 71; Ellyson to H. C. Genung of the Curtiss company, 10 Dec 1912.

14. Towers to the navy secretary, 12 Jan 1913, Chambers papers.

15. Foster oral transcript, 71–72; A-2 log, 18, 27 Feb and all Mar 1912; Towers to Chambers, 23 Jan 1913; Towers' weekly report of 1 Feb 1913; unit log, 6–12 Jan 1913, courtesy of P. E.

Coletta; Towers' medical reports, 13 Jan, 26 Feb 1913. Towers had to discipline Pat after one smoker (Coletta, *Bellinger,* 57).

16. Towers to Chambers, 1, 8 Feb 1913; unit log, 22, 27 Jan 1913; Towers to Ellyson, 6 Feb 1913. For the week ending 1 Feb, ninety-nine flights were made, and in the A-2, thirty-three; A-3, nineteen; B-1, twenty-three; B-2, ten; and C-1, fourteen.

17. "Assignment of Planes" at the beginning of the unit log.

18. Towers to Chambers, 1 Feb 1913; van Deurs, *Wings,* 77–80; Bellinger, "Gooney Bird," 29; Bellinger, "Sailors," 282.

19. Towers to Herbster, 6 Feb 1913; Towers to Chambers, 27 Dec 1912, and 30 Jan 1913 describing this "little controversy"; Hoover oral transcript, 76–78; Towers to Ellyson, 28 Jan 1913.

20. Chambers to Ellyson, 4 Oct 1912; C-1 log, 1 Mar 1913.

21. Towers to Ellyson, 6 Feb 1913, recounting his letters to Harry Genung of Curtiss about the C-1's problems; Mrs. C. R. Miller, "Flying with the Navy"; C-1 log, 26, 28 Feb 1913; unit log, especially 25 Feb 1913.

22. Unit log, Feb 1913; Towers' reports to Chambers, 23 Jan, 1, 8 Feb, 5 Mar 1913; Towers to the navy secretary, 5 Mar 1913; Nimitz to Badger (copies to Towers), 1, 7 Mar 1913; Bellinger, "Gooney Bird," 39–40.

23. Towers to Ellyson, 6 Feb 1913; C-1 log, 4 Feb 1913; Towers to Chambers, 12 Feb 1913.

24. Towers to Ellyson, 20 Feb 1913.

25. Ibid., including Badger's cable to the Navy Department.

26. Towers to Ellyson, 28 Feb, 4 Mar 1913, Chambers papers.

27. Ibid.; C-1 log, 6, 30 Jan and 5, 13 Mar 1913; Mustin flights, Jan–Mar 1913, listing the A-2 as the AX-1, the C-1 as the AB-1, their later designations, Mustin papers; Chambers to Towers, 13 Feb 1913; Hoover oral transcript, 76–78; Foster oral transcript, 73; Towers' report to the navy secretary and Chambers, 15 Mar 1913, listing all passengers given rides, Chambers papers; Chambers [unsigned] report, "Aviation," [1 Aug 1913], 4. In the C-1 or the A-2 Towers flew future aviator Lieutenant (jg) Newton H. White, future battleship admirals Lieutenant Commander Ridley McLean '94 and Ensign Morton L. Deyo '11, and World War II carrier logistics commander Ensign W. R. Carter '08. Herbster flew World War II leader Lieutenant H. Kent Hewitt '07 in the B-2, and in the B-1 Cunningham gave hops to future aviator-explorer Ensign Richard E. Byrd '12 and World War II air admiral Ensign J. W. Reeves, Jr., '11.

28. Towers to Ellyson, 4 Mar 1913.

29. Towers' report to the navy secretary and Chambers, 7 Mar 1913; *The Cuba Review,* 24–27, quoted in Miller chronology for Mar 1913; C-1 log, 6 Mar 1913.

30. *The Cuba Review,* Mar 1913; C-1 log, 10, 11 Mar 1913; Chambers, "Naval Aviation at Guantamano Bay," 20 Mar 1913. On Padgett, see Albion, *Makers,* 152.

31. C-1 log, 11 Mar 1913; unit log, 13–18 Mar 1913; *Neptune* log, Mar 1913; Towers' orders of Mar 1913.

32. Philadelphia *Public Ledger,* 20 Apr 1913; *Leslie's,* 10 July 1913.

33. Van Deurs, *Ellyson,* 147–51.

34. Unit log, Apr, 13 June 1913; C-1 log, Apr 1913; B-2 log, 22, 24, 26 Apr 1913; van Deurs, *Wings,* 81; A-2 log, 3 May 1913.

35. C-1 log, 6, 9 May 1913; Roseberry, 347–48; Breckinridge oral transcript, 142–43; Breckinridge diary, 6 Aug 1914, Breckinridge papers; John B. Semple to Chambers, [14 Apr 1913]; Casey, 121; *Aero and Hydro* (17 May 1913): 129 (gives 169 miles).

36. C-1 log, 20, 21 May 1913; unit log, 20, 21 May 1913; Baltimore *Sun* interview of Towers, 13 July 1913; Towers report to Chambers, 24 May 1913; Daniels, *Years of Peace,* 288, 290, in which Daniels mistook Towers' rank as commander; *New York Times,* 22 May 1913; Daniels diary, 21 May 1913, Daniels papers; logs of the unit, B-2 and A-2, all for 21 May 1913.

37. Daniels, *Years of Peace,* 293; FDR diary, 25 May 1913, RG 10, FDR Library. Towers erred in later years, recalling he had given FDR a ride during Daniels' visit on 21 May; no record indicates FDR was even present.

38. Towers to mother, 1 June 1913.

39. This account is taken from the interview with Towers, Baltimore *Sun,* 13 July 1913; *Aero and Hydro* (28 June 1913): 248; Chambers' report of the investigation, June 1913; Blakeslee, 4.

40. *Fleet Admiral King,* 86, which, however, is incorrect in claiming that King "found Towers"; Herbster report to Chambers, 21 June 1913; Chambers, "Aviation" [1 Aug 1913]: 9.

41. Chevalier letter, late June 1913, from Godfrey Chevalier memorial in *Medford* [Massachusetts] *Historical Society Publications* 43 (Mar 1940); Byrd, "It's Safe to Fly," 7. In Blakeslee, 4, Towers recalled that a kidney had been ruptured and his liver torn loose.

42. Chambers, "Aviation"; Herbster to Chambers, 23, 26, 28 June 1913; Chambers to V. B. Billingsley, the late pilot's father, 24 June 1913; Herbster to navy secretary, 25 June 1913; Chevalier to Chambers, 27 June 1913; Foulois, 74, 81; *New York Times* editorial, 23 June 1913.

43. Van Deurs, *Wings,* 86–87.

44. Towers' medical examinations, 20 June–8 July 1913; Daniels diary, 2 July 1913, Daniels papers; Baltimore *Sun* interview, 13 July 1913; Casey, 121–22; Daniels, *Years of Peace,* 292, in which he confused Bellinger with Billingsley; *Aero and Hydro* (28 June 1913): 246–47.

45. Holland, 4, 7–15.

46. Van Deurs, *Wings,* 89; Chambers to Towers, 4 July 1913.

47. Mustin to his wife, 3 Apr, 8 May, 7 Sep 1913, Mustin papers; Chambers, "Aviation" [1 Aug 1913]: 103. Rounded off in hours, the other flying times were Smith, 84; Herbster, 72; Bellinger, 69; Chevalier, 67; Ellyson, 53; Cunningham, 43; Rodgers, 36; Billingsley, 31; Isaac F. Dortch and L. N. McNair, 11 each; Murray and Richardson, 9 each; and Mustin, 8.

48. Chambers to Towers, 23 Sep 1913.

49. Towers to Chambers, 8 Oct [1913]; B-3 log, Sep–Nov 1913, Chambers papers; Chambers to Towers, 23 Sep 1913; Chambers, "Aviation" [1 Aug 1913]: 9; Gould, part 3, 270–72.

50. Chambers, "Aviation" [1 Aug 1913]: 4–6; Towers to Chambers, 2 Oct 1913; Chambers to Towers, 23 Sep 1913.

51. Towers to Chambers, 2, 8 Oct 1913. None of those rejected ever rose above the rank of commander.

52. Towers' reports to Chambers of 4, 11, 18, 25 Oct and 1, 15 Nov 1913; FDR to Chambers, 9 Oct 1913; Towers to Chambers board, 17, 24 Oct 1913, quoted in Miller chronology. The nonflying members of the board were Commander (later Rear Admiral) C. B. Brittain of BuNav, Commander (later Admiral) S. S. Robison of BuEng, and Lieutenant (later Rear Admiral) M. H. Simons of BuOrd.

53. Chambers memorandum (no addressee), 21 Nov 1913; van Deurs, *Wings,* 94.

54. Report of a board on naval aeronautics, presented by Daniels on 5 Feb 1914, House Naval Affairs Committee hearings of 1914, 794–803; Towers to navy secretary and Chambers, 4 Dec 1913; van Deurs, *Wings,* 99–100, 103–4; Towers' reports to Chambers, 22 Nov 1913 (signed by Murray) and 29 Nov 1913 (signed by R. C. Saufley); unit log, 21 Nov 1913.

55. Towers' reports of 6, 13, 20, 27 Dec 1913 and 3, 10 Jan 1914; unit log, Dec 1913, Jan 1914; Towers' orders of 3 Jan 1914.

56. Towers to Bristol, 20 Jan, 15 Feb 1914; Mustin to Bristol, 22 Jan, 31 Mar, 29 Apr 1914; Bristol to Mustin, 4 Apr 1914; interview of Corinne Mustin Murray by Pierre Towers about 1960. Mustin talked Towers into agreeing on four instead of two students per instructor for a course of one year; the syllabus was officially adopted in June.

57. Van Deurs, *Wings,* 104–7; Bristol to Rear Admiral Victor Blue, chief of BuNav, 19 Feb 1914; Towers to Lord, 9 Feb 1946; Bristol to Mustin, 26 Mar 1914; Rollins, 117, 130–31, 133; Wilson Brown, 146–48, FDR Library. Howe's title was secretary, upgraded in 1914 to special assistant.

58. Unit log, Feb 1914; van Deurs, *Wings,* 106; Callan to H. C. Genung, 3 Feb 1914, copied in L. C. Callan diary, Callan papers; Callan diary, [mid-Feb 1914].

59. Towers, "Record of Proceedings" over the accident, 16 Feb 1914; unit log, Feb–Apr 1914; van Deurs, *Wings,* 107; Chambers to E. L. Jones, 20 Feb 1914; Chambers to A. A. Merrill, 26 Feb 1914; Bristol to Mustin, 28 Apr, 23 May 1914.

60. Chambers to Burgess Company, Jan 1914, quoted in Miller chronology, 48; Mustin to

Bristol, 31 Mar 1914; Raleigh, vol. 1, 464–65; Duval, 47; Studer, 327–29; *New York Times,* 5, 6 Feb, 28 June 1914; *Aero and Hydro* (14 Feb 1914).

61. Bristol to Blue, 17 Feb 1914; *Hammondsport Herald,* 18 Feb 1914.

62. *New York Times,* 24 Feb, 28 June 1914; *Hammondsport Herald,* 18 Feb 1914.

63. Towers to Fiske, 10 Mar 1914.

64. Van Deurs, *Wings,* 107–8; Mustin to Bristol, 31 Mar 1914; unit log, Feb–Apr 1914; Towers to Woodhouse, 21 Mar 1914, in Woodhouse, "Policies," 169. On 27 March the Navy Department gave the navy's planes new designations to avoid confusion with the names of submarines ("the present system might have D-1 or E-2 *submarines* flying over the Gulf of Mexico!" Bristol commented to Mustin on 16 January 1914). But the airmen continued to use original designations through the spring.

65. Clipping, "From the Popular Magazine," dating some time after the Billingsley accident of June 1913; Blakeslee, 4. "The Naval Aviator" was copyrighted 16 May 1914 by the American Film and Manufacturing Company (courtesy National Air and Space Museum).

66. Mustin to Bristol, 27 Mar 1914; Bristol to Mustin, 17, 31 Mar, 9 Apr 1914. The exec, Lieutenant Commander Walter G. Roper, was finally replaced by John J. Hyland, anchor man in the Class of '98.

67. Van Deurs, *Wings,* 108; Bristol to Mustin, 13 Apr 1914; Wheeler, *Pratt,* 81; unit log, 19 Apr 1914; Turnbull and Lord, 36.

68. Mustin to Bristol, 29 Apr 1914.

69. Coletta, *Bellinger,* 77; *Aero and Hydro* (2 May 1914): cover and 58.

70. Sweetman, *Veracruz,* 105, 117–18; Lord, 118; Mustin to Bristol, 29 Apr 1914; Foster oral transcript, 74; *Aeronautics* (15 May 1914): 136.

71. Bristol to Mustin, 28 Apr, 11 June 1914; van Deurs, *Wings,* 110–11; Wheeler, *Pratt,* 81.

72. Unit log, May–June 1914; Mustin's weekly report of flights to Bristol, 30 May 1914; Mustin to Bristol, 14 May 1914.

73. Mustin to his wife, 3 June 1914; draft of Coletta's Bellinger biography. An aviator water polo team of Mustin, Towers, Chevalier, Bellinger, Stolz, and Bronson defeated the correspondents, 8–0.

74. In March 1912 James H. Hare had made the first aerial reconnaissance photos for the military along the Mexican border near Laredo, Texas, but with a civilian pilot and in a Wright plane on loan from Robert J. Collier (Foulois, 82–84).

75. Van Deurs, *Wings,* 110–11; Sweetman, *Veracruz,* 154–55; Mustin to wife, 3 June 1914; Connally, 12–13, 32–33.

76. Daniels to Woodhouse, 19 May 1914, in Woodhouse, *Textbook,* 137; *Hammondsport Herald,* 10 June 1914.

77. Baldwin, 82–91; Mustin report to Bristol, 28 June 1914; Mustin to Bristol, 14 May, 29 June 1914; Bristol to Mustin, 13 Apr, 23 May, 25 June 1914; Towers orders and Daniels telegram, 19 June 1914.

78. Curtiss to Towers, 5 May 1914.

79. Knott, *Flying Boat,* 26; Towers reminiscences; Towers, "Great Hop," 9.

80. *New York Times,* 19, 21, 24, 28 June 1914; *Aero and Hydro* (11 July 1914), reporting 7 July 1914 story.

81. Swarthout, 9, 22; *Hammondsport Herald,* 8 July 1914; Studer, 329–31; *New York Times,* 24, 28 June 1914.

82. *New York Times,* 21, 23 June 1914; Casey, 183–86.

83. Lord, 123; Studer, 335; Towers telegrams to Bristol, 25 June, 13 July 1914; Towers letter of 3 July 1914; Bristol telegram to Towers, 26 June 1914; Howard Huntington, secretary of the Aero Club, to Bristol, probably 28 June 1914; *Hammondsport Herald,* 1, 8, 22, 29 July 1914; *Aero and Hydro* (11 July 1914): 179; A. F. Zahm, " 'The America's' Trip Postponed," *Scientific American* (8 Aug 1914), reprinted in Zahm papers, 377. Towers corrected Markey when the latter wrote that Towers did all the testing because Porte fell ill (Towers to Markey, 21 Feb 1945).

84. Zahm papers, 377–78; *New York Times,* 2, 7, 9, 11, 16, 18, 19, 24–26 July 1914; *Hammondsport Herald,* 29 July 1914.

85. Unit log, July 1914; *North Carolina* log, July 1914; Towers orders of 10 July 1914; *New York Times,* 30 July, 3 Aug 1914; Towers, "Great Hop," 9.

86. Towers telegram to Bristol, 3 Aug 1914; Towers orders of 3 Aug 1914.

87. Bristol telegram and letters to Mustin, 5, 16, 17 Aug 1914; Bristol to Towers, 30 Aug 1914.

88. *Tennessee* log, 5 Aug 1914.

89. Van Deurs, *Wings,* 116. The skipper of the *North Carolina* was Captain Joseph W. Oman; Mustin became the exec.

90. *Tennessee* log, 5–7 Aug 1914; *New York Times,* 5–7 Aug 1914, which reported the figure at almost $6 million in gold coins distributed between both ships. According to the Breckinridge diary, 6 Aug 1914, the *Tennessee* carried $3 million provided by New York banks and $1.5 million allotted by Congress.

91. *Tennessee* log, 6–7 Aug 1914.

92. Casey, 185.

93. Van Deurs, *Wings,* 130–33.

CHAPTER 4. LEARNING FROM THE BRITISH, 1914–16

1. Breckinridge diary, 6, 13 Aug 1914, which then recalled the secretary's earlier flight with Towers as well as Towers' dramatic survival during the Billingsley crash. Others on the voyage included Treasury Department and banking agents, diplomats, Red Cross officials, and two dozen army officers. Commander Reginald R. Belknap was Breckinridge's naval aide during the voyage.

2. Ibid., which includes the *Tennessee*'s list of officers; Hoover oral transcript, 92–94. Benton had taught mathematics and had served in the Discipline Department. The executive officer was jovial Lieutenant Commander Earl P. Jessop, a classmate of Mustin's in '96.

3. Breckinridge diary, 13 Aug 1914; *Tennessee* log, Aug 1914; Captain B. C. Decker, "Aeronautics: Information Sent to Naval War College Based upon Conversations with Lieutenant Towers on Board the *Tennessee,*" in Rear Admiral Austin M. Knight memo, 3 Sep 1914, Naval War College.

4. *Tennessee* log, 16 Aug 1914; *New York Times,* 7, 17, 18 Aug 1914; Breckinridge diary, 13, 16 Aug 1914.

5. *New York Times,* 18 Aug 1914; *Tennessee* log, 18 Aug 1914. Breckinridge praised the embassy's work in his diary entry of 16 Aug 1914 but also observed, "I am sorry to say that many of my countrymen made asses of themselves in the first few days of panic in their unreasoning clamor for transportation and protection and everything else. Such neurotic and unrestrained individuals are always to be found."

6. Bristol to Towers, 30 Aug 1914; Breckinridge diary, Aug–Oct 1914.

7. Mustin to Daniels, 24, 29 Aug 1915; Bristol to Daniels, 16 June 1914, Daniels papers; Herbster to Bristol, 30 Aug, 9 Nov 1914; *North Carolina* log, 29 Aug 1914.

8. Dorwart, *ONI, 1865–1918,* 101; McCrary to Bristol, 5 Aug 1914, with Bristol's endorsement.

9. Gilbert, vol. 3, 66–67; Herbster to Bristol, 30 Aug 1914, relating conversation with Towers; Belknap to Bristol, 5 Nov 1914, relating conversation with Towers.

10. Towers to Bristol, 10 Sep 1914; Hezlet, 24–27 (italics in original).

11. Hines to Colonel Edward M. House, President Wilson's chief adviser, 22 Sep 1914, in Hendrick, vol. 1, 327. Norman Graham Thwaites, former New York *World* reporter, had joined the Fourth Royal Irish Dragoon Guards.

12. Towers to Bristol, 10 Sep 1914.

13. Ibid.; Towers' reminiscences (italics in original).

14. Hoover oral transcript, 97–98; White, 69. Instead of taking the walking test, the examinee could opt to ride a horse seventy-five miles or a bicycle a hundred miles in three days—choices probably ruled out by the on-foot constables.

15. Towers to Bristol, 16 Oct 1914.

16. Herbster to Bristol, 9 Nov 1914.

17. Towers' bimonthly assistant attaché report of 2 Nov 1914; Belknap to Bristol, 5 Nov 1914.

18. Symington to FDR, 23 Dec 1914, RG 10, FDR Library.

19. Bristol to Belknap, about 18 Nov 1914; Bristol to Herbster, 8 Dec 1914; Stolz to Bristol, [?] Mar 1915.

20. Towers to Bristol, 30 Nov, 11 Dec 1914; Bristol to Towers, 16 Feb 1915.

21. Studer, 339–40; Towers to Bristol, 11 Dec 1914; Bristol to Towers, 16 Feb 1915; Gilbert, vol. 3, 66–67, 123.

22. Towers to Bristol, 11 Dec 1914, and undated Bristol reply.

23. Towers to Bristol, 14 Dec 1914, 29 Jan, 1 Feb 1915; Herbster to Bristol, 25 Jan 1915; Dorwart, *ONI, 1865–1918,* 101–2; Hezlet, 29–30.

24. Towers to Bristol, 22 July 1915; Chambers, "Confidential Memorandum of Inspection on March 17, 1915," in which, after a secret inspection of British dirigible facilities, he suggests Towers ought to be warned about the clandestine nature of the dirigibles' tests.

25. Towers to Bristol, 1 Feb 1915. Constructor McBride, who held the equivalent line rank of lieutenant commander, had graduated number 7 (Ernie King was number 4) in the Class of '01.

26. Towers to Bristol, 22 Mar 1915.

27. *New York Times,* 3 May 1915.

28. Webb was acting director of trade division at the Admiralty.

29. Dorwart, *ONI, 1865–1918,* 102–3. In later years Towers erred in recollecting, notably in a newspaper interview in the mid-1930s (clipping from unidentified newspaper, Towers scrapbook) and in a letter to reporter Philip H. Patchin in 1943, that the first lord at the time of the *Lusitania*'s sinking was Arthur J. Balfour. Churchill held the post until 25 May.

30. Towers to Bristol, 21 June 1915; *New York Times,* 27, 28 May, 6–8 Sep 1915; Hendrick, vol. 2, 30, 40.

31. Patchin to Towers, 1 Feb, 7 Sep 1943, and undated Towers reply; Tokyo attaché report, 10 Oct 1914, among others, Naval War College. The report told of Lieutenant Yamada, one of John McClaskey's Curtiss students, bombing ships at Kiaochow, China. Yamada's report of 20 October described his bombing of Tsingtao on the tenth (RG 72, National Archives).

32. Towers to Bristol, 21 June 1915; Raleigh, vol. 1, 461–62, 484; Roskill, *Documents,* vol. 1, 195–200; Duval, 48–57; Jones, vol. 4, 16–18; Towers to Bristol, 2 Sep 1915; Towers to ONI on the Hall conversation, 5 Oct 1916, RG 72, National Archives.

33. Towers to Bristol, 21 June 1915.

34. Ibid., 1 Feb, 22 Mar, 13 Apr, 5, 21 June, 8, 22 July 1915; Bristol to Towers, 16 Feb 1915.

35. Bristol to Mustin, 16 Apr, 24 June 1915; Towers to Bristol, 22 July 1915. In the latter Towers also stated his preference for "the V (vertical) type of water-cooled engine over the rotary and radial types," though he reported that all standard British engines—the Gnomes and Samsons—lacked the 200 horsepower the pilots wanted. They would in fact get 225-hp Wight and Short tractors before the end of the war.

36. Bristol to Towers, 16 Feb, 7 July 1915; Towers to Bristol, 14, 21 June 1915; E. F. Johnson, 141; Towers to the Aero Club of America, 31 May 1915; Herbster to Bristol, 16 June 1915.

37. Towers to Bristol, 21 June, 8, 22 July 1915; Bristol to Towers, 7, [about 30] July 1915.

38. Fontanne to Towers, 14 Oct 1939, from the Pabst Theater in Milwaukee; Page to Towers, 20 Sep 1915; Towers' personal identification record, 14 Aug 1915; medical bill of 11 Feb 1916 for treatment of boils, 14 Sep to 26 Dec 1915; conversation with Mrs. Eleanor Ring Storrs, 1985. The Manners house probably belonged to the family of actor J. Hartley Manners, who performed in America from 1902 to 1914.

39. Charles S. Carstairs' obituary, *New York Times,* 11 July 1928; Jordan, vol. 2, 869–75; Mervine, vol. 1, 118–31; conversations in 1985 with Charles S. and Lois Towers and Lynne L. Riley, respectively Towers' son, daughter-in-law, and granddaughter. Lily was born on 2 November 1891. Charles Stewart (1778–1869), her great-granduncle, had served on active duty for sixty-three years, from 1798 to 1861, becoming the first rear admiral on the retired list in 1862 (for his service record, see Reynolds, *Admirals,* 332–33). Another forebear had been a surgeon on two Revolutionary War privateers. Charles Haseltine "Hake" Carstairs was Yale '08, Carroll Carstairs Yale '13 and later the

author of *A Generation Missing* (1930); Lily's younger brother Stewart Carstairs was a budding artist. Lily sought a husband partly to escape an unhappy domestic situation, namely, a young stepmother.

40. Towers to Bristol, 17 Jan 1914.

41. Ibid., 2 Aug, 26 Oct 1915.

42. Raleigh, vol. 1, 485–87; Jones, vol. 2, 355; Towers to Bristol, 15 Jan 1916.

43. Bristol to Towers, 7 Oct 1915.

44. Towers to Bristol, 2 Aug, 26 Oct, 7 Dec. 1915; conversation with Pierre Towers in 1983.

45. Towers to Bristol, 7, 14, 15 Dec 1915, and 15, 28 Jan 1916; C. L. Vaughn-Lee pass of 8 Dec 1915.

46. "Hearing of Lieutenant J. H. Towers, U.S.N., before the Executive Committee of the General Board on the development of Aeronautics in England," 6 Oct 1916, 9, 16–17.

47. Towers to Bristol, 26 Nov 1915; Raleigh, vol. 1, 465–66, 471–72; Jones, vol. 2, 430–33.

48. Towers to Bristol, 28 Jan 1916; Bristol to Towers, 19 Feb 1916 (italics original). Towers repeated his apprehensions to Bristol on 17 Mar 1916 and on the 29th requested sea duty. Symington turned him down because of his unique contacts with British officers.

49. Symington papers, "Notes from Fleet Diary," Apr–July 1916, especially entry of 13 July 1916.

50. Ibid., 24 May–1 June 1916. Marder makes no mention of this document, rather that Jellicoe was highly conservative in his tactics (vol. 2, 446–47). Also, Jellicoe claimed that fear of the United States entering the war *against* Britain made him even less inclined to risk the fleet—a feeble rationale for his tactics (vol. 3, 10).

51. Symington papers, "Notes from Fleet Diary," 15 July 1916.

52. Towers General Board hearing, 6 Oct 1916; Marder, vol. 4, 10–15. The one British seaplane ship at Jutland was the *Engadine*. See Young, *Rutland of Jutland*.

53. CNO to director, ONI, Captain James H. Oliver, 3 July 1916.

54. Towers' diplomatic pass of 21 July 1916 and Foreign Office certifications, 10–11 Aug 1916; conversations with Charles and Lois Towers; O. Murray of the Admiralty, "To the Officials of the South Eastern and Chatham Railway and All Whom It May Concern," 26 Aug 1916, Towers papers; Marjorie Towers' birth certificate, 30 July 1916 (copy of 9 Aug); Towers, orders of 31 July 1916.

55. Jones, vol. 2, 431, 434–35, 442–44.

56. Squadron Commander Spenser Grey No. 5 Wing daily report, 7 Sep 1916, and Wing Captain Charles L. Lambe, Royal Naval Air Services daily summary, 7 Sep 1916, Public Records Office, London, courtesy of Nigel P. Quinney. The quotations are from Towers' recollections in the early 1950s. Anderae and Towers were nowhere mentioned in the official reports used to reconstruct the events of this date.

57. Towers' General Board hearing, 6 Oct 1916, 14, 16.

58. Jones, vol. 2, 444ff.

CHAPTER 5. TOWERS AT WAR, 1916–18

1. E. F. Johnson, 163; Bronson to Bristol, 23 May 1916. See Klachko and Trask, 39, for McKean.

2. Van Deurs, *Wings*, 140–42; Bronson to Bristol, 22, 23 May 1916.

3. The following is from Towers' General Board hearing, 6 Oct 1916, 1–20.

4. Mustin testimony of 12 Oct 1916; Towers to General Board, 20 Oct 1916.

5. Table of 15 Nov 1916 and board recommendations of 24 June 1916; Lord, 219, 254.

6. FDR to Mustin, 15 June 1916; Swanborough, 98–105; Turnbull and Lord, 55; Towers' orders of 8 Jan 1917; CNO 909–17, 5 Apr 1917; Towers to Curtiss, 4 Apr 1917; Studer, 350.

7. Lord, 223–41, 269; Woodhouse, *Textbook*, 172–75; Gould, part 4, 277; Bellinger, "Gooney Birds," 128–31.

8. Paine, vol. 1, 78–80.

9. Ibid., 80–82, 288.

10. Lord, 259–60; Van Wyen, *Aeronautical Board,* 2–3, 29–30.

11. Taylor to secretary of the navy, 16 Sep 1916; Roland, vol. 1, 4–6, 32; Hunsaker historical paper on NACA in Hunsaker to Moffett, 19 Nov 1922, National Archives; Towers to McKean, 19 Jan 1917, saying he was filling in after the departure of Bristol. Roland gives his date of appointment as 10 Jan 1917 (vol. 2, 429). See also Holley, *Ideas,* 111.

12. Turnbull and Lord, 57; Fulton, 157n; Roland, vol. 1, 37–43, 329; Lord, 312.

13. Hunsaker paper to Moffett, 19 Nov 1922; Lord, 264–66 and passim. The army members were pilot Charles deF. Chandler and engineer Virginius E. Clark.

14. S. Wilson of the *Seattle* to Paymaster Grinnel of the *Mississippi,* 2 Feb 1917; Towers to Lieutenant Commander Joy Bright Hancock, 15 Jan 1944; Towers to McCrary, 7 Apr 1917; Van Wyen, *World War I,* 175; Miller chronology, 7 Sep 1917. Earle Johnson recalled that the insignia were obtained "through the initiative of Lieutenant Commander Towers" (173).

15. Lord, 255–56; Towers to the Commission on Navy Yards and Naval Stations, 3 Nov 1916; Bristol to the commission, 4 Dec 1916.

16. Benson to Daniels, 5 Feb 1917; Towers to McKean, 25 Jan 1917; Towers to Daniels, 1 June 1917; Lord, 260–61, 271–73; Daniels to the Cognizance Board, 12 Feb 1917; the Cognizance Board to Daniels, 14 Feb 1917; Lord, 261–63, 272–74; Towers' address at NAS Norfolk, 18 Jan 1954; Towers to Earle Johnson, 8 Mar 1917, in E. F. Johnson, 166.

17. Emme, 6.

18. Byrd, 80; Towers to brother William [winter 1918]. Towers did most of the talking before the General Board on 20 Aug 1917, and, a year later, 4 Sep 1918, Irwin testified, "I am sorry that my assistant is not here who has complete information in regard to [aircraft production]" (General Board hearings of those dates).

19. Towers to Lord, 13 Mar 1946; Lord, 288–89; *Fleet Admiral King,* 101–2; Smith, *First Across!,* 248n; Fulton, 164.

20. Clark, 2–5; E. F. Johnson, 171; Paine, vol. 1, 273; Gould, 5, 39.

21. Numerous correspondence between FDR, Howe, and Towers, 1917–18, including Howe to Towers, 3 Nov 1917. Irwin observed to FDR that thirty was the normal upper-age limit for pilot trainees (7 Sep 1917, RG 10, FDR Library).

22. Lord, 285.

23. Benson to Daniels, 5 Feb 1917; Towers to Daniels, 15 Feb 1917; Towers to Benson, 1 June 1917; E. F. Johnson, 174–75.

24. Towers to Irwin, 13 Aug 1917.

25. Turnbull and Lord, 108, 110; Lord, 302–7; Holley, *Ideas,* 40–41.

26. Foulois, 143–47; Lord, 284–85, 304, 308, 312–13; Technical Board to the secretaries of navy and war, 29 June 1917; Holley, *Ideas,* 41–45.

27. Irwin (Towers) to CNO, 22 June 1917; Lord, 308–10.

28. Lord, 242, 246, 270–71, 311–16, 325–35, 349, 351–52, 469–71; Featherstone, 40–41; Holley, *Ideas,* 53–59, 134–35; Towers, "Operations of Naval Aircraft," 374; Raleigh, vol. 1, 465–66; Jones, part 4, 18–19, 64–65; Swanborough, 106–11, 114–16; Duval, 56–66.

29. Lord, 321–25, 355ff; Towers to Irwin, 20 Sep 1917.

30. House Naval Affairs Committee hearings, 13 Feb 1918, 520–23; E. F. Johnson, 176; Sudsbury, 38–47.

31. Lord, 387–89; E. F. Johnson, 171; Paine, vol. 1, 273.

32. Wysong oral transcript, 18–20.

33. E. F. Johnson, 172.

34. Conversation with Tony Doherty in 1985, recalling Towers' visit to Tony's parents at Hammondsport in 1939 and their reminiscing about the war. See also Towers to Pierre, 17 Oct 1926.

35. CNO weekly bulletin, weeks ending 8, 29 Dec 1917; Towers' memo to brother William [early 1918].

36. Towers, "Operations of Naval Aircraft," 376.

37. General Board hearings, 14 Feb 1918; Lord, 396–406.

38. Lord, 407–11; Foulois, 157–71; Holley, *Ideas,* 138–40.

39. Wheeler, *Pratt,* 125; Holley, *Ideas,* 69ff; Arnold, 72ff; Towers' orders of 6 Sep 1918 (he executed the oath on 16 Sep).

40. Lord, 423–30.

41. Sims, 332.

42. Lord, 244, 472, 498–507; Swanborough, 117–19. Two 18-T or "Kirkham" fighters were built, one setting the world speed record of 163 mph in August 1918.

43. Lord, 473–74, 484, 519; Hezlet, 101.

44. Lord, 518–24; Emme, 9.

CHAPTER 6. BRIDGING THE ATLANTIC, 1918–19

1. Towers reminiscences; Towers to Benson, 31 Oct 1918.

2. Smith, *First Across!,* 11, 13–37; Towers to Benson, 31 Oct 1918; Tompkins board report, 4 Feb 1919.

3. Smith, *First Across!,* 15–28; Westervelt, 1530–31, 1550; Westervelt et al., 94ff, 109ff; Hunsaker in *Automotive Industries* [10 July 1919], including Taylor to Hunsaker, 25 Aug 1917, 69–70, [17 July 1919], 122, and [24 July 1919], 176.

4. Tompkins' board report, 4 Feb 1919; Duval, 71–73. The largest airplane in 1919 was the Curtiss Model T triplane flying boat, built three years before, with four engines and a wing span of 133 feet. Porte's wing span was 123 feet.

5. Towers, "Great Hop," 10; Steirman, 31; Westervelt et al., 93–94.

6. Smith, *First Across!,* 29–34; Wilbur, 11–12; Westervelt et al., 128–30.

7. Tompkins' board report, 4 Feb 1919; Towers and Richardson telephone conversation transcript, 18 Apr 1919; Towers to Hunsaker, 18 Apr 1919.

8. Tompkins' board report, 4 Feb 1919; Wilbur, 13; Steirman, 43.

9. Towers, "Great Hop," 10–11; Towers orders of 12 Feb 1919; Wilburn, 12–14.

10. Towers to Irwin, 14 Feb 1919.

11. Towers' orders were issued 21 Apr 1919, though McKean had authorized them in a memo to him three days before. Towers also wanted Earle Johnson, who, however, was about to leave the navy (Towers to Johnson, 5, 18 Mar 1919, in E. F. Johnson, 213–15); Byrd to CNO (aviation), 9 July 1918, and first endorsement by Captain Frank M. Bennett, commandant, NAS Pensacola, same date, Byrd papers; Byrd to Irwin, 4 Dec 1918; Byrd, 78–84, in which he called Towers "a student, quiet and reserved and methodical." As of yet Byrd had little pull in government, although his family was influential in Virginia State Democratic politics (brother Harry was a state senator), and he was admired by Secretary Daniels. On 14 May 1919, Bellinger wrote, Byrd edited, and Towers approved and endorsed a statement detailing Byrd's key role in the NC expedition to that date; Bellinger appended it to his special fitness report on Byrd of that date, Byrd papers.

12. Minutes of transatlantic flight conference, 15 Feb 1919; Towers to Hunsaker, 18 Apr 1919; Towers' 1954 speech, question and answer period.

13. Destroyer Force U.S. Fleet, operations order no. 1, 15 Apr 1918; Towers, "Aircraft Navigation," 1–2.

14. Smith, *First Across!,* 44–46; Howeth, 278; Lavender, 1601–2, 1605.

15. Smith, *First Across!,* 127; A. L. Johnson, 188; Wilbur, 17; White, 72–73. Sweet had worked with the navy's seaplane radios before taking command of the U.S. Navy radio detachment in France in July 1918.

16. Towers, "Aircraft Navigation," 2–3; Lavender, 1604.

17. Towers, "Aircraft Navigation," 4–5; Wright, 13, 32–33, 106.

18. Towers, "Aircraft Navigation," 3–4; Smith, *First Across!,* 40–44; Wright, 105–7; Byrd's fitness report, 14 May 1919, written by Bellinger.

19. Hunsaker, [24 July 1919], 172.

20. Ibid.; Towers, "Aircraft Navigation," 5–7; Byrd's fitness report, 14 May 1919.

21. Smith, *First Across!*, 50–53; Lord, 587; Laning, 264–65.

22. Towers, "Great Hop," 11.

23. Smith, *First Across!*, 53–60; Wilbur, 16; *Lucky Bag*, 1907, 99; Read to his wife, 2 May 1919, in Bess Read, 11.

24. Towers, "Great Hop," 11.

25. Navy News Bureau press release of 8 May 1919; Towers–Richardson telcon transcript, 18 Apr 1919; Read to his wife, 3 May 1919, Read papers.

26. Towers quoted in *Washington Post*, 19 May 1919.

27. Smith, *First Across!*, 64–66; *New York World*, 7 May 1919; Towers, "Great Hop," 11; FDR to Towers, 5 May 1919, RG 10, FDR Library; Read to wife, 6 May 1919, in Bess Read, 11.

28. M. H. McIntyre, Office of the Assistant Secretary of the Navy, to Towers, 7 May 1919, and enclosed letters from FDR to Walter H. Long, first lord of the Admiralty; Vice Admiral Harry S. Knapp, commanding U.S. naval forces in European waters; Rear Admiral Richard H. Jackson, commanding U.S. naval forces in the Azores; and the Portuguese minister of marine in Lisbon, 8 May 1919. Towers apparently never delivered the letters, which had stipulated delivery only if the flight was successful, for the originals were returned to the files (RG 10, FDR Library).

29. *Flight Across*, 32–33; Smith, *First Across!*, 67–68; Read to his wife, 7 May 1919, Read papers.

30. *Flight Across*, 34; Smith, *First Across!*, 68–69; *New York Times*, 9 May 1919; Richardson NC-3 pilot's log, 12 May 1919, Richardson papers.

31. *Flight Across*, 35; Smith, *First Across!*, 70; navy press release, 8 May 1919, and Richardson pilot's log.

32. Richardson log; Lavender, 1607; Towers, "Great Hop," 12.

33. Byrd, 85–86; Towers, "Great Hop," 12.

34. Towers, "Great Hop," 12–13; Towers, "Aircraft Navigation," 7–9; navy press release, 8 May 1919; Navy Department message log, 8 May 1919; Towers' Seaplane Division 1 report, 28 July 1919, 1, National Archives; Towers' NC-3 report, 8 July 1919, 12, National Archives; Richardson log; Richardson to mother and sister, 11 May 1919, Richardson papers; Byrd, 86–87; "Operations Orders and Special Instructions for Surface and Air-Craft Taking Part in the Transatlantic Flight," approved 15 Apr 1919; Smith, *First Across!*, 70–75; Wilbur, 20; Steirman, 60–61, 65–67; Richardson in Westervelt et al., 257–58.

35. Wanamaker to Towers, 9 May 1919.

36. Smith, *First Across!*, 75–78; Towers, "Great Hop," 13; navy press releases, 10, 12 May 1919.

37. Byrd, 87–89; Towers' NC-3 report, 12; Towers, "Great Hop," 13–14.

38. Byrd, 88; Towers, "Great Hop," 14.

39. Byrd, 88; Richardson to mother and sister, 11 May 1919; Richardson log.

40. Towers, "Aircraft Navigation" 8–9; navy press releases, 10, 12 May 1919; Richardson log; Towers NC-3 report, 13; Smith, *First Across!*, 77–78; Wilbur, 21; Towers, "Great Hop," 14; Steirman, 82; commander Pacific Division to Office of the Chief of Naval Operations, 12 May 1919, quoting Towers, RG 10, FDR Library; Richardson in Westervelt et al., 267–68.

41. FDR to Towers, radio message, 14 May 1919.

42. Smith, *First Across!*, 85–86.

43. Richardson log; Towers, "Great Hop," 15.

44. Towers, "Great Hop," 14.

45. Smith, *First Across!*, 78–79, 99, 101.

46. Ibid., 76–77, 99–101; Towers, "Aircraft Navigation," 9; Towers, "Great Hop," 14–15; *Baltimore Evening Sun*, 13 May 1919; Byrd, 89–90.

47. Tinker in the *Aroostook* to the Office of the Chief of Naval Operations; 13 May 1919, RG 10, FDR Library; Towers, "Great Hop," 15.

48. Smith, *First Across!*, 88–92; Navy Department message log, 14 May 1919.

49. Smith, *First Across!*, 86–87, 92–96, 102; Navy Department press release, 15 May 1919.

50. *Flight Across,* 39.

51. Smith, *First Across!,* 102–4; *Washington Post,* 19 May 1919; Steirman, 97–98.

52. Smith, *First Across!,* 105; *Flight Across,* 41; Towers, "Aircraft Navigation," 9; Steirman, 99, 108; Towers, "Great Hop," 15; Gregg to Towers [16 May 1919], Towers scrapbook.

53. Smith, *First Across!,* 105; Navy Department message log, 16 May 1919.

54. Smith, *First Across!,* 106; Wilburn, 25; Steirman, 105–6; Navy Department message log, 16, 17 May 1919; Hunsaker [24 July 1919], 175; Lavender, 1604.

55. Navy Department message log, 16 May 1919.

56. "Operations Orders and Special Instructions"; Read in *Washington Post,* 19 May 1919; Towers NC-3 report, 13; Towers, "Great Hop," 74; McCulloch to Navy Department, 23 May 1919, RG 10, FDR Library; Richardson log; Read in Westervelt et al., 200.

57. Richardson log; Towers NC-3 report, 13–14; NC-3 plotting chart, Towers scrapbook; Smith, *First Across!,* 111, and radio report of Ensign Herbert C. Rodd of the NC-4, 30 June 1919, contained therein, 226–27.

58. *Flight Across,* 43; "Operations Orders and Special Instructions"; Wilbur, 26; McCulloch to Navy Department, 23 May 1919; Smith, *First Across!,* 109–10, and Rodd report therein, 226; Clark, 5.

59. McCulloch to Navy Department, 23 May 1919; Richardson log; Richardson in Westervelt et al., 280; Towers, "Great Hop," 74; Smith, *First Across!,* 111–12, and Rodd report therein, 227; Read in *Washington Post,* 19 May 1919; Navy Department message log, 16, 17 May 1919; Towers NC-3 report, 14; Towers' Seaplane Division 1 report, 2; Steirman, 117–18; NC-3 plotting charts, Towers scrapbook; Towers to Office of the Chief of Naval Operations, 19 May 1919, RG 10, FDR Library.

60. *Flight Across,* 43; Towers manuscript released to New York *World,* 1; Towers, "Aircraft Navigation," 9; "Operations Orders and Special Instructions"; Towers, "Great Hop," 74; Richardson log.

61. NC-3 plotting charts; Towers, "Great Hop," 74; Smith, *First Across!,* 114–15; A. L. Johnson, 188. The NC-4 picked up signals from the transport *George Washington* 1,800 miles away.

62. Richardson log; Towers, "Great Hop," 74; NC-3 plotting charts.

63. NC-3 plotting charts; Read in *Washington Post,* 19 May 1919; Navy Department message log, 20 May 1919; Towers' NC-3 report, 14; Rodd report in Smith, *First Across!,* 228; Richardson log; Richardson in Westervelt et al., 282; Towers' New York *World* manuscript, 1–5; Towers' Associated Press interview, 20 May 1919; Towers, "Aircraft Navigation," 10–14, and "Great Hop," 74.

64. Laning, 267; Towers' Seaplane Division 1 report, 4.

65. Towers' NC-3 report, 14; Towers, "Great Hop," 74; McCulloch to Navy Department, 23 May 1919; Richardson log.

66. Navy Department message log, 17 May 1919; Towers' NC-3 report, 14; Rear Admiral R. H. Jackson to ComNav, 7:09 PM, 17 May 1919, RG 10, FDR Library.

67. Towers, "Great Hop," 74; Steirman, 120; McCulloch to Navy Department, 23 May 1919.

68. Towers, "Great Hop," 74; Richardson log.

69. Towers, "Great Hop," 74; McCulloch to Navy Department, 23 May 1919; Towers' NC-3 report, 15; Richardson log; Lavender, 1606; Steirman, 124, 126–27.

70. Richardson in Westervelt et al., 288. Reports on flying time, which vary slightly, are reckoned here from NC-3's liftoff at 2206 of 16 May to touchdown at 1330 on the seventeenth.

71. This account is taken largely from Towers' NC-3 report, 16–19; "Great Hop," 75; and his reminiscences in the early 1950s. See also Richardson's log, Steirman, 157, and Richardson in Westervelt et al., 288ff.

72. One plane had already set the record for mileage aloft, 1,350 miles, and another for staying airborne twenty-four hours, but both had been endurance efforts in confined areas, as had Towers' effort in the A-2 in 1912 (Wilbur, 7).

73. Smith, *First Across!,* 142–43.

74. Towers, "Great Hop," 75; Navy Department message log, 19 May 1919.

75. *Washington Post,* 17, 19 May 1919; *New York Times,* 19 May 1919.

76. Howard Shepherd to Mrs. Towers, 19 May 1919; Edward Wilson Edwards to Mrs. Towers, 20 May 1919.

77. *A Republica,* 21 May 1919; *New York Times,* 21 May 1919.

78. Smith, *First Across!,* 142, 149–52, 159–60.

79. "Operations Orders and Special Instructions," 15 Apr 1915; Towers to Daniels, 19 Sep 1919, quoting relevant messages of 20–21 May 1919.

80. Steirman, 169, 172; Towers to Daniels, 19 Sep 1919, quoting Read radio report of 20 May 1919.

81. Jackson to Office of the Chief of Naval Operations, 20 May 1919; Towers to Daniels, 19 Sep 1919, including relevant radio messages of 20 May 1919.

82. Knapp to Office of the Chief of Naval Operations, 20 May 1919; Towers to Daniels, 19 Sep 1919, including relevant messages of May 1919; *New York Times,* 28 May 1919; Smith, *First Across!,* 154–56; Daniels, *Years of War,* 568–70.

83. Steirman, 172–74. Bess Read remembered that being in Washington at the time "I was in the middle of this. There were friends of mine who were actually taking up sides on the matter" (13). Wrote Towers to Earle Johnson, 17 July 1919, "Needless to say, I was terribly disappointed" (E. F. Johnson, 217).

84. Towers to Navy Department, 21 May 1919; Towers' Seaplane Division 1 report, 3.

85. Steirman, 174; Towers, "Great Hop," 78; Smith, *First Across!,* 163–72, 177–78; Daniels, *Years of War,* 570.

86. Smith, *First Across!,* 179–86; *Flight Across,* 69.

87. Towers, "Great Hop," 78; Smith, *First Across!,* 187–88; *Atlanta Journal Magazine,* 24 Feb 1946; Towers to Daniels, 19 Sep 1919.

88. Smith, *First Across!,* 188–89; New York *World,* 29 June 1919; Towers, "Great Hop," 78; Read to wife, 10 June 1919, Read papers.

89. Smith, *First Across!,* 191–92; Gibbs-Smith, 180.

90. New York *Evening World,* 19 June 1919; Smith, *First Across!,* 192–93.

91. Smith, *First Across!,* 194–96; *New York Times,* 28 June 1919.

92. Towers' Seaplane Division 1 report, 7.

93. Smith, *First Across!,* 196; Lord, 594; Wilburn, 35; Bellinger to Pierre Towers, 3 Mar 1962; Read to Pierre Towers, [about Mar 1962]; Curtiss telegram to Byrd, 7 July 1919, Byrd papers. The telegram said, "Dinner given in honor of Comdr Raed [*sic*] and yourself as member of the N C one three and four crews. . . ." Towers wore his watch until he lost it years later while helping to raise the anchor of a large flying boat in San Pedro Harbor.

94. Smith, *First Across!,* 196, 201; navy secretary to Towers, 9 Dec 1935. Winner of the design competition was Catherine G. Barton of Englewood, New Jersey.

95. Daniels to Chairman Thomas S. Butler, 30 June 1919, in House Naval Affairs Committee hearings, vol. 1, 1919. By the bill, Read would have been jumped 267 numbers and Bellinger 4. See also 1920 hearings, vol. 2, 2955.

96. Plunkett to Benson, 16 July 1919; Towers to Daniels, 19 Sep 1919.

97. Benson's endorsement of Towers to Daniels, 19 Sep 1919; Daniels' endorsement and BuNav to Towers, 21 Oct 1919. In a letter of 3 Mar 1944 to Thomas A. Morgan, president of the Sperry Corporation, Daniels averred that he had "never had to decide a question which gave me more concern" and repeated his arguments for having Read go on without Towers. Also, Daniels claimed, during his first flight with Towers in 1913 "a lasting friendship was born between us." If so, it apparently did not last beyond his decision.

98. Bess Read, 18–19.

99. Towers, "Great Hop," 78.

100. Quoted in *Atlanta Journal Magazine,* 7 Sep 1919. The senator was William J. Harris.

101. Ibid.; Rome (evening) *Tribune News,* 7 Oct 1919. The *Journal* also published a photograph of "Towers and the crew of the NC-3," which was in fact Bellinger and the crew of the NC-1! Towers' field was soon swallowed up by urban sprawl.

CHAPTER 7. PEACETIME BATTLES AND BILLY MITCHELL, 1919–25

1. A minor index of Towers' fame was his being invited to attend a "High Jinx" affair at the celebrated Bohemian Club of the rich and famous near San Francisco, probably during 1920 or 1921 (Towers to Pierre, 11 Mar 1928).

2. Towers, Report of Medical Survey, 23 Aug 1933; Towers' medical history, 1926, 26 Apr 1927, 3 Jan 1928, and 8 Jan 1929; *Atlanta Journal Magazine,* 7 Sep 1919; Wilson, *Slipstream,* 115.

3. Towers remarked to Pierre on his religion, "I am not much of anything" (30 March 1926). See also letters of 15 Nov 1926 and 1 Jan 1927; van Deurs, oral transcript, 110–11. The first time he registered and voted was for a Republican Congressional candidate in San Diego in 1932. Clipping from unidentified clipping, Towers scrapbook.

4. Towers to Pierre, 6 Dec 1925, and 2 Jan, 15 Aug, 22 Nov 1926. Russell recalled an incident in 1945: "I have never seen anyone read so fast as Admiral Towers" (oral transcript, 226).

5. Towers, "Operations of Naval Aircraft," 382–85.

6. General Board hearings, 20 Aug 1917, 30, and 27–28 Mar 1919, 370; Lord, 570.

7. General Board hearings, 27–28 Mar 1919, 364–75, 381, 392.

8. Sudsbury, 59; Lord, 625–26.

9. Towers to Craven, 28 Aug 1919; *Aroostook* log, Dec 1919; Sudsbury, 50–51, 60–61, 64; Mustin diary, Dec 1919 and 6 Feb 1920, Mustin papers; Lord, 600–2; Taylor, *Mitscher,* 68; Turnbull and Lord, 155; Sudsbury, 64; Arpee, 51; Moffett to Sellers, 9, 27 Jan 1923 (hereafter all Moffett correspondence is from the Moffett papers). Towers relieved Lieutenant Commander Frank R. Berg '08 as exec.

10. Mustin diary, Dec 1919 and Feb 1920; Lord, 626; conversation with Lieutenant Commander Verne W. "Pappy" Harshman, former *Aroostook* crewman, in 1977; Lieutenant S. B. Fry to Tomb, 6 Dec 1920, Symington papers; Sudsbury, 75.

11. Mustin diary, Dec 1919–Apr 1920; Eileen Jackson, "Coronado Reported First in Affections of Duke and Duchess of Windsor," San Diego *Union,* 4 Aug 1946; Bocca, 31, 37, 44, 47; Duchess of Windsor, 72–81, 86. In 1920 the duke was pursuing one Geraldine Graham. Wallis' second married name was Simpson.

12. Mustin diary, Apr–June 1920; Arpee, 51–52; Taylor, *Mitscher,* 68–69; Sudsbury, 63, 69–70; *Aroostook* log, 1920; Lord, 647; Gibbs-Smith, 177n.

13. Lord, 633; Mustin diary, June–July 1920; *Aroostook* log, Aug 1920; Twining to Mustin, 26 Aug 1920; Mustin to Twining, 28 Aug, 20 Dec 1920; Rodman to Mustin, 9 Oct 1920; "Report of Board: Use of Naval Aircraft in Connection with Control of Gun Fire" [autumn 1920] Mustin papers; Towers to Mustin, tactical instructions for aircraft, 26 Oct 1920.

14. *Aroostook* log, Dec 1920; *Mugford* log, Dec 1920; *Lucky Bag, 1908,* 71; Knott, *Flying Boat,* 76.

15. Account taken from *Mugford* log, Dec 1920–Jan 1921; Mustin to Rodman, "Report of Flight from San Diego, Calif., to Balboa, Canal Zone," 19 Jan 1921; and Towers' medical reports, 4–20 Jan 1921.

16. Knott, *Flying Boat,* 76–77; Sudsbury, 77–78; Mustin, "Journal Balboa–San Diego Flight, Air Force Pacific Fleet 1921." Towers wrote to his brother William on 14 November 1943, "The only unpleasant after effects [of the operation] suffered was a bad deeply depressed scar, due to [the] fact I was so sick and weak I was left on my back for many weeks."

17. Morrow board hearings of 1925, 1638.

18. Sudsbury, 80–83.

19. Lord, 657, 687–88, 700–721, 852–53; Arpee, 83–96; Clark, 36; Melhorn, 69.

20. Lord, 646; E. F. Johnson, 232; Towers to brother William, 16 Sep 1921 and 2 Mar 1922.

21. Towers to brother William, 16 Sep 1921; Towers to BuNav, 15 Nov 1921. Jack sold the Cole automobile he had had at San Diego and had a new Templar delivered to Pensacola.

22. Marjorie called her father Mig or Miglet (Lynne L. Riley to the author, 29 Sep 1985).

23. *Navy Directory,* 1 Sep 1922.

24. Ketcham, oral transcript, 68; Doyle interview by Pierre Towers, about 1960; Clark, 10–11; Land, 117. Eight doctors also reported aboard in 1922 to train as the navy's first flight surgeons.

25. Lord, 762–68; Melhorn, 64–65, 72, 84–85; Roskill, *Naval Policy*, vol. 1, 322–24; "Naval Bases and Naval Stations, Pensacola," ZE file, Naval Historical Center. Pensacola's Station Field was renamed for Chevalier in 1936 (Coletta, *Domestic Bases,* 471).

26. Arpee, 124; Towers to Moffett, 11 July 1922; NAS Pensacola quarterly reports, 1 Jan–1 July 1922; Mustin to BuNav, 18 July 1922, Towers' BuAer file, National Archives; Land, 110.

27. Conversation with Pierre Towers in 1983; Towers' service file; Towers to brother William, 2 Mar, 15 Apr, 19 June 1922; Moffett to Christy, 17 Jan 1923; Christy to Moffett, 20 Jan 1923, National Archives.

28. Towers' physical exam for flying, 3 Feb 1923. Towers' color blindness went unnoticed.

29. Towers service file; Moffett to BuNav, 24 Jan 1923; Towers' orders of 13 Feb 1923; BuNav to Towers, 20 Feb 1923.

30. Mustin's orders of 30 July 1923 and first endorsement, 22 Aug 1923.

31. Holland, 20–22; Dorwart, *Conflict of Duty,* 38–41; Roskill, *Naval Policy,* vol. 1, 245, 529–30; General Board hearings of 1925, 402, 411–12.

32. Navy secretary to Towers, 20 Mar 1923; Towers to Lane Lacy, chief clerk of BuAer, 20 Apr, 8 May 1923; Lacy to Towers, 22 May 1923, Towers personnel file; O'Neil, 86–87; Swanborough, 121–22, 331–33; Arpee, 100.

33. BuAer to BuNav, 12 June 1923, Towers personnel file; Robinson and Keller, 137; Towers to Pierre, 4, 9 Sep 1925 and 7 June 1926.

34. Calhoun, vol. 3, 179, 199, 255, 271; Blake, 130, 150; Lily Towers to Towers, 17 May 1924; Towers to Pierre, 5 Feb 1926. Towers continued to find diversion through reading and maintained an account at Hatchard's bookstore in London (Towers to Pierre, 8 Nov 1925).

35. Towers to Pierre, 5 Nov 1925; conversation with Pierre Towers, 1983. Colonel Pierre de Grandmont had served with the marine infantry in colonial Tonkin (Indochina) and Senegal (Africa) before returning to France, transferring into the army, and getting married. He was killed in the Argonne while in command of the Thirteenth Infantry, 27 November 1914. Pierre was born 10 April 1902.

36. General Board hearings of 1925, 402–11, 413, 415–16; Roskill, *Naval Policy,* vol. 1, 248–49, 250ff, 356ff, 471ff; Towers to Fulton, 22 May [1924]; Lily Towers to Towers, 17 May 1924; Potter, *Halsey,* 119–22; Towers to Pierre, 2 Mar 1927; Towers' orders of 30 July 1923 for *Agamemnon* tests. His orders to Berlin, dated 4 April 1924, detached him from Rome 4 September, though the latter event did not actually occur until 8 November. Sec Nav Edwin Denby to Towers, 18 Apr 1923, gave Towers a $200 a month allowance "to cover extraordinary expenses."

37. Moffett to director of naval intelligence, 16 Mar 1925, Towers BuAer file, National Archives; Towers' orders of 19 May 1925; Towers to Pierre, 1, 6, 29 Oct and 6, 8 Dec 1925.

38. General Board hearings of 1925, 412.

39. Towers to Pierre, 25–29 Aug 1925; Pierre to Towers, 24 Aug 1926.

40. Towers to Pierre, 31 Aug, 1 Sep 1925.

41. Towers to Pierre, 1, 4 Sep 1925.

42. General Board hearings of 1925, 402–17, especially 411, 414–15; Melhorn, 93–94, 96.

43. Hurley, 90–101; Clark, 16–17; Arpee, 102–4.

44. Towers to Pierre, 15, 17 Sep 1925; Towers' orders to *Shenandoah* court, 15 Sep 1925.

45. Towers to Pierre, 4, 7, 9, 15 Sep, 1, 7, 19 Oct, 21 Nov, 14 Dec 1925. "Life with children is certainly complicated," he wrote her on 16 October.

46. Ibid., 1, 6 Oct, 25 Dec 1925; Robinson, 111ff. The *Shenandoah* court's findings were made public on 16 Jan 1926.

47. The eight members were Stanford University professor William F. Durand; Senator Hiram Bingham; retired Admiral Frank F. Fletcher; automotive-aeronautical engineer Howard Coffin; Congressman Carl Vinson; General James G. Harbord, president of RCA; circuit court judge Arthur C. Denison; and Congressman James C. Parker, an advocate of commercial aviation.

48. Towers to Pierre, 1, 6, 7 Oct 1925.

49. Moffett to Symington, 16 Feb 1925, in Arpee, 99; Hurley, 102–3.

50. Towers to Pierre, 7 Oct 1925. Mitchell had reverted to his permanent rank of colonel.

51. Melhorn, 95–97; Lord, 921; *New York Times*, 6, 7 Oct 1925.

52. Wilson, *Slipstream*, 62–65; Lord, 919–20; Moffett to Lieutenant Commander D. C. Ramsey, 13 Nov 1928, cited in Arpee, 117. By Commander Wilson's account, he and Lieutenant Commander Laurence T. DuBose, both on duty at BuAer but neither aviators, did the final editing of Moffett's prepared remarks. Wilson earned his wings the next year.

53. Towers to Pierre, 7, 14, 15 Oct 1925.

54. The *New York Times* ran the inaccurate headline "Towers Says Navy Unready for War" (17 Oct 1925). This account is taken from the statement of Commander John H. Towers, *Hearings before the President's Aircraft Board*, 16 Oct 1925, vol. 4, 1626–42 (author's italics).

55. Towers to Pierre, 7, 18, 29 Oct 1925.

56. Ibid., 15, 18, 19, 22, 27, 29 Oct 1925. The navy's two entries in the Schneider Cup did not finish owing to engine trouble. The army's Jimmy Doolittle won the competition.

57. Hurley, 101, 103–5; Towers to Pierre, 29 Oct, 2 Nov 1925.

58. Towers to Pierre, 2, 13 Nov 1925.

59. Ibid., 2, 4, 5, 8, 13, 19, 21, 22, 30 Nov, 1, 2, 8, 21 Dec 1925.

60. Ibid., 8, 13, 16 Nov, 14 Dec 1925.

61. Ibid., 13, 16, 19, 22 Nov, 8, 14 Dec 1925; *New York Times*, 15–18 Nov 1925. See Hook, 197–201.

62. Towers to Pierre, 22 Nov 1925. On 28 March 1935 Towers wrote to Congressman Carl Vinson, "As a matter of fact I have never before disclosed, I worked in Mr. Morrow's apartment many nights, assisting in the writing of the recommendations, after the Board had concluded its hearings." Durand only mentions the hotel room meetings (104).

63. Towers to Pierre, 22, 27 Nov, 1 Dec 1925.

64. Ibid., 1 Dec 1925, 12 Jan 1926; *New York Times*, 29 Nov 1925; *Washington Post*, 29 Nov 1925.

65. "Report of President's Aircraft Board," 30 Nov 1925, especially 5–6, 8, 12–14, 19–21, 23–26. Rear Admiral Harry E. Yarnell wrote to the CNO, Admiral William V. Pratt, on 4 April 1933, "I know for a fact that he [Towers] was mainly responsible for the writing of the Morrow Board Report . . ." (Standley papers). That "fact," however, had no doubt been provided by Towers, in 1933 Yarnell's own chief of staff. On 30 June 1943 Towers wrote to Vice Admiral F. J. Horne, "I was largely responsible for saving the day during the times of the Morrow Board" (Naval Historical Center). The only allusion to Mitchell in the report was the statement "We are not primarily concerned with questions of Army discipline," which had to "be dealt with through the ordinary channels," although the board inferred Mitchell was guilty of negligence in not preventing crashes of the army planes he criticized as being "flaming coffins" (3, 18–19).

66. Morrow Board report, 24–25.

67. Towers to Pierre, 1, 6, 14, 16 Dec 1925 and 21 Sep 1926, in which he noted Warner as his own recommendation.

68. Arpee, 114–17; Lord, 938.

69. Towers to Pierre, 1, 14 Dec 1925 and 29 Apr 1926.

70. Ibid., 21, 25 Dec 1925; Hurley, 105–7; Lord, 809–11.

71. Towers to Pierre, 8, 14, 16, 21, 25, 28 Dec 1925.

72. Ibid., 25 Dec 1925.

73. Ibid., 25, 28, 31 Dec 1925.

CHAPTER 8. CARRIER TACTICIAN, 1926–28

1. Towers to Pierre, 28 June, 9, 12 Jan 1926; Tate, 64.

2. Towers had given Jackson a ride in the old C-1 back in 1913 (C-1 log, 28 Feb 1913).

3. Administrative History 36, 5, 9; *Class of 1906*, 125; Arpee, 114–15; Moffett to Shoemaker,

19 Nov 1926, revealing promises made "six months ago", Towers' BuAer file, National Archives; Potter, *Nimitz,* 136–37. In E. J. King's view, Robison was "a great friend of Nimitz" and "helped him along, but in ability just so so" (King's comments to Whitehill in King papers, 31 July 1949, 5).

4. *Lucky Bag, 1909,* dedication page; Hayes, part 1, 51–52; Andrews, 97–100; Land oral transcript, 126; Wilson oral transcript, 352, 356–60.

5. Hayes, part 1, 52–53; Andrews, 107–13; Towers to Pierre, 18 Jan 1926; *Langley* log, 15–18 Jan 1926.

6. Towers to Pierre, 9 Jan, 5 Feb 1926 (he thought the "sea routine" was still "rather a dull life"); *Langley* log, Jan 1926; Friedman, *Aircraft Carriers,* 36; Tate, 64–68; *Langley* log, Jan 1926; Wilson, *Slipstream,* 116–17. All the fundamental features of the navy's first carrier had been the work primarily of Ken Whiting, Chevy Chevalier, and Lieutenants A. M. Pride and F. W. Pennoyer, Jr.

7. Towers to Pierre, 12 Jan 1926.

8. Ibid., 9, 12, 21, 27, 28, 31 Jan, 5 Feb, 7 June 1926; Towers' "annual and flying physical examinations," 26 Jan 1926, approved by BuMed, 6 Feb 1926.

9. Towers to Pierre, 21, 27, 31 Jan, 5, 8, 10, 15, 24, 25 Feb 1926; *Langley* log, 16, 17 Feb 1926; Potter, *Nimitz,* 139–41.

10. Towers to Pierre, 24, 25 Feb 1926; *Langley* log, 23 Feb 1926; Administrative History 36, 13–15.

11. Towers to Pierre, 3, 5, 14 Mar 1926; *Langley* log, 1, 4, 6, 8, 11 Mar 1926.

12. Towers to Pierre, 30 Mar, 14 Apr 1926.

13. Ibid., 7 June 1926, 29 Oct 1925 and 5, 25 Feb, 30 Mar, 5, 14, 22 Apr, 21 May 1926; conversations with Pierre Towers, 1985–86. Her mother counseled her, "If you marry a foreigner, you marry a country as well as the man."

14. Towers to Pierre, 5 Feb, 5, 9, 19, 29 Apr, 17, 21 May, 7, 28 June, 17 July 1926. Retired as lieutenant commander, Wead joined MGM studios in 1929.

15. Ibid., 22 Apr, 12 May 1926.

16. Hughes quoted in *Bellinger,* "Gooney Bird," 217–19.

17. Towers to Pierre, 9, 12, 17 May 1926.

18. Moffett to Shoemaker, 19 Nov 1926; Towers to Pierre, 3, 7 June 1926; Rear Admiral Ben Scott Custer, aide to McCrary when he commanded NAS Pensacola in 1933–34, to the author, 30 Sep 1986. Custer wrote, "Frank McCrary was the finest Naval officer I ever knew: a splendid sailor, a good naval aviator, an imperturbable administrator, with wide and broad experience. He was wise and judicious in his decisions and possessed of the highest integrity of anyone I've known."

19. Pierre to Towers, 2, 12 May 1926; *New York Times,* 28 Aug 1926.

20. *Langley* log, May 1926. In 1926 VF-1 included future wartime carrier skippers Lieutenants Ernest W. Litch, John Perry, Felix L. Baker, W. G. Tomlinson, Carlos W. Wieber, and Lieutenant (jg) Frank Akers.

21. Towers to Pierre, 31 May, 3, 14 June 1926; Zogbaum, 421; Pride, 32; *Langley* log, May 1926.

22. Towers to Pierre, 3, 7, 14, 19, 28 June, 23 July 1926; *Langley* log, June 1926. Towers moved into a house at 1121 Alameda, Coronado, late in June, where Tyke got into many scraps. As Towers wrote Pierre, wire-haired terriers "are perfect devils for fighting and getting into all kinds of trouble" (5 Mar 1926).

23. *Langley* log, July–Aug 1926; Towers to Pierre, 13, 17 July 1926; *Navy Directory, 1926–27.* Included were future wartime carrier captains H. B. "Beauty" Martin, S. J. Michael, George H. Seitz, Ben H. Wyatt, and G. B. H. Hall. With Ellyson to observe was Lieutenant Commander Wadleigh Capehart, also assigned to the *Lexington*'s fitting-out detail.

24. Towers to Pierre, 17, 29 July 1926.

25. Ibid., 20, 23 July 1926.

26. Ibid., 28 June, 6, 13, 17, 20, 23 July, 1, 24 Aug 1926.

27. Ibid., 6, 10 Aug 1926; Swanborough, 128–29; Towers to Moffett, 10 Nov 1926, Towers BuAer files, National Archives; Sudsbury, 120; Bogan, 98; *Langley* log, Aug 1926.

28. Towers to Pierre, 10, 15 Aug, 1 Sep 1926; Hayes, part 1, 53–54; van Deurs, *Ellyson*, 220; *Langley* log, Aug 1926; Oliver Jensen's notes on Ramsey, 24 Feb 1944, Jensen papers. Ramsey relieved Lieutenant Commander H. F. Floyd on 20 August; he was married on the twenty-fifth.

29. *Langley* log, Sep 1926; Towers to Pierre, 21, 25 Sep 1926.

30. Towers to Pierre, 1, 8, 21, 25 Sep, 9, 15, 25 Oct, 15 Nov, 3 Dec 1926.

31. Sudsbury, 120; Towers to Pierre, 25, 29 Oct 1926; *Langley* log, Oct 1926; Andrews, 113–15; Love, 52. VF-5 was simultaneously experimenting with dive bombing on the East Coast, and the marines were using the technique against Nicaraguan insurgents.

32. Towers to Pierre, 29 Oct, 9, 15, 18, 22, 28 Nov, 15 Dec 1926 and 10 Jan 1927.

33. Sudsbury, 120; *Langley* log, Oct–Nov 1926; Towers to Pierre, 9, 18, 22, 28, 29 Nov 1926; Melhorn, 99.

34. Towers to Pierre, 29 Nov, 3, 9, 15, 20, 28, 31 Dec 1926 and 1 Jan 1927; Moffett to Shoemaker, 19 Nov 1926; Towers' orders of 8 Dec 1926.

35. Wilson, *Slipstream,* 115; Zogbaum, 420; Towers to Pierre, 30 Mar 1926.

36. Towers to Pierre, 4 Jan 1927; *Langley* log, Jan 1927.

37. Towers to Pierre, 10, 19 Jan, 3, 10, 16 Feb 1927; *Langley* log, Jan–Feb 1927; Towers' medical history, 19 Jan 1927; Swanborough, 56–57.

38. Towers to Pierre, 22 Feb, 2, 3 Mar 1927.

39. Hayes, part 1, 55; Administrative History 36, 16–18; Towers to Pierre, 4 Mar 1927; Pierre to the author, 9 Dec 1978.

40. Towers to Pierre, 18 Mar 1927; *Langley* log, Mar–Apr 1927; *Class of 1906,* 28. Towers visited with the commandant of Guantanamo Bay, Commander Charles S. Soule, Jr., and his wife, "great friends," and with his cousin's husband, Captain Kenneth Castleman, skipper of the repair ship *Vestal.*

41. Loening, 101–3; *Langley* log, Mar–Apr 1927; Administrative History 36, 16–18; Melhorn, 59.

42. *New York Times,* 21 Dec 1927; Marconigrams, Towers to Pierre on SS *Olympic,* 30 Apr, 3 May 1927; conversation with Pierre in 1985. They had been separated in London on 25 August 1925.

43. Conversation with Pierre in 1985; Towers to Pierre, 22 July, 11, 20 Sep, 17 Oct 1927.

44. *Langley* log, May 1927; Lord, 995–97; Sudsbury, 121.

45. *Langley* log, May–Sep 1927; Towers to Pierre, 25, 27, 29 May, 2, 8, 18, 25 June, 6, 9, 18 July 1927; Sudsbury, 121; flight logs, June–Sep 1927, Molten papers.

46. Towers to Pierre, 30 June, 4, 9, 11, 15, 18, 22, 26 July, 14 Oct 1927; conversation with Pierre in 1985.

47. *Langley* log, 17 Aug 1927; Towers to Pierre, 17, 25 Aug 1927; Sudsbury, 121–22; conversation in 1985 with Mrs. Eleanor Storrs, who as Mrs. Morton T. Seligman had been present at the party. The crew of the *Langley,* originally 305 men, eventually swelled to 468 with the full air complement aboard.

48. *Langley* log, Aug–Sep 1927; Towers to Pierre, 25 Aug 1927; Molten flight log, 21 Aug 1927; Sudsbury, 121–22. In September Towers served as senior member of a board of inquiry into the details of an incident in which two navy pilots were killed. Their plane crashed on takeoff from North Island en route to Oakland to enter the Dole race.

49. *Langley* log, Aug–Sep 1927; Towers to Pierre, 29 Aug, 3, 20 Sep 1927; Wilbur to Towers, 15 Sep 1927, endorsed by Reeves, 27 Sep 1927.

50. Towers to Pierre, 18 July, 20 Sep, 8, 11 Nov 1927; *Langley* log, Sep–Nov 1927; Wilson oral transcript, 352–53. See Young on one Japanese agent in southern California during the 1930s (89ff).

51. Towers to Pierre, 14, 17 Oct 1927; *Langley* log, Oct 1927.

52. Towers to Pierre, 17, 22 Oct 1927; conversation with Herman "Gene" Northway, former *Langley* crewman, in 1986.

53. Wilson, *Slipstream,* 111–12; Towers to Pierre, 31 Oct 1927.

54. Wilson oral transcript, 258; Wilson, *Slipstream,* 116; Andrews, 130.

55. Wilson oral transcript, 258–59, 354; Wilson, *Slipstream,* 116–19.

56. Towers to Pierre, 11, 16, 20 Sep, 22, 31 Oct, 5, 8 Nov, 9, 17 Dec 1927 and 4 Jan 1928; Lily to Towers, 7 July 1927.

57. Towers to Pierre, 8, 30 Nov, 6, 9, 14, 17 Dec 1927; *Langley* log, Nov–Dec 1927.

58. Towers to Pierre, 25 Oct 1927. He noted the use of electric dinner candles to minimize the risk of fire.

59. *Langley* log, 20 Dec 1927; Long Beach *Independent,* 21 Dec 1927, Wilson papers; Towers to Pierre, 28 Dec 1927; *New York Times,* 21 Dec 1927.

60. Towers to Pierre, 26, 28, 31 Dec 1927 and 4 Jan 1928; conversation with Gene Northway in 1986; *New York Times,* 21 Dec 1927; chief of C&R, endorsement to court of inquiry, 21 May 1929.

61. Secretary of the Navy C. F. Adams to BuNav chief R. H. Leigh, 29 June 1929; Secretary of the Navy Claude A. Swanson to Towers, 15 Apr 1935. The court of inquiry was headed by Lieutenant Commander Alva D. Bernhard and included Lieutenant Commanders Bogan and J. E. Ostrander, Jr., and Lieutenant Ward C. Gilbert.

62. Wilson oral transcript, 355–56; Ramsey to Land, 9 Apr 1928, Ramsey papers.

63. Wilson oral transcript, 390; Towers to Pierre, 17 Jan 1928, enclosed message of 16 Jan from commander in chief Battle Fleet; from Towers to Pierre, 20, 23 Jan 1928; Towers' medical history for 24 Jan 1928; BuNav to Towers, physical waiver of 10 July 1928; Towers to Moffett, 10 Feb 1928; Melhorn, 101; Ramsey to Land, 9 Apr 1928; Towers to Board of Medical Survey, 4 Mar 1936. The civilian physician was a Dr. Hosmer of San Diego.

64. Towers to Pierre, 31 Jan, 4, 11, 17 Mar 1928. Ken Whiting was especially anxious to relieve him but did not (Ramsey to Land, 16 Apr 1928).

65. Towers to Pierre, 23 Feb, 2 Mar 1928; Ramsey to Land, 24 Feb 1928; *Langley* log, Feb 1928; Taylor, *Mitscher,* 82–84; CNO to AlNav, 12 Jan 1928, National Archives; van Deurs, *Ellyson,* 229–34. Towers made no mention of Ellyson's death in his surviving correspondence.

66. See Friedman, *Aircraft Carriers,* 43–44, for the increase of the *Saratoga* and *Lexington* displacements above the 33,000 tons allowed by the Washington Treaty.

67. Towers to Pierre, 27 Mar 1927; Wilson oral transcript, 363–64a (390–91); Andrews, 130–31.

68. Wilson oral transcript, 364a (392); Towers to Pierre, 31 Mar 1928; Wilson, *Slipstream,* 123–24.

69. Ramsey to Land, 9 Apr 1928; Towers to Pierre, 5, 9 Apr 1928.

70. Ramsey to Land, 16 Apr 1928; Towers to Pierre, 9, 12 Apr 1928; *Langley* log, Apr 1928; Wilson, *Slipstream,* 122–25.

71. Towers to Pierre, 17, 22, 26 Apr 1928; Administrative History 36, 19–22; Wilson, *Slipstream,* 125.

72. Towers to Pierre, 31 Mar, 22, 26 Apr 1928; *Langley* log, Apr 1928; Sudsbury, 125.

73. Towers to Pierre, 11, 15, 18, 24 May, 1, 9 June 1928; Wilson, *Slipstream,* 125–27; Wilson oral transcript, 315–16 (396–97); Administrative History 36, 21–22; *Langley* log, Apr–June 1928; Hayes, part 1, 54.

74. Towers to Pierre, 18, 24 May, 9 June 1928; Wilson, *Slipstream,* 127; Hayes, part 1, 55; Andrews, 131–34.

75. Towers to Pierre, 4, 7, 11 May, 9, 20 June, 25 July 1928.

76. William A. Riley, Jr., 149–51. The official change of VF-5B and VF-6B to VB-1B and VB-2B respectively took place 1 July 1928.

77. BuAer (King) to BuNav, 10 Sep 1928; Wilbur to Reeves, 15 Sep 1928; Reeves to Towers, 15 Oct 1928; BuNav (Leigh) to Towers, 22 Oct 1928; Moffett to Towers, 30 Oct 1928; Towers to Pierre, 25 July, 13 Aug 1928; *Langley* log, July–Aug 1928; Andrews, 234.

78. Herbert Hoover to Towers, 4 Sep 1929.

79. Towers to Pierre, 24 May, 11 July, 3, 13 Aug 1928; Towers to brother William, 15 May 1929; Sudsbury, 132.

80. Sudsbury, 128, 130, 132; Towers to Pierre, 19 Aug, 7 Sep 1928; *Langley* log, Aug, Oct

1928; Towers' orders of 16 Aug 1928, and Reeves' endorsement of 25 Aug 1928. Towers' permanent relief on the *Langley* in October was Captain A. B. Cook, a new pilot.

CHAPTER 9. CHIEF OF AIR STAFFS, ASHORE AND AFLOAT, 1928–33

1. Wilson oral transcript, 351.
2. Towers to Pierre, 20 Sep 1928; Towers to Moffett, 7 July 1933.
3. Chandler, 345, 484–86; Captain Timothy J. O'Brien to Thomas B. Buell, 11 Aug 1974, King papers; Wilson oral transcript, [249].
4. Towers book review, 1139–40. Moffett wrote to W. K. Wrigley on 7 May 1928, "I enjoy a fight and am perfectly willing to keep it up as long as I can accomplish results. . . ."
5. Moffett to Wrigley, 11 Feb 1925; Towers to Pierre, 25 Jan, 4 Feb 1929; Moffett to Navy Secretary Wilbur, 17 Jan 1929, endorsed by chief of BuNav Leigh, 18 Jan 1929; Wilbur to House Committee on Naval Affairs, 24 Jan 1929; Washington *Daily News*, 12 Dec 1928.
6. Moffett to Wrigley, 13 Oct 1928; Wilson oral transcript, [438]. For an overview of Moffett, see Reynolds, "Moffett."
7. Towers to Moffett, "Comment on Report of Standley Board," 2 Oct 1928; Arpee, 117–20. The fatality had occurred in November 1927 to Lieutenant Commander M. B. McComb.
8. Towers to Pierre, 20 Sep, 8, 26 Oct 1928.
9. General Board hearings of 25 Sep 1928, 287–89, of 2 Oct 1928, 295–96, and of 9 Oct 1928, 306–10.
10. Moffett to Senator Joseph T. Robinson, 7 Feb 1931; Moffett to Wrigley, 26 Jan 1929; Moffett to Ramsey, 13 Nov, 11 Dec 1928; Ramsey to Moffett, 7 Dec 1928; Arpee, 153.
11. Towers to Pierre, 14 Nov 1928 and 16, 25 Jan, 4, 9 Feb 1929; *New York Times*, 28 Jan 1929; Arpee, 149.
12. Wilson oral transcript, [265, 327]; Palmer, 36; Daniel V. Gallery to Thomas B. Buell, 21 Aug 1974, King papers.
13. Hayes, part 2, 51–56; Wilson oral transcript, 353–54, 409–15.
14. Ramsey to Wilson, 7 Nov 1928, Ramsey papers; King's comments to Whitehill, 31 July 1949, 5, and on Towers specifically, 3 July 1950, King papers; Arpee, 154; *Washington Post*, 19 Apr 1929; Towers' orders of 16 Apr 1929; Towers to brother William, 15 May 1929. Towers relieved King on 24 April 1929. In addition to King, Towers' predecessors as assistant BuAer chief were Mustin, Albert W. Johnson, Whiting, Rodgers, and Land.
15. Towers to Pierre, 20, 22, 29, 30 Sep, 3, 13 Oct, 24, 28 Nov 1928 and 3, 18, 25 Jan, 4 Feb 1929; Towers to brother William, 15 May 1929; *New York Times*, 21 Feb 1929; conversation with Pierre in 1985. On 20 February 1929 Lily married Martin B. Saportas, a wealthy banker of New York whose Reno divorce had been completed earlier the same month. He would lose everything in the stock market crash, whereupon Lily would open a successful dress shop in New York. They lived on Fifth Avenue.
16. Towers to Pierre, 26 Oct, 28 Nov, 3 Dec 1928 and 16, 18 Jan, 13, 18 Feb 1929; Towers' medical history, exam of 8 Jan 1929; Ceres to BuNav, 15 Jan 1929, third endorsement by Moffett, 30 Jan 1929; BuMed reply of 16 Feb 1929; BuNav to Towers, 1 Mar 1929, with Towers' penciled comments, Towers' BuAer file, National Archives; Towers to BuMed, 4 Mar 1936. The civilian physician was a Dr. Greene of Washington, the same doctor who had assisted in the original examination of the injured eye in 1906.
17. Molten to Ingalls, 20 Mar 1930, Molten papers; Moffett to Land, 25 Nov 1929; Moffett to Wrigley, 26 Nov 1929; Moffett to Porter Adams, 14 Nov 1929; Moffett to Towers, 25 Mar 1930; Wilson, *Slipstream*, 81–89; Clark, 31–32; Moffett to Captain J. H. Gunnell, 3 June 1930; Ramsey to Land, and Ramsey to Harry F. Guggenheim, 20 Apr 1929; Land to Ramsey, 29 Apr 1929, Ramsey papers.

18. Towers quoted in Arpee, 158; Moffett to Towers, 17 Feb 1930; W. J. Allen, 36; Molten to Ingalls, 29 Jan 1936, Molten papers. Towers also renewed his acquaintance with Assistant Secretary of War (Aeronautics) F. Trubee Davison, sparkplug of the wartime First Yale Unit (Davison to Towers, 9 June 1931).

19. Dyer, vol. 1, 107–8; *Navy Directory,* 1 Apr 1929, 1 July 1930; Towers to Moffett, 24 Jan 1930; Moffett to Towers, 10 Feb 1930.

20. Towers to Moffett, 24 Jan, 12 Feb 1930; Moffett to Towers, 10 Feb 1930; Moffett to White, 29 Mar 1930; Wheeler, *Pratt,* 283.

21. Moffett to Rear Admiral J. L. Latimer, 3 May 1930; Moffett to King, 8 Aug 1930; King to Towers, 3 Feb 1930, King papers.

22. King to Towers, 3 Feb 1930; Towers to King, 10 Feb 1930, King papers. Between 1929 and 1931 the number of pilots went from 520 to 737 (officers) and from 173 to 330 (enlisted). In fiscal 1929, 203,731 flights were made, totaling more than 203,000 hours. Each pilot averaged 216 hours (compared with 182 the previous year and 72 in 1922). During the year the total flying hours per fatal accident increased from 7,226 to 11,288. Eighteen fatalities in fiscal 1930 set a low record of 19,070 hours per accident (BuAer annual report of 1929, 9–10, 49; of 1930, 8; and of 1931, 1; Dyer, vol. 1, 108).

23. BuAer annual report of 1929, 3–4, 17, 48; of 1930, 1; and of 1931, 1; Trimble, 175–98; Moffett to Lieutenant A. R. Mead, 2 Apr 1930; Turnbull and Lord, 226–27. In 1928–29 the navy accepted 423 new planes and 900 engines: 68 fighters, the F4B and F8C; 181 scouts, the O2U and OL-8; 46 flying boats, mostly the Martin PM; 23 torpedo bombers, mostly the Great Lakes TG; and 103 trainers, mostly the Consolidated NY. These figures do not include a few experimental and obsolete planes. The engines were mostly Wright Cyclones and Pratt and Whitney Hornets and Wasps.

24. Navy Secretary Adams to President Hoover, 5 July 1929; Towers' orders of 24 Oct, 26 Nov 1929; Roland, vol. 2, 429; *History of NACA,* 2–5; Molten to Ingalls, 20 Mar 1930; Sudsbury, on Towers in the budget hearings, 17 Mar 1930, 142–43.

25. King to BuNav, 7 Sep 1928; Towers' orders of Oct 1928, 28 Feb, 12 June 1929, and May 1930; Towers to Pierre, 3 Oct 1928.

26. Moffett log book, Aug 1929, Smithsonian copy; Towers' orders of May 1929 and May 1930; *New York Times,* 30 Nov 1929, in which Towers paid tribute to the "rare courage and unusual qualities of leadership" Dick Byrd demonstrated in his recent flight to the South Pole.

27. Clark, 33–34; Hayes, part 2, 53–55; Towers to Moffett, 24 Jan, 3, 17 Feb 1930; Moffett to Towers, 17, 28 Feb 1930; Moffett to Gunnell, 3 June 1930; Ingalls to Moffett, 6 Feb 1930; Moffett to Ingalls, 30 Sep 1931.

28. Towers to BuAer chief, 23 Apr 1930; Towers' orders of 24 Apr 1930; Moffett to Towers, 3, 17 Feb 1930; Lord, 998–1003.

29. General Board hearings of 2, 9 Oct 1928 and 6 Feb 1929, 18–19; of 23 Apr 1929, 102; of 1 Oct 1929, 234–35, 247–51; of 27 Nov 1929, 298–99; of 23 June 1930, 228–32; of 30 Dec 1930, 716–21; and of 20 Apr 1931, 80–82, 91, 93–94, 96, 98, 103, 106–8, 110. See also Hone and Mandeles, 88–92.

30. General Board hearings of 1 May 1931, 152. In this hearing, when one officer complained about having to use the awkward terms "heavier than air" and "lighter than air," Towers explained, "Those terms are used internationally. I don't think myself they are very happy selections but I have no substitute to offer" (141).

31. For Towers' assistance to Moffett before he left, see Ibid., 151, 153; and 27 May 1931, 190; Lord, 946–47, 989–1000; and Clark, 36–37.

32. Towers to Moffett, 7 Feb 1930; House appropriations subcommittee hearings of 1930, 494–621. Among the key witnesses were Kelly Turner, Sidney Kraus, and Garland Fulton.

33. French to Moffett, 12 Mar 1930; Pugh to Moffett, 8 Feb 1930. See Albion, *Makers,* 472.

34. Moffett to Pugh, 28 Feb 1930; Ingalls to Moffett, 6 Feb 1930; Moffett to Ingalls, 24 Feb 1930; Moffett to Towers, 23 Jan, 17 Feb 1930; Moffett to Mead, 2 Apr 1930.

35. Moffett to Towers, 23 Jan, 3, 16, 17, 24 Feb, 31 Mar 1930; Arpee, 169–70; Towers to Moffett, 7 Feb 1930; Towers to Pierre, 9 Feb 1930.

36. Moffett to Towers, 2 Apr 1930; Moffett to Gunnell, 3 June 1930; Moffett to Ingalls, 30 Sep 1931; Moffett to Murray, 4 June 1930; Moffett to Land, 1 July 1930; O'Connor, *Equilibrium,* 76–77; Arpee, 173–77; General Board hearings of 4 Dec 1930, 641–70; of 23 Dec 1930, 716–21; and of 27 May 1931, 189–91; Lord, 1001–3.

37. Undated clipping, probably *Washington Post; New York Times,* 24 May 1930.

38. *Washington Post,* 7 June 1930; conversation with Pierre Towers in 1985; *Washington Post* feature story on Towers, 24 Nov 1929; Curtiss to Towers, 30 June 1930; Towers to Curtiss, 14 Jan 1930; *New York Times,* 1 Aug 1930.

39. Towers' orders of 28 June, 24 July 1930; Towers to Pierre, probably 14 July 1930; Roseberry, *Curtiss,* 455–56; Towers, "Twenty Years of Naval Aviation," 1931, 15, unpublished manuscript apparently written at the instigation of journalist Phil Patchin; Towers to Patchin, 15 Sep 1931.

40. Towers' service record of 16 June 1944; Towers' receipt of commission, 3 Jan 1931, also to date from 1 July 1930.

41. Lily to Towers, 7 July 1927; Towers to Pierre, 29 Apr 1928, and 19, 20 Nov 1929; conversation with Pierre in 1986; *New York Times,* 10 Aug 1930. Pierre strongly denied later claims (Jensen, 38) that five navy planes flew overhead during the ceremony (conversation in 1986). The other groomsmen were Commander A. H. "Gus" Gray, head of BuAer administration and a submariner; Lieutenant Commander John E. Ostrander, who had flown for Towers off the *Langley;* Lieutenants Ralph Ofstie and A. P. "Putt" Storrs, both top pilots; Lieutenant Commander J. Holmes Magruder; and Colonel T. C. "Tommy" Turner and Major Burdette Wright, Marine Corps aviators.

42. Towers to Slocum, 19 Aug 1930; Towers' orders of 10, 29 Aug 1930; conversation with Pierre in 1985; Jensen notes.

43. Jensen file; miscellaneous clippings, probably from the *Washington Post,* early 1931, and "These Fascinating Ladies," Feb 1939.

44. *New York Times,* 4 Nov 1930; Towers' endorsement of 23 Nov 1930 to orders of 1 Nov 1930; Towers to Moffett, 10 Nov 1930; Zogbaum, 421. The streamlined two-seat F8C-4 Helldiver had a 600-horsepower Wright Cyclone engine and a special cowling to give it a high speed of 180 mph; the cockpit was enclosed and lined for warmth, even at night. The plane was designated the XO2C-2.

45. Zogbaum, 421–28.

46. Heinlein to Thomas B. Buell, 3–13 Oct 1974, 36, King papers. Heinlein believed the incident to have indeed occurred in the Caribbean, with Towers in command of the *Langley.* However, November 1930 was the only time King and Heinlein were on the *Lexington* and Towers on the *Langley* when the two ships passed one another (*Fleet Admiral King,* 217–18).

47. Sudsbury, 147–48; Zogbaum, 421–28.

48. Moffett to King, 8 Aug 1930; Moffett to Towers, 9 Sep 1930; Moffett to Ingalls, 12 Sep, 10 Nov 1930; Moffett to Frank A. Tichenor of *Aero Digest,* 14 Jan 1931; House appropriations subcommittee hearings, 23 Jan 1931, 450–55. Towers paper, "Modern Development of Aircraft," Washington, 23 Apr 1931, 7. At the hearings Towers testified only on maintenance and repair of arresting gear and landing fields at NAS San Diego. Woodhouse shows contrasting Army Air Corps appropriations in millions at $24 in 1929, $34 in 1930, $36 in 1931, and $31 in 1932 ("Policies," 174).

49. *New York Times,* 31 Jan, 12 Mar 1931; Hayes, Part 1, 56–57; part 2, 55–56; Towers' orders of 18 May 1931; Towers to Joseph S. Ames of NACA, 21 May 1931; General Board hearing of 27 May 1931; Moffett to Towers, 16 July 1931; Towers to Moffett, 7 July 1931; Towers to Molten, 17 July 1931; Molten to Towers, 25 July 1931, Molten papers.

50. Towers to Moffett, 7 July 1931; Molten to Towers, 25 July 1931; Moffett to Towers, 22 Aug 1931. Still, Moffett wrote to Towers on 16 July 1931, "Cook has taken hold excellently and his knowledge of Fleet operations is proving to be very valuable. This is unusual."

51. Commander Archer M. R. Allen, "Across the Continent by Automobile," March 1931, Naval War College; Pierre to author, 9 Dec 1978; conversation with Pierre in 1985; Towers' endorsements to orders of 18 May 1931; Towers to Moffett, 7 July 1931.

52. *Navy Directory,* 1 July 1931; Towers to Molten, 17 July 1931; Towers to Moffett, 13 July

1932. Rodd was later killed in a cross-country flight and replaced by Kleber S. Masterson (Masterson oral transcript, 31).

53. Fredericks, n.p., ZE files, Naval Historical Center; Towers to Molten, 14 Sep, 21 Oct 1931; Towers to Moffett, 14 Oct 1931.

54. Radford, "Aircraft Battle Force," 18; Zogbaum, 450.

55. Conversation with former *Saratoga* crewman John Nevin in 1986; Towers to Molten, 21 Oct 1931; Riley, "Light Bombing," 150; Towers to Moffett, 14 Oct 1931; *Navy Directory,* 1 July 1931; *Saratoga* log, 1931; Clark, 46.

56. H. S. Duckworth to Buell, 6 Aug 1974; Heinlein to Buell, 3 Oct 1974; Thomas J. Nixon III to Buell, 1 Aug 1974; Robert J. Beebe to Buell, 2 Oct 1974, King papers; conversation with Paul Pihl in 1981; Clark, 44–45, 47–48; Radford, "Aircraft Battle Force," 18–19; *Fleet Admiral King,* 219.

57. Towers to Molten, 14 Sep 1939; Molten to Towers, 21 Oct 1931; Molten to Sherman, 22 June 1931, Molten papers; Towers to Moffett, 17 Aug 1931; Sudsbury, 157, 160–61. *Lexington* pilot Lieutenant George D. Price's wife had been fatally injured falling from her hotel window after an attempted rape, causing a furor that tied up the senior carrier staffs for two weeks in August (Heinlein to Buell, 3 Oct 1974; *New York Times,* 24, 25 Aug 1931).

58. Molten to Towers, 19 Nov 1931.

59. Radford, "Aircraft Battle Force," 19; Markey, 65; Loening, 189; Ballentine oral transcript, 176.

60. Ballentine oral transcript, 177–80, 184; Radford, "Aircraft Battle Force," 19; *Fleet Admiral King,* 228–29; Read oral transcript, 433; Loening, "On Board U.S.S. SARATOGA," 12 Feb 1932, mimeographed on board, 14 Mar 1932; Towers' Princeton '26 talk.

61. Administrative History 36, 97–104; Ballentine oral transcript, 185–89; *Fleet Admiral King,* 229–31; King report, 20 Mar 1932, King papers.

62. Administrative History 36, 104–7; Towers to Moffett, 25 Mar 1932; Moffett to Towers, 31 Mar 1932.

63. Administrative History 36, 107; Towers to Moffett, 16 June 1932.

64. Radford, "Aircraft Battle Force," 20–22.

65. Moffett to Towers, 29 Apr 1932; Towers to Pierre, 16 May 1932; Towers' medical survey, 23 Aug 1933.

66. Moffett to Yarnell, 7 May 1932; Moffett to Upham, 9 May 1932, Towers BuAer file, National Archives; Towers' orders of 11 May 1932, with endorsements; Towers to Pierre, 17 May 1932.

67. Towers to Moffett, 16 Nov 1932; Towers to Pierre, 16, 17, 19 May 1932. In these three letters Towers gave a detailed account of how he adroitly solicited and obtained the support of Ingalls and several senators and representatives. Towers wrote to Horne on 30 June 1943, "When I was Chief of Staff to Admiral Yarnell in 1932 Admiral Moffett brought me to Washington for temporary duty to fight another battle, which I did" (Naval Historical Center).

68. Towers to Moffett, 19 July, 16 Nov 1932.

69. Towers to Pierre, 16, 19 May 1932; Towers' physical exams, 8 Jan, 15 Dec 1932, 27 Jan 1932, and 13 Jan 1933.

70. Moffett to Yarnell, 22 Jan 1932; Towers to Pierre, 16, 17, 19 May 1932; Moffett to Towers, 10, 30 Aug 1932.

71. Towers' orders of 31 May 1932 and endorsements; Moffett to Vinson, 22 Nov 1932; Towers to Pierre, 16 May 1932; Towers telegram to Pierre, 15 May 1932; Moffett to Yarnell 11 June, 19 July 1932; Towers to Moffett, 16 June, 13 July 1932; Yarnell to Upham, 16 June 1932, Yarnell papers; Molten to Towers, 3 June 1932; Molten to Ingalls, 19 Sep 1932, Molten papers.

72. Moffett to Towers, 9 July 1932, reporting conversations of 8, 9 July; Moffett to Ingalls, 26 July 1932.

73. Moffett to Towers, 9, 25 July 1932; Towers to Moffett, 9, 19 July 1932; Moffett to Yarnell, 19 July 1932.

74. Moffett to Ingalls, 7 Sep 1932; Zogbaum, 444, 447. The *Saratoga* ran aground off Sunset Beach, California, on 18 August 1932. Rear Admiral William D. Leahy, commanding scouting force

destroyers, sat on the court-martial and on 14 October 1932 wrote to Rear Admiral Tom Craven, "The accident was one of those D— things that happen because of an unexpected current and deceptive visibility that was not bad enough to insure the use of available navigational mechanisms." Leahy held Steele in high regard. The navigator, Commander Wadleigh Capehart, also found his career ruined (Craven papers).

75. Yarnell to Rear Admiral J. K. Taussig, chief of staff to commander Battle Force, 27 Mar 1932, with attached handwritten memo, Towers to Yarnell, 1 June 1932, Yarnell papers; Ballentine oral transcript, 175–76; Towers to Moffett, 14 Oct 1932.

76. CINCUS annual report of 1932–33, 23; Towers to Moffett, 16 June 1932; Towers to Molten, 13 June 1932, Molten papers; Sudsbury, 165.

77. Dyer, vol. 1, 116–18.

78. Conversations with Mrs. Eleanor Storrs and William Towers Maddox in 1985 and with Pierre in 1983 and 1986; *Darlington* magazine (winter 1984–85), 16. Eleanor divorced aviator Morton T. Seligman in 1930, married Ring the next year, and after the latter's death many years later married Putt Storrs. She recalled how Towers had been a source of comfort and a counselor during her marital difficulties, writing her a long, sympathetic letter.

79. Conversation with Pierre in 1983. Her instructor was Paul Tyce, a native of Poland.

80. Moffett to Standley, 19 Dec 1932; King to Moffett, 27 Oct 1932; Moffett to King, 18 Nov 1932, in which Moffett told King he had recommended him for command of NAS Pensacola; Moffett to Vinson, 22 Nov 1932; Moffett to Towers, 13 Jan 1933; King to Molten, 23 Dec [1932], Molten papers.

81. Towers to Moffett, 16, 29 Nov 1932 and 10 Jan 1933; Moffett to Towers, 21 Nov, 15 Dec 1932 and 13 Jan, 6, 14 Mar 1933; Towers to Vinson, 29 Nov 1933; Ingalls to Towers, 3 Jan 1933; Moffett to Reeves, 27 Jan 1933; Byrd to Towers, 21 Apr 1933; Moffett to Yarnell, 28 Feb 1933; Moffett to Adams, 28 Feb 1933; Adams to Moffett, 4 Mar 1933.

82. "Raid on Oahu," annex A to operation order 1-33 of Fleet Problem XIV, National Archives; Administrative History 36, 108–11.

83. This account is drawn from Administrative History 36, 108–19, and CINCUS (Leigh) report of Fleet Problem XIV, 20 Apr 1933, National Archives.

84. CINCUS to fleet, 31 Jan 1933, National Archives; Towers to Moffett, 3 Mar 1933; Yarnell to Moffett, 23 Feb 1933; Administrative History 36, 114–18. Umpire Reeves was also chagrined at the undermanned and undertrained ships, there being a lack of funds for personnel and fuel oil (Hayes, part 2, 56–57).

85. Administrative History 36, 117–18.

86. Towers to George Wheat of United Aircraft Corporation, 18 Mar 1933; Pierre to author, 9 Dec 1978; Ballentine oral transcript, 193–96. Lieutenant (jg) Sharp's apartment lost its front wall and "a whole lot of home brew," which spilled and exploded (Sharp oral transcript, 27–28).

87. Towers to Moffett, 3, 27 Mar 1933; Moffett to Towers, 6, 14, 20 Mar 1933; FDR to Moffett, 11 Mar 1933; Moffett to Swanson, 13 Mar 1933; and Moffett to McIntyre, 17 Mar 1933; FDR Library, OF 18i.

88. Towers to Moffett, 20 Mar 1933; FDR to Moffett, 11 Mar 1933, FDR Library, OF 18i; Daniels, *Years of War*, 570; Taylor, 90–91; Arpee, 238–45; Smith, *Airships*, 80ff.

89. Yarnell to Pratt, 4 Apr 1933, Standley papers; Senator William Gibbs McAdoo telegram to FDR, 11 Apr 1933, citing Cohen's strong endorsement; Swanson to FDR, 15 Apr 1933; Loening to FDR, 17 Apr 1933, FDR Library, OF 18i; Zogbaum, 455. Among the *Akron* dead were the skipper, Commander Frank McCord, Towers' navigator on the *Langley* for a year, and a passenger, "Cash" Cecil, head of the flight division during Jack's last year at BuAer.

90. Towers to Vinson, 28 Mar 1935. Towers wrote, "I am told that fact [of King and H. L. Roosevelt having been classmates] more than any other, kept me out" of the post of chief of BuAer. See also Towers to J. O. Richardson, 28 Mar 1935, and *Fleet Admiral King*, 261–62n.

91. King to navy secretary, 13 Apr 1933, and Pratt endorsement, 14 Apr 1933; Swanson to FDR, 19 Apr 1933; Buell, *King*, 96–97. None of the many letters of congratulations to King came from Towers (King papers).

92. Standley quoted in Towers to Standley, 30 Mar 1935; Towers to Foulois, 28 Apr 1933, Foulois papers.

93. Foulois to Towers, 24 May 1933, Foulois papers.

94. The eligible observers and older pilots thus eliminated were Rear Admirals J. J. Raby, John Halligan, A. W. Marshall, A. W. Johnson, and Henry V. Butler.

95. King's exec on the *Lexington,* for example, had been dour Vic Herbster and equally uncongenial John Hoover. He had wanted the gentle Lieutenant Commander Charles A. Pownall for the job.

96. King to chief of BuNav, 8 May 1933, Towers BuAer file, National Archives; Towers' orders of 16 May 1933.

97. Zogbaum, 456–57.

98. Towers' physical exam, 13 Jan 1933; Towers to navy secretary, "Appeal for Redress" [Mar 1937]; Rossiter to Upham, 1 May 1933; Captain R. P. Craft of BuNav to Towers, 5 May 1933; Yarnell to Towers, 12 May 1933; report of Board of Medical Survey of Towers, 23 Aug 1933; Towers to Board of Medical Survey, 4 Mar 1936.

99. Towers' orders of 10 June 1933, with endorsements; conversation with Pierre, 1985.

100. Commander of the Newport naval hospital to Towers, 9 Aug 1933; Towers telegram to Pierre, 22 Aug 1933; report of Board of Medical Survey, 23 Aug 1933; Towers' medical history sheet, Aug 1933. The vision in his left eye was 20/20. His color blindness continued to be overlooked throughout 1932–34 and generally thereafter.

101. Towers to navy secretary, "Appeal for Redress"; Towers to Board of Medical Survey, 4 Mar 1936.

102. Leahy and Swanson endorsements of 25 Aug 1933 to report of Board of Medical Survey on Towers, 23 Aug 1933.

CHAPTER 10. CARRIER STRATEGIST, 1933–38

1. Vlahos, *Blue Sword,* 32, 40, 43, 46–53, 59, and passim; Captain Dudley W. Knox, "National Strategy," lecture of 1933, Naval War College, RG 15.

2. Naval War College roster, Class of '34; Towers to Molten, 1 May [1934], Molten papers; Hattendorf, 138–40; Laning and Wheeler, 83–84; Harriet Towers Bjelovcic to the author, 31 May, 13 June 1985; conversation with Donald Beaton, 1985. Harriet, about ten at the time, also attended a circus with "Cousin John," who was dressed in a "bowler and Chesterfield overcoat," and "Cousin Pierre," who impressed her as "very very pretty and absolutely charming and elegant."

3. Vlahos, *Blue Sword,* 71–75, 155, and passim. The works were Clausewitz, *On War;* Corbett, *Some Principles of Maritime Strategy;* Mahan, *The Influence of Sea Power upon History, 1660–1783* and other selections; and Richmond, *National Policy and Naval Strength.*

4. Vlahos, "Wargaming," 10–16; Vlahos, *Blue Sword,* 119–20, 145–46; Laning, "The Naval Battle," revised to May 1933, especially 20–22 and diagram IX; Douglas, "Elements of Air Tactics," lecture, 23 Oct 1933; John F. Molony, "Naval Aircraft and Their Operation in Connection with the War College Course," lecture, 3 Dec 1933, Naval War College; Hattendorf, 143 (italics original).

5. Vlahos, *Blue Sword,* 85–90; Buell, "Kalbfus," 31–32 and passim; Cullen, 16–17.

6. Vlahos, *Blue Sword,* 119–21, 145–46; Vlahos, "Wargaming," 16–17 (Vlahos' sources quote the Class of '33 rather than the Dec 1933 critique); *Fleet Admiral King,* 239–40, 242. In the 1933 games, Admiral Laning preferred a more southern route, against King's wishes, and so Blue was defeated off New Guinea. During World War II Towers would support the southern route.

7. Senior class '34 tactical problems, Department of Operations program, 1933–34, Naval War College, RG 4; Vlahos, *Blue Sword,* 172–73.

8. Vlahos, *Blue Sword,* 75ff; Kennedy, 250–53; Hattendorf, 142. Among other preserved theses of the Class of '34 are those by Captain Joe Richardson (see Richardson, 109–12) and Commander Roy C. Smith on the general wartime relationships of naval strategy, tactics, and

command. The policy and strategy of the British in the Seven Years War and in the later Napoleonic wars, of the Americans in the War of 1812, and of the Japanese against China and Russia were the subject of theses by, respectively, Commander Franklin Van Valkenburgh, Commander Elliott P. Nixon, army Major Russel P. Harris, and Commander Ellis M. Zacharias.

9. Towers, "The Relationship between French Policy and Strategy in the War of the Coalition, 1777–1783, and Its Lessons to Us," class of '34 thesis, Naval War College, 1–2 and passim.

10. Ibid., 14–15, 19, 21, 26–27 and passim.

11. Ibid., 27–28; Towers, "The Influence of Aircraft on Naval Strategy and Tactics," Class of '34 thesis, Naval War College, 3–4.

12. Towers, "French Policy," 28; Towers, "Influence of Aircraft," 4; Vlahos, *Blue Sword,* passim; Wheeler, *Pratt,* 348–50. Supporters of a global policy included Pratt, Bristol, and Yarnell; opponents included Meigs Taylor, Brooks Upham, Frank Schofield, and William Leahy.

13. Turnbull and Lord, 284ff; Reynolds, "King," 57–64. In "Influence of Aircraft" Towers wrote, "Those responsible for Policy may or may not have an intimate knowledge of Strategy" (8).

14. Towers, "Influence of Aircraft," 1–3, 8.

15. Ibid., 13–14, 16–18, 25.

16. Ibid., 12–13, 17–18, 22–24, 26.

17. Ibid., 8–10, 15–16.

18. Ibid., 7, 10, 19–22, 25 and passim.

19. Towers, "French Policy," 18–19; Symington diary, 15 Apr 1916; Towers, "Influence of Aircraft," 18.

20. Towers, "Influence of Aircraft," 27; Zacharias thesis, quoted in Kennedy, 253.

21. Towers, "Influence of Aircraft," 27.

22. McNamee, "The Mission and Organization of the U.S. Naval War College," 1 June 1934, thesis, preliminary draft, Naval War College; Hattendorf, 151.

23. "Reports of Physical Examination and for Flying," 4 Dec 1933, and Rossiter endorsement of 21 Jan 1934; King endorsement of 10 Feb 1934, Towers BuAer file, National Archives; Rossiter to chief of BuNav, 21 Jan 1934; Whitehill conversation of 3 July 1950 with King, King papers; *Fleet Admiral King,* 260–61, 261n; Leahy to Towers, 6 Mar 1934.

24. King to Leahy, 16 Jan 1934, Towers BuAer file, National Archives; Towers' orders of 10 Mar 1934, with endorsements; Towers to Molten, 1 May, 15 Aug 1934, Molten papers. Towers' humor showed forth in a postscript of the first letter to Molten: "I'll bite, why should a Russian Ice breaker have female stewardesses?—To keep the crew hot?"

25. Lord, 1105–12; conversations with Pierre in 1966 and 1985. Two of the *Ranger's* four squadrons would be transferred from the *Langley,* making a net addition of two new squadrons to North Island. Tarrant recalled Towers as "one of the best naval leaders. There's been a good deal of discussion about him, pro and con. A good many people don't like him and a good many do, but I thought he was an excellent officer in every way. . . ." (oral transcript, 43). Cinders would also be called Windy for his Kennel Club name, Marnwood Windy Gust (Pierre to the author, 21 Nov 1986).

26. Sudsbury, 177–78, 180–81, 183, 187, 189–90. Among Towers' more prominent officers at San Diego during 1934–36 were Lieutenant Commanders V. F. Grant, David Rittenhouse, and Valentine H. Schaeffer and Lieutenants Stanhope C. Ring and Braxton Rhodes, the person he had bounced from the flight crew of the NC-3 at Trepassey.

27. Van Deurs oral transcript, 110, 279, 282–83, 325.

28. Ibid., 277, 280, 286, 325. After being passed over the third time, said van Deurs, "I had some calling cards printed: 'Lieutenant, PA—Permanent Appointment' " (278).

29. Conversation with Vice Admiral Robert B. Pirie in 1987; Rear Admiral J. W. Boundy letter to Pierre, 20 Dec 1961.

30. Sudsbury, 175–76, 180, 190–91, 194–95; McCrary to King, 15 June 1934, and related documents, Towers BuAer file, National Archives; 1936 annual report of the chief of BuAer, 4.

31. Towers to J. O. Richardson, 31 Mar 1935; conversations with Pierre in 1966 and 1983.

32. Towers quoted by Admiral James S. Russell in Russell oral transcript, 225; Russell to John T. Mason, Jr., 28 Sep 1976, King papers.

33. Whitehill interview with King, 3 July 1950, King papers; "Physical Examination for Flying," 22 Nov 1934, with Rossiter endorsement, 23 Jan 1935; King endorsement of 4 Feb 1935 with covering memo by Paunack to Towers; Leahy to Towers, 7 Feb 1935, Towers BuAer file, National Archives. At the time, on the eve of his retirement, Paunack headed the flight division.

34. *Fleet Admiral King,* 260.

35. Towers to Vinson, 28 Mar 1935; Towers to Standley, 30 Mar 1935; Towers to Richardson, 31 Mar 1935.

36. Towers to Richardson, 31 Mar 1935; Towers to Vinson, 28 Mar 1935 (italics original). Henry Latrobe Roosevelt, an apparent foe, died in February 1936. Post flew around the world alone in eight and a half days in 1931 and just under eight days in 1933. He and Will Rogers were killed on a flight over Alaska in 1935.

37. Towers to Richardson, 31 Mar 1935; Towers to Vinson, 28 Mar 1935.

38. Towers to Vinson, 28 Mar 1935; Towers to Standley, 30 Mar 1935; Standley to Towers, 16 Apr 1935. Towers had probably become acquainted with Andrews at Annapolis in 1911–13 when the latter was aide to the superintendent, a friendship possibly continued off Vera Cruz in 1914 where Andrews was gunnery officer of the *Michigan.* Perhaps only coincidentally, Towers' portrait graced the cover of the journal of *U.S. Air Services,* Aug 1935.

39. Standley to Towers, 15 Apr 1935; *Fleet Admiral King,* 265. In unsolicited letters, Captain Elwood A. Cobey, aircraft squadrons supply officer, wrote to his old friend Colonel Marvin H. McIntyre, secretary to the president, recommending both Cook and Towers for consideration as King's relief (25 Nov, 30 Dec 1935, FDR Library, OF 18i).

40. Towers to Barkan, rough draft, Sep 1935; Towers to Vinson, 28 Mar 1935; "Captain J. H. Towers—Circumstances Relating to Eye Trouble of," memorandum, 27 Feb 1936; Towers to navy secretary, "Appeal for Redress" [Mar 1937].

41. Barkan to Towers, 20 Nov, 3 Dec 1936; Towers to Board of Medical Survey, 4 Mar 1936.

42. "Report of Physical Examination," 6 Jan 1936; Towers to navy secretary, "Appeal for Redress"; acting BuMed chief O. J. Mink to chief of BuMed, 16 Jan 1936; Andrews to Towers, 24 Jan 1936; Andrews to chief of BuMed, 22 July 1936, Towers BuAer file, National Archives. See also Molten, exec of the *Saratoga,* to Ingalls, 29 Jan 1936, Molten papers, on Towers being earmarked for the *Lexington.*

43. Towers to navy secretary, "Appeal for Redress"; report of Board of Medical Survey on Towers, 12 Feb 1936.

44. Rossiter endorsement of 21 Feb 1936; Towers to Reeves, 5 Mar 1936; Towers to Board of Medical Survey, 4 Mar 1936; report of Board of Medical Survey on Towers, 5 Mar 1936; Towers, "Appeal for Redress."

45. Ferrell, 214; Custer to the author, 30 Sep 1986, relating his conversation with McCrary; Towers to Reeves, 5 Mar 1936.

46. Reeves to Andrews, n.d., quoted in Towers, "Appeal for Redress"; an unnamed congressman quoted in the San Diego *Union,* 15 June 1941.

47. Reeves to Andrews, n.d.; King to Andrews, 9 Mar 1936; Towers, "Appeal for Redress"; Standley to Towers, 16 Apr 1935; chief of BuMed to commander Aircraft Battle Force, 29 Jan 1937.

48. King to Andrews, 7 Apr 1936; Nimitz to Towers, 20 Apr 1936; conversation with Pierre in 1985; Towers' orders of 11 Mar 1936.

49. Towers' fitness reports of 30 Sep 1934, 30 Mar, 30 Sep 1935, and 4 Apr 1936 by Tarrant and 9 June 1936 by Butler.

50. Duncan oral transcript, 254, on Butler; *Saratoga* log, 1936; Molten to Ramsey, 28 May 1937; Foley, oral transcript, 51.

51. Administrative History 36, 151–53; Towers' fitness report of 9 June 1936 by Butler; *Saratoga* cruise book of 1936, 18–19, 21, 34–35.

52. Duncan oral transcript, 238–39, 244; *Navy Directory,* 1 Jan 1937; *Saratoga* log, 1936–37; Clark, 60–61; van Deurs oral transcript, 318–19. Dixie Kiefer was staff engineer and C. Wade McClusky, Jr., flag lieutenant.

53. Towers to Molten, 8 July, 11 Aug 1936; Molten to Ramsey, 28 May 1937, Molten papers; Towers' fitness report by Horne, 30 Sep 1936.

54. Towers to Molten, 11 Aug 1936 and 27 Jan, 5 Feb 1937, Molten papers; Ralph R. Teeter to King, 15 May 1936, King papers; Molten to Towers, 24 Dec 1936; [Ostrander], "Modifications to Dive Bombing Technique," memorandum, 3 Feb 1937, Molten papers; Horne to commander Battle Force, data for CINCUS annual report, 18 May 1937, National Archives; Swanborough, 71, 146, 165, 202–3, 205, 357–58, 399.

55. "Report of Physical Examination," 16 Dec 1936, and Horne endorsement, 15 Jan 1937; Rossiter to Cook, 6 Feb 1937, and Cook endorsement of 15 Feb 1937; Andrews to Towers, 18 Feb 1937; Towers, "Appeal for Redress," especially 9 (he wrote, "As a result of the Surgeon General's attitude, I am informed that I will not be given a command"); Horne endorsement of 19 Mar 1937; Potter, *Halsey,* 131.

56. Cook to navy secretary, 24 Mar 1937.

57. Keen, 12.

58. Towers to Yarnell, 14 Oct 1937; report of Board of Medical Survey on Towers, 7 Apr 1937, with Rossiter endorsement of same date; Andrews endorsement, 10 Apr 1937; Cook to Andrews, 7 Apr 1937; Towers' orders of 21 Apr 1937; Rossiter to Andrews, 11 June 1937; Towers to Andrews, 10 July 1937; Andrews to Towers, 3 Aug 1937, Towers BuAer file, National Archives; King conversation with Whitehill in 1950, King papers. The man in charge of officer personnel at BuNav during 1936–37 was one of Towers' classmates, Captain Alexander "Sandy" Sharp. Assistant chief of BuAer was Putty Read.

59. Administrative History 36, 157–59; Duncan oral transcript, 240.

60. Administrative History 36, 159–61; Duncan oral transcript, 243.

61. Administrative History 36, 162–63; *Fleet Admiral King,* 274; Duncan oral transcript, 240–41.

62. Administrative History 36, 163–64; Molten to Ramsey, 28 May 1937, Molten papers. For Adolphus Andrews' similar views on keeping the carriers with the battleships, see Buell, *King,* 109–10.

63. Administrative History 36, 164; Molten to Ramsey, 28 May 1937; Towers to Yarnell, 6 Dec 1938, Yarnell papers; Bogan oral transcript, 42.

64. Sudsbury, 201; Towers to Halsey, 4 Aug 1936, Halsey papers; Molten to N. H. White, 23 Dec 1938, Molten papers; *Navy Directory,* 1 Sep 1937; *Saratoga* log, 1937; Jurika oral transcript, 302.

65. *Plane Talk* (the *Saratoga's* newspaper), 19, 26 June, 3 July, 2 Oct 1937; Towers to Yarnell, 14 Oct 1937, Yarnell papers; Clark, 63; conversations with Gene Northway in 1985 and with Rear Admiral John G. Crommelin in 1978; Custer to the author, 8, 30 Sep 1986; undated clippings from Los Angeles newspapers, 1937; Towers' medical examination, 10 Feb 1936; "Physical Examination for Flying," 1 Dec 1937, and Rossiter endorsement, 17 Jan 1938; Dyer, vol. 1, 1933. Jack mourned his oldest brother Reuben, who passed away in May 1938 at age sixty-two.

66. "Physical Examination for Flying," 1 Dec 1937; "Status of Naval Aircraft," BuAer monthly report, 31 Oct 1937; *Saratoga* annual report, 11 May 1938, National Archives; Swanborough, 399; Sudsbury, 202–3, 206. In October VF-3 included seventeen F3F-1s, one SBC-3, and two OSU-1s; VB-3, fourteen BFC-2s, one SBU-1, two O3U-2s, and one SB2U-1; VS-3, eighteen SBC-3s; VT-3, fifteen TG-2s, eighteen TBD-1s "from contract"; the utility unit, three O3U-3s, two J2F-1s, and one N2Y two-seater trainer; and the flag unit, one SOC, one SBU, and one F3F. The *Saratoga's* new squadrons were, formerly, VF-6B (now VF-3, Felix the Cat emblem), VB-2B (now VB-3, High Hat), VS-2B (now VS-3, Pointer Dog), and VT-2B (now VT-3, Dragon on Torpedo).

67. Towers to Yarnell, 6 Dec 1938, Yarnell papers; Cook to Andrews, 28 Jan 1938; Towers' orders of 17 Feb 1938, Towers BuAer file, National Archives; *Los Angeles Times, New York Times,* and New York *Herald Tribune* clippings, 20 Feb 1938.

68. Dyer, vol. 1, 129–33, which notes that Admiral A. K. Doyle and others had thought Towers kept Turner from getting a carrier. Doyle, an admirer of Towers, was happy to learn later of Dyer's evidence to the contrary. For an example of Turner's brusque manner, which Turner thought hurt

his chances, see Clark, 56–57. Ballentine recalled how everyone on the *Saratoga* had been "scared to death" of Turner (oral transcript, 496).

69. Van Deurs oral transcript, 318; Jurika oral transcript, 303–4.

70. Van Deurs oral transcript, 319–23.

71. Ibid., 319–20, 323, 326; Buell, *King,* 110–12; "Relations of *Saratoga* and 'Flag,' " King to staff, 21 Mar 1938, quoted in Coletta, *Bellinger,* 196; conversation with Crommelin, 1978; Duncan oral transcript, 245–47; *Fleet Admiral King,* 280.

72. *Saratoga* annual report, 11 May 1938; *Fleet Admiral King,* 281.

73. Administrative History 36, 116–71; Duncan oral transcript, 245–46.

74. Van Deurs oral transcript, 328–31.

75. Administrative History 36, 172–76, 178; *Fleet Admiral King,* 281–82; Duncan oral transcript, 248.

76. Administrative History 36, 175–77; "The Case for the Naval Aviator," 17, 60; Leahy to M. H. McIntyre, 27 June, 14 July 1938; R. Hutchinson to FDR, 24 June 1938, quoting letter from a frustrated pilot; FDR memo to McIntyre, 27 June 1938; McIntyre to Leahy, 6 July 1938, FDR Library, OF 18i; *New York Times,* 1 Apr 1938.

77. Administrative History 36, 178–85; *Fleet Admiral King,* 282–83; *Saratoga* annual report, 11 May 1938, which also notes how all personnel drilled in the use of gas masks during battle problems.

78. Administrative History 36, 184.

79. Towers to Yarnell, 6 Dec 1938, Yarnell papers; Towers to King, 1 Sep 1938; King to Towers, 6 Sep 1938, King papers. The quoted inspecting officer was Rear Admiral George F. Neal.

80. Faulk oral transcript, 18; Nixon to Buell, 11 Aug 1974, King papers; conversation with Gene Northway, who had served under Towers on the *Langley* and *Saratoga,* 1985; Adcock, 342; *New York Sun,* 19 Sep 1942.

81. Towers to Yarnell, 6 Dec 1938.

82. *Saratoga* log, May–June 1938; Towers BuAer file, National Archives. The automobile trip lasted 16–28 June, overlapped by leave, 25 June–2 July 1938.

CHAPTER 11. MOBILIZING AVIATION FOR DEMOCRACY, 1938–40

1. Towers to Pierre, 9, 18, 23 Aug 1938; conversation with Pierre, 1985. Ballentine remembered Cook as positive in his thinking, a "ripsnorter" and fine officer but sometimes hard to deal with (oral transcript, 308).

2. Towers to Pierre, 9, 18, 23 Aug 1938; *Look,* 2 Aug 1938, 4; Towers to brother William, 21 Sep 1943; *Washington Post,* 26 Feb 1939; conversation with Riley, 1966.

3. Blakeslee, 3; "Presenting Admiral Towers," 21; "Physical Examination for Flying," 20 Dec 1938, endorsed by Surgeon-General McIntire, 6 Jan 1939 (this found him fit, as did all subsequent physicals through 1947); Atlanta *Constitution,* 17 Mar 1939; New York *Sun,* 19 Sep 1942; Public Information Office wartime summary, Jensen papers. According to Pierre, her husband kept a favorite book of recipes of punches and other mixed drinks (conversation with the author, 1985).

4. Conversation with Pierre, 1985.

5. *Army-Navy Journal,* 23 July 1939, 1023, 1038, and 5 Nov 1938, 198; "The Case for the Naval Aviator," 14–15; Towers to Yarnell, 6 Dec 1938, Yarnell papers. Ben Scott Custer noted Custer's conversation about this time with retired Captain Frank McCrary, who had said to Ernie King and others, "Let's quit letting the medical people dominate the assignments of people in the Navy. This is the man who has the experience and the respect" (Custer oral transcript, 296). McCrary urged Towers' appointment. The other board members were Walton R. Sexton, John D. Wainwright, Cyrus W. Cole, and Arthur P. Fairfield.

6. *Army-Navy Journal,* 26 Nov 1938; conversation with Pierre, 1983.

7. *Army-Navy Journal,* 3 Dec 1938, 291 and 17 Dec 1938, 1. One of the selectees was fifty-five, four were fifty-four, one was fifty-three, and three were fifty-two. Towers was fifty-three.

8. Quote from clipping, probably *Washington Post,* in Mar 1939; Towers to Yarnell, 6 Dec 1938; conversation with Pierre, 1983.

9. Towers to Yarnell, 6 Dec 1938; *Army-Navy Journal,* 3 Dec 1938, 300; clipping, probably *Washington Post,* Mar 1939; Keen, 12.

10. *U.S. Air Services,* Jan 1939, editorial page.

11. FDR quoted in Richardson diary, entry of 23 Mar 1938, in J. O. Richardson, 121–22; FDR conversation with Towers, which Pierre repeated to author in 1983 and 1986. The meeting, which Pierre thought was the very morning after the announcement, was not logged in FDR's diaries and itineraries, but this was not unusual since many of the president's meetings were not logged. FDR may have discussed the Towers situation when he met with Leahy on 9 December 1938 and with Richardson on the twenty-second.

12. J. O. Richardson, 125; Assistant Navy Secretary Charles Edison to FDR, 15 Feb, 7 Mar 1939; memo with U.S. Maritime Commission letterhead [no doubt from Land], n.d.; Daniel J. Callaghan, memo, White House letterhead, n.d. and no addressee, FDR Library, PSF. On 25 March 1940 Josephus Daniels, ambassador to Mexico, wrote to both FDR and Towers recommending that Commander Andy Crinkley not be retired. In the letter to FDR, he said that the man "is in almost the same boat as Towers was when you stretched out your arm and saved Towers" (FDR Library, OF). Crinkley was not retired.

13. Arnold to Towers, 7 Jan 1939; Towers to Arnold, 9 Jan 1939, Arnold papers.

14. Towers' office diary, beginning 1 Feb 1939 (hereafter cited as "diary"). One example setting out the purpose of the diary is explained in the entry of 13 March 1940: "This . . . is . . . a record of the interview because of my short observation of Mr. [Maxwell] Brown [trying to sell certain aircraft to the navy]. I feel that he is going to . . . create the impression that the result of the interview was otherwise than as outlined above."

15. Edison to FDR, 7 Mar 1939; Richardson to Towers, 24 May 1939. An unsigned, undated memo, probably written by presidential aide Callaghan at FDR's behest in January or February and entitled "Prospective Changes in Chiefs of Bureau," said, "BuAero—President has expressed no decision or definite inclination" (FDR Library, PSF).

16. *Army-Navy Journal,* 18 Mar 1939, 655; *Washington Post,* 16, 18 Mar 1939; Atlanta *Constitution,* 17 Mar 1939.

17. Towers to King, 23 Mar 1939, King papers; *Fleet Admiral King,* 288–94; Buell, *King,* 117–19; *New York Times,* 16 Mar 1939. King's letter of congratulations to Towers does not survive.

18. Richardson to Towers, 24 May 1939; *Army-Navy Journal,* 16 Dec 1939, 338; Towers' acceptance memo to BuNav, 3 Jan 1940; chief of BuNav to Towers, 9 Feb 1940; assistant chief of BuPers to Towers, 21 Oct 1942.

19. Baltimore *Sun,* 16 Sep 1942; *Newsweek,* 28 Sep 1941. By the end of 1941 his salary would be $10,838—$6,000 base pay, $3,000 flight pay, $1,400 rental expenses, and $438 sustenance allowance for his dependents. Elevated to the upper half, this jumped to $13,878—$8,000, $4,000, $1,440, and $438 respectively (*Flying,* Jan 1942, 230).

20. Albion, *Makers, 170–71*; Albion and Connery, 45, 60; Edison to FDR, 7 Mar 1939, and related documents, FDR Library; Ferrell, 203; Administrative History 48, 11–12, 143.

21. Diary, 29 Feb 1940; Albion and Connery, 45, 60.

22. Millis, 269, 40–41; Beebe oral transcript, 15; Eaker oral transcript, 82; Spaatz oral transcript, 47–48; Lovett oral transcript, 16, 68; Towers, "My Friend Hap," 9. Admiral Cook and Congressman Maas were thwarted in their attempts to create a separate navy flight corps early in 1939 (*Army-Navy Register,* 18 Mar 1939).

23. Diary, 17 July 1939.

24. General Board hearings, 29 Dec 1939, 476ff, 26 Jan 1940, 68–92 and 19 Feb 1940, 96–122. Attention was also given to the use of catapults from tenders, but Towers doubted whether they could be developed for such heavy planes, and they were not. As for patrol plane costs, Towers gave production costs of $156,000 for one PBY-5, $262,000 for the PBM, $925,000 for the PB2Y, and $1 million for each projected PB2M.

25. General Board hearings, 2 July 1940, 215; Administrative History 48, 87; diary, 27 June 1940. The destroyer idea originated with the navy war plans division in the fall of 1939 and was pushed by Stark.

26. Diary, 2 Mar, 9, 10 May, 30 June, 26 Sep 1939; Callaghan to FDR, 4 June 1940; FDR to Edison, 11 June 1940, FDR Library, OF 18i; Smith, *Flying Aircraft Carriers,* 165, 167, 169–70, 217 n24. In November 1939 Towers also had to ward off a character with a fantastic scheme for a combination airplane-airship (diary, 8–9 Nov 1939). King tried to resurrect the rigid in January 1942, but Goodyear had already retooled for aircraft components.

27. CNO annual report, 31 July 1939; General Board hearings, 17 July 1939, 138.

28. Diary, 1 Mar 1939; Lord, 1170ff; General Board hearings, 28 Aug 1939, 246–50; Friedman, *Aircraft Carriers,* 111–14.

29. General Board hearings, 19 Jan 1939, 8; 17 July 1939, 138–40, 153; 18 Jan 1940, 8–9; Friedman, *Aircraft Carriers,* 140; Studenmund, 19.

30. General Board hearings, 17 July 1939, 140–41, 153, 169; 31 Oct 1939, 335–38; Friedman, *Aircraft Carriers,* 141–42, 211; Russell, "Early Days," 25–27; Russell, "Mess Treasurer," 54–57.

31. General Board hearings, 31 Oct 1939, 338–39; 13 Nov 1939, 390ff, 409; 18 Jan 1940, 7–9, 14; Friedman, *Aircraft Carriers,* 141–44, 214. Towers, however, wanted the 8-inch guns retained on the *Lexington,* figuring they might be engaged by 8-inch heavy cruisers while undertaking independent operations; the guns were kept until the outbreak of war (General Board hearings, 12 Dec 1940, 498–501; Friedman, *Aircraft Carriers,* 50–53, 207). The *Essex* also had the ability to steam twenty knots astern in order to launch over the stern in case of battle damage forward.

32. Friedman, *Aircraft Carriers,* 114–17, 211–14; General Board hearings, 12 Nov 1939, 394–96, 405–6. McCain's small carrier would have had an armored deck.

33. Turnbull and Lord, 301; Coletta, *Overseas Bases,* 150–51; Albion, *Makers,* 254; Administrative History 58, 8–14; 30; Administrative History 47a, 541–44; diary, 27 Apr, 16, 24 June, 17 July 1939.

34. Administrative History 49, 4–9, 17; BuAer *Manual,* 1940, 6–7 and passim.

35. BuAer *Manual,* 1940, 7; Stroop oral transcript, 66–68, 78. On Vinson's years on the committee, see Enders, 5–116.

36. Administrative History 41, 323–30; Pierre to author, 9 Dec 1978 and conversation, 1985; Mercer oral transcript, 5–6.

37. Administrative History 41, 35–3, 125, 131–33; Administrative History 40, 69–70, 77–80; "The Case for the Naval Aviator," 14–16; "Mutual Problems in Air Transportation—Military and Commercial," Towers speech, National Defense Day Meeting, Society of Automotive Engineers, Detroit, 11 Jan 1939; Lord, 1125ff, 1152; J. O. Richardson, 191–95; Featherstone, 44–45; Administrative History 59, 123–25; diary, 15 June 1939; House Naval Affairs Committee hearings, 29 Apr 1940, 3039–43.

38. Administrative History 41, 32–35; Administrative History 40, 23–25; Lord, 1131–32, 1156; Pisano, 21–25; diary, 20 Apr 1939; Senate commerce subcommittee hearings, 20 Apr 1939, 89–92, courtesy of Dominic A. Pisano.

39. Diary, 15 Feb 1940; Towers to Halsey, 6 Mar 1940; Halsey to Towers, 13 Dec 1940, Halsey papers; Read oral transcript, 67–73; Taylor, "Synthetics—Part I," 36–37. Lieutenant Commander W. W. Harvey of Fighting 3 died in a crash at Anacostia on 12 December 1940.

40. Towers' orders, 11 Jan 1939; Towers' Detroit speech, 11 Jan 1939; Roland, vol. 1, 160, 360–61; diary, 5 Apr 1939; Lindbergh diary, entries of 9, 23, 38 June, 18, 20 July, 14 Sep, 19 Oct 1939, 214–15, 233, 254–55, 276–77; *History of NACA,* 5–6. The Sunnyvale lab was later renamed Ames Aeronautical Laboratory in honor of Dr. Joseph S. Ames, NACA chairman, 1927–39.

41. BuAer annual report, 1939; Lindbergh, 276; Roland, vol. 1, 160–61; *History of NACA,* 6; John F. Victory to FDR, 2 JAN 1942, FDR Library, OF 18i; Towers' Detroit speech, 11 Jan 1939; Towers to brother William, 8 June 1940.

42. Hunsaker to FDR, 1 Oct 1942, and endorsement of Towers to Hunsaker, 28 Sep 1942, FDR Library, OF 249a; House appropriations subcommittee hearings, 8 Jan 1940, 490.

43. *New York Times,* 12, 21 May, 21 June 1939; Roseberry, *Skies,* 431–32; Knott, 152; Towers'

orders to 20 May 1939. Articles under Towers' name appeared in *Aero Digest* (Feb 1940), *National Aeronautics* (July 1940), and *Insignia* (1941) (AIAA file, National Archives).

44. Diary, 2 Feb, 8 Mar, 6, 14 Apr, 17 July 1939; Mitscher telegram to Towers, 12 July 1939; Towers to navy secretary, 25 July 1939, Towers BuAer file, National Archives.

45. Diary, 21 Aug 1939; Towers to Stark, 28, 31 Aug 1939, FDR Library, PSF; Administrative History 48, 84–85, 180.

46. Towers to J. V. Forrestal, 6 Oct 1942, quoted in Administrative History 48, 39–40.

47. Wagner, 213.

48. Diary, 6, 14 Sep, 25 Oct 1939; Administrative History 48, 41; Administrative History 91, 65. Of the 200 planes, 167 would be PBY-5 flying boats, 33 PBY 5A amphibians with wheels (Creed, 46). The exact cost of each was $90,354.

49. Administrative History 48, 41; Creed, 46; Langer and Gleason, 206ff.

50. Administrative History 41, 13–25; Administrative History 58, 29–32; diary, 1, 24 Nov 1939; Towers to Pierre, 17 Nov, and telegram, 20 Nov 1939; conversation with Riley in 1966, who recalled that during this and all trips Towers preferred to fly "contact" rather than on instruments; Towers to brother William, 24 Nov 1939. "This sleeping alone," Jack wrote his wife during the junket on the seventeenth, "is not so *hot,* expressed in slang terms" (italics original).

51. House Naval Affairs Committee hearings, 2 Apr 1940, 2766–72.

52. Markey, 65–66; Coffey, 191 (he tells an anecdote about Hap Arnold's son at Annapolis); diary, 29 Dec 1939.

53. Towers' orders and telegram to BuAer, 25 Oct 1939; Towers' orders, 10 Feb 1940; Towers to Mayor Fiorello LaGuardia, 23 Mar 1940, Towers BuAer file, National Archives; Atlanta *Constitution,* 27 Oct 1939; clipping on SAE election [1940]. Towers spoke before the NROTC at Georgia Tech in Oct 1939, appeared at FDR's side when the Herbert Schiff Trophy for unit performance was awarded to VP-11 in November, spoke at the Defense Week dinner in Cincinnati in February, with Stark dedicated Pan American Airways' international seaplane base in New York in March, and was elected honorary 1940 president of Sigma Alpha Epsilon fraternity, to which he had belonged at Georgia Tech.

54. *Time,* 23 June 1941, 20; Read oral transcript, 728; brother William to Towers, 30 Nov 1939.

55. *Flying,* Jan 1942, 35.

56. Administrative History 60, 8–22; Administrative History 47a, 544–56; Administrative History 48, 42–44; diary, 14 Sep, 1 Nov 1939. In addition to the 200 PBYs, Towers, Captains Mitscher, Kraus, and Ramsey, and Commander Laurence Richardson decided on 100 OS2U seaplanes with land gear, 138 SB2U seaplanes (57 for the marines), and 100 N3N trainers.

57. Lord, 1103, 1174; Turnbull and Lord, 285; J. P. Miller, 163–66; Connery, 267–68; Administrative History 47a, 136; Towers' testimony, House Naval Affairs Committee hearings, 23 Jan 1940, 1954–63.

58. McCarthy, 167–70, 173; Rae, 115–16; Gibbs-Smith, 194–95, 200–203; Towers quoted in Stanley M. Udale, letter to *Washington Post,* 31 Aug 1943. See Wilson, *Slipstream,* 196–203, for the Air Corps attempt to push liquid-cooled engines in the United States during 1937–39.

59. Wilson, *Slipstream,* 182, 195, 202; Towers to Wilson, 10 May 1940, Wilson papers. Towers congratulated Wilson on succeeding Donald L. Brown as president. One of United's advertising agents, John Monsarrat, recalled that "it was through him [Wilson] that I first heard of Towers and learned how greatly he was respected" (letter to the author, 17 Oct 1985). Army aviation relied chiefly on Republic, North American, Lockheed, and Boeing.

60. Thruelsen, 118; Towers quoted in Wagner, 294; conversation with Pierre, 1985.

61. Thruelsen, 92, 100–103, 106–8, 119–20, 125; Swanborough, 71–72, 205–6, 403; Halsey to Towers, 11 July 1940; Towers to Halsey, 25 July 1940, Halsey papers; Wilson, *Slipstream,* 193–94; McCarthy, 173.

62. Swanborough, 73–74, 150–52, 167–69, 357–58, 417; Halsey to Towers, 11 July 1940; Towers to Halsey, 25 July 1940. The navy had also accepted the Martin PBM Mariner before a prototype flew.

63. Swanborough, 143–45, 148–49, 165–66, 213–16, 393–96, 401–2, 421; diary, 3 Nov 1939; Thruelsen, 123; Halsey to Towers, 11 July 1940; Towers to Halsey, 25 July 1940. Early in 1942 the contract for the TBU was shifted to Consolidated, where the plane became the TBY.

64. Diary, 27 Feb, 1, 11 Mar, 26 Sep 1939; Allen, 38; Administrative History 48, 109–11; Daley, 8, 108ff, 172ff, 200–201, 224ff, 256ff; Solberg, 54, 243–45, 265. The CAA and Towers also cooperated in developing aviation safety measures, notably in the use of coastal lighthouses (Administrative History 48, 116–17).

65. Wilson, *Slipstream,* 191–94, 219; diary, 24 July 1939.

66. Diary, 2, 8, 10, 13 Feb, 5, 13 Apr, 8 Nov 1939; Wilson, *Slipstream,* 217–19; Arnold, 185.

67. Diary, 8 Nov 1939; Blum/Morgenthau, 116.

68. Diary, 8 Nov 1939; Wilson, *Slipstream,* 218–28; Connery, 84; Wagner, 213–14. Belgium, Norway, and Sweden also ordered American military aircraft.

69. Diary, 10–13 Dec 1939 and 2, 4–6 Mar 1940; Administrative History 64a, 7; conversation with Rear Admiral Paul Pihl in 1981.

70. Diary, 29, 30 Nov 1939 and 4, 8, Jan 1940; Administrative History 60, 19.

71. Diary, 9 Dec 1939.

72. Ibid., 29 Dec 1939 and 3 Jan, 20 Feb, 6, 26 Mar 1940; Arnold, 184–86; Blum/Morgenthau, 115–16.

73. Towers to Stark, 13 Jan 1940, quoted in Administrative History 48, 98.

74. Diary, 17 Jan 1940; Langer and Gleason, 291; Blum/Morgenthau, 115–16.

75. FDR to Naval Aide Callaghan, for Towers, 8 Feb 1940; Towers to Callaghan, for FDR, 9 Feb 1940; Callaghan to FDR, 10 Feb 1940, FDR Library, PSF. Callaghan agreed completely with Towers: "As I see it, the smaller companies . . . have neither the experience nor the *equipment* to go into production of the larger powers required" (italics original).

76. Administrative History 60, 19; Towers' testimony, House Naval Affairs Committee hearings of 23 Jan 1940, 1965, 1979–80. The eighty-one VSBs had been the choice of the CNO when the Senate insisted on cuts of some kind.

77. House Naval Affairs Committee hearings of 23, 31 Jan 1940, 1950–86, 2141–59; *New York Times,* 25 Jan 1940; diary, 24, 25, 29, 31 Jan, 14, 15 Feb 1940; Administrative History 60, 20–24.

78. Administrative History 60, 24.

79. House Naval Affairs Committee hearings of 23 Jan 1940, 1962, 1964–65.

80. Diary, 5, 6 Mar 1940.

81. Ibid., 6 Mar 1940; Coffey, 10.

82. Diary, 13 Mar 1940; Coffey, 10; Arnold, 185–86; Blum/Morgenthau, 117–19. Morgenthau began his diary account of the meeting, "Oh boy, did General Arnold get it!"

83. *New York Times,* 14 Mar 1940. This referred to the Norden bombsight.

84. Diary, 14 Mar 1940. The board of officers handling the sales consisted of Collins, Admiral Spear, and the acting quartermaster general of the army, Colonel Edmund B. Gregory.

85. Ibid.

86. Ibid., 14, 15 Mar, 5 Apr 1940; Kraus to Towers, 18 Mar 1940; Thruelsen, 111–12, 119; Swanborough, 206; Blum and Morgenthau, 119–20.

87. Diary, 20 Mar 1940; Administrative History 60, 24–26.

88. Diary, 20 Mar 1940. The other senators present were Henry Cabot Lodge of Massachusetts, Rufus C. Holman of Oregon, Theodore G. Green of Rhode Island, and ex officio, Peter G. Gerry, also of Rhode Island.

89. Ibid., 26 Mar 1940.

90. Ibid.; Air Corps decree of 19 Mar 1940, quoted in Arnold, 197.

91. Diary, 27, 29 Mar 1940. The aircraft engine manufacturers were briefed on the twenty-ninth, with Kraus representing BuAer.

92. Ibid., 2 Apr 1940. The working committee, in existence since 1919, had not become permanent until 1937 (Administrative History 49, 16–17, and Van Wyen, *Aeronautical Board,* passim).

93. Diary, 5, 10, 15, 19 Apr 1940; Administrative History 48, 99.

94. Diary, 10, 15, 19, 25 Apr 1940; *New York Times,* 20 Apr 1940; Senate Naval Affairs Committee hearings, 10, 15, 19 Apr 1940; J. O. Richardson, 307ff, 320. Most of the critical questioning was done by Senators Walsh, Frederick Hale of Maine, Lodge, and Hiram Johnson of California. Charles Lindbergh dropped by Towers' office on 19 April to discuss American naval aviation (Lindbergh, 337).

95. A. K. Doyle interview with Pierre Towers, about 1960; diary, 22–24, 30 Apr 1940; Towers to Pierre, 2 May 1940; Riley oral transcript, 110–11, 116–23. A United Airlines DC-3 paced the navy plane on the trip, its major trouble being that all twenty-one passengers got airsick! The defects of the R4O were corrected in the follow-on R5O Lodestar and army Hudson light bombers.

96. Diary, 9, 10 May 1940; Administrative History 41, 27.

97. J. O. Richardson, 463–64.

98. Diary, 11 May 1940.

99. Ibid., 13 May 1940.

100. Ibid., 14 May 1940; Enders, 126–27.

101. Rae, 113; *New York Times,* 16 May 1940; Arnold, 197; Goldberg, 48; Beasley, 229–30; House Naval Affairs Committee hearings of 22 May 1940, 3419.

102. Diary, 21 May 1940.

103. Ibid.; House Naval Affairs Committee hearings of 22 May 1940. 3418; Administrative History 30, 24–25; *New York Times,* 22 May 1940. The *New York Times* ran a picture of Stark, Towers, and Moreell at the White House in natty civilian attire.

104. House Naval Affairs Committee hearings of 22 May 1940, 3394–405.

105. Ibid., 3413–14.

106. Ibid., 3405–8. See also Administrative History 41, 44–46.

107. Diary, 23, 24 May 1940; *New York Times,* 24 May 1940.

108. *New York Times,* 23 May 1940; Senate Naval Affairs Committee hearings, reproduced in Administrative History 91, 61–68.

109. Administrative History 91, 68–72; *New York Times,* 25 May 1940.

110. *New York Times,* 27 May 1940; diary, 26 May 1940. That night Towers publicly affirmed naval aviation progress in a radio round table forum with moderator Ernest K. Lindley, General Barton Yount of the Air Corps, Robert Hinckley of the CAA; Colonel John Jouett of the Aeronautical Chamber of Commerce, NACA head Vannevar Bush, and aviation editor Gill Robb Wilson. Towers' toughness as a negotiator is revealed in the diary entry for 14 June 1940, when a paper mill representative lied to him about a water survey in connection with the expansion of Pensacola. Towers "accused him openly of endeavoring to conceal facts," whereupon the man relented.

111. Diary, 27 May 1940.

112. Albion, *Makers,* 413, 421–37; Rae, 114; Wilson, *Slipstream,* 237–38; Beasley, 234–41; Chandler, 496; Read oral transcript, 117; Albion and Connery, 5, 33–34.

113. Diary, 31 May 1940. The training planes were the Naval Aircraft Factory's N3N, Stearman N2S, North American SNJ, Vultee SNV, and Curtiss SNC.

114. Administrative History 58, 34–36; Administrative History 30, 31–32; Towers to Nimitz, 3 June 1940, quoted in Administrative History 41, 27–30. The supplemental national defense appropriation bill was passed on 26 June 1940. The CNO's letter to naval facilities was dated 25 June 1940.

115. Diary, 5 June 1940; Blum/Morgenthau, 155–56. The latter includes an account of Morgenthau's successful efforts to find bombs to go with the planes.

116. Diary, 7 June 1940.

117. Ibid., 10 June 1940; House Naval Affairs Committee hearings of 10 June 1940, 3495ff, 3512–19, 3527–32; Administrative History 59, 162–64; Administrative History 41, 47–49a. The Naval Aviation Personnel Act became law on 27 August 1940.

118. Administrative History 30, 29–30; Administrative History 48, 45–46; diary, 20 June 1940. The authorized carriers would eventually be named *Yorktown* (CV-10), *Intrepid* (CV-11), and *Hornet* (CV-12), the first and last named for carriers lost in battle.

119. Albion, *Makers,* 514–16; Enders, 126–27, reveals that Walsh played no role in the creation of the two-ocean navy bill.

120. Blum/Morgenthau, 282–89; Enders, 124; J. P. Miller, 166–67; Connery, 267–68.

121. *New York Times,* 20, 21 June 1940; diary, 19 June 1940; Rae, 115; Connery, 66–67.

122. House Naval Affairs Committee hearings of 20 June 1940, 3605–16; diary, 20 June 1940.

123. Diary, 3 July 1940; Administrative History 41, 30–31; Albion, *Makers,* 516. The new *Essexes* would eventually be named *Franklin* (CV-13), *Ticonderoga* (CV-14), *Randolph* (CV-15), *Lexington* (CV-16), *Bunker Hill* (CV-17), *Wasp* (CV-18), and *Hancock* (CV-19). The first of the light carriers would be the *Independence* (CVL-22).

124. Diary, 5, 8, 9 July 1940; Wilson, *Slipstream,* 245; Connery, 96.

125. Diary, 8, 18, 19 JULY 1940; Administrative History 30, 35–36; Administrative History 60, 34; House Appropriations subcommittee hearings of 23 July 1940, 94–95, 98, 245.

126. Diary, 23, 24 July 1940; Read oral transcript, 78–79; Rae, 115.

127. Diary, 26 July, 6 Aug 1940; Wilson, *Slipstream,* 243; J. P. Miller, 113–16; Beasley, 248ff. Stearman, a subsidiary of Boeing, produced the N2S Kaydet (army PT-17).

128. Diary, 26, 27 July 1940. FDR's views were expressed to Stettinius, who relayed them to Towers. See also Blum/Morgenthau, 290–91.

129. Diary, 18, 30, 31 July 1940; Read oral transcript, 112–16.

130. Diary, 18, 29 July, 1, 6 Aug 1940; Wilson, *Slipstream,* 229–31. Fleet also tried to talk Towers into letting Consolidated and other companies build a trainer for the navy, though Towers had no need of another model and learned that Fleet had a 5 percent royalty attached to the trainer design he offered (diary, 25 June 1940).

131. Diary, 6 Aug 1940; Wilson, *Slipstream,* 228, 243, 245.

132. Read oral transcript, 82–87, 120–23; diary, 7, 14 Aug 1940.

133. Diary, 8, 13 Aug 1940; Towers BuAer file, National Archives; Towers to brother William, 5 Aug 1940; Administrative History 30, 37; Administrative History 60, 35–36; Senate appropriations subcommittee hearings of 13 Aug 1940, 162ff.

134. Diary, 22 Aug 1940. For an Air Corps appreciation of Patterson, see Arnold, 195.

135. Diary, 27–29 Aug, 6 Sep 1940; Wilson to Midshipman Ira R. Hanna, 30 Oct 1956, courtesy of P. E. Coletta; Wilson oral transcript, 880; Read oral transcript, 82–87; Wilson, *Slipstream,* 243–44; Blum/Morgenthau, 292–96; J. P. Miller, 167–70; Connery, 268–73.

136. Wilson, *Slipstream,* 231–34, 239–42; Goldberg, 49; Towers before House Naval Affairs Committee hearings, 20 June 1940, 3607; Wagner, 214–15.

137. Diary, 12 Sep 1940; Wagner, 294.

138. Arnold, 196–97; diary, 3 Sep 1940.

139. Diary, 12 Sep 1940; Albion, *Makers,* 386, 531–32; Connery, 74–75, also 130–31 for Forrestal's streamlining of statistical information.

140. Nimitz, BuNav memo, 6 May 1941, quoted in Administrative History 59, 160–61; Administrative History 41, 79–82.

141. Administrative History 48, 112–13; Administrative History 41, 37, 72–75; House Naval Affairs Committee hearings of 20 June 1940, 3609; Pisano, 21–29, 33; diary, 13, 17 June, 11 July, 27 Aug, 3 Sep, 8, 16 Oct 1940 and 18 July, 10 Oct 1941.

142. New York *World Telegram,* 2 Aug 1940, probably from an interview with reporter Charles T. Lucey.

143. Arnold, 199; Goldberg, 49; diary, 5, 10 Sep 1940. No record exists, however, of any such "further conversation."

144. Diary, 11 Sep 1940.

145. Ibid., 5 June, 13 Sep 1940; Administrative History 30, 37–38; Administrative History 60, 36.

146. Diary, 17 Oct 1940. In this entry Towers wrote, "General Arnold and I left [a meeting with Knudsen] with the impression that somewhere behind the scenes there is a big effort being made to establish a large center of aviation industry in the State of Ohio and in the Detroit area, although there was nothing said by Mr. Knudsen that would indicate he was a participant in such a plan." See also diary, 21, 21 Dec 1940.

147. Buchanan, vol. 1, 25, 120–21; diary, 2–3 Oct 1940; *New York Times,* 3, 4 Oct 1940. The

latter includes an editorial that noted, as one aspect of their visit, the growing importance of the single radial air-cooled engine in the F4U alongside twin-engine army and foreign fighters.

148. Towers' fitness report for 25 June–30 Sep 1940, dated 22 Nov 1940.

CHAPTER 12. ARCHITECT OF NAVAL POWER, 1940–41

1. Quoted in *New York Times,* 26 Oct 1940.

2. Albion, *Makers,* 550–52; O'Connor, "Perspective," 176–77; Dyer, vol. 1, 156–61; J. O. Richardson, 378–79, 383–85, 395–96, 398–402, 423ff; diary, 11 July 1940.

3. Fanton, 18–20, 39, 55; *New York Times,* Lovett obituary, 8 May 1986; conversation with Pierre, 1985. Lovett had been with Brown Brothers Harriman, Gates with the New York Trust Company as its president. The regular assistant secretaries of the navy and of war became, respectively, Ralph A. Bard in February 1941 and John J. McCloy in April 1941. For an appreciation of Lovett, see Arnold, 195–96.

4. New York *World Telegram,* 2 Aug 1940; Administrative History 41, 167–68; Sherman to King, "The Case Against the United Air Force," 7 Apr 1941, with copies to Reeves, Walton R. Sexton, Horne, and Towers, King papers; Arnold, 206; Goldberg, 51.

5. Joint Board records.

6. BuAer memo to BuPers, 19 Feb 1941, in Administrative History 48, 50–54, 168–69. Aviation flag officers were Horne (an observer), King, Bristol, Cook, Halsey, McWhorter, and McCain. JCL carrier skippers were Ted Sherman of the *Lexington,* Ernest Gunther of the *Yorktown,* and Black Jack Reeves of the *Wasp.* Early airmen were Hugh Douglas of the *Saratoga;* Alfred Montgomery of the *Ranger;* and Baldy Pownall of the *Enterprise.* In the next rotation, JCL Elliott Buckmaster got the *Yorktown,* early airmen George Murray the *Enterprise* and W. Keen Harrill the *Ranger.*

7. J. O. Richardson, 220, 222–32; Commander Miles Browning to Halsey, 5 July 1940; Towers to Stark, 31 July 1940, commander Aircraft Battle Force, General Administrative File, National Archives; Halsey to Towers, 11 July 1940, Halsey papers.

8. Nimitz to Kimmel, 28 Feb 1941, Nimitz papers.

9. Hoover oral transcript, 88, 258–60, 311–12; conversation with Pierre, 1983.

10. Diary, 9 July, 13 Aug, 23, 25 Sep 1940; Langer and Gleason, 749–69; Creed, 48–49. Towers' diary reveals that PBY-5 and B-17 aircraft were inadvertently left out of the trade, to the chagrin of Cordell Hull and Morgenthau (17 Sep 1940). RADAR was an acronym for radio direction and ranging.

11. Administrative History 38b, 39–40; Administrative History 31, 29–31; Holley, *Buying Aircraft,* 263–65; diary, 19, 20 Sep, 7 Nov 1940. The navy members of the standardization committee were Commander F. W. Pennoyer, Jr., and Lieutenant Commander Dale Harris. In his diary, Towers for many months referred to JAC as the Joint Standardization and Allocations Committee. The highly technical minutes of JAC meetings are filed in RD 72 (entry 19C), National Archives.

12. Diary, 17–19 Sep, 7, 17, 21 Oct 1940; JAC "Case No. 217," 3 Mar 1941, National Archives. Towers, Brett, and Arnold attended a luncheon on Sep 18 at which RAF officers discussed British techniques of bombing and repelling bombing attacks. The British preferred 250-pound bombs on external racks, the Americans 500- or 1,000-pound bombs on internal racks for larger targets like heavy ships.

13. New York *Herald Tribune,* 26 Oct 1940. The night of the Young Men's luncheon meeting Towers also addressed some four hundred members of the University Club (diary, 25 Oct 1940). After these Friday speeches, Jack and Pierre spent the weekend in New York on a rare visit with brother Fullton and his wife Edna and attended the Yale-Navy football game at New Haven. "Strangely enough, although we are just a few hours apart, we see very little of each other, as we are both terribly busy" (Towers to brother William, 19 Oct 1940).

14. Diary, 31 Oct 1940; Connery, 92–95.

15. Diary, 4, 7, 11, 15 Nov, 12, 16, 19 Dec 1940.

16. Ibid., 7, 9, 11 Oct, 1, 7, 23 Nov, 3, 4 Dec 1940; Fleet to Towers [?] Dec 1940, quoted in Wagner, 234; Holley, *Buying Aircraft*, 265; Connery, 96–98.

17. Holley, *Buying Aircraft*, 265–66; Nelson, 116–22; Beasley, 299ff; diary, 23 Dec 1940; Administrative History 38b, 42–49; Administrative History 37a, 51; Albion, *Makers*, 413; Connery, 98–102; minutes of JAC meeting, 10–11 Mar 1941, National Archives. Fullton Towers remained on the OPM only until May 1941 (*New York Times*, 19 Feb 1942).

18. Albion, *Makers*, 552–53; Morison, vol. 1, 36–45, 51; DYER, VOL. 1, 160–61; diary, 2, 3 Jan 1941; Creed, 49.

19. Diary, 14, 15 Oct, 15 Nov 1940; BuAer annual report 1940, 24 and passim; *New York Times*, 6 Dec 1940; Baltimore *Sun*, 20 Dec 1940. De Seversky's Sikorsky four-engine flying boat—XPBS Flying Dreadnought, or VS-44A commercial liner—had lost out to Consolidated's PB2Y Coronado. His book, *Victory through Air Power*, in which he attacked naval aviation, appeared in 1942, while his column was syndicated in the press (see Sherry, 127ff).

20. House Naval Affairs Committee hearings, 7 Jan 1941; *New York Times*, 8 Jan 1941 (two stories, one carrying the byline of Hanson W. Baldwin); New York *Herald Tribune*, 8 Jan 1941.

21. Diary, 7, 9–11 Jan 1941; Associated Press story, 9 Jan 1941; Arnold, 245–46.

22. House Naval Affairs Committee hearings of 9–10 Jan 1941, 248–50, 311ff, 2055–64; Administrative History 41, 55, 184–86; Administrative History 58, 37–41; Administrative History 59, 164–83; New York *Herald Tribune*, 10 Jan 1941; Associated Press release, 10 Jan 1941; diary, 9, 10 Jan 1941. Actually, the existing reserve training station at Opa Locka was absorbed into the new NAS Miami complex, making a total of twenty. The other existing reserve stations were Philadelphia, Squantum (Rhode Island), Floyd Bennett Field (New York City), Anacostia (Washington, D.C.), Seattle, Oakland, Long Beach, Grosse Ile (Michigan), Glenview (Chicago), Minneapolis, St. Louis, and Kansas City (later renamed Olathe). Top priority for the new ones was given to New Orleans, Dallas, and Atlanta, with sites for ten more listed. On 10 August 1941 the Mason board on reserve air stations submitted its report, which was immediately approved by Towers. The major airlines to be tapped for pilots were Pan Am and Transcontinental and Western Air (TWA). Their callup was later delayed from June to September when the army refused to participate in the action jointly.

23. Administrative History 60, 37–44, 51–52; BuAer annual report of 1941, 31; Haynes, 19; Albion, *Makers*, 482. Towers appeared before the House appropriations naval subcommittee on 14, 24 February, 12 March, and 14, 15 July 1941; the Bureau of the Budget on 21 October, 4 November 1940 and 16, 27 January, 14 February, 18 July, and 3, 15 November 1941, the House Naval Affairs Committee on 16, 17, and 22 July 1941, and the Truman Committee investigating the war during the spring.

24. Diary, 8 Feb, 12, 18 Mar, 3 Apr, 15, 16, 22, 24 May 1941; Towers to brother William, 8 May 1941. Scrugham at least succeeded in getting the army to establish a bombing and gunnery training base at Las Vegas.

25. Aldo Joseph Draghi to the author, Feb 1987, and, for the XPB2M Martin Mars flying boat, "Presenting: Admiral John H. Towers," 21.

26. Draghi to the author, Feb 1987; Towers to brother William, 8 May 1941; "Presenting Admiral Towers," 21; diary, 29 Jan 1941. Riley was flag lieutenant to Bristol, then flag secretary to McCain.

27. Morison, vol. 1, 45; Slessor, 353–56. Slessor especially admired Ramsey.

28. Diary, Jan–Mar 1941 (this records the Greek fighter discussions in detail); Administrative History 64a, 40; Slessor, 356–59; Morison, vol. 1, 48–49, especially 49n.

29. Connery, 84; Administrative History 38b, 50–51; Nelson, 122–23; JAC minutes, 10–11 Mar 1941, National Archives; Holley, *Buying Aircraft*, 266–67; Administrative History 64a, 24–25, 42–43; Self oral transcript, 56.

30. Administrative History 64a, 41–47; diary, 6, 7 Mar, 15, 23 Apr, 5 May 1941; Towers to brother William, 8 May 1941; Los Angeles *Times*, 26 Apr 1941; San Diego *Union*, 28 Apr 1941.

Accompanied by Commander Cal Durgin, head of the flight division at BuAer, Towers inspected the new base at Oakland and NAS Alameda and stayed with Marjorie at Coronado during his trip of 23–29 April 1941. The final naming of all navy planes did not occur until 1 October 1941.

31. Diary, 19, 26, 28 Feb, 19, 21, 22, 26 Mar, 7, 14, 15 Apr 1941. Towers also had to calm FDR's fear that workers at the Naval Aircraft Factory might be laid off for lack of airplane orders. Towers assured him that the slowdown was due only to shortages of materials for the N3N trainers and that work was soon to begin on NAF versions of the OS2U (OS2N) and PBY (PBN) (FDR to Callaghan, 24 Feb 1941; Towers to Callaghan, 26 Feb 1941; Callaghan to FDR, 26 Feb 1941, FDR Library, PSF).

32. Diary, 24 Jan, 17 Feb, 7, 9, 20 Mar, 14 May 1941; conversation with Paul Pihl in 1981; Harris oral transcript, 35. Two naval aviators were also sent to Australia.

33. Friedman, *Aircraft Carriers,* 161–62; Towers to King, 30 July 1946; Towers to Lieutenant Commander C. L. Duval, 28 Nov 1945, from the *New Jersey,* Tokyo Bay, and copied in Forrestal diary, 21 Jan 1946, Naval Historical Center. Towers wrote, "It might be interesting to know that that very ship [the *Long Island*] came into Tokyo Bay yesterday, and is anchored close by." FDR's decision was reinforced by a recommendation from Halsey in December 1940 for just such a ship, though for the purpose of aircraft transport and pilot training (Lord, 1180).

34. FDR to Forrestal, 7 Mar 1941, copy in Towers diary; diary, 9 Mar, 6, 14 May 1941; Friedman, *Aircraft Carriers,* 162ff; Duncan oral transcript, 269–77.

35. Diary, 23 May 1941.

36. *Time,* 23 June 1941, 21; Towers to chairman of the General Board, 3 Apr 1941, quoted in Administrative History 52, 27–29.

37. Towers to brother William, 8 May 1941 (italics original); *New York Times,* 8 Feb 1942; diary, 8, 9, 19–21, 28 May 1941; Morison, vol. 1, 49ff. On 8 May 1941 the chief of the naval staff of Uruguay personally requested five OS2Us from Towers, who agreed.

38. Diary, 27, 29, 31 May, 12, 16, 17, 25 June 1941; Administrative History 48, 66–67; Arnold, 245; Towers to Arnold, 8 May 1941; Arnold to Towers, 9 May 1941, Arnold papers; Towers' KBE (Knight of the British Empire) citation.

39. *Time,* 23 June 1941, cover, 19–21.

40. Diary, 25 June 1941; Towers' fitness report, 9 Feb 1942. The British admirals were H. A. Little and J. W. S. Dorling. Towers' famous World War II contemporaries would not grace the cover of *Time* until well into the fighting, starting with Nimitz in May 1942.

41. Arnold, 234–35; Van Wyen, *Aeronautical Board,* 10; Roland, vol. 1, 189–91; C. G. Abbott to Goddard, 30 Apr 1940; Towers to Goddard, 14 July 1941; Goddard to Harry F. Guggenheim, 19, 25 July 1941; Goddard to Towers, 24 July 1941. All correspondence to and from Goddard in Goddard papers, 1307, 1406–7, 1409, 1410–12.

42. Arnold, 245, 264; Fanton, 62–63; Beasley, 308ff; Connery, 112.

43. Arnold, 195–96; Fanton, 32–33, 44, 52, 63.

44. Diary, 27 June 1941 (paragraphing added). Fanton gives Lovett's similar recollection of the meeting in a letter from Lovett to Stimson, 2 July 1941, 63–64.

45. Diary, 28 June, 1–3 July 1941; Associated Press release, 22 July 1941; Fanton, 64–65, 140–42.

46. Diary, 8 July 1941; Joint Board files, National Archives.

47. Arnold, 245; FDR's social appointments file, 25 Aug 1941, FDR Library; Administrative History 52, 49–50; Joint Board, "Estimate of United States Overall Production Requirements," 11 Sep 1942.

48. Wagner, 235; diary, 11 June 1941; Wilson, *Slipstream,* 247.

49. Diary, 9 July, 4 Aug 1941; OPM and army-navy position papers of 9 July 1941, copies in Towers diary. See also Fanton, 126–30.

50. Administrative History 49, 27–28.

51. Connery, 113; Administrative History 49, 22–24, 32–34; Administrative History 52, 34–35; Administrative History 47a, 431–32; Turnbull and Lord, 266–67. Pihl recommended the new division be called the coordination division, but Captain Webster suggested production division on 31 July 1941.

52. Booz, Fry, Allen, and Hamilton, "Survey of Administration, Bureau of Aeronautics, Navy Department," 16 Aug 1941, quoted in Administrative History 49, 25–36.

53. Ibid., 26–27.

54. Ibid., 38; Administrative History 55, 38ff; diary, 6 Oct 1941.

55. Administrative History 49, 27ff, 38–41; Administrative History 52, 34–43; Administrative History 47a, 567–69; Connery, 128–30; Read oral transcript, 125–26; conversation with Loomis, 1987. By 6 October 1941 the former divisions were administration, financial, plans, flight, personnel, progress, defense aid (Lend-Lease), production, and—under the material branch—engineering, procurement, maintenance, and airship. Towers had the benefit of three excellent secretaries—Gertrude E. Baker, Paula Gillespie, and a Miss Gallant.

56. Read oral transcript, 126–31; Administrative History 47b, 220–22; Administrative History 59, 364–66; Hancock oral transcript, 47–48; Taylor, "Synthetics," part 1, 32; Hubbell, 60.

57. Administrative History 59, 366–68; Taylor, "Synthetics," part 1, 39. Or $16.80 cash.

58. Administrative History 49b, 223–24; Administrative History 59, 376; Taylor, "Synthetics," part 1, 32, 39. Special devices became a division of BuAer in 1944 with a budget of $57 million for 1944–45 (*Naval Aviation News,* Apr 1961, 8). Taylor describes de Florez's "dice box for indecisive admirals, a simple device consisting merely of a leather cup and a number of suitably inscribed ivory cubes. On one side of a cube, for example, will appear 'Yes' and on the opposite side 'No.' Other cubes are labelled 'Sink' and 'Swim,' 'Damn the Torpedoes' and 'Watch the Torpedoes,' and so on. De Florez has presented sets to several admirals, who received them with various degrees of enthusiasm" (38).

59. Administrative History 41, 177–80, 186–88; Administrative History 47b, 179–80; Doyle interview by Pierre Towers, typescript, about 1960.

60. Administrative History 41, 40–43, 52ff, 82ff, 100ff, 129ff; conversation with John Monsarrat in 1985; Hancock oral transcript, 49–50; New York *Journal-American,* 23 May 1940; Potter, *Nimitz,* 170–72.

61. Administrative History 41, 181–82; diary, 14 July, 6 Oct 1941; conversation with John Crommelin, 1978.

62. Doyle oral transcript, 17–19; Administrative History 49, 41–42; Administrative History 41, 182–83; Administrative History 59, 281, 368n; diary, 31 Oct, 4 Nov 1941; Anderson oral transcript, 157.

63. Diary, 17 Sep 1940 and 16 Jan, 11, 16, 17 Apr, 14 June 1941; Administrative History 60, 43–44; Administrative History 30, 34, 53–54; House appropriations subcommittee hearings of 22 July 1941, 220.

64. Administrative History 66, 4–7, 18–19; Administrative History 52, 43; Administrative History 61, 11–15; Administrative History 63, 10–14; Administrative History 65, 68–69; Administrative History 57, 27–33; Administrative History 126, 2–5, 9–15, 23ff; Werrell, 23–24; Administrative History 91, 24–25, 45–47, 58–59; diary, 12 Nov 1940 and 2 Jan, 9 Oct 1941; Read oral transcript, 142–47; Coletta, *Domestic Bases,* 374–75.

65. Diary, 3 June, 11, 24–30 July 1941; *Time,* 23 June 1941, 20; Towers to Pierre, 25 July 1941.

66. Diary, 30, 31 July, 1, 2, 4, 6–8, 13 Aug 1941; Baltimore *News-Post,* 6 Aug 1941. On 13 August Towers discussed possible development of the autogiro with the Pipcairn company, but it never matured, the helicopter holding more promise.

67. Diary, 3–5, 22–29 Sep, 13 Oct 1941; Wagner, 241–43. Towers flew to Roanoke, Virginia, on 13–14 October to help dedicate the new Clifton Woodrum Airport, named for the chairman of the House appropriations subcommittee—a politically astute appearance by Towers.

68. Wagner, 236–37; diary, 1, 4, 9 Oct 1941; Connery, 268.

69. Wagner, 236–37; diary, 16, 17 Oct 1941.

70. Diary, 16 Oct 1941.

71. Ibid., 17 Oct 1941; Wagner, 237.

72. Diary, 18, 20, 21, 24, 25, 27 Oct 1941; San Diego *Union,* 21 Oct 1941; conversation with John Crommelin, Lumley Lyster's U.S. aide, 1978. The California newspapers referred to Consolidated as the company itself often did, Consair. Towers' interest in the lessons of combat was

insatiable. When John Monsarrat wrote a fifty-two-page report for United Aircraft on air operations he had studied in England, Gene Wilson sent a copy to Towers, who then invited Monsarrat to discuss it with him. During their meeting at BuAer in November, Towers had Monsarrat give details about "the 'Intruder Tactic' developed by British night fighters; the favorable performance of Pratt & Whitney engines vis-a-vis the liquid-cooled Rolls Royce engines with respect to length of time between overhauls and vulnerability to machine gun and antiaircraft fire; and the widespread and effective use of women in British armed services and supporting organizations" (Monsarrat to the author, 17 Oct 1985).

73. Diary, 31 Oct, 1, 3–5, 7 Nov 1941; memorandum for files of 31 Oct 1941, inserted in diary; Wagner, 241–43. Towers telephoned Fleet at his Beverly Hills home and at an Arizona hideaway.

74. Diary, 5, 6, 13, 18, 26, 27 Nov 1941.

75. Ibid., 24 Oct, 12–14, 19 Nov, 2, 5 Dec 1941; Connery, 105–6, 118–21.

76. Administrative History 30, 57–58; Administrative History 60, 45; diary, 3, 15, 19 Nov 1941; House appropriations subcommittee hearings of 17 Nov 1941, 31.

77. "Memorandum of Conference in the Office of the CNO," 27 Nov 1941, Navy Historical Center; diary, 27 Nov 1941; Morison, vol. 3, 210–11.

78. Towers to Knox, 27 Nov 1941; diary, 3–5 Dec 1941; Administrative History 60, 45–46.

79. Diary, 7 Dec 1941; Johnson oral transcript, 54.

80. Crosby Maynard, quoted in *December 7*, 187–88, courtesy of Paolo E. Coletta.

CHAPTER 13. AIR CHIEF OF THE WARTIME NAVY, 1941–42

1. Joint Board minutes, 8 Dec 1941, National Archives; Anderson oral transcript, 73–75; diary, 8 Dec 1941.

2. Draghi to Pierre [Feb 1987]; Arnold, 269–73; Joint Board minutes, 9 Dec 1941; diary, 9, 10, 13 Dec 1941; *New York Times*, 27 Jan 1942.

3. Administrative History 60, 44–46; FDR diaries and itineraries, 13 Dec 1941, FDR Library, PPF; diary, 11 Dec 1941.

4. Anderson oral transcript, 76; diary, 16 Dec 1941; Dyer, vol. 1, 196; Hoyt, 7–15.

5. Conversations with Crommelin, 1978 and 1984.

6. Ibid.; conversation with Pierre Towers, 1985; Buell, *King*, 152.

7. Diary, 16 Dec 1941.

8. Ibid.; Buell, *King*, 152–53; Potter, *Nimitz*, 8–9.

9. *Class of '06*, passim. Towers' academy roommate, Captain Tommy Lew Atkins, passed over for flag, was assistant director, shore establishments division, under Assistant Secretary Bard.

10. Morison, vol. 3, 235ff; diary, 26 Jan, 8 July 1942; Yarnell diary, 26 Jan 1942, Yarnell papers, courtesy of Robert J. Cressman.

11. Towers, "The Navy Spreads Its Wings," *Shipmate* (Jan 1942), 6–7; diary, 26, 29 Jan, 2 Feb 1942.

12. Alnav 31 of 30 Jan 1942; Pownall to Mitscher, 3 Feb 1942; Towers to Mitscher, 30 Jan 1942; Mitscher to Towers, 4 Feb 1942, Mitscher papers; Spruance to wife Margaret, 7, 10 Feb, 21 Mar, 4 Apr 1942, Spruance papers. Spruance knew so little about these aviators that he spelled Mitscher's name *M-i-t-c-h-e-r*.

13. CCS minutes, 24 Dec 1941–14 Jan 1942, copy in Arnold papers; diary, 24 Dec 1941; Davis, vol. 1, 222–39, 248–50. Other members of the council were General Holcomb of the marines and Brigadier General L. T. Gerow of army war plans.

14. Arnold, 276–83 (some dates and figures are inaccurate); diary, 19 Dec 1941; Ambrose, vol. 1, 141; CCS minutes, 24 Dec 1941.

15. Joint Board records; Buell, *King*, 180–85; Albion, *Makers*, 383–84; Arnold to Towers, 1 Jan 1942, Arnold papers; Administrative History 49, 74. The Joint Board held its last full-scale meeting on 16 March 1942 but was not officially dissolved until 1947.

16. Albion and Connery, 88–93; Buell, *King*, 143 and passim; John L. McCrea draft memoirs, item 5, FDR Library.

17. Diary, 22–24 Jan 1942; Albion and Connery, 94–96; Albion, *Makers*, 416.

18. Diary, 14 Jan 1942.

19. Somehow, details of the streamlined Victory Program of the previous September were leaked to the press on the eve of Pearl Harbor, leading to an investigation of the source by the FBI. Towers could shed no light when interviewed by agents on 27 January (diary, 27 Jan 1942; Dyer, vol. 1, 197). The two new *Essexes* would become *Bennington* (CV-20) and *Boxer* (CV-21).

20. Rae, 141–42; Towers to Knox, 2 Jan 1942; Stark endorsement of 7 Jan 1942; Towers to Knox, 2 Jan 1942, with FDR's penned "OK" of the twelfth; FDR to Knox, 9 Jan 1942; Towers to King, 29 Aug 1942, FDR Library, OF 18i; diary, 8, 9 Jan 1942; Administrative History 30, 58–62, 72–77; Administrative History 31, 35–36; Administrative History 47a, 58–61; Administrative History 48, 55–56; Administrative History 60, 47, 61–62; Riley oral transcript, 145, 150–51; Fanton, 74–77. McJimsey shows that Harry Hopkins also thought FDR's aircraft figures too high (223, and see Anderson oral transcript, 90–91).

21. Diary, 26 Dec 1941; Administrative History 48, 55–56; Administrative History 60, 47–57. Towers testified before the following committees or subcommittees during 1942: House naval affairs, 8 Jan, 9, 16 June, 21 July; House appropriations, 13 Jan, 17, 18 Mar, 24 Sep; Senate naval affairs, 29 Jan, 2 Feb; Senate appropriations, 1 Apr, 5 June; and Bureau of the Budget, 9, 27 Jan, 11 Mar.

22. Rae, 142–45, 147–48; Johnson oral transcript, 54–55; conversation with Paul Pihl, 1981; Wilson, *Slipstream*, 252–55.

23. Rae, 144; diary, 23 Dec 1941, 27, 31 Mar, 26 Aug 1942. Girdler had previously been board chairman of Republic Steel.

24. Towers to Grumman, 31 July 1942, quoted in Administrative History 56, 106–9, with an account of "Spare Parts Board," 109–12; Lundstrom, 140ff; Thruelsen, 134–35, 382; Riley oral transcript, 167; Anderson oral transcript, 103–4; Grumman to Towers, 7 Oct 1942; Towers to Grumman, 17 Oct 1942. The AAF officer was Lieutenant Colonel Eddie Langmead.

25. Diary, 14, 18, 25 Mar, 20 Apr, 4, 5, 8, 12 May, 31 July, 12 Sep 1942; *New York Times*, 12 Feb 1942. Only half of the F3As were completed when the navy closed down Brewster in July 1944 (courtesy of George R. Inger).

26. Diary, 18 Mar 1942; Albion and Connery, 96–97; Administrative History 49, 74; Vinson to FDR, 14 Apr 1942; FDR to Knox, 15 Apr 1942; Knox to FDR, 23 Apr 1942; FDR to Vinson, 4 May 1942, FDR Library, OF 18i.

27. Administrative History 48, 14–15; Administrative History 49, 75–77; Albion and Connery, 97–101; diary, 1, 20, 21 May, 9, 10 June 1942; *New York Times*, 9, 15 May 1942 (front-page story on the reorganization authored by Hanson Baldwin).

28. Riley oral transcript, 148; Administrative History 41, 192, 196–98. FDR ordered the CAA's civilian pilot training program committed wholly to military uses on 12 Dec 1941 (Pisano, 31ff).

29. Administrative History 58, 78–81, 88–91; several "pork barrel" letters Jan to July 1942 FDR Library, OF 18i; diary, 23, 24 Jan, 17 Feb, 23 Mar, 9, 11 Apr, 5 May, 11, 13, 17, 18, 25, 27, 31 July 1942.

30. Administrative History 47b, 197–200; Newton and Rae, 19–20.

31. Read oral transcript, 160–89, 203; Administrative History 66, 8–10, 19–28, 35–56; conversation with Loomis, 1987; diary, 26 Feb, 9, 10 Apr 1942; Custer to author, 19 Sep 1986; G. Willing Pepper to author, 16 Aug 1966. Custer describes Ragsdale as "a very worrisome kind of fellow" (oral transcript, 306). The ACIO program eventually produced over seventeen hundred graduates.

32. Hancock, 48–56, 59–67, 185–86, 189; Hancock oral transcript, 49–50; McAfee Horton oral transcript, 13–14; diary, 16 Sep 1942; Anderson oral transcript, 79–80. Walsh's aide was Joseph McIntyre.

33. Monsarrat, 9–16; Phillips, 20–25.

34. Monsarrat, 19; conversation with Monsarrat, 1985.

35. Johnson oral transcript, 56–59, 64, 66–67; diary, 7 Jan, 8, 19 Sep 1942. Of the other planes Towers wanted to receive cannon, the Brewster SB2A Buccaneer and F2A-3 Buffalo soon proved to be obsolete, the Douglas SB2D never evolved beyond the experimental stage, the Curtiss SB3C was never completed, and only late-model F6F Hellcats and F4U/F3A Corsairs received two cannon in place of two of their six .50-caliber machine guns.

36. Diary, 10 Feb, 6 May, 13 June, 21 July 1942; Swanborough, 497–501; Howeth, 490–91; Fahrney, 56–58; Werrell, 24–25. See Administrative History 39 for the ill-conceived marine glider program, which Towers supported.

37. Administrative History 49, 47–48; Administrative History 60, 49–50, 58–59; Swanborough, 506, 512; diary, 16, 18, 21 Apr, 2, 22 July 1942. Only 167 blimps were completed.

38. Administrative History 48, 87–90, and Towers to Stark, 12 Dec 1941, reproduced therein, 187; diary, 20 Dec 1941, 14 Jan 1942; *New York Times,* 9 Oct 1942.

39. Diary, 21, 22, 24 Jan, 16 June 1942; General Board hearings, 6 Mar 1942. The new *Essexes,* mostly postwar as it turned out, would become the *Bon Homme Richard* (CV-31), *Leyte* (CV-32), *Kearsarge* (CV-33), *Oriskany* (CV-34), *Antietam* (CV-36), *Princeton* (CV-37), *Shangri-La* (CV-38), *Lake Champlain* (CV-39), and *Tarawa* (CV-40); not completed was the *Reprisal* (CV-35). The *Midways* would become the *Midway* (CVB-41), *Franklin D. Roosevelt* (CVB-42), and *Coral Sea* (CVB-43); CVB-44 was never laid down.

40. Diary, 25 Feb 3, 4 March, 20 July 1942; Towers to Ramsey, 17 Mar 1942. Halsey and the *Enterprise* then struck Wake and Marcus islands as well.

41. Towers to Yarnell, 2 Mar 1942; Towers to Forrestal, 3 Mar 1942; diary, 20 Mar, 7 Apr 1942.

42. Diary, 14, 24 Apr, 1, 13 May 1942; Towers to Douglas, 14 Nov 1941, 5 Feb 1942, Douglas papers; Towers to Byrd, 12 Feb 1942; Byrd to Towers (two letters), 14 Feb 1942, Byrd papers; Studenmund, 20.

43. Diary, 1 May 1942.

44. Hayes, *JCS,* 129; Matloff and Snell, 223–24.

45. Administrative History 31, 49–56; Administrative History 47a, 63–68 (italics original); Administrative History 48, 100–104, and reproduced therein, Stimson to Knox, 30 Mar 1942, Knox to Towers, 31 Mar 1942, Towers to Knox, 4 Apr 1942; Craven and Cate, vol. 1, 538ff; Morison, vol. 1, 237ff; diary, 31 Mar 1942; Fanton, 183ff.

46. Matloff and Snell, 206–10; Slessor, 404–6; Arnold, 304–7; Hayes, *JCS,* 155; Fanton, 151–52.

47. Diary, 6, 8, 15, 19 May 1942; Churchill to FDR, 12 May 1942, and FDR to Churchill, 19 May 1942, copies in Arnold papers; Arnold, 306–7; Slessor, 406–7.

48. Diary, 20 May 1942; minutes of White House Conference, 20 May 1942, Arnold papers; Arnold, 307–8.

49. Diary, 20 May 1942; Administrative History 48, 83–84, 179, reproducing Towers to FDR, 6 June 1942.

50. Diary, 21, 23, 24–26 May 1942; Arnold log, "Trip to England," 23–26 May 1942, Arnold papers; Arnold, 308; Anderson oral transcript, 82.

51. Arnold log, 26 May 1942; diary, 26 May 1942.

52. Arnold log, 26, 27 May 1942; diary, 26–28 May 1942; London *Evening Standard,* 26 May 1942; London *Daily Telegraph and Morning Post,* 27 May 1942; London *Times,* 27 May 1942.

53. Arnold log, 28 May 1942; diary, 28 May 1942.

54. Diary, 28–30 May 1942; Arnold log, 28–30 May 1942; Arnold, 312–15; Slessor, 407–10; Craven and Cate, vol. 1, 566–67.

55. Arnold, 312.

56. Diary, 30 May 1942; Beebe oral transcript, 56; Arnold log, 30 May 1942; Arnold, 316; conversation with William M. Towers, III, Jack's nephew, in 1985; Anderson oral transcript, 92–93.

57. Arnold, 318; Arnold log, 31 May 1942; Anderson oral transcript, 92; Beebe oral transcript, 57–58. Beebe notes that rumors quoted Mrs. Churchill as having said, "My word, do all American admirals act like that?" Grover Loening later sent *The Snow Goose* and a second book as a gift from the Towers to Mrs. Churchill (Clementine Churchill to Pierre, 25 Sep 1942).

58. Diary, 31 May–4 June 1942; Arnold log, 1–3 June 1942; Slessor, 410–11.

59. Craven and Cate, vol. 1, 567–71, and vol. 6, 407–8; Administrative History 64a, 73n; Matloff and Snell, 226–27, 248–49; Hayes, *JCS*, 156–63; diary, 20 June 1942. The agreement was somewhat modified in December.

60. Atlanta *Constitution,* 19 June 1942; diary, 18, 23, 25 June, 2, 10 July 1942; Matloff and Snell, 266–73.

61. Forrestal to Donald Nelson, 10 Aug 1942, Towers papers; Towers to Captain W. R. Smedberg, 6 Feb 1947, Forrestal papers, National Archives; George W. Anderson to Captain J. L. Pratt, 27 Jan 1947, Towers papers; Anderson oral transcript, 98; diary, 14 Feb 1939. According to Towers' diary, the original Budd proposal was for a large flying boat comparable to the four-engine PB2Y Coronado.

62. Wilson, *Slipstream,* 255; Administrative History 48, 60–61; diary, 23 Mar, 18–20 May, 10 June 1942.

63. Administrative History 48, 61–63; Towers to Smedberg, 6 Feb 1947, which includes relevant entries from the diary from July 1942.

64. Diary, 23, 27 July 1942; Morison, vol. 10, 41; *Time,* 27 July 1942; Barton, 54–55; Foster, 183. Of Towers' emergency cargo planes, only seventeen RBs were completed.

65. Diary, 7–13 Aug 1942; Barton, 55–56; Forrestal to Nelson, 10 Aug 1942; Foster, 179–83; Towers' statement before Brewster committee on Kaiser-Hughes contract, 28 July 1947.

66. Diary, 12 Aug, 3, 4 Sep 1942, 7 Feb 1944, when Towers visited Hughes; Towers quoted in *New York Times,* 9 Oct 1942; Towers' statement before Brewster committee, 28 July 1947, with Towers to Nelson and Lovett to Nelson, 12 Sep 1942, attached; Barton, 56–59; Read oral transcript, 451; Foster, 184. Hughes called his big boat the H-4 Hercules, which made its one flight in November 1947.

67. Diary, 6, 11 Aug, 2 Sep 1942; Daley, 345.

68. Monsarrat, 19; Markey, 66. The latter was based on an interview with Towers late in 1944.

69. Vinson to FDR, undated (received at the White House on 4 July 1942); FDR to Knox, 6 July 1942; Knox to FDR, 7 July 1942, FDR Library, PSF 11 and OF 18i; diary, 7 July 1942.

70. Diary, 7, 8 July, 12 Sep 1942.

71. Clipping from unidentified newspaper [Sep 1942]; diary, 23 Apr 1942.

72. Towers' fitness reports, 14 July, 15 Oct 1942; diary, 29, 30 July 1942; Bogan conversation with Pierre, transcribed, Towers papers.

73. Towers' medical abstract.

74. Diary, 20 July 1942; *Washington Post,* 15 July 1942; Hancock oral transcript, 44, 45; *Washington Star,* 1 Mar 1942; *Flying and Popular Aviation,* Jan 1942, 35.

75. Hancock oral transcript, 45; *Washington Post,* 19 July 1942; *New York Times,* 19 July 1942; diary, 20, 22, 23, 31 July 1942. Colonel Jouett also visited Towers for his views on a possible publicity campaign to promote the aircraft industry, but Towers discouraged it.

76. Diary, 20 July 1942; Buell, *King,* 176, 178.

77. King-Nimitz conference notes, 4 July, 8 Sep, 11–13 Dec 1942 (on the latter two occasions King tried to get Nimitz to take Hoover); diary, 23, 24 July, 14, 26 Aug 1942; Albion and Connery, 97, which notes that BuPers chief Jacobs was King's "man."

78. Reynolds, *Fast Carriers,* 32; Morison, vol. 10, 58; Pierre Towers to author, 9 Dec 1978, quoting her husband.

79. Fletcher to Nimitz, 24 Sep 1942, Naval Historical Center, courtesy of Michael Lowe. For a defense of Fletcher, see Regan.

80. Diary, 14, 25, 26, 31 Aug, 3 Sep 1942.

81. Administrative History 31, 35–37; Towers to King, 29 Aug, 3 Oct 1942; King to FDR, 2 Sep 1942; diary, 21 Sep 1942; Fanton, 78–85.

82. Buell, *King,* 364; Pearson in *Washington Post,* 24 Sep 1942; unidentified newspaper clipping [Sep 1942]; Pierre to author, 19 Jan 1978.

83. Diary, 29 Aug, 21, 30 Sep 1942; *New York Times,* 16 Sep 1942; conversation with Monsarrat in 1985; *Washington Post,* 7 Oct, and editorial of 9 Oct 1942.

84. Administrative History 149a, 21; Administrative History 48, 56; Stroop oral transcript, 166.

85. King-Nimitz conference notes, 7–8 Sep 1942; Potter, *Nimitz*, 186–87; Potter, *Halsey*, 154–57; Stroop oral transcript, 166. Halsey officially became ComAirPac on 19 September 1942, Fitch commander Air Force South Pacific on the twentieth.

86. Diary, 10–12 Sep 1942; Arnold, 350; Lovett oral transcript, 68. Read, in a transcribed interview by Pierre about 1960, strongly asserted that Gates had been the real culprit in convincing Knox to transfer Towers: Gates "had a little czar complex" from being the youngest bank vice president in New York, and "Jack couldn't stand Gates." Read tended to exaggerate, but the Towers-Gates tension apparently did exist.

87. Pearson in *Washington Post*, 24 Sep 1942; Monsarrat, 20; Riley oral transcript, 160; conversation with Riley, 1966; *Time*, 5 Oct 1942; Anderson oral transcript, 94.

88. Towers to Arnold, 17 Sep 1942, Towers papers. Arnold's letter does not survive. Yarnell to Towers, 19 Sep 1942, said, "Before the war is over you will be C in C" in the Pacific.

89. Reynolds, *Fast Carriers*, 30–32; San Diego *Union*, 16 Sep 1942; Towers to Nimitz, 21 Sep 1942, and undated reply, Nimitz papers. Admiral Leigh Noyes was sacked for losing the *Wasp*.

90. *U.S. Air Services*, Sep 1942, 8–9; "Let's Get Two-Fisted," *Collier's*, 24 Oct 1942, 86; *Time*, 28 Sep 1942; Pearson column in *Washington Post*, 24 Sep 1942; *New York Times*, 16, 20 Sep 1942; *Washington Post*, 16 Sep 1942; Charlotte (North Carolina) *News*, 16 Sep 1942; *Newsweek*, 28 Sep 1942; Baltimore *Sun*, 16 Sep 1942.

91. Knox to Nimitz, 13 Oct 1942, Nimitz papers.

92. Morgenthau to Towers, 16 Sep 1942; Towers to Morgenthau, 17 Sep 1942, FDR Library, Morgenthau collection; Symington to King, 18 Sep 1942; King to Symington, 23 Sep 1942, King papers.

93. *New York Times*, 9 Sep 1942; Louis E. Denfeld to Pierre, 6 Mar 1942; Knox to Pierre, 14 Mar 1942; Forrestal to Pierre, 26 Sep 1942; Pierre to Forrestal, received 3 Oct 1942, Ship Name and Sponsor file, Naval History Center, courtesy of Robert J. Cressman; diary, 25 Sep 1942. Perfectly reasonable though the change was, it was still a bit of a dirty trick, since Knox did not even invite the first lady to christen the CV-10 until December 1942.

94. Diary, 2 Oct 1942; Read oral transcript, 220–22; Towers' personnel file, 16 June 1944.

95. Read oral transcript, 732; Charlotte *News*, 16 Sep 1942.

96. Meigs to Towers, 7 Oct 1942. Meigs had a dinner conversation with Knudsen on the sixth in which the latter shared his appraisal of Towers.

CHAPTER 14. AIR CHIEF AGAINST JAPAN, 1942–43

1. Swanborough, 416; Pirie oral transcript, 92; Read oral transcript, 222–24.

2. Read oral transcript, 223–24; Morison, vol. 5, 184; conversation with Crommelin, 1978; Gwenfread Allen, 113; Pirie to the author, 23 June, 21 July 1987. "Dim-out" meant that only 25-watt light bulbs, usually Christmastree lights, could be used at night.

3. Towers to Nimitz, 21 Sep 1942, Nimitz papers; Nimitz quoted in Potter, *Nimitz*, 189; Mercer oral transcript, 5–6; Pirie to the author, 21 July 1987.

4. *Lucky Bag, 1907*, 107.

5. Nimitz to King, 12 Oct 1942, Nimitz papers; Taylor, *Mitscher*, 140; Pirie to author, 21 July 1987.

6. Towers to Nimitz, 28 Oct 1942.

7. Hoyt, 161, 166; conversation with Admiral George Anderson, 1964, in which he said that Towers "hated" Kinkaid; Towers to Nimitz, 9 Nov 1942; Read oral transcript, 288.

8. Read oral transcript, 730; Morison, vol. 5, 291; Hoyt, 195, 198.

9. ComAirPac History, 12–14; Reynolds, *Fast Carriers*, 33–35. The fourth *Cimarron*, the *Santee*, came out later.

10. Towers to Nimitz, 12 Jan, 14 Apr 1943, Naval Historical Center; Reynolds, *Fast Carriers,* 34–35.

11. Halsey to Fitch, 23 Dec 1942, Halsey papers; Taylor, *Mitscher,* 141.

12. Reynolds, *Fast Carriers,* 29; ComAirPac to AirPac, 1 Sep 1942; Navy Department press release, 14 Sep 1942; Johnson oral transcript, 65; Busch, 83; Read oral transcript, 223, 236, 436.

13. Anderson to author, 31 Jan 1985; Pierre to author, [19 Jan 1978]; conversation with Pierre, 1985 (italics original). Buell, however, asserts, "Nimitz came to hate Towers. . . ." (*King,* 336).

14. Towers' fitness report, 8 Oct 1942 to 31 Mar 1943, dated 13 May 1943.

15. Read oral transcript, 225–26; conversation with Pierre, 1985; Towers to brother William, 21 Sep 1943.

16. Pirie oral transcript, 92–93, 102; staff directory, 1 July 1943, in ComAirPac History.

17. Towers to brother William, 10 Mar 1943; ComAirPac History, 118–26; conversation with Monsarrat, 1985; Hoyt, 183; conversations with Pirie and Loomis, 1987; Pennoyer to author, 7 Apr 1969; Allen, "Ingalls," 38–39; Pepper to author, 16 Aug 1966. Towers also brought his driver, Joe Draghi, from Washington to ComAirPac. Pepper eventually became president of Scott Paper Company.

18. *Lucky Bag, 1918,* 194; Read oral transcript, 225.

19. Conversation with Monsarrat, 1985; Read oral transcript, 227–33, 248–49; San Diego *Union,* 13 June 1943, date of the *McFarland* ceremony.

20. Jurika oral transcript, 304.

21. Ramage to author, 20 Dec 1986.

22. Pennoyer to author, 7 Apr 1969; Pirie to author, 21 July 1987; Pirie oral transcript, 92–95; Johnson oral transcript, 65–66; Halsey to McCain, 28 Apr 1943, Halsey papers; Towers to McCain, 2 May 1943.

23. Towers to Gates, 31 May 1943; Horne to Moreell, 5 June 1943; Pirie oral transcript, 92, 101; diary, 2, 17 Mar 1944; King-Nimitz conference notes, 21 Feb, 25–28 Sep 1943, Naval Historical Center; Towers to Nimitz, 14 Nov 1942, on the F4F-7s; Swanborough, 208; Hutchings, 42–44, on the magnetic anomaly detection device; Sherrod, 325–26.

24. Read oral transcript, 234–35.

25. Pirie to author, 21 July 1987.

26. Towers to brother William, 10 Mar, 17 Apr, 21 Sep 1943; Towers to Grumman, 13 Jan 1943; Halsey to Nimitz, 11 Jan 1943, Nimitz papers; Clark, 103.

27. Towers to Grumman, 13 Jan 1943; Pirie to author, 21 July 1987; conversation with Pirie, 1987; Potter, *Nimitz,* 214–15.

28. Glover, 41–43.

29. Coronado *Journal,* 1 Apr 1943; Loening to Pierre, 23 Aug 1943, including copy of his laudatory report on the project to his boss, Donald M. Nelson, head of the War Production Board; Keen, " 'Feeder' Factories," in which Pierre is pictured at work, 26–27, 96; Towers to brother William, 10 Mar 1943; Towers to William, 17 Apr 1943; conversations with Pierre Towers and Billy Maddox, 1985; *New York Times,* 9 Sep 1943.

30. Taylor, *Mitscher,* 144ff; Halsey to Towers, 10 June 1943, Halsey papers; Read oral transcript, 251–52, 272. Charlie Mason, then Pete Mitscher, commanded Solomons air forces.

31. Halsey to Towers, 10 June 1943; Reynolds, *Fast Carriers,* 35, 355; Read oral transcript, 266–68.

32. Reynolds, *Fast Carriers,* 35, 303–4; Read oral transcript, 262–65; Smeeton to author, 17 May 1966.

33. Reynolds, *Fast Carriers,* 41–44.

34. Towers to Gates, 30 May 1943; Gates to King, 12 June 1943, reproduced in Administrative History 24, appendix.

35. Towers to Horne, 30 June 1943; Pepper to author, 16 Aug 1966; McCain to Towers on Pepper, 12 Aug 1943.

36. Reynolds, *Fast Carriers,* 44–47.

37. Towers to brother William, 10 Mar, 17 Apr 1943; Potter, *Halsey,* 193–194 (italics and capitals original).

38. Morison, *Two-Ocean War,* 580; *Fleet Admiral King,* 362, 419–20, 541–42, 575, 605n; Reynolds, "King," 59.

39. Potter, *Nimitz,* 210–11; conversation with Beakley, 1965; Riley to Pierre, 19 July 1961, recalling Beakley's account of the Towers-Price discussion; conversation with Pierre, 1987.

40. Potter, *Nimitz,* 189, 237; Buell, *Spruance,* 161; Towers to Ghormley, 9 June 1943.

41. Buell, *Spruance,* 160–62; Potter, *Nimitz,* 237–38.

42. Towers to Nimitz, 28 Apr 1943, Halsey papers.

43. Browning to Halsey, 1 May 1943, Halsey papers.

44. Morison, vol. 7, 80–82.

45. Buell, *Spruance,* 163; Towers to Horne, 30 June 1943, recounting the sudden change of heart "just two weeks ago"; King-Nimitz conference notes, 28 May–1 June, 30 July–1 Aug 1943. Towers wanted Sherman promoted to the one-star rank of commodore, but King preferred to minimize the number of officers holding that rarely used rank.

46. Morison, vol. 7, 82–84; Potter, *Nimitz,* 243, 245; Buell, *King,* 358–59; Buell, *Spruance,* 163–65; Dyer, vol. 2, 613–14, 616–17.

47. Reynolds, *Fast Carriers,* 72–73.

48. Spruance to wife, 4 July 1943, Spruance papers.

49. Buell, *Spruance,* 174, 184; Reynolds, *Fast Carriers,* 70–71; Potter, *Nimitz,* 238–40; Spruance to wife, 4 July 1943; Hedding interview; conversation with Morse, 1966.

50. Halsey to Towers, 10 June 1943, Halsey papers; Taylor, 160; Towers to McCain, 2 May 1943.

51. F. C. Sherman diary, June–July 1943.

52. Towers to Nimitz, 17 July, 13 Aug 1943; conversation with Radford, 1964. McFall became chief of naval air operational training at Jacksonville in August 1943.

53. Towers to Nimitz, 17, 26 July 1943; Knox to FDR, and FDR's approval, 29 July 1943, FDR Library, OF 18i.

54. Reynolds, *Fast Carriers,* 73–74; Hoover oral transcript, 325–26; *Lucky Bag, 1907,* 107; Bryan, *Aircraft Carrier,* 63–64; Nimitz to McCain, 2 Sep 1943, Nimitz papers.

55. Spruance to wife, 23 Aug, 3 Oct 1943, on Kinkaid, whom Towers blamed for losing the *Hornet.*

56. Forrestel, 69; Towers to Nimitz, 8 Aug 1943, Nimitz papers.

57. ComAirPac History, 14; Towers to Nimitz, 13 Aug 1943.

58. King to Nimitz, 12 Aug 1943, Naval Historical Center.

59. Nimitz to Towers, 16 Aug 1943, Nimitz papers; Reynolds, *Fast Carriers,* 75–76.

60. Forrestal to Towers, 2 Aug 1943; Towers to Forrestal, 18 Aug 1943.

61. Towers to Nimitz, 21 Aug 1943; Reynolds, *Fast Carriers,* 76.

62. Yarnell to Nimitz, 4 Aug 1943; Yarnell to Towers, 4 Aug 1943; Towers to Yarnell, 7 Sep 1943; Reynolds, *Fast Carriers,* 46. Towers did not receive his letter from Yarnell until 29 August.

63. Towers to Horne, 30 June 1943; Towers to Nimitz, 22 Aug 1943; diary, 23 Aug 1943; Towers to Yarnell, 7 Sep 1943; Reynolds, *Fast Carriers,* 76–77.

64. Moore oral transcript, 808, 813–14.

65. Pacific Command history, 55, 61, 65, 70–71; diary, 25–26, 31 Aug, 3–6 Sep 1943.

66. Diary, 10–17 Sep 1943, noting Towers to Nimitz, 16 Apr, 21 Aug 1943; Reynolds, *Fast Carriers,* 83; Read oral transcript, 404–11.

67. Diary, 8, 18, 21–22 Sep 1943.

68. Ibid., 8–9, 11–12, 26 Sep 1943; Towers to McCain, 21 Sep, 24 Oct 1943, detailing Fairlamb's case; Reynolds, *Fast Carriers,* 80–85; Reynolds, *Fighting Lady,* 31–43; Mitscher to Towers, 13 Sep 1943, Mitscher papers.

69. Diary, 10, 19 Sep 1943; Reynolds, *Fast Carriers,* 87–88.

70. Towers to brother William, 21 Sep, 14 Nov 1943.

71. Ibid. (Italics original).

72. Diary, 26 Sep 1943; ComAirPac History, 121–22; Read oral transcript, 414.

73. Diary, 8, 10 Nov 1943; Howeth, 492ff; Fahrney, 58–59. King's three key COMINCH aviation advisers at the end of 1943 were assistant chief of staff (operations), Rear Admiral Davis;

assistant planning officer (air), Rear Admiral Duncan; and assistant operations officer (air), Captain Beakley. His CNO air advisers were deputy CNO (air), Vice Admiral McCain, and assistant deputy CNO (air), Rear Admiral Frank Wagner. Rear Admiral Ramsey was chief of BuAer.

74. Pepper to author, 16 Aug 1966.

75. Diary, 10, 21 Sep, 6 Nov 1943; conversation with George Anderson, 1964; Buell, *Spruance,* 179. Read claims that he had discussed with Forrest Sherman T. E. Lawrence's tactics of bypassing Turkish strongpoints in the Middle East during World War I (oral transcript, 430–31).

76. Conversation with Radford, 1964; Buell, *Spruance,* 184–85; Towers to Nimitz, 21 Sep 1943; Anderson oral transcript, 131–33.

77. Towers to brother William, 21 Sep 1943; Potter, *Nimitz,* 252; Dyer, vol. 2, 617–19; Buell, *Spruance,* 179–80; diary, 22, 23, 25–28, 30 Sep 1943; King-Nimitz conference notes, 25–28 Sep 1943; ComAirPac History, 20–21; Buell, *King,* 411.

78. Diary, 29 Sep 1943.

79. Ibid., 30 Sep 1943.

80. Ibid., 1–5 Oct 1943. Dyer notes that others remembered Towers' "elephant guns against rabbits" statement to be, "Spruance wants a sledgehammer to drive a tack." Perhaps he said both (vol. 2, 629).

81. Reynolds, *Fast Carriers,* 44–49, 88–89; Towers to Nimitz, 4 Oct 1943; Towers to brother William, 21 Sep, 14 Nov 1943; Sudsbury, 249. Towers also saw Pierre during his visit to San Diego; they now purchased and sublet a house in Washington as an investment.

82. Sherman to Nimitz, 8 Sep 1943, in Yarnell report files, Naval Historical Center; Reynolds, *Fast Carriers,* 47, 88–89; Sherman diary, 6–9 Oct 1943.

83. King conversation with Whitehill, 31 July 1949, King papers, 5; Buell, *King,* 361; diary, 9, 11 Oct 1943; Nimitz to Towers, 11 Oct 1943, Nimitz papers; Reynolds, *Fast Carriers,* 89.

84. Diary, 12 Oct 1943. The *Indiana* collided with the *Washington* early in 1944, blame for which Nimitz assigned to Steele (diary, 8 Feb 1944).

85. Towers to Nimitz, 13 Oct 1943, Nimitz papers.

86. Pepper to author, 16 Aug 1966.

87. Reynolds, *Fast Carriers,* 87–88, 93–94; diary, 8, 14 Oct 1943; Potter, *Nimitz* 254; Jurika and Radford, 15–16.

88. Diary, 17 Oct 1943.

89. Ibid., 20, 25, 28 Oct 1943.

90. Ibid., 23, 26 Oct 1943; Buell, *Spruance,* 217–18.

91. Morison, vol. 7, 201–2; diary, 23 Oct 1943; King to Nimitz, 21 Oct 1943; Towers to Nimitz, 23 Oct 1943.

92. Reynolds, *Fast Carriers,* 94–96.

93. Towers to Nimitz, 1 Nov 1943. Halsey supported Towers' views on obtaining good photo reconnaisance "under cover of a heavy strike," particularly at Truk (Halsey to Nimitz, 18 Nov 1943, Nimitz papers).

94. Reynolds, *Fast Carriers,* 96–99.

95. Diary, 5–6 Nov 1943.

96. Ibid., 6–8 Nov 1943.

97. Ibid., 7–8, 11 Nov 1943; Potter, *Nimitz,* 255.

98. Diary, 24 Oct, 11 Nov, 5 Dec 1943; Towers to McCain, 24 Oct 1943; Ramsey to Carney, 12 Aug 1943; Towers to Nimitz, 16 Aug 1943. The latter two documents relate to the Hardison case. Forrest Sherman had been earmarked for the escort carriers before being assigned to Nimitz's staff.

99. Reynolds, *Fast Carriers,* 99–101; Towers to Ramsey, 21 Nov 1943.

100. Diary, 13–15 Nov 1943.

101. Ibid., 15, 22 Nov 1943.

102. Ibid., 20 Nov 1943.

103. Ibid., 21 Nov 1943; Reynolds, *Fast Carriers,* 103–4.

104. Towers to McCain, 3 Dec 1943; diary, 24–25 Nov, 3 Dec 1943; Potter, *Nimitz,* 259. The captain of the *Liscome Bay,* Captain I. D. Wiltsie, was also lost.

105. ComAirPac History, 21–22; Reynolds, *Fast Carriers*, 105, 130–31; conversation with Radford, 1964.

106. Reynolds, *Fast Carriers*, 106–8; Clark, 138–40; conversations with Clark, 1963–67; Reynolds, *Fighting Lady*, 68ff; Hoyt, 316–18; conversations with Loomis, 1987; Towers to Nimitz, 17 Dec 1943; Anderson oral transcript, 120–21, 123; Pownall oral transcript, 129 (Pownall "couldn't see the justification for a second strike with tired pilots, tired airplanes"). See also Jurika and Radford, 13. The *Yorktown* officer sent home was Lieutenant Herman S. Rosenblatt.

107. Diary, 26 Nov, 2–5, 29 Dec 43.

108. Ibid., 4, 8–10, 13–18, 23 Dec 1943; Towers to Pierre, 19 Dec [1943].

109. Diary, 23, 25 Dec 1943; Buell, *Spruance*, 216.

110. Diary, 25 Dec 1943; Towers to brother William, 17 Jan [1944]; Read oral transcript, 441.

111. Towers to Nimitz, 27 Dec 1943; diary, 2, 20 Dec 1943. Horne to King, 28 July 1944; Sherman and McMorris to Nimitz [28 July 1944]; Towers to Nimitz, 1 Aug 1944, Naval History Center. When Rear Admiral Putty Read asked Towers' endorsement for a carrier division command, Towers turned him down (George Anderson's comments to Read's son-in-law, Charles Cunningham; Cunningham to author, 22 Oct 1988).

112. Diary, 27 Dec 1943; Reynolds, *Fast Carriers*, 40ff; Potter, *Nimitz*, 267–68; Reynolds, *Fighting Lady*, 40–45.

113. King-Nimitz conference notes, 3–4 Jan 1944, King papers; Spruance to Forrestal, 9 Feb 1963; Spruance to Moore, 25 June 1964, Spruance papers; Moore oral transcript, 1030–31; Buell, *Spruance*, 216; Read oral transcript, 443; Yarnell "Report on Naval Aviation," 6 Nov 1943, especially 11, Naval Historical Center.

114. King-Nimitz conference notes, 3–4 Jan 1944; Pepper to author, 16 Aug 1966; McMorris to Nimitz, 31 Dec 1943, Nimitz papers; diary, 6 Jan 1944; Potter, *Nimitz*, 267; Reynolds, *Fast Carriers*, 119.

115. Diary, 6 Jan 1944; Gardner to author, 21 May 1966; Gardner transcribed interview with Pierre, about 1960; Towers to brother William, 17 Jan [1944] (italics original).

116. "Georgia and the Flat Tops," Atlanta *Constitution*, 14 Dec 1943; Forrestal to Towers, 10 Jan 1944. Secretary Knox told the press simply, "Admiral Towers is a man of wide experience, especially in the air. The Commander in Chief (Admiral Nimitz) is not an air man and thus it is appropriate that his deputy should be experienced in that line" (quoted in *New York Times*, 12 Feb 1944).

CHAPTER 15. STRATEGIST-ADMINISTRATOR OF THE PACIFIC OFFENSIVE, 1944

1. Diary, 19 Dec 1943; Reynolds, *Fast Carriers*, 113–14; Buell, *King*, 391, 427–29.

2. Matloff, 377; diary, 20 Dec 1943; Reynolds, *Fast Carriers*, 114; Pogue, vol. 3, 323–24.

3. Markey, 66. This information is drawn from Markey's interview of Towers late in 1944. Towers proofread Markey's draft carefully but found errors relating only to Pierre and the *America* project of 1914 (Towers to Markey, 21 Feb 1945).

4. Markey, 66; Holland Smith, 111, 141; Reynolds, *Fast Carriers*, 115–16; Potter, *Nimitz*, 264–65; Buell, *Spruance*, 211; Morison, vol. 7, 203, 206; Jurika and Radford, 21.

5. Towers to Nimitz, 5 Jan 1944; Reynolds, *Fast Carriers*, 116–17; Buell, *King*, 441.

6. King-Nimitz conference notes, 4 Jan 1944, King papers.

7. Holland Smith, 156.

8. Morison, vol. 7, 206; diary, 30 Dec 1943; McMorris to Nimitz, 30 Dec 1943, Nimitz papers. Reynolds confuses Spruance's objections as being to D minus 2 instead of D minus 9, a misreading of Towers' diary (*Fast Carriers*, 124).

9. Diary, 31 Dec 1943, 1–4 Jan 1944; McMorris to Nimitz, 1 Jan 1944 [misdated as 1943], Nimitz papers.

10. Diary, 5–8 Jan 1944; Potter, *Nimitz,* 267; Hedding interview; Read oral transcript, 443.

11. Hoover to Nimitz, 3 Jan 1944, Nimitz papers; Morison, vol. 7, 343–50; diary, 9, 11, 14, 21, 23 Jan 1944.

12. Diary, 13, 14 Jan 1944; Jurika and Radford, 22.

13. Reynolds, *Fast Carriers,* 117–18; Potter, *Nimitz,* 281.

14. Diary, 17 Jan, 9, 22 Feb 1944 (italics original).

15. Ibid., 24 Jan 1944.

16. Ibid., 25 Jan 1944; Potter, *Nimitz,* 280.

17. Diary, 25, 27, 28 Jan 1944; Kenney, 347–49; Carney oral transcript, 11–12, courtesy of E. B. Potter; Potter, *Nimitz,* 280–81; Grace Hayes, 547; Reynolds, *Fast Carriers,* 118–19. Halsey, delayed by weather in the United States, did not arrive until 29 January.

18. Buell, *King,* 440–42; Potter, *Nimitz,* 282–83; King to Nimitz, 8 Feb 1944, King papers; King to Fletcher, 10 Feb 1944, on the North Pacific, Nimitz papers.

19. Diary, 2–4 Feb 1944 (kept by Radford), 7 Feb 1944; Jurika and Radford, 22–23.

20. Diary, 8 Feb 1944; Reynolds, *Fighting Lady,* 95; Buell, *Spruance,* 231; Jurika and Radford, 23–24.

21. *New York Times,* 11 Feb 1944; Spruance to wife, 23 Feb 1944, Spruance papers; diary, 6 Jan, 7, 9 Feb 1944; conversation with Radford, 1964.

22. Diary, 9 Feb 1944.

23. Ibid., 15 Feb 1944; Towers to Baldridge, 16 Feb 1944.

24. Reynolds, *Fast Carriers,* 136–41; Morison, vol. 7, 316–31; Reynolds, *Fighting Lady,* 94–108.

25. Diary, 17, 23 Feb 1944; Potter, *Nimitz,* 283–84; Buell, *King,* 442. Nimitz informed Towers of his impending trip to Washington on the twenty-third.

26. Diary, 19, 22 Feb 1944; Towers to Nimitz, 22 Feb 1944; Spruance to wife, 23 Feb 1944, Spruance papers. Nimitz spent time in Washington 2–15 March, Australia 23–29 March, Kwajalein 7–10 April, and San Francisco 3–8 May 1944.

27. Diary, 25 Feb 1944; Towers' Legion of Merit.

28. Diary, 28 Feb 1944.

29. Ibid., 23, 29 Feb 1944; Reynolds, *Fast Carriers,* 141–42; Buell, *Spruance,* 241, 243.

30. Reynolds, *Fast Carriers,* 142–43; King-Nimitz conference notes, 6–7 Mar 1944; Potter, *Nimitz,* 287–88; Buell, *King,* 444; JPS 467 (revised), 8 June 1944, study for Russian entry into the war; Reynolds, "King," 59–60; Reynolds, "MacArthur," 83.

31. Diary, Mar, Apr, 9 May 1944; Anderson oral transcript, 125–26, 139. In his diary Towers wrote, "I advised the Flag Secretary [Mercer] that I intended to devote a considerable amount of time in having chased down and acted upon correspondence which is being unduly delayed . . ." (1 Mar 1944).

32. Diary, 20, 21 Mar, 14 Apr, 7, 13 May 1944; Potter, *Nimitz,* 230; Moore oral transcript, 1031; Hoyt, 369–71; Anderson oral transcript, 130–31.

33. Anderson oral transcript, 127–28; diary, 14 Feb (kept by Radford), 17, 20 Mar, 10, 15, 19, 29 Apr–5 May 1944; Reynolds, *Fighting Lady,* 110–19; Reynolds, *Fast Carriers,* 149–51.

34. Diary, Feb–Mar 1944; Anderson oral transcript, 129.

35. Diary, 11–16 Mar 1944; Buell, *Spruance,* 244–51.

36. Diary, 19, 30 Mar, 1, 3, 21 Apr 1944.

37. Diary, 12 Feb (kept by Radford), 19 Apr 1944; Nimitz to McCain, 21 Mar 1944, Nimitz papers.

38. Reynolds, *Fast Carriers,* 146–54; diary, 5–6 May 1944.

39. Diary, 21–23 May 1944.

40. Ibid., 24, 26, 28 May 1944.

41. United Press story, 26 May 1944, in unidentified newspaper clipping of the following day; ComAirPac History, 86.

42. Diary, 30 May 1944; *New York Times,* 6 June 1944.

43. Diary, 1–5, 11 June 1944; Towers to brother William, 21 June 1944. Riley was assigned to the Office of the Deputy CNO (Air) at the time.

44. Diary, 6–8 June 1944; Towers to brother William, 21 May 1944; Pierre to Denfeld, n.d.; Denfeld to Pierre, 18 Feb, 7 June 1944, Naval Historical Center; Markey, 66; Towers to Arnold, 28 Sep 1944; Lieutenant General Barney M. Giles to Lieutenant General Carl Spaatz, 6 Oct 1944; Arnold to Towers, 12 Oct 1944, Arnold papers. In the autumn, Towers went through Hap Arnold to obtain gasoline for Pierre's sister and brother-in-law so they could return from the south of France to newly liberated Paris.

45. Diary, 9–11 June 1944; Buell, *King*, 445–46. For the events that followed, see Reynolds, *Fast Carriers*, 156ff; Buell, *Spruance*, 259ff; Potter, *Nimitz*, 298ff.

46. Diary, 13–15 June 1944; conversation with George Anderson in 1964; Anderson oral transcript, 139–40.

47. Moore oral transcript, 1030–31, quoting Leavey from conversation in 1959; Pierre's notation in 1970 on her copy of Hoyt, 395 (italics original).

48. Towers to brother William, 21 June 1944; Towers speech of 1953 or 1954 (unknown audience) "Strategic Employment of Naval Forces as the Essential Element of World War II in the Pacific"; Hopkins, 146; Moore oral transcript, 1030; Hoyt, 428–29; Read oral transcript, 731; Buell, *Spruance*, 277; Reynolds, *Fast Carriers*, 204–6; Reynolds, *Fighting Lady*, 147–48, 156.

49. Towers, "French Policy," 18–19. For my fuller treatment of the controversy, see *Fast Carriers*, 204–10. My discussion in 1968 of Rodney at the Saints thus antedated by twenty years my discovery of Towers' similar discussion in his thesis. For two defenses of Spruance, see Buell, *Spruance*, 277–80, and Potter, *Nimitz*, 303–5. On greeting Spruance in July 1944, King said to him simply, "Spruance, you did a damn good job there. No matter what other people tell you, your decision was correct" (quoted in Buell, *King*, 466).

50. Diary, 26, 29 June, 18 July, 19, 20 Aug 1944.

51. Gwenfread Allen, 260; conversation with W. T. Maddox in 1985; diary, 10 Mar, 10 July 1944.

52. Morison, vol. 11, 7; diary, 19, 20, 29, 30 June 1944.

53. Diary, 1–3 July 1944.

54. Ibid., 5 July 1944.

55. Ibid., 23, 24 June, 6, 8, 13, 14 July 1944; Forrestal to Nimitz, 9 July 1944, Nimitz papers; F. C. Sherman diary, 20 Nov 1944.

56. Reynolds, *Fast Carriers*, 236–37; diary, 22, 31 July 1944; F. C. Sherman diary, 21 Dec 1944.

57. Forrest Sherman to Nimitz [undated], endorsement of Towers to Nimitz, 1 Aug 1944, Nimitz papers (italics original). Wood was thereupon transferred from Seattle as commander Fleet Air to Kodiak, Alaska, as Com 17, where he finished the war.

58. Diary, 13, 14 July 1944; Towers to brother William, 12 Aug 1944.

59. King-Nimitz conference notes, 13–22 July 1944; King conversation with Whitehill, 3 July 1950, King papers; Reynolds, *Fast Carriers*, 238; Moore oral transcript, 1064–64. Moore said that McCain's "ideas were screwball in a great many ways."

60. King-Nimitz conference notes, 13–22 July 1944.

61. Ibid.; diary, 20–22 July 1944; Buell, *King*, 466–68; Dyer, vol. 2, 974; Potter, *Nimitz*, 314–15. Towers to Pierre, 4 Oct 1944: "In the July conference here K, N. & Co. would hardly listen to me, but I stuck out (before a selected group of about 30 officers from Wash. & this staff). Mick Carney supported me. This is something."

62. Diary, 24–26 July 1944; conversation with W. T. Maddox, 1985; Potter, *Nimitz*, 316–17; Morison, vol. 11, 8–9.

63. Diary, 26–29 July, 3 Aug 1944; conversation with W. T. Maddox, 1985; Potter, *Nimitz*, 317–20.

64. Diary, Aug–Nov 1944; Anderson oral transcript, 136, 142, 154.

65. Nimitz to King, 18 Sep 1944, Nimitz papers; Towers' fitness report, 1 Mar 1945; diary, 7, 8, 14 Aug, 6–8, 16 Sep, 1, 7, 10, 11, 20 Oct, 9 Nov, 2, 10–12, 29 Dec 1944 and 3, 6 Jan, 27 Mar, 3 June 1945; Anderson oral transcript, 127–28. Towers recounted telling staff member Captain R. C. Bourne, USNR, "very bluntly that he was not carrying out his instructions and was causing me considerable embarrassment" (diary, 4–5 Mar 1945). A committee of aviator captains, Stanhope C.

Ring, air logistician Jim Boundy, and Joseph L. Herlihy (Supply Corps), also played watchdog over fleet logistics for Towers.

66. Diary, 19 Aug, 4, 18, 20 Sep, 5, 10 Oct, 16, 17 Nov, 6 Dec 1944 and 3, 11, 16 Jan 1945; Hancock, 68, 196–203; Gwenfread Allen, 327ff; Towers to brother William, 19 Nov [1944]. Towers was involved in a great uproar over "war dogs" in Hawaii not having veterinarians (Nimitz to Towers, 29 Nov 1944, Nimitz papers).

67. Diary, 14, 24 Aug, 27, 29 Sep, 3, 10 Nov 1944 and 3 Jan 1945 and passim; Craven and Cate, vol. 5, 514–15; Ketcham oral transcript, 292.

68. Diary, 28 Nov, 9 Dec 1944; "Reorganization of National Defense," Towers' statement, 9 Dec 1944; Reynolds, *Fast Carriers*, 351–52.

69. Diary, 20, 22 Aug, 12, 19 Oct, 10 Dec 1944; Sherrod, 327–29.

70. Diary, 19, 28 Aug, 27 Sep, 10, 19 Nov 1944.

71. Ibid., Aug–Dec 1944; brother William to Towers, 4 Dec 1944; conversation with W. T. Maddox, 1985. On 16 November 1944 Towers was presented a "plank" from the *Saratoga;* he was on board for her seventeenth anniversary festivities.

72. Diary, 8, 9, 14–16, 21, 22 Aug, 2, 3, 5 Oct 1944; Clark, 193–97; Buell, *King,* 492–93; Halsey to Nimitz, 6 Oct 1944; Towers to Nimitz, 9 Oct 1944, Nimitz papers.

73. Diary, 19, 23–25 Aug, 7 Sep 1944; Reynolds, *Fast Carriers,* 244–46.

74. Morison, vol. 11, 13–16; Towers to Pierre, 15 Sep 1944; diary, 8–15 Sep 1944. Hoover commented on Towers and his inspection party that "their backsides are sore from two days of jeep riding around Saipan" (letter to Nimitz, 12 Sep 1944, Nimitz papers). There Towers learned that Hoover had monopolized officers clubs for his own staff and flagship, causing a minor furor. When Towers dutifully reported this, Hoover wrote to Nimitz, "Towers apparently alarms you unduly in regard to civil affairs here. It is hard to see how he could get such definite ideas" on such a complex subject from such a short visit. Nimitz and Spruance, Hoover wrote, "are the only ones to whom I feel I can write fully with confidence and understanding" (5 Oct 1944).

75. Morison, vol. 11, 17–18; Potter, *Nimitz,* 326–27; Towers to Pierre, 21 Sep, 4 Oct 1944 (italics original); diary, 23, 24, 26 Sep, 3, 4 Oct 1944.

76. Reynolds, *Fast Carriers,* 259–61; diary, 12, 15 Oct 1944.

77. Diary, 24 Oct 1944; *New York Times,* 25 Oct 1944 (author's italics).

78. Conversation with George Anderson, 1964. For the details of and debate over the battle, see especially Morison, vol. 11, 193ff; Reynolds, *Fast Carriers,* 255ff; Potter, *Halsey,* 286ff; Potter, *Nimitz,* 330ff; and Reynolds, "Halsey." Towers interviewed several senior air admirals involved in the battle at his office on 20 November 1944.

79. Diary, 11–13 Nov 1944; Towers to brother William, 21 Nov 1944. Former Ambassador to Japan Joseph C. Grew counseled the staff on both Japan and China and discussed the possible exchange of American and Japanese civilian internees.

CHAPTER 16. THE INDISPENSABLE TOWERS, 1944–45

1. Diary, 21 Nov, 4–6, 8 Dec 1944; King-Nimitz conference notes, 29 Sep–1 Oct, 24–26 Nov 1944; Reynolds, *Fast Carriers,* 320–24; Dyer, vol. 2, 1059–64, 1075–76, 1108–9; Reynolds, "MacArthur," 82–84; Buell, *Spruance,* 364–66.

2. Ballentine, 252; King-Nimitz conference notes, 24–26 Nov 1944.

3. Diary, 7, 28–29 Oct 1944, 22, 23 Feb 1945.

4. Ibid., 13–17 Dec 1944. On the movie, see Reynolds, *Fighting Lady,* 13, 182, 185, 206, 222–24, 262, 325.

5. Diary, 18 Dec 1944; Reynolds, *Fast Carriers,* 325–27.

6. Diary, 19 Dec 1944; Ballentine, 248.

7. Diary, 19–22 Dec 1944, Forrestal to Towers, 17 Dec 1944, Forrestal papers, National Archives; Forrestal diary, 19 Dec 1944, Naval Historical Center, Towers to brother William, 19

Nov [1944]; Markey in *Liberty,* 17 Feb 1945, 24–25, 65–66; brother William to Towers, 15 Feb 1945, citing Elmer Grant. The *Liberty* article was subsequently condensed in *Reader's Digest.* An article on Nimitz and his advisers in *Time* remarked on "the florid, polished" Towers (26 Feb 1945, 28).

8. Diary, 28, 31 Dec 1944, 8 Jan, 18 Mar, 24 May 1945; Reynolds, *Fast Carriers,* 282ff, 312ff.

9. King-Nimitz conference notes, 24–26 Nov 1944; Hoyt, 458; diary, 15, 16, 21 Jan 1945; conversation with Radford, 1964.

10. Diary, 5, 25, 30 Jan 1945; Austin oral transcript, 297–98.

11. McMorris to Towers, 14 Mar 1945.

12. Diary, 26, 27 Feb, 6–10 Mar 1945; Towers to Nimitz, 12 June 1945, Nimitz papers.

13. Diary, 12, 13 Feb, 7 Mar 1945; Forrestal diary, 12, 13 Feb 1945, Naval Historical Center.

14. Diary, 28 Feb, 1 Mar 1945; Forrestal diary, 1, 2 Mar 1945.

15. Towers to brother William, 11 Mar [1945]; diary, 13 Mar 1945.

16. Diary, Mar–Apr 1945.

17. Towers to brother William, 27 Sep [1945]; diary, 30 Mar, 30 May 1945; Towers to Nimitz, and Nimitz to King dispatches, 1 June 1945, Naval Historical Center.

18. Diary, 6 Apr 1945; Towers to Nimitz, 6 Apr 1945; Nimitz to Towers, 17 Apr 1945, Nimitz papers; Ballentine, 255ff, Potter, *Nimitz,* 378–79.

19. Ballentine, 255, 263; diary, 12, 15 Apr 1945; Towers to brother William, 25 June [1945]; Pierre to Forrestal, n.d.; Captain E. B. Taylor to Forrestal, 7, 16 Apr 1945; Forrestal to Pierre, 19 Apr 1945, Forrestal papers, National Archives. The third CVB, no. 43, was named *Coral Sea.*

20. Diary, 19–26 Apr 1945; Reynolds, *Fast Carriers,* 343; Potter, *Nimitz,* 379–80.

21. Nimitz dispatches to King, 26, 27 Apr, 5, 22 May 1945. The incumbent commander Hawaiian Sea Frontier, Vice Admiral D. W. Bagley, would be transferred stateside under this scheme.

22. King to Nimitz, 26, 27 Apr, 1 May 1945; Nimitz to King, 18, 26, 29 Apr 1945, all dispatches.

23. Diary, 26–30 Apr 1945.

24. Ballentine, 263–73; Nimitz to Towers, 26 Apr 1945; King dispatches to Nimitz, 4–6 May 1945; Nimitz dispatches to King, 5, 7 May 1945; diary, 1–6 May 1945.

25. Diary, 7–9 May 1945; Towers to brother William, 25 June [1945]; Canaga (who rode in the R5D flight) to Pierre, 4 Nov 1958.

26. Diary, 10 May–7 June 1945; Riley oral transcript, 212–14; Towers to brother William, 25 June [1945]. Admiral Kent Hewitt settled in temporarily as part of an investigation of the Pearl Harbor attack.

27. King to Nimitz dispatch, 18 May 1945; Nimitz to King, 22 May 1945.

28. Diary, 24, 31 May, 2–5, 11, 13, 16–22, 25, 26 June 1945; Ballentine, 282–85; Forrestal diary, 4 July 1945; Austin oral transcript, 297–98.

29. Towers to Nimitz, 24 May 1945, Nimitz papers; diary, 22, 23 May, 1, 9, 10, 20 June 1945; Craven and Cate, vol. 5, 533; Arnold diary, 9, 10, 12, 14 June 1945.

30. Read oral transcript, 694–700; diary, 1 June 1945; Reynolds, *Fast Carriers,* 345–46.

31. King dispatches to Nimitz, 5 May, 5 June 1945.

32. King dispatches to Nimitz, 8, 10 June 1945; Nimitz dispatches to King, 9, 13 June 1945; diary, 11, 12 June 1945; Towers to Nimitz, 12 June 1945.

33. King dispatch to Nimitz, 15 June 1945; Nimitz dispatch to King, 17 June 1945.

34. Diary, 19 June 1945; Towers to brother William, 25 June [1945]; Sherman diary, 26 June 1945; Reynolds, *Fast Carriers,* 361.

35. CINCPAC-CINCPOA joint staff study Olympic, 25 June 1945; Olympic operation plans 10-45 of 8 Aug 1945 and 11-45 of 9 Aug 1945, Naval Historical Center; Reynolds, *Fast Carriers,* 363–71.

36. Diary, June–July 1945; Arnold diary, June 1945. He also hosted veteran war correspondent Frederick Palmer, whom he had known on the *Kentucky.*

37. Towers to brother William, 23 July 1945; Whitehill conversation with King, 27 Aug 1950, King papers; Towers' fitness report, 16 Aug 1945; Towers' DSM, transmitted 7 Dec 1945.

38. Diary, 26 July 1945; conversation with Admiral J. J. Clark in 1965; King to Nimitz, 12 May 1945; Russell oral transcript, 228–29. Forrestal also did not want Soc McMorris to greet visitors.

39. Towers to brother William, 23 July 1945; Reynolds, *Fast Carriers*, 362. The flag lieutenant was Lieutenant J. P. Sheftall.

40. Towers to brother William, 27 Sep [1945]; diary, 4, 7, 8 Aug 1945; Russell oral transcript, 227–28.

41. Diary, 13, 14, 17, 19 Aug 1945; Potter, *Halsey*, 350; Sherman diary, 24 Aug 1945.

42. Towers to brother William, 27 Sep [1945]; diary, 20, 22–31 Aug, 1 Sep 1945; Task Force 38 war diary, 22–23 Aug 1945; *Shangri-La* log, 22 Aug, 1 Sep 1945; *Shangri-La* war diary, 1 Sep 1945.

43. Diary, 2 Sep 1945.

CHAPTER 17. SHAPING THE NEW ORDER OF AIR-SEA POWER, after 1945

1. See Sprouts, *Toward a New Order of Sea Power;* Kansas City *Times*, 10 Dec 1947; Reynolds, *Command*, 321ff, 545ff.

2. Towers 1953/54 speech, "Strategic Employment of Naval Forces as the Essential Element of World War II in the Pacific."

3. Diary, 16–19 Sep 1945; *Shangri-La* war diary, 5, 16, 18 Sep 1945; Towers to brother William, 27 Sep [1945]. The active typhoon season had also visited Jerry Bogan's task group in late August, inflicting much damage on the carriers and their escorts. According to Herb Riley, Bogan was to blame for turning into the storm, but Towers chose to overlook his culpability (conversation with author, 1966).

4. Towers interview, Jan 1946, recalled in Kansas City *Times*, 10 Dec 1947; brother William to Towers, 16 Oct 1945. During the autumn of 1945, Fullton Towers accepted an army and navy "E" on behalf of Ford, Bacon, and Davis, of which he was now president, for its role in constructing the physical facilities used in building the bomb.

5. Towers to brother William, 27 Sep [1945]; diary, 25 Sep 1945.

6. Diary, 19, 20, 28 Sep 1945; *Shangri-La* war diary, Sep 1945.

7. Towers to brother William, 27 Sep [1945].

8. Diary, 1–23 Oct 1945; *Shangri-La* war diary, Oct 1945; commander Task Force 38 war diary, Oct 1945; Jackson oral transcript, 137–38; Los Angeles *Times*, 22 Oct 1945; Los Angeles *Examiner*, 23 Oct 1945. En route, the task designation switched to Task Group 38.1.

9. BuPers to CINCPAC, 18 Oct 1945; Buell, *King*, 501–2; *New York Times*, 5 Dec 1945; King to Forrestal, "General Slate of Flag Officers," n.d. (but written before 10 Oct, the date the title of COMINCH was abolished, for the memo was addressed from COMINCH-CNO to the navy secretary), King papers; Potter, *Nimitz*, 400–404. See also, Forrestal to Towers, 20 Oct 1945; Forrestal to Truman, 23 Oct 1945, requesting confirmation, Forrestal papers, National Archives.

10. BuPers to Towers, 25 Oct 1945; diary, 24–29 Oct 1945; King quoted by Whitehill in conversation, 3 July 1950, King papers; Buell, *King*, 502; Potter, *Nimitz*, 406–9; Taylor, *Mitscher*, 3–6; Buell, *Spruance*, 378–79; Spruance to his wife, 12, 14 Nov 1945, Spruance papers.

11. Forrestal quoted in *New York Times*, 5 Dec 1945; Potter, *Nimitz*, 413.

12. *Time*, 17 Dec 1945, 8; Dayton *Daily News*, 7 Dec 1945.

13. King conversation with Whitehill, 3 July, 27 Aug 1950, King papers.

14. *Shangri-La* war diary, 31 Oct 1945; commander Task Force 38 war diary, 31 Oct 1945; diary, 31 Oct–8 Nov 1945; Spruance's change of command remarks. Towers received his official temporary designation as admiral on 28 December 1945, to date from 8 November, when he actually put on his fourth star (BuPers to Towers, 28 Dec 1945; BuPers to CINCPAC, 3 Jan 1946). He was advanced to the permanent rank of admiral in May 1946 (*New York Times*, 21 May 1946).

15. Diary, 8 Nov–7 Dec 1945; Fifth Fleet war diary, Nov–Dec 1945; Buell, *Spruance*, 378.

16. Diary, 7–31 Dec 1945; Pogue, vol. 4, 58–60; Towers to Pierre, "Christmas Eve" [1945]. Also agreeing with Towers and Spruance on China was MacArthur's new chief of staff, Major General Richard T. Marshall.

17. Diary, 1–18 Jan 1946; Fifth Fleet war diary, Jan 1946.

18. Diary, 18–29 Jan 1946; Wellborn oral transcript, 259; Stroop oral transcript, 221; John Riley, 7; Towers to brother William, 12 Feb 1946. Young John later flew for Eastern Airlines until his untimely death in an automobile accident in 1984. Forrestal had held the admiral over in Washington to confer on the highly controversial hearings concerning the loss of the cruiser *Indianapolis*, sunk by a Japanese sub in the last week of the war.

19. Diary, 1 Feb 1946; Towers' fitness report, 4 Feb 1946; Spruance's change of command address, 1 Feb 1946; Buell, *Spruance*, 386ff; Felt oral transcript, 179–82; conversation with Felt, 1966.

20. Busch, 83; Schoeffel oral transcript, 277–78; Towers to brother William, 12 Feb 1946; conversation with Pierre, 1985; Pierre to author, 3 Dec [1986]. The mounted penis was later stolen.

21. Pogue, vol. 4, 58–62, 63ff; Palmer, 13–22.

22. Leffler, 349–59, 365–69; Messer, 82, 148, 156ff, 181 and passim; Dingman, 8–11; Spanier, 30–39; Blum, 4–7; Schnabel, vol. 1, 158ff; Palmer, 22, 27–28.

23. Dyer oral transcript, 438–43; diary, 22–27 Feb, 16 Apr 1946.

24. See Wellborn oral transcript, 264, for an appraisal of Towers as "highly capable."

25. Diary, 16, 21, 27 May, 24–28 June, 16 Aug 1946; Towers to brother William, 19 June 1946; Forrestal diary, 25, 29 June 1946. Towers, with Nimitz's concurrence, rejected Blandy's recommendation for a third test because it would have taxed Pacific Fleet resources too much.

26. Diary, 11, 27 May 1946.

27. Towers to Nimitz, 19 May 1945, Nimitz papers; Wellborn oral transcript, 265–68.

28. Diary, 29, 30 Apr, 16, 20 May, 4–9 June, 14, 18–27, 31 Aug, 3, 25, 26 Sep 1946; *New York Times*, 26 Sep, 1, 4 Oct, 9 Nov 1946; Towers to Nimitz, 3 Sep 1946.

29. Honolulu *Advertiser*, 26 Oct 1946; diary, 30 Sep 1946; *New York Times*, 5 Aug 1946. Ickes had written a critical article in *Collier's* magazine.

30. Diary, numerous entries, 1944–45, also 19 Feb, 17 May, 1, 28 Aug, 1, 4 Oct, 7 Nov 1946 and 7, 22, 29 Jan, 14 Feb 1947. Most of Towers' dealings with Pan Am were through its representative in the Pacific, William Mullahey.

31. Diary, 1, 23 Apr, 29 June, 2 Dec 1946.

32. Atlanta *Constitution*, 1 Oct 1946; *New York Times*, 4 Oct 1946; diary, 27 June 1946.

33. Albion, *Makers*, 602; James, vol. 3, 68–71; *New York Times*, 4, 5 Aug 1946; diary, 8 Feb, 30 Apr, 21 May 1946; Eisenhower to Towers, 25 May 1946; Reynolds, "MacArthur," passim.

34. Conversation with W. T. Maddox, 1985; diary, 18 June 1946; conversation with John Monsarrat, 1985; Slocum to Monsarrat, 6 Nov 1985. Captain Lanny Callan was also a member of Blandy's staff.

35. Smith-Hutton oral transcript, 603–4; diary, 27, 28 May 1946.

36. Pogue, vol. 4, 75, 108; Wellborn oral transcript, 269; diary, 5, 20 Mar, 6 Apr, 21 May, 19 July 1946; Towers to Nimitz, 3 Sep 1946.

37. Albion, *Makers*, 604–11; Connery, 451.

38. Albion, *Makers*, 611–16; diary, 20 Mar, 28 June, 7 July 1946; Caraley, 127–43.

39. Diary, 7–9 July 1946; Towers' statement before the Senate Naval Affairs Committee, 9 July 1946; Caraley, 144ff.

40. Diary, 9, 10 July 1946; Goldberg, 101–2.

41. Forrestal diary, 21 Aug, 24 Sep 1946; diary, 3, 4, 23, 25–29 Sep 1946; *New York Times*, 23 Sep 1946; James, vol. 3, 71–72; Atlanta *Constitution*, 1 Oct 1946; Towers to brother William, 31 Oct 1946.

42. Diary, 30 Sep 1946; Forrestal diary, 30 Sep 1946; conversation with W. T. Maddox, 1985; *New York Times*, 1 Oct 1946.

43. Schnabel, vol. 1, 171ff; diary, 30 Sep 1946; James, vol. 3, 72; *Washington Post*, 17 Dec 1946. The other theater commands were European, Atlantic Fleet, Caribbean, Northeast, and Alaskan, plus the Strategic Air Command.

44. Towers to Nimitz, 31 Dec 1946; diary, 20, 21, 24, 26, 27, 30 Dec 1946; *New York Times,* 13 Nov 1946, 1 Jan 1947; Towers to brother William, 9 Jan 1947.

45. Diary, 24 Oct, 16, 19 Dec 1946, 6, 10–15 Jan, 14, 17 Feb 1947; Towers to Nimitz, 3 Sep 1946; Pogue, vol. 4, 139–44.

46. Diary, 21–23, 25–31 Mar, 3, 6 Apr 1946; Moore oral transcript, 1118. The retirement board also included, for the staff corps, Vice Admiral E. L. Cochrane, Vice Admiral Ross T. McIntire, Vice Admiral Ben Moreell, and Rear Admiral W. J. Carter.

47. Read oral transcript, 734–35. Read rather fancifully blamed King for lowering the retirement age just to punish Towers: "That was the last dirty trick that King could play on Towers."

48. Diary, 10 July, 25, 26 Sep 1946; Towers to Nimitz, 8 Aug 1946; *New York Times,* 25 Sep 1946. Forrestal replied to Towers' criticism by saying that nothing was firm yet, but as it turned out Fechteler got the job. During 1946 Fechteler was commander Battleships and Cruisers Atlantic.

49. Towers to Nimitz, 8 Aug 1946.

50. Forrestal, "Comments on Recommendations of the Interdepartmental Committee on International Civil Aviation," 14 Nov 1943; Wilson, *Slipstream,* 260–77; Forrestal to Towers, 27 July 1946; Towers to Forrestal, 6 Aug 1946; diary, 25, 30 Sep, 27 Nov 1946.

51. Albion, *Makers,* 93; Forrestal to Towers, 21 May 1946; Towers to Forrestal, 27 May 1946; diary, 12–27 Nov 1946; Forrestal to Truman, 13 Dec 1946 (approved on the sixteenth), Forrestal papers, National Archives. Such retention on active duty was allowed by Public Law 305. The appointment to the General Board was announced on 30 December (*New York Times,* 31 Dec 1946). On nuclear-powered ships, see Hewlett and Duncan.

52. Albion, *Makers,* 616–20; diary, 18 Nov 1946; Caraley, 150; Jurika and Radford, 99.

53. Diary, 19–28 Nov 1946, 20 Jan 1947; Albion, *Makers,* 617–18.

54. Diary, Jan–Feb 1947; Towers to brother William, 9 Jan 1947.

55. Towers' fitness reports, 31 Aug 1946, 28 Feb 1947; Diary, 28 Feb 1947.

56. Diary, Mar 1947; Towers to brother William, 9 Jan 1947; Towers to Smedberg, 6 Feb 1947; Towers to Forrestal and reply, 12 Mar 1947, Forrestal papers, National Archives; conversation with Pierre, 1985.

57. *New York Times,* 25 May 1947; diary, 7 Aug 1947.

58. Albion, *Makers,* 453–59; diary, 3, 10, 14, 15, 17 Apr, 20, 22, 27 May, 2, 13, 16 June (on 12 June Naval War College meeting), 1 July 1947; Schnabel, vol. 1, 169, 186; Palmer, 29–31.

59. Towers to Forrestal, 22 May 1947, Forrestal papers, National Archives; diary, 7, 14, 15 May, 16, 21, 22, 29, 30 July 1947.

60. Diary, 11 Mar 1947; General Board hearings, 3 July 1947, 248–49.

61. Diary, 10–12 Mar, 2, 4, 13, 14, 16 Apr, 22 July 1947; Burke oral transcript, 17ff. Secretaries of the board during Towers' chairmanship were Captain S. W. DuBois until 8 July and Commander J. M. Lee from 22 August 1947.

62. Albion, *Makers,* 442–47; diary, 13 Mar, 9, 11 Apr, 1, 5 May, 24 June, 7 July, 1 Aug 1947; General Board hearings, 23 July 1947, 388–89, 415–16.

63. Diary, 23 June, 5 Aug 1947; General Board hearings of 1947, passim.

64. Caraley, 152–60; diary, 28 Mar, 4 Apr 1947.

65. Caraley, 160ff; diary, 16, 20, 24 Apr 1947.

66. Diary, 5, 19, 22 May, 4 June 1947; Towers to Cole, 29 May 1947. For the AAF's role, see Kirkendall.

67. Caraley, 160–77; diary, 28, 30 June 1947.

68. Caraley, 178–82; diary, 18, 22, 24, 26 July 1947; Forrestal diary, 22 July 1947; Anderson oral transcript, 169–70.

69. Caraley, 182; diary, 28 July, 20 Aug 1947; Connery, 454–56.

70. Solberg, 303ff, 323ff; Daley, 378–86; diary, 10, 27 Mar, 9, 14, 16, 17, 28 Apr, 21, 25, 27, 30 July 1947; *New York Times,* 31 July 1947; Warner, 30–44; Ryan, 45–66. "TWA" stood for Transcontinental and Western Air, later changed to Trans World Airlines.

71. Diary, 25 July, 25 Aug, 25, 26, 30 Sep, 1, 2, 31 Oct 1947.

72. Ibid., 30, 31 Oct, 3, 4, 13 Nov 1947; Hinshaw to Towers, 1 Mar 1948.

73. Diary, 13 Oct 1947; Haynes, 120–24; Coletta, *Unification,* 29, 47–58. On 10 October Towers attended the funeral of his World War I London compatriot, Captain Lewis McBride.

74. Diary, 12 June, 1, 17, 18 Nov 1947; Forrestal diary, 12 Nov 1947; Clark, 253, 293.

75. Chief of naval personnel to Towers, 5 June 1947; Towers' fitness report, 17 Sep 1947. Forrestal gave him the highest marks except in "technical competence," namely, flying, for which Towers received the lowest rating.

76. Diary, Aug–Nov 1947; Burke oral transcript, 58–61, 70; conversation with Burke, 1985; Clark, 256–57; Friedman, *Aircraft Carriers,* 239ff; Coletta, *Unification,* 31. Towers spent 8–19 August on leave at Fort Ticonderoga, New York; had broken glass removed from his foot in early September; remained in the hospital recuperating until the eighteenth; and sat for another portrait. He gave the Navy Day address at San Antonio, Texas, on 27 October and with Pierre attended the Navy–Georgia Tech football game on 8 November 1947.

77. Towers to brother Fullton, 14, 20 Nov 1947; diary, 11, 17 Nov 1947; Forrestal diary, 11 Nov 1947.

78. New York *Herald Tribune,* 1 Dec 1947; diary, 28 Oct 1946, 22 Oct, 20 Nov 1947; Neilson Abeel, Pacific War Memorial secretary, to Towers, 6 Nov 1947; Towers to Abeel, 20 Nov 1947; Towers to brother William, 14 Nov 1947; Towers to navy secretary, 20 Nov 1947. He replaced Archibald B. Roosevelt, a son of Teddy.

79. Diary, 26–30 Nov, 1 Dec 1947; *New York Times,* 30 Nov 1947; Towers' fitness report, 1 Dec 1947.

80. Forrestal diary, 1 Dec 1947; conversation with John Crommelin in 1978.

81. *New York Times,* 6 Dec 1947; Kansas City *Times,* 10 Dec 1947; Forrestal to Towers, 7 Dec 1947.

82. H. V. Markham, Admiralty, to "Vice-Admiral John Henry Towers, K.B.E., U.S.N.," 11 Dec 1945; H. R. F. Brett, British embassy, to Towers, 15 July 1947; *New York Times,* 22 July 1948; *Debrett's Peerage, Baronetage, Knightage and Companionage, 1952; Class of '06,* 151.

83. The two others who paid for *Class of '06* were L. L. "Chip" Ewell, who had resigned upon graduation, and Commander C. M. "Pip" Lynch, a turnback to '07 (*Class of '06,* 1, 3).

84. Towers to brother William, 14, 17 Nov 1947; Towers to brother Fullton, 20 Nov 1947; conversations with Tony Doherty and Lynne Riley, 1985; *Class of '06,* 151; Towers to Pacific War Memorial board of directors, 24 Mar 1948; diary, 24–28 Mar 1948. Marjorie had left the raising of her daughter to Herb's mother in Baltimore.

85. Reprinted in the New York *Herald Tribune,* 8 Mar 1948.

86. Diary, 1948–50.

87. Ibid., 18, 20 May 1948; Connery, 458.

88. Diary, 23, 25 May, 29 June, 28 July 1948; Connery, 458.

89. Diary, 19 July 1948.

90. Ibid., 4–6, 11, 12, 17, 18 Aug 1948; Forrestal to Towers and Spaatz, 9 Aug 1948; Millis, 468–69, 476; Forrestal to Towers, 19 Aug 1948.

91. Millis, 476–77; diary, 1, 9–11, 17, 20 Sep, 5, 6, 14, 18, 19, 29, 30 Oct, 6, 21, 27, 28 Dec 1948 and 5 Jan, 3 Feb 1949; Riley oral transcript, 323–25; Connery, 458–59.

92. Towers to Ingalls, 13 July, 19 Aug 1948; diary, 1948–50; Daley, 387–95. On a stillborn idea of Forrestal's for Towers and Ike to study the defense organization, see Eisenhower to Forrestal, 21 Dec 1948, in Galambos and Eisenhower, vol. 10, 382.

93. Diary, Dec 1948, Mar 1949.

94. Ibid., 8 May 1949.

95. Diary, 25 May 1949; Alsop, "Matter of Fact: A Dark Lesson," New York *Herald Tribune,* 25 May 1949.

96. Diary, June–Nov 1949; Connery, 459–60.

97. Goldberg, 116; Coletta, *Unification,* 169ff; Potter, *Nimitz,* 447–48; Towers to Sherman, 2 Nov 1949; Sherman to Towers, 11 Nov 1949, Sherman's CNO papers. See also Palmer, passim.

98. Diary, Nov 1949–Jan 1950 and 18 Mar 1950. Riley eventually attained the rank of vice admiral.

99. Reynolds, "Forrest Sherman," 209ff; diary, 10, 17, 18, 29 Mar, 10 May, June 1950.

100. George Rhodes in San Francisco *Call-Bulletin*, 17 Aug 1950; Towers to Pierre, n.d. [probably 22 Mar 1951].

101. Greenwich, Connecticut newspaper clipping, [late 1951]; Princeton '26 address [1952?].

102. Address to Aviation Commandery of New York, 24 Oct 1952.

103. Towers to brother William, 27 May 1953.

104. Address to General Electric employees, 9 Feb 1953; Towers' orders of 18 Sep 1950; Towers to brother William, 5 June 1952.

105. Princeton '26 talk; Friedman, *Aircraft Carriers*, 255ff.

106. Towers to brother William, 5 Aug 1953; conversation with Tony Doherty, 1985.

107. Clipping from a Norfolk or Newport News paper, 12 Dec 1954. The *Forrestal* was commissioned on 1 October 1955.

108. Conversation with Ernestine Towers, 1985; Canaga, Jr, to Pierre, 4 Oct 1954; Towers to "Marge," 18 Feb 1955 (brother William's copy). Bruce Canaga, Sr, had retired as captain in 1940 but returned to active duty during the war. He died in 1966.

109. Towers to Marge, 18 Feb 1955; conversations with Pierre, 1983, and Lynne Riley, 1986; Towers' medical report, 6 May 1955; *New York Times*, 1 May 1955.

110. Rome *News-Tribune*, 1 May 1955; *New York Times*, 2, 4 May 1955; *Washington Post* and *Times Herald*, 3 May 1955; *Washington Post*, 4 May 1955.

111. Atlanta *Journal* and *Constitution*, 1 May 1955; *New York Times* editorial, 2 May 1955; Norfolk *Pilot*, 3 May 1955; Norfolk *Despatch-Ledger*, 3 May 1955; *Shipmate*, June 1955, 16.

112. Seattle *Post-Intelligencer*, 24 Apr 1959, 7 June 1961, and related documents, courtesy of Commander R. V. Burrow, captain of the *Towers* in 1986; Jacksonville *Journal*, 6, 9 Sep 1960; *Naval Aviation News*, Jan 1967, 6–7, and Nov 1968, 3; Navy Secretary John H. Warner to Pierre, 20 Feb 1973. An entire issue of *Aeronautica* (Apr–June 1955) was dedicated to Towers.

113. Morison mentioned Towers only three times in his great fifteen-volume history, in volume 7, on pages 91, 104, and 208.

BIBLIOGRAPHY

PRIMARY SOURCES

Documentary Collections

Library of Congress

The papers of John Henry Towers, now housed with the Naval Historical Foundation Collection, manuscript division, Library of Congress, consist of personal letters to his family (1906–10), his fiancée and wife Pierre (1925–30, 1938–45), and his brother Will (1906–55), the latter donated by Will's son Billy during the writing of this book. Official correspondence, orders, photographs, clippings, speeches, and mementos are carefully preserved in notebooks. Included are reproductions of the logs of the A-1, A-2 (AX-1), B-1, B-2, and C-1.

Most valuable are the "memoranda for files" or daily logs or diaries—the several designations Towers gave his nightly dictations to his yeoman. They begin in early 1939 and end in mid-1950, with a large gap from October 1942 to August 1943. In addition, Towers' own reminiscences are, according to Pierre (letter to author, 9 December 1978), "his notes and notes dictated to me, and accounts of our talks scribbled on whatever paper I had, at St. Albans," in 1955.

Included in the collection are copies of many of the documents, notes of interviews, and correspondence gathered for this book. Notable among them are the diaries of Reuben S. Norton (1830, 1861–67, 1888–95), courtesy of Abner A. Towers and W. T. Maddox; the "War Reminiscences of W. M. Towers of Forrest's Escort," April 1900, courtesy of Robert Towers; and the manuscript memoirs of Rome, Georgia, by Elmer P. Grant.

Given Towers' family past and his extensive reading of history, it is ironic that he never made any effort to write about his career (save for the NC adventure). The navy's two senior wartime civilian historians visited him at Pearl Harbor: Samuel

Eliot Morison paid his respects while passing through on 2 March and 16 June 1945, and Robert G. Albion had a long discussion with him on 27 June 1945. But neither man seems to have encouraged his sense of history, nor were they impressed sufficiently to devote any attention to him in their histories of World War II. Towers toyed with the idea of writing an autobiographical history of naval aviation in the early 1950s, but nothing came of it.

The following papers are also housed in the Library of Congress. Those marked with asterisks are part of the Naval Historical Foundation Collection.

American Institute of Aeronautics and Astronautics (extensive biographical clipping files, especially boxes 116 and 119 for Towers).
H. H. Arnold
*Harry A. Baldridge
Henry S. Breckinridge
J. Lansing Callan
*Washington Irving Chambers (including copies of T. G. Ellyson papers)
*Thomas T. Craven
Josephus Daniels
Benjamin D. Foulois
*William F. Halsey, Jr.
*H. Kent Hewitt
*Frederick J. Horne
*Ernest J. King
*Robert P. Molten, Jr.
*Henry C. Mustin
*Chester W. Nimitz
*Dewitt C. Ramsey
*Holden C. Richardson
*John Rodgers and family
*Powers Symington (especially "Notes from Fleet Diary," 1916)
*Harry E. Yarnell

National Archives

Record Group (RG) 24   Ships' logs (hull numbers date from 1920)

Aroostook (CM 3)	*New Jersey* (BB 62)
Kentucky (BB)	*North Carolina* (ACR)
Langley (CV 1)	*Saratoga* (CV 3)
Michigan (BB)	*Shangri-La* (CV 38)
Mugford (DD 105)	*Tennessee* (ACR)
Neptune (AC)	

RG 38   Chief of Naval Operations; Security Classified General Corre-
     spondence, 1929–42 (including Towers' BuAer OO file)

RG 45   CNO (aviation) files, 1911–14; Transatlantic Flight

RG 72   BuAer annual reports; Confidential Correspondence, 1922–44;
     Joint Aircraft Committee

RG 72–73   Historical Papers Submitted (to BuAer)

RG 80   Army-Navy Joint Board minutes; Secretary of the Navy James
     V. Forrestal correspondence, 1940–47

RG 118   Transatlantic Flight

RG 313   Records of naval operating forces (including Aircraft Battle
     Force)

RG 405   U.S. Naval Academy Academic and Conduct Records of Cadets,
     vol. 25 (1902–1906)

Naval Historical Center
Washington Navy Yard
Washington D.C.

General navy official records, World War II
General Board hearings, 1916–47
Commander Air Force Pacific Fleet History
Commander in Chief Pacific Fleet Command History
Commander in Chief U.S. Fleet, series 4, administrative files (zero-zero) (including
     message files 14 and 25)
Forrest P. Sherman CNO files
Photographic section

Naval War College
Newport, Rhode Island

RG 8   Intelligence and Technical Archives (including naval attaché re-
     ports, 1914–16)

RG 10   Academic Calendars

RG 12   Student Problems and Solutions

RG 13   Student Theses and Research Papers

RG 14   Faculty and Staff Presentations

RG 15   Guest Lecturers

RG 18   Selected Readings

RG 29   Staff and Faculty

RG 35   Naval War Gaming

Archibald Hugh Douglas papers
Ernest J. King papers (including the biographical research materials collected by
     Walter Muir Whitehill and Thomas B. Buell)

Bibliography

Raymond A. Spruance papers (including the biographical research materials collected by Thomas B. Buell)

Franklin D. Roosevelt Library
Hyde Park, New York

Franklin D. Roosevelt Collection
  Alphabetical File
  Assistant Secretary of the Navy File, 1913–20
  Official File (OF)
  President's Personal File (PPF)
  President's Secretary's File (PSF)
Louis M. Howe papers
John L. McCrea draft manuscript
Henry Morgenthau Collection
Eleanor Roosevelt papers

Miscellaneous

Mrs. Frederick W. Bellinger papers, portions of which—notably the aviation unit log, 1913–15—were shared with me by Bellinger's biographer, Paolo E. Coletta
Richard E. Byrd papers, Byrd Polar Research Center, Ohio State University
Alfred A. Cunningham papers, history and museums division, headquarters, U.S. Marine Corps
Georgia Institute of Technology archives
Glenn H. Curtiss Museum of Local History, Hammondsport, New York
Oliver Jensen papers, privately held
Captain Robert F. Jones papers on wartime target drones, privately held
William A. Moffett papers, Nimitz Library, U.S. Naval Academy
National Personnel Records Center, Military Personnel Records, St. Louis
Public Records Office, London: Admiralty Record Office Papers, Adm. 137 (War Histories)
A.C. Read papers, courtesy of Charles Cunningham (copy in Towers collection)
Frederick C. Sherman papers. These were utilized in the 1960s when they were deposited with California Western University in San Diego, a university that is now defunct. The present location of the papers is unknown.
William H. Standley papers, University of Southern California, courtesy of Robert J. Cressman
Eugene E. Wilson papers, Nimitz Library, U.S. Naval Academy

Congressional Hearings

The published hearings of congressional committees and subcommittees are printed by the Government Printing Office immediately following their completion. Rather than give the long and redundant titles of bound volumes, which were consulted at the Navy Department Library, Washington Navy Yard, I list hearings by date only.

House Naval Affairs Committee, 1918–19, 1919–21, 1925, 1940, 1941, 1942
House Committee on Appropriations Subcommittee, 1930–31, 1939–40, 1941
Senate Commerce Subcommittee, 1939
Senate Appropriations Subcommittee, 1940, 1941
Senate Naval Affairs Committee, 1940, 1941

Oral History Transcripts

These superb resources are useful not only for the reminiscences but also for the careful questions asked by interviewers employed by the three collections. Transcripts are listed by collection, along with the year of the interview.

U.S. Naval Institute, Annapolis, Maryland

Admiral George W. Anderson, Jr., 1980
Vice Admiral Bernard L. Austin, 1970
Vice Admiral Gerald F. Bogan, 1969
Admiral Arleigh A. Burke, 1979
Vice Admiral Austin K. Doyle, 1970
Vice Admiral George C. Dyer, 1970
Captain (Chaplain Corps) Roland W. Faulk, 1974
Admiral Harry D. Felt, 1972
Rear Admiral Francis D. Foley, 1984
Vice Admiral Paul F. Foster, 1966
Captain Joy Bright Hancock, 1969–70
Captain Mildred McAfee Horton, 1969
Admiral Roy L. Johnson, 1980
Vice Admiral Andrew McB. Jackson, 1971–72
Captain Stephen Jurika, Jr., 1976
Vice Admiral Dixwell Ketcham, 1983–84
Admiral David L. McDonald, 1974–76
Vice Admiral Charles P. Mason, 1970
Vice Admiral Kleber S. Masterson, Sr., 1972–73
Captain Charles M. Melhorn, 1970
Rear Admiral P. V. Mercer, 1969
Vice Admiral Robert B. Pirie, 1972–73
Vice Admiral Charles A. Pownall, 1970
Admiral Alfred M. Pride, 1970, 1984
Vice Admiral Herbert D. Riley, 1971
Admiral James S. Russell, 1974
Rear Admiral Malcolm F. Schoeffel, 1979
Admiral U. S. G. Sharp, 1969–70

Captain H. H. Smith-Hutton, 1974
Vice Admiral P. D. Stroop, 1969
Rear Admiral George van Deurs, 1969
Vice Admiral Charles Wellborn, Jr., 1971–72
Commander E. E. Wilson, 1962
Forrest E. Wysong, 1970

Columbia University, New York, New York

Admiral J. J. Ballentine, 1964
Colonel Eugene Beebe, 1959
Henry S. Breckinridge, 1953
Rear Admiral Ben Scott Custer, 1965
Admiral Donald B. Duncan, 1969
Vice Admiral Paul F. Foster, 1969
Air Marshal Arthur T. Harris, 1959
Admiral John H. Hoover, 1964
Vice Admiral A. W. Johnson, 1964
Vice Admiral Emory S. Land, 1963
Robert A. Lovett, 1973
Rear Admiral C. J. Moore, 1964
Rear Admiral W. A. Read, 1964
Admiral James S. Russell, 1970
Sir Henry Self, 1960
Vice Admiral William T. Tarrant, 1964
Commander E. E. Wilson, 1962

Headquarters, U.S. Marine Corps, Washington Navy Yard, Washington D.C.

Admiral Robert B. Carney, 1973

Interviews with Author

Admiral George W. Anderson, Jr., 1964
Vice Admiral Wallace M. Beakley, 1965
Donald G. Beaton, 1985
Admiral J. J. Clark, 1963–67
Rear Admiral John G. Crommelin, Jr., 1976, 1978
William E. Doherty, Jr., 1985, 1986
Admiral Harry D. Felt, 1966
Lieutenant Commander Verne D. Harshman, 1976
Vice Admiral Truman J. Hedding, 1976
A. Lee Loomis, Jr., 1986
William T. Maddox, 1985

John Monsarrat, 1985
Rear Admiral Robert W. Morse, 1966
John S. Nevins, 1986
Herman Northway, 1986
Rear Admiral Paul E. Pihl, 1981
Vice Admiral Robert B. Pirie, 1987
Admiral Arthur W. Radford, 1964
Vice Admiral Herbert D. Riley, 1966
Lynne L. Riley, 1985
Eleanor R. Storrs, 1985
Charles and Lois Towers, 1985–87
Ernestine (Mrs. W. M.) Towers, 1985
Pierrette Anne (Mrs. John H.) Towers, 1966, 1983, 1985–87
William T. Towers, III, 1985
Commander Eugene E. Wilson, 1967

Official U.S. Navy Administrative Histories

Two sets of official, in-house aviation history monographs were written after World War II. The first, prepared by the aviation history unit of the deputy CNO (air), includes thirty volumes covering the years 1898 to 1945. The second, a narrative history of BuAer, covers 1921 to 1947 in twenty volumes. Both focus on World War II and necessarily overlap, sometimes verbatim. Several of the volumes quote from and cite "Admiral Towers Official Tracers, 1939–42," although a diligent search by the National Archives staff failed to locate that file.

A complete listing of these "admin" volumes is included in *Guide to United States Naval Administrative Histories of World War II* (Navy Department: Naval History Division, 1976). They are cited in the notes by their numerical listing in this source, although each set has its own sequential listing by volume number as well.

Office of the Deputy Chief of Naval Opertions (Air)

27 "Aviation in the Office of the Chief of Naval Operations," vols. 1
 and 2
30 "Financial and Legislative Planning, 1911–45," vols. 8 and 9
31 "Aviation Planning," vol. 10
32 "Aviation Shore Establishments," vol. 11
34 "Aviation Training, 1940–45," vol. 14
35 "The Civil Aeronautics Administration War Training Service (Navy)
 Flight Training Program," vol. 15
36 "Aviation in the Fleet Exercises, 1911–39," vol. 16
38 "Procurement of Naval Aircraft, 1940–45," vols. 18 and 19
39 "The Navy's Transport Glider Program, 1941–43," vol. 20
40 "Aviation Personnel, 1911–39," vol. 21
41 "Aviation Personnel, 1939–45," vol. 22

44 "Development of Fleet Air Wings," vol. 27
—"Carrier Warfare," vol. 28
126 "Naval Air Test Center, Patuxent River, Maryland," vol. 12

Bureau of Aeronautics

47 "Summary," 2 vols.
48 "Background," vol. 1
49 "Organization and Administration," vol. 2
50 "Operational Responsibilities," vol. 3
52 "Aviation Planning," vol. 5
54 "Naval Aviation Inspection," vol. 7
55 "Maintenance," vol. 8
56 "Material and Supply," vol. 9
57 "Research, Technical Developments and Engineering," vol. 10
58 "Aviation Shore Establishments," vol. 11
59 "Aviation Personnel and Training," vol. 12
60 "Budget Planning and Administration," vol. 13
61 "Naval Aviation Photography and Motion Pictures," vol. 14
63 "Publications," vol. 16
64 "Foreign Aid," vol. 17
66 "Air Intelligence," vol. 19

Bureau of Supplies and Accounts

91 "Supplying the Aeronautical Establishment"

SECONDARY SOURCES

Aero Club of America *Bulletin* (Feb–Mar 1912).
Aero Club of America 1910 (yearbook). New York, 1910.
"Aeronautics in the Navy," *The Navy* (Oct 1911): 10.
Albion, Robert Greenhalgh. *Makers of Naval Policy, 1798–1947.* Annapolis: Naval Institute Press, 1980.
———, and Robert H. Connery. *Forrestal and the Navy.* New York: Columbia University Press, 1962.
Alden, John D. *The American Steel Navy.* Annapolis: Naval Institute Press, 1972.
Allen, Archer M. R. "Across the Continent by Automobile." Manuscript essay, Naval War College archives, Mar 1931.
Allen, Gwenfread. *Hawaii's War Years, 1941–1945.* Honolulu: University of Hawaii Press, 1950.

Allen, William J. "David Ingalls: First of the Navy's Aces." Naval Aviation Museum *Foundation* 2, no. 1 (Mar 1981): 33–39.

Ambrose, Stephen E., ed. *The Papers of Dwight D. Eisenhower: The War Years.* 5 vols. Baltimore: The Johns Hopkins University Press, 1970.

Anderson, Frank W., Jr. *Orders of Magnitude: A History of NACA and NASA.* Washington: National Aeronautics and Space Administration, 1981.

Andrews, Adolphus, Jr. "Admiral with Wings: The Career of Joseph Mason Reeves." Senior thesis, Princeton University, 1943. Virtually an autobiography, based on interviews with Reeves.

Arnold, H. H. *Global Mission.* New York: Harper and Brothers, 1949.

Arpee, Edward. *From Frigates to Flat-tops: The Story of the Life and Achievements of Rear Admiral William Adger Moffett, U.S.N.* Privately published, 1953.

Arthur, Reginald Wright. *Contact! Careers of U.S. Naval Aviators Assigned Numbers 1 to 2000.* Washington: Naval Aviator Register, 1967.

Aycock, Roger. *All Roads to Rome.* Rome, Ga.: Rome Area Heritage Foundation, 1981.

Baldwin, Hanson W. "The End of the Wine Mess." U.S. Naval Institute *Proceedings* 84, no. 8 (Aug 1958): 82–91.

Ballentine, Duncan S. *U.S. Naval Logistics in the Second World War.* Princeton: Princeton University Press, 1947.

Barbey, Daniel E. *MacArthur's Amphibious Navy.* Annapolis: Naval Institute Press, 1969.

Bartley, Numan V. *The Creation of Modern Georgia.* Athens, Ga.: University of Georgia Press, 1983.

Barton, Charles. *Howard Hughes and His Flying Boat.* Fallbrook, Ca.: Aero, 1982.

Battey, George Magruder, Jr. *A History of Rome and Floyd County, 1540–1922.* Atlanta: Webb and Vary, 1922.

Beasley, Norman. *Knudsen: A Biography.* New York: McGraw-Hill, 1947.

Beigel, Harvey M. "The Battle Fleet's Home Port: 1919–1940." U.S. Naval Institute *Proceedings* (historical supplement, 1985): 54–63.

Bellinger, P. N. L. "The Gooney Bird." Manuscript autobiography, 1960. Mrs. Frederick A. Bellinger papers.

———. "Sailors in the Sky." *National Geographic* (Aug 1961): 276–96.

Bilstein, Roger E. *Flight Patterns: Trends of Aeronautical Development in the United States, 1918–1929.* Athens, Ga.: University of Georgia Press, 1983.

Blake, Nelson Manfred. *The Road to Reno: A History of Divorce in the United States.* New York: Macmillan, 1962.

Blakeslee, Victor F. "Our Chief of Aeronautics." *Shipmate* (Dec 1939): 3–4, 6.

Blum, John Morton. *From the Morgenthau Diaries: Years of Urgency.* Vol. 2. Boston: Houghton-Mifflin, 1965.

Blum, Robert M. *Drawing the Line: The Origins of American Containment Policy in East Asia.* New York: W. W. Norton, 1982.

Bocca, Geoffrey. *The Woman Who Would Be Queen.* New York: Rinehart, 1954.

Bogan, Gerald F. "The Navy Spreads Its Golden Wings." U.S. Naval Institute *Proceedings* 87, no. 5 (May 1961): 97–101.

Bonnalie, Allan F. "We View the Passing of Another Pioneer." *U.S. Air Services* (July 1955): 10–11.

Brown, Jerold E. "From the Ground Up: Air Planning in the Office of the Chief Signal Officer, 1917–1918," *Aerospace Historian* 33 (Sep 1986): 176–82.

Bryan, J. III. *Aircraft Carrier.* New York: Ballantine, 1954.

Bryan, T. Conn. *Confederate Georgia.* Athens, Ga.: University of Georgia Press, 1953.

Buchanan, A. Russell. *The United States and World War II.* 2 vols. New York: Harper, 1964.

Buck, Paul H. *The Road to Reunion, 1865–1900.* Boston: Little, Brown, 1937.

Buel, C. C. and R. W. Johnson. *Battles and Leaders of the Civil War.* 4 vols. New York: Appleton, Century, 1887.

Buell, Thomas B. "Admiral Edward C. Kalbfus and the Naval Planner's 'Holy Scripture': *Sound Military Decision.*" *Naval War College Review* (May–June 1973): 31–44.

———. *Master of Sea Power: A Biography of Fleet Admiral Ernest J. King.* Boston: Little, Brown, 1980.

———. *The Quiet Warrior: A Biography of Admiral Raymond A. Spruance.* Boston: Little, Brown, 1974.

Bureau of Aeronautics Annual Report, 1941.

Burns, James MacGregor. *Roosevelt: The Soldier of Freedom.* New York: Harcourt, Brace, Jovanovich, 1970.

Busch, Noel F. "Admiral Chester Nimitz." *Life* (10 July 1944): 82–92.

Butcher, M. E. "Admiral Frank Jack Fletcher: Pioneer Warrior or Gross Sinner?" *Naval War College Review* 40, no. 1 (winter 1987): 69–79.

Byrd, Richard E. "It's Safe to Fly." *Collier's* (3 Sep 1927): 7–8, 43.

———. *Skyward.* New York: G. P. Putnam's, 1928.

Cagle, Malcolm W. "Arleigh Burke, Naval Aviator," Naval Aviation Museum *Foundation* 2, no. 2 (Sep 1981): 2–11.

———. "The Four Read Brothers." Naval Aviation Museum *Foundation* 8, no. 1 (spring 1987): 13–23.

———. "Mr. Wu." Naval Aviation Museum *Foundation* 8, no. 1 (spring 1987): 46–52; 10, no. 2 (fall 1989): 43–51.

Calhoun, Arthur W. *A Social History of the American Family.* 3 vols. Cleveland: Arthur H. Clarke, 1919.

Caraley, Demetrios. *The Politics of Military Unification.* New York: Columbia University Press, 1966.

"The Case for the Naval Aviator." *Popular Aviation* 25, no. 3 (Sep 1939): 14–17, 60, 84.

Casey, Louis S. *Curtiss: The Hammondsport Era, 1907–1915.* New York: Crown, 1981.

Chandler, Alfred D., Jr. *The Visible Hand: The Managerial Revolution in American Business.* Cambridge: Harvard University Press, 1977.

"Chronology of U.S. Naval Aviation." Compiled by Harold Blaine Miller, assisted by Joy Bright Hancock, n.d., but annotated during the late 1950s. A. B. Cook's copy in Towers papers.

Clark, J. J., with Clark G. Reynolds, *Carrier Admiral*. New York: David McKay, 1967.

The Class of 1906. Annapolis: U.S. Naval Institute, 1954.

Class of 1907, United States Naval Academy, 1903–1924. Baltimore, n.p., n.d.

Coffey, Thomas M. *HAP*. New York: Viking, 1982.

Coletta, Paolo E. *Patrick N. L. Bellinger and U.S. Naval Aviation*. Lanham, Md.: University Press of America, 1987.

———. *The United States Navy and Defense Unification, 1947–1953*. Newark: University of Delaware Press, 1981.

———, and K. Jack Bauer, eds. *United States Navy and Marine Corps Bases*, 2 vols.: *Overseas* and *Domestic*. Westport, Ct.: Greenwood Press, 1985.

Connally, James B. "The Seagoing Flyers." *Collier's* (20 June 1914): 12–13, 32–33.

Connery, Robert H. *The Navy and the Industrial Mobilization in World War II*. Princeton: Princeton University Press, 1951.

Conway, Alan. *The Reconstruction of Georgia*. Minneapolis: University of Minnesota Press, 1966.

Coontz, Robert E. *From the Mississippi to the Sea*. Philadelphia: Dorrance, 1930.

Copp, DeWitt S. *A Few Great Captains*. Garden City: Doubleday, 1980.

Craven, T. T. "Director of Naval Aviation." U.S. Naval Institute *Proceedings* 79, no. 3 (Mar 1953): 293–301.

———. "Naval Aviation." U.S. Naval Institute *Proceedings* 46, no. 2 (Feb 1920): 181–91.

Craven, Wesley Frank, and James Lea Cate, eds. *The Army Air Forces in World War II*. 5 vols. Chicago: University of Chicago Press, 1948–1953.

Creed, Roscoe. *PBY: The Catalina Flying Boat*. Annapolis: Naval Institute Press, 1985.

"The Crossing of the Atlantic: The Hydroplane No. 3 Arrived at Ponta Delgada, After a Heroic Trip." *A Republica* (May 1919). Translated in National Archives RG 45.

Cruise of the U.S.S. Saratoga, 1937.

Cullen, Charles W. "From the Kriegsacademie to the Naval War College: The Military Planning Process." *Naval War College Review* (Jan 1970): 6–18.

Cummings, Damon E. *Admiral Richard Wainwright and the United States Fleet*. Washington: Government Printing Office, 1962.

Cunningham, Frank. *Sky Master: The Story of Donald Douglas*. Philadelphia: Dorrance, 1943.

Curtiss Aeroplanes. 1912 catalogue.

Daley, Robert. *An American Saga: Juan Trippe and His Pan-Am Empire*. New York: Random, 1980.

Daniels, Josephus. *The Wilson Era: Years of War and After, 1917–1923*. Chapel Hill: University of North Carolina Press, 1946.

———. *The Wilson Years: Years of Peace, 1910–1917*. Chapel Hill: University of North Carolina Press, 1944.

Davenport, William Wyatt. *Gyro! The Life and Times of Lawrence Sperry*. New York: Charles Scribner's Sons, 1978.

Davis, Vernon E. *The History of the Joint Chiefs of Staff in World War II.* 2 vols. Washington: Joint Chiefs of Staff, 1972.

December 7: The First Thirty Hours. New York: Alfred A. Knopf, 1942.

Debrett's Peerage, Baronetage, Knightage and Companionage, 1952.

Dictionary of American Naval Fighting Ships. 8 vols. Washington: Naval Historical Center, 1959–81.

Dingman, Roger. "Strategic Planning and the Policy Process: American Plans for War in East Asia, 1945–1950." *Naval War College Review* (Nov–Dec 1979): 4–21.

Donald, David. *The Politics of Reconstruction, 1863–1867.* Baton Rouge: Louisiana State University Press, 1965.

Dorwart, Jeffrey M. *Conflict of Duty: The U.S. Navy's Intelligence Dilemma, 1919–1945.* Annapolis: Naval Institute Press, 1983.

————. *The Office of Naval Intelligence: The Birth of America's First Intelligence Agency, 1865–1918.* Annapolis: Naval Institute Press, 1979.

Douhet, Giulio. *The Command of the Air.* Washington: Office of Air Force History, 1985. Reprint.

Durand, W. F. *Adventures: A Life Story.* New York: American Society of Mechanical Engineers, 1953.

Duval, G. R. *British Flying-Boats and Amphibians, 1909–1952.* London: Putnam, 1966.

Dyer, George Carroll. *The Amphibians Came to Conquer: The Story of Admiral Richmond Kelly Turner.* 2 vols. Washington: Government Printing Office, 1972.

Ellicott, J. M. "Japanese Students at the United States Naval Academy." U.S. Naval Institute *Proceedings* 73, no. 3 (Mar 1947): 303–7.

Emme, Eugene M. *Aeronautics and Astronautics . . . 1915–1960.* Washington: NASA, 1961.

Enders, Calvin W. "The Vinson Navy." Ph.D. diss., Michigan State University, 1970.

Evans, Robley D. *An Admiral's Log.* New York: D. Appleton, 1911.

Fahrney, Delmar S. "The Birth of Guided Missiles." U.S. Naval Institute *Proceedings* 106, no. 12 (Dec 1980): 54–60.

Fanton, Jonathan Foster. "Robert A. Lovett: The War Years." Ph.D. diss., Yale University, 1978.

Featherston, Frank H. "A.E.D.O.: A History and a Heritage." U.S. Naval Institute *Proceedings* 94, no. 2 (Feb 1968): 33–45.

Ferrell, Henry C., Jr. *Claude A. Swanson of Virginia: A Political Biography.* Lexington: University of Kentucky Press, 1985.

The Flight across the Atlantic. N.p., n.d.

Flynn, Charles L., Jr. *White Land, Black Labor: Caste and Class in Late Nineteenth-Century Georgia.* Baton Rouge: Louisiana State University Press, 1983.

Forrestel, E. P. *Admiral Raymond A. Spruance, USN: A Study in Command.* Washington: Government Printing Office, 1966.

Foster, Mark S. *Henry J. Kaiser: Builder in the Modern American West.* Austin: University of Texas Press, 1989.

Foulois, Benjamin D., with C. V. Glines. *From the Wright Brothers to the Astronauts: Memoirs.* New York: McGraw-Hill, 1968.

"Four Darlington Alumni Enjoy an Unforgettable Trip to the Olympic Games in Los Angeles (in 1932)." *Darlington* (winter 1984–85): 14–17.

Fredericks, Edward H. C. "The U.S. Navy in San Diego Prior to World War II." Manuscript history, National Historical Center, ZE file, n.d.

Friedman, Norman. *Carrier Air Power.* London: Conway, 1981.

———. *U.S. Aircraft Carriers: An Illustrated Design History.* Annapolis: Naval Institute Press, 1983.

Fulton, Garland. "The General Climate for Technological Developments in Naval Aeronautics on the Eve of World War I." *Technology and Culture* 4, no. 2 (spring 1963): 154–65.

Furlong, William Rea. *Class of 1905, U.S. Naval Academy.* Annapolis: U.S. Naval Academy, 1930.

Galambos, Louis, ed. *The Papers of Dwight D. Eisenhower: Columbia University.* Vol. 10. Baltimore: Johns Hopkins University Press, 1984.

Gibbs-Smith, Charles Harvard. *Aviation: An Historical Survey.* London: Her Majesty's Stationery Office, 1970.

Gilbert, Martin. *Winston S. Churchill.* Vol. 3. Boston: Houghton Mifflin, 1971.

Glover, Cato D. *Command Performance—With Guts.* New York: Greenwich, 1969.

Goddard, Esther C., ed. *The Papers of Robert H. Goddard.* 3 vols. New York: McGraw-Hill, 1970.

Godfrey Chevalier Memorial, in Medford (Mass.) *Historical Society Publications* 43 (Mar 1940).

Goldberg, Alfred, ed. *A History of the United States Air Force, 1907–1957.* Princeton: D. Van Nostrand, 1957.

Gould, Bartlett. "The Burgess Story." *American Aviation Historical Society Journal* part 1, 1910 (summer 1965): 79–87; part 2, 1911–12 (winter 1965): 241–49; part 3, 1913–14 (winter 1966): 270–78; part 4, 1915–16 (winter 1967): 273–80; part 5, 1917–18 (spring 1968): 37–42.

Grant, Elmer P. "I Knew Them All." Manuscript history, Sara Hightower Regional Library, Rome, Ga., 1956.

Gray, George W. *Frontiers of Flight: The Story of NACA Research.* New York: Alfred A. Knopf, 1948.

"Greatest Meet Ever Held Ends Happily." *Aero* (26 Aug 1911): 453–59.

[Green Bowl Society.] *List of Members, Classes 1909 to 1930.*

Greene, Fred C. "The Military View of American National Policy, 1904–1940." *American Historical Review* 46, no. 2 (Jan 1961): 354–77.

Hahn, Steven. *The Roots of Southern Populism: Yeoman Farmers and the Transformation of the Georgia Upcountry, 1850–1890.* Oxford: Oxford University Press, 1983.

Halsey, William F., and J. Bryan III. *Admiral Halsey's Story.* New York: McGraw-Hill, 1947.

Hancock, Joy Bright. *Lady in the Navy.* Annapolis: Naval Institute Press, 1972.

Hart, Caroline Brownson. *From Frigate to Dreadnought: Willard Herbert Brownson, USN.* Sharon, Ct.: King House, [1973].

Hart, Robert A. *The Great White Fleet*. Boston: Little, Brown, 1965.

Hattendorf, John B., B. Mitchell Simpson, and John R. Wadleigh. *Sailors and Scholars: The Centennial History of the U.S. Naval War College*. Newport: Naval War College Press, 1984.

Hayes, Grace Person. *The History of the Joint Chiefs of Staff: The War against Japan*. Annapolis: Naval Institute Press, 1982.

Hayes, John D. "Admiral Joseph Mason Reeves." *Naval War College Review* (Nov 1970): 48–57; (Jan 1972): 50–64.

Haynes, Richard F. *The Awesome Power: Harry S. Truman as Commander in Chief*. Baton Rouge: Louisiana State University Press, 1973.

Heinrichs, Waldo. *Threshold of War: Franklin D. Roosevelt and American Entry into World War II*. New York: Oxford University Press, 1988.

Hendrick, Burton J. *The Life and Letters of Walter H. Page, 1855 to 1918*. 2 vols. Garden City: Garden City Publishing Company, 1927.

Henry, Ralph Selph. *"First with the Most" Forrest*. Indianapolis: Bobbs-Merrill, 1944.

Hesseltine, William B. *Confederate Leaders in the New South*. Baton Rouge: Louisiana State University Press, 1950.

Hewlett, Richard G., and Francis Duncan. *Nuclear Navy, 1946–1962*. Chicago: University of Chicago Press, 1974.

Hezlet, Sir Arthur. *Aircraft and Sea Power*. New York: Stein and Day, 1970.

Higham, Charles. *The Duchess of Windsor: The Secret Life*. New York: McGraw-Hill, 1988.

Hoaglund, Roland W., ed. *The Book of Aviation*. Los Angeles: Hoaglund, 1932.

Holland, Maurice, with Thomas M. Smith. *Architects of Aviation*. New York: Duell, Sloan and Pearce, 1951.

Holley, I. B. *Buying Aircraft: Materiel Procurement for the Army Air Forces*. Washington: Government Printing Office, 1964.

———. *Ideas and Weapons*. 1953. Reprint. Washington: Office of Air Force History, 1983.

Hone, Thomas C. "Battleships vs. Aircraft Carriers: The Patterns of U.S. Navy Operating Expenditures, 1932–41. *Military Affairs* 41, no. 3 (Oct 1977): 133–41.

———, and Mark Daniel Mandeles. "Managerial Style in the Interwar Navy: A Reappraisal." *Naval War College Review*, (Sep–Oct 1980): 88–101.

Hook, Thom. *Shenandoah Saga*. Annapolis: Air Show, 1973.

Hopkins, Captain Harold, RN. *Nice to Have You Aboard*. London: Allen and Unwin, 1964.

Hovgaard, William. *Modern History of Warships*. 1920. Reprint. Annapolis: Naval Institute Press, 1971.

Howard, Frank, and Bill Gunston. *The Conquest of the Air*. New York: Random House, 1972.

Howeth, L. S. *History of Communications-Electronics in the United States Navy*. Washington: Navy Department, 1963.

Hoyt, Edwin P. *How They Won the War in the Pacific: Nimitz and His Admirals*. New York: Weybright and Talley, 1970.

Hubbell, John G. "How Our Troops Trained for Combat." *Reader's Digest* (Oct 1961): 57–61.

Hunsaker, J. C. "How American Ingenuity Designed the NC Boats." *Automotive Industries* 41 (10 July 1919): 68–72.

———. "How the NC Boats Were Built under Pressure of War Need." *Automotive Industries* 41 (17 July 1919): 120–23.

———. "How the NC Boats Were Equipped for the Pioneer Flight." *Automotive Industries* 41 (24 July 1919): 172–75.

Huntington, Samuel P. *The Soldier and the State.* Cambridge: Harvard University Press, 1957.

Hutchings, Curtis. "Patrol Squadron Sixty-Three." Naval Aviation Museum *Foundation* 4, no. 2 (fall 1983): 42–51.

Inger, George R. "The Rise and Fall of the Brewster Aeronautical Corporation, 1932–1944." To be published.

James, D. Clayton. *The Years of MacArthur.* Vol. 3. Boston: Houghton-Mifflin, 1985.

Janowicz, Morris. *The Professional Soldier: A Social and Political Portrait.* [New York:] Free Press, 1960.

Jentschura, Hansgeorg, Dieter Jung, and Pieter Mickel. *Warships of the Imperial Japanese Navy, 1869–1945.* London: Arms and Armour Press, 1977.

Johnson, Allen L. "Two Hundred Years of Airborne Communications." *Aerospace Historian* 31, no. 3 (Sep 1984): 185–93.

Johnson, Earle Freeman. "Some Navy Years, 1903–1919." Manuscript, Naval Historical Center, 1963.

Johnson, Edward C. *Marine Corps Aviation: The Early Years, 1912–1940.* Washington: U.S. Marine Corps, 1977.

Jordan, John W. *Colonial and Revolutionary Families of Pennsylvania.* Vol. 2. New York, 1911.

Jurika, Stephen, Jr., ed. *From Pearl Harbor to Vietnam: The Memoirs of Admiral Arthur W. Radford.* Stanford: Hoover Institution Press, 1980.

Keen, Harold. " 'Feeder' Factories." *Flying* (Feb 1944): 26–27, 96.

———. "Navy's No. 1 Flier Passed Over for Promotion—Many Puzzled." San Diego *Tribune Sun,* 6 Dec 1938.

Kennedy, Gerald John. "United States Naval War College, 1919–1941: An Institutional Response to Naval Preparedness." Research thesis, Naval War College, 1975.

Kenney, George C. *General Kenney Reports.* New York: Duell, Sloan and Pearce, 1949.

King, Ernest J., and Walter Muir Whitehill. *Fleet Admiral King: A Naval Record.* New York: W. W. Norton, 1952.

Kinsey, Gordon. *Seaplanes—Felixstowe: The Story of the Air Station, 1913–1963.* Suffolk, England: Terence Dalton, 1978.

Kirkendall, Richard S. "Harry S. Truman and the Creation of the Air Force." *Aerospace Historian* 34, no. 3 (fall 1987): 176–84.

Klachko, Mary, and David F. Trask. *Admiral William S. Benson: First Chief of Naval Operations.* Annapolis: Naval Institute Press, 1987.

Knott, Richard C. *The American Flying Boat: An Illustrated History.* Annapolis: Naval Institute Press, 1979.

Land, Emory Scott. *Winning the War with Ships: Land, Sea and Air—Mostly Land.* New York: Robert M. McBride, 1958.

Langer, William L., and S. Everett Gleason. *The Challenge to Isolation, 1937–1940.* New York: Harper Brothers, 1952.

Laning, Harris. "An Admiral's Yarn." Manuscript, Naval Historical Center, c. 1938.

Lavender, Robert A. "Radio Equipment on NC Seaplanes." U.S. Naval Institute *Proceedings* 46, no. 10 (Oct 1920): 1601–7.

Leffler, Melvyn P. "The American Conception of National Security and the Beginnings of the Cold War, 1945–48." *American Historical Review* 89, no. 2 (Apr 1984): 346–81.

"Let's Get Two-Fisted." *Colliers* (24 Oct 1942): 86.

Leutze, James. *A Different Kind of Victory: A Biography of Admiral Thomas C. Hart.* Annapolis: Naval Institute Press, 1981.

"Lieutenant Towers Wins Pilot's License." *Aero* (23 Sep 1911): 534.

Link, Arthur S. *The Papers of Woodrow Wilson.* Vol. 30. Princeton: Princeton University Press, 1979.

———. *Wilson: The New Freedom.* Princeton: Princeton University Press, 1956.

———. *Wilson: The Struggle for Neutrality.* Princeton: Princeton University Press, 1960.

Loening, Grover. *Amphibian: The Story of the Loening Biplane.* Greenwich, Ct.: New York Graphic Society, 1973.

———. *Our Wings Grow Faster.* Garden City: Doubleday, Doran, 1935.

Lord, Clifford L. "History of Naval Aviation." 4 vols. Manuscript, Naval Historical Center, 1946. Typewritten copy by Pierre Towers, in Towers papers.

Lowry, Frank J. "The End of the Green Bowlers." *Shipmate* (Jan 1955): 3–4.

Lucky Bag [U.S. Naval Academy yearbook]. U.S. Naval Academy: 1903, 1904, 1905, 1906, 1907, 1908, 1909, 1918.

Lundstrom, John B. *The First Team.* Annapolis: Naval Institute Press, 1984.

MacDonald, Scot. *Evolution of Aircraft Carriers.* Washington: Government Printing Office, 1964.

Marder, Arthur J. *The Anatomy of British Sea Power: A History of British Naval Policy in the Pre-Dreadnought Era, 1880–1905.* New York: Knopf, 1940.

———. *From the Dreadnought to Scapa Flow: The Royal Navy in the Fisher Era, 1904–1919.* 5 vols. New York: Oxford University Press, 1961–70.

Markey, Morris. "Naval Aviator No. 1." *Liberty* (12 Feb 1945): 24–25, 65–66.

Mason, John T., Jr. *The Atlantic War Remembered.* Annapolis: Naval Institute Press 1990.

Matloff, Maurice, and Edwin M. Snell. *Strategic Planning for Coalition Warfare, 1941–1942.* Washington: Office of the Chief of Military History, 1953.

McCarthy, Charles J. "Naval Aircraft Design in the Mid-1930's." *Technology and Culture* 4, no. 2 (spring 1963): 165–74.

McJimsey, George. *Harry Hopkins.* Cambridge: Harvard University Press, 1987.

McMath, Robert C., Jr. *Engineering the New South: Georgia Tech, 1885–1985.* Athens: University of Georgia Press, 1985.

Melhorn, Charles M. *Two-Block Fox: The Rise of the Aircraft Carrier, 1911–1929.* Annapolis: Naval Institute Press, 1974.

Mervine, William M., ed. *The Genealogical Register.* Vol. 1. Philadelphia, 1913.

Messenger, Charles. *"Bomber" Harris and the Strategic Bombing Offensive, 1939–1945.* New York: St. Martin's Press, 1984.

Messer, Robert L. *The End of an Alliance: James F. Byrnes, Roosevelt, Truman, and the Origins of the Cold War.* Chapel Hill: University of North Carolina Press, 1982.

Messimer, Dwight R. *No Margin for Error: The U.S. Navy's Transpacific Flight of 1925.* Annapolis: Naval Institute Press, 1981.

Miller, Harold Blaine. *Navy Wings.* Rev. ed. New York: Dodd, Mead, 1942.

Miller, John Perry. *The Pricing of Military Procurements.* New Haven: Yale University Press, 1949.

Miller, Mrs. C. R. "Flying with the Navy: An Ill-fated Biplane." *Leslie's Illustrated Weekly Newspaper* (10 July 1913).

Millis, Walter, and Eugene S. Duffield, eds. *The Forrestal Diaries.* New York: Viking, 1951.

Monsarrat, John. *Angel on the Yardarm: The Beginnings of Fleet Radar Defense and the Kamikaze Threat.* Newport: Naval War College Press, 1985.

Moran, Gerard P. *Aeroplanes Vought.* Temple City, Ca.: Historical Aviation Album, 1978.

Morehouse, Harold E. "The Flying Pioneers." Biographies of early aviators in the *American Aviation Historical Society Journal,* 1960s.

Morison, Elting E. *Admiral Sims and the Modern American Navy.* Boston: Houghton-Mifflin, 1942.

Morison, Samuel Eliot. *History of United States Naval Operations during World War II.* 15 vols. Boston: Little, Brown, 1947–63.

———. *The Two-Ocean War.* Boston: Little, Brown, 1962.

[Morrow Board.] *Hearings before the President's Aircraft Board.* 4 vols. Washington: Government Printing Office, 1925.

Musicant, Ivan. *U.S. Armored Cruisers.* Annapolis: Naval Institute Press, 1985.

Nelson, Donald M. *Arsenal of Democracy: The Story of American War Production.* New York: Harcourt, Brace, 1946.

Newton, Wesley Phillips, and Robert R. Rea, eds. *Wings of Gold: An Account of Naval Aviation Training in World War II.* Tuscaloosa: University of Alabama Press, 1987.

O'Connor, Raymond G. "The American Navy, 1939–1941: The Enlisted Perspective." *Military Affairs* 50, no. 4 (Oct 1986): 173–78.

———. *Perilous Equilibrium: The United States and the London Naval Conference of 1930.* Lawrence: University of Kansas Press, 1962.

Official Records of the Union and Confederate Armies in the War of the Rebellion. 70 vols. Washington: Government Printing Office, 1880–1901.

O'Neil, Paul. *Barnstormers and Speed Kings.* Alexandria, Va.: Time-Life Books, 1981.

Paine, Ralph D. *The First Yale Unit: A Story of Naval Aviation, 1916–1919.* 2 vols. Cambridge, Ma.: Riverside Press, 1925.

Palmer, Michael A. *Origins of the Maritime Strategy: American Naval Strategy in the First Postwar Decade.* Washington: Government Printing Office, 1988.

Peck, S. E. "Lighter-Than-Air." *Flying* (Jan 1942): 94ff.

Phillips, Christopher. *Steichen at War.* New York: Harry N. Abrams, 1981.

Pirie, Robert B. "Return to Midway, 1934." Naval Aviation Museum *Foundation* 7, no. 1 (spring 1986): 25–30.

Pisano, Dominick A. "A Brief History of the Civilian Pilot Training Program, 1939–1944," in *National Air and Space Museum Research Report, 1986.* Washington: Smithsonian Institution Press, 1986.

Pogue, Forrest. *George C. Marshall.* Vols. 3 and 4. New York: Viking, 1973, 1987.

Potter, E. B. *Bull Halsey.* Annapolis: Naval Institute Press, 1985.

———. *Nimitz.* Annapolis: Naval Institute Press, 1976.

Pratt, Fletcher. *Fleet against Japan.* New York: Harper and Brothers, 1946.

———. "Nimitz and His Admirals." *Harper's* (Feb 1945): 209–17.

Prendergast, Curtis. *The First Aviators.* Alexandria, Va.: Time-Life, 1980.

"Presenting: Admiral John H. Towers." *Pathfinder* Washington News Weekly (14 June 1941): 21.

Radford, Arthur W. "Aircraft Battle Force," in Paul Stillwell, ed., *Air Raid: Pearl Harbor! Recollections of a Day of Infamy.* Annapolis: Naval Institute Press, 1981.

Rae, John B. *Climb to Greatness: The American Aircraft Industry, 1920–1960.* Cambridge: MIT Press, 1968.

Raleigh, Walter, and H. A. Jones. *The War in the Air.* 6 vols. Oxford: Clarendon, 1922–37.

Read, Bess Burdine. "The Private Letters of Putty Read." Naval Aviation Museum *Foundation* 7, no. 1 (spring 1986): 9–19.

Reckner, James R. *Teddy Roosevelt's Great White Fleet.* Annapolis: Naval Institute Press, 1988.

Regan, Stephen D. "In Bitter Tempest: The Battles of Admiral Frank Jack Fletcher." To be published by Iowa State University Press.

"Remarkable Rome, Illustrated." Rome [Ga.] *Tribune-Herald,* Dec. 1911.

Reynolds, Clark G. "Admiral Ernest J. King and the Strategy for Victory in the Pacific." *Naval War College Review* 28, no. 3 (winter 1976): 57–64.

———. *Civil War.* New York: Mallard, 1991.

———. *Command of the Sea: The History and Strategy of Maritime Empires.* Rev. ed., 2 vols. Malabar, Fl.: Robert Krieger, 1983.

———. "Confederate Romans and Bedford Forrest: Civil War Roots of Admiral John H. Towers." *The Georgia Historical Quarterly,* forthcoming: 77, no. 1 (Spring 1993).

———. *Famous American Admirals.* New York: Van Nostrand Reinhold, 1978.

———. *The Fast Carriers: The Forging of an Air Navy.* New York: McGraw-Hill, 1968. Reprint. Annapolis: Naval Institute Press, 1992.

———. *The Fighting Lady: The New Yorktown in the Pacific War.* Missoula, Mt.: Pictorial Histories, 1986.

———. "Forrest Percival Sherman," in Robert William Love, ed., *The Chiefs of Naval Operations.* Annapolis: Naval Institute Press, 1980.

————. *History and the Sea: Essays on Maritime Strategies.* Columbia: University of South Carolina Press, 1989.

————. "MacArthur as Maritime Strategist." *Naval War College Review* 38, no. 2 (Mar–Apr 1980): 79–91.

————. "William A. Moffett: Steward of the Air Revolution," in James C. Bradford, ed., *Admirals of the New Steel Navy.* Annapolis: Naval Institute Press, 1989.

————. "Writing on Naval Flying." *Aerospace Historian* 31, no. 1 (Mar 1984): 21–29. Bibliographical.

Richardson, J. O., as told to George C. Dyer. *On the Treadmill to Pearl Harbor: The Memoirs of Admiral James O. Richardson.* Washington: Naval History Division, 1973.

Riley, John. "From Georgia Rowboat to Admiral's Flagship." *The Atlanta Journal Magazine* (24 Feb 1946): 6–7.

Riley, William A., Jr. "The Navy's Light Bombing Wing." *American Aviation Historical Society Journal* 3 (July–Sep 1958): 148–51.

Robinson, Douglas H., and Charles L. Keller. *"Up Ship!" A History of the U.S. Navy's Rigid Airships, 1919–1935.* Annapolis: Naval Institute Press, 1982.

Rodgers, C. R. J. "The Pony Road: Bath and Hammondsport." Manuscript, Corning Library, New York, n.d.

Roland, Alex. *Model Research: The National Advisory Committee for Aeronautics, 1915–1958.* 2 vols. Washington: NASA, 1985.

Rollins, Alfred B., Jr. *Roosevelt and Howe.* New York: Knopf, 1962.

Roseberry, C. R. *The Challenging Skies . . . 1919–1939.* Garden City: Doubleday, 1966.

————. *Glenn Curtiss: Pioneer of Flight.* Garden City: Doubleday, 1972.

Roskill, S. W. *Documents Relating to the Naval Air Service.* Vol. 1. London: Naval Records Society, 1969.

————. *Naval Policy between the Wars.* 2 vols. London: Collins, 1968, 1976.

"Roster of American Aviation Pilots." *Aero and Hydro* (19 Apr 1913): 38–40.

Russell, James S. "The Early Days of Carrier Aviation and the Design of the *Essex*-Class Carrier." Naval Aviation Museum *Foundation* 3, no. 2 (fall 1982): 17–31.

————. "Mess Treasurer of the *Essex* Class." U.S. Naval Institute *Proceedings* (historical supplement 1986): 54–63.

————. "The *Ranger:* Atavistic Anomaly." U.S. Naval Institute *Proceedings* (historical supplement 1986): 52–53.

Ryan, Oswald. "Recent Developments in United States International Air Transport Policy." *Air Affairs* 1 (Sep 1946): 45–66.

Saunders, Frances Wright. *First Lady between Two Worlds: Ellen Axson Wilson.* Chapel Hill: University of North Carolina Press, 1985.

Scheppler, Robert H. *Pacific Air Race.* Washington: Smithsonian Institution, 1988.

Schnabel, James F. *The History of the Joint Chiefs of Staff.* Vol. 1. Wilmington, De.: Michael Glazer, 1979.

Seversky, Alexander P. de. *Victory through Air Power.* New York: Simon and Schuster, 1942.

Sherman, Forrest. "Air Warfare." U.S. Naval Institute *Proceedings* 52, no. 1 (Jan 1926), 62–71.

Sherrod, Robert. *U.S. Marine Corps Aviation in World War II.* Washington: Combat Forces Press, 1952.

Sherry, Michael S. *The Rise of American Air Power: The Creation of Armageddon.* New Haven: Yale University Press, 1987.

Sherwood, Robert E. *Roosevelt and Hopkins: An Intimate History.* New York: Harper and Brothers, 1950.

Shiner, John F. "The Air Corps, the Navy, and Coast Defense, 1919–1941." *Military Affairs* 45, no. 3 (Oct 1981): 113–20.

———. *Foulois and the U.S. Army Air Corps, 1931–1935.* Washington: Office of Air Force History, 1983.

Sims, William S. *The Victory at Sea.* Garden City: Doubleday, 1920.

Sizer, Theodore R. *Secondary Schools at the Turn of the Century.* New Haven: Yale University Press, 1964.

Slessor, Sir John. *The Central Blue: Recollections and Reflections.* London: Cassell, 1956.

Small, Ernest G. "The U.S. Naval Academy: An Undergraduate's Point of View." U.S. Naval Institute *Proceedings* 38, no. 12 (Dec 1912): 1397–403.

Smith, Holland M., and Percy Finch. *Coral and Brass.* New York: Charles Scribner's Sons, 1949.

Smith, Myron, Jr. *Passenger Airliners of the United States, 1926–1986: A Pictorial History.* Missoula, Mt.: Pictorial Histories, 1986.

Smith, Richard K. *The Airships* Akron *and* Macon. Annapolis: Naval Institute Press, 1965.

———. *First Across! The U.S. Navy's Transatlantic Flight of 1919.* Annapolis: Naval Institute Press, 1973.

Solberg, Curl. *Conquest of the Skies: A History of Commercial Aviation in America.* Boston: Little, Brown, 1979.

Spanier, John. *American Foreign Policy since World War II.* 7th ed. New York: Praeger, 1977.

Sprout, Harold, and Margaret Sprout. *The Rise of American Naval Power, 1776–1918.* Princeton: Princeton University Press, 1939.

———. *Toward a New Order of Sea Power, 1918–1922.* Princeton: Princeton University Press, 1940.

Steirman, Hy, and Glenn D. Kittler. *Triumph.* New York: Harper and Row, 1961. Must be used with care because of journalistic license, but the authors interviewed many participants of the NC flight.

Studenmund, W. Russell. "A President's Admiral: William D. Leahy." Naval Aviation Museum *Foundation* 7, no. 2 (fall 1986): 16–21.

Studer, Clara. *Sky Storming Yankee: The Life of Glenn Curtiss.* New York: Stackpole Sons, 1937.

Sudsbury, Elretta. *Jackrabbits to Jets: The History of North Island, San Diego, California.* San Diego: Neyenesch, 1967.

Swanborough, Gordon, and Peter M. Bowers. *United States Naval Aircraft since 1911.* 2d ed. Annapolis: Naval Institute Press, 1976.

Swarthout, Laura L. *A History of Hammondsport to 1962.* Corning, N.Y.: Painted Post Historical Society, n.d.

Sweetman, Jack. *The Landing at Veracruz, 1914.* Annapolis: U.S. Naval Institute, 1968.

———. *The U.S. Naval Academy: An Illustrated History.* Annapolis: Naval Institute Press, 1979.

Tate, Jackson R. "We Rode the Covered Wagon." U.S. Naval Institute *Proceedings* 104, no. 10 (Oct 1978): 62–69.

Taylor, Robert Louis. "Captain among the Synthetics." *The New Yorker* (11 Nov 1944): 32–39; (18 Nov 1944): 28–39.

Taylor, Theodore. *The Magnificent Mitscher.* New York: W. W. Norton, 1954.

Thayer, Frederick C., Jr. *Air Transport Policy and National Security.* Chapel Hill: University of North Carolina Press, 1965.

Thetford, Owen. *British Naval Aircraft since 1912.* 2nd ed. London: Putnam, 1962.

Thompson, C. Mildred. *Reconstruction in Georgia, 1865–1872.* 1915. Reprint. Freeport, N.Y.: Books for Libraries Press, 1971.

Thompson, Ernest Trice. *Presbyterians in the South.* 3 vols. Richmond: John Knox Press, 1973.

Thruelsen, Richard. *The Grumman Story.* New York: Praeger, 1976.

Tillman, Stephen F. *Man Unafraid.* Washington: Army Times, 1958.

Towers, John H. "The Great Hop: The Story of the American Navy's Transatlantic Flight." *Everybody's Magazine* 41 (Nov 1919): 9–15, 74, 76, 78.

———. "The Influence of Aircraft on Naval Strategy and Tactics." Thesis, Naval War College, 1934.

———. "My Friend 'Hap' Arnold." *The Bee-Hive* (United Aircraft Corporation) (spring 1950): 8–9.

———. [Probably ghostwritten by Joy Bright Hancock.] "Naval Aviation Policy and the Bureau of Aeronautics." *Aero Digest* (Feb 1940): 34ff.

———. [Probably ghostwritten by Joy Bright Hancock.] "The Navy Spreads Its Wings." *Shipmate* (Jan 1942): 6–7, 19, 61–63.

———. "Operations of Naval Aircraft." *Transactions of the Society of Automotive Engineers* 14 (1919): 373–85.

———. "The Relationship between French Policy and Strategy in the War of the Coalition, 1777–1783, and Its Lessons to Us." Thesis, Naval War College, 1934.

———. Review of Arpee's *From Frigates to Flat-tops,* in U.S. Naval Institute *Proceedings* 79, no. 10 (Oct 1953): 1139–40.

"Training Legacy of Luis de Florez." *Naval Aviation News* (Apr 1961): 6–10.

Trimble, William F. "The Naval Aircraft Factory, the American Aviation Industry, and Government Competition, 1919–1928." *Business History Review* 60, no. 2 (summer 1986): 175–98.

Turnbull, Archibald D., and Clifford L. Lord. *History of United States Naval Aviation.* New Haven: Yale University Press, 1949.

"Twentieth-Century Rome." Rome [Ga.] *Tribune,* special industrial edition, Oct 1902.

United States Naval Aviation, 1910–1980. Washington: Deputy Chief of Naval Operations (Air Warfare), 1981.

Van Deurs, George. *Anchors in the Sky: Spuds Ellyson, The First Naval Aviator.* San Raphael: Presidio, 1978.

———. *Wings of the Fleet: A Narrative of Naval Aviation's Early Development, 1910–1916.* Annapolis: U.S. Naval Institute, 1966.

Van Wyen, Adrian O. *The Aeronautical Board, 1916–1947.* Washington: Deputy Chief of Naval Operations (Air), 1969.

———. *Naval Aviation in World War I.* Washington: Chief of Naval Operations, 1969.

Vlahos, Michael. *The Blue Sword: The Naval War College and the American Mission, 1919–1941.* Newport: Naval War College Press, 1980.

———. "Wargaming, An Enforcer of Strategic Realism: 1919–1942." *Naval War College Review* (Mar–Apr 1986): 7–22.

Wagner, Ray. *Reuben Fleet and the Story of Consolidated Aircraft.* Fallbrook, Ca.: Aero, 1976.

Wallace, Robert B., Jr. *Dress Her in White and Gold: A Biography of Georgia Tech.* Atlanta: Georgia Tech Foundation, 1963.

Warner, Edward. "Notes from PICAO Experience." *Air Affairs* 1 (Sep 1946): 30–44.

Warren, Marion E., and Mame Warren. *"The Train's Done Been and Gone": An Annapolis Portrait, 1859–1910.* Annapolis: M. E. Warren, 1976.

Werrell, Kenneth P. *The Evolution of the Cruise Missile.* Maxwell Air Force Base, Al.: Air University Press, 1985.

Westervelt, G. C. "Design and Construction of the NC Flying Boats." U.S. Naval Institute *Proceedings* 55, no. 9 (Sep 1919): 1529–31.

———, H. C. Richardson, and A. C. Read. *The Triumph of the NC's.* Garden City: Doubleday, Page, 1920.

"What Does the Towers Promotion Portend?" *U.S. Air Services* (Oct 1942): 8–9.

Wheeler, Gerald E. *Admiral William Veazie Pratt, U.S. Navy: A Sailor's Life.* Washington: Naval History Division, 1974.

———, ed. "The War College Years of Admiral Harris Laning, U.S. Navy." *Naval War College Review* (Mar 1969): 69–87.

White, Lillian C. *Pioneer and Pilot: George Cook Sweet, Commander, USN, 1877–1953.* Delray Beach, Fl.: Southern, 1963.

Who Was Who in American History: The Military. Chicago: Marquis Who's Who, 1975.

Whyte, William H., Jr. *The Organization Man.* Garden City: Doubleday Anchor, 1956.

Wilbur, Ted. *The First Flight across the Atlantic, May 1919.* Washington: National Air and Space Museum, 1969.

Wiley, Henry A. *An Admiral from Texas.* Garden City: Doubleday, 1934.

Wilkerson, Ethel. *Rome's Remarkable History.* Georgia: n.p., 1968.

Wilson, Eugene E. *Slipstream: The Autobiography of an Air Craftsman.* New York: McGraw-Hill, 1950.

Windsor, The Duchess of. *The Heart Has Its Reasons.* New York: David McKay, 1956.

Woodhouse, Henry. *Textbook of Naval Aeronautics.* New York: Century, 1917. Reprint. Annapolis: Naval Institute Press, 1991.

———. "U.S. Naval Aeronautical Policies, 1904–1942." U.S. Naval Institute *Proceedings* 68, no. 2 (Feb 1942): 161–75.

Woodward, C. Vann. *Origins of the New South, 1877–1913.* Baton Rouge: Louisiana State University Press, 1951.

Wright, Monte Duane. *Most Probable Position: A History of Aerial Navigation to 1941.* Lawrence, Ka.: University Press of Kansas, 1972.

Young, Desmond. *Rutland of Jutland.* London: Cassell, 1963.

Zahm, Alfred F. *Aeronautical Papers, 1885–1945.* 2 vols. Notre Dame: University of Notre Dame Press, 1950.

Zogbaum, Rufus F. *From Sail to Saratoga: A Naval Autobiography.* Rome, Italy: Tipografia Italo-Orientale, 1961.

ACKNOWLEDGMENTS

The genesis of this book lay in the decision of Pierrette Anne Towers to write a biography of her husband soon after his death. She had diligently preserved all his papers, in spite of his own disinterest in them, and during the late 1950s began organizing them, doing additional research, interviewing and corresponding with his former associates, and typing a clean copy of his many letters to his family and to her in the years before their marriage.

In the midst of her project, the early 1960s, Mrs. Towers generously allowed me to utilize her husband's wartime diary for my doctoral dissertation, which was eventually published as *The Fast Carriers*. Eventually the task grew too formidable for her, and in the mid-1970s she agreed to allow me to undertake the biography as soon as I could. This was not possible for yet another decade, although we remained in close touch as I gathered materials.

Like her husband, Pierre Towers was a pragmatic, unpretentious individual whose sharp intellect and memory never faltered over the years. She gave me carte blanche to tell her husband's story however I desired. She turned over all his papers to me with the understanding that, upon completion of this book, they be deposited with the Naval Historical Foundation at the Library of Congress. This has been done. My debt of gratitude to this amazing woman is therefore boundless. Without her tireless assembling of the Towers papers, the task would have been daunting indeed and this book certainly not possible in its final form. Regrettably, Pierre Towers passed away in August 1990.

I am also indebted to other members of the Towers family, to many of his colleagues and friends, and to historians and archivists who facilitated and enhanced my research. All are listed below. Special thanks are due to Naval Academy professor Paolo E. Coletta, who kept pressing me to write and then complete this book by sending me information on Towers encountered during the course of his own research in naval history. To him and all those listed below, my heartfelt thanks.

Acknowledgments

A research grant from the Air Force Historical Foundation provided partial support for this project and for which I am grateful.

Dean C. Allard, director, Naval Historical Center, and his energetic staff
Peter J. Anderson, Byrd Polar Research Center, Ohio State University
Adolphus Andrews, Jr., biographer of Joseph Mason Reeves
Donald G. Beaton, the "adopted" son of J. Fullton Towers
Harriet Towers Bjelovcic, Towers' second cousin
Constance Buchanan, copy editor
Thomas B. Buell, commander, biographer of King and Spruance
B. V. Burrow, commander, captain of the USS *Towers*
Malcolm W. Cagle, vice admiral, Naval Aviation Museum Foundation
Mary Rose Catalfano, Nimitz Library, U.S. Naval Academy
James W. Cheevers, U.S. Naval Academy Museum
Evelyn M. Cherpak, Naval Historical Collection, Naval War College
Ernest E. Christensen, rear admiral, son of an NC-1 crewman
Alice S. Creighton, Nimitz Library, U.S. Naval Academy
Robert J. Cressman, Naval Historical Center, biographer of Yarnell
Ben Scott Custer, rear admiral, naval aviator
William E. "Tony" Doherty, Jr., son of Gink Doherty
Aldo Joseph Draghi, Towers' former driver
Lindsley Dunn, Glenn H. Curtiss Museum
Phil Edwards, National Air and Space Museum
William R. Emerson, Franklin D. Roosevelt Library
Benis M. Frank, Marine Corps oral historian
Paul E. Garber, National Air and Space Museum
Peggy Graham of Rome, Georgia, and Hammondsport, New York
Charles S. Haberlein, Naval Historical Center
John B. Hattendorf, Ernest J. King Chair, Naval War College
Charles Higham, biographer of the Duchess of Windsor
John W. Huston, major general, air force historian
George R. Inger, historian of Brewster Aeronautical Corporation
Barry D. Ives, grandnephew of Victor D. Herbster
Patricia H. Johnson, typist
Stanley Kallkus, Navy Department Library
Charles Kelley, manuscripts division, Library of Congress
Martha J. Kennedy, Shorter College Alumni Association
Monica Knudsen, National Air and Space Museum
William M. Leary, University of Georgia

Acknowledgments

James Lee, Naval Historical Foundation

A. Lee Loomis, Jr., Towers' former aide

Lois Lovisolo, historian, Grumman Aerospace Corporation

William Towers "Billy" Maddox, Towers' nephew

John F. Marszalek, Mississippi State University

Maurice Maryanow, lieutenant colonel, U.S. Air Force Historical Research Center

John T. Mason, oral historian

John Monsarrat, former BuAer officer

John S. Nevins, USS *Saratoga* Association

Herman Northway, former *Langley* and *Saratoga* crewman

Robert Parks, Franklin D. Roosevelt Library

G. Willing Pepper, former staff officer of commander, Air Force, Pacific

Robert B. Pirie, vice admiral, naval aviator

Dominick A. Pisano, National Air and Space Museum

E. B. Potter, U.S. Naval Academy, biographer of Nimitz and Halsey

Jane H. Price, Nimitz Library, U.S. Naval Academy

Nigel Quinney, British researcher

J. D. "Jig Dog" Ramage, rear admiral, naval aviator

Rhoda Ratner, Smithsonian Institution Library

Connie Reynolds, my wife and typist, chief of logistics

Lynne L. Riley, Towers' granddaughter

Alex Roland, Duke University

James S. Russell, admiral, naval aviator

Robert N. Sheridan, naval bibliographer

Anne Atkins Staley, daughter of Tommy Lew Atkins

Merrill Stickler, Glenn H. Curtiss Museum

Paul Stillwell, U.S. Naval Institute oral historian

Eleanor Reynolds (Seligman) (Ring) Storrs, navy wife

Abner A. Towers, Towers' cousin

Charles S. Towers, Towers' son

Ernestine (Mrs. William M., Jr.) Towers, Towers' sister-in-law

Lois (Mrs. Charles S.) Towers, Towers' daughter-in-law

William M. Towers III, Towers' nephew

John Vadja, Navy Department Library

Richard E. von Doenhoff, National Archives

INDEX

Shiptype and hull-number abbreviations (adopted in 1920) follow. (For aircraft abbreviations, see squadrons.)

ACR   armored cruiser
AV   seaplane tender
BB   battleship
CA   heavy cruiser
CL   light cruiser
CV   aircraft carrier
CVA   attack carrier

CVB   battle carrier
CVE   escort carrier
CVL   light carrier
DD   destroyer
SS   submarine
ZR, ZRS   dirigible (airship), scout

About the Author

Clark G. Reynolds is author of several books on naval history, including *The Fast Carriers*, *Command of the Sea: The History and Strategy of Maritime Empires*, *Famous American Admirals*, *History and the Sea: Essays in Maritime Strategies*, and *War in the Pacific*. He received a Ph.D. from Duke University and is currently professor of history at the College of Charleston in South Carolina.

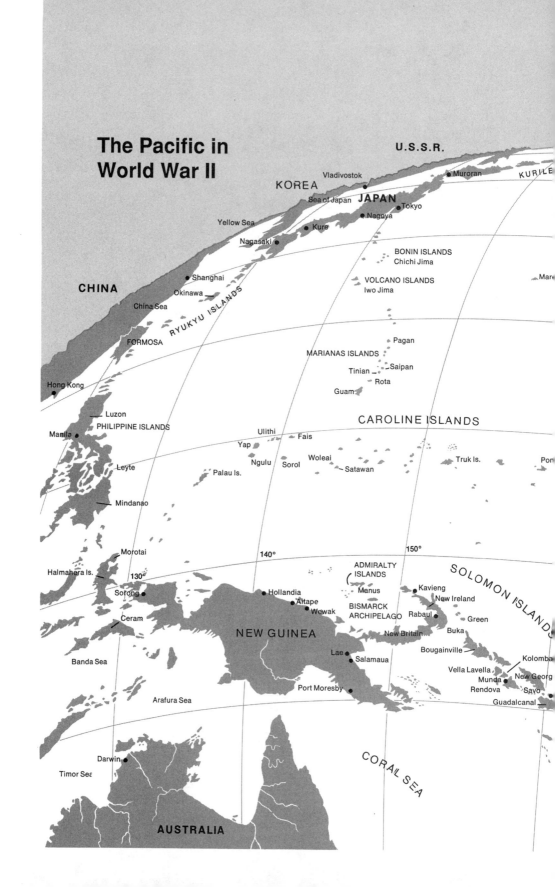

The Pacific in World War II

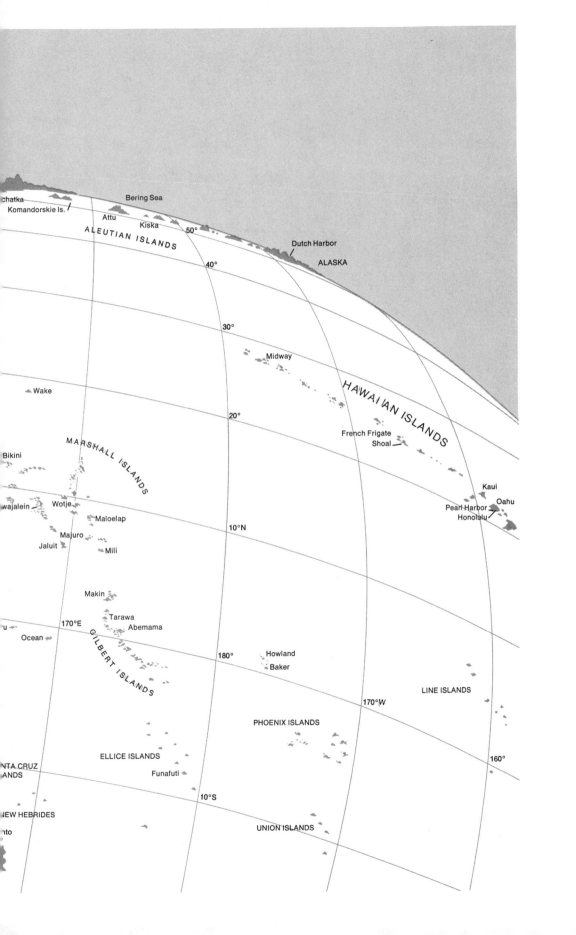

chatka
Komandorskie Is.
Bering Sea
Attu
Kiska
ALEUTIAN ISLANDS
50°
Dutch Harbor
ALASKA
40°

30°

Midway

Wake

20°

HAWAIIAN ISLANDS

MARSHALL ISLANDS

French Frigate
Shoal

Bikini

Kaui

wajalein
Wotje
Oahu
Pearl Harbor
Honolulu

Maloelap

10°N

Majuro

Jaluit
Mili

Makin

Tarawa
170°E
Abemama

Ocean

GILBERT ISLANDS

180°
Howland
Baker

LINE ISLANDS

170°W

PHOENIX ISLANDS

160°
ELLICE ISLANDS

NTA CRUZ
ANDS
Funafuti

10°S

NEW HEBRIDES

nto
UNION ISLANDS

The **Naval Institute Press** is the book-publishing arm of the U.S. Naval Institute, a private, nonprofit professional society for members of the sea services and civilians who share an interest in naval and maritime affairs. Established in 1873 at the U.S. Naval Academy in Annapolis, Maryland, where its offices remain today, the Naval Institute has more than 100,000 members worldwide.

Members of the Naval Institute receive the influential monthly magazine *Proceedings* and discounts on fine nautical prints, ship and aircraft photos, and subscriptions to the quarterly *Naval History* magazine. They also have access to the transcripts of the Institute's Oral History Program and get discounted admission to any of the Institute-sponsored seminars regularly offered around the country.

The Naval Institute's book-publishing program, begun in 1898 with basic guides to naval practices, has broadened its scope in recent years to include books of more general interest. Now the Naval Institute Press publishes more than sixty new titles each year, ranging from how-to books on boating and navigation to battle histories, biographies, ship and aircraft guides, and novels. Institute members receive discounts on the Press's more than 375 books.

Full-time students are eligible for special half-price membership rates. Life memberships are also available.

For a free catalog describing the Naval Institute Press books currently available, and for further information about U.S. Naval Institute membership, please write to:

Membership & Communications Department
U.S. Naval Institute
118 Maryland Avenue
Annapolis, Maryland 21402-5035

Or call, toll-free, (800) 233-USNI. In Maryland, call (301) 224-3378.

THE NAVAL INSTITUTE PRESS
ADMIRAL JOHN H. TOWERS
The Struggle for Naval Air Supremacy

Designed by Alan Carter

Set in Garamond #3
by TCSystems, Inc.
Shippensburg, Pennsylvania

Printed on 50-lb. Finch Opaque Smooth White
and bound in ICG Arrestox B and DSI Permalin
by The Maple-Vail Book Manufacturing Group
Binghamton, New York